EVIDENCE LAW

ASPEN CASEBOOK SERIES

Evidence Law

Practice, Problems, and Policy

Laurie L. Levenson
Professor of Law and
David W. Burcham Chair in Ethical Advocacy
Loyola Law School

Hon. Brian M. Hoffstadt
Associate Justice
California Court of Appeal

To contact Customer Service, e-mail customer.service@aspenpublishing.com, call 1-800-950-5259, or mail correspondence to:

Aspen Publishing
Attn: Order Department
PO Box 990
Frederick, MD 21705

Printed in the United States of America.

2 3 4 5 6 7 8 9 0

ISBN 978-1-5438-2598-5

Library of Congress Cataloging-in-Publication Data application is in process.

About Aspen Publishing

Aspen Publishing is a leading provider of educational content and digital learning solutions to law schools in the United States and around the world. Aspen provides best-in-class solutions for legal education through authoritative textbooks, written by renowned authors, and breakthrough products such as Connected eBooks, Connected Quizzing, and PracticePerfect.

The Aspen Casebook Series (famously known among law faculty and students as the "red and black" casebooks) encompasses hundreds of highly regarded textbooks in more than eighty disciplines, from large enrollment courses such as Torts and Contracts to emerging electives such as Sustainability and the Law of Policing. Study aids such as the *Examples & Explanations* and the *Emanuel Law Outlines* series, both highly popular collections, help law students master complex subject matter.

Major products, programs, and initiatives include:

- **Connected eBooks** are enhanced digital textbooks and study aids that come with a suite of online content and learning tools designed to maximize student success. Designed in collaboration with hundreds of faculty and students, the Connected eBook is a significant leap forward in the legal education learning tools available to students.
- **Connected Quizzing** is an easy-to-use formative assessment tool that tests law students' understanding and provides timely feedback to improve learning outcomes. Delivered through CasebookConnect.com, the learning platform already used by students to access their Aspen casebooks, Connected Quizzing is simple to implement and integrates seamlessly with law school course curricula.
- **PracticePerfect** is a visually engaging, interactive study aid to explain commonly encountered legal doctrines through easy-to-understand animated videos, illustrative examples, and numerous practice questions. Developed by a team of experts, PracticePerfect is the ideal study companion for today's law students.
- The **Aspen Learning Library** enables law schools to provide their students with access to the most popular study aids on the market across all of their courses. Available through an annual subscription, the online library consists of study aids in e-book, audio, and video formats with full text search, note-taking, and highlighting capabilities.
- Aspen's **Digital Bookshelf** is an institutional-level online education bookshelf, consolidating everything students and professors need to ensure success. This program ensures that every student has access to affordable course materials from day one.
- **Leading Edge** is a community centered on thinking differently about legal education and putting those thoughts into actionable strategies. At the core of the program is the Leading Edge Conference, an annual gathering of legal education thought leaders looking to pool ideas and identify promising directions of exploration.

About the Authors

Laurie L. Levenson is a professor of law and David W. Burcham Chair in Ethical Advocacy at Loyola Law School, Los Angeles. From 1996 to 1999, Professor Levenson was the Associate Dean for Academic Affairs. She teaches evidence, criminal law, criminal procedure, ethics, and trial advocacy. She is the founder of Loyola's Project for the Innocent.

Professor Levenson received her A.B. from Stanford University and her J.D. from UCLA School of Law, where she was the Chief Articles Editor at the UCLA Law Review. Following law school, Professor Levenson clerked for the Honorable James Hunter III of the U.S. Court of Appeals for the Third Circuit. From 1981 to 1989, she was an Assistant U.S. Attorney for the Central District of California.

Brian M. Hoffstadt is an Associate Justice on the California Court of Appeal. He has served on the Court of Appeal since 2014 and served as a judge of the Los Angeles Superior Court from 2010 until 2014. As an adjunct professor at various law schools, he has taught evidence, criminal procedure, and trial advocacy. He is a faculty member of the California Judicial College and has taught numerous judicial education courses.

Justice Hoffstadt received his B.S. from California Polytechnic University and his J.D. from UCLA School of Law. Following law school, Justice Hoffstadt clerked for the Honorable Cynthia Holcomb Hall on the U.S. Court of Appeals for the Ninth Circuit and for the Honorable Sandra Day O'Connor on the U.S. Supreme Court. Prior to his appointment to the bench, Justice Hoffstadt worked as a Special Counsel to the Federal Communications Commission; as Senior Counsel in the Office of Policy Development for the U.S. Department of Justice in Washington, D.C.; as an Assistant U.S. Attorney for the Central District of California; and as a partner in the Issues & Appeals practice group at Jones Day.

To Doug and my children—Nothing would be possible without you. To my amazing friend—Justice Nora M. Manella—thank you for always inspiring and standing by me. And to my incredible co-author, Brian, thank you for making this possible.

Laurie L. Levenson

To my wife, Coreen, and our children, Matthew and Lia. I am blessed to have you in my life and love nothing more than to spend my time with you. Thank you for letting me spend some of that precious time on this book.

Brian M. Hoffstadt

Summary of Contents

Contents

Preface

Our goal is to write a student-friendly book that sets forth in a straightforward manner the rules of evidence, the rationale for them, how they are applied, and the challenging issues that can arise in their application. Both of us have been teaching evidence for decades, and we draw on our experiences in the classroom and courtrooms to help students learn both the theory and application of evidence law. From our collective experience on both sides of the bench, our aim is to capture how both lawyers and judges view the law of evidence.

Evidence Law: Practice, Problems, and Policy is part of a teaching package that professors can individualize for the needs of their class. There is the basic textbook that sets forth the evidence rules, the rationale for them, examples of their applications, cases demonstrating their use in civil and criminal litigation, and plenty of problems for classroom discussion and review. Many chapters have summary charts and diagrams to help students follow the requirements and apply the rules.

Additionally, this book comes with a companion supplement containing an assortment of review questions that professors and students can use to reinforce the students' understanding of the evidence rules. There is a teacher's manual, sample syllabi, and a deck of PowerPoint slides for professors to use in teaching their courses. We will include within these materials links to readily accessible videos that can be helpful in understanding how the rules are used in court.

We recognize that professors have different approaches to teaching evidence. Therefore, we have created an evidence book that should work with any approach. The cases have been edited so that the application of the rules can be seen in context without students being overwhelmed by their class reading assignments. To make the book particularly approachable, differently shaded boxes are used so that students can quickly identify the language of the rules, examples, and review problems.

Finally, this book and its supplement contain short readings regarding cutting-edge areas of evidence law, such as the impact of new science; sensitivity to racial, economic, and cultural biases; constitutional developments; and strategic choices that arise in using evidence during trial proceedings.

We welcome your comments and suggestions regarding the book. Our goal is to provide the best possible teaching tool for evidence, one of the most critical courses for upcoming lawyers.

Laurie L. Levenson
Brian M. Hoffstadt

Acknowledgments

The authors wish to express their sincerest gratitude to Amy Powell, who spent hours tirelessly reviewing drafts of the textbook and related materials, tracking edits, and filling in gaps where needed; the book is better for her involvement. We also wish to thank the professors who took time to review earlier versions of the textbook; their input was very helpful. And we wish to thank Paul Sobel, Dena Kaufman, and all the staff at The Froebe Group, for their dedication to ensuring that the book and accompanying materials are of the greatest use to professors and students alike.

Evidence Law

Chapter 1

Introduction

PART A: THE RULES OF EVIDENCE AND THEIR PURPOSE

In years past, societies looked to trial by ordeal or trial by combat to resolve disputes. In England, trial by divine ordeal was common until 1215: There was the ordeal of cold water, by which an accused was adjudged "innocent" if he sank into a pool of water and "guilty" if he floated, although being innocent but drowned was likely little consolation. There was also the ordeal by fire, by which an accused was burned with a hot poker and guilt or innocence was determined by how the wound healed. Both types of ordeal were overseen by priests, who would interpret whether God had intervened to side with the accused. This practice ended in 1215 with a papal council decree against further Church involvement; the right to a trial by petit jury was decreed by King Henry III just four years later. Trial by combat was used to settle civil disputes, with the verdict going to the party who bested the other in battle. Parties could have a "champion" fight in their stead, which tended to tip the scales in favor of the party who could hire the burliest champion. Trial by combat was not outlawed until 1819.

Today, disputes are resolved by presenting them to a neutral body—sometimes a jury, sometimes a judge—who considers the facts underlying the dispute and renders a verdict as to how the dispute should be resolved.[1] Because post-verdict review is very limited, it is critical that the process be designed to lead to a fair and accurate verdict.

For the most part, juries and judges decide cases on the basis of *evidence*,[2] and the rules governing their consideration of that evidence are called the *rules of evidence.* A trial is supposed to be a "search for the truth," but the reality is that the truth of a verdict depends greatly on the evidence presented to the jury and how the jury interprets that evidence.

---

1. Jury trials in early America bore little resemblance to trials of today. Parties argued their own cases, and the admissibility of evidence varied greatly among judges. Even today, there is enormous variety between the Anglo-American approach to evidence law and the Continental European approach. United States courts are wedded to the adversarial system; the inquisitorial system governs in many other countries. *See* The Legal Concept of Evidence, Stanford Encyclopedia of Philosophy (2015).

2. It is hard to imagine a trial without evidence. However, some proceedings, such as impeachment trials, may proceed without witnesses or even subpoenaed evidence. These types of proceedings have led to debates over whether they should be considered "trials" in the same manner as courtroom proceedings.

The law of evidence accordingly addresses two crucial issues in the decision making process that leads to a verdict: (1) What information will the decision maker be allowed to use—and for what purpose(s) will the decision maker be permitted to use that information—in deciding that case, and (2) in what form may that information be presented to the decision maker?

1. *The Purpose and Policy Goals of the Federal Rules of Evidence*

The goal of the Federal Rules of Evidence is to create a set of rules that will ensure that the decision maker has sufficient, pertinent information to decide a case, but not allow a trial to become an unruly, inefficient free-for-all where any information, no matter how remote or prejudicial, may be presented.

Thus, the rules of evidence are crafted so as:

(1) To ensure that the case proceeds in an orderly and efficient manner by admitting only evidence that is *relevant*;
(2) To have accurate decision making by admitting evidence that is *reliable*;
(3) Where appropriate, to implement *substantive policy* that reflects societal judgments regarding the use of certain facts as evidence at trial; and
(4) To assist in the *orderly presentation* of evidence, which serves to protect the parties' rights under the Constitution and common law.

2. *Is Evidence Law Neutral?*

As with all aspects of the law, evidence law reflects the biases and culture of the justice system that developed it. Different cultures hold different types of proceedings to resolve their disputes. For example, in some countries, trials may be more informal, with the court conducting the examinations. In other countries, the presentation of a case is guided by religious traditions. The rules of evidence in the United States are not without their own inherent biases. For example, impeachment rules that permit the introduction of prior convictions can have a disproportionate impact on racial groups who may have been targeted by the criminal justice system. Other rules use a "reasonable person" standard to determine when silence is deemed to be an admission, but can define that "reasonable person" by reference to the dominant group in a community. Yet another example is when flight may reasonably be considered consciousness of guilt.[3] Historically, there have been many aspects of evidence that were dominated by biases, such as gender and racial restrictions regarding who was competent to testify as a witness. As you study the rules of evidence, consider to what extent the evidence rules and cases reflect these biases and what can be done to create a more "neutral" approach in deciding cases.

---

3. *See* Jules Epstein, *Is Evidence Law Race "Neutral?"* https://www2.law.temple.edu/aer/is-evidence-law-race-neutral; Jasmine B. Gonzales Rose, *Toward a Critical Race Theory of Evidence*, 101 Minn. L. Rev. 2243 (2018).

3. The Origin and Evolution of the Federal Rules of Evidence

Originally, the law of evidence was governed by common law. Judges' opinions governed the admissibility of evidence. New York largely continues to follow this common law approach.

However, in the 1900s there was a movement to codify the rules to create more clarity and uniformity for the courts. The first code of evidence was drafted by Professor John Wigmore in 1909. That code was not adopted, but the American Law Institute proposed a Model Code of Evidence in 1942, which led to the first draft of the Uniform Rules of Evidence in 1953.[4]

Eventually, states began to use these proposed codes to adopt their own rules of evidence. In 1965, California adopted the California Evidence Code, which modernized many of the evidentiary rules and included them in a comprehensive set of statutes governing the admissibility of evidence.

In 1975, the Federal Rules of Evidence ("FRE" or "Federal Rules") were adopted by Congress and the United States Supreme Court.[5] The timing of their adoption affected their content. The rules were proposed just as the Watergate scandal was breaking. President Richard Nixon had been asserting executive privilege during the Watergate hearings, and Congress thought that it was politically unwise to adopt rules of evidence that contained privilege rules. Thus, and as discussed more fully in Chapter Fifteen, the Federal Rules that were adopted left to the common law the issue of evidentiary privileges. FRE 501. Despite the codification of most of the rules of evidence, they are based originally in common law and were created by judges who came from elite, homogenous backgrounds, which also creates a potential for ongoing bias in the rules.

The Federal Rules apply to most of the civil and criminal matters occurring in federal courts except for specifically enumerated proceedings within those matters. FRE 1101(a)-(d). They are also merely the default rules, as they can be modified by Congress's enactment of a statute or by rules promulgated by the United States Supreme Court. FRE 1101(e). Specifically, FRE 1101 provides as follows:

FRE 1101. Applicability of the Rules

(a) To Courts and Judges. These rules apply to proceedings before:

- United States district courts;
- United States bankruptcy and magistrate judges;
- United States courts of appeal;

4. The Uniform Rules were revised again in 1989 and 1999. The earlier incarnations became the template for the Federal Rules of Evidence.

5. Briefly, the process for adopting and amending federal rules is for a committee to draft proposed rules with advisory notes and reports. Those are transmitted to the Supreme Court for its consideration. If the rules are adopted, they are transmitted to Congress for adoption pursuant to the Enabling Act, 28 U.S.C. § 2072. The rules are regularly reviewed and amended by the Court and Congress.

- the United States Court of Federal Claims; and
- the district courts of Guam, the Virgin Islands, and the Northern Mariana Islands.

(b) To Cases and Proceedings. These rules apply in:

- civil cases and proceedings, including bankruptcy, admiralty, and maritime cases;
- criminal cases and proceedings; and
- contempt proceedings, except those in which the court may act summarily.

(c) Rules on Privilege. The rules on privilege apply to all stages of a case or proceeding.

(d) Exceptions. These rules—except for those on privilege—do not apply to the following:

(1) the court's determination, under Rule 104(b), on a preliminary question of fact governing admissibility;

(2) grand-jury proceedings; and

(3) miscellaneous proceedings such as:

- extradition or rendition;
- issuing an arrest warrant, criminal summons, or search warrant;
- a preliminary examination in a criminal case;
- sentencing;
- granting or revoking probation of supervised release; and
- considering whether to release on bail or otherwise.

(e) Other Statutes and Rules. A federal statute or a rule prescribed by the Supreme Court may provide for admitting or excluding evidence independently from these rules.

Although the Federal Rules are the primary mechanism governing the admissibility of evidence in federal proceedings, they are not the sole mechanism. In criminal cases, constitutional considerations such as the right of confrontation under the Sixth Amendment, the privilege against self-incrimination under the Fifth and Fourteenth Amendments, and the right to due process under the Fifth and Fourteenth Amendments will also affect the admissibility of evidence. The impact of these Amendments will be addressed in the discussion of the rules regulating relevance and hearsay.

4. *The Scope of the Rules of Evidence*

The rules of evidence, as their name suggests, explain what "evidence" may be admitted, what "evidence" must be excluded, and how admissible "evidence" is to be presented to the decision maker. The Federal Rules do not specifically define "evidence." However, a common understanding is that "evidence" means "testimony, writings, material objects, or other things presented to the senses that are offered to prove the existence or nonexistence of a fact."[6] "Evidence" encompasses

6. Cal. Evid. Code § 140.

both proof that a fact exists as well as proof that a fact does not exist (which is called "negative evidence").

Not everything a jury or judge sees or hears inside or outside the courtroom is "evidence" regulated by the rules of evidence:

- *Statements of counsel.* Trial counsel are not under oath while they perform most of the functions of counsel, such as questioning prospective jurors during *voir dire*, making opening statements, examining testifying witnesses, and making closing arguments. Thus, counsel do not satisfy the prerequisites for being a competent witness, and none of the attorney's statements made during the above-referenced tasks at trial are "evidence." The same is true when a defendant acts as his or her own attorney; the self-represented defendant's opening and closing arguments are not "evidence" because, at the time they are made, the defendant is not under oath.
- *What jurors see happening in the courtroom.* As a general rule, how litigants conduct themselves in the courtroom when not on the witness stand is *not* evidence (because they are not under oath).
- *What witnesses say, how witnesses look, and how they act while on the stand.* Assuming a witness has been found competent to testify, what she says while testifying is evidence. This is true as to what the witness herself says as well as to the content of the questions her answers adopt. (Thus, if a witness is asked, "Were you present at the Rave Club on Saturday, October 28, 2021?" and the witness answers, "Yes," the evidence is that the witness was present at the Rave Club on that date.) A witness's appearance and conduct while on the stand—that is, whether she is sweating, whether she speaks quickly or haltingly, whether she looks nervous or confident—is called demeanor evidence and is a form of evidence (which, as discussed in Chapters Two and Eleven, is relevant to the believability or credibility of the witness).
- *Jury views.* Sometimes, litigants wish to have the jurors travel to a location outside the courtroom to view a scene (such as the scene of a murder or the location of a property line dispute). The federal courts are currently split over whether a jury view constitutes "evidence." The majority rule is that a jury view is *not* evidence, *United States v. Gray*, 199 F.3d 547, 548 (1st Cir. 1999), with a minority holding that it *is* evidence, *Devin v. DeTella*, 101 F.3d 1206, 1208 (7th Cir. 1996).
- *Stipulations and matters subject to judicial notice.* Stipulations are matters that the parties agree the jury may accept as true during the proceeding; they constitute evidence. Matters that have been judicially noticed by a court are also considered evidence. FRE 201(f); Cal. Evid. Code § 457.
- *Post-verdict statements of jurors.* These statements are considered evidence for post-trial motions, but their admissibility is heavily regulated, as discussed more fully in Chapter Ten. FRE 606; Cal. Evid. Code § 1150.

Although these enumerated items certainly add to the "theater of the courtroom,"[7] the rules regulate only the "evidence" the jury may use in reaching its decision.

---

7. *See* Laurie L. Levenson, *Courtroom Demeanor: The Theater of the Courtroom*, 29 Minn. L. Rev. 573 (2008).

5. *Interpreting the Rules of Evidence*

When a trial or appellate judge is called upon to apply a rule to a particular piece of evidence and, in the process of doing so, to interpret the rule, the judge typically looks to the following key sources: (1) the language of the actual rule, (2) the Advisory Committee Notes for that rule, and (3) any applicable case law. FRE 102 also sets forth an interpretive maxim to use in construing the rules:

> **FRE 102. PURPOSE**
>
> These rules should be construed so as to administer every proceeding fairly, eliminate unjustifiable expense and delay, and promote the development of evidence law, to the end of ascertaining the truth and securing a just determination.

An additional theme that threads its way through many different rules is the notion that a "just determination" that leads to the "ascertainment of truth" is, in part, a function of ensuring that the parties to litigation do not abuse the rules of evidence in a way that skews what is presented to the trier of fact. For example, as discussed below, a party who introduces one snippet of a conversation cannot object when the opposing party seeks to introduce a different portion of that same conversation so as to prevent the snippet from creating a misleading impression to the trier of fact. Similarly, as also discussed below, a criminal defendant who introduces evidence of his own "good" character trait cannot object when the prosecutor seeks to respond by introducing evidence of the defendant's "bad" character on that same trait. This scenario, generally referred to as "opening the door," is a common theme of many doctrines under the Federal Rules.

6. *The Influence of the Federal Rules*

States and other sovereign entities within the United States, such as Native American tribes, remain free to adopt their own rules of evidence. However, many of those jurisdictions have opted to use the Federal Rules as their model. Such states include Illinois, Texas, and Florida. *See* Ill. Rules of Evidence (2011); Tex. Rules of Evidence (1998); Fla. Stat. §§ 90.101-90.958 (1977). In this book, the focus is primarily on the Federal Rules. Where some of the larger jurisdictions (such as California, New York, Texas, Illinois, and Florida) have different rules, those deviations will be identified.

In civil cases, parties often agree—either before a dispute arises (through contractual arbitration agreements) or after a dispute arises (through stipulation)—to present a case to a third-party neutral, such as an arbitrator. Arbitration is often more flexible, less formal, and faster than litigation in the federal or state court systems. Even so, the parties often agree that the arbitrator must use the Federal Rules during the arbitration.

PART B: THE LITIGATION AND TRIAL PROCESS

Because the Federal Rules of Evidence apply only to certain portions of civil and criminal proceedings and because the context of their application is always important, it is helpful to have a good understanding of civil and criminal litigation proceedings before studying the rules themselves. The players through the process are the parties to the case, the judge, and the decision maker or "trier of fact" (which can be either the judge or the jury).

The Federal Rules assign the trial judge specific tasks:

- Making preliminary, pretrial evidentiary rulings;
- During trial, deciding whether the threshold requirements for admitting evidence have been met;
- During trial, ruling on objections made to exclude evidence and entertaining offers of proof from parties seeking to admit evidence; and
- After trial, deciding challenges to the verdict.

1. *Initiating Civil and Criminal Proceedings*

A civil lawsuit is started when a party (who is called the *plaintiff*) files a complaint that (1) identifies who is being sued (who are called the *defendants*), (2) makes factual allegations regarding the defendants' conduct, and (3) specifies the legal claims (or causes of action) that entitle the plaintiff to relief (whether it be money damages, an injunction, or some other form of equitable relief) from the defendants.

There are two ways to initiate a criminal case, which is also called a criminal prosecution. First, the prosecutor may seek an indictment from a grand jury. The grand jury is an ex parte body: The only ones present are the prosecutor, the grand jurors, the witness, and a court reporter who transcribes what is said; no judge presides over the proceeding, and the defendant has no right to be present. The prosecutor presents evidence to the grand jurors (through witness testimony or documents), and the grand jurors' task is to determine whether that evidence establishes probable cause to believe that the defendant has committed the crime(s) the prosecutor alleges. If so, the grand jury returns an indictment as to those charges. In federal criminal prosecutions, the Fifth Amendment guarantees a defendant the right to indictment by grand jury. The Federal Rules of Evidence do not apply to grand jury proceedings. FRE 1101(d)(2).

Second, the prosecutor may file a criminal complaint, which alleges the crime(s) the prosecutor believes the defendant has committed. Then the matter proceeds to a preliminary examination (which is also called a preliminary hearing). A preliminary examination is an adversarial proceeding in which the prosecutor introduces evidence to a judge, the defendant is present and may challenge that evidence or present additional evidence, and the judge then decides whether there is probable cause to believe that the defendant committed the crimes charged in the complaint; if the judge so concludes, the prosecutor files an information containing those charges. Because the Fifth Amendment right to a grand jury has not been incorporated to apply to the states, *Hurtado v. California*, 110 U.S. 516 (1884), many states—especially those west of the Mississippi—often employ the preliminary examination model. The Federal Rules of Evidence also do not apply to preliminary hearings. FRE 1101(d)(3).

2. *Pretrial Litigation*

Before trial, parties to a pending case engage in discovery to identify the evidence they will want to introduce to prove their case and to decide what evidence they will want to exclude when offered by the other side. In civil cases, discovery focuses on depositions (examination of witnesses outside the courtroom), requests for interrogatories and admissions, and subpoenas for documents. In the criminal arena, prosecutors obtain evidence in a variety of ways, ranging from witness interviews and interrogation of defendants to grand jury investigations. They also conduct searches and obtain physical evidence. Defense lawyers may do their own investigations. Separate discovery rules govern the exchange of information in criminal proceedings.

Once the parties have identified the evidence they wish to admit or to exclude, they may ask the trial judge to issue rulings on whether to admit or exclude evidence (which will affect how the parties then shape the presentations they wish to make to the trier of fact). Some of the evidence rules, such as the rule governing the admissibility of prior bad acts (FRE 404(b)), *require* notice in advance of the presentation of evidence so as to give the opposing party the opportunity to obtain a ruling on the admissibility of that evidence before trial. The proponent of the evidence bears the burden of establishing the threshold admissibility of that evidence.

The usual mechanism for obtaining a pretrial evidentiary ruling as to whether a particular piece of evidence is to be admitted or excluded at trial is called a *motion in limine.* The trial judge may nevertheless decline to issue a pretrial ruling, preferring instead to "see how the trial plays out." What is more, pretrial rulings are necessarily tentative; trial is fluid, so the basis for a pretrial ruling may be eroded by what happens at trial. Motions in limine are typically heard before a jury is selected (and thus outside the jury's presence). However, the Federal Rules of Evidence only *require* that a motion in limine be heard outside the jury's presence when (1) the motion regards the admissibility of a confession in a criminal case, FRE 104; (2) the defendant in a criminal case is the witness and so requests, *id.*; (3) when "justice requires," *id.*; or (4) the jury might otherwise hear "inadmissible evidence," FRE 103(d).

When deciding motions in limine, the rules of evidence *do not apply* except for the rules regarding privilege. FRE 1101(d)(1), 104(a). If the judge believes that it is appropriate, the judge may hold pretrial hearings to determine the admissibility of evidence. This occurs, for example, in determining whether witnesses can testify as expert witnesses (so-called *Daubert* hearings).[8]

In ruling on the admission or exclusion of evidence, the trial judge may categorically admit a piece of evidence, categorically exclude a piece of evidence, or admit it for a limited purpose (or against some parties but not all parties) under FRE 105. Specifically, FRE 105 provides:

8. See Chapter Twelve.

FRE 105. Limiting Evidence That Is Not Admissible Against Other Parties or for Other Purposes

If the court admits evidence that is admissible against a party or for a purpose—but not against another party or for another purpose—the court, on a timely request, must restrict the evidence to its proper scope and instruct the jury accordingly.

Limiting instructions are commonplace in trials. Sometimes, evidence against one party cannot be used against another party or the evidence against one party may be used for only a limited purpose (such as impeachment or to address a particular issue in a case) and not for other purposes. In these situations, the court will give a limiting instruction directing the triers of fact how they may consider this evidence. Are these limiting instructions effective? In other words, do jurors heed them? Courts generally presume that jurors do, *Richardson v. Marsh,* 481 U.S. 200, 211 (1987); *United States v. Nance,* 767 F.3d 1037, 1043 (10th Cir. 2014), but whether they do as an empirical matter is a different question altogether. When a trial judge believes that a limiting instruction may not be effective, the judge usually has the discretion to exclude the evidence due to the danger of how the evidence may be misused.

3. *Trial*

The main event of litigation in civil and criminal cases is the trial. Due to the possibility of settlement or plea, and the prevalence of both (indeed, more than 90% of civil cases settle, and 95% of criminal cases end in a plea), trial is a relatively rare event. Even so, the assessment of whether to settle a case often relies heavily on what evidence is likely to be admitted at a trial. Further, for those cases that *do* proceed to trial, it is critical to understand the trial process.

(a) Jury Selection

If a jury is going to decide a case, the parties start the trial by selecting the jury. In criminal cases, the right to a jury trial is guaranteed under the Sixth Amendment for all "serious" offenses, which means offenses whose maximum authorized penalty is more than six months. In civil cases in federal court, the Seventh Amendment provides for the right to a jury trial "in Suits at common law, where the value in controversy shall exceed twenty dollars."

Jury selection begins with a *venire* (panel) of jurors being called for trial. The parties then have an opportunity to *voir dire* (question) the jurors. Depending on the court, the questioning may be done by the lawyers directly, the judge, or a combination of both. Lawyers may exercise *challenges for cause* and *peremptory challenges.* Once the jury is selected and sworn, trial begins.

(b) Opening Statements

Each side gives an overview of their case in an *opening statement.* The plaintiff (or, in a criminal case, the prosecutor) goes first. In a criminal case, the defense can reserve its opening statement until after the prosecution's presentation of the case.

As noted above, the lawyer's statements throughout the case, especially during opening statement and closing argument, are *not evidence.* Rather, an opening statement recites what the lawyers expect (or hope) the evidence will show during trial. Opening statements can be brief or can be detailed outlines as to which witnesses will testify and what exhibits will be presented. Part of the lawyers' goals is to create a connection and credibility with the jury.

(c) Presentation of Proof

The *order* of proof at trial turns on who bears the *burden* of proof:

- The plaintiff in a civil case, and the prosecution in a criminal case, bears the burden of proof and will go first in its presentation of the case. This is referred to as the plaintiff's or prosecution's *case-in-chief.* Once the plaintiff or prosecution *rests,* the court may entertain a motion by the defendant to end the trial at that point by issuing a directed verdict in a civil case or a verdict for acquittal in a criminal case. A directed verdict or acquittal is appropriate if the court finds that a reasonable jury viewing the plaintiff's or prosecution's evidence could not return a verdict in the plaintiff's or prosecution's favor. Ordinarily, such motions are denied.
- The defense then presents its case, if it so chooses. The defendant can opt (and in criminal cases, often does opt) not to present any evidence of its own, particularly if the plaintiff's or prosecution's case is weak.
- Once the defense rests, the plaintiff or prosecution may present a *rebuttal case.* Rebuttal cases are generally limited and should be in direct response to evidence presented by the defense. On rare occasion, the court will allow the defense to present *surrebuttal* evidence after the plaintiff's or prosecution's rebuttal case.

During these various steps of the trial, parties may present any of the following:

- Witness testimony;
- Documentary evidence (such as the contract at issue in a business dispute or a business record);
- Physical (or real) evidence (such as the murder weapon or the drugs seized from the defendant);
- Demonstrative evidence (such as a demonstration or illustration of what happened during a scuffle or a computer reconstruction of the event at issue);
- Stipulations of the parties, by which the parties agree to certain facts; and
- Requests for judicial notice, which if granted require a civil jury and permit a criminal jury to accept certain well-known and undisputable facts as being true.

(i) Witness testimony

The Federal Rules specify a number of requirements that govern how witness testimony is to be presented:

- *Direct examination.* When a party calls a witness, the initial examination is called the "direct examination." The scope of direct examination is limited chiefly by relevance. As a general rule, a witness on direct examination may only be asked questions in a *nonleading* manner. Leading questions are questions that suggest the answer being elicited (that is, questions that effectively put words in the witness's mouth). By contrast, nonleading questions are more open-ended so that the witness can use his or her own words to describe the events. Leading questions are permitted during the direct examination of a so-called hostile witness (that is, a witness who has signaled that she does not favor the position of the party calling her), an adverse party, or a witness "identified with an adverse party." FRE 611(c)(2).

Examples

Q: Did the defendant grab $500 from you when he entered the bank?
[*Leading*]

Q: What, if anything, did the defendant do when he entered the bank?
[*Nonleading*]

Q: You never told the police that the defendant took $500 from you, right?
[*Leading*]

- *Cross-examination.* During cross-examination, the party who did not call a witness has the opportunity to challenge the witness's testimony. Leading questions are allowed during cross-examination because it is assumed that the witness—who was called by the other side—will be reluctant to provide answers to the cross-examiner. By using leading questions, the cross-examiner can better control the witness and challenge the witness's testimony. The scope of cross-examination is narrower than direct. It is generally limited to (1) any substantive topics discussed during a witness's direct examination and (2) topics bearing on the witness's credibility (that is, questions aimed at impeaching the witness's credibility).

Examples

Direct Examination

Q: What happened when the defendant saw you in the bank?
A: He grabbed $500 from me.

Cross-Examination

Q1: Don't you usually wear glasses, but you weren't wearing them that day?
[*Permitted; goes to witness's credibility*]

Q2: You like to use your money to buy fancy clothes, don't you?
[*Not permitted; outside the scope of direct examination*]

- *Redirect and further examination.* Redirect examination, in turn, can generally cover (1) only those substantive topics discussed during cross-examination and (2) rehabilitating the witness's credibility. FRE 611(b). A trial judge can deviate from these rules by allowing a party to "reopen" direct examination (or cross-examination) by getting into substantive topics not touched on during cross-examination (or during redirect examination); however, a party needs the court's permission to do so if there is an objection. *Id.*

As this description indicates, the examination of testifying witnesses is designed to start broad (constrained by the rules regarding relevance) and to grow increasingly narrower as the examination of the witness proceeds:

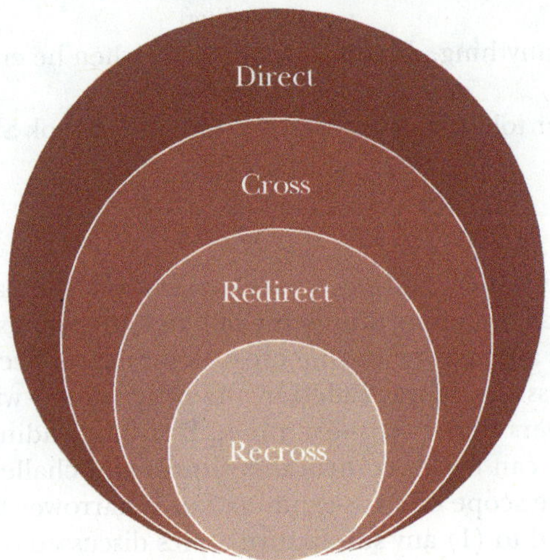

These rules governing the party examination of testifying witnesses are set forth in FRE 611, as follows:

FRE 611. Mode and Order of Examining Witnesses and Presenting Evidence

(a) Control by the Court; Purposes. The court should exercise reasonable control over the mode and order of examining witnesses and presenting evidence so as to:

(1) make those procedures effective for determining the truth;

(2) avoid wasting time; and

(3) protect witnesses from harassment or undue embarrassment.

(b) Scope of Cross-Examination. Cross-examination should not go beyond the subject matter of the direct examination and matters affecting the witness's credibility. The court may allow inquiry into additional matters as if on direct examination.

(c) Leading Questions. Leading questions should not be used on direct examination except as necessary to develop the witness's testimony. Ordinarily, the court should allow leading questions:

(1) on cross-examination; and

(2) when a party calls a hostile witness, an adverse party, or a witness identified with an adverse party.

- *Examination by the trial judge.* The trial judge is not wholly passive. Although judges usually allow the parties to examine witnesses without any intervention from them, judges have the right to ask questions, as long as they do so in a neutral fashion and ask questions aimed at clarifying the testimony elicited by the parties. The judge may also call witnesses *not* called by the parties—whether they be lay witnesses or expert witnesses. Judges rarely exercise the power to call witnesses, but that power exists. It is set forth in FRE 614. The power to appoint and call expert witnesses is covered in FRE 706 and is discussed in Chapter Twelve.

FRE 614. Court's Calling or Examining a Witness

(a) Calling. The court may call a witness on its own or at a party's request. Each party is entitled to cross-examine the witness.

(b) Examining. The court may examine a witness regardless of who calls the witness.

(c) Objections. A party may object to the court's calling or examining a witness either at that time or at the next opportunity when the jury is not present.

- *Questions posed by jurors.* Some trial judges allow jurors to present questions to witnesses. Most judges prefer to screen the questions (that is, to have the jurors submit possible questions to the judge, which are then discussed with the parties before being posed to the witness); screening ensures that the questions asked are designed to elicit admissible evidence. This procedure was followed in *United States v. Hernandez*, 176 F.3d 719, 722-26 (3d Cir. 1999). However, some judges allow jurors to directly ask questions of witnesses, with the parties and judge intervening if a particular question is inappropriate or would lead to inadmissible evidence. There is no Federal Rule governing this practice, and it is within the general authority and discretion of the judge to have "reasonable control" of the proceedings.

(ii) Exclusion and ordering of witnesses

Exclusion of witnesses. During the presentation of proof, the trial judge also has the power and duty to regulate who is present in the courtroom. Why? If the third witness to be called in a case sits in the courtroom and listens to the testimony of the first and second witnesses, the third witness's testimony might be colored by what that witness heard from the previous witnesses. FRE 615 (known as the rule of "sequestration") provides for exclusion of witnesses to avoid precisely this problem, but has exceptions for (1) the parties themselves; (2) the parties' representatives, if a party is not a "natural person"[9]; (3) persons authorized by statute to be present; and (4) persons shown to be "essential to presenting the party's claim or defense." FRE 615. Typically, the second category includes the lead investigating officer or "case agent" in a criminal case, and the last category includes expert witnesses whose opinions turn on what the percipient witnesses relate during testimony at the trial. In full, FRE 615 provides as follows:

FRE 615. Excluding Witnesses

At a party's request, the court must order witnesses excluded so that they cannot hear other witnesses' testimony. Or the court may do so on its own. But this rule does not authorize excluding:

(a) a party who is a natural person;

(b) an officer or employee of a party that is not a natural person, after being designated as the party's representative by its attorney;

(c) a person whose presence a party shows to be essential to presenting the party's claim or defense; or

(d) a person authorized by statute to be present.

Interestingly, FRE 615 does not specifically prohibit a party from telling excluded witnesses what other witnesses have stated while testifying and does not specifically prohibit a party from sharing a transcript of that testimony. The federal courts are split over whether an exclusion order reaches such conduct. *See United States v. McClendon*, 362 Fed. Appx. 475, 483 (6th Cir. 2010) (concluding it does not). A pending amendment to FRE 615 would, if adopted, clarify that an exclusion order under FRE 615 "operates only to exclude witnesses from the courtroom," but that the trial judge may also, "by order," "prohibit disclosure of trial testimony to witnesses who are excluded from the courtroom" or "prohibit excluded witnesses from accessing trial testimony." Even as currently drafted, FRE 615's bar only applies to the evidentiary portion of the trial; it does not apply to opening statements. *United States v. West*, 607 F.2d 300, 306 (9th Cir. 1979).

9. A pending amendment to FRE 615, if adopted, would explicitly limit the entity's representative to "*one* officer or employee."

Order of witnesses. Although the parties choose which witnesses to call and usually choose the order in which to call them, a trial judge has the authority to alter that order if needed for the convenience of the witnesses, the jury, the parties, or the court. Thus, a court may allow a defense expert who is only available on a Tuesday afternoon to be called as a witness in the middle of the plaintiff's case-in-chief. This is not uncommon given how busy many people are these days. The jury is simply informed of what is happening.

(d) Jury Instructions

Throughout the trial, the court gives instructions to the jury. They may include introductory instructions to explain to the jurors their duties during the trial, instructions during the trial to limit how jurors use evidence (*limiting instructions*), and even instructions by the court to cure previous erroneous rulings (*curative instructions*). At the end of trial, there are *closing instructions* that direct the jurors on what the law is and how to evaluate the evidence, and that spell out the jurors' duties and responsibilities during deliberations. These closing instructions typically set forth the elements required to prove a claim, as well as definitions of the burden of proof and types of evidence (such as direct and circumstantial evidence).

(e) Closing Arguments

Once all of the proof is submitted, the parties have an opportunity to present closing arguments. Like opening statements, closing arguments are not evidence. Rather, they are the lawyers' efforts to persuade the jury (or the trial judge in a bench trial) why the evidence presented in the case supports the verdict they seek. During argument, the parties will use the evidence at trial, as well as inferences from that evidence, to argue why they should win. Typically, closing arguments are more dramatic—a moment of courtroom theater where the lawyer convinces the jury of the "just" verdict. Plaintiffs and prosecutors will argue why they have met the burden of proof; defense counsel will argue why that burden has not been met.

As discussed more fully in Chapter Fourteen, the *burden of proof* depends on what kind of case is before the court. In a *criminal case*, the prosecution must prove its case *beyond a reasonable doubt.* In a *civil case*, the burden of proof is ordinarily by a *preponderance of the evidence* (that is, more likely than not), although it can be by *clear and convincing evidence* in some types of actions (such as actions involving the rights of parents over their children).

The plaintiff or prosecutor gets to make the initial closing argument. Then, the defense will argue. Following that, the plaintiff or prosecutor gets one more shot at the jury through rebuttal argument. On rare occasions, judges can allow surrebuttal arguments as well.

(f) Deliberations and Rendering of the Verdict

Jurors deliberate cases behind closed doors. They may ask questions of the court during their deliberations, and the court answers those questions with both sides present. If the jury cannot reach a verdict, it is a *hung jury*, and the case may be retried. If there is a verdict, it is taken in open court, and the jurors may be *polled* (asked individually) whether they agree with the verdict.

(g) Sentencing

In criminal cases after the rendering of a guilty verdict, there is a second phase to the proceedings: The defendant must be sentenced. In a capital case where the defendant is facing the death penalty, this second phase is called the "penalty phase" and has all the trappings of the first, "guilt" phase insofar as the rules of evidence apply and the phase is also tried to a jury. However, in noncapital cases, sentencing is pronounced by the judge, and the rules of evidence (except for privileges) do not apply.

4. *Post-Trial Litigation*

Judgment is entered by the court after a verdict. If the court disagrees with the verdict, it may grant a post-verdict acquittal or, in a civil case, grant a judgment notwithstanding the verdict. In a criminal case, a final judgment is entered at the time of sentencing.

5. *The Appeal*

The trial is the main event in litigation, but the party who loses at trial has a statutory right to appeal the verdict. On appeal after judgment is entered, a party can argue that the trial judge erred in the evidentiary rulings and that these errors warrant a new trial. (A party can *also* try to seek appellate review of an evidentiary ruling in the middle of the trial by seeking an interlocutory appeal. Such appeals are discretionary with the appellate court and are rarely granted to review evidentiary issues except for those involving privileges, where an erroneous ruling requiring the disclosure of privileged material may be impossible to remedy after trial or where a witness who claims a privilege has been held in contempt for failing to testify and would have to remain in custody pending trial if interlocutory review is not granted.)

(a) Was the Alleged Evidentiary Error "Preserved"?

One of the most important functions of a lawyer at trial is to make a clear record as to the evidence being offered and why it is or is not admissible. That is because a party can argue that a trial judge's evidentiary ruling was wrong only if the party properly *preserved* its disagreement with that ruling during the trial. Although it has some exceptions, the preservation requirement ensures that disagreements are brought to the trial judge's attention at a time when the judge can consider the issue and make a ruling that obviates the need for an appeal and reversal. The preservation requirement also discourages parties from "sandbagging" by sitting silently while the trial judge makes an improper ruling with the expectation that they will either (1) win at trial or (2) lose at trial, but raise the issue on appeal and get a retrial. The preservation requirement also acknowledges that the appellate court is limited to the record of proceedings in the trial court—that is, the exhibits that were admitted and the reporter's transcript of what was said. New evidence cannot generally be presented on appeal.

What must a party do to properly preserve its disagreement? If the party is seeking to *exclude* evidence, the party must object to the evidence's admission before it may appeal a trial judge's ruling *overruling* that objection. (If the objection is *sustained,* the trial judge has agreed with the objection and the evidence is kept out, obviating any basis to appeal that ruling.) An objection may be either oral or in writing. An *objection* calls to the trial judge's attention a party's intention to exclude evidence. To be valid, an objection must be (1) timely (that is, made before the witness answers the question) and (2) specific (that is, made on a specific ground). FRE 103(a)(1). If the judge *sustains* the objection, the answer is not permitted. If the judge *overrules* the objection, an answer is allowed.

Trial judges do not want objections that are long speeches that essentially argue before the jury why the evidence should not be admitted; accordingly, a brief reference to the applicable rule or short statement of the basis for objection is preferred. Judges also do not want to have the trial proceedings repeatedly interrupted by objections after every question when those objections are based on the same reasons. Thus, the rules provide that if a party has objected or made an offer of proof once, they do not need to renew that objection. FRE 103(b). When a witness answers a question so quickly that a party does not have a chance to object, the judge has discretion to entertain the late objection and, if requested, can also strike the witness's answer from the record and tell the jury to disregard it and not consider it during deliberations. Trial judges may make and sustain their own objections to evidence, although they rarely do so in civil cases.

Here is a list of the *standard objections* (along with the Federal Rule that provides the basis for that objection) that parties make when attempting to exclude evidence:

- Irrelevant (FRE 401)
- Unduly prejudicial (FRE 403)
- Improper character evidence (FRE 404)
- Asked and answered
- Assumes facts not in evidence
- Beyond the scope of direct examination (FRE 611)
- Argumentative (FRE 611)
- Leading the witness (FRE 611)
- Calls for speculation (FRE 602)
- Calls for a narrative
- Calls for hearsay (FRE 801)
- Ambiguous
- Lacks a foundation (FRE 902)
- Compound
- Cumulative
- Improper impeachment (FRE 608, 609)

If the party is seeking to *admit* evidence, the party must make an *offer of proof.* Typically, a party asks the judge if they can make an offer of proof, explains what the evidence is (usually, outside the jury's presence), and explains why the evidence is admissible under the rules of evidence. FRE 103(a)(2). If the trial judge sustains the other party's objection to the introduction of the evidence, the evidence is excluded and the proffering party can appeal that ruling. (If the trial judge overrules the objection, the evidence is admitted, and the proffering party got what she wanted, obviating any need to appeal that ruling.) Offers of proof may be made during trial or prior to trial in a motion in limine. The failure to make an offer of proof means that the party's objection to exclusion of this evidence is not preserved for appeal, although that is not an absolute rule in criminal cases.

The judge can quickly rule on these objections or ask for further explanation (including an offer of proof by the party trying to introduce the evidence) at a *sidebar* outside of earshot of the jurors. If the witness has already answered an objectionable question, the opposing party may move to *strike the answer*, and the judge may instruct the jury not to consider the witness's answer.

FRE 103 spells out the rules on how to properly preserve adverse evidentiary rulings for appeal.

RULE 103. RULINGS ON EVIDENCE

(a) Preserving a Claim of Error. A party may claim error in a ruling to admit or exclude evidence only if the error affects a substantial right of the party and:

(1) if the ruling admits evidence, a party, on the record:

(A) timely objects or moves to strike; and

(B) states the specific ground, unless it was apparent from the context; or

(2) if the ruling excludes evidence, a party informs the court of its substance by an offer of proof, unless the substance was apparent from the context.

(b) Not Needing to Renew an Objection or Offer of Proof. Once the court rules definitively on the record—either before or at trial—a party need not renew an objection or offer of proof to preserve a claim of error for appeal.

(c) Court's Statement About the Ruling; Directing an Offer of Proof. The court may make any statement about the character or form of the evidence, the objection made, and the ruling. The court may direct that an offer of proof be made in question-and-answer form.[10]

(d) Preventing the Jury from Hearing Inadmissible Evidence. To the extent practicable, the court must conduct a jury trial so that inadmissible evidence is not suggested to the jury by any means.

(e) Taking Notice of Plain Error. A court may take notice of a plain error affecting a substantial right, even if the claim of error was not properly preserved.

---

10. In this situation, rather than counsel explaining to the judge what the evidence would show, there is an examination of the witness outside the presence of the jury so that the judge can decide whether the evidence should be allowed. If it is allowed, the examination is then repeated for the jury.

An error that was not properly preserved falls into one of two categories. *Forfeited* errors are errors that a party did not properly preserve. *Waived* errors (or *invited* errors) are those rulings that the party knowingly and intelligently requested—often, for tactical reasons.

When a party affirmatively agrees with an evidentiary ruling, the party will be deemed to have waived any objection to that error or invited it. It is *very* difficult if not impossible for a party to attack on appeal an error that is waived or invited.

(b) Was There Evidentiary "Error"?

The purpose of an appeal is not to grade a judge on the evidentiary rulings. Although the Federal Rules often define the boundaries of when evidence is admissible and when it is not, there is plenty of gray area in between. Trial judges are accorded a fair deal of discretion in dealing with that gray area, and a trial judge "errs" only when the judge *abuses that discretion* by making a ruling that constitutes an unreasonable application of the law of evidence to the facts of the case.

(c) Does the Error Warrant Reversal of the Verdict?

Whether an evidentiary error that is properly preserved warrants reversal of the verdict turns on whether it constitutes *harmless error* or *reversible error.* The test that separates the two depends on whether (1) the error is based on a constitutional provision or instead on statute-based law and (2) the underlying case is civil or criminal. When an alleged evidentiary error (of either constitutional or statutory dimension) occurs in a civil case, or when a statute-based evidentiary error occurs in a criminal case, appellate courts ask whether the error in admitting or excluding evidence "affect[ed] a substantial right" of the party complaining about it on appeal. FRE 103(a). Appellate courts will ask: Did this error *matter* to the outcome of the case, or was it so tangential or the evidence supporting the verdict otherwise so overwhelming that the error did not really matter? If the error mattered, it is *reversible error*; if it did not, it is *harmless error.* Where an alleged evidentiary error of constitutional dimension occurs in a criminal case, the error is presumed to be harmful unless the prosecution can prove—*beyond a reasonable doubt*—that the error was harmless (because it did not affect the verdict). *Chapman v. California,* 386 U.S. 18, 24 (1967). This standard is very difficult to meet: If it is not met, the error is reversible error; if it is, the error is harmless error.

Whether an evidentiary error that is forfeited or waived warrants reversal turns on whether it constitutes *plain error,* at least in federal court. Because plain error is defined as an error that "affect[s] a substantial right," plain error is necessarily reversible error. FRE 103(a); Fed. R. Crim. P. 52(b). But appellate courts have *discretion* whether to correct plain errors, so the threshold question is whether an appellate court will exercise that discretion in a particular case. Although they can, appellate courts rarely recognize plain errors in civil cases. *Walker v. Groot,* 867 F.3d 799, 807 (7th Cir. 2007); *Acevedo-Garcia v. Monroig,* 351 F.3d 547, 570 (1st Cir. 2003). In criminal cases, courts are to exercise their discretion to correct plain errors only when the error that is found to be plain "seriously affect[s] the fairness, integrity or public reputation of judicial proceedings." *United States v. Olano,* 507 U.S. 725, 732 (1993), internal quotations omitted.

The following table sets forth the various standards for granting relief for errors with evidentiary rulings and when they apply.

	Preserved	Forfeited	Waived/Invited
Civil cases	Reviewed for *harmless error,* which means the error would likely have affected the outcome	NON-REVIEWABLE, although in theory have power to review for *plain error*	NON-REVIEWABLE
Constitutional error in criminal case	Error is presumptively *reversible error,* although prosecutors may prove harmlessness by showing that the error was harmless beyond a reasonable doubt	Reviewed for *plain error*	Reviewed for *plain error,* but likely treated as issue of ineffective assistance of counsel
Non-constitutional error in criminal case	Reviewed for *harmless error,* which means that the error would likely have affected the outcome	Reviewed for *plain error*	Reviewed for *plain error,* but likely treated as issue of ineffective assistance of counsel

PART C: USING THIS BOOK

With this basic understanding of the litigation and trial process in mind, it is now time to turn to the rules of evidence. We suggest the following approach to learning the law of evidence. As set forth in each chapter:

(1) Read the rule;
(2) Review examples of how the rule is used;
(3) Study the requirements of the rule and issues that arise in its application, and in this regard, the Advisory Committee Notes can often serve as a helpful guide;
(4) Read how a rule was used in a case and the case's clarification of the rule;
(5) Try review problems in this book and the Supplement;
(6) Use diagrams and summary charts to help make your own personal study guide.

This book intentionally focuses chiefly on the Federal Rules of Evidence because these rules are applied in courtrooms across the United States, although there are mentions to other jurisdictions where the evidence rules are different. It focuses not only on how the rules are meant to operate in theory, but also how they work in practice, day in and day out. The pace of trial often leaves little time for lawyers to deliberate over the application of the rules. You can develop the understanding and instincts you need for applying these rules by working through each chapter's problems, as well as the additional problems in the companion Supplement. The focus here is often more practical than theoretical. To explore the more theoretical underpinnings of the Rules of Evidence and whether they achieve their stated goals, see Bennett Capers, *Evidence Without Rules*, 94 Notre Dame. L. Rev. 867 (2019).

In addition, this book addresses the various rules of evidence one at a time. However, in any given proceeding, the presentation of evidence, even with the same witness, may raise multiple issues that interact with one another. Therefore, although you may learn the rules separately, the book's final chapter will show you how the rules can come together during a proceeding. Also, as you learn the rules one at a time, think about the policies those rules implement and how, when those rules combine with others, the differing policies underlying the rules interact.

Review Questions

1. **Suppression hearing.** The court is conducting a suppression hearing, and Prosecutor wants to call an officer to summarize the statements of four witnesses he interviewed. The defense objects because, as we will learn, these are hearsay statements.

   Sustained or overruled?

2. **Motion in limine.** Prior to trial, the defense files a *motion in limine* to preclude Plaintiff from calling an expert. The court holds a hearing and decides to grant the defense's motion. Must the defense renew its objection in front of the jury if the court has given a definitive ruling?

   Yes or no?

3. **Beyond the scope.** Defendant is charged with unlawful transportation of stolen vehicles across state lines.[11] On direct examination, Prosecutor asks a witness about six cars he bought from Defendant in Iowa. The witness testifies to the six purchases. On cross-examination, defense counsel asks the witness about purchases from third parties of other cars beyond the date of the indictment that were not asked about on direct examination. Prosecutor objects.

   Sustained or overruled?

4. **Leading question.** Prosecutor calls her star witness—a coconspirator in the case. Worried that the witness would not come across well to the jury, Prosecutor asks the following question.

11. *See United States v. Lawinski*, 195 F.2d 1 (7th Cir. 1952).

Q: Mr. Snitch, now it was Defendant's idea to put together the drug transaction, correct?

Defense counsel objects.

Sustained or overruled?

5. **Appeal.** During trial, Prosecutor asks the case agent whether she tried to interview Defendant, but Defendant insisted on asserting her Fifth Amendment privilege against self-incrimination. Defense counsel failed to object, but appellate counsel raises the issue on appeal.

Is the appellate court permitted to consider the issue, and if so, under what standard?

Test Your Understanding

To test your understanding of the material in this chapter, turn to the Supplement for additional practice problems.

Chapter 2

Relevance

Perhaps the most important rule of evidence is that evidence must be *relevant* to be admissible. As FRE 402 plainly spells out, "[i]rrelevant evidence is not admissible."

To a great degree, relevance is a matter of common sense. Introducing information that has nothing to do with the case will not help the decision maker in reaching a verdict and can be both misleading and a waste of time. For example, assume that you are deciding whether you should go to law school. Having someone tell you whether green zucchini is better than yellow zucchini is unlikely to help you make your decision. For this reason, the rules of evidence embodying the relevance requirement help ensure that trials are orderly and efficient, which is one of the key goals of the rules of evidence explained in Chapter One.

This chapter discusses the definition of relevance *generally*. Chapters Three and Four set forth the special rules of relevance applicable to specific types of testimonial and documentary evidence, and Chapter Thirteen's discussion of the authentication requirement sets forth the special rules of relevance applicable to documentary and physical evidence.

In general, relevance is a function of two questions. First, is the item of evidence being considered relevant *as a matter of logic*—that is, does that item "advance the ball," and does that particular "ball" matter to this case? Second, even if the item has *some* so-called logical relevance, is that item relevant *as a practical matter*—that is, is the degree to which it advances the ball worth the time and effort it takes at trial to introduce it, and does it risk confusing or misleading the jury? These questions have "practical relevance."

This chapter explains these general rules of relevance. Part A discusses *logical relevance* under FRE 401. Part B then discusses *practical relevance* under FRE 403. The remainder of the chapter deals with more specialized aspects of the relevance rules. Part C discusses when the relevance of an item of evidence depends on the existence (or nonexistence) of some other fact. Because the relevance of the item is conditioned on that other fact, it is known as *conditional relevance.* Part D discusses the *rule of completeness,* which permits a court to allow a party to introduce an otherwise inadmissible portion of a document or conversation after its opponent has introduced some other part—all to guarantee that the relevant and undistorted whole is put before the jury. Part E discusses the admissibility of *probabilistic evidence,* which is evidence aimed at assessing the mathematical probability of a particular fact being true.

PART A: LOGICAL RELEVANCE [FRE 401]

Many issues arise in a case. Every case, civil or criminal, requires that a party prove certain *elements* to win the case. In a criminal case, the prosecutor will have to prove the elements that prove the charged crime(s) beyond a reasonable doubt. In a civil case, the plaintiff will have to prove the elements of the claims by either a preponderance of or by clear and convincing evidence. Even defenses have elements. However, beyond that, evidence may also be relevant because it helps the trier of fact decide what evidence to believe. Such evidence is considered *credibility evidence.* Thus, to start your analysis of relevance, you need to determine what is at issue in a case and how it will be proved or disproved. Once that is done, arguing relevance is a matter of describing for the court how the evidence being offered tends to prove something at issue in the case.

For example, let us say that a prosecutor charges a defendant with bank robbery. The defendant wishes to put on an alibi defense by calling his girlfriend as a witness to say that the two of them were out bowling. This evidence is relevant because (1) an alibi is a defense to the charge because, if established, it means that the defendant was not the perpetrator, and (2) the girlfriend's testimony helps prove that defense because it constitutes evidence that the defendant was not at the bank at the time it was robbed.

As this example illustrates, whether a particular item of evidence is relevant turns on two closely related considerations. The first consideration asks what the evidence is meant to prove. Is it meant to prove an element or a defense or perhaps to try to get the jury to believe or disbelieve a witness or other piece of evidence? For instance, if the defendant called a witness to testify that his favorite type of ice cream is rocky road, that fact is not relevant because it has nothing to do with the crime of bank robbery. Often, courts address this first consideration by asking whether the evidence is *material* to any issue in the case. The second consideration asks whether the proffered evidence—assuming that it is meant to prove some material element or defense or question of credibility—actually helps prove it. For instance, if the defendant's girlfriend testified that she and defendant spent Thursday night bowling, but the bank robbery happened on a Saturday morning, the girlfriend's testimony is not relevant because it does not help prove the alibi. Often, courts address this second consideration by asking whether the evidence is *probative.*

1. Is It Material?

In determining whether an item of evidence is material to the issues in a case, it is critical to know what those issues are:

- *The elements the plaintiff or prosecution must prove.* Every case, civil or criminal, requires a party with the burden of proof to prove certain *elements* to win its case. Evidence that is probative to prove or disprove any of these elements satisfies the materiality requirement.
- *The elements of any defenses.* If the defendant seeks to establish any defenses (such as an alibi defense in a criminal case or the comparative negligence

of the other driver in a personal injury case), evidence that is probative to prove or disprove the elements of those defenses also satisfies the materiality requirement.

- *Credibility of witnesses and hearsay declarants.* Whether the witnesses who testify at trial are telling the truth or instead lying or shading the truth is always material to a case. The same is true as to persons whose out-of-court statements are properly admitted at trial.

Thus, to know whether a particular item of evidence is material, you need to determine what is at issue in a case and how it will be proved or disproved. Thus, materiality is case dependent. The same fact might be material in one case, but not another. Thus, a defendant's wealth is not relevant to prove he committed a murder, but may be relevant in a civil case where he is being sued for wrongful death and the plaintiffs are seeking punitive damages. Arguing materiality is a matter of describing for the court how the evidence being offered tends to prove something at issue in a case.

Does evidence lose its materiality if the opposing party decides not to dispute the fact that the evidence tends to prove? Under the Federal Rules of Evidence, the answer is "no."[1] The Advisory Committee Notes specify that the evidence does not need to be directed at an issue "in dispute." Thus, for example, even if it is undisputed that the defendant signed the bounced check, the prosecution can still put on evidence of that fact if it makes it more probable that the defendant is responsible for check kiting. But this rule is not universal. In some states, such as California, relevant evidence is limited to evidence that goes to an issue "in dispute," Cal. Evid. Code § 210.

Example

Assume that the defense in a criminal case has evidence that the prosecution's witness is lying because he got a deal on another case. Defendant wants to introduce evidence showing that the witness is a liar. This evidence is relevant because it helps disprove the case against Defendant. For a discussion of the rules governing how such "impeachment evidence" is to be admitted, see Chapter Eleven.

2. *Is It Probative?*

In determining whether an item is probative of the fact at issue in the proceeding, one needs to know: How probative does that item have to be to satisfy this part of the definition of relevance? The drafters of the Federal Rules of Evidence had a number of possible definitions available to them:

---

1. The same rule is followed in Illinois, Florida, New York, and Texas. Ill. R. Evid. 401; Fl. Stat. § 90.401; *People v. Stevens,* 76 N.Y.2d 833, 835 (N.Y. 1990); Tex. R. Evid 401.

(1) *An item of evidence is probative only if that item, by itself, proves the fact at issue is more probably true than not.* This is a very high standard because it would bar evidence that otherwise might, in combination with other evidence, help prove issues in the case.

(2) *An item of evidence is probative, even if it does not by itself more probably than not prove the fact at issue, only if it is the best evidence available to prove that act.* This standard has several problems. For example, how do you know what is the best evidence in a case until the evidence is presented? Also, wouldn't this strict standard bar from consideration valuable evidence that is simply limited in how it helps prove a case?

(3) *An item of evidence is probative only if the judge, as a gatekeeper, first finds that the evidence is sufficiently probative.* The problem with this standard is that it shifts much of the decision making in a case from the jury to the judge. Although the rules of evidence reflect a certain reservation in trusting jurors to properly consider all evidence that the parties may want to present in a case, there is a concern with the court screening too much of the evidence from the jury.

(4) *An item of evidence is probative as long as a jury could conclude that it makes the fact at issue more or less probable than it would be without the evidence.* This approach to relevance is the most lenient. All a party must show is that the proffered evidence is a "brick in the wall" or "part of the puzzle" that will prove a case. As long as it "moves the needle" a little, it is considered to be probative. Under this approach, the evidence need not be the most important evidence or better than other evidence offered in the case.

The Federal Rules of Evidence selected the fourth option:

FRE 401. Test for Relevant Evidence

Evidence is relevant if:

(a) it has any tendency to make a fact more or less probable than it would be without the evidence; and

(b) the fact is of consequence in determining the action.

Excerpts from Advisory Committee Notes to FRE 401

- Relevancy is not an inherent characteristic of any item of evidence but exists only as a relation between an item of evidence and a matter properly provable in the case.
- The fact to be proved may be ultimate, intermediate, or evidentiary; it matters not, so long as it is of consequence in the determination of the action.
- The fact to which the evidence is directed need not be in dispute.

The Advisory Committee Notes confirm FRE 401's text. On the one hand, the Notes recognize that the courtroom is a theater in which the presentation of a case may be enriched by photographs, physical evidence, and other demonstrative evidence that help tell the story of the case. Such evidence may be helpful, even if other evidence can, and may, also be used to prove the case. What is more, because "[i]t is not to be supposed that every witness can make a home run," the Notes reject the more stringent standards for relevance as "unworkable and unrealistic."

Whether evidence is probative turns on whether the evidence tends to prove or disprove the fact *to any degree*. For these purposes, it does not matter if the fact might be explained away or is far from conclusive. As long as it moves the proverbial needle—even a little bit—either way, it is probative. For example, is the fact that law enforcement investigated other suspects besides the charged defendant probative of the defendant's innocence? The courts have taken various approaches. Some jurisdictions, such as California, deem such evidence to be probative only if there is evidence—beyond "motive or opportunity to commit the crime"—that "links the third person either directly or circumstantially to the actual perpetration of the crime." The federal courts have taken a broader view and will deem "someone else may have done it" evidence to be probative even if it consists solely of evidence that there were similar crimes in the same geographical area and same time frame at a time when the defendant could not have committed those crimes, without requiring the identification of a specific third person or evidence tying that specific third person to the perpetration of the charged crime.

Examples

1. Defendant is charged with bank robbery. Prosecutors will have to prove that Defendant was at the bank and took the money. They offer evidence that his car was seen pulling into the parking lot of the bank a few minutes before it was robbed by a masked assailant. Although this testimony alone may not be sufficient to prove the case, it is a piece of the puzzle that can help prove the case. Another way to think about it is that it is another "brick in the wall" that the prosecution is constructing to prove its case.
2. Defendant is charged with embezzling funds. Prosecutors offer evidence that Defendant had recently fallen on financial hard times. Although needing money doesn't necessarily prove that Defendant embezzled funds, the trier of fact may be asked to make the inference that it was Defendant who took the funds because she was desperate.

3. Direct Versus Circumstantial Evidence

Although television shows often make an issue of it, the probativeness of an item of evidence does *not* turn on whether it directly proves a fact at issue (*direct evidence*) or instead proves that fact indirectly and inferentially (*circumstantial evidence*).

In reality, circumstantial evidence is far more prevalent than direct evidence, especially when it comes to proving a person's intent. A person who kills another person rarely pens a diary entry the night before a killing saying, "I intend to kill my archenemy tomorrow." Instead, the defendant's intent to kill is proven by the manner of the killing and the possible motive for the killing. From the accused's intense dislike of the victim, the jury can infer that the accused was more likely the person who committed the killing and that he did so intentionally. Similarly, the killing itself is usually proven circumstantially. Unless you have a video of the murder, an eyewitness to the killing, or a confession, the evidence will largely be circumstantial—someone can testify that the defendant was present at the location of the murder around the time it happened, someone can testify the defendant's DNA was found on the murder weapon, or someone can testify that the defendant had a motive.

* * *

Because the threshold for relevance under FRE 401 is very low, courts are usually reluctant to exclude evidence as "irrelevant." As long as the party proffering the evidence can show that the evidence is probative of some issue being decided, it is likely to be deemed logically relevant.

Relevance is a *necessary* condition for admissibility, but it is not sufficient by itself. This rule is embodied in FRE 402.

FRE 402. General Admissibility of Relevant Evidence

Relevant evidence is admissible unless any of the following provides otherwise:

- the United States Constitution;
- a federal statute;
- these rules; or
- other rules prescribed by the Supreme Court.

Irrelevant evidence is not admissible.

Not all evidence has the same degree of logical relevance; some evidence is *very* probative, and other evidence is marginally so. Fortunately, the rules of evidence grant judges the means to keep out evidence that is only tangentially relevant or may, for other reasons, be inappropriate for admission in a case. Perhaps the proffered evidence is too inflammatory; perhaps it is cumulative of other evidence already presented. Perhaps the proffered evidence will actually confuse the jury or take so long that its marginal probative value is eclipsed by the need to keep a trial on track. Thus, in addition to logical relevance, evidence must satisfy the requirement of "practical relevance" under FRE 403. As you will see, "what Rule 401 giveth, Rule 403 can taketh away."

PART B: DISCRETION TO EXCLUDE RELEVANT EVIDENCE [FRE 403]

Although FRE 401 opens the door widely for the admissibility of evidence even if it has marginal relevance to a case, the drafters were keenly aware that evidence can have such little relevance that its usefulness in proving a fact can sometimes be greatly outweighed by factors favoring its exclusion.

Examples

1. What if the jury has heard eight witnesses testify to the same information? The party wants to call eight more. The judge has the discretion to exclude these additional witnesses unless there is some reason that their testimony would be qualitatively different from the prior witnesses.
2. What if a trial involves a shooting? Prosecutor has many gruesome pictures of the victim. No one really disputes that the victim is dead, but Prosecutor wants to offer color pictures of the fatal injuries. Defendant is afraid that the jurors will be so inflamed by the photos that they will set aside their reason and simply want to convict someone of the horrible crime. The judge has the discretion to limit what kind of photos and how many photos will be admitted in an effort to accommodate both sides' interests.

Even though the evidence offered in both examples has some tendency to make a point more probable than not, its value may be outweighed by other factors expressed in FRE 403.

FRE 403. Excluding Relevant Evidence for Prejudice, Confusion, Waste of Time, or Other Reasons

The court may exclude relevant evidence if its probative value is substantially outweighed by a danger of one or more of the following: unfair prejudice, confusing the issues, misleading the jury, undue delay, wasting time, or needlessly presenting cumulative evidence.

Excerpt from Advisory Committee Notes to FRE 403

- "Unfair prejudice" within its context means an undue tendency to suggest decision on an improper basis, commonly, though not necessarily, an emotional one.

The case of *Langenbau v. Med-Trans Corp.* is an illustration of the approach courts take in deciding whether to admit evidence that may have logical relevance under FRE 401, but is excludable under FRE 403.

Langenbau v. Med-Trans Corp.

167 F.Supp.3d 983 (N.D. Iowa 2016)

STRAND, Judge.

FACTS

On January 2, 2013, an air ambulance helicopter crashed in central Iowa just minutes after takeoff. At the time of the crash, weather forecasts for the area included a potential for icy conditions, in which the helicopter was not certified to fly. All three members of the helicopter crew—a pilot, a nurse, and a paramedic—were killed in the crash. The survivors of the nurse have brought this case, involving negligence claims, against the owner and operator of the air ambulance service. [T]he plaintiffs have requested that the jury be allowed to view the wreckage of the helicopter.

1. Arguments of the parties

The plaintiffs argue that a federal court has the inherent power to permit a jury to view places or objects outside of the courtroom. They argue that there is no better evidence of the nature and extent of the crash, the dynamics of impact, and the physical trauma suffered to the occupants than the helicopter wreckage itself and that photos and descriptions are a distant second. They argue that the facts that the wreckage will not fit in the courtroom and that a view of the wreckage tends to prove facts in question more conclusively than other evidence are not valid objections to permitting the jurors to view the wreckage.

In response, Med-Trans argues that the plaintiffs have failed to meet their burden to show that viewing the helicopter wreckage will aid the jury in resolving any disputed issues of fact in this case or provide anything of greater evidentiary value than the evidence that can be presented in the courtroom. Indeed, they contend that the plaintiffs have not even identified or substantiated any factual issue, theory, or other dispute that viewing the wreckage might resolve, where there is no dispute among the parties, their experts, or the National Transportation Safety Board (NTSB) that maintenance and mechanical issues did not cause this crash. Med-Trans argues that, consequently, the disputed areas of fact in this case involve piloting and procedures, on which a view of the wreckage has slight, if any, relevance, and certainly no more probative value than the expert testimony and other evidence that can be presented in the courtroom. Med-Trans argues that, under these circumstances, viewing the wreckage is unduly expensive, burdensome, time-consuming, and inconvenient.

2. Applicable standards

Rule 401 of the Federal Rules of Evidence defines relevant evidence as evidence that "(a) . . . has any tendency to make a fact more or less probable than it would be without the evidence; and (b) the fact is of consequence in determining the action." Rule 402 provides that relevant evidence is generally admissible, but irrelevant evidence is not. Rule 403 provides for exclusion of even relevant evidence on various grounds, as follows:

> The court may exclude relevant evidence if its probative value is substantially outweighed by a danger of one or more of the following: unfair prejudice, confusing the issues, misleading the jury, undue delay, wasting time, or needlessly presenting cumulative evidence.

Fed. R. Evid. 403. The Eighth Circuit "give[s] great deference to the district court's Rule 403 determinations."

[U]nder Rule 403, the [challenged evidence's] probative value must be *substantially* outweighed by *unfair* prejudice. "Evidence is not unfairly prejudicial because it tends to prove guilt, but because it tends to encourage the jury to find guilt from improper reasoning. Whether there was unfair prejudice depends on whether there was an undue tendency to suggest decision on an improper basis."

3. Analysis

Here, while I clearly have the discretion to allow a jury view of the wreckage of the air ambulance helicopter, I conclude, first, that such a view has only slight probative value. See Fed. R. Evid. 401. As Med-Trans points out, the plaintiffs have explained only in vague terms the supposed relevance and probative value of a view of the helicopter wreckage, pointing to "the nature and extent of the crash, the dynamics of impact, and the physical trauma suffered to the occupants."

[Moreover], whatever probative value a view of the wreckage might have is vastly outweighed by the potential waste of time, confusion of the issues, misleading the jury, delay, logistical difficulties, and the needless presentation of cumulative evidence, which are pertinent factors under both Rule 403 and case law standards specifically pertaining to a jury view. Where the plaintiffs have identified only vaguely the issues on which a view of the wreckage might be probative, the jurors would likely be confused or misled about the purpose of viewing the wreckage and would likely give undue weight to evidence involving so much time, logistical difficulties, and travel outside of the courtroom. Indeed, the plaintiffs have not demonstrated why evidence that can be presented in the courtroom, including expert testimony and photographs, some of which are already in the record, will not be more than sufficient to resolve the issues that they claim a view of the wreckage will help resolve, if those issues are relevant. There is also serious potential for Rule 403 "prejudice" from such a view, as viewing wreckage—particularly when it otherwise has, at best, slight evidentiary value—might encourage a damages award on the improper basis of an emotional response. I have concerns that this is the true purpose of the request for a view of the helicopter wreckage, here, in light of the poor demonstration of the probative value of such a view to any matter actually in dispute and relevant to disposition of the plaintiffs' claims.

The plaintiffs' motion for jury view of subject helicopter wreckage is denied.

Most relevancy and FRE 403 objections arise during trial as evidence is offered, so the judge may not have the benefit of pretrial briefing on the issues. In this situation, the party objecting to relevant evidence must argue why the probative value of the evidence is substantially outweighed by the considerations weighing against its admission into evidence. Those considerations include:

- *Unfair prejudice.* The most commonly asserted basis for excluding evidence under FRE 403 is unfair prejudice. To be excluded on this basis, it is not enough that the evidence is prejudicial to the objector. Almost every piece of evidence a party objects to is *prejudicial* to that party; if it were not, the party likely would not be objecting. FRE 403 therefore looks to whether the evidence is *unfairly* prejudicial. To be unfairly prejudicial, the Advisory Committee Notes indicate, the evidence must "have an undue tendency to suggest decision on an improper basis, commonly, though not necessarily, an emotional one."
- *Confusing the issues or misleading the jury.* These considerations come into play when the proffered evidence is probative as to more than one fact and at least one of those facts is not material to the case at issue such that its admission may end up diverting the jury's attention away from the material issues the jury needs to decide.
- *Undue delay, wasting time, or needlessly presenting cumulative evidence.* These considerations ask: Is the probative value of this evidence worth the time it will take at trial to prove it? For instance, as discussed in Chapter Three, a defendant's prior conduct in distributing cocaine may be probative to rebut the defense he offers in a pending drug distribution case that he thought he was selling powdered sugar. But how long will it take to prove this prior conduct? If he was previously convicted of distributing cocaine, introducing the conviction will not take much time. But if the prior drug dealing is to be proven by witnesses who saw him do it, the result may be a "trial within a trial" that may take up a considerable amount of trial time.

Although FRE 403 empowers trial judges to exclude otherwise relevant evidence based on any of these considerations, FRE 403 tips the balance decidedly in favor of admitting this evidence because exclusion under FRE 403 is appropriate only if the probative value of the evidence is *substantially outweighed* by these other considerations. In other words, the probative value of the evidence is accorded greater weight when balancing it against the other considerations. These considerations have to greatly outweigh probative value to justify excluding the evidence:

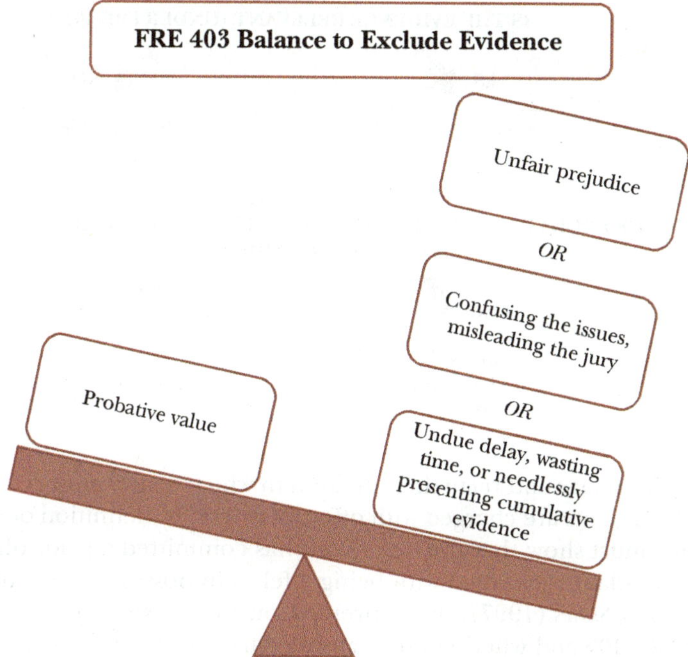

Ultimately, trial judges have *broad discretion* in conducting this balance. That makes sense, because there are many cases where the balance will tip in different directions depending on the trial judge's assessment of the probative value of the item of evidence (is it greatly probative or only mildly so?) and of the unfair prejudice (is it slight or great?).

Trial judges also have broad discretion in how they mitigate the harmful aspects of evidence. FRE 403 is not an all-or-nothing statute. A trial court may exclude a piece of evidence entirely, but it may also decide to admit only a portion of the proffered evidence (four crime scene photos rather than 16), to modify how the evidence is to be presented (requiring the photos to be black and white or of a particular size), or to give an instruction limiting the jury's consideration of the evidence to specific purposes. Thus, although the drafters took the approach that as much evidence as possible should be considered by the trier of fact, they tempered that approach by giving the court discretion to limit the presentation of evidence when necessary to ensure the fairness of the trial.

FRE 403's evaluation and balancing look at the probative value and competing considerations for each piece of evidence proffered (and challenged on this ground). In some circumstances, the rules of evidence have effectively undertaken this balancing in advance—and for an entire category of evidence. We discuss these categorical rules—namely, the rules governing the admission of character evidence and a handful of other specific categories—in Chapters Three and Four, respectively.

The interaction between FRE 403's practical relevance and FRE 401's logical relevance is graphically illustrated as follows:

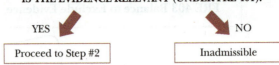

STEP #1
IS THE EVIDENCE RELEVANT (UNDER FRE 401)?

YES — NO

Proceed to Step #2 | Inadmissible

STEP #2
IS THE PROBATIVE VALUE OF THE EVIDENCE SUBSTANTIALLY OUTWEIGHED BY FRE 403 CONSIDERATIONS?

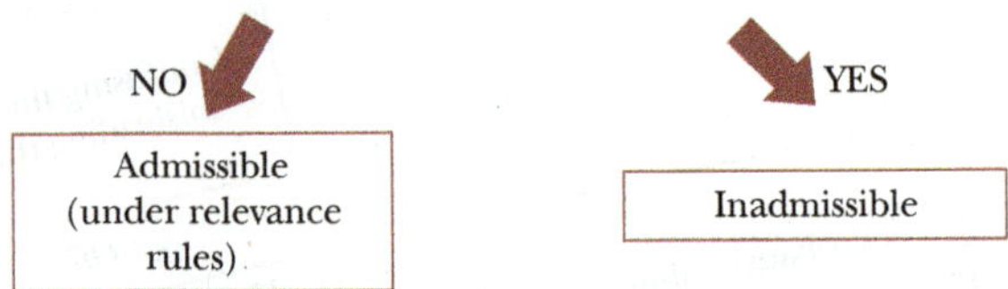

One particular and recurring situation in which courts must consider FRE 403 is when defendants are charged with offenses where, by definition of the crime, the prosecutor must show that the defendant has committed a prior offense, such as when a defendant is charged with being a felon in possession of a firearm. In *Old Chief v. United States* (1997), the Supreme Court discussed the application of FRE 401 and FRE 403 and whether an opposing party's stipulation to a fact makes that evidence "irrelevant" and, if not, how the stipulation might affect the balancing under FRE 403.

Old Chief v. United States

519 U.S. 172 (1997)

JUSTICE SOUTER delivered the opinion of the Court.

In 1993, petitioner, Old Chief, was arrested after a fracas involving at least one gunshot. [Defendant was charged with assault with a dangerous weapon and using a firearm in a crime of violence. He was also charged with being a convicted felon in possession of a firearm, in violation of 18 U.S.C. § 922(g)(1). A felony is an offense punishable by more than one year in prison. Old Chief's prior felony conviction was for assault causing bodily injury. In order to prevent the jury from hearing about his prior assault, Old Chief offered to stipulate that he had been convicted of a prior felony.]

Before trial, he moved for an order requiring the Government "to refrain from mentioning [any evidence] regarding the prior criminal convictions of the Defendant, *except* to state that the Defendant has been convicted of a crime punishable by imprisonment exceeding one (1) year." He said that revealing the name and nature of his prior assault conviction would unfairly tax the jury's capacity to hold the Government to its burden of proof [and that his] offer to stipulate to the fact of the prior conviction rendered evidence of the name and nature of the offense inadmissible under Rule 403 of the Federal Rules of Evidence, the danger being that unfair prejudice from that evidence would substantially outweigh its probative value.

The Assistant United States Attorney refused to join in a stipulation, insisting on his right to prove his case his own way, and the District Court agreed. At trial, over renewed objection, the Government introduced the order of judgment and commitment for Old Chief's prior conviction. This document disclosed that on December 18, 1988, he "did knowingly and unlawfully assault Rory Dean Fenner, said assault resulting in serious bodily injury," for which Old Chief was sentenced to five years' imprisonment. The jury found Old Chief guilty on all counts, and he appealed.

[The Ninth Circuit held that "the district court did not abuse its discretion by allowing the prosecution to introduce evidence of Old Chief's prior conviction to prove that element of the unlawful possession charge."]

II

A

As a threshold matter, there is Old Chief's erroneous argument that the name of his prior offense as contained in the record of conviction is irrelevant to the prior-conviction element, and for that reason inadmissible under Rule 402 of the Federal Rules of Evidence. Rule 401 defines relevant evidence as having "any tendency to make the existence of any fact that is of consequence to the determination of the action more probable or less probable than it would be without the evidence." To be sure, the fact that Old Chief's prior conviction was for assault resulting in serious bodily injury rather than, say, for theft was not itself an ultimate fact, as if the statute had specifically required proof of injurious assault. But its demonstration was a step on one evidentiary route to the ultimate fact, since it served to place Old Chief within a particular subclass of offenders for whom firearms possession is outlawed. A documentary record of the conviction for that named offense was thus relevant evidence in making Old Chief's [felon] status more probable than it would have been without the evidence.

Nor was its evidentiary relevance under *Rule 401* affected by the availability of alternative proofs of the element to which it went, such as an admission by Old Chief that he had been convicted of a crime "punishable by imprisonment for a term exceeding one year" within the meaning of the statute. The 1972 Advisory Committee Notes to *Rule 401* make this point directly:

> "The fact to which the evidence is directed need not be in dispute. While situations will arise which call for the exclusion of evidence offered to prove a point conceded by the opponent, the ruling should be made on the basis of such considerations as waste of time and undue prejudice (see Rule 403), rather than under any general requirement that evidence is admissible only if directed to matters in dispute."

B

The principal issue is the scope of a trial judge's discretion under Rule 403, which authorizes exclusion of relevant evidence when its "probative value is substantially outweighed by the danger of unfair prejudice, confusion of the issues, or misleading the jury, or by considerations of undue delay, waste of time, or needless presentation of cumulative evidence." Old Chief relies on the danger of unfair prejudice.

The term "unfair prejudice," as to a criminal defendant, speaks to the capacity of some concededly relevant evidence to lure the factfinder into declaring guilt on a ground different from proof specific to the offense charged. "'Unfair prejudice' within its context means an undue tendency to suggest decision on an improper basis, commonly, though not necessarily, an emotional one." Advisory Committee's Notes on Fed. Rule Evid. 403.

Such improper grounds certainly include the one that Old Chief points to here: generalizing a defendant's earlier bad act into bad character and taking that as raising the odds that he did the later bad act now charged. As then-Judge Breyer put it, "Although . . . 'propensity evidence' is relevant, the risk that a jury will convict for crimes other than those charged—or that, uncertain of guilt, it will convict anyway because a bad person deserves punishment—creates a prejudicial effect that outweighs ordinary relevance."

In dealing with the specific problem raised by § 922(g)(1) and its prior-conviction element, there can be no question that evidence of the name or nature of the prior offense generally carries a risk of unfair prejudice to the defendant. That risk will vary from case to case, . . . but will be substantial whenever the official record offered by the Government would be arresting enough to lure a juror into a sequence of bad character reasoning. Where a prior conviction was for a gun crime or one similar to other charges in a pending case the risk of unfair prejudice would be especially obvious, and Old Chief sensibly worried that the prejudicial effect of his prior assault conviction, significant enough with respect to the current gun charges alone, would take on added weight from the related assault charge against him.

The District Court was also presented with alternative, relevant, admissible evidence of the prior conviction by Old Chief's offer to stipulate, evidence necessarily subject to the District Court's consideration on the motion to exclude the record offered by the Government. Although Old Chief's formal offer to stipulate was, strictly, to enter a formal agreement with the Government to be given to the jury, even without the Government's acceptance his proposal amounted to an offer to admit that the prior-conviction element was satisfied, and a defendant's admission is, of course, good evidence.

Old Chief's proffered admission would, in fact, have been not merely relevant but seemingly conclusive evidence of the element. [A]lthough the name of the prior offense may have been technically relevant, it addressed no detail in the definition of the prior-conviction element that would not have been covered by the stipulation or admission. Logic, then, seems to side with Old Chief.

There is, however, one more question to be considered before deciding whether Old Chief's offer was to supply evidentiary value at least equivalent to what the Government's own evidence carried. In arguing that the stipulation or admission would not have carried equivalent value, the Government invokes the familiar, standard rule that the prosecution is entitled to prove its case by evidence of its own choice, or, more exactly, that a criminal defendant may not stipulate or admit his way out of the full evidentiary force of the case as the Government chooses to present it.

This is unquestionably true as a general matter. The "fair and legitimate weight" of conventional evidence showing individual thoughts and acts amounting to a crime reflects the fact that making a case with testimony and tangible things not only satisfies the formal definition of an offense, but tells a colorful story with descriptive richness. Evidence thus has force beyond any linear scheme of reasoning, and as its pieces come together a narrative gains momentum, with power not only to support conclusions but to sustain the willingness of jurors to draw the inferences, whatever they may be, necessary to reach an honest verdict. This persuasive power of the concrete and particular is often essential to the capacity of jurors to satisfy the obligations that the law places on them. Jury duty is usually unsought and sometimes resisted, and it may be as difficult for one juror suddenly to face the findings that can send another human being to prison, as it is for another to hold out conscientiously for acquittal. When a juror's duty does seem hard, the evidentiary account of what a defendant has thought and done can accomplish what no set of abstract statements ever could, not just to prove a fact but to establish its human significance, and so to implicate the law's moral underpinnings and a juror's obligation to sit in judgment. Thus, the prosecution may fairly seek to place its evidence before the jurors, as much to tell a story of guiltiness as to support an inference of guilt, to convince the jurors that a guilty verdict would be morally reasonable as much as to point to the discrete elements of a defendant's legal fault.

But there is something even more to the prosecution's interest in resisting efforts to replace the evidence of its choice with admissions and stipulations, for beyond the power of conventional evidence to support allegations and give life to the moral underpinnings of the law's claims, there lies the need for evidence in all its particularity to satisfy the jurors' expectations about what proper proof should be. "If [jurors'] expectations are not satisfied, triers of fact may penalize the party who disappoints them by drawing a negative inference against that party."

In sum, the accepted rule that the prosecution is entitled to prove its case free from any defendant's option to stipulate the evidence away rests on good sense. A syllogism is not a story, and a naked proposition in a courtroom may be no match for the robust evidence that would be used to prove it. People who hear a story interrupted by gaps of abstraction may be puzzled at the missing chapters, and jurors asked to rest a momentous decision on the story's truth can feel put upon at being asked to take responsibility knowing that more could be said than they have heard. A convincing tale can be told with economy, but when economy becomes a break in the natural sequence of narrative evidence, an assurance that the missing link is really there is never more than second best.

This recognition that the prosecution with its burden of persuasion needs evidentiary depth to tell a continuous story has, however, virtually no application when the point at issue is a defendant's legal status. As in this case, the choice of evidence for such an element is usually not between eventful narrative and abstract proposition, but between propositions of slightly varying abstraction, either a record saying that conviction for some crime occurred at a certain time or a statement admitting the same thing without naming the particular offense. The most the jury needs to know is that the conviction admitted by the defendant falls within the class of crimes that Congress thought should bar a convict from possessing a gun, and this point may be made readily in a defendant's admission and underscored in the court's jury instructions.

Given these peculiarities of the element of felony-convict status, there is no cognizable difference between the evidentiary significance of an admission and of the legitimately probative component of the official record the prosecution would prefer to place in evidence. For purposes of the Rule 403 weighing of the probative against the prejudicial, the functions of the competing evidence are distinguishable only by the risk inherent in the one and wholly absent from the other. In this case, as in any other in which the prior conviction is for an offense likely to support conviction on some improper ground, the only reasonable conclusion was that the risk of unfair prejudice did substantially outweigh the discounted probative value of the record of conviction, and it was an abuse of discretion to admit the record when an admission was available.

The judgment is reversed.

JUSTICE O'CONNOR, with whom THE CHIEF JUSTICE, JUSTICE SCALIA, and JUSTICE THOMAS join, dissenting.

The Court today announces a rule that misapplies Federal Rule of Evidence 403 and upsets, without explanation, longstanding precedent regarding criminal prosecutions. I do not agree that the Government's introduction of evidence that reveals the name and basic nature of a defendant's prior felony conviction in a prosecution brought under 18 U.S.C. § 922(g)(1) "unfairly" prejudices the defendant within the meaning. Perhaps petitioner's case was damaged when the jury discovered that he previously had committed a felony and heard the name of his crime. But I cannot agree with the Court that it was *unfairly* prejudicial for the Government to establish an essential element of its case against petitioner with direct proof of his prior conviction.

The structure of § 922(g)(1) itself shows that Congress envisioned jurors' learning the name and basic nature of the defendant's prior offense. Even more fundamentally, in our system of justice, a person is not simply convicted of "a crime" or "a felony." Rather, he is found guilty of a specified felony. The name and basic nature of petitioner's crime are inseparable from the fact of his earlier conviction and were therefore admissible to prove petitioner's guilt. Any incremental harm resulting from proving the name or basic nature of the prior felony can be properly mitigated by limiting jury instructions.

A jury is as likely to be puzzled by the "missing chapter" resulting from a defendant's stipulation to his prior felony conviction as it would be by the defendant's conceding any other element of the crime. The jury may wonder why it has not been told the name of the crime, or it may question why the defendant's firearm possession was illegal, given the tradition of lawful gun ownership in this country.

I cannot agree that it "unfairly" prejudices a defendant for the Government to prove his prior conviction with evidence that reveals the name or basic nature of his past crime. Like it or not, Congress chose to make a defendant's prior criminal conviction one of the two elements of the § 922(g)(1) offense. [T]he Government may not be forced to accept a defendant's concession to an element of a charged offense as proof of that element. I respectfully dissent.

As noted in *Old Chief,* evidence is not automatically irrelevant simply because the opposing party is willing to stipulate to it. However, a stipulation may reduce the probative value of the evidence and thus shift the balance between the probative value of that evidence and its and prejudicial effect under FRE 403.

Another recurring situation in which FRE 403 issues come up is in deciding whether to admit evidence of a defendant's "flight." Evidence that a defendant has fled or attempted to flee from a crime scene is relevant to show her *consciousness of guilt*—that is, that she was aware that what she did was wrong and was thus seeking to avoid punishment for it. But is evidence of flight too prejudicial under FRE 403? Courts make this determination on a case-by-case basis, recognizing that flight has a relatively "weak" probative value (because there is reason to question the wisdom that "the wicked flee when no man pursueth, but the righteous are as bold as a lion") but also recognizing that consciousness-of-guilt evidence is rarely substantially more prejudicial than probative. *See United States v. Dillon*, 870 F.2d 1125, 1126-27 (6th Cir. 1989); *United States v. Cody*, 498 F.3d 582, 591-92 (6th Cir. 2007) (discussing this analysis).

Review Questions

1. **Rap song.** Defendant is charged with murder. On his social media site, Defendant has posted lyrics for a gangster rap song that closely parallel the prosecution's allegations of Defendant's commission of the murder. Defendant objects to introduction of the lyrics.
2. **Bank fraud.** Defendant is charged with bank fraud. He calls several character witnesses to testify that he is an honest person who, in their opinion, would never engage in deceitful conduct. After calling six character witnesses, Defendant seeks to call *TIME* magazine's "Person of the Year" winner. The prosecutor objects.
3. **Gym jeopardy.** Plaintiff sues her neighborhood gym after she suffers an injury exercising on its equipment. She has witnesses who will testify how they heard the machine crash down on her at the time of the accident. Defendant-gym is willing to stipulate that Plaintiff injured herself on the equipment. The defense is assumption of the risk. Should the witnesses be allowed to testify?
4. **Autopsy photo.** Defendant is charged with murder. Prosecutor seeks to admit the following photograph. Defendant objects, "403"!

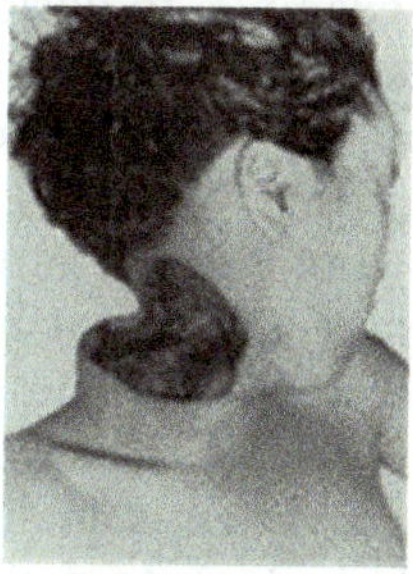

a. Does it matter if the cause of death is contested or uncontested?
b. Does it matter if the mechanism of death (for example, a machete, an axe) is contested or uncontested?

PART C: CONDITIONAL RELEVANCE [FRE 104]

Sometimes, evidence is relevant only if other evidence will be offered that links the evidence to the issues at hand. For example, assume that the defendant is charged with possessing cocaine. Prosecutors call a narcotics officer to testify that her drug-sniffing canine alerted on two suitcases at the airport and that a subsequent residue test showed that those suitcases had contained cocaine. That testimony is only relevant if the suitcases can be connected to the defendant. But the rules of evidence do not require the evidence connecting the defendant to the suitcase to be admitted at trial *prior to* the evidence of the canine alert. Instead, under FRE 104(b), the court may allow the officer's testimony on the condition that there later will be evidence presented linking the defendant to the suitcases. Because we want judges to have the maximum flexibility in the order of the presentation of evidence, evidence may be admitted even though its relevance is conditioned on other evidence.

FRE 104. Preliminary Questions

(b) Relevance That Depends on a Fact. When the relevance of evidence depends on whether a fact exists, proof must be introduced sufficient to support a finding that the fact does exist. The court may admit the proposed evidence on the condition that the proof be introduced later.

Closely related to the issue of conditional relevance are preliminary facts. The rules of evidence in many instances require that certain prerequisites be met before evidence may be admitted. For example, to decide whether a statement qualifies under the coconspirator exception to the hearsay rule, there must be a preliminary determination that the statement was made by a coconspirator during the course of and in furtherance of the conspiracy. FRE 801(d)(2). Or, to allow an expert to testify, the court will need to preliminarily determine whether the facts show that the witness can qualify as an expert. FRE 702. Unless these prerequisites are met, the evidence is relevant—but still not admissible.

At times, these preliminary questions of admissibility are entrusted to the trial judge alone (as it is with whether a witness is qualified to testify, whether a privilege exists, or whether evidence is admissible). In such instances, the judge must assess whether any preliminary facts are proven by a preponderance of the evidence, FRE 104(a); *Huddleston v. United States*, 485 U.S. 681 (1988). For example, a trial judge deciding whether a witness is competent to testify will decide whether, by a preponderance of the evidence, the witness's mental illness is so severe as to impede the witness's ability to perceive or recollect the subject of his proffered testimony. Other times, the preliminary questions of admissibility are entrusted to the jury. In such instances, the trial judge's role is simply to assess whether there is sufficient evidence for a reasonable jury to find the preliminary facts to be true by a preponderance of the evidence, FRE 104(b); *United States v. Beechum*, 582 F.2d 898, 913 (5th Cir. 1978). Thus, a trial judge deciding whether a telephone call came from the defendant will decide whether there is sufficient evidence for a reasonable jury to find that defendant's voice was on the other end of the line, even if the evidence on that point is disputed.

No matter what the division, however, it is important to realize that if there are preliminary questions of fact, the court is not bound by all the rules of evidence (except the rules governing privileges) in making that determination. The court can generally use any information it chooses to rely on to make the determination.

FRE 104. Preliminary Questions

(a) In General. The court must decide any preliminary question about whether a witness is qualified, a privilege exists, or evidence is admissible. In so deciding, the court is not bound by evidence rules, except those on privilege.

Review Questions

1. **Agent provocateur.** Plaintiff sues Defendant for defamation. Plaintiff seeks to introduce evidence that Defendant's niece made defamatory remarks about Plaintiff. Defendant objects, "Hearsay." Plaintiff responds, "Judge, the niece is Defendant's employee and agent." Who decides whether the niece's statements can be attributed to Defendant? In other words, who decides whether the niece is Defendant's employee or agent?
2. **Valid methodology?** Plaintiff sues Defendant for injuries suffered by a defective product. Plaintiff seeks to call an expert witness to opine about the product's defects. Defendant objects, "This proposed expert's methodology is invalid." Who decides the question of whether the methodology is sufficiently reliable?

PART D: RULE OF COMPLETENESS [FRE 106]

It is important that the trier of fact consider evidence in context. Thus, the rules of evidence do not permit a party to present only a portion of a written or recorded statement when it is unfair for the trier of fact not to consider other parts of that or another writing or recording at the same time. In other words, if one part of the statement is "relevant," other parts of that statement—or related statements—that are needed to put the initial portion in context are admissible as well.

FRE 106. Remainder of or Related Writings or Recorded Statements

If a party introduces all or a part of a writing or recorded statement, an adverse party may require the introduction, at that time, of any other part—or any other writing or recorded statement—that in fairness ought to be considered at that time.

The Supreme Court applied this rule in the case of *Beech Aircraft Corp. v. Rainey* (1988).

Beech Aircraft Corp. v. Rainey

488 U.S. 153 (1988)

Justice Brennan delivered the opinion of the Court.

This litigation stems from the crash of a Navy training aircraft at Middleton Field, Alabama, on July 13, 1982, which took the lives of both pilots on board, Lieutenant Commander Barbara Ann Rainey and Ensign Donald Bruce Knowlton. Because of the damage to the plane and the lack of any survivors, the cause of the accident could not be determined with certainty. The two pilots' surviving spouses brought a product liability suit against petitioners Beech Aircraft Corporation, the plane's manufacturer, and Beech Aerospace Services, which serviced the plane under contract with the Navy. The plaintiffs alleged that the crash had been caused by a loss of engine power, known as "rollback," due to some defect in the aircraft's fuel control system. The defendants, on the other hand, advanced the theory of pilot error, suggesting that the plane had stalled during the abrupt avoidance maneuver.

One piece of evidence presented by the defense was an investigative report prepared by Lieutenant Commander William Morgan on order of the training squadron's commanding officer. This "JAG Report" [made findings of fact that will be discussed when we study the Public Reports exception to the hearsay rules.]

Among his "opinions" Lieutenant Commander Morgan stated, in paragraph 5, that due to the deaths of the two pilots and the destruction of the aircraft "it is almost impossible to determine exactly what happened to Navy 3E955 from the time it left the runway on its last touch and go until it impacted the ground." He nonetheless continued with a detailed reconstruction of a possible set of events, based on pilot error, that could have caused the accident. The next two paragraphs stated a caveat and a conclusion:

> "6. Although the above sequence of events is the most likely to have occurred, it does not change the possibility that a 'rollback' did occur.
> "7. The most probable cause of the accident was the pilots [sic] failure to maintain proper interval."

Five or six months after the accident, plaintiff John Rainey, husband of the deceased pilot and himself a Navy flight instructor, sent a detailed letter to Lieutenant Commander Morgan. Based on Rainey's own investigation, the letter took issue with some of the JAG Report's findings and outlined Rainey's theory that "[t]he most probable primary cause factor of this aircraft mishap is a loss of useful power (or rollback) caused by some form of pneumatic sensing/fuel flow malfunction, probably in the fuel control unit."

At trial Rainey did not testify during his side's case in chief, but he was called by the defense as an adverse witness. On direct examination he was asked about two statements contained in his letter. The first was to the effect that his wife had unsuccessfully attempted to cancel the ill-fated training flight because of a variety of adverse factors including her student's fatigue. The second question concerned a portion of Rainey's hypothesized scenario of the accident [and was being offered to prove that it was pilot error]:

> "Didn't you say, sir, that after Mrs. Rainey's airplane rolled wings level, that Lieutenant Colonel Habermacher's plane came into view unexpectedly at its closest point of approach, although sufficient separation still existed between the aircraft. However, the unexpected proximitely [sic] of Colonel Habermacher's plane caused one of the aircrew in Mrs. Rainey's plane to react instinctively and abruptly by initiating a hard right turn away from Colonel Habermacher's airplane?"

Rainey admitted having made both statements. On cross-examination, Rainey's counsel asked the following question [designed to show the cause of the accident was the plane's malfunction]: "In the same letter to which Mr. Toothman made reference to in his questions, sir, did you also say that the most probably [sic] primary cause of this mishap was rollback?" Before Rainey answered, the court sustained a defense objection [and] questioning along this line was cut off.

We have no doubt that the jury was given a distorted and prejudicial impression of Rainey's letter. The theory of Rainey's case was that the accident was the result of a power failure, and, read in its entirety, his letter to Morgan was fully consistent with that theory. While Rainey did discuss problems his wife had encountered the morning of the accident which led her to attempt to cancel the flight, and also agreed that her airplane had violated pattern integrity in turning left prematurely, the thrust of his letter was to challenge Morgan's theory that the crash had been caused by a stall that took place when the pilots turned sharply right and pitched up in attempting to avoid the other plane.

The common-law "rule of completeness," which underlies Federal Rule of Evidence 106, was designed to prevent exactly the type of prejudice of which Rainey complains.

> "When a writing or recorded statement or part thereof is introduced by a party, an adverse party may require the introduction at that time of any other part or any other writing or recorded statement which ought in fairness to be considered contemporaneously with it."

[W]e hold that on the facts of this litigation the District Court abused its discretion in restricting the scope of cross-examination of respondent Rainey by his counsel, and to that extent we affirm the Court of Appeals' judgment. The case is remanded for further proceedings consistent with this opinion.

Does the rule of completeness authorize a court to admit evidence that might otherwise be inadmissible? For instance, if the prosecutor introduces one snippet of the defendant's *Mirandized* interrogation by police that is misleading, does the rule of completeness allow the court to introduce other necessary portions—which might otherwise be hearsay—to put the snippet in its proper context? Sometimes, ensuring that the picture is not distorted requires that evidence that might otherwise be inadmissible is admitted. Most federal courts recognize this reality, although a few resist this conclusion. *Compare United States v. Sutton*, 801 F.2d 1346, 1368-69 (D.C. Cir. 1986) (rule of completeness allows for admission of otherwise inadmissible evidence) *with United States v. Mitchell*, 502 F.3d 931, 965 n.9 (9th Cir. 2007) ("Rule 106 does not render admissible otherwise inadmissible hearsay"). This open issue regarding whether the rule of completeness overcomes a possible hearsay objection may be resolved if a pending amendment to FRE 106 is adopted.[2] However, even with an amended rule, the rule of completeness will not go so far as to open the door for a defendant to introduce his own self-serving statements to police officers just because prosecutors offer against him portions of his confession. The rule of completeness is designed just to prevent a distortion of the evidence presented to the court, as *United States v. Vallejos*, 742 F.3d 902 (9th Cir. 2014), illustrates.[3]

---

2. The Advisory Committee on Evidence Rules sought public comment on amending FRE 106 to add a further sentence to the Federal Rules of Evidence: "The adverse party may do so over a hearsay objection."

3. *United States v. Castro-Cabrera*, 534 F. Supp. 2d 1156, 1160 (C.D. Cal. 2008); *United States v. Coughlin*, 821 F. Supp. 2d 8, 30 (D.D.C. 2011); *United States v. Bucci*, 525 F.3d 116, 133 (1st Cir. 2008).

United States v. Vallejos

742 F.3d 902 (9th Cir. 2014)

GOULD, Judge.

Defendant-Appellant Eric Paul Vallejos appeals his conviction and sentence under 18 U.S.C § 2252(a)(2) for receipt of material involving the sexual exploitation of minors. Specifically, Vallejos appeals the district court's decision to deny his requests that (1) his unedited confession be shown to the jury under the Rule of Completeness, Fed. R. Evid. 106. On September 16, 2010, police detective Arthur Hively used a computer program to discover that Vallejos was making available on a peer-to-peer file-sharing network dozens of files whose names "were consistent with child pornography."

Three weeks later, police officers executing a search warrant discovered dozens of child pornography images and videos, and a peer-to-peer file sharing program called LimeWire, on Vallejos's computer. After the search, Vallejos admitted to officers that "he was responsible for the child pornography that was on the computer," and he voluntarily gave the police an audio- and video-recorded statement to that effect. The district court played an edited version of this statement at trial. After a two-day trial, a jury found Vallejos guilty of receipt of material involving the sexual exploitation of minors.

We review the district court's decision on the Rule of Completeness for an abuse of discretion.

Federal Rule of Evidence 106 codified the common law Rule of Completeness, which exists to avert "misunderstanding or distortion" caused by introduction of only part of a document. The Rule does not, however, require the introduction of any unedited writing or statement merely because an adverse party has introduced an edited version. Rather, "it is often perfectly proper to admit segments of prior testimony without including everything, and adverse parties are not entitled to offer additional segments just because they are there and the proponent has not offered them." In other words, if the "complete statement [does] not serve to correct a misleading impression" in the edited statement that is created by taking something out of context, the Rule of Completeness will not be applied to admit the full statement.

Vallejos contends that the redacted version of his confession misled the jury because it left out parts concerning, among other things, his prior prison sentence, his drug history, and his church. This argument misunderstands the Rule's purpose. The district court properly concluded that the Rule of Completeness is not so broad as to require the admission of all redacted portions of a statement, without regard to content. The district court explained that "[j]ust because somebody is putting in part of a transcript . . . does not mean for the sake of completeness, everything comes in," and it properly rejected Vallejos's argument that the redacted portions should be admitted to show the jury the "flavor of the interview," to "humanize" Vallejos, to prove his "character," and to convey to the jury the voluntariness of the statement. The district court did not abuse its discretion when it determined that—while this evidence might be relevant to "sympathy" and sentencing—the redacted statement was not misleading and therefore that the Rule of Completeness did not require admission of the full statement into evidence.

FRE 106 is limited to "writing[s] or recorded statement[s]." It currently does not apply to unrecorded, oral conversations,[4] *Mitchell*, 502 F.3d at 965 n.9, although many federal courts invoke the U.S. Supreme Court's decision in *Beech Aircraft Corp.* to recognize a common law rule of completeness that, in conjunction with FRE 611, reaches unrecorded oral statements. *See, e.g., United States v. Williams*, 930 F.3d 44, 58-59 (9th Cir. 2019); *accord, Beech Aircraft Corp.*, at 171-72.

Review Questions

1. **Refused entry.** Defendant is charged with false statements to the border authorities. At trial, Prosecutor introduces a statement on the immigration form in which Defendant stated that he was an American citizen. Prosecutor does not offer, however, a statement on the next page of the form in which Defendant states, "seeking to become an American citizen." How, if at all, does FRE 106 apply to the second page of the statement?
2. **Good motive, bad acts.** A bank sues Teller A for embezzlement. In its case-in-chief, the bank offers the first paragraph of Teller A's termination statement in which she states that she took approximately $8,500 from the bank. Teller A seeks to introduce a later paragraph in the statement in which she explains, "I took the money because I had so many student loans to pay." How, if at all, does FRE 106 apply to the second page of the statement?

PART E: PROBABILISTIC EVIDENCE

It is the job of the trier of fact to decide how likely it is that the defendant committed the charged crime or that the plaintiff showed by a preponderance (more likely than not) that the alleged acts occured. However, parties sometimes want to prove their case by presenting statistical evidence that will allegedly show that there was a high probability that things occurred as they have alleged. This evidence is referred to as *probabilistic evidence.*

To what extent is evidence of probabilities relevant to a case? If it is relevant under the liberal standard of FRE 401, can such evidence be misleading and confusing? To some extent, courts are generally willing to accept some statistical evidence of probabilities. For example, as discussed in Chapter Twelve, expert witnesses may

4. This statutory limitation may be eliminated if the currently pending amendment is ultimately adopted, as that amendment would extend FRE 106 to any "written or oral statement." Doing so would bring the Federal Rules of Evidence into conformity with the law in many states. In California, for example, the rule of completeness reaches any "act, declaration, conversation or writing." Cal. Evid. Code § 356.

testify as to the probability that a DNA sample matches a particular person's genetic profile. However, courts tend to balk at an approach in which the parties rely on such evidence to prove their entire case. Not only is there the concern that the statistics offered may be wrong because of faulty assumptions or inaccurate comparison, but there is also the concern as to whether the jurors' task can be reduced to a mathematical formula.

Consider, for example, the next case, *People v. Collins.* To understand *Collins,* it is helpful to have a little background about statistics. The "odds" of an event occurring depend in part on whether the variables at issue are dependent on one another or are totally independent of one another. When events are totally independent, the odds of both events happening are calculated by multiplying the odds together (using what is called the product rule). For instance, what are the odds of picking the queen of hearts out of a deck of 52 cards? The probability of selecting a queen is 1 in 13 (because there are 4 queens in the 52-card deck), and the probability of selecting a hearts card is 1 in 4 (because there are 13 hearts in a 52-card deck). Because the face value of the card is independent of its suit, the probability of selecting the queen of hearts is 1 in 52—that is, 1/13 multiplied by 1/4, which makes sense because the odds of selecting a particular card out of a 52-card deck are 1 in 52. But what happens if the variables are *not* independent? Is an opinion based on using the product rule in this situation relevant? That is what was at issue in *Collins.*

People v. Collins

68 Cal. 2d 319 (Cal. 1968)

SULLIVAN, Justice.

We deal here with the novel question whether evidence of mathematical probability has been properly introduced and used by the prosecution in a criminal case. While we discern no inherent incompatibility between the disciplines of law and mathematics and intend no general disapproval or disparagement of the latter as an auxiliary in the fact-finding processes of the former, we cannot uphold the technique employed in the instant case. As we explain in detail, the testimony as to mathematical probability infected the case with fatal error and distorted the jury's traditional role of determining guilt or innocence according to long-settled rules. Mathematics, a veritable sorcerer in our computerized society, while assisting the trier of fact in the search for truth, must not cast a spell over him. We conclude that on the record before us defendant should not have had his guilt determined by the odds and that he is entitled to a new trial. We reverse the judgment.

A jury found defendant Malcolm Ricardo Collins and his wife defendant Janet Louise Collins guilty of second degree robbery.

On June 18, 1964, about 11:30 a.m. Mrs. Juanita Brooks, who had been shopping, was walking home along an alley in the San Pedro area of the City of Los Angeles. She was pulling behind her a wicker basket carryall containing groceries and had her purse on top of the packages. She was using a cane. As she stooped down to pick up an empty carton, she was suddenly pushed to the ground by a person whom she neither saw nor heard approach. She was stunned by the fall and felt some pain. She managed to look up and saw a young woman running from the scene. According to Mrs. Brooks the latter appeared to weigh about 145 pounds, was wearing "something dark," and had hair "between a dark blond and a light blond," but lighter than the color of defendant Janet Collins' hair as it appeared at trial. Immediately after the incident, Mrs. Brooks discovered that her purse, containing between $35 and $40 was missing.

About the same time as the robbery, John Bass, who lived on the street at the end of the alley, was in front of his house watering his lawn. His attention was attracted by "a lot of crying and screaming" coming from the alley. As he looked in that direction, he saw a woman run out of the alley and enter a yellow automobile parked across the street from him. He was unable to give the make of the car. The car started off immediately and pulled wide around another parked vehicle so that in the narrow street it passed within six feet of Bass. The latter then saw that it was being driven by a male Negro, wearing a mustache and beard. At the trial Bass identified defendant as the driver of the yellow automobile. However, an attempt was made to impeach his identification by his admission that at the preliminary hearing he testified to an uncertain identification at the police lineup shortly after the attack on Mrs. Brooks, when defendant was beardless.

In his testimony Bass described the woman who ran from the alley as a Caucasian, slightly over five feet tall, of ordinary build, with her hair in a dark blonde ponytail, and wearing dark clothing. He further testified that her ponytail was "just like" one which Janet had in a police photograph taken on June 22, 1964.

On the day of the robbery, Janet was employed as a housemaid in San Pedro. Her employer testified that she had arrived for work at 8:50 a.m. and that defendant had picked her up in a light yellow car about 11:30 a.m. On that day, according to the witness, Janet was wearing her hair in a blonde ponytail but lighter in color than it appeared at trial.

There was evidence from which it could be inferred that defendants had ample time to drive from Janet's place of employment and participate in the robbery. Defendants testified, however, that they went directly from her employer's house to the home of friends, where they remained for several hours.

In the morning of June 22, Los Angeles Police Officer Kinsey, who was investigating the robbery, went to defendants' home. He saw a yellow Lincoln automobile with an off-white top in front of the house. He talked with defendants. Janet, whose hair appeared to be a dark blonde, was wearing it in a ponytail. Malcolm did not have a beard. The officer explained to them that he was investigating a robbery specifying the time and place; that the victim had been knocked down and her purse snatched; and that the person responsible was a female Caucasian with blonde hair in a ponytail who had left the scene in a yellow car driven by a male Negro. He requested that defendants accompany him to the police station at San Pedro and they did so. There, in response to police inquiries as to defendants' activities at the time of the robbery, Janet stated, according to Officer Kinsey, that her husband had picked her up at her place of employment at 1 p.m. and that they had then visited at the home of friends in Los Angeles. Malcolm confirmed this. Defendants were detained for an hour or two, were photographed but not booked, and were eventually released and driven home by the police.

Late in the afternoon of the same day, Officer Kinsey, while driving home from work in his own car, saw defendants riding in their yellow Lincoln. Although the transcript fails to disclose what prompted such action, Kinsey proceeded to place them under surveillance and eventually followed them home. He called for assistance and arranged to meet other police officers in the vicinity of defendants' home. Kinsey took a position in the rear of the premises. The other officers, who were in uniform and had arrived in a marked police car, approached defendants' front door. As they did so, Kinsey saw defendant Malcolm Collins run out the back door toward a rear fence and disappear behind a tree. Meanwhile the other officers emerged with Janet Collins whom they had placed under arrest. A search was made for Malcolm who was found in a closet of a neighboring home and also arrested. Defendants were again taken to the police station, were kept in custody for 48 hours, and were again released without any charges being made against them.

Officer Kinsey interrogated defendants separately on June 23 while they were in custody and testified to their statements over defense counsel's objections. According to the officer, Malcolm stated that he sometimes wore a beard but that he did not wear a beard on June 18 (the day of the robbery), having shaved it off on June 2, 1964. He also explained two receipts for traffic fines totaling $35 paid on June 19, which receipts had been found on his person, by saying that he used funds won in a gambling game at a labor hall. Janet, on the other hand, said that the $35 used to pay the fines had come from her earnings.

At the seven-day trial the prosecution experienced some difficulty in establishing the identities of the perpetrators of the crime. In an apparent attempt to bolster the identifications, the prosecutor called an instructor of mathematics at a state college. Through this witness he sought to establish that, assuming the robbery was committed by a Caucasian woman with a blond ponytail who left the scene accompanied by a Negro with a beard and mustache, there was an overwhelming probability that the crime was committed by any couple answering such distinctive characteristics.

Applying the product rule to his own factors the prosecutor arrived at a probability that there was but one chance in 12 million that any couple possessed the distinctive characteristics of the defendants.[5] Accordingly, under this theory, it was

---

5. Here are the statistics the prosecution offered to support its argument that the defendants were probably—beyond a reasonable doubt— the robbers in the case.

If "Pr" represents the probability that a certain distinctive combination of characteristics, hereinafter designated "C," will occur jointly in a random couple, then the probability that C will *not* occur in a random couple is (1 Pr). Applying the product rule (see fn. 8, *ante*), the probability that C will occur in *none* of N couples chosen at random is (1—Pr) N, so that the probability of C occurring in *at least one* of N random couples is [1—(1—Pr) N].

Given a particular couple selected from a random set of N, the probability of C occurring in that couple (i.e., Pr), multiplied by the probability of C occurring in none of the remaining N—1 couples (i.e., (1—Pr) N—1), yields the probability that C will occur in the selected couple and in no other. Thus the probability of C occurring in any particular couple, and in that couple alone, is [(Pr) × (1—Pr) N—1]. Since this is true for each of the N couples, the probability that C will occur in precisely *one* of the N couples, without regard to which one, is [(Pr) × (1—Pr) N—1] added N times, because the probability of the occurrence of one of several *mutually exclusive* events is equal to the *sum* of the individual probabilities. Thus the probability of C occurring in *exactly one* of N random couples (*any* one, but *only* one) is [(N) × (Pr) × (1—Pr) N—1].

to be inferred that there could be but one chance in 12 million that defendants were innocent and that another equally distinctive couple actually committed the robbery. Objections were timely made to the mathematician's testimony on the grounds that it was immaterial, that it invaded the province of the jury, and that it was based on unfounded assumptions. The objections were "temporarily overruled" and the evidence admitted subject to a motion to strike. When that motion was made at the conclusion of the direct examination, the court denied it, stating that the testimony had been received only for the "purpose of illustrating the mathematical probabilities of various matters, the possibilities for them occurring or re-occurring."

[Specifically, the mathematician calculated the following odds:

(1) Partly yellow car – 1 out of 10
(2) Man with a mustache – 1 out of 4
(3) Woman with a ponytail – 1 out of 10
(4) Woman with blonde hair – 1 out of 3
(5) Black man with a beard – 1 out of 10
(6) Interracial couple in a car – 1 out of 1,000

TOTAL odds of all six being true at the same time (by multiplying each denominator) – 1 out of 12 million]

Defendant [argues that] the introduction of evidence pertaining to the mathematical theory of probability and the use of the same by the prosecution during the trial was error prejudicial to defendant.

As we shall explain, the prosecution's introduction and use of mathematical probability statistics injected two fundamental prejudicial errors into the case: (1) The testimony itself lacked an adequate foundation both in evidence and in statistical theory; and (2) the testimony and the manner in which the prosecution used it distracted the jury from its proper and requisite function of weighing the evidence on the issue

---

By subtracting the probability that C will occur in *exactly one* couple from the probability that C will occur in *at least one* couple, one obtains the probability that C will occur in *more than one* couple: [1—(1—Pr) N]—[(N) × (Pr) × (1—Pr) N—1]. Dividing this difference by the probability that C will occur in at least one couple (i.e., dividing the difference by [1—(1—Pr) N]) then yields *the probability that C will occur more than once in a group of N couples in which C occurs at least once.*

Turning to the case in which C represents the characteristics which distinguish a bearded Negro accompanied by a ponytailed blonde in a yellow car, the prosecution sought to establish that the probability of C occurring in a random couple was 1/12,000,000—i.e., that Pr = 1/12,000,000. Treating this conclusion as accurate, it follows that, in a population of N random couples, the probability of C occurring *exactly once* is [(N) × (1/12,000,000) × (1—1/12,000,000) N—1]. Subtracting this product from [1—(1—1/12,000,000) N], the probability of C occurring in *at least one* couple, and dividing the resulting difference by [1—(1—1/12,000,000) N], the probability that C will occur in at least one couple, yields the probability that C will occur more than once in a group of N random couples of which at least one couple (namely, the one seen by the witnesses) possesses characteristics C. In other words, the probability of *another* such couple in a population of N is the quotient A/B, where A designates the numerator [1—(1—1/12,000,000) N]—[(N) × (1/12,000,000) × (1—1/12,000,000) N—1], and B designates the denominator [1—(1—1/12,000,000) N].

of guilt, encouraged the jurors to rely upon an engaging but logically irrelevant expert demonstration, foreclosed the possibility of an effective defense by an attorney apparently unschooled in mathematical refinements, and placed the jurors and defense counsel at a disadvantage in sifting relevant fact from inapplicable theory.

We initially consider the defects in the testimony itself. As we have indicated, the specific technique presented through the mathematician's testimony and advanced by the prosecutor to measure the probabilities in question suffered from two basic and pervasive defects—an inadequate evidentiary foundation and an inadequate proof of statistical independence. First, the prosecution produced no evidence whatsoever showing, or from which it could be in any way inferred, that only one out of every ten cars which might have been at the scene of the robbery was partly yellow, that only one out of every four men who might have been there wore a mustache, that only one out of every ten girls who might have been there wore a ponytail, or that any of the other individual probability factors listed were even roughly accurate. But, there was another glaring defect in the prosecution's technique, namely an inadequate proof of the statistical independence of the six factors. No proof was presented that the characteristics selected were mutually independent, even though the witness himself acknowledged that such condition was essential to the proper application of the "product rule" or "multiplication rule."

We now turn to the second fundamental error caused by the probability testimony. Quite apart from our foregoing objections to the specific technique employed by the prosecution to estimate the probability in question, we think that the entire enterprise upon which the prosecution embarked and which was directed to the objective of measuring the likelihood of a random couple possessing the characteristics allegedly distinguishing the robbers, was gravely misguided. At best, it might yield an estimate as to how infrequently bearded Negroes drive yellow cars in the company of blonde females with ponytails.

The prosecution's approach, however, could furnish the jury with absolutely no guidance on the crucial issue: *Of the admittedly few such couples, which one, if any, was guilty of committing this robbery*? Probability theory necessarily remains silent on that question, since no mathematical equation can prove beyond a reasonable doubt (1) that the guilty couple *in fact* possessed the characteristics described by the People's witnesses, or even (2) that only *one* couple possessing those distinctive characteristics could be found in the entire Los Angeles area.

Review Question

The problems with *Collins*. What were the chief gaps in logic that doomed the probabilistic evidence in *Collins*? Were the assumptions of the expert's statistical model valid? Did the model ignore the overlap and interdependence of the factors it identified? Did the probabilities calculated by this model make it any more likely that the two charged defendants were guilty of the charged crime?

Test Your Understanding

To test your understanding of the material in this chapter, turn to the Supplement for additional practice problems.

Chapter 3

Character Evidence

The rules of evidence embrace the idea that a person's liability—whether criminal or civil—should be grounded in what that person has done (or not done), not on the type of person they are. If a person is found standing outside a bank after it has been robbed, should evidence that the person has robbed a bank before be admitted to prove that the person has the propensity or disposition to rob banks and thus is guilty of this bank robbery as well? The rules of evidence generally say "no."

Character evidence is evidence that suggests that a person acted in a certain manner on a particular occasion at issue in the pending case because of a personality trait or a penchant for engaging in certain acts. *Character evidence* suggests that because a person has done something before, *he or she is the type of person who does such things* and hence is more likely to have done it again. It is the inference highlighted in italics—that the person acted in accordance with their immutable character—that makes evidence *character evidence*. Character evidence can pertain to a person's character as a whole (for example, "he is a good man" or "she is a law-abiding citizen") or to specific character traits such as one's character for violence, peacefulness, carefulness, promiscuity, or truth and veracity.

Examples

1. Plaintiff sues Defendant for causing a car accident. Plaintiff offers proof that Defendant is known as a "careless" driver to prove Defendant caused the accident.
2. Prosecution charges Defendant with robbing a bank. Prosecutor offers evidence that Defendant is known as a thief to prove Defendant robbed the bank.
3. Prosecution charges Defendant with murder. Prosecutor offers a character witness to testify that Defendant is a violent person to prove that Defendant is the murderer.

Graphically, the chain of logic that relies upon an inference of propensity—which is what defines character evidence—can be illustrated as follows:

For the reasons discussed more fully in Part A of this chapter, the rules of evidence generally exclude character evidence. This exclusion is a departure from the common law tradition, when courts used the compurgator system where jurors were literally the peers of the defendant and would decide the case based in large part on what they knew about the defendant's character. The general rule restricting character evidence is set forth in FRE 404(a)(1). FRE 404(a)(2) sets forth some of the exceptions to the rule; the remaining exceptions are set forth in FRE 412 through 415. FRE 404(a)(3) sets forth the exception that applies when the character trait at issue is the trait for honesty (or dishonesty) and when the trait is being used to show that a witness should (or should not) be believed; how to use evidence of a witness's character for truth and veracity is discussed separately in Chapter Eleven. Even when character evidence may be admitted under these specialized rules, a trial judge may still exclude it through the rules of practical relevance under FRE 403 if the judge concludes that the probative value of the character evidence is substantially outweighed by unfair prejudice, undue consumption of time, and the like. See Chapter Two.

FRE 404. Character Evidence, Other Crimes, Wrongs, or Acts

(a) Character Evidence.

(1) ***Prohibited Uses.*** Evidence of a person's character is not admissible to prove that on a particular occasion the person acted in accordance with the character or trait.

(2) ***Exceptions for a Defendant or Victim in a Criminal Case.*** The following exceptions apply in a criminal case:

(A) a defendant may offer evidence of the defendant's pertinent trait, and if the evidence is admitted, the prosecutor may offer evidence to rebut it;

(B) subject to the limitations in Rule 412, a defendant may offer evidence of an alleged victim's pertinent trait, and if the evidence is admitted, the prosecutor may:

(i) offer evidence to rebut it; and

(ii) offer evidence of the defendant's same trait; and

(C) in a homicide case, the prosecutor may offer evidence of the alleged victim's trait of peacefulness to rebut evidence that the victim was the first aggressor.

Part B examines the basic prohibition against the use of character evidence in civil cases. FRE 404(a)(1).

Part C examines the rules regarding the use of character evidence in criminal cases. Those rules generally prohibit prosecutors from using character evidence against the defendant until the defendant opens the door by presenting good character evidence about the defendant or bad character evidence about the victim. FRE 404(a)(2).

Part D focuses on the *methods* of proving character. Character evidence is typically proven in one of three ways: (1) testimony from witnesses relaying that the person has a reputation in the relevant community for having a certain type of character (*reputation evidence*), (2) testimony from witnesses giving their opinion that the person has a certain type of character (*opinion evidence*), and (3) evidence recounting specific instances when the person has exhibited his or her character (*specific instance evidence*). When character evidence is allowed, it is generally, but not always, limited to opinion or reputation evidence. FRE 405(a), (b).

Part E addresses two types of evidence closely related to character evidence, but which are not themselves character evidence—namely, (1) evidence that a person acted in a specific manner on a different occasion when used to prove a fact *other than* his or her character under FRE 404(b), and (2) habit evidence. These types of evidence are discussed here because they can be easily misused as character evidence by the trier of fact, so it is critical to understand what qualifies as these permissible types of evidence and how to guard against misuse.

Part F concludes the chapter by explaining how the rules apply when the character trait at issue is one's character for promiscuity or for sexual violence. These rules include what are commonly referred to as rape shield laws, and are designed to effectuate additional public policies aside from the policies animating the rules of character evidence generally.

PART A: RATIONALE FOR LIMITING CHARACTER EVIDENCE

In everyday life, we often judge people by what they have done before and what their acts say about what type of person they are, and we use this information to predict how they will act in the future. Thus, the problem with character evidence is that there is a real danger that jurors will view it as being *too* relevant. To guard against this danger, the rules of evidence have supplanted the usual rules allowing for the balancing of probative value against unfair prejudice with a near categorical prohibition on the use of character evidence—subject to a handful of narrowly defined exceptions. But that begs the question: Why is it a problem to admit character evidence in legal proceedings if our practical experience tells us that it is such useful information? Three reasons have emerged.

First, it is far from clear that the generalized belief that "if they did it once, they'll do it again" is empirically accurate. People can and often do change their conduct and approaches to life. Without some assurance of accuracy, there is a risk that the inference that character evidence necessarily asks jurors to draw will be incorrect and will lead to inaccurate and unjust verdicts. In the face of this uncertainty, the legal system has opted to err on the side of being aspirational in adopting rules that rest on the notion that people change.

Second, even if there is some empirical truth underlying the use of character evidence, there is still a danger that jurors will decide cases just on the assumption that a person of a certain ilk is likely to have committed the charged conduct—and will do so without focusing on any assessment of the evidence beyond what they think of the defendant. Thus, evidence of a person's bad character could eclipse other evidence that is offered in a case. As the Advisory Committee Notes to FRE 404 observe: "Character evidence . . . tends to distract the trier of fact from the main question of what actually happened on the particular occasion. It subtly permits the trier of fact to reward the good man and to punish the bad man because of their respective characters despite what the evidence in the case shows actually happened."

Third, the inquiry into one's character may itself be denigrating to the litigants. Consider the following explanation:

> Is it possible that our system of litigation and proof is so contentious and so coarse, and the human internal operating system so complex and submerged, that it is just not possible for our system of litigation and proof to produce reliable verdicts about a matter so subtle and complex as human character? The American system of litigation and proof is both contentious and adversarial. Is it possible and probable that large amounts of character evidence—such as detailed life histories—are peculiarly and excessively susceptible to manipulation and distortion in an adversary and contentious system of litigation and proof such as ours? In short, is it the case that large amounts of character evidence—detailed personal histories, for example—are peculiarly susceptible to manipulation and that in our adversary and contentious system of proof otherwise nuanced evidence of human character—evidence, that is, of the complex internal operating system that we call human character—would surely be corrupted and degraded and that the necessary nuances about character would be obliterated in the heat of courtroom warfare?
>
> It bears repeating that human character is elusive as well as complex. That is in part because character is deep within each one of us; that is, there are many components of character that are hidden from the immediate view of strangers and even of ourselves. This suggests a question of the utmost importance: Is it the case that meaningful—that is, detailed—evidence of character must peer so deeply into the human heart and soul, into the inner recesses of the mind and soul, that such evidence ought to be regarded as so demeaning and degrading that such evidence ought to be prohibited for that reason alone?[1]

---

1. Peter Tillers, *What Is Wrong with Character Evidence*, 49 Hastings L. J. 781, 832-34 (1998).

PART B: RULES FOR CHARACTER EVIDENCE IN CIVIL CASES [FRE 404(a)(1)]

The general rule barring the use of character evidence is stated in FRE 404(a)(1): "Evidence of a person's character is not admissible to prove that on a particular occasion the person acted in accordance with the character or trait."

1. General Rule: Character Evidence Is Prohibited

On its face, FRE 404(a)(1)'s prohibition on character evidence rule applies to both civil and criminal cases. Where they differ is with the pertinent exceptions. Whereas FRE 404(a)(2) lists exceptions to allow character evidence under certain circumstances in criminal cases, there are no similar exceptions for civil cases. Thus, character evidence when offered to prove behavior in a specific incident is generally *not admissible* in civil cases unless those cases involve sexual assault or child molestation, or character is an element of a claim of defense.

Examples

1. In a car accident, Plaintiff sues Defendant for driving negligently. Plaintiff cannot introduce evidence that Defendant is known as a bad, careless driver, and Defendant cannot put on evidence that he is known as a good, careful driver.
2. In a wrongful termination case, Plaintiff sues Defendant for terminating him without cause. Defendant cannot introduce evidence that Plaintiff has the reputation of being a disloyal friend, and Plaintiff cannot introduce evidence that he is known as a loyal friend.
3. In a civil assault case, Plaintiff sues Defendant for pushing him at a party. Plaintiff cannot introduce evidence that Defendant is known as a temperamental hothead, and Defendant cannot introduce evidence that Plaintiff is known as a violent person and Defendant is known as a peace-loving "saint."

2. Exception: When Character Relates to an Element of the Claim or Defense [FRE 405(b)][2]

Character evidence is not barred in a civil case when an essential element of a charge, claim, or defense at issue in that case relates to a person's character. This exception is set forth in FRE 405(b).

---

2. Some states have additional exceptions in civil cases. In Texas, for instance, a party in a civil case "accused of conduct involving moral turpitude may offer evidence of [its] pertinent trait" and a party in a civil case "accused of assaultive conduct" may "offer evidence of the victim's trait of violence to prove self-defense"; if it does so, evidence from the other party to rebut these character traits is also admissible. Tex. R. Evid. 404(a)(2)(B), (a)(3)(C).

FRE 405. Methods of Proving Character

(b) By Specific Instances of Conduct. When a person's character or character trait is an essential element of a charge, claim, or defense, the character or trait may also be proved by relevant specific instances of the person's conduct.

There are certain types of civil cases where a party's character is an essential part of the case. Specifically:

(1) *Defamation.* An element of the civil claim of defamation is that the defendant made false statements about the plaintiff's character that hurt the plaintiff's reputation. To prove this claim, the plaintiff needs to present evidence of her reputation. Likewise, the defense has a right to argue that the plaintiff did not have a good reputation or that the defendant's statements did not diminish that reputation.

(2) *Negligent entrustment.* To prove the tort of negligent entrustment, the plaintiff must prove that the defendant improperly entrusted the plaintiff's property with someone who they should have known would put the property at risk. To prove this claim—or defend against it—the parties may need to show the character of the person to whom the property was entrusted. If that person's character was known as negligent, the entrustment would be improper. If that person's character was known as careful, a negligent entrustment action may not stand.

(3) *Child custody.* In child custody cases, the ultimate issue is which parent has the better character to be the parent with custody of the child.

(4) *Wrongful death damages.* Finally, damages in wrongful death cases are based on the "worth" of the decedent. To show that worth, or to contest it, the parties need to be free to present evidence of that person's character.

In civil cases in which character is a part of the claim or defense, not only is character evidence admissible, but the parties may prove character by any of the three acceptable types of evidence—namely, reputation, opinion, or specific instance(s). FRE 405(a), 405(b).

The exception for when character is at issue is still subject to the court examining whether the probative value of specific items of evidence is substantially outweighed by the danger of unfair prejudice or any of the other considerations set forth in FRE 403, as is illustrated by the case discussed next.

World Wide Ass'n of Specialty Programs v. Pure, Inc.

450 F.3d 1132 (10th Cir. 2006)

Tacha, Chief Judge.

I. BACKGROUND

World Wide is an association of residential treatment programs for troubled and at-risk teenagers. It does not own or operate schools; rather, it markets its members' schools to parents who might be interested in them. Ms. Scheff was one such parent. Her daughter attended a World Wide member school for nine months before Ms. Scheff decided to remove her from the program. Less than a year later, Ms. Scheff founded PURE. Like World Wide, PURE provides information about programs for families seeking help for their children; PURE-affiliated schools compete with the schools associated with World Wide. PURE schools pay Ms. Scheff a substantial sum whenever a child enrolls in its program based on her recommendation.

After the creation of PURE, Ms. Scheff used various fictitious names to post negative messages about schools for at-risk teenagers on an internet forum. Several of the schools Ms. Scheff disparaged were schools affiliated with World Wide.

Ms. Scheff and Mr. Berryman were also both members of an e-mail listserve whose members spread unfavorable information about World Wide schools to parents searching for programs for troubled teens. [In their postings, they mentioned alleged incidents of abuse at the schools.]

After discovering the postings and e-mails sent by Ms. Scheff and Mr. Berryman, World Wide filed this suit against them seeking damages and an injunction for defamation per se. The District Court granted Mr. Berryman's motion for summary judgment and dismissed the entire complaint against him. Ms. Scheff stood trial, and the jury returned a unanimous verdict for her on every claim. World Wide then filed this appeal, arguing that the District Court erred[, inter alia,] in admitting into evidence media reports about abuse and neglect at World Wide schools.

II. DISCUSSION

The Federal Rules of Evidence permit the introduction of opinion evidence, reputation evidence, and specific instances of conduct when the character of a person is an element of the claim or defense or is otherwise at issue. Although Utah has never so stated, it is well-established in other jurisdictions that the character of the plaintiff in a defamation case is at issue.

World Wide [also] argues that the media evidence should have been excluded because its probative value was substantially outweighed by the danger of unfair prejudice and confusion of the issues. See Fed. R. Evid. 403. We find no abuse of discretion here. We . . . note that it was relevant to whether Ms. Scheff acted with actual malice because the reports, if relied on by Ms. Scheff, support a finding that she had a reasonable belief when making the statements. As to the question of whether the evidence was unfairly prejudicial under Rule 403, the District Court observed that in the context of the entire trial, during which both parties offered media evidence (including a television program praising World Wide programs), the media evidence "largely cancelled each other out." We conclude that the potential for prejudice and confusion was not so substantial that the District Court abused its discretion in allowing these media accounts.

PART C: RULES FOR CHARACTER EVIDENCE IN CRIMINAL CASES [FRE 404(a)(2)]

1. General Rule: Character Evidence Is Prohibited

FRE 404(a)(1)'s general prohibition on character evidence applies in criminal cases. However, there are several exceptions to this prohibition in criminal cases. FRE 413 and FRE 414 make character evidence admissible in cases where the defendant is being prosecuted for sexual assault and child molestation, but those exceptions are discussed separately in Part F of this chapter. The other exceptions are discussed next.[3]

2. Exception: When the Defendant Opens the Door

The rules of evidence grant criminal defendants—but not the prosecution—the option of introducing evidence regarding a pertinent trait of their own character or of the alleged victim of their crime. Once a criminal defendant opens that door, however, the prosecution may provide character evidence in response. For example, a defendant who is charged with fraud should be able to argue to the jury that he is known as an honest person and therefore is unlikely to have committed the offense; but if he does, the prosecution can introduce evidence that the defendant has a character for deceit. Similarly, a defendant might argue that he is a nonviolent person and therefore would not have killed the victim but in self-defense; if he does, the prosecution may respond with evidence of his character for violence.

Although, as stated above, it is debatable whether the inference the defendant is asking the trier of fact to make is accurate, because we want to give the defendant every opportunity to defend himself, the rules of evidence provide that the defendant (but not the prosecutor) has the option of opening the door to character evidence by presenting evidence on pertinent traits. This practice of allowing criminal defendants to use character evidence to defend themselves is sometimes called the "mercy rule."

Even though the drafters approved of adopting this common law approach, they were reluctant to bog down a trial into a minitrial over the defendant's or victim's character. Accordingly, character evidence is limited to pertinent traits, and the methods by which the defendant's character may be proved are also limited.

(a) Evidence of the Defendant's "Good" Character Trait(s) [FRE 404(a)(2)(A)]

FRE 404(a)(2)(A) empowers a criminal defendant to introduce evidence of a pertinent character trait and for the prosecution to respond in kind. Specifically, it provides:

---

3. In some jurisdictions, there are additional exceptions. For instance, California and Illinois authorize the prosecution to introduce a defendant's prior specific instances of domestic violence to prove that he has the character for violence and hence is more likely to have committed a charged domestic violence offense. Cal. Evid. Code § 1109; 725 Ill. Comp. Stat. Ann. 5/115-7.4(a).

FRE 404. Character Evidence; Other Crimes, Wrongs, or Acts

(a) Character Evidence.

. . .

(2) ***Exceptions for a Defendant or Victim in a Criminal Case.*** The exceptions apply in a criminal case:

(A) a defendant may offer evidence of the defendant's pertinent trait, and if the evidence is admitted, the prosecutor may offer evidence to rebut it.

Examples

1. Defendant is on trial for assault. He seeks to call a character witness who will testify that Defendant has a reputation of being a peaceful individual. If Defendant calls this character witness, the prosecution can call a character witness to testify that Defendant has a reputation for being a violent individual.
2. Defendant is on trial for insurance fraud. She seeks to call a character witness who will testify that, in the character witness's opinion, Defendant is an honest person. If the defense opens the door by calling the good character witness, the prosecution will be able to call a character witness to testify that, in that witness's opinion, Defendant is a dishonest person.

The rule permitting a criminal defendant to present good character evidence has two key requirements: (1) the character evidence must go to a "pertinent trait," FRE 404(a)(2)(A); and (2) this pertinent trait may only be proven with opinion or reputation evidence. FRE 405(a). A defendant may *not* introduce evidence of prior specific instances in which he has exhibited the trait; inquiry into specific instances is only permitted during cross-examination of that character witness. FRE 405(b). Without these limitations, the evidence of defendant's character might distract the jury into considering irrelevant information or waste valuable time going into every instance in which the defendant exhibited the trait at issue. Once the defendant introduces reputation or opinion evidence of his pertinent character trait, the proverbial door is open for the prosecution to introduce evidence to respond in kind—that is, by introducing reputation or character evidence of the defendant's character for the opposing trait (for example, character for violence after defendant elicits his character for peacefulness). Thus, there are significant risks for the defense in relying on character witnesses.

(i) Pertinent character trait

What constitutes a "pertinent" character trait? The Rule and Advisory Committee Notes do not answer that question, but common sense and court decisions can. To determine what kind of character evidence is relevant, one must look at the issues in the case.

If the case involves alleged violence by the defendant, evidence of peacefulness would serve to contest that. However, evidence that the defendant is fun or generous do not really provide information on any issue in that case. Similarly, if a defendant is charged with a crime of fraud, evidence that the defendant is violent does not help decide the relevant issues of honesty in the case. Rather, they are likely an effort to claim that the defendant is a bad person so that the jury should vote to convict him.

When defense counsel offers character evidence, counsel must be prepared to argue why such evidence is pertinent to the charges in the case. Consider the pertinent character evidence for the following types of crimes:

(1) *Narcotics offenses.* Is honesty pertinent? (A drug dealer may be an honest drug trader.) Is peacefulness pertinent? (A drug dealer may be peaceful.) Is being philanthropic pertinent? (A drug dealer may give money to others.)
(2) *Possessing unregistered weapons.* Is honesty pertinent? (Is failing to register a weapon a dishonest act?) Is being civic-minded pertinent? (Do civic-minded persons nonetheless violate registration laws?)
(3) *Car burglary.* Is honesty pertinent? (Is it dishonest to openly break into someone else's car?) Is peacefulness pertinent? (What if the burglary is accomplished with a coat hanger instead of breaking a window?)

Whether a trait is pertinent under the rules is a decision that a judge makes before allowing the evidence. If the evidence is only marginally pertinent, the court can also use FRE 403 to exclude it.

How about vague character evidence such as the defendant is known as a "good guy" in the community? Courts are generally reluctant to allow such evidence because it provides little guidance to the jury and redirects the jurors to deciding the case based on their feelings about the defendant as a person, rather than on whether they believe the defendant committed the charged conduct. What about evidence that the defendant is widely known to be a "law-abiding" person? Although being law-abiding is a very broad character trait, many courts, like the court in *United States v. Angelini*, discussed next, will allow it. The defense takes the risk, however, that in questioning the character witness, the prosecution will be allowed to ask about any violation of the law that the defendant has committed—no matter how small or egregious—so as to challenge the character witness's testimony.

United States v. Angelini

678 F.2d 380 (1st Cir. 1982)

CAMPBELL, Judge.

Victor Angelini was convicted after a jury trial of possessing with intent to distribute and distributing methaqualone, a controlled substance, in violation of 21 U.S.C. § 841(a)(2), 18 U.S.C. § 2. The evidence presented against him at trial consisted primarily of the testimony of Drug Enforcement Administration Special

Agent Keefe. Agent Keefe testified that, while working undercover, he met with one Samuel Jacobs on October 7, 1980, at which time Jacobs informed him of a new drug source from Florida. Jacobs arranged for Keefe to meet the source on October 14. Angelini was introduced as the drug source at this meeting. According to Keefe, Angelini stated that he could obtain various drugs. Angelini also asked Keefe about a small sample of drugs he, Angelini, had given Jacobs. Angelini went on to quote a price for shipments of the drugs.

The defense consisted chiefly of Angelini's denials of what Keefe said transpired at the October 14 meeting. Angelini sought to introduce evidence through three character witnesses that he was law-abiding. The district court refused to allow the witnesses to take the stand on the basis that law-abidingness was not relevant to the case. We hold that the court erred in excluding evidence concerning Angelini's character as a law-abiding person.

Federal Rule of Evidence 404(a) states that an accused may introduce "evidence of a pertinent trait of his character." The word "pertinent" is read as synonymous with "relevant." Thus, the basic issue is whether the character trait in question would make any fact "of consequence to the determination" of the case more or less probable than it would be without evidence of the trait. See Fed. R. Evid. 401.

Under this analysis, evidence of law-abidingness should have been admitted. Evidence that Angelini was a law-abiding person would tend to make it less likely that he would knowingly break the law. Such evidence has long been recognized as relevant. In *Michelson v. United States* (1948), the Supreme Court stated that "possession of . . . characteristics (including law-abidingness) would seem . . . incompatible with offering a bribe to a revenue agent," which was the crime charged.

In a case directly on point, *United States v. Hewitt*, 634 F.2d 277 (5th Cir. 1981), the Fifth Circuit held that evidence of a defendant's law-abiding character was erroneously excluded in a trial for unlawful possession or receipt of firearms. In the course of its analysis, the court stressed the relevancy of such evidence. As it noted, however, this inquiry does not end the matter. While the *Hewitt* court went on to ask whether law-abidingness is a "specific" or a "general" trait of character, we think the issue may be better framed as whether it qualifies as a trait at all, or is so diffuse as to be merely synonymous with good character generally, which is not admissible. Rule 404 permits evidence of traits only; an earlier draft was modified, deleting language that would have allowed the introduction of evidence of a defendant's character generally. See Advisory Committee's Note to Rule 404. Under the common law, there was a similar distinction made between general good character and particular traits of character. Since Rule 404 was intended to restate the common law rule, it is useful to examine the cases to determine whether evidence of law-abidingness was normally held to be admissible.

With very few exceptions, the cases hold that evidence of a defendant's character as a law-abiding person is admissible. We hold, therefore, that the trait of law-abidingness was relevant and admissible under Rule 404(a). We cannot say that the exclusion of this evidence was harmless error. Cf. *Michelson v. United States*, (evidence of good character may in itself raise a reasonable doubt as to defendant's guilt). We therefore remand for a new trial.

(ii) Form of character evidence

As noted above and discussed more fully in Part D of this chapter, a defendant's proof of his or her good character trait is limited to calling character witnesses who will testify regarding defendant's reputation with regard to that character trait or the character witness's opinion of the defendant's character. FRE 405(a). The defendant will not be allowed to ask for specific examples demonstrating defendant's character. However, the prosecutor will be allowed to ask on cross-examination of those witnesses about specific bad acts by the defendant to challenge the defense character witness's testimony. FRE 405(b). When the prosecution introduces its own evidence of the opposing character trait of the defendant, the prosecution is also limited to reputation and opinion evidence. FRE 405(a).

Example

Defendant, who is charged with assault, can call his spouse to testify to her opinion that he is a peaceful person. Although *Defendant* cannot elicit from the spouse examples of when Defendant avoided the use of violence (because those would be specific instances), on cross-examination the *prosecution* can ask the spouse about specific instances in which Defendant was violent and can also call witnesses to testify about Defendant's reputation for violence and their opinion as to his violent character.

(b) Evidence of the Victim's "Bad" Character Trait(s) [FRE 404(a)(2)]

Under FRE 404(a)(2), not only can the defense present good evidence of the *defendant's* character trait, but it also can present bad character evidence regarding a *victim* on a pertinent trait.

FRE 404. Character Evidence; Other Crimes, Wrongs, or Acts

(a) Character Evidence.

...

(2) ***Exceptions for a Defendant or Victim in a Criminal Case.*** The following exceptions apply in a criminal case:

(B) subject to the limitations in Rule 412, a defendant may offer evidence of an alleged victim's pertinent trait, and if the evidence is admitted the prosecutor may:

(i) offer evidence to rebut it; and

(ii) offer evidence of the defendant's same trait; and

(C) in a homicide case, the prosecutor may offer evidence of the alleged victim's trait of peacefulness to rebut evidence that the victim was the first aggressor.

Consider an assault case in which the defendant claims that he acted in self-defense. A key issue in such a case would be who was the aggressor. Although the defendant might want to offer good character evidence that he is a peaceful person, he may also want to introduce evidence that the victim is known as an aggressive person. As with the exception for evidence of the defendant's "good" character, evidence of the victim's "bad" character is also limited to a pertinent character trait and to proof by opinion or reputation evidence. FRE 405(a). *United States v. Abrahamson* discusses how this limitation works in practice.

United States v. Abrahamson

2018 U.S. Dist. LEXIS 231416 (E.D. Wa. 2018)

Rice, Chief Judge.

ORDER GRANTING IN PART UNITED STATES' MOTION IN LIMINE TO LIMIT REFERENCE AND EXAMINATION INTO VICTIM'S ALLEGED PRIOR ACTS OF VIOLENCE

Background

Defendant Eugene D. Abrahamson is charged with Assault with Intent to Commit Murder and Assault Resulting in Serious Bodily Injury. Defendant allegedly assaulted L.W. by stabbing her multiple times with a knife. In the instant motion, the Government requests the Court issue an order limiting references and examination at trial on the issues of the alleged prior acts of L.W.

Discussion

Under Federal Rule of Evidence 404(a), "[e]vidence of a person's character or character trait is not admissible to prove that on a particular occasion the person acted in accordance with the character or trait." Fed. R. Evid. 404(a)(1). In a criminal case, "a defendant may offer evidence of an alleged victim's pertinent trait." Fed. R. Evid. 404(a)(2)(B). Under Federal Rule of Evidence 405, character may be proved be either reputation or opinion evidence, or specific instances of conduct. Fed. R. Evid. 405. Specific instances of conduct is an appropriate method of proving character when "a person's character or character trait is an essential element of a charge, claim, or defense." Fed. R. Evid. 405(b).

The Ninth Circuit [in *United States v. Keiser*] has held that evidence should be limited to opinion or reputation when character is not an essential element to the charge, claim, or defense. In a crime of assault, a "victim's violent nature is not essential to a successful claim of self-defense," meaning that only opinion or reputation evidence is admissible.

Here, the Court finds that collateral proof of L.W.'s alleged violent nature is not an essential element of Defendant's charges or his claim of self-defense. Similar to *Keiser*, L.W.'s alleged violent character does not constitute an element of Defendant's claim that he acted in self-defense. The Court finds that opinion or reputation evidence is then admissible [but that specific instances are not] and the Court considers below whether any of the relevant exceptions apply to this rule.

When a defendant introduces evidence of the victim's "bad" character trait, that choice opens the door for the prosecution to rebut that evidence (1) with evidence of the *victim's* character for the opposing trait *and* (2) with evidence of the *defendant*'s character for the same "bad" character trait. FRE 404(a)(2)(B). Thus, once a defendant introduces evidence that the victim had a character for violence, the prosecution would be able to introduce evidence that the victim was peaceful and, as in *United States v. Abrahamson,* character evidence that the defendant was violent. Like the defendant, the prosecution's rebuttal evidence is limited to opinion and reputation evidence—except that the prosecution may elicit specific instances on cross-examination of the defendant's character witnesses. FRE 405(a), (b). In earlier versions of the rule, the prosecutor could not attack the defendant's character unless the defendant had introduced evidence of his or her good character. The change in the rule was designed to "give a more balanced presentation of character evidence when an accused chooses to attack the character of the alleged victim."

Graphically, FRE 404(a)(2)(B) can be illustrated as follows:

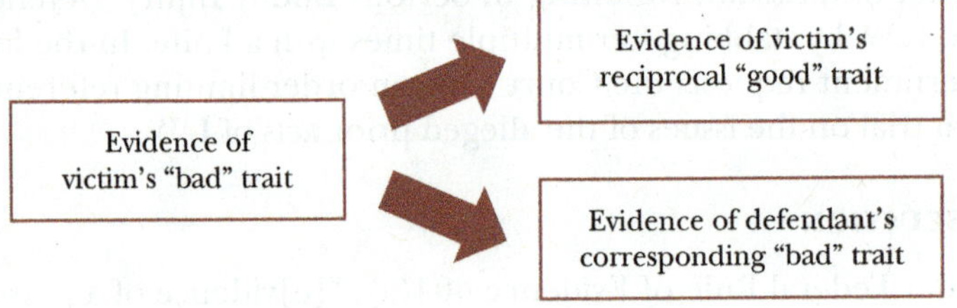

In a homicide case, the rule goes one step further. If the defendant is going to claim that the victim was the aggressor, the prosecution does not have to wait for the defense to call character witnesses to testify that the victim had the character for aggression or violence. *Any* evidence that the defense offers that the victim was the aggressor, including evidence that comes out on cross-examination of the prosecution's witnesses, will open the door for the prosecution to present evidence that the victim was peaceful. FRE 404(a)(2)(C).

Example

Prosecution witness: I saw the fight between Defendant and the victim.
Defense cross: And, didn't you see the victim pull out a knife first and lunge at Defendant?

At this point, the door is open for the prosecution to present character evidence that the victim is a peaceful person.

3. Exception: When Character Relates to an Element of the Claim or Defense [FRE 405(b)]

As in civil cases, character evidence is admissible when a criminal defendant's character is an element of a claim or defense. FRE 405(b). This exception does not arise in criminal cases as often as it does in civil cases, but it still occasionally applies, such as when a defendant raises the defense of entrapment, which turns on his predisposition to commit the charged offense. Otherwise, as *United States v. Keiser* illustrates, this exception is narrowly construed.

United States v. Keiser

57 F.3d 847 (9th Cir. 1995)

HOLCOMB HALL, Judge.

[Defendant appeals his conviction for assault resulting in serious bodily injury.]

The regrettable events giving rise to this prosecution occurred early in the morning of December 19, 1992, in Wolf Point, Montana. A group of people gathered at a home across the street from the home of the defendant, Ronald Keiser. The gathering was raucous. Members of the group had been drinking at various bars and the drinking apparently was continuing at the after-hours party.

Keiser went across the street to complain about the party. Testimony regarding the details of what happened next is conflicting, but it appears that several arguments ensued. Keiser may have slapped a woman; a scuffle began; a guest tried to throw Keiser out of the house; Keiser pulled a chunk of hair out of the head of one of the guests.

Keiser then returned home and was quite upset. His girlfriend was unable to calm him down, so she called the defendant's brother, Randy Keiser, to come over. Randy came and was successful in calming the defendant down. Randy then left the defendant's house and returned to his pickup truck, which was parked on the street between the two houses.

At around the same time as Randy was leaving, however, Victor Romero, the brother of the girl whom the defendant allegedly slapped, arrived at the house across the street. Angered that someone had slapped his sister, Romero set off across the street with two companions. En route, they encountered Randy, the brother of the defendant, sitting in his pickup truck as it warmed up. Romero saw Randy in the truck and, thinking it was Randy who had slapped his sister, began hitting and shoving Randy, who was still sitting in the driver's seat of his truck.

The defendant watched these events from inside his house. He testified that he saw one of the two men who were with Romero remove a gun from the back of a parked Ford Escort station wagon, place it in the back of his pants, and head in Randy's direction. He therefore feared the three men were about to kill his brother. Ronald retrieved a rifle from his bedroom. When he saw what he thought was a gun being used in the assault on his brother, he shot at the people by the truck, hitting Romero.

The bullet passed through Romero's kidney, colon, and small intestine, and lodged in his spine. Romero is now paralyzed from the waist down, and uses a wheelchair and a colostomy bag.

Keiser was arrested four days later and indicted on the charge of violating 18 U.S.C. § 113(f). His theory at trial was that he had acted in defense of his brother, who he reasonably believed was in danger because of the assault by three armed and angry men.

During the second day of trial, the defense called the defendant's brother, Randy Keiser. Defense counsel began to ask Randy about an incident that had occurred the day prior in the lobby outside the courtroom. The prosecutor objected to the line of questioning as irrelevant and the court sustained the objection.

Counsel then approached the bench and defense counsel made an offer of proof:

> [Y]esterday afternoon Victor Romero [the victim] was with his family and friends in the presence of court security. He looked at this witness and he said words to the effect, there he is, that's the fucker's brother. And he had to be taken out of there, he was screaming. I think that's indicative of . . . his actions on the night in question. This is not the sympathetic individual that comes in here and says he was very calm and collected. I think it is relevant.

The court again sustained the objection.

Keiser's only defense in this case was that he was justified in shooting into the muster because he was acting in defense of his brother, whom Romero was assaulting at the time of the shooting. Keiser sought to introduce testimony about this incident outside the courtroom in order to bolster his self-defense claim. He argues on appeal that the incident "tends to show the character of Mr. Romero for anger and violence."

The Federal Rules of Evidence provide an exception to the general rule against character evidence as propensity evidence in the case of "evidence of a pertinent trait of character of the victim of the crime offered by an accused." Fed. R. Evid. 404(a)(2). The advisory committee's note to this rule indicates that a victim's "violent disposition" is exactly the sort of evidence this rule was intended to encompass.

Thus, whether Romero is a violent and angry person is certainly relevant to the defendant's claim that he was acting in defense of his brother: Romero's violent character makes it more likely that his behavior on the night of the shooting was violent—which supports the defendant's defense that he was shooting to protect his brother—than it would be if Romero were peaceable.

The government, however, argues that because the incident occurred *after* the shooting, it has no bearing on whether the defendant acted reasonably at the time of the shooting. It reasons that, at the time of the shooting, the defendant did not "have personal knowledge of the victim[']s character."

This argument misapprehends the purpose of presenting testimony regarding the victim's character. Rule 404(a)(2) provides one of the few instances in which character evidence *is* admissible to allow the jury to infer that a person acted on a specific occasion in conformity with his character. The rule does not contemplate that the character evidence will somehow reveal the defendant's state of mind at the time he acted in self-defense.

These cases suggest a common understanding in the federal courts that "personal knowledge" of the victim's propensity for violence is simply not a prerequisite for admission of victim character evidence under Rule 404(a)(2). We therefore hold that Romero's violent nature is relevant to Keiser's theory of defense of his brother.

Form of the excluded testimony

Despite its relevance, the testimony regarding the altercation outside the courtroom was properly excluded. Under the Federal Rules of Evidence, only reputation or opinion evidence is proper to show that the victim of an assault had a propensity toward violence. The excluded testimony, on the other hand, would have constituted paradigmatic "specific act" evidence.

Methods of Proving Character

(a) *Reputation or opinion*
In all cases in which evidence of character or a trait of character of a person is admissible, proof may be made by testimony as to reputation or by testimony in the form of an opinion. . . .

(b) *Specific instances of conduct*
In cases in which character or a trait of character of a person is an *essential element* of a charge, claim, or defense, proof may also be made of specific instances of that person's conduct. Fed. R. Evid. 405.

Our object in this case, therefore, is to determine whether Romero's violent character is an "*essential element*" of Keiser's defense. We conclude, by reference to the model instruction we expressly approved in Part II, that Romero's violent character does not constitute an *essential element* of Keiser's claim that the shooting was justified because he was acting in defense of his brother. Even had Keiser proven that Romero is a violent person, the jury would still have been free to decide that Romero was not using or about to use unlawful force, or that the force Romero was using was not likely to cause death or great bodily harm, or that Keiser did not reasonably believe force was necessary, or that he used more force than appeared reasonably necessary. On the other hand, a successful defense in no way depended on Keiser's being able to show that the Romero has a propensity toward violence. A defendant could, for example, successfully assert a claim of self-defense against an avowed pacifist, so long as the jury agrees that the defendant reasonably believed unlawful force was about to be used against him. Thus, even though relevant, Romero's character is not an *essential element* of Keiser's defense. Thus, exclusion of the proffered testimony regarding the verbal altercation outside the courtroom was proper because the victim's violent nature is not essential to a successful claim of self-defense. Keiser's claim of self-defense neither rises nor falls on his success in proving that Romero has a penchant for violent outbursts. Thus, Keiser had no right to introduce evidence of the incident outside the courtroom to buttress his defense. We therefore affirm the district court's exclusion of the testimony.

PART D: METHODS OF PROVING CHARACTER

There are three theoretical ways to introduce evidence regarding a person's character:

(1) *Reputation evidence.* A witness testifies that the witness is familiar with the defendant's or victim's reputation in the community and relays that reputation to the trier of fact.

(2) *Opinion evidence.* A witness testifies that the witness is familiar with the defendant or victim and shares the witness's opinion about the person's character.

(3) *Specific acts.* A witness testifies as to individual acts that demonstrate a defendant's or victim's character.

Although the drafters were willing to admit character evidence in limited circumstances, they were wary of having such evidence dominate the proceedings. In particular, they were concerned that "specific instances of conduct (although the most convincing) . . . possesses the greatest capacity to arouse prejudice, to confuse, to surprise, and to consume time." Advisory Committee Notes, FRE 405. Accordingly, the Federal Rules of Evidence generally limit character evidence to opinion and reputation testimony.

FRE 405. Methods of Proving Character

(a) By Reputation or Opinion. When evidence of a person's character or character trait is admissible, it may be proved by testimony about the person's reputation or by testimony in the form of an opinion. On cross-examination of the character witness, the court may allow an inquiry into relevant specific instances of the person's conduct.

(b) By Specific Instances of Conduct. When a person's character or character trait is an essential element of a charge, claim, or defense, the character or trait may also be proved by relevant specific instances of the person's conduct.

As stated in FRE 405, except where a person's character or character trait is an essential element of a charge, claim, or defense, if a party calls a character witness, that witness is limited to offering reputation or opinion testimony. Here are examples of opinion and reputation testimony:

Examples

1. "I have known Defendant for ten years, and I believe that he is an honest person." [*Opinion testimony*]
2. "I live and work in the same community as Defendant and he is generally known as being a peaceful person." [*Reputation testimony*]

As you can see, such testimony can be short and sweet. Once the lawyer establishes the foundation as to how the witness knows the defendant or why the witness is qualified to report on the defendant's reputation, the actual statement as to the defendant's reputation or the witness's opinion is brief.

That is not the end of the story, however. The rules allow the opposing party to challenge the character witness's testimony by asking about specific instances of conduct. Under FRE 405(a): "On cross-examination of the character witness, the court may allow an inquiry into relevant specific instances of the person's conduct." It is this part of the rule that makes it particularly risky for a criminal defendant to call character witnesses.

Consider what might happen when a defendant calls a character witness.

Examples

1. "Ms. Witness, you testified that you believe Defendant is an honest person, correct? Would your opinion of Defendant be the same if you knew he regularly lied to his employer about where he was on sick days? Would your opinion be the same if you knew Defendant cheated on his income taxes?"
2. "Mr. Witness, you testified that Defendant has the reputation of being a peaceful person, correct? Would your testimony be the same if you knew that Defendant was known as an abuser and accused of hurting his family members and pets?"

Rule 405(a) allows the opposing party to ask about particular instances of conduct pertinent to the trait in question. The only requirement is that there be a good faith basis for the question. The witness may stick to his or her opinion or reputation testimony, but presentation of these specific instances of conduct may tarnish the defendant nonetheless.

Critically, FRE 405 does *not* allow the defendant to respond by asking the character witness about specific instances related to good character. The court can control the attacks on the defendant's character by invoking FRE 403, but there is no guarantee that the questions about specific instances regarding character might not both undermine the character witness's testimony and the jurors' view of the defendant. Whether a particular fact is a specific instance (rather than part of the defendant's reputation) is explained in *United States v. Brown.*

United States v. Brown

503 F.Supp.2d 239 (D.C.D.C. 2007)

KOLLAR-KOTELLY, Judge.

[Defendants were police officers, and the charges related to their employment.] The Court shall herein set out the proper legal framework in which it may permit Defendants to introduce character evidence and the Government to cross-examine Defendants based on specific incidents demonstrating character traits which relate to character evidence offered by Defendants.

I. Character Evidence in the Form of Opinion or Reputation May Be Offered by Defendants Which Demonstrates Truthfulness and/or Other Appropriate Character Traits

A. Defendants may introduce relevant character evidence

Pursuant to Federal Rule of Evidence 404(a), "[i]n a criminal case, evidence of a pertinent trait of character [may be] offered by an accused[.]" Generally, where a character trait is relevant to the issues raised at trial, a defendant may offer evidence of a character trait through reputation or opinion testimony: While character witnesses (rather than defendants themselves) are typically used to provide reputation or opinion testimony as to a defendant's character, defendants in certain instances may themselves offer evidence as to their good character and accordingly open the door to cross-examination on those same traits. However, unless the case is one "in which character or a trait of character of a person is an essential element of a charge, claim, or defense," in which case a defendant may provide proof of "specific instances of that person's conduct," see Fed. R. Evid. 405(b), a defendant may only offer character evidence via opinion or reputation testimony.

In determining which character traits may be relevant to the instant case, the Court notes that Defendants have been charged with obstruction of justice and making false statements. The Court concludes that such charges implicate the truthfulness and veracity of Defendants, and accordingly Defendants may offer character evidence with respect to these character traits.

B. Commendations constitute character evidence

Character evidence encompasses evidence of a defendant's prior commendations and awards. Such information is not "background evidence" because the only purpose for offering such information would be to portray a defendant in a positive light by demonstrating recognition of certain character traits or actions that demonstrate such character traits. Such information is even more character-oriented than details regarding a defendant's family composition, which have been held to be properly excluded by this circuit on the grounds that such information constitutes character evidence irrelevant to the charges in a particular case that would be used only to make the defendant appear more sympathetic. *See Harris*, 491 F.3d 440, 446-47 ("The district court's toughest evidentiary rulings, those against the mother and girlfriend, show one persistent aim: to prevent testimony whose purpose was, in the court's judgment, purely or mainly to cast [the defendant] in the sympathetic light of a dedicated family man who spent the evening before his criminal adventure talking with his mother, playing with his son, and caring for his girlfriend").

Two circuit court cases dealing specifically with defendants' requests to introduce their commendations as police officers have rejected such requests. In

United States v. Washington (D.C. Cir. 1997), a defendant charged with narcotics and bribery offenses sought to have his prior police commendations admitted as character evidence, proffered to rebut instances of criminal activity raised by the government and to disprove predisposition. The D.C. Circuit held that the district court did not abuse its discretion in refusing to admit the defendant's commendations, as defendant's "dedication, aggressiveness, and assertiveness" in investigating drug dealing and carjacking (for which he received the commendations at issue) was neither "pertinent" to the crimes charged nor "an essential element" of supposed lack of predisposition to engage in corrupt criminal activity. In *United States v. Nazzaro* (1st Cir. 1989), the defendant was charged with and convicted of mail fraud conspiracy and perjury related to the purchase of police officer promotion exams and answers. Affirmed by the circuit court, the trial court did not permit the defendant to offer into evidence either his resume or anecdotal proof of commendations received while in military service and as a police officer.

However, the charges at issue in *Washington* and *Nazzaro* relate to acts (drug dealing, stealing exams) committed by police officers outside of their scope of duty, such that the manner in which the defendants in those cases performed their professional duties was not at issue. The instant case, however, is less clear-cut, as the conduct at the heart of the charges against Defendants has been cast in trial to date as part and parcel of Defendants' professional diligence and involves their duties as police officers.

But while the traits exemplified by Defendants' commendations may be *relevant* to the instant case, commendations themselves are arguably neither opinion nor reputation testimony and accordingly are more akin to specific instances of conduct which may only be offered "[i]n cases in which character or a trait of character of a person is an essential element of a charge, claim, or defense." Fed. R. Evid. 405(b). *See Cudlitz* ("[Defendant's] good character evidence [by testifying on direct examination that, when previously faced with an unprofitable business venture, he had dutifully paid has debts and had not had any fire connected with that enterprise, nor made a claim for insurance for fire damage on any other of his properties] was improper in form since the rules limit the proponent to offering an opinion or reputation witness rather than testifying to specific instances or events."). No argument has been made by Defendants thus far that this is a case "in which character or a trait of character of a person is an essential element of a charge, claim, or defense."

II. The Government may cross-examine Defendants about specific instances for which it has a good faith basis and which demonstrate either truthfulness or lack of professional diligence only if these traits are raised by character evidence offered by Defendants' witnesses

Pursuant to Federal Rule of Evidence 404(a), "[i]n a criminal case, evidence of a pertinent trait of character [may be] offered by an accused, or by the prosecution to rebut the same[.]" The prosecution may inquire into specific instances of

Defendants' conduct relevant only to character testimony offered by Defendants themselves on cross-examination: "In all cases in which evidence of character or a trait of character of a person is admissible, proof may be made by testimony as to reputation or by testimony in the form of an opinion. On cross-examination, inquiry is allowable into relevant specific instances of conduct." Fed. R. Evid. 405(a).

Cross-examination of a witness regarding specific incidents relevant to the character traits about which that witness testified is permitted in order to test the credibility of the witness:

> The probe on cross-examination may extend to those matters, among others, which legitimately affect the witness' knowledge of the accused's community reputation for the character trait or traits which he confirms. Accordingly, it is well settled, both here and elsewhere, that it may become appropriate on cross-examination to ask a good-character witness whether he has heard reports of particular events, including prior convictions or arrests of the accused, which are inconsistent with the reputation to which he has testified. Questions of this sort are permitted as a test of the credibility of the witness, for the good-reputation testimony may be doubted if the witness has heard the report, and the witness' acquaintance with the accused's community reputation may be disbelieved if he has not heard. The inquiry is indulged solely for that purpose, and the jury must be instructed to limit consideration of the interrogation to an assessment of the worth of the witness' testimony.

In order to cross-examine a witness about a particular incident, a good faith basis must exist that the relevant incident occurred.

III. FEDERAL RULE OF EVIDENCE 403 APPLIES TO CHARACTER EVIDENCE AND CROSS-EXAMINATION RELATED THERETO

Of course, with respect to the admission of character evidence or cross-examination related thereto, the Court must balance whether the probative value of such evidence is substantially outweighed by any unfair prejudice pursuant to Federal Rule of Evidence 403. "Although relevant, evidence may be excluded if its probative value is substantially outweighed by the danger of unfair prejudice, confusion of the issues, or misleading the jury, or by considerations of undue delay, waste of time, or needless presentation of cumulative evidence." The time frame in which specific incidents occurred may affect the Court's calculation of their probative value versus any unfair prejudice or confusion cross-examination on such incidents may cause.

Accordingly, the Court herein has set forth the legal framework under which it shall consider proffered character evidence and any incidents proffered as the subject of cross-examination related thereto.

Character Evidence
Methods of Proof
Summary Chart

<table>
<tr><td>GENERAL RULE:</td><td colspan="2">Defendant's and victim's character evidence is inadmissible</td></tr>
<tr><td colspan="2">EXCEPTIONS:</td><td>Type of Evidence</td></tr>
<tr><td colspan="3">CIVIL</td></tr>
<tr><td></td><td>A party's character or trait of character, if it is an element of a claim or defense
[Defamation, negligent entrustment, child custody, wrongful death damages]</td><td>• Reputation
• Opinion
• Specific instances</td></tr>
<tr><td colspan="3">CRIMINAL</td></tr>
<tr><td></td><td>A party's character or trait of character, if it is an element of a claim or defense
[Entrapment]</td><td>• Reputation
• Opinion
• Specific instances</td></tr>
<tr><td></td><td>A criminal defendant's pertinent trait of character (by either the prosecution or defense) if:
(1) defendant first introduces evidence of that pertinent trait of character, or
(2) defendant first introduces evidence of the same trait in his or her victim</td><td>• Reputation
• Opinion
(BUT: Prosecution may inquire into specific instances on cross-examination)</td></tr>
<tr><td></td><td>A victim's pertinent trait of character (by either the prosecution or defense) if:
(1) defendant first introduces evidence of that pertinent trait of character or
(2) defendant introduces evidence that victim was the aggressor, then the victim's trait for peacefulness</td><td>• Reputation
• Opinion
(BUT: Prosecution may inquire into specific instances on cross-examination)</td></tr>
</table>

Review Questions

Scenario 1: Fraud Allegations

1. **"I think she's . . ."** Defendant is being sued for business fraud. There is also a criminal case pending against Defendant. In the civil case, Plaintiff calls Defendant's business partner to testify that, in his opinion, Defendant is a cheat. Should the testimony be allowed?
2. **No Scrooge.** In her civil case, Defendant calls the president of the chamber of commerce to testify that Defendant is a respected member of the business community who is known as being generous with everyone and, just last Christmas, gave out free laptops to local school kids.
3. **Bad reputation.** In her criminal case, the prosecution seeks to call Defendant's business partner who will testify that Defendant has a reputation for being a dishonest businessperson.
4. **Unfair dealings.** In her criminal case, the prosecution calls the president of the chamber of commerce to testify that, in his opinion, Defendant is stingy and dishonest and has cheated repeatedly in business dealings.
5. **A stand-up partner.** In her criminal case, Defendant calls her prior business partner who will testify that Defendant was very careful in all her business dealings, was completely trustworthy, and paid him back the one time she made a mistake in her accounting.
6. **Bit by bit.** Defendant sues her business partner for defamation. To show that her reputation has been damaged, Defendant calls a series of businesspersons who will testify regarding individual transactions in which Defendant was scrupulously honest.

Scenario 2: Assault Allegations

1. **Bellicose neighbor.** Defendant is sued for assaulting his neighbor, Joe. Defendant seeks to introduce evidence that Joe has started many fights with other neighbors on their block.
2. **Quick to fight.** Defendant is charged with criminal assault. Prosecutor calls several of Defendant's other neighbors to testify that Defendant is known as a hothead who will start a fight over anything.
3. **Laid back.** Defendant is charged with criminal assault. Defendant calls his other neighbors to testify that he is a peaceful and fun neighbor, but that Joe has repeatedly picked fights with them.
4. **Lawlessness.** After the neighbors testify, Prosecutor calls a witness to testify that Joe is a peaceful guy, but that Defendant doesn't care which laws he breaks.

PART E: OTHER SIMILAR ACTS AND HABIT EVIDENCE [FRE 404(b), 406]

Although the Federal Rules of Evidence do not generally allow a party to use propensity evidence to argue that just because someone did something before, they must have done it again, the rules do allow the introduction of other acts to prove more specific points, such as the defendant's motive, knowledge, intent, plan, modus operandi, identity, absence of mistake, or lack of accident. This is a more surgical approach to using other conduct by a party as evidence in a case. Unlike regular character evidence that can be used to say that someone's inherent traits will cause them to act in a particular manner, FRE 404(b) allows the use of other acts to prove up specific issues in a case.

1. *Other Act Evidence [FRE 404(b)]*

Not all evidence of a defendant's other conduct is excluded as *character evidence.* For example, evidence that a defendant previously was convicted of distributing cocaine could be introduced for one of two reasons. First, it could be used to prove the defendant's propensity for drug dealing. Second, it could be used to prove that the defendant knows what cocaine looks and tastes like to rebut the defense—in a case prosecuting him for drug possession—that he thought that he received a shipment of powdered sugar. Introduced for the first purpose, it is character evidence and inadmissible. But if introduced for the second purpose, it is not propensity evidence and may be admissible. As discussed next, the rules of evidence generally permit parties to introduce other acts to prove something *other than* propensity.

(a) Other Act Evidence Is Generally Admissible

FRE 404. Character Evidence; Other Crimes, Wrongs, or Acts

(b) Crimes, Wrongs, or Other Acts.

(1) ***Prohibited Uses.*** Evidence of a crime, wrong, or other act is not admissible to prove a person's character in order to show that on a particular occasion the person acted in accordance with the character.

(2) ***Permitted Uses.*** This evidence may be admissible for another purpose, such as proving motive, opportunity, intent, preparation, plan, knowledge, identity, absence of mistake, or lack of accident.

(3) ***Notice in a Criminal Case.*** In a criminal case the prosecutor must:

(A) provide reasonable notice of any such evidence that the prosecutor intends to offer at trial, so that the defendant has a fair opportunity to meet it; [and]

. . .

(C) do so in writing before trial – or in any form during trial if the court, for good causes, excuses lack of pretrial notice.

Examples

1. Defendant is on trial for distributing cocaine. Defendant plans to argue that he did not know that the white substance he delivered was cocaine. Prosecutor seek to introduce evidence that Defendant had previously distributed cocaine

in order to prove that Defendant likely knew that the substance was cocaine. FRE 404(b) might allow this evidence to show Defendant's knowledge.

2. Defendant is on trial for distributing cocaine. Only a small sample is found on him at the time of arrest. He claims that it was for personal use. Prosecutor seek to introduce evidence that Defendant previously distributed cocaine and used the same size sample found on him to provide to his customers. FRE 404(b) might allow this evidence to prove Defendant's intent to distribute.
3. Defendant is charged with robbing Security Pathetic Bank. The bank video shows a person wearing a joker's mask. Defendant has previously been caught robbing other banks wearing a joker's mask. FRE 404(b) might allow this evidence as evidence of modus operandi so as to identify Defendant as the robber.
4. Defendant is charged with embezzlement. Prosecutor wants to introduce evidence that Defendant had fallen behind in payments that she owed on an illegal gambling debt. FRE 404(b) might allow this evidence as evidence of motive.
5. Defendant is being sued for employment discrimination. Defendant claims that it was just an oversight that Plaintiff, who is Hispanic, was passed over for a promotion. Plaintiff wants to introduce evidence that Defendant previously and illegally withheld bonuses from non-white employees at the business. FRE 404(b) might allow this evidence to show lack of accident or intent.

The trial judge has broad discretion in admitting other acts under FRE 404(b). However, because this evidence can so easily be misused as character evidence, it is critical that judges carefully weigh its probative value for permissible purposes against the danger that it might be misused as propensity evidence. Under FRE 403, the judge may exclude other acts that are unduly prejudicial. Typically, if a defendant does not contest an issue, the probative value of other act evidence introduced to prove that issue may be minimal, and the court will be more reluctant to allow evidence of other acts because those acts may be viewed more as evidence showing a propensity to engage in wrongful behavior rather than to prove a specific disputed issue in the case. On the other hand, if there are contested issues, the FRE 404(b) evidence may be allowed.

Consider the approach that the court takes in *United States v. Byers* in deciding whether to admit the FRE 404(b) evidence in light of considerations under FRE 403.

United States v. Byers

649 F.3d 197 (4th Cir. 2011)

Traxler, Chief Judge.

Patrick Albert Byers, Jr., and Frank Keith Goodman were convicted on charges stemming from a 2007 conspiracy and murder of a witness to prevent him from testifying against Byers in an upcoming state murder trial. Byers and Goodman appeal, challenging evidentiary rulings by the district court.

A.

The government presented strong evidence tying Byers and Goodman to the killing of Carl Lackl and offered a motive for the killing: Lackl was the prosecution's primary witness in the upcoming murder trial of Byers for the March 2006 murder of Larry Haynes, and Lackl was expected to be the only witness to place Byers at the scene of that murder. Byers attempted to refute the purported motive by attacking the strength of the state's case against him for the 2006 Haynes murder and the reliability of Lackl as an eyewitness. Thus, the identity of Byers as the person at the scene of the Haynes murder became a critical part of the Lackl case. In response to Byers's strategy, the government sought to bolster Lackl's credibility and value as a witness by introducing evidence to prove identity, and hence motive, that Byers had previously shot another person in a drug dispute in the same block on North Montford Street where Haynes was killed.

B.

Byers argues that the district court abused its discretion in admitting testimony under Rule 404(b) that in 2004 Byers shot Carlile Coleman on the same North Montford Street block where Haynes was killed. We disagree.

Rule 404(b) prohibits evidence of "'other crimes, wrongs, or acts'" solely to prove a defendant's bad character, but "[s]uch evidence . . . may 'be admissible for other purposes, such as proof of motive, opportunity, intent, preparation, plan, knowledge, identity, or absence of mistake or accident.'"

For prior bad acts to be admissible under Rule 404(b), the proffered evidence (i) "must be . . . relevant to an issue other than character," such as identity or motive. . . . In addition, "the probative value of the evidence must not be substantially outweighed by its prejudicial effect," which "involves a Rule 403 determination." We review the district court's decision to admit evidence under Rule 404(b) for abuse of discretion.

The district court concluded that the 2004 Coleman shooting was important to several critical issues at trial, particularly Byers's identity at the Haynes murder scene. The court noted that Byers's defense to the Lackl murder charges was largely focused on eroding Byers's purported motive to shoot Lackl by showing that "Lackl had mistakenly identified him as the person fleeing from the [Haynes] murder scene in possession of a firearm" and posed little threat to Byers as a witness. The district court reasoned the Coleman evidence was relevant to establish identity in light of the similarities between the Coleman shooting and the Haynes murder:

> There are significant similarities between the Coleman shooting and the Haynes murder, and such similarities are especially significant to the relevance inquiry under Rule 404(b). In both situations, Byers asserted control over his drug turf through the close range use of a semi-automatic handgun in broad daylight. Moreover, both incidents are closely linked by their geographical proximity. The Coleman shooting occurred at 506 North Montford Ave., which is less than a block away from where Haynes was shot and directly across the street from the alley where Lackl saw Byers discard his gun.

The district court also found that the Coleman evidence was "necessary" within the meaning of Rule 404(b) to counter Byers's strategy of negating motive by attacking Lackl's identification. The court explained that

> [t]he challenged evidence does not address collateral issues, but instead supports the government's theory that Byers was an established drug dealer in the vicinity of 506 North Montford Avenue and that he used firearms to control his domain. More specifically, . . . the evidence is necessary to reinforce the government's claim . . . that Byers was correctly identified as discarding a gun near the scene of the Haynes murder.

Byers next contends that the probative value of the Coleman evidence was outweighed by its prejudicial effect. Evidence sought to be admitted under Rule 404(b) must satisfy Rule 403's requirement that the probative value of the evidence must not be "substantially outweighed by the danger of unfair prejudice, confusion of the issues, or misleading the jury, or by considerations of undue delay, waste of time, or needless presentation of cumulative evidence." Fed. R. Evid. 403. "[G]eneral prejudice, however, is not enough to warrant exclusion of otherwise relevant, admissible evidence. Evidence may be excluded under Rule 403 only if the evidence is unfairly prejudicial and, even then, only if the unfair prejudice substantially outweighs the probative value of the evidence." In turn, unfair prejudice exists "when there is a genuine risk that the emotions of a jury will be excited to irrational behavior, and this risk is disproportionate to the probative value of the offered evidence." Generally speaking, "bad acts" evidence, admissible under Rule 404, is not barred by Rule 403 where such evidence "did not involve conduct any more sensational or disturbing than the crimes with which [the defendant] was charged."

Here, the Coleman shooting evidence is actually less sensational than the murder of Haynes, which was clearly admissible, or the murder of Lackl, which was carefully planned and carried out in front of Lackl's daughters for the purpose of precluding Lackl's testimony and evading punishment for the murder of Haynes. With regard to the Coleman shooting, the evidence suggests that the incident was spontaneous and not the result of an elaborate plan. And, of course, the shooting did not result in Coleman's death.

Furthermore, the possibility of unfair prejudice from the Coleman testimony was abated by the two limiting instructions offered by the district court—one immediately before the Coleman evidence was presented to the jury and one immediately before jury deliberation. In the charge to the jury, the district court instructed "you may not consider the evidence of this alleged [Coleman incident] as a substitute for proof that the defendant committed a crime charged in the indictment. Nor may you consider this evidence as proof that the Defendant Byers is a criminal personality or bad character." Accordingly, we reject this argument as well.

In sum, we conclude that the district court did not abuse its discretion in admitting the Coleman evidence. The district court admitted the evidence in question for permissible purposes under Rule 404(b) and not merely to show general criminal disposition.

(b) Approach for Admitting FRE 404(b) Evidence

In admitting FRE 404(b) evidence, courts use the following four-part approach derived from the U.S. Supreme Court's decision in *Huddleston v. United States*, 485 U.S. 681 (1988):

(1) Is the other similar act evidence being offered for a proper FRE 404(b) purpose?
(2) How probative is that evidence of the proffered purpose?
(3) Is the probative value of the evidence substantially outweighed by its unfair prejudice?
(4) Has a party requested a limiting instruction regarding the evidence?

(i) Proper 404(b) purposes

FRE 404(b) lists several "permitted uses" that other acts may be admitted to prove in criminal or civil cases:

- *Motive.* Evidence of motive tends to make it more likely that a person did the conduct at issue and more likely that they did so intentionally. Typically, uncharged acts can prove motive in one of two ways. First, the other act can be the motive for the charged act. For instance, if the defendant is charged with assaulting the victim, evidence that the victim previously assaulted the defendant or the defendant's family members would give the defendant a motive for the assault. Second, the other act can be used to illustrate a common motive that underlies both the uncharged act and the charged act. For instance, if the defendant is charged with a gang-related shooting, evidence that the defendant previously engaged in violence against the same gang is evidence of the common motive underlying both acts—namely, a hatred of the rival gang and its members.
- *Opportunity.* Other acts that demonstrate that a party had the opportunity to engage in the alleged acts are admissible under FRE 404(b).
- *Intent.* Intent is an element of nearly every criminal offense. Evidence that the defendant had engaged in similar acts in the past makes it more likely that she did so intentionally a second or third time.
- *Preparation.* Evidence that a person engaged in other acts in preparation for the act at issue in a case makes it more likely that he or she did so.
- *Plan.* Closely related to preparation, evidence showing that a person planned to engage in the conduct at issue tends to show that the person executed that plan. Like motive evidence, plan evidence can also come in two types—in the first, the other act is evidence that the plan is being executed; in the second, the other act is evidence of the plan itself. Stealing a car to be used in the upcoming bank robbery is the first type; evidence that a defendant has tried the plan previously and failed is the second type.
- *Knowledge.* Other acts that demonstrate a person's knowledge can be relevant to prove that he or she had the knowledge and skills to commit the charged crime and is thus more likely to be the perpetrator.
- *Modus operandi/identity.* To be admitted as proof of identity, the other act must be sufficiently distinctive to tie the known other act of the person to

the charged act where identity is yet to be proven. For example, if there has been a rash of robberies by robbers wearing purple clown wigs and the defendant can be linked to one of the robberies, the unique modus operandi might link the defendant to the other robberies. However, the more generic the other act, the less likely it is to be admitted as proof of identity. For example, if the only modus operandi is that the defendant wore a wig, that fact might be insufficient. Acts tending to show that the defendant was *not* the perpetrator of the charged crime can also qualify for admission under FRE 404(b); when it does, it is called "reverse 404(b) evidence." Thus, evidence that a very similar crime was committed by someone *other than the defendant* can be used to establish that the defendant was *not* the perpetrator of the charged crime.

- *Absence of mistake/lack of accident.* When a defendant claims that the charged incident was a mistake or an accident, evidence showing that the defendant had previously engaged in the same conduct tends to negate the claim of mistake or accident. But accidents do happen, so the question of admissibility turns on the trial judge's assessment of how likely it is that the defendant was unlucky twice or was instead acting intentionally both times.

This list is not exclusive. Evidence may be admitted under FRE 404(b) for purposes not specifically enumerated in that rule. Sometimes a defendant's other acts are relevant to give the narrative of defendant's conduct a complete explanation. This explanation is often referred to as "res gestae" (evidence that is "part and parcel" of the transaction). For example, if the defendant is charged with participating in a scheme to defraud that involves buying a yacht, inflating its value through sham transactions, obtaining insurance on the yacht, and then scuttling the yacht to obtain the insurance proceeds, evidence that the defendant had previously lost three boats off of the same stretch of coast is relevant to explain why the defendant engaged in the elaborate scheme he did (such as why he had to engage in the elaborate machinations to use false names and other information to obtain insurance coverage on which he could later make a claim). It may also occur that a defendant refers to other acts during the current criminal activity. For example, if a drug dealer tells the prospective buyer, "I'll sell you five kilos of drugs, just like I did in our last three transactions," the reference to the prior sales is a part of the narrative.

(ii) Probativeness

Consistent with the general definition of logical relevance set forth in Chapter Two, how probative other act evidence ends up being is a function of (1) the tendency of the uncharged act to prove a fact at issue and (2) the materiality of that fact to the current litigation. The first consideration is usually a function of how similar the other act is to the conduct at issue in the current case. The more similar, the more probative it is. For example, a defendant's prior conduct in selling drugs is relevant to show that he possessed drugs on this occasion with the intent to distribute, but it is less relevant to show that he robbed a bank. The extent of similarity required to make another act probative depends on the facts it is being used to prove. For example, a prior drug transaction with cocaine may be sufficient to make that transaction probative for purposes of proving knowledge of the drug at issue or intent to distribute, but it is not enough by itself to prove that the defendant was the person who committed the drug transaction at issue if the question of identity is disputed; where identity is at issue, the two acts have to be similar enough almost as to be a "signature" or *modus operandi.*

The *degree of similarity* required for each type of proper purpose is identified in this graphic:

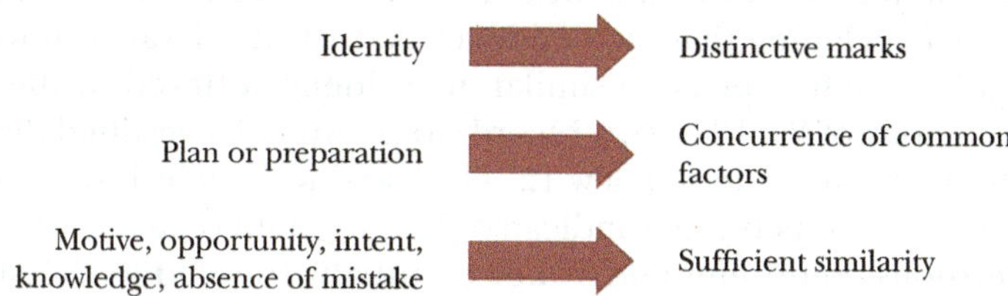

(iii) FRE 403 considerations

The final two *Huddleston* considerations are both grounded in FRE 403: Is the probative value substantially outweighed by the unfair prejudice, and has the party requested a limiting instruction telling the jury to consider the evidence for only the proper purpose (and not to consider it as propensity evidence)?

(iv) Responsibility for admitting FRE 404(b) evidence

There remains a procedural question: What preliminary showing must a party make before a judge will admit "other act" evidence? This question is addressed in *Huddleston.*

Huddleston v. United States

485 U.S. 681 (1988)

Chief Justice Rehnquist delivered the opinion of the unanimous Court.

This case presents the question whether the district court must itself make a preliminary finding that the Government has proved the "other act" by a preponderance of the evidence before it submits [Rule 404(b)] evidence to the jury. We hold that it need not do so.

Petitioner, Guy Rufus Huddleston, was charged with one count of selling stolen goods in interstate commerce and one count of possessing stolen property in interstate commerce. The two counts related to two portions of a shipment of stolen Memorex video cassette tapes that petitioner was alleged to have possessed and sold, knowing that they were stolen.

The evidence at trial showed that a trailer containing over 32,000 blank Memorex video cassette tapes with a manufacturing cost of $4.53 per tape was stolen from the Overnight Express yard in South Holland, Illinois, sometime between April 11 and 15, 1985. On April 17, 1985, petitioner contacted Karen Curry, the manager of the Magic Rent-to-Own in Ypsilanti, Michigan, seeking her assistance in selling a large number of blank Memorex video cassette tapes. After assuring Curry that the tapes were not stolen, he told her he wished to sell them in lots of at least

500 at $2.75 to $3 per tape. Curry subsequently arranged for the sale of a total of 5,000 tapes, which petitioner delivered to the various purchasers—who apparently believed the sales were legitimate.

There was no dispute that the tapes which petitioner sold were stolen; the only material issue at trial was whether petitioner knew they were stolen. The District Court allowed the Government to introduce evidence of "similar acts" under Rule 404(b), concluding that such evidence had "clear relevance as to [petitioner's knowledge]." The first piece of similar act evidence offered by the Government was the testimony of Paul Toney, a record store owner. He testified that in February 1985, petitioner offered to sell new 12" black and white televisions for $28 a piece. According to Toney, petitioner indicated that he could obtain several thousand of these televisions. Petitioner and Toney eventually traveled to the Magic Rent-to-Own, where Toney purchased 20 of the televisions.

The second piece of similar act evidence was the testimony of Robert Nelson, an undercover FBI agent posing as a buyer for an appliance store. Nelson testified that in May 1985, petitioner offered to sell him a large quantity of Amana appliances. Petitioner was arrested shortly after he arrived at the parking lot where he and Nelson had agreed to transfer the appliances. A truck containing the appliances was stopped a short distance from the parking lot, and Leroy Wesby, who was driving the truck, was also arrested. It was determined that the appliances were part of a shipment that had been stolen.

Petitioner testified that the Memorex tapes, the televisions, and the appliances had all been provided by Leroy Wesby, who had represented that all of the merchandise was obtained legitimately. Petitioner maintained that all of the sales for Wesby had been on a commission basis and that he had no knowledge that any of the goods were stolen.

In closing, the prosecution explained that petitioner was not on trial for his dealings with the appliances or the televisions. The District Court instructed the jury that the similar acts evidence was to be used only to establish petitioner's knowledge, and not to prove his character.

A divided panel of the United States Court of Appeals for the Sixth Circuit initially reversed the conviction, concluding that because the Government had failed to prove by clear and convincing evidence that the televisions were stolen. The panel subsequently granted rehearing to address the decision in [another case], in which a different panel had held: "Courts may admit evidence of prior bad acts if the proof shows by a preponderance of the evidence that the defendant did in fact commit the act."

We granted certiorari to resolve a conflict among the Courts of Appeals as to whether the trial court must make a preliminary finding before "similar act" and other Rule 404(b) evidence is submitted to the jury. We conclude that such evidence should be admitted if there is sufficient evidence to support a finding by the jury that the defendant committed the similar act.

Federal Rule of Evidence 404(b)—which applies in both civil and criminal cases—generally prohibits the introduction of evidence of extrinsic acts that might adversely reflect on the actor's character, unless that evidence bears upon a relevant issue in the case such as motive, opportunity, or knowledge. Extrinsic acts evidence may be critical to the establishment of the truth as to a disputed issue, especially when that issue involves the actor's state of mind and the only means of ascertaining that mental state is by drawing inferences from conduct. The actor in the instant case was a criminal defendant, and the act in question was "similar" to the one with which he was charged.

Petitioner acknowledges that this evidence was admitted for the proper purpose of showing his knowledge that the Memorex tapes were stolen. He asserts, however, that the evidence should not have been admitted because the Government failed to prove to the District Court that the televisions were in fact stolen.

Petitioner argues from the premise that evidence of similar acts has a grave potential for causing improper prejudice. For instance, the jury may choose to punish the defendant for the similar rather than the charged act, or the jury may infer that the defendant is an evil person inclined to violate the law. Because of this danger, petitioner maintains, the jury ought not to be exposed to similar act evidence until the trial court has heard the evidence and made a determination under Federal Rule of Evidence 104(a) that the defendant committed the similar act. According to petitioner, the trial court must make this preliminary finding by at least a preponderance of the evidence.

We reject petitioner's position. The Advisory Committee specifically declined to offer any "mechanical solution" to the admission of evidence under 404(b). We conclude that a preliminary finding by the court that the Government has proved the act by a preponderance of the evidence is not called for under Rule 104(a). This is not to say, however, that the Government may parade past the jury a litany of potentially prejudicial similar acts that have been established or connected to the defendant only by unsubstantiated innuendo. Evidence is admissible under Rule 404(b) only if it is relevant. In the Rule 404(b) context, similar act evidence is relevant only if the jury can reasonably conclude that the act occurred and that the defendant was the actor. In the instant case, the evidence that petitioner was selling the televisions was relevant under the Government's theory only if the jury could reasonably find that the televisions were stolen.

In determining whether the Government has introduced sufficient evidence to meet Rule 104(b), the trial court neither weighs credibility nor makes a finding that the Government has proved the conditional fact by a preponderance of the evidence. The court simply examines all the evidence in the case and decides whether the jury could reasonably find the conditional fact—here, that the televisions were stolen—by a preponderance of the evidence. The trial court has traditionally exercised the broadest sort of discretion in controlling the order of proof at trial. Often the trial court may decide to allow the proponent to introduce evidence concerning a similar act, and at a later point in the trial assess whether sufficient evidence has been offered to permit the jury to make the requisite finding. If the proponent has failed to meet this minimal standard of proof, the trial court must instruct the jury to disregard the evidence.

We emphasize that in assessing the sufficiency of the evidence under Rule 104(b), the trial court must consider all evidence presented to the jury. In assessing whether the evidence was sufficient to support a finding that the televisions were stolen, the court here was required to consider not only the direct evidence on that point—the low price of the televisions, the large quantity offered for sale, and petitioner's inability to produce a bill of sale—but also the evidence concerning petitioner's involvement in the sales of other stolen merchandise obtained from Wesby, such as the Memorex tapes and the Amana appliances. Given this evidence, the jury reasonably could have concluded that the televisions were stolen, and the trial court therefore properly allowed the evidence to go to the jury.

We share petitioner's concern that unduly prejudicial evidence might be introduced under Rule 404(b). We think, however, that the protection against such unfair prejudice emanates not from a requirement of a preliminary finding by the trial court, but rather from four other sources: first, from the requirement of Rule 404(b) that the evidence be offered for a proper purpose; second, from the relevancy requirement of Rule 402—as enforced through Rule 104(b); third, from the assessment the trial court must make under Rule 403 to determine whether the probative value of the similar acts evidence is substantially outweighed by its potential for unfair prejudice; and fourth, from Federal Rule of Evidence 105, which provides that the trial court shall, upon request, instruct the jury that the similar acts evidence is to be considered only for the proper purpose for which it was admitted.

Affirmed.

As *Huddleston* holds, another act may be admitted if its proponent proves to the trial judge as a preliminary matter that the jury could find the act to have occurred by a preponderance of the evidence. It is ultimately up to the jury to decide whether it is more likely than not that the other act occurred and whether it supports the inference for which it is being offered.

Several interesting questions can arise in the application of FRE 404(b). First, if the prosecution seeks to use acts for which the defendant was acquitted, why doesn't the Double Jeopardy Clause bar their use as FRE 404(b) evidence? The Supreme Court answered the question in *Dowling v. United States*, 493 U.S. 342 (1990), holding that there was no constitutional violation. Since the use of the other act for FRE 404(b) purposes only requires proof by a preponderance of the evidence, it doesn't matter that the prosecution could not prove beyond a reasonable doubt that the other acts constituted a crime.

Second, is there any particular way that the prosecution must present the FRE 404(b) evidence? The answer is "no." Sometimes, prosecutors can call witnesses who will describe the acts; sometimes they can use documents, including prior criminal records.

Third, what if the others acts occurred *before* the defendant's trial, but *after* the acts that are at issue in the trial occurred? Do these other acts still qualify under FRE 404(b)? The rule does not limit such acts from being used as long as they are relevant to a FRE 404(b) purpose. The rule only speaks of "evidence of a crime, wrong, or other act." It does not state that it has to occur before the events that led to the trial.

Finally, are there any scenarios in which FRE 404(b) might benefit the defendant? The answer is "yes." As noted above, this practice is sometimes called "reverse 404(b) evidence." Imagine a situation in which the defendant blames a third party for the crime. The defendant may seek to show that the crime with which the defendant is charged was committed by someone else as shown by other act evidence that links the third party to similar offenses. A good example is a defendant trying to prove that the modus operandi used to commit a bank robbery can be linked to a third party because there are prior acts of the third party using that same modus operandi.

Review Questions

1. **Ingredients for success.** Defendant is charged with possessing the ingredients of methamphetamine with intent to manufacture. The prosecution seeks to introduce the following items of evidence. Which are admissible under FRE 404(b), and why?
   a. A piece of paper found in the garage next to some of the ingredients that has the "recipe" for how to cook methamphetamine.
   b. Defendant's prior conviction for manufacturing methamphetamine.
   c. A receipt from a pool supply warehouse showing that Defendant purchased 40 gallons of hydriodic acid (a key ingredient of methamphetamine) two weeks before the police executed a search warrant and recovered just four remaining gallons.
2. **Unlucky by design?** Defendant is sued for insurance fraud after his business burned to the ground. The insurance company wishes to introduce evidence that Defendant filed insurance claims for his prior business, which also burned down. What if the insurance company had evidence that Defendant's last two businesses burned down? His last three?

2. *Habit Evidence [FRE 406]*

Habit evidence is another type of evidence that resembles character evidence, but is distinct from it. For example, evidence that a person had the habit of locking his sports car every time he walked away from it is relevant to show that, on the occasion when the car was burglarized, he had followed his usual practice of locking it (such that the defendant entered into a *locked* car, which is an aggravated offense).

This example is of so-called habit evidence, and its admissibility is governed by FRE 406.

FRE 406. Habit; Routine Practice

Evidence of a person's habit or an organization's routine practice may be admitted to prove that on a particular occasion the person or organization acted in accordance with the habit or routine practice. The court may admit this evidence regardless of whether it is corroborated or whether there was an eyewitness.

Excerpts from Advisory Committee Notes to FRE 406

- "Habit" . . . describes one's regular response to a repeated specific situation.

- A habit . . . is the person's regular practice of meeting a particular kind of situation with a specific type of conduct.
- Equivalent behavior on the part of a group is designated "routine practice of an organization" in the rule.

The rules of evidence treat habit evidence differently than character evidence for two reasons. First, habit evidence is typically thought to be a better predictor of future conduct and hence more probative. People *are* creatures of habit, the thinking goes, such that the more routine and almost instinctual conduct is, the more likely it will be admissible as habit evidence. Second, a person's truly habitual behavior is an unthinking act or series of acts routinely undertaken and hence does not require the same probing and possibly demeaning inquiry into a person's character.

As set forth above, the Advisory Committee Notes define a "habit" as "describ[ing] one's regular response to a repeated specific situation." Before a person's (or organization's) conduct will achieve the status of being a habit, courts will examine (1) how specific it is, (2) how frequently it occurs, (3) how often the person or organization deviates from the habitual conduct, and (4) whether its regularity can be confirmed (although, as the text of FRE 406 makes clear, this last consideration is not an *absolute* requirement). For example, a company seeking to prove that it did not receive a letter from the plaintiff may introduce evidence of how it processes incoming mail to establish that it would have documented receiving a letter had one been sent.

PART F: CHARACTER EVIDENCE IN SEX OFFENSE CASES

Sex offense cases are different because they involve different public policy considerations. Reflecting this difference, the rules of evidence governing character evidence carve out special exceptions for cases involving sexual conduct in two significant ways. First, FRE 404(a)(2)(B), as discussed above, allows a criminal defendant in other types of cases to introduce a pertinent trait of a victim's character. This general rule would ostensibly allow a defendant charged with rape to introduce evidence of the victim's character trait for promiscuity to prove that, because she often consents to sex with others, she likely consented to having sex with defendant (thereby absolving the defendant of liability for rape). Admission of this type of evidence is problematic for a number of reasons, so the rules generally—and, in FRE 404(a)(2)(B), explicitly—prohibit such evidence except in very specific situations delineated in FRE 412. Second, the general rule of FRE 404(a)(1) prohibits the admission of character evidence in criminal cases. Despite this general prohibition, and for public policy reasons discussed below, the rules (specifically, FRE 413, 414 and 415) permit prosecutors and civil plaintiffs to introduce evidence of a defendant's propensity for engaging in sexual conduct to prove that the defendant did so on the occasion at issue in that case.[4]

---

4. By definition, these rules of evidence apply in cases involving sexual conduct and, in many cases, sexual abuse. The underlying facts can be disturbing. To minimize the negative impact of these facts on the reader, we have tried to describe only those facts necessary to illustrate the legal concepts.

1. The Victim's Other Sexual Conduct (Rape Shield Statutes) [FRE 412]

For a long time, a victim's sexual history was ostensibly admissible in criminal cases under FRE 404(a)(2)(B) as evidence of the victim's trait for promiscuity. As scholars have explained:

> The law traditionally insisted that the sexual history of a woman who alleged that she was raped was relevant to the truth of her allegation. A chaste woman was considered more likely to have resisted the defendant's sexual advances and to have lodged a legitimate claim of rape. By contrast, an unchaste woman was considered more likely to have succumbed willingly to the defendant's sexual advances and to have lied about it later.
>
> Historically, rape law portrayed consent to sexual intercourse as a kind of temporally unconstrained permission that could be imprecise as to act and even transferable to other people . . . if a woman consented to sexual intercourse with men to whom she was not married, she was deemed indiscriminate in her sexual life. As a result, her sexual consent lost its differentiated and unique nature and she was considered to have functionally consented to sex with others. A rape defendant was able to question a complainant in detail about her prior sexual behavior, looking for evidence that she failed to personify a model of sexual modesty. These questions allowed the defendant to suggest that the complainant was routinely unchaste and "asking for it" on the night in question. "Isn't it true that you have acted lewdly with other men in the late hours at bars when you were in a drunken state?" "Isn't it true that you have been known to kiss men at public parties?" "Isn't it true that you have had sexual intercourse many times before with a number of different men?" Having been unchaste with other men before was enough to suggest functional consent to sexual intercourse with the defendant himself.
>
> [In the late 1970s], rape shield laws emerged on the legal landscape. . . . They circumscribed defendants' abilities to cross-examine rape complainants about their sexual histories and to proffer evidence on the same matter. Almost all jurisdictions in the United States adopted some form of rape shield statute. Legislators concluded that it was illogical to assume that the complainant consented to sexual intercourse with the defendant, or was more likely to lie under oath, simply because she had previously consented to sexual intercourse with someone else.[5]

The justification for these rape shield laws is largely uniform. First and foremost, admitting evidence of a victim's sexual history constitutes an invasive violation of the victim's right to privacy and personhood. For far too many years, the victims of sexual assaults were essentially put on trial when they came forward with their allegations. During rape trials, the victims would be subject to aggressive cross-examination about

---

5. Michelle J. Anderson, *From Chastity Requirement to Sexuality License: Sexual Consent and a New Rape Shield Law*, 70 Geo. Wash. L. Rev. 51 (2002). For a further discussion of the policies underlying rape shield laws, see Harriett R. Galvin, *Shielding Rape Victims in the State and Federal Courts: A Proposal for the Second Decade*, 70 Minn. L. Rev. 763 (1986), and Erin Wilson, *Let's Talk Specifics: Why STI Evidence Should Be Treated As a "Specific Instance" Under Rape Shield Laws*, 98 N.C. L. Rev. 689 (2020).

their own sexual behavior and background. Victims were blamed for putting themselves in the "wrong" situation, and defendants would argue that the victim's provocative behavior, dress, or lifestyle invited the defendant's sexual actions. These persons were victimized once by the crime at issue; dredging up and walking through their entire sexual history victimized them again. Second, and as a direct result of the first reason, the prospective of such withering treatment while testifying discouraged victims of sexual assault from coming forward to report crimes and thus allowed more rapists to escape justice. Some reports documented that fewer than 20 percent of individuals who had been the victim of sexual assault were willing to come forward with their allegations.

The rape shield law in the Federal Rules of Evidence is FRE 412. It now provides for the following:

FRE 412. Sex-Offense Cases: The Victim's Sexual Behavior or Predisposition

(a) Prohibited Uses. The following evidence is not admissible in a civil or criminal proceeding involving alleged sexual misconduct:

(1) Evidence offered to prove that a victim engaged in other sexual behavior; or

(2) Evidence offered to prove a victim's sexual predisposition.

(b) Exceptions.

(1) ***Criminal Cases.*** The court may admit the following evidence in a criminal case:

(A) evidence of specific instances of a victim's sexual behavior, if offered to prove that someone other than the defendant was the source of semen, injury, or other physical evidence;

(B) evidence of specific instances of victim's sexual behavior with respect to the person accused of the sexual misconduct, if offered by the defendant to prove consent or if offered by the prosecutor; and

(C) evidence whose exclusion would violate the defendant's constitutional rights.

(2) ***Civil Cases.*** In a civil case, the court may admit evidence offered to prove a victim's sexual behavior or sexual predisposition if its probative value substantially outweighs the danger of harm to any victim and of unfair prejudice to any party. The court may admit evidence of a victim's reputation only if the victim has placed it in controversy.

Excerpts from Advisory Committee Notes to FRE 412

- Past sexual behavior connotes all activities that involve actual physical conduct, i.e., sexual intercourse and sexual contact, or that imply sexual intercourse or sexual contact.
- In addition, the word "behavior" should be construed to include activities of the mind, such as fantasies and dreams.
- [E]vidence such as that relating to the alleged victim's mode of dress, speech, or life-style will not be admissible.

Additionally, there are procedural requirements that a party intending to offer such evidence must file a motion 14 days before trial and that there must be an *in camera* hearing on the issues. FRE 412(c).

(a) Rape Shield Law in Criminal Cases

As FRE 412(a) states, the general rule in a criminal case is that a victim's sexual background is inadmissible. Sexual background covers a wide range of issues, including marital status or history, mode of dress, sexual practices, dating habits, sexual innuendos, flirting, viewing of or participation in pornography, work or hobby as an exotic dancer, living arrangements, sexual identity, and sexual fantasies. None of these activities is a basis for a defendant to argue that the victim somehow invited or consented to sexual conduct.

Under FRE 412(b), there are three exceptions that would allow a defendant to admit evidence related to the victim's sexual behavior in a criminal case:

(1) Who assaulted the victim? If there is a question of who had sex with the victim, the defendant can introduce evidence of the victim's sexual behavior with another person to show that the defendant was not the source of the semen, injury, or other physical evidence that is found. FRE 412(b)(1)(A). If there is no question that the defendant was the one who had sex with the victim, this exception does not come into play.[6]

(2) Did the victim consent? If the issue is whether the victim consented, either side can offer specific incidences of prior sexual conduct between the victim *and the defendant.* FRE 412(b)(1)(B). This evidence is limited to the victim's sexual conduct with the defendant, not anyone else. For example, the defendant may argue that the defendant and the victim had an ongoing sexual relationship that led the defendant to believe that the victim consented to the sexual behavior. The prosecution is still free to argue that just because the victim consented before does not mean that the victim continued to consent to sexual acts.

(3) Is the defendant constitutionally entitled to introduce the evidence to show the victim's motive for making a false charge against the defendant? This statutory exception is not technically required because a defendant's constitutional rights always trump the rules of evidence, but the drafters nevertheless acknowledged the importance of a defendant's constitutional rights by specifically allowing for admission of victim-related evidence when its admission is constitutionally compelled. FRE 412(b)(1)(C). In *Olden v. Kentucky*, 488 U.S. 227 (1988), which is specifically mentioned in the Advisory Committee Notes for FRE 412, the victim claimed rape because she did not want others to know that she was having a cross-racial relationship. In that situation, the court was willing to admit evidence of the prior relationship. Courts have similarly allowed evidence of other taboo relationships, such as those involving incest.

---

6. In the high-profile allegations against the late basketball great Kobe Bryant, for example, there was an issue of whether Bryant caused the victim's injuries. If this case had gone to trial, Bryant would likely have been allowed to offer evidence of the victim's sexual encounters with other individuals near the time the injuries were sustained.

Olden v. Kentucky

488 U.S. 227 (1988)

Per Curiam.

Petitioner James Olden and his friend Charlie Ray Harris, both of whom are black, were indicted for kidnaping, rape, and forcible sodomy. The victim of the alleged crimes, Starla Matthews, a young white woman, originally told the police that she had been raped by four men. Later, she claimed that she had been raped by only petitioner and Harris. At trial, she contended that petitioner was the sole rapist. Further, while Matthews testified at trial that petitioner had threatened her with a knife, she had not previously alleged that petitioner had been armed. Petitioner and Harris asserted a defense of consent. According to their testimony, Matthews propositioned petitioner as he was about to leave the bar, and the two engaged in sexual acts behind the tavern. [Ultimately], the men . . . dropped Matthews off, at her request, in the vicinity of Bill Russell's home.

[Other defense witnesses] corroborated the defendants' account of the evening. . . . Although Matthews and Russell were both married to and living with other people at the time of the incident, they were apparently involved in an extramarital relationship. By the time of trial the two were living together, having separated from their respective spouses. Petitioner's theory of the case was that Matthews concocted the rape story to protect her relationship with Russell, who would have grown suspicious upon seeing her disembark from Harris' car. In order to demonstrate Matthews' motive to lie, it was crucial, petitioner contended, that he be allowed to introduce evidence of Matthews' and Russell's current cohabitation. Over petitioner's vehement objections, the trial court nonetheless granted the prosecutor's motion *in limine* to keep all evidence of Matthews' and Russell's living arrangement from the jury. Moreover, when the defense attempted to cross-examine Matthews about her living arrangements, after she had claimed during direct examination that she was living with her mother, the trial court sustained the prosecutor's objection.

Based on the evidence admitted at trial, the jury acquitted Harris of being either a principal or an accomplice to any of the charged offenses. Petitioner was likewise acquitted of kidnaping and rape. However, in a somewhat puzzling turn of events, the jury convicted petitioner alone of forcible sodomy. He was sentenced to 10 years' imprisonment.

Petitioner appealed, asserting, *inter alia*, that the trial court's refusal to allow him to impeach Matthews' testimony by introducing evidence supporting a motive to lie deprived him of his Sixth Amendment right to confront witnesses against him. Here, Matthews' testimony was central, indeed crucial, to the prosecution's case. Her story, which was directly contradicted by that of petitioner and Harris, was corroborated only by the largely derivative testimony of Russell, whose impartiality would also have been somewhat impugned by revelation of his relationship with Matthews. Finally, as demonstrated graphically by the jury's verdicts, which cannot be squared with the State's theory of the alleged crime, the State's case against petitioner was far from overwhelming. In sum, we find it impossible to conclude "beyond a reasonable doubt" that the restriction on petitioner's right to confrontation was harmless.

Review Questions

1. **Prior sexual encounters.** A star hockey player is charged with sexual assault on a woman in his hotel room. He claims that the woman consented. The woman had sexual injuries when she was examined by the doctor. The hockey player wants to introduce the woman's prior sexual encounters with other persons in the weeks and months before the alleged sexual assault. Is that evidence admissible?
2. **Proving consent.** A Hollywood producer is charged with sexual assault on a young actress seeking a role in his movie. The producer seeks to introduce evidence that the actress repeatedly engaged in sexual acts with the producer after the alleged assault to show consent. Is the evidence admissible?
3. **Polygamous relationships.** Defendant lives in a community of "free love" and polygamous relationships. The victim alleges that Defendant sexually assaulted him. Defendant seeks to introduce evidence that the victim regularly engages in consensual sexual acts with Defendant and other members of their close community. Is the evidence admissible?

(b) Rape Shield Law in Civil Cases

FRE 412's rape shield law also applies in civil cases, although not in the same way. Rather than go with the approach adopted in FRE 412 for criminal cases that erects a rule against admitting evidence of a victim's sexual traits subject to a few specific exceptions, FRE 412 for civil cases sets up a "reverse FRE 403" balancing test that provides that evidence of a victim's "sexual behavior or sexual predisposition" is admissible if its probative value *substantially outweighs* "the dangerous of harm to any victim or of unfair prejudice to any party." FRE 412(b)(2). (This test is largely the inverse of the FRE 403 test, which calls for the admission of evidence *unless* its probative value is substantially outweighed by the danger of unfair prejudice and other considerations.) Evidence of the "victim's reputation," however, only comes in "if the victim has placed it in controversy."

Consider a situation in which a woman is suing for sexual harassment and the defense wants to introduce evidence that she has dated many people in the office and tells off-color jokes at holiday parties. Before the defense can use this evidence, it must convince the court that the probative value of the evidence substantially outweighs the danger of harm to the victim and unfair prejudice to a party. That was the issue in the next case.

Wilson v. City of Des Moines

442 F.3d 637 (8th Cir. 2006)

BEAM, Judge.

Mary Wilson sued the City of Des Moines, raising claims of sexual discrimination, sexual harassment and retaliation under Title VII of the Civil Rights Act of

1964. Wilson appeals from the district court's denial of her motion for new trial following a jury verdict in favor of the City. We affirm.

I. BACKGROUND

Wilson began working for the City of Des Moines in 1995 and moved to its Public Works Department in 1998. The Public Works director at the time was William Stowe. Roger Jaschke supervised Wilson in the sidewalk division and Keith McLey led Wilson's crew. Wilson trained with Thomas Carrington in the sewer division. The City terminated Wilson in June 2003.

The testimony of her supervisors revealed that Wilson was an employee who had a pattern of lodging complaints only when her own work performance would come under scrutiny. The City further established that Wilson was an employee who did not take responsibility for her own misconduct, instead blaming others and coming up with excuses. Further evidence detailed Wilson's own engagement in sexually explicit language and behavior in the workplace. She talked about vibrators and men's sex organs, among other comments and actions. Indeed, Wilson's workplace behavioral problems extended to sleeping on the job, which the City alleged demonstrated her motive for lying about sexual harassment.

Wilson complained of Jaschke's sexual discrimination in January 2001 based on the difference in treatment she received in work assignments and in the way he treated Wilson. The City investigated the complaint. That investigation revealed some personal differences between Jaschke and Wilson (e.g., he disliked Wilson because Wilson perpetuated a rumor about Jaschke) and Jaschke was disciplined for some unequal work assignments. Wilson was likewise disciplined for spreading the rumor.

Wilson also alleged that she was sexually harassed by McLey, her crew chief on the sidewalk crew. Wilson testified that McLey's offensive behavior began within the first week of working with him, in the spring of 2000. Once the City learned of Wilson's complaint, it separated Wilson and McLey into different crews and the two never worked together again. The City concluded that McLey had indeed acted inappropriately and issued a leave of absence of one day for McLey.

Stowe testified that the City ultimately fired Wilson for misconduct by being several miles off her work route, for damaging a City vehicle and then engaging in a cover-up, in addition to being absent without leave.

On appeal, Wilson cites a very different set of facts. She claims that she was viewed as a productive employee but was exposed to sexual harassment and discrimination in a male-dominated workplace. She claims that McLey subjected her to repeated, vulgar workplace discussions that were sexually offensive and that he touched her inappropriately on a number of occasions. Wilson argued that the City was determined to terminate her, watching her for any problems, and that they ultimately did terminate her as planned.

The jury, as indicated, ruled in favor of the City and against Wilson. [Among other issues], Wilson challenges McLey's allegations about her sexual language and behavior under Federal Rule of Evidence 412, [as well as] the admission of Roxanne Sikes's testimony under Rule 412. Sikes was a coworker of Wilson's who testified that Wilson spoke in a lewd, rude and unlady-like fashion.

II. DISCUSSION

Rule 412 Evidence—Admission and Notice Provisions

Wilson challenges the fact that the district court failed to hold a hearing as required by Federal Rule of Evidence 412 concerning the testimony about Wilson's alleged sexual behavior or sexually charged comments in the workplace and that the district court improperly admitted certain testimony of McLey and Sikes.

Rule 412 excludes, in civil or criminal proceedings involving alleged sexual misconduct, any evidence about a victim's sexual behavior unless certain conditions are met. Fed. R. Evid. 412(a). Among other things, the rule contains procedural requirements—that the party intending to offer such evidence must file a motion specifically describing the evidence and its purpose fourteen days before trial. Fed. R. Evid. 412(c)(1)(A). Then, the court must hold an in camera hearing that allows "the victim and parties" the right to be heard. Fed. R. Evid. 412(c)(2). There was no motion or hearing here. In a civil case, though, Rule 412 allows the admission of evidence "if it is otherwise admissible under [the Federal Rules of Evidence] and its probative value substantially outweighs the danger of harm to any victim and of unfair prejudice to any party." Fed. R. Evid. 412(b)(2).

In past cases we have refrained from expressly determining whether Rule 412 applies to sexual harassment lawsuits. However, advisory committee notes clearly contemplate that "Rule 412 will . . . apply in a Title VII action in which the plaintiff has alleged sexual harassment." Fed. R. Evid. 412 advisory committee's notes. Here, the testimony at issue addressed "other sexual behavior" as contemplated by Rule 412(a)(1). Even so, we believe that the evidence was properly admitted as an exception under Rule 412(b)(2), and the court struck an acceptable balance between the danger of undue prejudice and the need to present the jury with relevant evidence.

At trial, the City offered evidence, by way of McLey's testimony, of sexually charged comments made by Wilson in the workplace. Sikes also testified over Wilson's rule 412 and 403 objections that Wilson used lewd, rude and unlady-like language, which evidence was offered by the City to demonstrate, among other things, why Wilson's coworkers did not socialize with her. The district court also admitted the evidence to establish that Wilson might have welcomed the alleged harassment, determining first that this was not Rule 412 testimony and that even if it was, the testimony was properly admitted because Wilson's behavior in the workplace was relevant to the issue of whether the sexual harassment was invited.

Wilson claims that this eviscerated the policies behind Rule 412 and only disparaged Wilson in an effort to focus the jury's attention on issues other than the evidence of sexual harassment. While we agree that the district court erred in mischaracterizing this evidence as non-Rule 412 evidence in the first instance, there was no danger of harm or prejudice to Wilson or any other party, and the district court correctly determined that it was admissible as relevant to the issues raised by Wilson's claims.

We recognize that an alleged victim's private sexual behavior does not change her expectations about her work environment. Even so, evidence of an alleged victim's particular behavior in the workplace may be probative of welcomeness. In that light, the district court carefully limited the testimony at issue to Wilson's workplace behavior and comments made while she worked with McLey and Sikes. As limited, it was highly probative of the question of whether the alleged harassment was unwelcome.

Rule 412 "aims to safeguard the alleged victim against the invasion of privacy, potential embarrassment and sexual stereotyping that is associated with public disclosure of intimate sexual details." Fed. R. Evid. 412 advisory committee's note. The evidence of Wilson's sexual comments and behavior in the workplace does not raise such concerns. Wilson had no intention to hide this behavior from others, for the comments and behavior at issue were conducted in public. Its probative value substantially outweighed any unfair prejudice that it might have produced.

Finally, the failure to follow the procedural requirements under Rule 412 was harmless in light of Wilson's knowledge that McLey would testify and her own submission of exhibit sixteen that contained facts substantially similar to the testimony adduced at trial.

For the reasons stated herein we affirm the district court's denial of Wilson's motion for new trial.

(c) Procedures for Rule 412 (In Civil or Criminal Cases)

Under FRE 412, if a party intends to offer evidence related to the victim's sexual behavior or predisposition, that party must file a motion at least 14 days before the trial that describes the evidence to be admitted and for what purposes. The victim must be notified of the hearing, and the court must conduct the hearing ex parte (not in public) so that the victim has an opportunity to be heard. A victim ordinarily does not have the right to address the court on evidentiary rulings, but in recognition of the impact of such evidence on victims, FRE 412 gives the victim a right to address the court directly. The record of the hearing must be sealed.

2. *Other Sexual Misconduct Evidence Against Defendants in Sexual Assault and Misconduct Cases [FRE 413, 414, 415]*

The other main way in which the rules governing character evidence deviate in cases involving sexual misconduct is that, in sexual misconduct cases, the civil or criminal accuser may introduce evidence of the defendant's prior sexual misconduct to prove the defendant's propensity to do it again. Congress adopted FRE 413, 414, and 415 in 1994 as part of a crime bill to address a range of issues relating to sexual offenses. These rules were not without controversy. *See* Christina E. Wells & Erin Elliott Motley, *Reinforcing the Myth of the Crazed Rapist: A Feminist Critique of Recent Rape Legislation*, 81 B.U. L. Rev. 127 (2001) (arguing that the rules feed into the "myth of the crazed rapist" and are "inconsistent with the feminist agenda regarding rape"). They were accordingly not adopted in a standard fashion and do not include any Advisory Notes. Moreover, there continues to be a debate as to whether the assumption—that a person who commits a sexual crime is likely to commit another—is an accurate assumption. Nonetheless, the rules provide, in pertinent part, as follows:

FRE 413. Similar Crimes in Sexual-Assault Cases

(a) Permitted Uses. In a criminal case in which a defendant is accused of a sexual assault, the court may admit evidence that the defendant committed any other sexual assault. The evidence may be considered on any matter to which it is relevant.

FRE 414. Similar Crimes in Child-Molestation Cases

(a) Permitted Uses. In a criminal case in which a defendant is accused of child molestation, the court may admit evidence that the defendant committed any other child molestation. The evidence may be considered on any matter to which it is relevant.

FRE 415. Similar Acts in Civil Cases Involving Sexual Assault or Child Molestation

(a) Permitted Uses. In a civil case involving a claim for relief based on a party's alleged sexual assault or child molestation, the court may admit evidence that the party committed any other sexual assault or child molestation. The evidence may be considered as provided in Rules 413 and 414.

Because these rules permit introduction of this evidence "on any matter to which it is relevant," other sex acts by a defendant may be used as propensity evidence in both criminal and civil cases. The prosecutor or plaintiff need not show an independent, nonpropensity purpose under FRE 404(b). The only limitation is that the evidence meet the definition of "sexual assault" evidence under FRE 413(d) for admission in an adult criminal or civil sexual assault case. In a criminal or civil child-molestation case, the prior acts must involve "child molestation," as defined by FRE 414(d)(2) as various sexually motivated crimes involving persons under the age of 14. This list of qualifying offenses includes not only physical contact with a child, but also the possession or distribution of child pornography (covered by 18 U.S.C. chapter 110). In some cases, the prosecution will seek to admit evidence of the defendant's other sexual conduct under *both* FRE 414 and 404(b). There must also be pretrial notice to the defendant that such evidence will be used. The evidence of the other acts may include convictions of the defendant for prior sexual assault or testimony regarding the incidents, even if they did not result in convictions.[7]

---

7. Not all states admit such evidence in criminal cases. Fl. Stat. § 90.404(2)(b), (2)(c); Tex. R. Evid. 412.

Examples

1. Defendant is charged with sexual assault. Prosecutor seeks to admit testimony that Defendant sexually assaulted another victim 20 years ago. This evidence is admissible under FRE 413.
2. Defendant is charged with child molestation. Prosecutor seeks to admit evidence that Defendant was previously convicted of sexually assaulting two adults. This evidence is inadmissible under FRE 414 because it is not "child molestation," but may be admissible under FRE 413.
3. Defendant is sued for sexual assault. Plaintiff wants to have witnesses testify that Defendant had assaulted them, although they never pursued cases against him. FRE 415 would allow such evidence for propensity purposes.

Given the impact of such propensity evidence, the issue has arisen as to whether a defendant may seek to preclude evidence under FRE 413, 414, and 415 because it is unduly prejudicial. The rules themselves state that the court "may" admit the evidence, not that it "must." Accordingly, the courts have held that the trial judge should entertain a motion under FRE 403 to preclude this type of propensity evidence. In fact, in some states, the courts have held that due process requires that the trial judge conduct such a balancing. The judge can consider many factors in determining whether the prejudice of introducing this evidence substantially outweighs the probative value, as illustrated in the next case.

United States v. Schaffer

2014 U.S. Dist. LEXIS 54325 (E.D.N.Y. 2014)

Ross, Judge.

Defendant Gregory John Schaffer ("Schaffer") is charged with four counts under 18 U.S.C. § 2422 relating to his alleged enticement of a minor to engage in illicit sexual activity. The government moved to admit at trial video evidence of Schaffer's prior sexual assaults on two minors under Federal Rule of Evidence ("FRE") 413 and his possession of child pornography under FRE 404(b).

BACKGROUND

According to the complaint, a 15-year-old girl ("Jane Doe") from Brooklyn, New York, notified law enforcement in March 2012 that she had been sexually assaulted by a 30 to 35-year-old man named "John." In late February or early March, Jane Doe had placed an advertisement on Craigslist indicating that she was a "Teen in need of a afterschool & weekend job (NYC)." An individual subsequently identified as Schaffer responded to the advertisement in an email stating that he was "looking for part time help in my store in Newport mall in jersey city."

On or about March 17, 2012, Jane Doe traveled to Schaffer's office in Jersey City, New Jersey, accompanied by a male friend who was also a minor (the "Friend"). After they arrived, Schaffer took Jane Doe into a private office area and closed the door, while the Friend remained in the waiting area. During the meeting, Schaffer told Jane Doe that she was probably going to work at the Victoria's Secret store, and he asked her whether she was sexually active or used drugs. He also gave her papers for her guardian, her great-grandmother, to sign.

When Jane Doe returned to Schaffer's office on or about March 18, 2012, Schaffer had her sign a "confidentiality agreement" and an employment contract. After she signed the documents, Schaffer informed Jane Doe that she had agreed to have sex with him by signing the contract. Schaffer then asked Jane Doe to try on outfits, including a bathing suit, and took photos of her. He told her that, if the job was important to her, she would try on the bathing suit. He tried to place her hands on his genitals, and she asked if she could get out of the contract. Schaffer then asked her if she had a boyfriend and, when she told him that her boyfriend was 17 years old, threatened to "report" the boyfriend if she tried to get out of the contract. He also threatened to sue her great-grandmother for breach of contract. Schaffer then had sexual intercourse with Jane Doe on his desk and used a condom from his desk drawer. Jane Doe tried to reach for her phone several times, but Schaffer blocked her hand.

While Jane Doe was in Schaffer's office, there was a black camera on a tripod in the office.

During the search of Schaffer's office on June 3, 2012, the items recovered by the agents included a computer, a camcorder, and a number of electronic storage devices. Agents subsequently obtained a search warrant for those devices. They discovered approximately 85 images of child pornography and four videos depicting Schaffer with two different minor girls.

The government seeks to admit as evidence at trial select portions of the four videos pursuant to FRE 413, and the court has reviewed those excerpts of the videos in camera. The government also seeks to admit clips from ten videos and three still images of child pornography recovered from Schaffer's computer under FRE 404(b). The court has also reviewed those materials, which depict explicit sexual contact involving girls who appear to be as young as 5 years old. While several of the videos involve girls who appear to be pre-teens or teenagers closer to age 15, a number of the videos involve girls who appear prepubescent and much younger than 15.

DISCUSSION

The government seeks to introduce portions of the four videos recovered from Schaffer's electronic devices as evidence of his prior sexual assaults on two other minor girls. Although propensity evidence is not generally allowed under FRE 404, it may be allowed in a sexual offense case under FRE 413. FRE 413 states:

> In a criminal case in which a defendant is accused of a sexual assault, the court may admit evidence that the defendant committed any other sexual assault. The evidence may be considered on any matter to which it is relevant.

Fed. R. Evid. 413(a). This rule "renders evidence of prior sexual assaults presumptively admissible in a federal prosecution for sexual assault." First, Schaffer does not appear to contest the government's characterization of the charges against him in this case as well as the prior acts evidenced by the videos as involving "sexual assault" within the meaning of FRE 413. This court agrees with the government that offenses under 18 U.S.C. § 2422 involving the enticement of a minor to engage in illegal sexual activity, as charged in this case, fall within the realm of crimes involving nonconsensual sexual contact defined as "sexual assault" under the rule.

Second, the video evidence is highly relevant to the charges against Schaffer. As part of its case, the government must prove that, when Schaffer enticed Jane Doe to travel across state lines, he had the intent to engage in sexual conduct with her. Schaffer's prior acts demonstrating his sexual interest in minor females are extremely relevant to the question of his intent here. This is particularly so because of the similarities between the conduct shown on the videos and Schaffer's alleged conduct with Jane Doe. The videos show a pattern of Schaffer's enticing girls into situations in which they are alone with him and making them try on swimsuits before forcing them to engage in sexual conduct. This pattern is highly probative of the question of his intent here.

Third, applying the FRE 403 balancing test after having reviewed the videos in camera, the court finds that the probative value of the portions of the videos that the government seeks to introduce are not substantially outweighed by the danger of unfair prejudice to Schaffer. As discussed above, the video evidence showing conduct with minors that occurred close in time and that is highly similar in pattern is extremely probative of Schaffer's intent in this case. Schaffer argues, however, that the probative value of the videos is outweighed by their potential prejudicial effect because they involve minors who are younger than Jane Doe (and therefore those prior acts are more serious or inflammatory). The Second Circuit has stated that prior acts of child molestation "may be highly prejudicial but not necessarily unfairly prejudicial." Here, having reviewed the videos, the court cannot conclude that the videos are more serious or inflammatory than the allegations that the defendant engaged in nonconsensual sexual intercourse with a 15-year-old girl. Although there is a slight age difference between Jane Doe and the other two girls, it is not great. They appear to be pre-teen or teenage, pubescent girls who could be attributed with an age range somewhere between 12 and 16. Even were slight differences in age discernible, the differences are not so inflammatory as to be unfairly prejudicial.

The government also seeks to introduce some of the child pornography recovered from Schaffer's devices as evidence of his intent pursuant to FRE 404(b). Having reviewed the child pornography that the government seeks to introduce, the court harbors serious concerns about the potential for unfair prejudice that could result from the introduction of the still images and video clips. These pornographic materials, while probative of Schaffer's intent, are of lesser probative value than the four videos discussed above because, unlike those videos, they do not demonstrate Schaffer's own actions and pattern of conduct with minor females. At the same time, the pornographic materials pose a greater risk of prejudice because they are extremely explicit and, in most cases, involve young girls who are visibly pre-pubescent.

The court declines to rule on the admission of the ten videos and three still images of child pornography prior to trial and reserves decision pending the presentation of evidence at trial.

Review Questions

1. **Propensity to molest.** Defendant is charged with molesting his seven-year-old cousin. Prosecutor seeks to introduce evidence that (1) Defendant was previously convicted of molesting a seven-year-old child, and (2) Defendant also molested a nine-year-old but was never criminally charged with that conduct.
   a. Defendant objects on the ground that the evidence should be admitted only to prove his intent and not to prove his propensity to molest. Is this objection well taken?
   b. Defendant objects on the ground that Prosecutor did not give him advance notice of her intent to introduce this evidence. Is this objection well taken?
   c. Defendant objects on the ground that the time it would take to prove the second, uncharged incident (by calling the victim and others that defendant would call to contradict the victim) would take up too much time under FRE 403. Is this objection well taken?
2. **Past harassment.** Plaintiff sues her boss for engaging in sexual harassment in the workplace. Plaintiff seeks to introduce evidence that her boss has been twice held liable for sexual harassment. Is this evidence appropriately admitted to prove the boss's propensity for engaging in sexual misconduct?

SUMMARY OF CHARACTER EVIDENCE

As explained in this chapter, the general rule is that trials are based on the parties' acts, not their character, but there are exceptions to that rule. First, if the defendant in a criminal case opens the door by presenting good character evidence, the prosecution can rebut with bad character evidence. The format of this character evidence is limited to opinion or reputation testimony. It must also relate to a pertinent character trait. Second, in the very limited group of civil cases in which character is an "element" of a claim, specific acts demonstrating an individual's character may be presented. Third, although general character evidence is inadmissible, under FRE 404(b), other act evidence is admissible in criminal and civil cases if it goes to a nonpropensity purpose. Finally, in cases involving sexual conduct, the general rule is that a victim's character is protected under FRE 412, except with limited exceptions, but the defendant's propensity for wrongful sexual conduct is admissible under FRE 413, 414, and 415.

GENERAL RULE:	**Character evidence is inadmissible**	
EXCEPTIONS:		**Type of evidence**
	CIVIL	
	A *party's* character or trait of character, if it is an element of a claim or defense [*Defamation, negligent entrustment, child custody, wrongful death damages*]	• Reputation • Opinion • Specific instances
	A *victim's* "sexual behavior or sexual predisposition" if the probative value of that evidence substantially outweighs the danger of harm to any victim or unfair prejudice	• Reputation • Opinion • Specific instances
	A *criminal defendant's* other acts of "sexual assault" and "child" molestation	• Specific instances
	CRIMINAL	
	A *party's* character or trait of character, if it is an element of a claim or defense [*Entrapment*]	• Reputation • Opinion • Specific instances
	A *criminal defendant's* pertinent trait of character (by either the prosecution or defense) if: (1) defendant first introduces evidence of that pertinent trait of character, or (2) defendant first introduces evidence of the same trait in his victim	• Reputation • Opinion (BUT: Prosecution may inquire into specific instances on cross examination)

GENERAL RULE:	Character evidence is inadmissible	
	A *victim's* pertinent trait of character (by either the prosecution or defense) if: (1) defendant first introduces evidence of that pertinent trait of character, or (2) defendant introduces evidence that victim was the aggressor, then the victim's trait *for peacefulness* EXCEPT: (1) evidence that a victim engaged in other "sexual behavior" or evidence of the victim's "sexual predisposition" is inadmissible except when: (a) Offered to prove that *someone else* was the source of semen, injury, or other physical injury to the victim (b) evidence that a victim has engaged in sexual behavior with the defendant to prove consent (c) evidence whose exclusion would violate the U.S. Constitution	• Reputation • Opinion (BUT: Prosecution may inquire into specific instances on cross-examination) • Specific instances as to exceptions when the victim's sexual behavior is permitted
	A *criminal defendant's* other acts of "sexual assault" and "child" molestation	• Specific instances

TEST YOUR UNDERSTANDING

To test your understanding of the material in this chapter, turn to the Supplement for additional practice problems.

CHAPTER 4

LIMITS ON EVIDENCE FOR POLICY REASONS

Although the Federal Rules of Evidence generally embrace a liberal approach to the admission of relevant evidence, in certain situations those rules will nevertheless exclude evidence — on relevance grounds — that otherwise satisfies the requirements of "logical relevance" under FRE 401 and "practical relevance" under FRE 403. As discussed more fully in Chapter Two, FRE 401 and FRE 403 examine the relevance of evidence on an item-by-item basis, examining each proffered item of evidence to assess whether it is both logically relevant and that its probative value is not substantially outweighed by other concerns such as unfair prejudice, confusing the issues, undue delay, and the like.

This chapter discusses specialized rules that mandate the exclusion of specific types of evidence *as a categorical matter* based on social policy concerns. These special rules of exclusion are FRE 407 through FRE 411. As to each, the special rule excludes evidence so as to avoid discouraging a practice that is deemed socially beneficial.

Understanding these rules requires us to ask two questions:

- What social policy is the special rule trying to advance? In other words, what practice is the special rule trying to encourage — or, at a minimum, *not* discourage?
- What are the requirements of the special rule? Most of the special rules (1) apply to certain, specified types of evidence (2) when that evidence is offered for a specific purpose. If the evidence falls outside the universe of evidence identified in the special rule or if the evidence is offered for purposes other than those identified as being prohibited by the special rule, the special rule does not apply. However, the evidence still remains subject to exclusion under FRE 403 on an item-by-item basis.

Part A discusses FRE 407, which requires the exclusion of evidence of subsequent remedial measures, when offered to prove liability.

Part B discusses FRE 408, which requires the exclusion of evidence of offers to settle a civil case, and statements made during the course of settlement negotiations, when offered to prove the validity of a pending, disputed claim.

Part C discusses FRE 409, which requires the exclusion of evidence that a person offered or did pay for medical, hospital, or similar expenses resulting from an injury, when offered to prove liability for that injury.

Part D discusses FRE 410, which requires the exclusion of evidence of a later-withdrawn plea in a criminal case, statements made during the in-court colloquy underlying the later-withdrawn plea, and statements made during plea negotiations, when offered for *any* purpose. Part D also discusses the exceptions to this special rule.

Last, Part E discusses FRE 411, which requires the exclusion of evidence that a person did or did not have liability insurance, when used to prove that the person acted negligently or wrongfully.

Because the rationales for these special rules categorically excluding evidence rest on social policy, it is not surprising that the federal courts have split over whether these rules are considered "substantive" or "procedural" rules within the meaning of *Erie Railroad Co. v. Tompkins*, 304 U.S. 64 (1938). Some courts have held that these rules are *substantive*, such that a federal court hearing a case grounded in the diversity jurisdiction must apply the relevant state's categorical exclusion rules rather than FRE 407 through FRE 411. *See Wheeler v. John Deere Co.*, 862 F.2d 1404 (10th Cir. 1988). Other courts have held that these rules are still mostly *procedural*, such that a federal court hearing a diversity case should apply FRE 407 through FRE 411 rather than the corresponding rule under state law. *See Flaminio v. Honda Motor Co., Ltd.*, 733 F.2d 463 (7th Cir. 1984). This distinction matters because, as discussed below, not all states have drafted their special relevance rules the same way as the Federal Rules of Evidence.

PART A: SUBSEQUENT REMEDIAL MEASURES [FRE 407]

From a public policy standpoint, do we want parties to be able to introduce evidence of what the other party did after the injury at issue to minimize the chances of that injury happening again? Consider the following examples.

Examples

1. Defendant owns a market. Plaintiff slips on the floor while shopping. Worried that the tile in the market might be too worn, Defendant changes the market's flooring the day after Plaintiff's fall. Plaintiff seeks to introduce evidence that Defendant changed the flooring to prove that the original flooring was negligently maintained.
2. Plaintiff has an accident while driving her Toyota sedan. She seeks to introduce evidence that after her accident, Toyota recalled her vehicle and changed the design of the brakes. Plaintiff files a product liability claim against Toyota for defective design in its brakes and wants to use the change of design to prove that Toyota's earlier design was defective.

FRE 407 generally bars the admission of subsequent remedial measures.

FRE 407. Subsequent Remedial Measures

When measures are taken that would have made an earlier injury or harm less likely to occur, evidence of the subsequent measures is not admissible to prove:

- negligence;
- culpable conduct;
- a defect in a product or its design; or
- a need for a warning or instruction.

But the court may admit this evidence for another purpose, such as impeachment or—if disputed—proving ownership, control, or the feasibility of precautionary measures.

1. *What Social Policy Does FRE 407 Serve?*

Rule 407 rests chiefly on two rationales. The first is a relevance-based rationale—namely, a person's decision to make something safer does not necessarily mean that it was *legally* unsafe to begin with or that the person should be somehow liable for injuries incurred before those additional measures were taken. As the Advisory Committee Notes to FRE 407 state, "The conduct is not in fact an admission, since the conduct is equally consistent with injury by mere accident or through contributory negligence." The second is a social policy-based rationale—namely, that even if one thought that the defendant's subsequent actions have some logical relevance to whether the defendant was responsible for the accident, we as a society do not want to discourage people and companies from taking steps to further public safety like making subsequent repairs, installing safety devices, changing company rules, and even discharging employees who inflict harm on others. Without a rule like FRE 407, people and companies would have a *disincentive* to make things safer. FRE 407 removes that disincentive and encourages the greater good.

2. *What Are the Requirements of FRE 407?*

By its text, FRE 407's prohibition applies as follows:

(1) To "subsequent remedial measures"—that is, (a) *measures* taken *after* an injury or harm has occurred (b) that "would have made [that] *earlier injury or harm less likely to occur.*"
(2) When offered to prove:
    (a) Negligence;
    (b) Culpable conduct;
    (c) "A defect in the product or its design"; or
    (d) "A need for a warning or instruction."

FRE 407	Prohibited Evidence	Prohibited Purposes	Permissible Evidence and Purposes
	(1) Subsequent remedial measures. (2) That would have made injury/harm less likely.	(1) Negligence. (2) Culpable conduct. (3) Product or design defect. (4) Failure to warn.	(1) Remedial measures taken *before* the harm/injury at issue. (2) Remedial measures that would not have reduced likelihood of harm/injury. (3) Subsequent remedial measures admitted to prove: (a) Ownership, (b) Control, or (c) Feasibility.

(a) What Is a "Subsequent Remedial Measure"?

Sandoval v. Ritz Developers

2006 U.S. Dist. LEXIS 2645 (S.D.S.D. 2006)

Simko, Judge.

[Plaintiff is suing a developer after she slipped on ice on the sidewalk in front of defendant's building.] The fall occurred during the time of the year when temperatures rise above freezing during the day so snow melts. Water is produced both from the snow on the ground in the area surrounding the low spot and from the roof of the motel where water runs through a down spout and drains onto the sidewalk. The water collects in the low spot on the sidewalk. During the evening the temperature drops below freezing and the water collected on the sidewalk turns to black ice. One of the motel employees had seen ice at that place on the sidewalk in prior years.

Defendant claims it was not negligent, but also that plaintiff overlooks her own contributory negligence. Ritz hired reputable and good contractors to build the motel and sidewalk and complete the landscaping. The property and sidewalk are in good condition. There are no cracks and no upheavals in the sidewalk. The levels of the sidewalk do not change. The owners did not notice any low areas in the sidewalk that would pool water. They did not receive any complaints about water pooling before plaintiff's fall. It is their practice to remove ice and snow upon discovery. On the day of the fall the sidewalk was clear and dry. There had been no new snow. It did not rain. The temperature "had been around freezing the entire day" and melting was not anticipated by motel employees. There was an area on the sidewalk where ice formed, but the employees were not aware of it until after plaintiff fell.

[Plaintiff claims it was error for the trial court not to allow plaintiff to introduce evidence that after the accident, one of defendant's employees put ice melt on the sidewalk where plaintiff fell. Defendants also added additional lighting to the area.]

There was no error in excluding the [evidence]. Rule 407 says so. [This rule bars the introduction of subsequent remedial measures.]

Plaintiff claims Federal Rule of Evidence 407 permits subsequent remedial measures evidence when offered for the purpose of impeachment. [But this exception does not apply]. The location of the fall and the presence of ice at that location on the sidewalk are not disputed. There is no evidence from the defendant to impeach. This is merely an attempt to circumvent FRE 407 to introduce subsequent remedial measures evidence to establish negligence.

The sentence about putting salt on the sidewalk does not tend to prove or disprove any issue in the case so it is not relevant evidence. That salt was placed on the sidewalk after plaintiff's fall would tend to prove there was ice on the sidewalk and that salt had not been applied before plaintiff's fall, both of which were undisputed. The proffered evidence, therefore, was not for the purpose of impeachment. Putting salt on the side walk is a subsequent remedial measure which is not admissible to prove negligence under FRE 407.

Plaintiff claims she should have been permitted to argue to the jury about lighting that showed on a video tape of the motel which was taken after the fall. The video tape was introduced into evidence by the defendant. The video tape showed that a double row of fluorescent bulbs existed under the soffit of the motel. Plaintiff was prohibited from pointing out to the jury that these lights did not exist on the building at the time of the fall. This allowed the jury to be misled about the lighting which existed at the scene of the fall at the time of the fall.

Defendant claims . . . the new lighting had been installed after plaintiff's fall for the purpose of drawing attention to the motel, not for the purpose of illumination. He testified those lights were not installed for the purpose of lighting the sidewalk.

The lights plaintiff claims she should have been able to point out to the jury did not exist at the time Mrs. Sandoval fell. They did not tend to prove or disprove any fact material to the outcome of the case. They did not lend significant light, if any at all, to the place where Mrs. Sandoval fell. In that sense, the lights were not even remedial measures. Nonetheless, giving plaintiff the benefit of the doubt about the light cast by these new lights under the soffit on the place where Mrs. Sandoval fell, they were subsequent remedial measures which could not be used to prove negligence. There was no other possible reason for plaintiff to point them out to the jury other than to try to prove defendant's negligence by reference to them.

[T]he rulings regarding subsequent remedial measures were correct.

FRE 407 covers a wide range of remedial *measures.* They may include physical improvements to a location where an accident has occurred, changes in a product design, new policies and regulations for employees to follow, additional warnings about a product, new security procedures, or any change that relates to the safety of a product, place, or practice. FRE 407 does not cover *statements.*

The measure must nevertheless be *subsequent* to the accident at issue. For example, assume the plaintiff buys a 2018 model of a car. In 2019, the manufacturer changes the design to make it safer but does not notify the 2018 owners. The accident occurs in 2020. If the remedial actions occur prior *to the injury*, they are not barred by FRE 407.

(b) What Is the Subsequent Remedial Measure Being Offered to Prove?

FRE 407 only prohibits subsequent remedial measures from being used to prove the defendant's negligence, culpable conduct, product defect or design, or the need for a warning. The last two categories were not added until 1997. Prior to that time, the federal courts were split on whether FRE 407's prohibitions on the use of subsequent remedial measures to prove "culpable conduct" encompassed products liability claims based on theories of strict liability.[1]

By its terms, FRE 407 does not apply when the measures are introduced for any other purpose. FRE 407 goes so far as to enumerate a few of those nonprohibited purposes:

- To impeach a witness, or
- *If disputed,* to prove ownership, control, or the feasibility of precautionary measures.

When admitted for these permissible purposes, however, and if there is a danger that the evidence might be considered for an impermissible purpose as well, a trial judge must give an instruction limiting the jury's consideration of the evidence to the permissible purpose if such an instruction is requested. FRE 105.

---

1. Many states have followed the lead of the Federal Rules of Evidence: Texas lists the same categories, Tex. R. Evid. 407(a); and Florida lists negligence, culpable conduct or "the existence of a product defect," Fla. Stat. § 90.407. As a matter of judicial precedent, Illinois bars subsequent remedial measure to prove negligence, but the Illinois courts are split on whether that prohibition applies in cases based on strict liability. *Herzog v. Lexington Township,* 167 Ill. 2d 288, 300 (Ill. 1995) (bar applies in negligence actions); *compare Davis v. International Harvester Co.,* 167 Ill. App. 3d 814, 822 (Ill. Ct. App. 1988) (bar applies in strict liability cases unless feasibility is disputed) *with Stallings v. Black & Decker (U.S.), Inc.,* 342 Ill. App. 3d 676, 684-85 (Ill. Ct. App. 2003) (bar does not apply in strict liability cases). Along similar lines, New York as a matter of judicial precedent applies the subsequent remedial measures bar in cases based on negligence and based on strict liability for design defects and failure to warn, but not in cases based on manufacturing defects. *See Haran v. Union Carbide Corp.,* 68 N.Y.2d 710, 711-12 (N.Y. 1986); *Cover v. Cohen,* 61 N.Y.2d 261, 274-75 (1984); *Caprara v. Chrysler Corp.,* 52 N.Y.2d 114, 123-26 (N.Y. 1981). California has ostensibly adopted a narrower rule because its rule does not explicitly cover strict liability-based claims, Cal. Evid. Code § 1151 (only reaching proof of "negligence or other culpable conduct"). To the extent a state allows evidence of subsequent remedial measures to be introduced to prove strict liability based claims, that policy choice is based on the notion that there are enough incentives for product manufacturers to make remedial changes, including the prospect of many more future actions, that an evidentiary bar against subsequent remedial measures to strict product liability cases is deemed unnecessary.

(i) Subsequent remedial measures to impeach

In *Sandoval*, the plaintiff tried to argue that she should be able to introduce evidence of subsequent remedial measures to "impeach" *the defendant's case generally*. But the impeachment exception to FRE 407 is not read so broadly. If it were, the exception would swallow the rule. Rather, the evidence must be offered *to directly contradict the testimony of a witness at the proceeding*. Thus, if the manager of the defendant's motel had said, "We have never used salt on our sidewalks because they never need it," the door would have been opened to evidence that the defendants put salt on the sidewalk after plaintiff slipped.

Likewise, experienced trial lawyers may caution their experts not to testify that the defendant's product had the "safest" design. Doing so could open the door to safer designs that were ultimately implemented by the defendant.

(ii) Subsequent remedial measures to show "feasibility"

Plaintiffs frequently argue that subsequent remedial measures are admissible to prove the "feasibility" of the defendant having a safer protocol, product, or design. However, this exception is also read narrowly and can only be used when the defendant disputes whether the precautionary measures could have been taken before the accident, not whether they "should" have been taken. For example, if the defense presented a witness who testifies that no other approach would have been "possible," the "feasibility" door may be opened under FRE 407. The next case discusses how the feasibility exception works in practice.

Tuer v. McDonald

701 A.2d 1101 (Md. Ct. App. 1997)

WILNER, Judge.

[Mary Tuer brought a medical malpractice suit against St. Joseph's Hospital and its cardiac surgeons, Garth McDonald and Robert Brawley, after her husband died of cardiac arrest while awaiting a coronary artery bypass graft surgery. Mr. Tuer was originally scheduled to have heart surgery on November 9, 1992, but on October 30, 1992, he began to experience chest pain. He was admitted to the hospital and prescribed Heparin, an anticoagulant, intended to prevent Mr. Tuer from having a heart attack. It was the standard procedure of the hospital at that time to discontinue Heparin three to four hours prior to surgery to reduce the risk of excessive bleeding. Mr. Tuer's surgery was moved up to November 2. Because Mr. Tuer's surgery was scheduled for 9:00 a.m., the hospital discontinued his Heparin at 5:30 a.m. However, Mr. Tuer's surgery was postponed for three to four hours and the doctors did not restart the Heparin. While he was waiting for his surgery, Mr. Tuer had a heart attack and died.

Mrs. Tuer argued that the trial court erred in not allowing her to introduce evidence that after Mr. Tuer's case, the defendants changed their surgical procedures and stopped their practice of discontinuing the drug Heparin to patients with Mr. Tuer's condition before surgery. She argued that the evidence was admissible (1) to prove the feasibility of restarting the Heparin and (2) to impeach Dr. McDonald's testimony.]

A. FEASIBILITY

Mrs. Tuer predicated her claim on proving that appellees' standard of care as of November 2, 1992 was negligent. Introducing evidence that, after Mr. Tuer died, appellees changed their procedure for administering Heparin to prove that it could have been administered to Mr. Tuer successfully would help establish appellees' negligence.

In th[is] case, there is no evidence that, at trial, appellees contested whether Heparin could have been restarted. In her brief, Mrs. Tuer admits that no defense witness testified that Heparin could not have been restarted. The testimony at trial supports Mrs. Tuer's concession and reveals that appellees and defense witnesses recognized that Heparin could have been restarted, but that Dr. McDonald did not restart Heparin because he believed the risks outweighed the benefits.

Mrs. Tuer insists that "feasibility was controverted by virtue of 'inferences' drawn from the defense's testimony." Arguing that a party chose not to perform a certain action because of the risk involved, however, is different than arguing that a party did not perform a task because it was physically unable to actually accomplish the task. "Where a defendant argues about the trade-off involved in precautionary measures, it is not placing feasibility in issue."

B. IMPEACHMENT

Mrs. Tuer argues that the change of procedure after Mr. Tuer's operation undermines Dr. McDonald's credibility with respect to his testimony that "it would have been unsafe to restart Mr. Tuer's heparin" after Mr. Tuer's surgery was postponed. Appellees counter that the subsequent change in procedure was not appropriate impeachment evidence.

Generally, impeachment evidence is used to attack the credibility of a witness by questioning a witness's personal veracity or the reliability of his testimony. Parties, however, are not allowed to use impeachment evidence as a ruse to get substantive evidence before the jury that the rules of evidence otherwise prohibit.

In the context of subsequent remedial measures, mere contradictory testimony is not enough to warrant the admission of subsequent remedial measures for impeachment purposes. "If 'impeachment' means simple contradiction, then the impeachment exceptions to Rule 407 would threaten to swallow the Rule itself." Thus, in order to avoid having the impeachment exception swallow Rule 407 like the great fish swallowed Jonah, courts have required more than mere contradiction in order to allow subsequent remedial measures to be used for impeaching a witness's credibility.

Parties may use subsequent measures to affect the credibility of a witness by showing "that the witness is wrong or spoke dishonestly with respect to the particular fact (here, that the condition was safe or had not been changed)." Additionally, when a defendant testifies in a superlative nature, *e.g.*, that "this is the safest practice known to medicine," subsequent remedial evidence provides more than mere contradiction and can, thereby, be used for impeachment purposes.

In this case, the change in administering Heparin prior to surgery had no bearing on Dr. McDonald's credibility as a witness. In order to impeach Dr. McDonald's statement, Mrs. Tuer had to demonstrate that Dr. McDonald thought that it was safe to restart Heparin. Instead, Dr. McDonald's statement evinces a doctor and a hospital that, as of November 2, 1992 and based on the scientific data and their professional opinion, believed that the risks of restarting Heparin outweighed the benefits. Additionally, Dr. McDonald's statement lacks the superlative tone that would otherwise warrant admitting subsequent remedial evidence for impeachment purposes.

(iii) Subsequent remedial measures to prove ownership or control

When *disputed*, subsequent remedial measures may also be used to prove who had ownership or control. Thus, for example, if a defendant claimed that it did not own or control the location at which an injury occurred, the plaintiff could use changes that the defendant made to that location to prove that the defendant did, in fact, have ownership or control.

Review Question

Virus prevention. Plaintiff sues his employer, Big Box Store ("BBS"), after he contracts a virus at work. Plaintiff claims that BBS did not implement sufficient protocols to protect its employees until they started to come down with the virus. After Plaintiff contracted the virus, BBS then mandated that the employees wear masks and installed an air filtration system for the store. Plaintiff wants to introduce evidence of the new protocols adopted by BBS. Admissible? How about if the owner of BBS testifies at trial that "he had no idea that there was a problem with virus transmission among his employees"? How about if the owner of BBS testifies that "he did the best he could when his employees came back to work, but given current city protocols, it wasn't really possible to require more"?

PART B: SETTLEMENT OFFERS AND NEGOTIATIONS [FRE 408]

From a public policy standpoint, do we want the evidence in any of these examples to be admitted?

Examples

1. A sues B for unlawful termination. At trial, B seeks to introduce evidence that A was originally willing to drop his lawsuit if B would pay him $10,000. As the trial approached, A increased his demand to $100,000. B wants to introduce evidence of A's original demand to show that his current claim of damages is inflated. Should the court admit the original demand?
2. A sues B for injuries he claims to have suffered in a car accident with B. B denies that he caused the action. B wants to introduce a letter from A that says, "If you don't pay me $15,000 by the end of the week, I will sue you." Should the court admit the letter?
3. At trial, A claims that he suffered $150,000 in damages. B wants to introduce a letter sent by A's counsel after he sued B saying that he would "resolve the matter" if B paid him $5,000. Should the court admit the letter?

FRE 408 generally prohibits admission of compromises or conduct during settlement negotiations as evidence if the case is not ultimately resolved and proceeds to trial.

FRE 408. Compromise Offers and Negotiations

(a) Prohibited Uses. Evidence of the following is not admissible—on behalf of any party—either to prove or disprove the validity or amount of a disputed claim or to impeach by a prior inconsistent statement or a contradiction:

(1) Furnishing, promising, or offering—or accepting, promising to accept, or offering to accept—a valuable consideration in compromising or attempting to compromise the claim; and

(2) Conduct or a statement made during compromise negotiations about the claim—except when offered in a criminal case and when the negotiations related to a claim by a public office in the exercise of the regulatory, investigative, or enforcement authority.

(b) Exceptions. The court may admit this evidence for another purpose, such as proving a witness's bias or prejudice, negating a contention of undue delay, or proving an effort to obstruct a criminal investigation or prosecution.

1. What Social Policy Does FRE 408 Serve?

Several reasons lie behind FRE 408's exclusion of compromise offers and negotiations for settlements. The first is relevance-based. It is not necessarily true that a party willing to settle is actually admitting that the opposing side is right in its claim. Many settlement offers are made just to make a claim go away, recognizing that the cost, time, and aggravation in fighting the claim might be greater than the financial burden of paying a monetary settlement. The second is policy-based. Public policy strongly supports the resolution of lawsuits without lengthy and contentious litigation. Not only are settlements more expeditious for the courts and parties, but compromise can often lead to greater acceptance of the outcome of the case. Indeed, the justice system itself wants to encourage settlement so as to reduce the burden on the courts and, it is hoped, resolve cases with less rancor between the parties. Without a rule like FRE 408, parties would be unlikely to negotiate candidly toward a settlement if their words and actions could later be used against them as admissions.[2]

2. *What Are the Requirements of FRE 408?*

By its text, FRE 408's prohibition applies when:

(1) Two people have a "disputed claim" between them;
(2) Either of those persons, or someone on behalf of each person:
  (a) Furnishes, promises, or offers something to settle or attempt to settle "a claim";
  (b) Accepts, promises to accept, or offers to accept a settlement offer; or
  (c) Engages in conduct or makes a statement *during compromise negotiations* about the claim, except when offered in a criminal case and when the negotiations are related to a claim by a public office in the exercise of its regulatory, investigative, or enforcement authority; and
(3) The settlement offer, acceptance, conduct, or statement is offered to:
  (a) Prove or disprove the validity of the disputed claim; or
  (b) The amount of the disputed claim; or
  (c) Impeach a party.

FRE 408	Prohibited Evidence	Prohibited Purposes	Permissible Evidence and Purposes
	(1) Offers to compromise, or offers to accept a compromise, to a disputed claim. (2) Conduct or statements during compromise negotiations.	(1) To prove/ disprove validity of claim. (2) To prove amount of disputed claim. (3) To impeach a party.	(1) Statements during compromise negotiations, if: (a) negotiations relate to government regulatory entity, and (b) are offered in a criminal case. (2) Offers and statements offered to: (a) Prove bias or prejudice of a witness, (b) Negate contention of undue delay in bringing suit, or (c) Prove effort to obstruct a criminal investigation or prosecution.

---

2. Indeed, some states have created a *privilege* that governs everything that is said during attempts to mediate a dispute. *See* Cal. Evid. Code §§ 1115-1129.

(a) Resolving a "Disputed" Claim

FRE 408 has a timing requirement. To be covered by FRE 408, an offer to compromise must be made after there is a "dispute." Thus, early interactions between the parties may not be seen as formal offers or promises to resolve a dispute. For example, on the street after a car accident, A may say to B, "Well, it looks like both our cars have damage. Tell you what. I'll pay you $3,000, and we'll just call this a day. I just don't want to hassle with my insurance company." Because there is no formal dispute yet, A's statement may be taken as an admission, rather an offer to resolve a formal dispute. Certainly, the timing requirement is met once a formal action is filed, but courts may also apply FRE 408 to statements made after one counsel writes an initial letter to the opposing counsel letting the opposing counsel know that the party is inclined to seek formal action unless a compromise is met.

Must the disputed claim be between the parties who ultimately become the plaintiff and defendant in the pending lawsuit? What if the defendant's subsidiary who is chiefly responsible for the plaintiff's injury makes statements in the course of trying to settle with a third party? Are the subsidiary's statements covered by FRE 408? They are certainly covered by the social policy underlying FRE 408 because the goal of FRE 408, as noted above, is to avoid discouraging settlements, and admitting the subsidiary's statements would discourage the subsidiary from trying to settle with the third party.

(b) Improper Use(s) of Settlement Offers and Negotiations

Not only are settlement offers and payments inadmissible to show who is at fault, but they are also inadmissible to *impeach* a witness or to prove or disprove the *amount* of a disputed claim. Settlement negotiations are inadmissible to impeach because, without this rule, any party who made a settlement offer or said anything during settlement negotiations would be subject to cross-examination about that offer and those statements if they took the stand to testify and asserted any position inconsistent with what they said or did during the settlement talks. Settlement offers and payments are also inadmissible to prove or disprove the amount of the disputed claim; thus, if a defendant at trial disputes the plaintiff's claim that he caused $150,000 in damages, the plaintiff cannot use a previous settlement offer by the defendant to pay $150,000 in exchange for the plaintiff dismissing the action. Such was the issue in *Pierce v. F.R. Tripler & Co.*

Pierce v. F.R. Tripler & Co.

955 F.2d 820 (2d Cir. 1992)

MESKILL, Judge.

[John Pierce sued his former employer, F.R. Tripler & Company, a subsidiary of Hartmarx, for age discrimination and failure to promote him to a manager's position.]

Pierce was 63 years old in 1986 and had been employed by Tripler, a wholly owned subsidiary of Hartmarx Specialty Stores, Inc., as its controller for approximately twenty years. In 1985 Hartmarx planned a companywide reorganization of its operations. As a result of this reorganization, Pierce's position was eliminated and in May 1986 he was discharged. The age discrimination charge here does not flow from that discharge, however. Rather, it stems from Tripler's failure to promote Pierce to the position of General Manager. That position was awarded to Peter Van Berg, age 39.

In May 1986 Pierce told the Hartmarx official responsible for the supervision of Tripler, that he was more qualified than Van Berg to be General Manager and that he should be hired for that position. During one discussion, the Hartmarx official told Pierce not to get angry with him because he, the official, was young.

Thereafter, Pierce's attorney, Debra Raskin, informed Tripler by mail that she believed that Pierce had a meritorious age discrimination claim in the denial of the promotion, but that Pierce was reluctant to litigate the matter. Raskin proposed a meeting with Tripler in order to "work out an amicable resolution of this matter." Carey Stein, General Counsel for Hartmarx Specialty Stores, answered Raskin, stating that while he did not believe that Pierce had a claim, he would be happy to speak to Raskin in order to arrive at "an 'amicable resolution' of any claim he [Pierce] may have."

In early June 1986 Raskin and Stein discussed Pierce's situation but did not come to any agreement. In late July 1986 Pierce filed a complaint with the Equal Employment Opportunity Commission (EEOC) alleging age discrimination. On September 25, 1986, Stein telephoned Raskin offering Pierce a financial position at the Long Island City warehouse of Wallachs, another Hartmarx subsidiary. This conversation engendered some confusion as to whether Pierce would be required to waive his age discrimination claim in order to accept the position.

After this conversation, Raskin wrote Stein stating: "If you are willing to make this offer of employment . . . without regard to the settlement of Mr. Pierce's claims, he would, of course, be willing to give it serious consideration." Stein responded by letter, stating that he was confused by Raskin's reference to the offer being "in exchange" for a release. He claimed that he had said that he would not offer the job "just for the purposes of settling the lawsuit," and that he still thought the lawsuit groundless. He further stated that, although the Wallachs position might already have been offered to someone else, if Pierce were still interested Raskin should call and Stein would check back at Wallachs.

This letter was followed a week later by another from Raskin restating her understanding of the telephone call, which was that the job was conditioned on a release of all claims against the company. Stein wrote back to Raskin, implying that the offer had not been conditioned on such a release, but that they should "agree to disagree about what was said in the phone conversation and get on with the lawsuit if that's what's to be." Pierce then initiated this action in the Southern District of New York.

EVIDENCE OF THE WALLACHS JOB OFFER

Hartmarx attempted before trial to have evidence of the subsequent job offer it made to *Pierce* ruled admissible. The district judge refused to allow the evidence, and Hartmarx contends on appeal that this disallowance was reversible error.

Hartmarx argued that the evidence was relevant for two purposes. First, Pierce's rejection of the job offer purportedly showed that *Pierce* had failed to take reasonable steps to mitigate his damages, thus limiting his claim for back pay. Second, evidence of the job offer made in September 1986 allegedly was relevant to Hartmarx's state of mind in May when it denied Pierce the General Manager position. Pierce opposed the introduction of the evidence, contending that the offer took place in the course of settlement negotiations and thus was inadmissible under Fed. R. Evid. 408. The district court held a hearing and determined that, because the offer was not "unambiguously unconditional," the evidence was not admissible for either purpose proposed by Hartmarx. The district court did not address the Rule 408 issue.

In order to show a failure to mitigate damages evidence of the failure must first be admissible. Fed. R. Evid. 408 states:

> *Evidence of* (1) furnishing or *offering* or promising *to furnish,* or (2) accepting or offering or promising to accept, *a valuable consideration in compromising or attempting to compromise a claim* which was disputed as to either validity or amount, *is not admissible to prove liability for or invalidity of the claim or its amount.* Evidence of conduct or statements made in compromise negotiations is likewise not admissible. This rule does not require the exclusion of any evidence otherwise discoverable merely because it is presented in the course of compromise negotiations. This rule also does not require exclusion when the evidence is offered for another purpose, such as proving bias or prejudice of a witness, negativing a contention of undue delay, or proving an effort to obstruct a criminal investigation or prosecution.

Evidence that demonstrates a failure to mitigate damages goes to the "amount" of the claim and thus, if the offer was made in the course of compromise negotiations, it is barred under the plain language of Rule 408. Under Fed. R. Evid. 104(a) preliminary factual questions concerning the admissibility of evidence, such as whether an offer was made in the course of settlement negotiations, are to be determined by the court.

It is often difficult to determine whether an offer is made "in compromising or attempting to compromise a claim." Both the timing of the offer and the existence of a disputed claim are relevant to the determination. *See, e.g., Cassino v. Reichhold Chemicals* (offer of severance pay conditioned on waiver of age discrimination claim made contemporaneous with discharge not protected by Rule 408), *Big O Tire Dealers v. Goodyear Tire & Rubber Co.* (correspondence between parties prior to the filing of an action held "business communications" rather than "offers to compromise" and thus outside scope of Rule 408). However, where a party is represented by counsel, threatens litigation and has initiated the first administrative steps in that litigation, any offer made between attorneys will be presumed to be an offer within the scope of Rule 408. The party seeking admission of an offer under those circumstances must demonstrate convincingly that the offer was not an attempt to compromise the claim.

The district court here did not make an explicit determination as to the admissibility of the evidence of the job offer under Rule 408. However, later in imposing Rule 11 sanctions on Hartmarx, the district court stated that the offer was conditioned on the release of Pierce's claims, which is another way of saying that the job offer was an attempt to compromise a claim. Therefore, under the plain language of Rule 408, evidence of the job offer was not admissible to show Pierce's failure to mitigate damages.

Hartmarx, however, urges us to look behind the language of Rule 408 to its purposes. The Advisory Committee on Proposed Rules stated that the exclusion of evidence of compromise offers "may be based on two grounds. (1) The evidence is irrelevant, since the offer may be motivated by a desire for peace rather than from any concession of weakness of position. . . . (2) A more consistently impressive ground is promotion of the public policy favoring the compromise and settlement of disputes." Hartmarx contends that neither of these policies would be advanced where, as here, it is the offeror seeking to introduce evidence of the offer. If the offeror is introducing the evidence, according to Hartmarx we should not worry that the evidence will be unfairly viewed as a concession of weakness of the offeror's position. Similarly, argues Hartmarx, parties will not be discouraged from free and frank settlement discussions by the knowledge that they may introduce their own statements at trial.

We believe that admission into evidence of settlement offers, even by the offeror, could inhibit settlement discussions and interfere with the effective administration of justice. As the circumstances under which this issue arose in the district court suggest, widespread admissibility of the substance of settlement offers could bring with it a rash of motions for disqualification of a party's chosen counsel who would likely become a witness at trial.

It is common for attorneys in pending litigation to be involved in efforts to settle the case before trial actually commences. It is also common that adverse parties have different memories as to what was said at such a meeting. If the substance of such negotiations were admissible at trial, many attorneys would be forced to testify as to the nature of the discussions and thus be disqualified as trial counsel. Indeed, one commentator has noted that the advocate-witness rule itself "means that no lawyer in a law firm that a client wished to serve as trial counsel in threatened litigation could safely attend negotiation sessions designed to avert trial or to renegotiate a contractual arrangement that had become unraveled, for fear of becoming a potential witness."

This undesirable result is largely avoided by excluding evidence of settlement negotiations. Hartmarx's interpretation of Rule 408 would discourage settlement discussions or encourage expensive and wasteful duplication of efforts by "negotiation counsel" and "trial counsel."

We prefer to apply Rule 408 as written and exclude evidence of settlement offers to prove liability for or the amount of a claim regardless of which party attempts to offer the evidence.

In a disparate treatment employment discrimination case the determinative question is whether, at the time of the adverse employment action, the defendant was motivated by impermissible factors. This is precisely the issue on which Hartmarx seeks to introduce the evidence of the job offer. Such evidence on the merits of the case goes to "liability for or invalidity of the claim" and thus does not fall within the "other purpose" exception to excludability under Rule 408.

The evidence of the Wallachs job offer was properly excluded by the district court, albeit for the wrong stated reason as we explain below. The evidence should have been excluded under Rule 408.

(c) Exceptions

(i) Compromise negotiations with public offices in criminal cases

Plea negotiations in criminal cases are covered by FRE 410. However, in some criminal cases, the defendant will also seek to settle a related civil case with government agencies that have regulatory, investigative or enforcement authority. Consider, for example, securities violations or environmental violations. The defendant may face both criminal and civil actions. In such situations, statements and conduct made during negotiations with the civil government authorities are admissible under FRE 408(a)(2). This exception was adopted in 2006. For example, if a defendant admitted fault during a civil securities enforcement action, this admission would be admissible against the accused in a subsequent criminal action for fraud. *See United States v. Prewitt*, 34 F.3d 436, 439 (7th Cir. 1994). The court still has the discretion under FRE 403 to bar the statement and may do so if defendant was unrepresented at the time of the negotiations with the civil authorities. Moreover, a defendant can seek an agreement with the civil regulator or attorney for the government not to use statements the defendant makes during negotiations.

Note that the rule *does* exclude civil settlements with private individuals from being admitted in criminal cases. For public policy reasons, we want defendants to be prepared to negotiate and reach settlements with private parties. However, government authorities have additional responsibilities of supervision and enforcement, so there are other policy interests served by providing an exception to FRE 408 for these types of enforcement-related civil settlements and allowing the use of statements made during them in related criminal proceedings.

(ii) Other express exceptions to FRE 408

Rule 408 also expressly provides exceptions for when compromise offers and negotiations are offered for purposes other than proving or disproving the validity of a claim or its amount. Thus, compromise negotiations may be used to prove a witness's bias, negate claims of undue delay, or prove an effort to obstruct a criminal investigation. Consider, for example, the defendant who claims that the plaintiff waited too long to bring a claim against the defendant. As it turns out, the delay was due to settlement discussions among the parties. The defendant has opened the door to evidence of the prior negotiations and the reasons for delay. Similarly, if prior negotiations show that the defendant plans to pay any judgment entered against his codefendant and the codefendant takes the stand during trial, the plaintiff may use the prior negotiations to show why the codefendant has a bias.

Review Questions

1. **Billionaires' designs.** Elon and Richard are threatening to sue each other over who owns the intellectual property rights to the design of the latest self-propellant vehicle. Elon's lawyer sent a letter to Richard's lawyer with the following language: "I know we both want to resolve this. Even if we created the car at the same time, I couldn't possibly owe you $1 billion.

I'll pay you $1 million to make this go away for both of us. Deal?" What if Elon sent the letter instead of his lawyer? What if Elon's lawyer sent the letter after Richard filed a lawsuit?

2. **Quenching fire damage.** Eastern Gas & Electric ("EG&E") is being sued by homeowners who claim that its transmission lines caused a recent, devastating wildfire. The matter is also being investigated by the state attorney general to determine if there were regulatory or criminal violations. During discussions with the attorney general, EG&E's representatives offered to pay the victims $100,000 each if they did not pursue their claims. The victims accept the settlement, but the attorney general brings criminal negligence charges against EG&E. Are EG&E's statements admissible?

PART C: OFFERS TO PAY MEDICAL AND SIMILAR EXPENSES [FRE 409]

Another category of relevant evidence that is excluded for public policy reasons are offers to pay medical and similar expenses.

FRE 409. Offers to Pay Medical and Similar Expenses

Evidence of furnishing, promising to pay, or offering to pay medical, hospital, or similar expenses resulting from an injury is not admissible to prove liability for the injury.

1. What Social Policy Does FRE 409 Serve?

FRE 409 rests on several rationales. The first rationale is relevance-based. As the Advisory Committee Notes explain, "[E]vidence of payment of medical, hospital, or similar expenses of an injured party by the opposing party" may be "made from humane impulses and not from an admission of liability." The second rationale is policy-based. Again, as the Advisory Committee Notes explain, allowing a party to admit the other party's humanitarian gestures into evidence would "tend to discourage assistance to the injured person" and thus would discourage the very type of conduct that might obviate the need or the motivation to sue to recover such expenses.

2. What Are the Requirements of FRE 409?

By its text, FRE 409 bars the admission of:

(1) "Evidence of furnishing, promising to pay, or offering to pay medical, hospital or other similar expenses resulting from an injury".

(2) When offered to prove the liability of the offeror for that injury.

FRE 409	Prohibited Evidence	Prohibited Purposes	Permissible Evidence and Purposes
	Evidence of furnishing, promising to pay, or offering to pay medical, hospital or other similar expenses resulting from an injury.	To prove liability of offeror for the injury.	(Rule does not reach admissions of liability and expressions of sympathy made in conjunction with evidence of furnishing, promising, or offering to pay expenses.)

Unlike FRE 408, FRE 409 does not require that there be a formal "claim" when the payment of medical or similar expenses are made. Anytime those expenses are paid, evidence of their payment is inadmissible. What is more, the rule bars introduction of not only the payment of the expenses, but also offers or promises to pay them.

Rule 409 does not list any exceptions. However, offers to pay medical expenses may be made in conjunction with other remarks, such as (1) admissions of liability and (2) expressions of sympathy. In these situations, the judge must determine which part of the statement is covered by FRE 409 and which part might be admissible as an admission.

Example

Jessie and Jackie are in a car accident. Jackie calls Jessie and says, "I am so sorry I hit your car. I feel so bad about it. Don't worry. I will pay your medical bills. I know it was my fault." Arguably, FRE 409 would only exclude the statement of "I will pay your medical bills."[3] Jackie would have to argue that, under FRE 403, the remaining statement should be excluded as well.

At times, statements may be covered by both FRE 408 and FRE 409. The court must examine each portion of the statement to determine which parts are excludable under these rules.

3. Some states, such as California, have a special relevance rule that also reaches—and excludes—expressions of sympathy. Cal. Evid. Code § 1160. New York, Illinois, Texas, and Florida do not bar the introduction of expressions of sympathy. *Grogan v. Dooley*, 211 N.Y. 30, 31-32 (N.Y. 1914); Ill. R. Evid. 410; 735 Ill. Com. Stat. § 5/8-1901; Tex. R. Evid. 409; Fla. Stat. § 90.409.

Example

Jessie and Jackie are in a car accident. Jackie sends Jessie a note: "I hope you won't pursue your lawsuit against me. I was just having a bad day when I hit you. If you release me from liability, I am happy to pay for time you missed from work, pay for your doctor bills, and fix your car." In this example, there has been a formal claim. Thus, it is more likely that more of the statements in the note can be excluded under FRE 408, including the offer to pay to fix Jessie's car. Offers to pay for the doctor bills fall clearly within FRE 409. Jackie's statement that "I was just having a bad day when I hit you" could be deemed an admission unless, under FRE 408, the entire statement is found to be part of settlement negotiations.

Review Questions

1. **Ruff offer.** Devan's dog bites Felipe. Devan feels terrible about it and offers to give Felipe a ride to the doctor and pay for any days Felipe misses from work. Devan also gives him $250 to take care of any other costs he had because of the dog bite. Felipe ends up suing Devan. Are Devan's offers and payment admissible?
2. **Free lunch.** Jayden gets sick while eating in Wally's restaurant. Wally doesn't want the bad publicity even though he thinks that Jayden probably got sick from a snack he ate before coming to the restaurant. Nonetheless, Wally offers to comp Jayden's bill and give him vouchers for free meals at the restaurant. If Jayden sues Wally, is this evidence admissible?

PART D: PLEAS, PLEA BARGAINING, AND PLEA AGREEMENTS IN CRIMINAL CASES [FRE 410]

Plea bargaining is the process of negotiations between the prosecutor and defense to resolve a criminal case. By plea bargaining, the parties can reach a compromise by which the defendant enters a guilty plea or nolo contendere plea to lesser charges or pleads guilty in exchange for a lesser sentence.

A guilty plea is the process by which a defendant admits to a crime, waives the rights related to trial, and resolves a case except for sentencing. A nolo contendere plea (which in some states is called a no contest plea) is a plea in which the defendant does not admit to commission of an offense, but the defendant agrees not to contest it. Once a defendant pleads nolo contendere, the defendant is subject to sentencing as if the defendant had pled guilty. However, unlike a guilty plea, a nolo contendere plea cannot be used as an admission in a civil case. An estimated 95 percent of criminal cases resolve with guilty or nolo contendere pleas.

In federal court, the entry of pleas is governed by Federal Rule of Criminal Procedure 11. At a guilty plea colloquy, a defendant will usually state or agree to facts that demonstrate the defendant committed a crime. Without FRE 410, guilty pleas and nolo contendere pleas would be admissible as party admissions against the defendant if the defendant later withdrew the guilty plea and decided to exercise the right to a trial.

FRE 410 governs the subsequent admissibility of plea negotiations, the pleas themselves, and the defendant's statements during a plea colloquy.

FRE 410. Pleas, Plea Discussions, and Related Statements

(a) Prohibited Uses. In a civil or criminal case, evidence of the following is not admissible against the defendant who made the plea or participated in the plea discussions:

(1) a guilty plea that was later withdrawn;

(2) a nolo contendere plea;

(3) a statement made during a proceeding on either of those pleas under Federal Rule of Criminal Procedure 11 or a comparable state procedure; or

(4) a statement made during plea discussions with an attorney for the prosecuting authority if the discussions did not result in a guilty plea or they resulted in a later-withdrawn guilty plea.

(b) Exceptions. The court may admit a statement described in Rule 410(a)(3) or (4):

(1) In any proceeding in which another statement made during the same plea or plea discussions has been introduced, if in fairness the statements ought to be considered together; or

(2) In a criminal proceeding for perjury or false statement, if the defendant made the statement under oath, on the record, and with counsel present.

1. What Social Policy Does FRE 410 Serve?

FRE 410 serves a policy-based purpose. As stated in the Advisory Committee Notes, "Exclusion of offers to plead guilty or nolo has as its purpose the promoting of disposition of criminal cases by compromise. . . . Effective criminal law administration in many localities would hardly be possible if a large proportion of the charges were not disposed of by such compromises." In other words, disposing of cases can better fine-tune resolution of cases to each defendant's situation. What is more, the criminal justice system is not set up to hold trials for all defendants. From the prosecution's perspective, plea bargaining provides a mechanism to obtain some accountability by the defendant and maybe even secure a defendant's cooperation in its investigation or prosecution of a case. From the defense's perspective, plea bargaining may mitigate the impact of a conviction. From the court's perspective, plea bargaining frees up the courts to try cases in which there is a dispute regarding the facts and the defendant's culpability. FRE 410 serves all these goals by eliminating a disincentive to engage in plea negotiations or to enter pleas. This disincentive applies whether the statement from the plea colloquy or plea negotiations is to be admitted for its truth or admitted to impeach; *both* are barred by FRE 410 (except, as noted below, defendants may waive the rule's protection as to impeachment). *See United States v. Lawson*, 683 F.2d 688, 691-93 (2d Cir. 1982) (reviewing legislative history of FRE 410). If a defendant knows that plea discussions could later be used to impeach her at trial, she may be reluctant to engage in plea negotiations.

2. *What Are the Requirements of FRE 410?*

By its plain text, FRE 410 bars in any civil or criminal case:

(1) Evidence of:
   (a) A guilty plea that was later withdrawn;
   (b) A nolo contendere plea;
   (c) A statement made during a plea colloquy;
   (d) Statements made "during plea discussions with an attorney for the prosecuting authority" if the discussion did not result in a plea or resulted in a plea that was subsequently withdrawn;[4]

(2) Against a defendant in a civil or criminal case;

(3) Except that statements from plea colloquys and during plea negotiations may be admitted if:
   (a) Another statement from the same colloquy or negotiations has been admitted and the statement at issue "in fairness" "ought to be considered"; or
   (b) The statement was made "under oath, on the record, and with counsel present," if the defendant is being prosecuted for perjury or making a false statement.

FRE 410	Prohibited Evidence	Prohibited Purposes	Permissible Purposes
	Withdrawn plea of guilty, a nolo contendere plea, statements during a plea colloquy, or statements to an attorney during plea negotiations, *if offered against the defendant.*	All purposes.	(1) If statement during colloquy or negotiations ought be considered "in fairness" with other statements from the same proceeding already admitted. (2) If statement was made under oath, on the record and with counsel present, and defendant is now being prosecuted for perjury or making a false statement. (3) Defendant waives FRE 410's protection.

4. Not all states with this policy-based special rule extend their rule to plea negotiations. California does not. Cal. Evid. Code § 1153. However, Illinois, Florida, and Texas bar plea negotiations. Ill. R. Evid. 410; Fla. Stat. § 90.410; Tex. R. Evid. 410.

(a) Plea Negotiations

For FRE 410 to protect a defendant, the plea discussions must be between the defense and a prosecutor. The rule refers to an "attorney for the prosecuting authority." Thus, if a defendant discusses a plea with a law enforcement officer, like an FBI agent, FRE 410 does not apply, even if the defendant has a good faith belief that the officer can help the defendant secure a plea deal.

(b) Exceptions to FRE 410

FRE 410 lists two exceptions to the general rule that a defendant's statements during a plea or during plea negotiations will be admissible in a later criminal proceeding on those charges.

First, under FRE 410(b)(1), if the defense seeks to introduce a statement from the plea or plea discussions, the prosecution may be able to introduce other statements "if in fairness the statements ought to be considered together." This exception operates like the rule of completeness discussed in Chapter Two. It is designed to prevent the defendant from misrepresenting what happened during any pleas or plea discussions with the government.

Second, FRE 410(b)(2) provides that if the defendant is later charged with perjury or false statement for statements he made under oath, on the record, and with counsel present, the defendant's statements during the plea colloquy or in plea discussions that did not lead to a plea agreement may be admitted. For example, when former National Security Advisor Michael Flynn sought to withdraw his plea for providing false statements to government officials, concerns were raised as to whether he could be charged with lying to the court during his plea that would lead to perjury charges and use of his plea statements against him. Before that issue could be resolved, he received a presidential pardon.

(c) Waiving FRE 410

In *United States v. Mezzanatto*, 513 U.S. 196 (1995), the Supreme Court addressed the issue of whether a defendant can waive FRE 410. This issue becomes important in cases in which the prosecution refuses to engage in plea bargaining unless the defendant agrees to waive FRE 410 if the parties do not reach a resolution. The Supreme Court held that like other protections in the Federal Rules of Evidence, a defendant could waive the protections of FRE 410.

United States v. Mezzanatto

513 U.S. 196 (1995)

JUSTICE THOMAS delivered the opinion of the Court.

Federal Rule of Evidence 410 and Federal Rule of Criminal Procedure 11(e)(6) provide that statements made in the course of plea discussions between a criminal defendant and a prosecutor are inadmissible against the defendant. The court below held that these exclusionary provisions may not be waived by the defendant. [W]e now reverse.

On August 1, 1991, San Diego Narcotics Task Force agents arrested Gordon Shuster after discovering a methamphetamine laboratory at his residence in Rainbow, California. Shuster agreed to cooperate with the agents, and a few hours after his arrest he placed a call to respondent's pager. When respondent returned the call, Shuster told him that a friend wanted to purchase a pound of methamphetamine for $13,000. Shuster arranged to meet respondent later that day.

At their meeting, Shuster introduced an undercover officer as his "friend." The officer asked respondent if he had "brought the stuff with him," and respondent told the officer it was in his car. The two proceeded to the car, where respondent produced a brown paper package containing approximately one pound of methamphetamine. Respondent then presented a glass pipe (later found to contain methamphetamine residue) and asked the officer if he wanted to take a "hit." The officer indicated that he would first get respondent the money; as the officer left the car, he gave a prearranged arrest signal. Respondent was arrested and charged with possession of methamphetamine with intent to distribute.

On October 17, 1991, respondent and his attorney asked to meet with the prosecutor to discuss the possibility of cooperating with the Government. The prosecutor agreed to meet later that day. At the beginning of the meeting, the prosecutor informed respondent that he had no obligation to talk, but that if he wanted to cooperate he would have to be completely truthful. As a condition to proceeding with the discussion, the prosecutor indicated that respondent would have to agree that any statements he made during the meeting could be used to impeach any contradictory testimony he might give at trial if the case proceeded that far. Respondent conferred with his counsel and agreed to proceed under the prosecutor's terms.

Respondent then admitted knowing that the package he had attempted to sell to the undercover police officer contained methamphetamine, but insisted that he had dealt only in "ounce" quantities of methamphetamine prior to his arrest. Initially, respondent also claimed that he was acting merely as a broker for Shuster and did not know that Shuster was manufacturing methamphetamine at his residence, but he later conceded that he knew about Shuster's laboratory. Respondent attempted to minimize his role in Shuster's operation by claiming that he had not visited Shuster's residence for at least a week before his arrest. At this point, the Government confronted respondent with surveillance evidence showing that his car was on Shuster's property the day before the arrest, and terminated the meeting on the basis of respondent's failure to provide completely truthful information.

Respondent eventually was tried on the methamphetamine charge and took the stand in his own defense. He maintained that he was not involved in methamphetamine trafficking and that he had thought Shuster used his home laboratory to manufacture plastic explosives for the CIA. He also denied knowing that the package he delivered to the undercover officer contained methamphetamine. Over defense counsel's objection, the prosecutor cross-examined respondent about the inconsistent statements he had made during the October 17 meeting.

Federal Rule of Evidence 410 provides:

> "Except as otherwise provided in this rule, evidence of the following is not, in any civil or criminal proceeding, admissible against the defendant

> who . . . was a participant in the plea discussions: . . . (4) any statement made in the course of plea discussions with an attorney for the prosecuting authority which do not result in a plea of guilty. . . ."

The Ninth Circuit noted that these Rules are subject to only two express exceptions, neither of which says anything about waiver, and thus concluded that Congress must have meant to preclude waiver agreements such as respondent's.

The Ninth Circuit's analysis is directly contrary to the approach we have taken in the context of a broad array of constitutional and statutory provisions. Rather than deeming waiver presumptively unavailable absent some sort of express enabling clause, we instead have adhered to the opposite presumption. A criminal defendant may knowingly and voluntarily waive many of the most fundamental protections afforded by the Constitution. Likewise, absent some affirmative indication of Congress' intent to preclude waiver, we have presumed that statutory provisions are subject to waiver by voluntary agreement of the parties.

The presumption of waivability has found specific application in the context of evidentiary rules. [A]t the time of the adoption of the Federal Rules of Evidence, agreements as to the admissibility of documentary evidence were routinely enforced and held to preclude subsequent objections as to authenticity. And although hearsay is inadmissible except under certain specific exceptions, we have held that agreements to waive hearsay objections are enforceable.

Indeed, evidentiary stipulations are a valuable and integral part of everyday trial practice. Prior to trial, parties often agree in writing to the admission of otherwise objectionable evidence, either in exchange for stipulations from opposing counsel or for other strategic purposes. Because the plea-statement Rules were enacted against a background presumption that legal rights generally, and evidentiary provisions specifically, are subject to waiver by voluntary agreement of the parties, we will not interpret Congress' silence as an implicit rejection of waivability.

Respondent also contends that waiver is fundamentally inconsistent with the Rules' goal of encouraging voluntary settlement. The Ninth Circuit expressed similar concerns, noting that Rules 410 and 11(e)(6) "aid in obtaining the cooperation" that is often necessary to identify and prosecute the leaders of a criminal conspiracy and that waiver of the protections of the Rules "could easily have a chilling effect on the entire plea bargaining process."

We need not decide whether and under what circumstances substantial "public policy" interests may permit the inference that Congress intended to override the presumption of waivability, for in this case there is no basis for concluding that waiver will interfere with the Rules' goal of encouraging plea bargaining. [A]lthough the availability of waiver may discourage some defendants from negotiating, it is also true that prosecutors may be unwilling to proceed without it. Prosecutors may be especially reluctant to negotiate without a waiver agreement during the early stages of a criminal investigation, when prosecutors are searching for leads and suspects may be willing to offer information in exchange for some form of immunity or leniency in sentencing. In this "cooperation" context, prosecutors face "painfully delicate" choices as to "whether to proceed and prosecute those suspects against whom the already produced evidence makes a case or whether to extend leniency or full immunity to some suspects in order to procure testimony against other, more dangerous suspects against whom existing evidence is flimsy or nonexistent." Because prosecutors have limited resources and must be able to answer "sensitive questions about the credibility of the testimony" they receive before entering into any sort of cooperation agreement, prosecutors may condition cooperation discussions on an agreement that the testimony provided may be used for impeachment purposes. If prosecutors were precluded from securing such agreements, they might well decline to enter into cooperation discussions in the first place and might never take this potential first step toward a plea bargain.

Indeed, as a logical matter, it simply makes no sense to conclude that mutual settlement will be encouraged by precluding negotiation over an issue that may be particularly important to one of the parties to the transaction. A sounder way to encourage settlement is to permit the interested parties to enter into knowing and voluntary negotiations without any arbitrary limits on their bargaining chips.

Finally, respondent contends that waiver agreements should be forbidden because they invite prosecutorial overreaching and abuse. Respondent asserts that there is a "gross disparity" in the relative bargaining power of the parties to a plea agreement and suggests that a waiver agreement is "inherently unfair and coercive."

The dilemma flagged by respondent is indistinguishable from any of a number of difficult choices that criminal defendants face every day. The plea bargaining process necessarily exerts pressure on defendants to plead guilty and to abandon a series of fundamental rights, but we have repeatedly held that the government "may encourage a guilty plea by offering substantial benefits in return for the plea."

The mere potential for abuse of prosecutorial bargaining power is an insufficient basis for foreclosing negotiation altogether. Instead, the appropriate response to respondent's predictions of abuse is to permit case-by-case inquiries into whether waiver agreements are the product of fraud or coercion. We hold that absent some affirmative indication that the agreement was entered into unknowingly or involuntarily, an agreement to waive the exclusionary provisions of the plea-statement Rules is valid and enforceable.

Does the Supreme Court's resolution of this issue in *Mezzanatto* undercut some of the effectiveness of FRE 410?

Review Questions

1. **Can we make a deal?** Bernardo is being prosecuted for money laundering. Initially, he thought that he would plead guilty, but he later changed his mind. In the meantime, Bernardo said to the investigating agent, "I was just a small fish in this scheme. If I make a deal with you, can you make me a witness and not send me to prison?" Can the prosecutor introduce this statement at trial?
2. **No contest.** Cecilia pleads nolo contendere to stealing from her boss. She is subsequently sued. Her boss wants to introduce Cecilia's no contest plea. Admissible?

3. **Perjury during plea.** Evie is facing a lengthy sentence for distributing drugs. During her guilty plea colloquy, Evie said that she delivered the drugs because her partner, Morgan, threatened to hurt her children if she didn't help with the drug delivery. Evie got probation, and Morgan was subsequently charged with conspiracy to distribute drugs. Prosecutors have now indicted Evie for lying about Morgan's alleged participation in the conspiracy. Can they use Evie's statements at her guilty plea colloquy?

PART E: LIABILITY INSURANCE [FRE 411]

From a public policy standpoint, do we want evidence of a party's decision to obtain insurance to be put before a jury?

Example

Doug, a local handyman, sues Laurie for injuries suffered when he was visiting her home. He seeks to introduce evidence that Laurie recently increased the amount of her homeowner's insurance when another guest had an injury. Is the evidence admissible?

FRE 411 excludes evidence that a person was or was not insured to prove whether the person acted negligently or otherwise wrongfully.

FRE 411. Liability Insurance

Evidence that a person was or was not insured against liability is not admissible to prove whether the person acted negligently or otherwise wrongfully. But the court may admit this evidence for another purpose, such as proving a witness's bias or prejudice or proving agency, ownership, or control.

1. What Social Policy Does FRE 411 Serve?

FRE 411 serves two purposes. As with many of the other special rules of relevance, the first purpose is relevance-based. Whether a person has (or does not have) insurance generally says little about whether they are being careless on a particular occasion. As the Advisory Committee Notes state, "At best the inference of fault from the fact of insurance coverage is a tenuous one, as is its converse." Most people and businesses do not become suddenly reckless simply because an insurance company may have to pay a claim; the fact that insurance companies typically raise their premiums if accidents are reported tends to mute any tendency to be reckless. The second purpose is policy-based. We generally want individuals and businesses to obtain insurance because insurance is a loss-spreading mechanism that is, as a general matter, good for the economy. If evidence of a person's or business's decision to get insurance were admissible to show negligence or wrongful conduct, people and businesses might forgo getting insurance. There is also the danger that jurors with knowledge of which party is insured (and which party is not) may be tempted to impose liability on the party with the "deep pocket" insurance coverage or to punish the party that "selfishly" forewent insurance coverage.

2. *What Are the Requirements of FRE 411?*

By its text, FRE 411 applies to:

(1) Evidence that a person was or was not insured against liability.[5]
(2) When admitted to prove the person acted negligently or otherwise wrongfully.

FRE 411	Prohibited Evidence	Prohibited Purposes	Permissible Evidence and Purposes
	(1) A person has liability insurance. (2) A person does not have liability insurance.	To prove liability.	Any other purpose, including: (1) Bias or prejudice of a witness. (2) Agency, ownership, or control over property.

Although evidence that a person was insured or not insured cannot be used to prove that the person acted negligently or wrongfully caused an accident, it can be used for other purposes, such as proving who owned a vehicle in an accident or that a witness has a bias.

Example

Santiago slips and falls on the driveway to an apartment complex. He sues the owner of the complex. However, the owner claims that the tenants are responsible for the condition of the driveway. Santiago wants to introduce an insurance policy that the owner has taken out for the driveway. Is the policy admissible?

---

5. Some states, like California, only exclude evidence that a party has insurance—not evidence that a party *lacked* insurance. Cal. Evid. Code § 1155. New York, Illinois, and Texas bar the absence of insurance as well, *Salm v. Moses*, 13 N.Y.3d 816, 817-18 (N.Y. 2009); Ill. R. Evid. 411; Tex. R. Evid. 411. As a matter of case law (rather than its rules), Florida bars evidence that a party is insured, *Barnett v. Butler*, 112 So. 2d 907 (Fla. Dist. Ct. App. 1959); it is not clear whether Florida would exclude evidence that a party was *not* insured.

SUMMARY CHART

FRE 407-411

Special Relevance Rule	General Rule	Exceptions
Subsequent remedial measures (FRE 407)	Measures taken *after* the incident at issue are inadmissible to prove: • Negligence and other culpable conduct • Strict liability for product defects or failure to warn	Admissible for other purposes, including: • Impeachment • *If disputed*, ownership, control, or feasibility of precautionary measures
Compromise offers and negotiation (FRE 408)	Offer to compromise or to accept a compromise to a disputed claim is inadmissible: • To prove/disprove the validity of that claim • The amount of the disputed claim • To impeach	Admissible: • In *any* case, if offered • To prove bias or prejudice of a witness • To negate a contention of undue delay in bringing suit • To prove an effort to obstruct a criminal investigation or prosecution • In a criminal case, if compromise negotiations relate to a government regulatory entity
Humanitarian gestures (FRE 409)	Evidence that a person offered or promised or did pay hospital, medical, or similar expenses resulting from an injury is inadmissible to prove the person's liability for that injury	Rule does not bar: • Admissions of liability, even if made with gesture • Expressions of sympathy, even if made with gesture
Pleas and plea negotiations (FRE 410)	In both civil and criminal cases, the following are inadmissible for any purpose: • A prior guilty plea that was withdrawn • A nolo contendere plea • Statements made to an attorney for the prosecution during plea negotiations, *if offered against the defendant*	Admissible: • In a civil or criminal case, if necessary, "in fairness," to put another statement from the plea colloquy or negotiations in proper context • If defendant is now being prosecuted for perjury or making a false statement, and prior statement was made on the record, under oath and with counsel present • In a civil or criminal case, if defendant waives FRE 410's protections

Special Relevance Rule	General Rule	Exceptions
Insurance (FRE 411)	Evidence that a person has or does not have liability insurance is inadmissible to prove liability	Admissible for any other purpose, including: • Bias or prejudice of a witness • Agency, ownership or control of property

Review Question

Exploding gas tanks. Ford, Inc. has a problem with one of its automobiles. It seems as if the Pinto model has a problem with its gas tank. Company engineers tell Ford's executives that it would be difficult and costly to build a stronger gas tank. Therefore, the executives continue to sell the Pinto model with gas tank problems. After thirty people are killed in exploding gas tank accidents, Ford finally redesigns its gas tank and orders a recall of its old Pintos so that it can repair their gas tanks.

Which, if any, of the following could the plaintiffs introduce in a products liability suit against Ford?

a. Evidence that after plaintiffs' accidents, Ford redesigned its gas tank.
b. Evidence of the redesigned gas tank if Ford's engineer testifies that it was not feasible to have another design.
c. Evidence that Ford took out an insurance policy for $100 million when it heard that its cars were exploding.
d. Evidence that Ford paid for many of the plaintiffs' medical bills.
e. Evidence that Ford's General Counsel called plaintiffs' lead counsel on the eve of trial with a very generous settlement offer.
f. Evidence that a Ford executive told an investigating FBI agent: "I'll do anything to put this mess behind me. I thought we might have problems, but I didn't think it would get this bad. I hope it is not too late to help and work this thing out with the prosecutor."
g. Evidence that counsel for Ford's executive told DOJ prosecutors that the president of the company would plead nolo contendere to submitting false engineering reports to the Department of Transportation if the prosecution did not charge the executive with manslaughter.

Test Your Understanding

To test your understanding of the material in this chapter, turn to the Supplement for additional practice problems.

Chapter 5

Hearsay

As recounted in Chapter One, the rules of evidence are designed not only to ensure that the trier of fact considers only *relevant* evidence, but also that the trier of fact considers only *reliable* evidence. No one would want to decide cases based on evidence no more reliable than rumor, innuendo, or unaccountable remarks. The hearsay rule is one of these reliability-focused rules.

Part A of this chapter focuses on the rationale for the hearsay rule. Part B sets forth the basic rule against hearsay. Part C explains the definition of hearsay and, importantly, what kind of statements do not fall under the hearsay rule and are instead "nonhearsay." Finally, Part D briefly discusses the issues of indirect hearsay and hearsay within hearsay. Hearsay "exceptions" will be covered in Chapters Six through Eight.

PART A: RATIONALE FOR THE HEARSAY RULE

If you have ever played the game of "Telephone," you will understand why there is a general rule against allowing hearsay evidence. In that game, one person whispers a word or phrase to another person. That person then whispers that word or phrase to another person, who whispers it to another, and so on. By the time it is circulated to several people, the word or phrase will probably have changed and no longer reflect what was initially observed or said. The rule against hearsay is a recognition that the court system wants information from the most reliable sources—the person at the head of the "telephone line" who directly observed or heard what happened.

Consider this further example. A car collided with a person riding a bicycle in an intersection. The bicycle rider has the option of calling three witnesses at his trial against the car driver for damages he suffered as a result of the collision:

- *The bystander.* The first witness was a person standing on the sidewalk near the intersection and who saw the accident happen.
- *The bystander's friend.* The second witness is the bystander's friend, who was looking at her cell phone when the accident happened, but who heard a crash and then heard the bystander say, "Wow, that car totally blew through that red light."

- *The police officer.* The third witness is the police officer who responded to the accident scene and who spoke with the bystander's friend (because the bystander left the scene to get to a doctor's appointment before the officer arrived). The bystander's friend recounted what the bystander told her about the accident.

Which witness is likely to be the most reliable in terms of determining what actually happened—the bystander who observed the accident or the witness who relates (second- or thirdhand) what the bystander said?

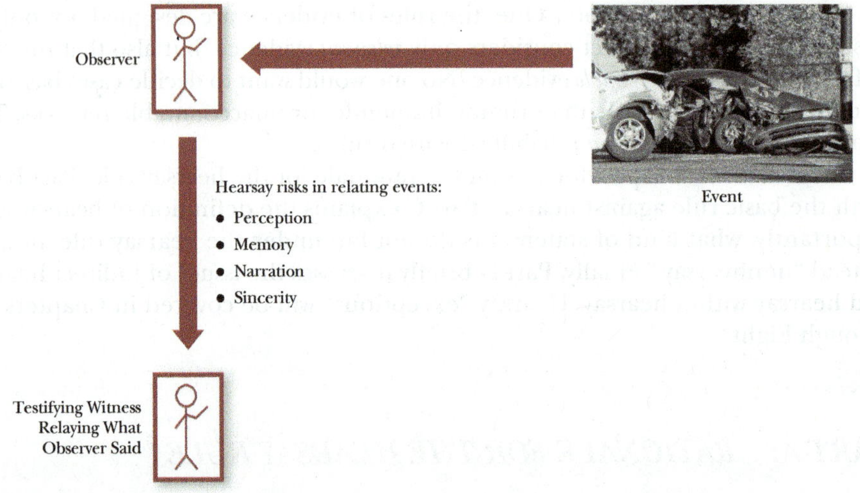

For the same reason that we generally are wary of getting information from people further down the "Telephone" line, the most reliable witness is the bystander. But why?

(1) *Perception.* The only person who saw and heard the accident—that is, the only percipient witness—was the bystander. Only *the bystander* can testify to what he observed and heard, including how he noticed that the traffic light had turned red for the car. Further, unless the bystander testifies, there is no way for the car driver to challenge the bystander's ability to perceive: Was the bystander distracted? Does he have impaired vision or hearing? Was he stumbling out of a bar just moments before? (In other cases, other senses may come into play, such as taste, touch, and smell.)

(2) *Memory.* The person in the best position to remember the accident itself is also the bystander. If there was any gap in time between the accident and the bystander's statement, was the bystander accurately remembering what he saw? Neither the bystander's friend nor the police officer saw the accident, so they can, at best, recount what the bystander said about it

(as to the friend) or what the friend said about it (as to the police officer). Yet with each further link in this "Telephone"-like chain, there is greater danger of getting the bystander's original observational statement wrong.

(3) *Narration.* By his statement, the bystander was narrating what he saw, yet only if the bystander is on the stand is there any way to test whether his narration to his friend was factually accurate. That is because only the bystander can testify to how long had the light been red for the car or where the bicycle was at the time of the collision.

(4) *Sincerity.* Because the bystander's account is the only percipient account, it is critical to know whether he was telling the truth. As we will discuss more fully in Chapter Ten, the traditional mechanism for assuring the sincerity of witness testimony is to have witnesses come into court and swear or affirm that they will tell the truth. Swearing in the bystander's friend or the police officer might assure us that what they report having heard was true, but that assurance says nothing about whether *the bystander* had been telling them the truth. Relatedly, having the bystander present in court is the only way for the trier of fact—whether it be the jury or the trial judge—to assess the bystander's demeanor while testifying: Does he look nervous and shifty? Is he hostile to one attorney over another? A further mechanism for assuring the sincerity of testimony is cross-examination, where the adverse party can test the witness's motives. Did the bystander know (and hate) the car's driver, or did he know (and like) the cyclist? Cross-examination is an important engine for getting at the truth and for criminal cases is secured by the Confrontation Clause itself, yet only cross-examining the bystander will ferret out any biases and ulterior motives.

Given these concerns, the law prefers having percipient witnesses—that is, the real observer of the events—as the witnesses in court to testify to the events. The general rule against hearsay implements this preference. If you want the most reliable evidence, get the person who had the most direct observations.

Review Questions

For each of these situations, identify why the testimony other than that of Witness A might be a problem.

1. **"I heard."** D is accused of killing V. D claims self-defense. Witness A saw the altercation and told Witness B, "All of a sudden, D was on top of V and stabbing him. I don't really think that it was V's fault. It upsets me just to think about it." The prosecution seeks to call Witness B at trial.
2. **Defendant's thoughts.** Same problem. After he is arrested, D tells Witness C, "What was I supposed to do? V started the fight. My life was in danger."

PART B: THE RULE AGAINST HEARSAY [FRE 802]

The basic rule against the use of hearsay long predates the Federal Rules of Evidence and, like many other rules of evidence, dates back to the English common law. Although there is a general prohibition against hearsay, we will see in the next chapters that there are an overwhelming number of exceptions to the rule. In this respect, the rule against hearsay is a lot like a slice of swiss cheese: It sets up a barrier, but has a number of "holes" (or exceptions). However, even to understand those exceptions, it is important to understand how the hearsay rule operates in the first place.

FRE 802. The Rule Against Hearsay

Hearsay is not admissible unless any of the following provides otherwise:

- A federal statute;
- These rules; or
- Other rules prescribed by the Supreme Court.

As FRE 802 indicates, whether evidence qualifies as "hearsay" is *the* threshold question. If evidence is not hearsay, no further thought need be given to the hearsay rule. But if evidence *does* qualify as hearsay, the rules governing hearsay apply.

The rules governing hearsay, however, are anything but absolute and have many, many exceptions. Some exceptions entirely exempt certain proceedings from the hearsay rule. Specifically, FRE 1101(d) provides that hearsay may be used in grand jury hearings, preliminary hearings, extraditions, arrest warrant proceedings, sentencing, probation or supervised release proceedings, and bail matters. Hearsay may also generally be used at suppression hearings to determine the preliminary admissibility of confessions and other evidence under constitutional provisions, *United States v. Raddatz*, 447 U.S. 667, 679 (1980), but courts at such hearings apply slightly greater scrutiny to ensure that the hearsay is sufficiently reliable. In suppression hearings and the other situations explicitly listed in FRE 1101(d), the trier of fact is a judge, not a jury. As such, there is less concern about the risks of using hearsay because it is believed that judges are already taking into account the possible problems with the reliability of the statements in their decision making. Additionally, some of these proceedings occur so early in the criminal justice process that it might be unrealistic to expect firsthand information to be available. Is hearsay inadmissible at a suppression hearing? *United States v. Raddatz*, 477 U.S. at 679, held that "[a]t a suppression hearing, the court may rely on hearsay and other evidence, even though that evidence would not be admissible a trial." *Accord, United States v. Collins*, 577 Fed. Appx. 180, 186 (4th Cir. 2014) ("It is well established . . . that hearsay testimony is admissible at a suppression hearing").

Even if the hearsay rule applies to the proceeding as a whole (as it does at civil and criminal trials), the rule has dozens of exceptions, which we examine in Chapters Six through Eight. Curiously, the Federal Rules of Evidence classify statements falling into a handful of the exceptions as being "not hearsay," even though those statements meet the general definition of hearsay. FRE 801(d). In other jurisdictions, those same statements are considered "hearsay" subject to hearsay exceptions. Why the unusual treatment of these hearsay-but-not-hearsay statements under the Federal Rules of Evidence? This category was created as a compromise during the drafting of the rules because the statements falling into those exceptions were so commonly admitted in proceedings and were considered to be sufficiently reliable as to not fall under the general prohibition against hearsay.

PART C: DEFINITION OF "HEARSAY" [FRE 801]

As noted above, the all-or-nothing threshold question that either allows a litigant to bypass the hearsay rules entirely or requires the litigant to find an applicable exception is: Does this evidence meet the definition of "hearsay"?

The Federal Rules define "hearsay" in FRE 801(c):

> **FRE 801. DEFINITIONS THAT APPLY TO THIS ARTICLE**
>
> **(c) Hearsay.** "Hearsay" means a statement that:
>
> **(1)** the declarant does not make while testifying at the current trial or hearing; and
>
> **(2)** a party offers in evidence to prove the truth of the matter asserted in the statement.

By its plain language, the rule has two components:

(1) Is the evidence a statement made by a declarant *other than* while testifying at the current trial or hearing? In other words, is it an out-of-court statement?

(2) If the answer to (1) is "yes," is that out-of-court statement being offered to prove the truth of the matter asserted in that statement? In other words, is the statement relevant *only if it is true*?

1. Is the Evidence a Declarant's Out-of-Court Statement?

As stated, the essence of hearsay is that a party is seeking to introduce a statement (oral or written) that was made outside the courtroom. As explained above, such a statement is suspect because the declarant (that is, the person who made the statement) was not under oath or subject to examination at the time the statement was said, and we cannot observe their demeanor, ability to perceive and recall, and sincerity when the statement was made. However, this definition requires that we define two key terms: (1) Who qualifies as a declarant? (2) What qualifies as a statement? FRE 801 helps us answer these key questions.

FRE 801. Definitions That Apply to This Article

(a) Statement. "Statement" means a person's oral assertion, written assertion, or nonverbal conduct, if the person intended it as an assertion.

(b) Declarant. "Declarant" means the *person* who made the statement.

Excerpt from Advisory Committee Notes to FRE 801

- The key to the definition [of hearsay] is that nothing is an assertion unless intended to be one.

(a) Who Qualifies as a "Declarant"?

The "declarant" is the person who made the statement sought to be introduced into evidence during a court proceeding. The declarant can be the same person who is testifying in the courtroom or someone different.

Examples

1. Talia testifies that Ian told her as they stood on the sidewalk that the blue car hit the red car. In this situation, Talia is the witness and Ian is the declarant.
2. Ian testifies that he told Talia, while they were standing on the sidewalk, that the blue car hit the red car. In this situation, Ian is both the witness and the declarant. Because he was not under oath when he made the statement to Talia, because we could not observe his demeanor, and because he was not subject to cross-examination at that time, his own statement outside the courtroom can be hearsay.

The rule provides that only a "person" can be a "declarant." Thus, information from animals and machines generally do not qualify. Because their responses are a product of training (as to animals), or internal calibration, calculation, or fixed processes (as to machines), we are not concerned that animals or machines will be motivated to skew their responses; in such cases, the chief concern is whether they are properly trained or calibrated, which is covered more fully in Chapter Thirteen discussing authentication.

Examples

1. Officer Sarah testifies that the dog "alerted" on Defendant's bag and the officer then found cocaine in the bag. As long as the dog is trained to provide such a response automatically, the alert is admissible. It is not a "statement" by a person.
2. Witness A testifies: "At the time I heard the shots, the clock said it was 2:00 p.m." Clocks are not people; they are machines. The clock's readout is not hearsay.

Many types of devices may qualify as machines that do not provide hearsay. They include calculators, thermometers, gauges, automatic telephone logs, e-mail logs, raw data by forensic labs, and clocks. If the information comes automatically from a preset function of the machine, it is not hearsay. However, if the information from the machine simply reflects information previously entered into the machine manually by a person, it may be hearsay.

Examples

1. The nurse testifies that the thermometer showed that the patient had a temperature of 104°F. The thermometer is not a declarant.
2. The gas tank showed that it was "empty" when the car was recovered. The gas gauge is not a declarant.
3. The phone logs showed that number (213) 736-1149 called (310) 839-9877 before the murder. The phone logs are automatically created by a machine and are not hearsay.
4. The website said, "We have 4,000 happy customers." In this situation, the website is not really the declarant. It is just posting what a person has said, and this may be hearsay.

United States v. Washington

498 F.3d 225 (4th Cir. 2007)

NIEMEYER, Judge.

[Dwonne Washington was convicted of driving on the Baltimore-Washington Parkway while under the influence of alcohol or drugs. At trial, the government offered, over Washington's objection, expert testimony to prove that a blood sample, taken from Washington the night of his arrest and tested at Dr. Levine's lab, contained phencyclidine ("PCP") and alcohol. The raw data generated by the forensic lab's diagnostic machines and relied on by the expert was not hearsay because it was generated by a machine.]

At 3:30 a.m. on January 3, 2004, Officer Gary Hatch of the United States Park Police was patrolling the Baltimore-Washington Parkway when he saw a car going approximately 30 miles per hour in an area posted with a speed limit of 55 miles per hour. Officer Hatch stated that it was "as though [the car] was almost standing still." Officer Hatch turned on his siren and flashing lights to pull the car over to find out "why they were going so slow," but the car did not stop. Accelerating and decelerating, pulling off onto the shoulder, and then back onto the road, the car continued to meander along the parkway as Officer Hatch pursued it with his siren and flashing lights. Only with the assistance of another park police officer, who maneuvered in front of the car, was Officer Hatch able to force the car to stop.

When Officer Hatch opened the door, he caught a "very strong smell of PCP." Officer Hatch removed Washington from the car [and] placed him in handcuffs. Based on the strong PCP odor and Washington's flat, unresponsive demeanor, Officer Hatch took Washington to a hospital where Washington agreed to give a blood sample for testing.

The Institute's Forensic Toxicology Laboratory subjected the blood sample to "headspace gas chromatography" to identify whether ethanol was in the blood and to "immunoassay or chromatography" to screen for the presence of amphetamine, barbiturates, benzodiazepines, cannabinoids, cocaine, opiates, and phencyclidine, using a Hewlett Packard HP 6890 Series gas chromatograph machine. After lab technicians subjected the blood sample to testing, the instruments printed out some 20 pages of data and graphs. Based on the data, the director of the lab and its chief toxicologist, Dr. Barry Levine, issued a report to the United States Park Police, stating that the blood sample tested positive for phencyclidine.

The raw data were mechanical computer printouts with each page headed by the date of the test, the machine operator, an identification of the sample, its dilution factor, and other similar information, and containing computer-generated graphs and data reporting the results produced by the chromatograph machine. In the case before us, the "statements" in question are "[t]he raw data generated by the diagnostic machines"; [they are] the statements of the machines themselves, not their operators.

Hearsay is understood to be "a statement, other than one made by the declarant while testifying at the trial or hearing, offered in evidence to prove the truth of the matter asserted." Fed. R. Evid. 801(c). "A declarant is a person who makes a statement." Fed. R. Evid. 801(b). Only a person may be a declarant and make a statement. Accordingly, "nothing 'said' by a machine . . . is hearsay." *United States v. Khorozian*, 333 F.3d 498, 506 (3d Cir. 2003) (automatically generated time stamp on a fax is not a hearsay statement); *People v. Holowko*, 109 Ill. 2d 187, 486 N.E.2d 877, 878-79 (Ill. 1985) ("printout of results of computerized telephone tracing equipment is not hearsay evidence" but rather "a self-generated record of its operations"). In short, the raw data generated by the machines do not constitute "statements," and the machines are not "declarants."

MICHAEL, Judge, dissenting.

The test results, although computer-generated, were produced with the assistance and input of the technicians and must therefore be attributed to the technicians. For this reason, the majority is mistaken in concluding that "[t]he raw data generated by the diagnostic machines [or computers] are the 'statements' of the machines themselves."

Unlike the header information on a web page or fax, computerized laboratory equipment cannot detect, measure, and record toxin levels in blood samples without the assistance or input of a trained laboratory technician. The toxicology tests on Washington's blood in this case were conducted by technicians at the Armed Forces Institute of Pathology. A technician conducting a blood toxicology test must follow a "step-by-step procedure." He must, among other things, calibrate the testing instrument; withdraw the appropriate portion of blood from the larger sample; insert, without contamination, the smaller test sample into the instrument; initiate the test; and monitor the instrument while the test is in progress. In light of the significant role that the technician plays in conducting the test and generating accurate results, the results cannot be attributed solely to the *machine*.

(b) What Is a "Statement"?

FRE 801(a) has a very specific definition of a statement. A statement may be oral, written, or nonverbal conduct, but it can qualify as hearsay only if it is intended as an assertion. Let's look at examples reflecting each situation:

Examples

1. Darius tells Julie: "I saw the blue car hit the red car."
2. Darius writes a note to Julie: "I saw the blue car hit the red car."
3. Darius writes in his journal: "I saw the blue car hit the red car."
4. Darius e-mails his friend: "I saw the blue car hit the red car."
5. When asked which car caused the accident, Darius points at the blue car.

Each of these examples qualifies as a "statement" under the Federal Rules of Evidence. The trickiest issue is with regard to conduct that may or may not be intended to assert a fact.

(i) Statements or conduct intended as an assertion

In the famous case of *Wright v. Doe d. Tatham*, 112 Eng. Rep. 488 (Exch. Ch. 1837), the court took a broader approach to what qualifies as a statement. In that case, Sandford Tatham, a family member of John Marsden, filed an action to set aside Marsden's will that left all his property to Marsden's steward, George Wright. Tatham argued that Marsden was of feeble mind when he wrote the will and was under the control of Wright. As evidence of this assertion, Tatham sought to introduce evidence that Marsden's staff treated him like a child, called him "Silly Marsden," and made remarks like, "There goes crazy Marsden." In response, Wright sought to introduce evidence that people treated Marsden with respect and tried to introduce letters sent to Marsden that referred to Marsden in respectful terms and asked for his input on important decisions.

In a decision written by Judge Baron Parke, the court found that the letters could not be introduced because they "imply a statement or opinion" of their authors, even if it was not a direct or intentional assertion. By this logic, any conduct that might be used to prove an inference would be hearsay. For example, if an employer promoted a worker, this information would be hearsay because it implies the employer's assertion that the employee did good work. Similarly, if a doctor puts a patient in intensive care, he is making an implied statement that the patient is not well.

The Federal Rules of Evidence rejected such a broad approach to hearsay, as the next case illustrates. Only conduct that is *intended* to be an assertion is a hearsay statement. The rationale for the narrower approach is that although we worry that implicit assertions by nonverbal conduct might be slanted and unreliable, those concerns are less pressing when action is taken for a purpose other than to communicate. That is not the universal rule; some states treat implied assertions as hearsay.

United States v. Zenni

492 F. Supp. 464 (E.D. Ky. 1980)

BERTELSMAN, Judge.

This prosecution for illegal bookmaking activities presents a classic problem in the law of evidence, namely, whether implied assertions are hearsay. The problem was a controversial one at common law. Although the answer to the problem is clear under the Federal Rules of Evidence, there has been little judicial treatment of the matter.

FACTS

While conducting a search of the premises of the defendant, Ruby Humphrey, government agents answered the telephone several times. The unknown callers stated directions for the placing of bets on various sporting events. The government proposes to introduce this evidence to show that the callers believed that the premises were used in betting operations. The defendants object on the ground of hearsay.

COMMON LAW BACKGROUND

At common law . . . there existed strong policy reasons for ruling that such utterances were hearsay.

The classic case, which is discussed in virtually every textbook on evidence, is Wright v. Tatham (Exch. Ch. 1837). Described as a "celebrated and hard-fought cause," *Wright v. Tatham* was a will contest, in which the will was sought to be set aside on the grounds of the incompetency of the testator at the time of its execution. The proponents of the will offered to introduce into evidence letters to the testator from certain absent individuals on various business and social matters. The purpose of the offer was to show that the writers of the letters believed the testator was able to make intelligent decisions concerning such matters, and thus was competent.

One of the illustrations advanced in the judicial opinions in *Wright v. Tatham* is perhaps even more famous than the case itself. This is Baron Parke's famous sea captain example. Is it hearsay to offer as proof of the seaworthiness of a vessel that its captain, after thoroughly inspecting it, embarked on an ocean voyage upon it with his family?

The court in *Wright v. Tatham* held that implied assertions of this kind were hearsay. This was the prevailing common law view, where the hearsay issue was recognized. But frequently, it was not recognized. Thus, two federal appellate cases involving facts virtually identical to those in the case at bar did not even discuss the hearsay issue, although the evidence admitted in them would have been objectionable hearsay under the common law view.

THE FEDERAL RULES OF EVIDENCE

The common law rule that implied assertions were subject to hearsay treatment was criticized by respected commentators for several reasons. A leading work on the Federal Rules of Evidence, referring to the hotly debated question whether an implied assertion stands on better ground with respect to the hearsay rule than an express assertion, states:

> "By the time the federal rules were drafted, a number of eminent scholars and revisers had concluded that it does. Two principal arguments were usually expressed for removing implied assertions from the scope of the hearsay rule. First, when a person acts in a way consistent with a belief but without intending by his act to communicate that belief, one of the principal reasons for the hearsay rule to exclude declarations whose veracity cannot be tested by cross-examination does not apply, because the declarant's sincerity is not then involved. In the second place, the underlying belief is in some cases self-verifying:
>
> > 'There is frequently a guarantee of the trustworthiness of the inference to be drawn . . . because the actor has based his actions on the correctness of his belief, i. e. his actions speak louder than words.'"

In a frequently cited article the following analysis appears:

> "But ought the hearsay rule be deemed applicable to evidence of conduct? As McCormick has observed, the problem 'has only once received any adequate discussion in any decided case,' i. e., in *Wright v. Tatham*, already referred to. And even in that case the court did not pursue its inquiry beyond the point of concluding that evidence of an 'implied' assertion must necessarily be excluded wherever evidence of an 'express' assertion would be inadmissible. But as has been pointed out more than once (although I find no judicial recognition of the difference), the 'implied' assertion is, from the hearsay standpoint, not nearly as vulnerable as an express assertion of the fact which the evidence is offered to establish.
>
> "This is on the assumption that the conduct was 'nonassertive;' that the passers-by had their umbrellas up for the sake of keeping dry, not for the purpose of telling anyone it was raining; that the truck driver started up for the sake of resuming his journey, not for the purpose of telling anyone that the light had changed."

A man does not lie to himself. Put otherwise, if in doing what he does a man has no intention of asserting the existence or non-existence of a fact, it would appear that the trustworthiness of evidence of this conduct is the same whether he is an egregious liar or a paragon of veracity. Accordingly, the lack of opportunity for cross-examination in relation to his veracity or lack of it, would seem to be of no substantial importance.

The drafters of the Federal Rules agreed with the criticisms of the common law rule that implied assertions should be treated as hearsay and expressly abolished it.

The Advisory Committee note concerning this problem states:

> "The definition of 'statement' assumes importance because the term is used in the definition of hearsay in subdivision (c). The effect of the definition of 'statement' is to exclude from the operation of the hearsay rule all evidence of conduct, verbal or nonverbal, not intended as an assertion. The key to the definition is that nothing is an assertion unless intended to be one."

Applying the principles discussed above to the case at bar, this court holds that the utterances of the betters telephoning in their bets were nonassertive verbal conduct. The language is not an assertion on its face, and it is obvious these persons did not intend to make an assertion about the fact sought to be proved or anything else.[21]

As an implied assertion, the proffered evidence is expressly excluded from the operation of the hearsay rule by Rule 801 of the Federal Rules of Evidence, and the objection thereto must be overruled.

(ii) Specific applications of this definition

Are questions "statements"? It depends. As a general matter, questions are not intended to assert a fact and thus are not "statements" capable of qualifying as hearsay. For example, if a person asks, "What time is it?" or "How do I get to the bus stop?" the declarant is not intentionally asserting, "I don't know what time it is" or "I am lost." However, some questions can contain intentional assertions, so be careful. For example, a question like, "Do you think Joe went to Bob's house to rob him again?" contains the intended assertion that Joe has robbed Bob before.

21. A somewhat different type of analysis would be required by words non-assertive in form, but which under the circumstances might be intended as an assertion. For example, an inspector at an airport security station might run a metal detector over a passenger and say "go on through." In the absence of the inspector, would testimony of this event be objectionable *hearsay*, if offered for the proposition that the passenger did not have a gun on him at that time?

Are actions by themselves "statements"? No. As we have seen, actions are not statements unless they are intended to convey specific information. The classic examples are pointing in response to a question or pantomiming a response. In those situations, the declarant is intentionally conveying information through signals. For example, Paul Revere signaled the arrival of British troops by the number of lanterns he displayed in the Old North Church Belfry. "Two if by sea" was an intentional signal that the British had landed by sea.

Can the failure to speak or failure to act constitute a "statement"? It depends. For example, consider a case in which a guest in a hotel is found dead from carbon monoxide poisoning. The hotel owners want to introduce evidence that they had never had complaints that their heaters were not working. Guests not complaining were not intentional assertions. However, if the guests were asked after the accident whether they ever had any complaints, their negative answers would be an assertion.

Review Questions

1. **Telling time.** To prove that it was 11:00 p.m. when the victim's home was burglarized, Prosecutor introduces testimony by the security company that the clock said 11:00 p.m. when the burglary alarm was activated.
2. **Finger pointing.** To prove Defendant was the burglar, Prosecutor introduces testimony by a police officer, who relays that when the officer asked the victim who had committed the robbery, the victim pointed at Defendant.
3. **Incentive to steal.** To prove that Defendant needed money and therefore that he committed the burglary, Prosecutor introduces testimony from Defendant's coworker that their boss said to Defendant the morning of the burglary, "You're fired."
4. **No complaints.** To prove that parents did not suspect a teacher of harming their children, the school district sued by the parents introduces testimony that no parent ever complained about the teacher.

2. *Is the Statement Being "Offered in Evidence to Prove the Truth of the Matter Asserted"?*

Probably the most critical—and also trickiest—part of determining whether a particular piece of evidence constitutes hearsay is trying to determine when a statement is being offered "to prove the truth of the matter asserted." To help us with that determination, let us look at a few examples. Then we will go through each example of a statement that does not qualify for the hearsay rule because it is offered for some purpose *other than* to prove that its content is true. These statements are often referred to as "nonhearsay."

Examples

1. At trial, the witness testifies that the blue car hit the red car. Prior to his testimony, and while speaking to investigators, the witness said that the red car hit the blue car. The defense can offer this statement to "impeach" the witness by showing that the witness changed his story and is therefore not to be believed. If the out-of-court statement is offered to prove that the red car hit the blue car, that purpose is achieved only if that statement is true; for this purpose, the statement is hearsay. However, if the statement is offered just to show that the witness has not been consistent in his statements, that purpose is achieved as long as the two statements are inconsistent—and whether or not the statement is true; for this purpose, the statement is not hearsay.
2. At trial, the witness testifies that Plaintiff offered to sell his car to Defendant for $2,000. Defendant said, "I accept." In this situation, the out-of-court statements have legal consequences just because they were said. Rather than narrating a past event, the words themselves are independent verbal acts forming a contract. They are nonhearsay.
3. At trial, Defendant claims that Plaintiff assumed the risk of using a certain product. Plaintiff claims that she had no idea that the product was dangerous. Defendant wants to introduce evidence that Plaintiff was told, "Be careful. That is a dangerous product." Clearly, Defendant is not offering that statement to prove that its own product was dangerous. Rather, the statement is being offered to prove that Plaintiff was on notice of the risk. This statement is nonhearsay.
4. The issue in a case is whether the victim survived a car crash and died later of malpractice in the hospital. To prove that the victim survived the accident, his next of kin offers testimony that the victim said after the crash, "Yikes, it is a miracle I am not dead." In this situation, it does not matter what the victim said. The fact that the victim spoke at all is what matters. It shows that the victim survived the crash. This statement is nonhearsay.

The best way to assess whether a statement is offered for the truth of the matter asserted is to determine two things: (1) What, if anything, is being directly asserted by the statement? (2) Is the statement only relevant because its content is true, or is it instead relevant regardless of whether that content is true or not?

Fortunately, statements admitted for purposes other than their truth generally fall into one of six categories: (1) statements that are "verbal acts" with independent legal significance; (2) statements offered to show the impact on the listener or viewer; (3) statements used to impeach; (4) statements offered as circumstantial evidence of the declarant's state of mind; (5) verbal objects; and (6) statements that are otherwise relevant just because they were said, regardless of whether they were true. We will review each in turn.

(a) Verbal Acts

Particularly in the fields of contracts and property law, words sometimes have significance simply because they are uttered—whether or not they are true. For example, a contract is an exchange of words:

Buyer: "I offer you $2,000 for your painting."
Seller: "I accept."

Neither of these statements constitutes hearsay. The words are being offered to show the making of the contract and thus have independent legal significance. Uttering these words is how you make a contract. Those words are called "verbal acts" or "legally operative facts." They create a contract whether or not they are true; as such, they are not offered for their truth and thus do not constitute hearsay.

Consider how the following exchange is different:

Seller: "You *agreed* to buy the painting for $2,000."
Buyer: "No, you *agreed* to sell it for $1,000."

These words are assertions regarding past events. They do not create a contract, but rather are assertions about whether a contract was formed at some time in the past. As such, they would not qualify as verbal acts. In fact, we would have every concern about whose recollection is correct, which is one of the reasons for the rule against hearsay.

(i) Civil cases

In the civil arena, common examples of verbal acts include the following:

- Contracts: Offers and acceptances
- Property: Words designating delivery ("Here are your goods") or whether something is a gift ("This book is a gift to you")
- Sexual harassment: Actionable, harassing words, such as "Give me a smooch; I can make you happy." Such words are not being offered to show that the declarant would make the victim happy. Rather, the words themselves *are the harassing conduct* and thus have independent legal significance.

Hanson v. Johnson

161 Minn. 229 (Minn. 1924)

Wilson, Chief Justice.

In an effort to prove that the corn was owned by plaintiff and that it was a part of his share, he testified, over the objection of hearsay and self-serving, that when the tenant was about through husking corn he was on the farm and the tenant pointed out the corn in question (and a double crib of corn) and said: "Mr. Hanson, here is your corn for this year, this double crib here and this single crib here is your share for this year's corn; this belongs to you, Mr. Hanson." A bystander was called and against the same objection testified to having heard the talk in substantially the same language.

There is no question but that plaintiff owned some corn. It was necessary to identify it. This division and identity was made by the acts of tenant in husking the corn and putting it in separate cribs and then his telling Hanson which was his share and the latter's acquiescence therein. The language of the tenant was the very fact necessary to be proved. The verbal part of the transaction between plaintiff and the tenant was necessary to prove the fact. The words were the verbal acts. They aid in giving legal significance to the conduct of the parties. They accompanied the conduct. There could be no division without words or gestures identifying the respective shares. This was a fact to be shown in the chain of proof of title. It was competent evidence. It was not hearsay nor self-serving. As between plaintiff and the tenant this evidence would be admissible.

(ii) Criminal cases

In the criminal field, common examples of verbal acts include the following:

- Threats: The threatening words are themselves the *actus reus* of the crime
- Bribes: Again, the words constituting the bribe are the *actus reus* of the crime
- Drug orders: The words asking for drugs are the conduct underlying a charge of distributing drugs
- Bookmaking: The words underlying the placement of bets shows gambling is occurring

The words in each of these circumstances are of independent legal significance just because they were said and no matter whether they are true.

Garner v. State

414 Md. 372 (Md. Ct. App. 2010)

Murphy, Judge.

[A] jury convicted Alphonso Garner, Petitioner, of possession of cocaine with intent to distribute. This case presents "a fascinating evidentiary issue." At the police station, Mr. Garner was stripped of his personal items, including his cell phone. [A] trooper subsequently answered the cell phone. [The trooper] was allowed to testify, over objection, that after he said "hello" a male caller replied, "can I get a 40," and then hung up when asked his name.

Petitioner [claims] that the Court should have sustained the "hearsay" objection to [the] Trooper's testimony about the call to Petitioner's cell phone. [We] hold that the rule against hearsay was not violated by [the] Trooper's testimony about the telephone call at issue.

The making of a wager or the purchase of a drug, legally or illegally, is a form of contract. There is an offer and an acceptance. The telephoned words of the would-be bettor or would-be purchaser are frequently categorized, therefore, as verbal parts of acts. They are not considered to be assertions and do not fall under the scrutiny of the Rules Against Hearsay.

While there may be an "implied assertion" in almost any question, in the case at bar, the only assertion implied in the anonymous caller's question was the assertion that the caller had the funds to purchase the drugs that he wanted to purchase. Because the caller's request did not constitute inadmissible hearsay evidence, the rule against hearsay does not operate to exclude evidence of the "verbal act" that established a consequential fact: Petitioner was in possession of a telephone called by a person who requested to purchase cocaine.

(b) Words Proving Effect on Listener or Reader

Sometimes words are relevant not because they are true, but rather because someone heard those words being uttered. In such cases, what is relevant is the effect that those words had on the reader or listener and, typically, whether the reader or listener gained knowledge or acted reasonably given the information conveyed by those words.

Examples

1. Defendant is charged with murder. She claims that she acted in self-defense because Jessica had told her that the victim was coming to kill her. Here, Defendant is offering Jessica's out-of-court statement to explain why Defendant reasonably feared for her life and used self-defense.
2. Plaintiff is suing his mechanic because Plaintiff had an accident when his brakes failed. Defendant is asserting "assumption of the risk" as a defense. Defendant seeks to have a witness testify that he heard the mechanic tell Plaintiff, "I fixed the axle, but your brakes still look pretty shot." The out-of-court statement is not being offered to prove that the mechanic fixed the axle or that the brakes were shot. Defendant wants to introduce the statement to show that Plaintiff was on notice that he should not drive his car.

Consider why the statement offered in *State v. Muller* was ruled not to be hearsay.

State v. Muller

2013 Ariz. App. Unpub. 1019 (Az. Ct. App. 2013)

DOWNIE, Judge.

Christopher Stuart Muller appeals his conviction and life sentence for conspiracy to commit first-degree murder. The conviction stems from an alleged plan by Muller to kill a former business associate and the associate's brother. The plot failed when the person Muller spoke to about arranging the murders notified the authorities. On appeal, Muller argues that error occurred in the admission of evidence. For reasons that follow, we affirm.

ADMISSION OF TESTIMONY REGARDING THREAT

Muller contends the trial court erred in admitting testimony regarding a threat made by one of the brothers. We review a ruling on the admissibility of evidence for an abuse of discretion. The State's theory was that Muller wanted to kill M.S. and his brother because they were threatening his businesses—including a crating business and a marijuana growing enterprise for use by medical dispensaries in California. At trial, M.S. testified about a telephone call his brother made to Muller. During the call, the brother "warned [Muller] that often times if you overload a grow house, a marijuana grow house, and overload the power system they have the ability to catch fire." M.S. testified that his brother's statement "almost sounded threatening." Muller argues this testimony should have been excluded because it was hearsay.

Hearsay is an out-of-court statement offered to prove the truth of the matter asserted and is generally inadmissible. The rule excluding hearsay, however, is inapplicable when the statement is offered for some valid purpose other than proving the truth of the matter asserted in the statement.

Here, testimony regarding the brother's "warning" was not offered to prove that overloading the power system on a grow house will cause a fire, but rather to show the effect of the statement on Muller vis-à-vis his motive for wanting the brothers killed. Hence, the testimony was properly admissible for a non-hearsay purpose.

Review Questions

The most effective way to understand this aspect of the hearsay rule—namely, that a statement may be relevant for its effect on the hearer or reader—is to review common situations in which out-of-court statements may be offered for this other purpose.

1. **Killer Fifi.** Sheila is charged with murder when her dog, Fifi, mauls the neighbor to death. In her defense, Sheila calls W, who will testify that he heard Fifi's trainer tell Sheila, "Fifi is the gentlest dog on earth." Is the trainer's out-of-court statement hearsay? For what purpose is it being offered?
2. **Heads up.** Plaintiff sues Defendant for negligence when she is hit by falling debris at Defendant's construction site. Defendant calls W to testify that he heard someone yell at P just before she was hit, "Watch out below. You're going to get hit." Hearsay or nonhearsay? For what purpose is the statement being offered?
3. **Hostile environment.** Plaintiff sues her employer for creating a hostile work environment. P calls W to testify that W heard the boss say, "She's really stupid, but I keep her around because she is so cute." Hearsay or nonhearsay? For what purpose is the statement being offered?

4. **Warning signs.** Plaintiff is suing the school district for failing to fire a teacher who was engaged in misconduct. The school district claims that it had no notice that the teacher was engaged in misconduct. Plaintiff wants to introduce a letter a parent sent to the president of the school board that stated, "You've got to get Mr. Jones out of the classroom. He is harming the kids." Hearsay or nonhearsay? For what purpose is the statement being offered?
5. **Wrong information.** Officer Steve is being sued for violating Plaintiff's civil rights. Plaintiff claims that Steve used excessive force during an arrest. Officer Steve calls W to testify, "When the arrest occurred, someone yelled, 'Be careful. This guy is on PCP.'" As it turns out, Plaintiff was not on PCP. Is the statement hearsay or nonhearsay? For what purpose is it being introduced?

(c) Statements Used to Impeach

A witness's prior out-of-court statement may be used to impeach the witness's credibility if that prior statement contradicts the witness's in-court testimony. If the prior, out-of-court statement is used *solely* to impeach, it does not matter which of the two statements is true; what matters for impeachment purposes is that the witness changed his or her story. Thus, the prior statement does not constitute hearsay.

Example

Alex sues Jasmine for hitting Alex's car. W testifies that Jasmine ran a red light and hit Alex's car. On cross-examination, Jasmine's lawyer asks W, "Isn't it true that you told our investigator that Alex was the one who ran the red light and hit Jasmine's car?" Jasmine's lawyer can ask about the out-of-court statement to the investigator if she is using it to show that W's testimony is unreliable; for that purpose, the statement is not hearsay. But if she used it as proof that Alex ran the red light and hit Jasmine's car, the statement would be hearsay.

Because the simultaneous permissible use of the statement for one purpose (impeachment) and impermissible use of the statement for another purpose (the truth) may be confusing to the jury, the court may have to give a limiting instruction that the out-of-court statement may only be used to assess W's credibility. If use of the statement may be too confusing to the jury, the court may use FRE 403 to exclude the statement. Alternatively, as we will learn, there may also be a hearsay exception that applies.

The case of *United States v. Lay* provides another example of an out-of-court statement that is nonhearsay when it is being used to impeach.

United States v. Lay

644 F.2d 1087 (5th Cir. 1981)

AINSWORTH, Judge.

Appellant James J. Lay was convicted in district court of possession of 96 pounds of marijuana with intent to distribute. Lay and a companion, Richard T. Broussard, were stopped at a border checkpoint as they drove from Mexico into the United States near Sarita, Texas. The border patrol agent, noticing that Lay, who was driving, appeared nervous, asked him to open the trunk of the car. Lay told the agent that he did not have the key to the trunk. The agent then gained access to the trunk by removing the back seat of the car and found 96 pounds of marijuana in the trunk.

At trial, Broussard was the key witness against Lay. Broussard testified that the marijuana transaction was Lay's idea and that they were jointly involved in the deal. Lay, on the other hand, testified that the car belonged to Broussard and that he knew nothing about the marijuana until Broussard told him about it just before they reached the border. Lay testified that Broussard had made statements to him which contradicted Broussard's testimony. The prosecutor objected.

The district judge excluded Lay's testimony about Broussard's statements and motives for two stated reasons: the testimony would relate to events which occurred after the commission of the crime and would therefore not be relevant, and reports of Broussard's statements would be hearsay. Neither of these reasons is appropriate. Lay apparently would have testified about statements made by Broussard after his arrest which were inconsistent with his trial testimony. Such statements are not offered to prove the truth of the matter asserted, but instead to cast doubt on the trial testimony in light of the inconsistency. They are therefore not hearsay. Under the Federal Rules of Evidence, extrinsic evidence of prior inconsistent statements of witnesses is admissible only if the witness is afforded an opportunity to explain or to deny making the prior statements. Fed.R.Evid. 613(b). Broussard was questioned about the statements he allegedly made to Lay and he denied making them. Thus, Lay's testimony, a form of extrinsic evidence, was admissible to impeach Broussard.

Review Questions

1. **Fair weather.** In court, W testifies that it was raining on the day of the accident. Out of court, the witness said that it was sunny. If the out-of-court statement is offered as evidence, is it hearsay?
2. **Hair color blind?** In court, W testifies that the robber had blond hair. Out of court, W told the police that the robber had black hair. As it turns out, Defendant has black hair. If the prosecution offers the out-of-court statement, is it hearsay?

3. **Touchdown alibi.** In a murder trial, W, Defendant's brother, testifies that Defendant was home with him watching a football game at the time of the murder. Prosecutors then call X, W's roommate, who testifies that on the night of the murder, W said, "I can't believe my brother didn't come over today to watch the football game with us."

(d) Statements Offered as Circumstantial Evidence of the Declarant's State of Mind

When an out-of-court statement is offered not to prove that its content is true, but rather as indirect (or circumstantial) evidence of the declarant's state of mind, it is not hearsay for this purpose. What is critical, however, is that the declarant's state of mind be *relevant* to the case; if it is not relevant to any issue in the case, it should be excluded under the rules regarding relevance.

Example

In a will contest, Plaintiff calls W to testify that at the time the deceased signed the will, he also yelled out, "I am Napoleon!" This statement is not being offered to prove that the deceased was really Napoleon. Instead, it is being offered to show circumstantially that he was incompetent to write his will (because he *thought* he was Napoleon). Because the decedent's state of mind is relevant to a will contest, the statement circumstantially showing the individual was not competent is both nonhearsay—and relevant.

It is important to note that this nonhearsay category is only applicable to *circumstantial* evidence of a declarant's state of mind. If the declarant had said, "I'm crazy," that *direct* statement regarding the declarant's state of mind would meet the definition of hearsay because its relevance turns on its truth. As we will see, there is a hearsay exception under FRE 803(3) for direct statements of a declarant's state of mind when that state of mind is relevant in the case. When the statement is only circumstantial evidence of one's state of mind, it is more likely to be inadvertent and hence more likely to be reliable; that is why it falls outside the definition of hearsay in the first place.

Review Questions

1. **Bias in the workplace.** Plaintiff is suing Company A for discrimination in hiring. Company A wants to call a witness to testify that Plaintiff regularly announced at the office meetings, "If you judge people by their color, you are not fit to make hiring decisions."

2. **Child's wishes.** The court is deciding whether to place a child in the custody of Parent 1 or Parent 2. Parent 1 wants to introduce testimony by the nanny that the child told her, "My life is over if I have to live with Parent 2."
3. **Cruisin'.** Plaintiff is suing Defendant after Defendant's car hit Plaintiff's car. Defendant claims that he was unaware that his brakes would fail. Defendant wants W to testify that the day before the accident, W heard Defendant say, "Let's take a cruise. My car has never run better."

(e) Verbal Objects and Markers

Words are everywhere in our society, but the mere fact that they are repeated by a witness on the stand does not make them hearsay. Consider the following examples.

Examples

1. Witness testifies that the bank robber was wearing a shirt that said "I Love Lucy." The words on the shirt are not being offered to prove that the wearer loves Lucy. They are being used to make an identification.
2. W1 testifies that the murderer was drinking from a can of Coke right before he shot the victim. W2 testifies that he saw Johnny with a Coke can right before the murder. Again, the wording on the Coke can is just being used for identification purposes. It is not being used to prove that there was Coke in the can.
3. W1 testifies that the assailant wore a "Pantages University" shirt. It would be hearsay if the label were being used to prove that the assailant attends Pantages University. However, if W1 can identify the person in the shirt as the assailant and if W2 can identify Defendant as the same person that W1 identified, the shirt's words are just a verbal marker.
4. Defendant is charged with murder. Prosecutor calls an eyewitness, who identifies Defendant in part based on the tattoo of a tear just below his left eye. Defendant objects, "Hearsay." If the tattoo is just used as a means of identifying Defendant, the fact that it may have a further meaning is irrelevant. Thus, there is no hearsay. *Accord Carter v. State*, 23 So. 3d 1238, 1243 (Fla. Dist. Ct. App. 2009); *People v. Iraheta*, 14 Cal. App. 5th 1228, 1248 (Cal. Ct. App. 2017).
5. Same as Example 4, except that Prosecutor seeks to call a gang expert to testify that the tear tattoo is meant to communicate that a person is a gang member who has killed at least one member of a rival gang. Defendant objects, "Hearsay." The tattoo here is relevant as a statement of Defendant, "I have killed a rival gang member." As such, it is hearsay. However, as explained in Chapter Six regarding hearsay exceptions, it would be admissible in this case as the statement of a party opponent.
6. Plaintiff sues a pipe distributor for manufacturing the asbestos-laden pipes that Plaintiff installed on a project, and further alleges that his

exposure to those pipes caused his mesothelioma years later. Plaintiff calls a witness who testifies that she remembers seeing a K-shaped logo made out of what looked like pipes, which was the distributor's logo. The distributor objects, "Hearsay." This objection should be overruled because the logo is used to prove the pipe supplier's identity (that is, as a verbal marker), not the truth of the logo. *Hart v. Keenan Properties, Inc.*, 9 Cal. 5th 442 (Cal. 2020).

7. Plaintiff sues defendant for false designation of origin and theft of trade secrets. Defendant seeks to introduce business records with a logo that purports to indicate their origin. Plaintiff objects, "Hearsay." Because the logos are being introduced as an assertion, "These are my business records," they are admitted for their truth and as such are hearsay. *McCaskill v. Ray*, 279 Fed. Appx. 913, 915 (11th Cir. 2008).

A verbal marker can be circumstantial evidence that an individual was in a location where they could obtain the object with that marking.

Examples

Prosecutors allege that Defendant repeatedly sold drugs at "Hamburger Hamlet." When police search Defendant's car, they find several bags and wrapping papers with the wording "Hamburger Hamlet." The words on the bag are being used as circumstantial evidence that Defendant was at one point at a place with the name "Hamburger Hamlet."

The burden is on the proponent of the evidence to articulate the nonhearsay purpose for which the evidence is being used. Once again, if there is any possible confusion, the trial judge can give a limiting instruction or use his or her discretion to exclude the statement under FRE 403.

Review Questions

1. **Stealing secrets.** Disney is suing a former employee for theft of trade secrets. W1 testifies that he saw a folder in Defendant's briefcase that had the label "Disney Property." If this testimony is the only evidence that the folder had trade secrets, is it hearsay? If another witness can identify the folder as one in which Disney trade secrets are held, is it hearsay?
2. **Ironic tees.** Defendant is on trial for arson. W1 testifies that the arsonist wore a T-shirt with "Hot Stuff" written on it. A T-shirt with this lettering is found at Defendant's house. Is it hearsay?

(f) Statements That Are Relevant Merely Because They Were Uttered Regardless of Their Truth

Many other statements could fall into this residual category of nonhearsay statements. What they all have in common is that the statements are relevant merely because they were said and irrespective of whether they are true. Here are some examples.

Examples

1. **Circumstantial evidence of memory or belief.** To prove that the plaintiff-accident victim did not black out immediately after the accident, Plaintiff seeks to introduce the witness's testimony that Plaintiff was able to describe what the ambulance driver wore. Here, the fact that Plaintiff said anything is relevant as to whether the plaintiff blacked out, regardless of whether his description was accurate.
2. **Lying.** To prove that Defendant's business partner was covering up for her fraud, Prosecutor elicits testimony by an FBI agent that when she interviewed Defendant's partner, the partner lied about whether he even knew Defendant. Prosecutor will not be seeking to introduce this testimony to show that the partners didn't know each other; instead, it is being introduced to prove exactly the opposite—namely, that the lying shows the cover-up.
3. **Willingness to say or omit.** Defendant is charged with rigging the play clock at the Super Bowl. When interviewed by investigators, Defendant admits that he was taught how to use the scoreboard. Defendant may want to introduce this testimony not to prove that he knew how to use the scoreboard, but to show that he did not have a guilty conscience because he was willing to admit that he knew how to conduct the fraud if he had wanted to do so.
4. **Questions.** In a contract dispute, Plaintiff wants the witness to testify to Plaintiff asking him, "Were the goods delivered?" Since the question does not assert that something occurred, it does not meet the hearsay definition. However, what if Plaintiff asked a different question, "Were the goods delivered to the same place as the last goods?" Within *that* question is an assertion (namely, that there had been a prior delivery), and to that extent it is hearsay.
5. **Putting other statements in context.** Occasionally, statements are admitted because they put other statements in context. For example, Prosecutor wants W to testify that he heard X ask Defendant, "How did you pull it off?" Defendant replied, "I used the same m.o. as my last robbery." Even though the question implies that Defendant committed the crime, its real purpose is to put Defendant's responsive answer in context.

People v. Turner

8 Cal. 4th 137 (Cal. 1994)

ARABIAN, Justice.

The jury found defendant guilty of two counts of first degree murder.

PROSECUTION EVIDENCE

On the night of July 11, 1979, defendant drove codefendant Teague Hampton Scott to the Torrance Airport, where defendant had worked as a security guard. While at the airport, defendant followed a 1979 yellow Mazda RX7 that Scott wanted to steal. The vehicle stopped outside a hangar. When the victims, Dr. George S. Hill, a surgeon, and Ms. Joella Champion, a schoolteacher, got out of the Mazda and entered the hangar, defendant and Scott got out of their car and followed them. A robbery ensued, during which the victims' jewelry was taken at gunpoint. The victims were then bound hand and foot, gagged, and forced to sit against the wall of the hangar. Each victim was shot in the head once at close range by a .38-caliber gun. Death was immediate.

Defendant made several inconsistent statements regarding his involvement. . . . Defendant stated that while he was at the airport when the murders occurred, he was not the one who pulled the trigger. Rather, he merely stood guard at the door of the hangar for Scott, and did not enter the hangar. Defendant [later] stated that on the night of the murders, he and Scott entered the hangar after defendant was unable to locate Champion's purse in the Mazda. Defendant bound the woman. Scott gave defendant the gun. Scott then tied up the man.

Scott told defendant to watch the victims, who were tied and sitting on their knees. After Scott had gathered all of the property, he told defendant to shoot. Defendant had already cocked the gun, which was pointed at the woman's ear and temple, and his finger was on the trigger. Scott said, "Remember what I told you, anybody we rob, we got to shoot, cuz we can't leave a witness behind." Scott kept hollering, "shoot her and get it over with so we can leave." Defendant stood shaking and trembling and would not pull the trigger. Scott grabbed defendant's hand, the gun went off, and Champion fell. Scott then took the gun and shot Hill in the head.

On August 13, 1979, Armand Vincent, who had been charged with misdemeanor violations of performing home repair and remodeling without a contractor's license, was on a jail bus to and from the Torrance courthouse with defendant and Scott as they conversed about the murders. Vincent was handcuffed to defendant. Scott was separated from defendant and Vincent by a screen. When Scott said, "I didn't have any idea we were going to kill anyone," defendant responded, "Well, you know, man, dead witnesses don't talk." In response to Scott's question, "How did you do it?" defendant said he "killed the man and then the woman" with two shots, and that the victims were tied with their hands behind their back.

ADMISSIBILITY OF VINCENT'S TESTIMONY

Defendant contends that the trial court erred in permitting jailhouse informant Armand Vincent to testify regarding Scott's statements in a conversation with defendant, during which defendant admitted shooting both victims. We conclude that Scott's statements were not hearsay and were properly admitted to supply context to defendant's statements.

Before the jury, Vincent testified that on August 13, 1979, he rode on a county jail bus with defendant and Scott to and from the Torrance courthouse. During the trip, defendant and Scott discussed the Torrance Airport murders. Scott began the conversation by saying, "I'm in jail for a double murder that I knew nothing about. This is cold." Scott said, "I thought that we were out just to do a little robbery at the Torrance Airport." "I didn't have any idea we were going to kill anyone." Turner responded, "Well, you know, man, dead witnesses don't talk."

Scott asked, "How did you do it?" Defendant said, "I killed the man and then the woman." He pointed his left index finger at his temple and said he shot them.

Scott said, "[Y]ou left the gun in my car and my fingerprints are all over it." Defendant said, "Well, you should have got rid of it." Defendant laughed and said, "[Y]ou take the rap for it, man."

After Vincent testified, the trial court instructed the jury that they were to consider the statements attributed to Scott "only to the extent that they give meaning to the statements of [defendant]. The statements of [Scott] are not to be considered for the truth of the matter asserted . . . [;] you are the sole judges as to whether [defendant] made the statements testified to and whether such statements are true in whole or in part."

Defendant asserts that Scott's statements were inadmissible hearsay, resulting in prejudice. As noted earlier, he does not assert that his own statements were improperly admitted [because a defendant's statements are admissible as admissions]. We conclude the trial court properly admitted Scott's statements to give meaning to defendant's statements and that allowing these statements for this limited purpose was within the trial court's discretion.

An out-of-court statement is properly admitted if a nonhearsay purpose for admitting the statement is identified, and the nonhearsay purpose is relevant to an issue in dispute. Here, Scott's identification of the location of the robberies and murders as the Torrance Airport, and inquiries regarding why and how defendant shot the victims, gave context to defendant's statements and tethered them to the crimes at issue in this case. Accordingly, we conclude that Scott's statements satisfied the requirements governing the admission of out-of-court statements for a *nonhearsay* purpose. We further conclude that the value of Scott's statements to give meaning to defendant's admissions substantially outweighed any probability of undue prejudice, or danger of confusing or misleading the jury.

Review Questions

For each of these problems, consider *carefully* what the statement is being offered to prove and whether it constitutes "hearsay" under the definition of hearsay in FRE 801(c).

1. **Quiet streets.** W testifies that there was no traffic on the street at the time of the accident. In a signed statement before trial, W stated, "The street was hectic and crowded when the accident occurred." If offered to prove that W cannot be believed, is the statement hearsay or nonhearsay?
2. **Explosive threats.** Defendant is charged with extortion. Prosecutors call W to testify that he received a call from Defendant's henchman, who said, "If you don't pay me $5 million, I'm going to blow up your business." Hearsay or nonhearsay?
3. **Unwilling conspirator.** Defendant is on trial for being an accomplice to bank robbery. He is asserting a duress defense. Defendant calls W to testify that he heard X tell Defendant, "You'd better be there with the getaway car or we will kill you and your family." Hearsay or nonhearsay?
4. **Best parent.** Parent 1 and Parent 2 are in a custody battle over their child. W testifies that she heard Parent 1 say, "No one can be a better parent than I can. The Memes told me so."
5. **Broken promises.** Plaintiff is suing Defendant for consumer fraud. Plaintiff calls W to testify that when W called Defendant's business, someone told him, "We give you a $100 guaranty." However, when the product was defective, the guaranty was not honored. Hearsay or nonhearsay?
6. **Doesn't add up.** Plaintiff claims that she worked as a bookkeeper for Defendant and he failed to pay her wages. To prove that she actually worked as a bookkeeper, Plaintiff calls W to testify, "Plaintiff described for me in detail the program and records kept by Defendant."
7. **Trade names.** Defendant is being prosecuted for selling a scam medical test for pregnancy. It is called "Baby101." To prove that the test that the victims used were the ones produced by Defendant, the victims testify that the kits had "Baby101" printed on them.

PART D: INDIRECT HEARSAY AND HEARSAY WITHIN HEARSAY

1. Indirect Hearsay

Sometimes, it is not immediately apparent that the testimony that will be presented will constitute hearsay, but a close examination of the statement will reveal that there is "indirect hearsay." Indirect hearsay is hearsay that is embedded in the question or narrative and, by answering the question, the witness will be testifying to hearsay information. There are times when we don't really care about indirect hearsay. For example, if a witness is asked, "When were you born?" the witness will only know this information through hearsay since the witness will have been too young to have firsthand knowledge. The witness's answer is therefore technically hearsay, but will rarely elicit a successful hearsay objection.

In other situations, however, indirect hearsay can be quite troubling.

Example

Defendant is being prosecuted for selling drugs. The prosecution wants the jury to hear the informant's out-of-court statements about Defendant's activities because the prosecution doesn't want to put the informant on the stand and subject him to cross-examination. Instead, the prosecution calls the investigating officer and asks that following questions:

Prosecutor: Officer Kluwer, were you in charge of this investigation?
Officer Kluwer: Yes.
Prosecutor: How did you learn that Defendant was selling drugs?
Officer Kluwer: The informant told me that he bought from Defendant.
Defense lawyer: Objection.
Judge: Sustained.
Prosecutor: During this investigation, did you work with an informant?
Officer Kluwer: Yes.
Prosecutor: After you spoke to the informant, who did you focus the investigation on?
Defense lawyer: Objection. Calls for indirect hearsay.

In this example, Officer Kluwer's answer to the question will necessarily imply that the informant told him that Defendant was selling drugs.

Indirect hearsay is impermissible, but only a lawyer who listens carefully may be able to detect it.

State v. Pratt

2018 Tenn. Crim. App. LEXIS 634 (Tenn. Ct. Crim. App. 2018)

Easter, Judge.

Defendant, Lloyd Rush Pratt, Jr., appeals from his convictions for driving as an habitual motor vehicle offender, driving under the influence, and failure to exercise due care. For the following reasons, we determine that the trial court erred in denying a mistrial and improperly admitting hearsay evidence. The judgments of the trial court are reversed and remanded.

At trial, Deputy Scott Bell testified that he was dispatched to a one vehicle accident in the "early morning hours" of February 15, 2015. When he arrived at the scene he observed one "white vehicle off to the left side of the road." According to Deputy Bell "there was a white male in the driver's seat and a female passenger in the passenger seat." The male identified himself as Defendant.

Deputy Bell was "not sure" if the vehicle was running when he arrived. He assessed Defendant and the female for injuries. Deputy Bell called Emergency Medical Services ("EMS") to respond to the scene. Deputy Bell went on to testify that Defendant "wasn't real sure" how the crash happened but that Defendant "said he was" driving. Again, counsel for Defendant objected, claiming that it was "a discovery issue" because Defendant had "no notice that [Defendant] made any statements to Deputy Bell."

At that point, the trial court excused the jury from the courtroom. After a jury-out hearing, the trial court determined that the State violated discovery rules by failing to disclose statements made by Defendant at the scene. The trial court informed the jury that they were not permitted to consider any portions of Deputy Bell's testimony relating to statements made by Defendant.

Counsel for Defendant moved for a mistrial, arguing that the "whole defense [was] that he never says he was driving" and that the officers "never asked him." The trial court determined that a curative instruction would suffice. Deputy Bell continued his testimony, explaining that he remained on the scene until EMS and the Tennessee Highway Patrol ("THP") arrived on the scene.

On cross-examination, Deputy Bell admitted that he did not see the car leave the roadway. [Trooper Allen then testified.] The following exchange occurred during the testimony of Trooper Allen:

[State]: Okay. And based on your investigation, you testified that [Defendant] was the driver. Was that what you determined?

[Trooper Allen]: Yes, I did come to the conclusion that he was the driver.

[State]: Okay. And what was that conclusion based on?

[Trooper Allen]: Statements that was told to me by the—by the passenger and by the sheriff. . . .

Counsel for Defendant objected, arguing that the State was not permitted to use the statements of the passenger.

Hearsay is "a statement, other than one made by the declarant while testifying at the trial or hearing, offered in evidence to prove the truth of the matter asserted." Indirect hearsay, a way to "get in hearsay through the back door," is still inadmissible hearsay unless it fits within the hearsay exceptions. In *State v. Robert Spencer* (Tenn. Crim. App. Jan. 27, 2016), this Court explained indirect hearsay. In *Robert Spencer*, a drug task force agent testified that "the house [on Olympic Street] and the [d]efendant matched the descriptions provided by the source." This testimony, in conjunction with the agent's testimony about his background in narcotics investigations, effectively "allowed the jury to learn what the source told [the agent], that the [d]efendant was selling cocaine from the house on Olympic Street." In other words, the agent's testimony "relayed the hearsay statements of the source."

Using that rationale in the case herein, we conclude that Trooper Allen's testimony that Defendant was the driver based on "statements" made by Ms. Reeves was indirect hearsay. Ms. Reeves, much like the confidential informant in *Robert Spencer*, did not testify at trial. As the parties stipulated, Ms. Reeves died shortly after the incident. The proof establishing that Defendant was the driver was largely circumstantial. No one testified that they actually saw Defendant driving the vehicle at the time of the crash. In fact, the only testimony that Defendant was the driver of the vehicle came from improperly admitted testimony during Deputy Bell's direct examination. In our view, therefore, the admission of the indirect hearsay, especially when combined with the improperly introduced testimony from Deputy Bell discussed above, more probably than not affected the judgment. Therefore, the admission of the evidence could not be harmless.

Review Questions

1. **Where are the witnesses?** Defendant is charged with assault. The investigating officer testifies, "I interviewed as many of the witnesses I could find as to who caused the fight and then asked Defendant for his side." Indirect hearsay?
2. **Puree fiction?** Plaintiff sued Company X for selling defective blenders. On the stand, Plaintiff is asked, "Why did you think the problem was with the blender, instead of how you used it?" Plaintiff answers, "Well, I did a lot of research, and it became clear to me from what I read that it must be a defective product." Indirect hearsay?

2. *Hearsay Within Hearsay*

At times, a single item of evidence can contain multiple layers of hearsay. Say, for example, that a witness in a civil case testifies that she spoke with the plaintiff's stepfather, who told the witness that the plaintiff had told her stepmother that she had had three glasses of wine prior to getting in the car accident at issue in that case. The witness's testimony involves three layers of hearsay: (1) what the stepfather told the witness, (2) what the stepmother told the stepfather, and (3) what the plaintiff told the stepmother. Each layer involves an out-of-court statement by a person that is relevant only if true. The witness would be allowed to provide this testimony only if *each layer* or *level* of hearsay is either (a) not hearsay or (b) falls into a hearsay exception.

The need to take a level-by-level or layer-by-layer approach is set forth in FRE 805.

FRE 805. Hearsay Within Hearsay

Hearsay included within hearsay is not excluded by the rule against hearsay if each part of the combined statements conforms with an exception to the rule.

Because of this rule, it is critical to examine evidence for whether it contains multiple levels of hearsay. This issue frequently arises in documents that contain statements. The document itself might have a hearsay exception (for example, FRE 803(6): Business Records exception), but the statements reported in that business record might be a second layer of hearsay.

Example

General Manufacturing, Inc. ("GM") conducts a regular audit of safety at its plant. In conducting the audit, GM speaks to many employees about their experiences on the production line. Assuming that there is a business record exception for the company report, there would still potentially need to be a hearsay exception for the individual accounts in the report.

Nair v. Columbus State Cmty. College

2008 U.S. Dist. LEXIS 90831 (S.D. Ohio 2008)

HOLSCHUH, Judge.

MEMORANDUM OPINION AND ORDER

Plaintiff Girija Nair filed this suit against Defendant Columbus State Community College alleging national origin discrimination under Title VII of the Civil Rights Act of 1964.

Motion in Limine

Objection to Exhibit 22

Exhibit 22 is a memorandum from Goldenetz and another instructor, Beth Barnett, to Dr. Kevin May, the chair of the DED when Plaintiff was initially hired. In the memorandum, Goldenetz and Barnett detail a long list of complaints about Plaintiff, including not complying with departmental rules and her "poor attitude within the department" and conflict with staff members. Plaintiff is correct that the document contains a considerable amount of hearsay within hearsay, such as reports of what other faculty and staff members said about Plaintiff that does not fall within any of the hearsay exceptions. Plaintiff's objection is SUSTAINED.

Objection to Exhibit 68

Plaintiff makes hearsay objections to Defendant's proposed Exhibit 68, a memorandum from Tom Erney to Erv Zitlow, Defendant's Director of Human Resources, that contains a log, recorded by Laughbaum, of numerous issues that faculty members raised about Plaintiff. The document itself is entirely hearsay because it does not come within Rule 803(6)'s business records exception, or any other hearsay exception. To satisfy Rule 803(6), the "regular practice of the business activity [must have been] to make the" record. FED. R. EVID. 803(6). In this memorandum, Erney clearly states that Laughbaum prepared the log at his request, not as a matter of regular practice.

Even if it could be considered a business record, however, the log is rife with *hearsay* statements from multiple members of Plaintiff's department, as well as complaints from students. These statements are not being offered to show their effect on any individual or to reveal a state of mind, but are being offered to prove their contents. Admitting such unreliable evidence would be unduly prejudicial to Plaintiff. Plaintiff's objection is SUSTAINED.

Review Questions

1. **FEMA facts.** Under the hearsay exception for public records (FRE 803(8)), the court agrees to admit a report by FEMA on fraud committed during a recent hurricane disaster. The report lists the number of fraud claims and includes specific accounts by witnesses to those frauds. Is there hearsay within hearsay?
2. **Side notes.** Defendant is sued for breach of contract. All parties agree that the contract at issue qualifies as nonhearsay as a verbal act that has independent legal significance. However, marked on the side of the contract is a notation: "We made an exception here—most folks won't do business with this guy." Is the notation admissible?

SUMMARY INTRODUCTION TO HEARSAY

Step 1

- What out-of-court statement is a party seeking to admit?

Step 2

- What is the nature of the statement?
  - If the statement is (1) oral, (2) written, or (3) nonverbal conduct intended as an assertion (that is, intended to communicate), *go to Step 3*
  - Otherwise, nonverbal conduct is *not hearsay*

Step 3

- Who or what made the statement?
  - If the statement was made by a person, *go to Step 4*
  - If the statement was made by a machine or animal, it is *not hearsay*

Step 4

- Is the statement being offered for the truth of the matter asserted? Consider the common nonhearsay purpose of statements:
  - Verbal acts
  - Effect on the listener or reader
  - Impeachment
  - Circumstantial evidence of state of mind
  - Verbal objects
  - Relevant just because statement was made
- If offered to prove truth, *hearsay*; if offered for some other purpose, *not hearsay*

Test Your Understanding

To test your understanding of the material in this chapter, turn to the Supplement for additional practice problems.

PREVIEW OF COMING ATTRACTIONS: HEARSAY EXCEPTIONS

Chapters Six through Eight focus on hearsay "exceptions." The Federal Rules of Evidence have labeled some of these as "Not Hearsay" and others as "Hearsay Exceptions." Here is some of what you will learn:

Chapter Six
FRE 801(d)(1): Declarant-Witnesses' Prior Statements ["Not Hearsay"]
(A) Prior Inconsistent Statements
(B) Prior Consistent Statements
(C) Statements of Identification
FRE 801(d)(2): Opposing Parties' Statements/Admissions ["Not Hearsay"]
(A) A Party's Own Statements
(B) Adopted Statements
(C) Statements by Spokespersons
(D) Statements by Employees and Agents
(E) Coconspirators' Statements

Chapter Seven
FRE 803: Exceptions Applicable Regardless of Declarant's Availability
(1) Present Sense Impressions
(2) Excited Utterances
(3) Statements of Then-Existing Mental, Emotional, or Physical Condition
(4) Statements for Medical Diagnosis or Treatment
(5) Past Recollection Recorded
(6)&(7) Business Records
(8)&(10) Public Records
(9),(11)-(23) Other Exceptions

Chapter Eight
FRE 804: Exceptions Applicable Only When the Declarant Is Unavailable
(a) Definition of "Unavailable"
(b) Exceptions
  (1) Former Testimony
  (2) Dying Declarations
  (3) Statements Against Interest
  (4) Statement of Personal or Family History
  (5) Forfeiture by Wrongdoing
FRE 807: Residual Exception

Chapter 6

Hearsay Exceptions Designated as "Not Hearsay"

The hearsay rule discussed in Chapter Five is sweeping, reaching all out-of-court statements sought to be admitted for their truth. However, the hearsay rule has numerous exceptions that operate to remove it as a barrier to admission. Chapters Six through Eight detail the exceptions to the hearsay rule. These exceptions fall into four broad categories.

(1) *FRE 801(d)—"NOT HEARSAY."* The Federal Rules of Evidence declare the statements listed in this provision to be "not hearsay," even though they meet the general definition of hearsay because they are out-of-court statements admitted for their truth under FRE 801(c)(2). The Federal Rules of Evidence label them as "not hearsay" (rather than as "hearsay exceptions") because they may be invoked only when the out-of-court declarant is on the stand or when offered against an opposing party. Either way, there is an opportunity to cross-examine the declarant or for the party to take the stand and explain the prior statement. This means that the reliability of these out-of-court statements can be tested in the current proceedings. Moreover, they are the type of statements—especially admissions—that were traditionally allowed at common law. Electing to label these exceptions "not hearsay" is an innovation of the Federal Rules of Evidence. Many states do not segregate these exceptions from the others and treat them as a species of hearsay *exceptions.* These categories of "not hearsay" will be discussed in this chapter.

(2) *FRE 803—HEARSAY EXCEPTIONS THAT MAY BE INVOKED ANYTIME,* regardless of whether the out-of-court declarant is shown to be unavailable as a witness at the proceeding at which the hearsay statement is to be admitted. These exceptions will be discussed in Chapter Seven.

(3) *FRE 804—HEARSAY EXCEPTIONS THAT MAY BE INVOKED ONLY WHEN THE DECLARANT IS UNAVAILABLE* as a witness at the proceeding at which the hearsay statement is to be admitted. These exceptions will be discussed in Chapter Eight.

(4) *FRE 807—RESIDUAL HEARSAY EXCEPTION,* grants a trial judge some latitude to admit hearsay statements for their truth even if there is no specific hearsay exception that applies. This exception will be discussed in Chapter Eight.

Rationale for Hearsay Exceptions

What justifies all these exceptions to the hearsay rule? Most trace their lineage to the English common law courts and persist today as a matter of tradition. Courts nevertheless offer two sometimes overlapping policy rationales for the various exceptions:

(1) *Necessity*. Some hearsay exceptions are just *necessary* as a practical matter. Hearsay statements often contain relevant and reliable information needed by the trier of fact. Strict adherence to the hearsay rule would deprive the trier of fact of that information and potentially result in less accurate verdicts. For instance, the dying words of a witness regarding who shot him are potentially the best evidence regarding the identity of his assailant. Without a hearsay exception for dying declarations, this statement would be inadmissible and lost to the trier of fact forever because the dead declarant is obviously no longer available to be called as a witness. Necessity-based hearsay exceptions exist to enable such evidence to be considered with the understanding that the trier of fact (whether judge or jury) will be able to appropriately assess that evidence and give it the weight that it deserves despite the lack of any opportunity to cross-examine the declarant.

(2) *Reliability*. Other hearsay exceptions recognize that the out-of-court statement may be *more* reliable than anything the declarant later says in court under oath. This heightened reliability typically exists because the out-of-court statement was made when the subject of the statement was fresher in the declarant's mind or said under circumstances that indicate less opportunity or incentive for guile. For instance, a percipient witness's outburst upon seeing a horrific accident regarding what happened, or a robbery victim's identification of his assailant within hours of the crime, may be *more* reliable than the witness's or victim's recounting months or years later.

Key Questions in Evaluating Hearsay Issues

In learning about the hearsay exceptions (whether classified as "not hearsay" or a hearsay "exception" under the Federal Rules), we will examine three primary questions:

(1) What are the prerequisites for each exception, and how have they been interpreted?
(2) Who decides whether these prerequisites are met, the trial judge or the jury?
(3) Does the exception raise any constitutional concerns unique to that exception?

As Chapter Nine discusses, some out-of-court statements, when used against a defendant in a criminal case, may violate the Confrontation Clause of the Sixth

Amendment even if there is an applicable hearsay exception. The "not hearsay" statements will not pose that risk because the declarant is available for cross-examination or the Confrontation Clause does not otherwise cover them.

"Not hearsay" falls into two categories discussed in this chapter.

First, and as discussed in Part A, FRE 801(d)(1)(A) covers the three exceptions for prior statements of a testifying witness:

(1) prior inconsistent statements;
(2) prior consistent statements; and
(3) prior identifications.

Second, and as discussed in Part B, FRE 801(d)(2)(B) covers the exceptions constituting admissions by an adverse party:

(1) admissions made by the adverse party;
(2) admissions adopted by the adverse party;
(3) admissions authorized by the adverse party;
(4) admissions made by the adverse party's employees and agents; and
(5) statements made by an adverse party's coconspirators.

PART A: HEARSAY EXCEPTIONS FOR A WITNESS'S PRIOR STATEMENTS [FRE 801(d)(1)]

Even if a witness is on the stand testifying, the witness's prior statements meet the definition of hearsay if those statements are being admitted for their truth.[1] Why is this so, given that the hearsay declarant is now a witness subject to cross-examination about that prior statement? The reason is that the prior statement may not have been made under oath and was certainly not made in front of a trier of fact capable of evaluating the speaker's demeanor at the time the statement was made.

These prior witness statements fall into three categories: (1) prior inconsistent statements, (2) prior consistent statements, and (3) prior identifications.

Examples

1. Witness is a bank teller who is called by Prosecutor and who testifies that the man who pointed a gun at her had one brown eye and one blue eye. On cross-examination, Defendant asks, "Didn't you tell the police, right after the robbery, that the gunman had blue eyes?" The teller's statement

1. If those statements are *not* being admitted for their truth—and are instead admitted solely to impeach or rehabilitate the witness's credibility—they do not meet the hearsay definition and need not satisfy the hearsay rule. Rules regarding the impeachment and rehabilitation of witnesses are set forth in Chapter Eleven.

to the police is an out-of-court statement. If it is admitted solely to cast doubt on the witness's credibility in identifying the gunman, it does not constitute hearsay and need not satisfy the hearsay rule. But if it is admitted to prove that the gunman had two blue eyes, it is being admitted for its truth and must satisfy the hearsay rule.

2. Witness was involved in a three-car pile-up accident. Defendant calls witness, and witness testifies that Plaintiff ran a red light. On cross-examination, Plaintiff asks witness, "Didn't you settle with Defendant last month and receive a pretty big settlement check?" On redirect examination, Defendant asks, "Didn't you tell the police officer who reported to the scene—and long before you settled the case with me—that Plaintiff ran the red?" Witness's statement to the police officer is a prior consistent statement offered to rebut Plaintiff's suggestion that witness's testimony is biased. If it is offered to prove that Plaintiff ran the red light (that is, for its truth), it is a hearsay statement and must satisfy the hearsay rule.
3. Defendant is on trial for robbery. The victim who was mugged in the alleyway testifies at trial that he cannot say one way or the other whether Defendant was the mugger. Prosecutor calls a police officer to testify that, hours after the mugging, the victim was able to pick Defendant out of a six-person lineup as his assailant. If this prior identification is being offered to prove that Defendant is the assailant, it is being offered for the truth and is a hearsay statement that must satisfy the hearsay rule.

Certain procedural requirements must be met before a testifying witness's prior statement may be introduced, whether the statement is being introduced for its truth or for impeachment or rehabilitation purposes. FRE 613 sets forth those requirements.

FRE 613. Witness's Prior Statement

(a) Showing or Disclosing the Statement During Examination. When examining a witness about the witness's prior statement, a party need not show it or disclose its contents to the witness. But the party must, on request, show it or disclose its contents to an adverse party's attorney.

(b) Extrinsic Evidence of a Prior Inconsistent Statement. Extrinsic evidence of a witness's prior inconsistent statement is admissible only if the witness is given an opportunity to explain or deny the statement and an adverse party is given an opportunity to examine the witness about it, or if justice so requires. This subdivision (b) does not apply to an opposing party's statement under Rule 801(d)(2).

FRE 613 provides that when the witness to be confronted with a prior statement is testifying at a hearing:

- The party impeaching the witness must show or disclose the contents of the statement to the adverse party's (that is, the party that is not confronting the witness with the prior statement) attorney, if that attorney so requests.
- The witness must be given an opportunity to explain or deny the statement, and the adverse party must be given an opportunity to examine the witness regarding the statement. This requirement does not apply when the prior statement is the admission of an adverse party (discussed in Part B of this chapter). Also, the trial judge retains the authority to dispense with this requirement "if justice so requires."
- The *witness* need not be shown the statement before being questioned about it. (This requirement is designed to prevent the witness from having time in advance to think about how to reconcile her testimony with her prior statement.)

It is for the trial judge to decide whether the prerequisites for prior inconsistent statements, prior consistent statements, and prior identifications have been met. FRE 104(a).

1. Prior Inconsistent Statements [FRE 801(d)(1)(A)]

Consider the situation when a witness says one thing on the witness stand but has said something inconsistent at some point prior to that testimony. For example, the witness testifies that the robber was wearing a blue jacket, but before trial told the police that the robber was wearing a red jacket. Certainly, the witness's prior statement to the police can be used to impeach the witness (that is, to show that the witness's in-court testimony regarding the color of the jacket is not to be believed). However, on occasion a party wants to argue that the truth is what was said previously, not what is now testified to on the stand. Introducing a prior inconsistent statement for its truth is sometimes called using it for "substantive" purposes (rather than "impeachment" purposes).

Examples

1. The witness testifies in trial that the red car hit the blue car. Out of court, the witness told a friend that the blue car hit the red car. If the statement to the friend is being offered to show that it really was the blue car that hit the red car, the statement is being offered for its truth and is hearsay unless it meets the requirements of the rule to be "not hearsay."
2. In a domestic violence case, the victim takes the stand and suddenly states that she does not remember who gave her the black eye. Out of court, she told the police that it was Defendant who hit her. Without this out-of-court statement, Prosecutor may not have other evidence to prove that

Defendant caused the injury. Prosecutor will want to admit the out-of-court statement for substantive purposes to prove that it was Defendant who caused the injury.

Because, as noted above, the trier of fact was not present when the witness made the prior statement and thus could not contemporaneously assess the witness's demeanor and credibility, the drafters of the Federal Rules of Evidence were reluctant to *automatically* allow the admission of the prior inconsistent statement for its truth. Instead, the drafters elected to limit the substantive use of prior inconsistent statements to a subset of the witness's out-of-court statements.

Specifically, FRE 801(d)(1)(A) provides the following:

FRE 801(d). Statements That Are Not Hearsay

(d) Statements That Are Not Hearsay. A statement that meets the following conditions is not hearsay:

(1) ***A Declarant-Witness's Prior Statement.*** The declarant testifies and is subject to cross-examination about a prior statement, and the statement:

(A) is inconsistent with the declarant's testimony and was given under penalty of perjury at a trial, hearing, or other proceeding or in a deposition[.]

Thus, the not hearsay exception for prior inconsistent statements has the following prerequisites:

Hearsay Exception for Prior Inconsistent Statements

(1) Out-of-court declarant is testifying and subject to cross-examination; *and*
(2) The prior statement is:
  (a) "inconsistent" with the witness's testimony, *and*
  (b) was given under penalty of perjury
  (c) at a trial, hearing, or other proceeding or in a deposition.

(a) When Is a Prior Statement "Inconsistent"?

The issue frequently arises as to how "inconsistent" the prior statement must be with the witness's current testimony. Does it need to be contrary in all aspects or just different *in general*?

Judges have discretion in making this determination. The Advisory Committee Notes do not define what constitutes an "inconsistent" statement, but case law gives some guidance. In *United States v. Williams*, 737 F.2d 594, 608 (7th Cir. 1984), the Court wrote:

> As long as people speak in nonmathematical languages such as English . . . it will be difficult to determine precisely whether two statements are inconsistent. But we do not read the word "inconsistent" in Rule 801(d)(1)(A) to include only statements diametrically opposed or logically incompatible. Inconsistency may be "found in evasive answers, . . . silence, or changes in positions." In addition, a purported change in memory can produce "inconsistent answers." Particularly in a case of manifest reluctance to testify, "if a witness has testified to [certain] facts before a grand jury and forgets . . . them at trial, his grand jury testimony . . . falls squarely within Rule 801(d)(1)(A)."

Thus, although there must be significant differences between the declarant's prior statement and current testimony in the courtroom, the two statements need not be completely opposite.

Two situations arise fairly often and delve more deeply into whether the witness's current testimony and her prior statement are "inconsistent."

(i) When the prior "statement" is the witness's silence

What if the witness, while in court, testifies to a fact that appears nowhere in her prior statement? Is her prior *omission* inconsistent with her current testimony? The answer is "yes," as long as the omitted fact is one that likely would have been included in the prior statement if it had been true. For example, if the plaintiff in an auto accident personal injury case calls a bystander who testifies that she saw the defendant get out his car swaying and stumbling in a way that indicated that he was intoxicated, the bystander's failure to include those observations in her statement to the responding police officers at the scene would likely be deemed a prior inconsistent statement because most people would expect a bystander to tell the police about the intoxication of one of the two people involved in a car crash.

(ii) When a witness feigns a lack of memory

A situation frequently encountered by trial judges is when a witness feigns a lack of memory at trial. Is that "inconsistent" with a witness's prior statement when there were no such problems with the witness's memory? For some courts, it does not matter if the witness's lack of memory at trial is real or feigned. They will find it to be inconsistent. *See, e.g., Wassilie v. State*, 57 P.3d 719 (Alaska Ct. App. 2002). However, some jurisdictions, such as California, will find a statement to be "inconsistent" only if the witness is just pretending not to remember. *See, e.g.*, Cal. Evid. Code § 1235; *People v. Green*, 3 Cal. 3d 981, 988-89 (Cal. 1971).

Evasive answers in the courtroom can also be considered "inconsistent" with statements previously made by the witness. This situation frequently occurs when the witness has second thoughts regarding testifying about a matter, as the next case illustrates.

United States v. Iglesias

535 F.3d 150 (3d Cir. 2008)

Hardiman, Judge.

In this appeal, Enrique Iglesias seeks to overturn his conviction on various drug and weapons charges. Early in the morning on August 19, 2004, law enforcement agents executed a search warrant at the home of Elliott Shisler and seized a small quantity of methamphetamine. Shisler agreed to cooperate with law enforcement and informed the agents that Iglesias had sold him the drug.

Iglesias asserts that the District Court erred when it admitted into evidence the statements that Shisler made at the hearing on Iglesias's motion to suppress. Although Shisler testified freely at the suppression hearing, he did an about-face at trial, apparently because he had second thoughts about the propriety of his cooperation with the government. [T]he District Court then admitted Shisler's prior testimony into evidence.

The government argues that the District Court properly admitted this prior testimony pursuant to Rule 801(d)(1)(A) of the Federal Rules of Evidence.

Rule 801(d)(1)(A) provides that a statement is not hearsay if "[t]he declarant testifies at the trial or hearing and is subject to cross-examination concerning the statement, and the statement is . . . inconsistent with the declarant's testimony, and was given under oath subject to the penalty of perjury at a trial, hearing, or other proceeding, or in a deposition. . . ."

Two days before Iglesias's trial began, the government called Shisler as a witness at the suppression hearing. Shisler testified under oath that he had bought methamphetamine from Iglesias "once or twice" in 2004 at the Red Lion Road apartment, that he sometimes would pay Iglesias for the drugs after he sold them to other people, and that Iglesias might have delivered drugs to Shisler's apartment.

At trial, the government called Shisler to testify again. Shisler conceded that he had a prior criminal record, admitted selling methamphetamine in 2004, and testified that he had persuaded his girlfriend to buy him a handgun because he knew that his status as a felon precluded him from doing so. When Shisler was asked to identify "who supplied you with the methamphetamine that you sold," however, Shisler responded: "I can't answer that question because it has been brought to my attention that charges may be brought against me."

On the facts presented in this case, we do not find that the District Court committed plain error in admitting Shisler's sworn testimony from the suppression hearing. The admissibility of this evidence turned on whether Shisler's prior testimony was "inconsistent" with his refusal to answer the same questions at trial. This Court has noted previously that "[t]he district court should have considerable discretion to determine whether evasive answers are inconsistent with statements previously given."

"In applying Rule 801(d)(1)(A), inconsistency is not limited to diametrically opposed answers but may be found in evasive answers, inability to recall, silence, or changes of position." Specifically, where a witness demonstrates a "manifest reluctance to testify" and "forgets" certain facts at trial, this testimony can be inconsistent under Rule 801(d)(1)(A). We agree with these courts such that when a witness who testifies frankly under oath subject to cross-examination only two days later states that he now "can't answer the question" and is otherwise evasive and vague, a district court may find that these statements are inconsistent and may admit the prior testimony under Rule 801(d)(1)(A).

In either situation, the witness's inability to recall or evasiveness raises a further question as to whether the prior inconsistent statement hearsay exception applies—namely, is such a witness "subject to cross-examination about [the] prior statement"? Can a witness be subject to cross-examination regarding a prior statement if the witness does not recall making that statement, does not recall the matters the witness discussed, or is evasive about it? The answer to this question has gone both ways. Some courts will answer that a witness is "subject to cross-examination" if the witness is on the stand and can be asked about the prior statement, regardless of whether the witness has a recollection. Others require that the witness have enough memory to be reasonably responsive in answering questions about the inconsistency. Even in criminal cases in which there is a constitutional right of confrontation, the standard for "subject to cross-examination" under FRE 801(d)(1) is still fairly minimal. In *United States v. Owens*, 484 U.S. 554 (1988), a prison guard had been attacked by Owens, an inmate at the prison. The prison guard could remember telling an FBI agent that Owens had attacked him, but he could not really recall the incident except that he recalled feeling blows to his head and seeing blood on the floor. The Supreme Court held that the prison guard had enough recollection to be "subject to cross-examination."

(b) When Is a Statement "Given Under Penalty of Perjury at a Trial, Hearing, or Other Proceeding"?

(i) "Penalty of perjury"

To be admissible as a prior inconsistent statement, the prior statement must have been given under the penalty of perjury. This requirement is almost always satisfied by the further requirement that the prior statement be made "at a trial, hearing, or other proceeding or in a deposition" because those proceedings almost always require the witness to be under oath. Critically, there is no requirement that the witness *be subject to cross-examination* at the prior proceeding.

(ii) "At a trial, hearing, or other proceeding"

To ensure that the prior statements have sufficient reliability to become substantive evidence in the current trial, the Federal Rules require that the prior proceeding was sufficiently formal enough that the importance of telling the truth was impressed on the witness.

A "trial" includes prior criminal and civil trials, as well as formal administrative trials. A "hearing" may include pretrial and other proceedings related to trials, such as a suppression hearing. However, an issue arises as to what qualifies as "other proceedings."

Do grand jury proceedings qualify? Yes, even though the defense is not present and did not have an opportunity to cross-examine during those proceedings.

Since the defense has an opportunity to confront the witness in the present proceeding about the earlier grand jury testimony, the requirements of the rule and constitutional right of confrontation are met.

Do administrative proceedings short of a trial qualify? Sometimes. Proceedings conducted by other government agencies may also qualify as "other proceedings" under the rules. Such proceedings may include immigration hearings, tax proceedings, hearings before a department of motor vehicles, inquests, military proceedings, or disciplinary hearings. Whether they qualify turns on whether such proceedings have the formality and structure to qualify under the rule. Thus, stationhouse interviews are unlikely to qualify as a "proceeding" even if they result in the witness signing an affidavit under oath or in front of a notary. The same is true of affidavits created by lawyers. *See Santos v. Murdock*, 243 F.3d 681 (2d Cir. 2001). The approach toward evaluating whether affidavits fall within "other proceedings" is set forth in *United States v. Dietrich.*

United States v. Dietrich

854 F.2d 1056 (7th Cir. 1988)

FLAUM, Judge.

John Dietrich was convicted of conspiring to sell counterfeit notes in violation of 18 U.S.C. § 371 and selling counterfeit notes in violation of 18 U.S.C. § 473. Dietrich contends that the district court committed plain error when [among other things] it admitted a witness's prior inconsistent statement as substantive evidence.

On October 11, 1985, Angel Thomas gave a written sworn statement to two Secret Service Agents. In her statement, Thomas indicated that she and her common-law husband, Charles Peek, had met with Dietrich and his wife. During the meeting Dietrich supposedly showed Thomas and Peek a number of counterfeit $100 federal reserve notes and assured them that the bills were easy to pass. According to Thomas' statement, Dietrich wanted Peek and Thomas to get rid of $10,000 worth of counterfeit currency. Thomas further stated that neither she nor Peek took any of the counterfeit money, and that she never saw Dietrich after their meeting.

At trial Thomas testified that she did not know John Dietrich. When the Assistant United States Attorney pointed to Dietrich in the courtroom, Thomas testified that she had never seen him before. As a result, the government sought to question Thomas on her prior inconsistent statement. In response to this line of questioning, Thomas admitted making the statement. She testified, however, that she had lied during the interview to help Peek, who was then awaiting trial on separate counterfeiting charges. Thomas further testified that the agents who took the statement pressured her into giving it by threatening to arrest her on charges of passing counterfeit currency unless she told them about Dietrich. According to Thomas, she made up the story about Dietrich to avoid arrest and to help her husband.

[T]he government claims that the statement was properly admitted under Federal Rule of Evidence 801(d)(1)(A). This Rule provides that:

> (d) Statements which are not hearsay. A statement is not hearsay if—

> (1) Prior statement by witness. The declarant testifies at the trial or hearing and is subject to cross-examination concerning the statement, and the statement is (A) inconsistent with the declarant's testimony, and was given under oath subject to the penalty of perjury at a trial, hearing, or other proceeding, or in a deposition . . .

(Emphasis added). If a prior inconsistent statement meets the requirements of Rule 801(d)(1)(A) it may be admitted as substantive evidence to establish the truth of the matter asserted. A prior inconsistent statement that does not meet one of the criteria of Rule 801(d)(1)(A), however, may be used only for the purpose of impeaching the witness.

Dietrich admits that Thomas' statement was inconsistent with her testimony at trial, and that the prior statement was given under oath subject to the penalties of perjury. Both parties admit that Thomas' interview with the Secret Service Agents did not occur during a trial, hearing, or deposition. Thus, the statement was properly admitted only if the interview constituted an "other proceeding" for purposes of Rule 801(d)(1)(A). We conclude that it did not.

The term "other proceeding" is not unlimited. A typical police station interrogation, for example, is not an "other proceeding" within the meaning of the Rule. "The Rule seems to contemplate situations in which an official verbatim record is routinely kept, whether stenographically or by electronic means, under legal authority."

The term "other proceeding" includes grand jury proceedings, even though the declarant is not subject to cross-examination during the grand jury proceeding. Fed. R. Evid. 801(d)(1)(A) (conference committee notes). An immigration proceeding also has been held to constitute an "other proceeding" under Rule 801(d)(1)(A). *United States v. Castro-Ayon*, 537 F.2d 1055 (9th Cir. 1976). The *Castro-Ayon* court concluded that the immigration proceeding was acceptable for purposes of the Rule because it contained many of the same procedural protections as a grand jury proceeding. For instance, both proceedings are "investigatory, ex parte, inquisitive, sworn, basically prosecutorial, held before an officer other than the arresting officer, recorded, and held in circumstances of some legal formality." In fact, as the court noted, a witness in an immigration proceeding is actually afforded more procedural protections than is a grand jury witness.

In contrast, Thomas gave her prior inconsistent statement during an interview with two Secret Service Agents in her home. No one was present during the interview except Thomas and the two agents, and the interview was not recorded. Thomas simply spoke to the agents who then wrote down what she had told them, and she signed the written statement verifying its truth.

Thomas' statement was given to the same agents who had the authority to arrest her, the interview was not prosecutorial, it was not recorded, and there were no indicia of legal formality. The circumstances surrounding Thomas' statement did not differ significantly from a typical police station interrogation. Thomas' interview therefore does not qualify as an "other proceeding" pursuant to Rule 801(d)(1)(A), and the admission of her statement was erroneous.

(iii) Absence of this requirement in other jurisdictions

Some states, like Florida and Texas, follow the Federal Rules of Evidence and require that the prior inconsistent statement be under oath. However, other states do not have this requirement. For example, California admits a prior inconsistent statement as substantive evidence even if the prior statement was not made under oath or at a prior proceeding. Cal. Evid. Code § 1235. New York admits a prior inconsistent statement that was not made under oath, but only in a civil proceeding and only if the prior statement has sufficient indicia of reliability. *Kaufman v. Quickway, Inc.*, 14 N.Y.2d 907, 908 (N.Y. 2010).[2]

The approach of states that do not require that the prior inconsistent statement be under oath can be key in cases, such as domestic violence prosecutions, where victims not infrequently change their testimony before trial and deny that the defendant hurt them. If the victim had said something differently to, for example, a police officer or friend, that statement can come in to prove the defendant was the assailant. Since there frequently are not other witnesses to such attacks, the prior inconsistent statement may be the only evidence (other than physical evidence) that the defendant committed the offense.

People v. Briggs

2006 Cal. App. Unpub. LEXIS 5940 (Cal. Ct. App. 2006)

King, Justice.

Defendant was charged with one count of willfully inflicting corporal injury on his live-in girlfriend of 18 years, Karen Harrison.

The prosecution presented evidence that, during the late evening of September 20, 2003, defendant beat his live-in girlfriend of 18 years, Karen Harrison, in the head and face while defendant was driving Karen home from a friend's house in Pomona. At trial, Karen denied that defendant beat her during the drive home. She specifically denied telling her daughter, Shawntee Kendrick, that defendant beat her, and said she did not recall telling San Bernardino County Police Officer Scott Mathews, that defendant beat her. Shawntee and Officer Mathews testified that, during the early morning hours of September 21, 2003, Karen told them defendant had beaten her. The defense theory was that Karen sustained her injuries in the auto accident, none of them from defendant.

At trial, Karen denied that defendant beat her during the drive home. She did not recall police coming to her house on September 21, or being interviewed by the police. She did not recall telling the police that defendant was upset that she had been in an accident that defendant beat her during the drive home, or anything else about what happened during the drive home. She also did not recall

---

2. Illinois admits a prior inconsistent statement if it was either (1) made under oath or (2) if not made under oath, the statement (a) describes an event or condition of which the declarant had personal knowledge, and (b) the prior statement was in writing, the declarant acknowledged the prior statement under oath, or it was recorded. Ill. R. Evid. 801(d)(1)(A).

signing a Domestic Violence Victim Advisory form. She specifically denied telling Shawntee that defendant beat her, and claimed she sustained all of her facial injuries, as depicted in the police photographs, in the car accident.

Defendant contends that Shawntee's and Officer Mathews's testimony that Karen told them defendant had beaten her was inadmissible hearsay and did not qualify under the prior inconsistent statements exception to the hearsay rule. (Evid. Code, §§ 770 & 1235.) We disagree. Both witnesses' testimony was properly admitted under the prior inconsistent statements exception to the hearsay rule.

A statement by a witness that is inconsistent with his or her trial testimony is admissible to establish the truth of the matter asserted in the statement under the conditions set forth in Evidence Code sections 1235 and 770. Those statutes, as relevant here, provide for the admission against a hearsay challenge of a prior statement by a witness "'if the statement is inconsistent with his testimony at the hearing and is offered in compliance with [Evidence Code] section 770.' (Evid. Code, § 1235.)" Defendant does not argue that the conditions of Evidence Code section 770 were not satisfied. Instead, he asserts that Karen's trial testimony was not inconsistent with her prior statements to Officer Mathews, because Karen testified that she could not recall ever having spoken to Officer Mathews.

Normally, the testimony of a witness that he or she does not remember an event is not inconsistent with that witness's prior statement describing the event. However, courts do not apply this rule mechanically. Inconsistency in effect, rather than contradiction in express terms, is the test for admitting a witness's prior statement, and the same principle governs the case of the forgetful witness. *When a witness's claim of lack of memory amounts to deliberate evasion, inconsistency is implied.* As long as there is a reasonable basis in the record for concluding that the witness's "I don't remember" statements are evasive and untruthful, admission of his or her prior statements is proper.

Here, there was a reasonable basis in the record for concluding that Karen was being evasive and untruthful when she testified that she did not recall ever speaking to Officer Mathews, or telling him that defendant had beaten her. Shawntee and Officer Mathews both testified that Karen was alert and oriented when she spoke to Officer Mathews. In addition, Karen was able to recall what happened in the car accident and that defendant left to retrieve her van shortly after he drove her home. In view of her ability to recall these events, it strained credulity to believe she could not recall speaking to Officer Mathews.

Karen flatly denied telling Shawntee that defendant had assaulted her. Thus, Shawntee's testimony that Karen told her defendant had beaten her was inconsistent with Karen's trial testimony, and was therefore admissible as a prior inconsistent statement. (Evid. Code, § 1235.)

The following graphic illustrates the rules governing the use of prior inconsistent statements as substantive evidence (because they fit within a hearsay exception) and as impeachment evidence (as discussed more fully in Chapter Eleven) in both federal and some state courts.

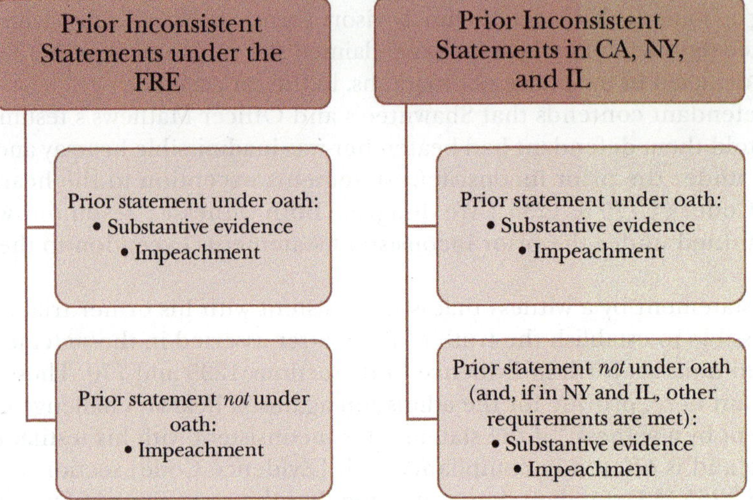

Review Questions

1. **Recanting cellmate.** Defendant is charged with assaulting his prison cellmate. When a third cellmate is first interviewed by the guards, he tells them that Defendant committed the assault. At trial, the third cellmate testifies that he "doesn't know anything about what those two guys were up to in the cell." Prosecutor seeks to introduce the third cellmate's statement to the guards.
   a. Under the Federal Rules of Evidence, is the cellmate's statement to the guards admissible and, if so, for what purposes? How about in California?
   b. What if the cellmate had made the statement in a prison disciplinary hearing under oath or in the grand jury?
2. **Promotional failures.** Henry has sued Gillian for employment discrimination. In an affidavit filed with the Equal Employment Opportunity Commission, witness Jesse stated under the penalty of perjury that Gillian would not promote Henry because of his religion. At trial, Jesse testifies that Henry was not promoted because he did subpar work.
   a. Under the Federal Rules of Evidence, is Jesse's affidavit admissible and, if so, for what purposes?
   b. In California, is Jesse's affidavit admissible and, if so, for what purposes?

2. *Prior Consistent Statements [FRE 801(d)(1)(B)]*

Consider the situation in which a witness testifies that "X is true." On cross-examination, the other party implies that the witness is lying. Evidence that the witness had, at some point in the past, made an earlier statement that "X is true" can tend to show under some circumstances that the witness has been consistent with her story the whole time and that her testimony in the current proceeding is thus more likely to be true. It can bolster her credibility. But can this prior consistent statement also be used to prove that X is, in fact, true?

The following examples highlight the two factual scenarios in which prior consistent statements are most typically used.

Examples

1. Kyle is charged with assaulting his neighbor, Rudy. Rudy claims that Kyle pushed him when Rudy accidentally picked up Kyle's newspaper. Kyle claims that Rudy started the fight. Kyle calls Petra as a witness. Petra testifies that she saw Rudy push Kyle first. On cross-examination, Prosecutor asks Petra, "Isn't it true that Kyle just gave you a beautiful ring for your birthday?" On redirect, Kyle's lawyer asks, "Isn't it true that even before Kyle gave you the ring you told the police that Rudy started the fight?"
2. Pauline sues Steven for breach of contract. She calls Sophie to testify that Steven had promised to pay Pauline $800 for a painting. On cross-examination, Sophie is asked, "Isn't it true that you never knew the amount Steven had promised to pay Pauline?" On redirect, Sophie is asked, "Isn't it true that the day the contract was made, you called a friend and said, 'Wow, I can't believe Steven is paying Pauline $800 for her painting'?"

In Example 1, the prosecutor is implying that Petra is lying on behalf of Kyle because he gave her a ring. To rebut that claim, Kyle's lawyer wants to introduce evidence that Petra said the same thing before she received the ring. In other words, the prior consistent statement is being offered to rebut an implication that Petra's testimony was improperly influenced and that she had a motive to lie on Kyle's behalf.

In Example 2, the prior consistent statement is being offered to rehabilitate Sophie's testimony by showing that she knew the price of the painting even though Steven had suggested by his question that Sophie never knew that information.

Whether the prior consistent statement can be admitted as independent proof that Rudy started the fight or that Steven offered to pay Pauline $800 for the ring turns on whether those prior consistent statements comply with FRE 801(d)(2)(B).

FRE 801(d). Statements That Are Not Hearsay

(d) Statements That Are Not Hearsay. A statement that meets the following conditions is not hearsay:

(1) *A Declarant-Witness's Prior Statement.* The declarant testifies and is subject to cross-examination about a prior statement, and the statement:

. . .

(B) is consistent with the declarant's testimony and is offered:

(i) to rebut an express or implied charge that the declarant recently fabricated it or acted from a recent improper influence or motive in so testifying; or

(ii) to rehabilitate the declarant's credibility as a witness when attacked on another ground[.]

Excerpt from Advisory Committee Notes to FRE 801

- [FRE 801(d)(1)(B)] retains the requirement set forth in *Tome v. United States*, 513 U.S. 150 (1995) that . . . a consistent statement offered to rebut a charge of recent fabrication of improper influence or motive must have been made before the alleged fabrication or improper inference or motive arose.

Thus, the hearsay exception for prior consistent statements has the following prerequisites:

Hearsay Exception for Prior Consistent Statements

(1) Out-of-court declarant is testifying and subject to cross-examination; *and*

(2) The prior statement is:

(a) "consistent" with the witness's testimony, *and*

(b) "is offered" either to:

(i) rebut a charge that the witness has recently fabricated her testimony or is testifying out of a recent improper influence or motive; *or*

(ii) rehabilitate the witness's credibility when it is attacked on some other ground.

Because the exception operates differently when the prior consistent statement is admitted to rebut a charge of recent fabrication or improper motive than when it is admitted to rehabilitate on any other ground, we examine each separately.

(a) When a Prior Consistent Statement Is Offered to Rebut a Claim That Witness Recently Fabricated Her Testimony or Is Testifying Out of an Improper Motive

Whether the hearsay exception applies in this context turns on *when* the prior consistent statement was made vis-à-vis when the motive to fabricate arose. For example, if the claim is that the witness is testifying favorably on behalf of a party, when did the witness acquire the motive to do so? Was it when Petra was given a ring? What if they were engaged before that happened? Wouldn't that have created a motive to fabricate at the time she provided the so-called prior consistent statement? Sometimes a party attacks a witness's credibility by showing that the witness has a grudge against the party. What caused that grudge, and when did that occur? Was the prior consistent statement made before the party upset the witness?

Whether the timing matters was addressed by the Supreme Court in *Tome v. United States.*

Tome v. United States

513 U.S. 150 (1995)

JUSTICE KENNEDY delivered the opinion of the Court, except as to Part II-B.

At issue is the interpretation of a provision in the Federal Rules of Evidence bearing upon the admissibility of statements, made by a declarant who testifies as a witness, that are consistent with the testimony and are offered to rebut a charge of a "recent fabrication or improper influence or motive." Fed. Rule Evid. 801(d)(1)(B). The question is whether out-of-court consistent statements made after the alleged fabrication, or after the alleged improper influence or motive arose, are admissible under the Rule.

I

Petitioner Tome was charged in a one-count indictment with the felony of sexual abuse of a child, his own daughter, aged four at the time of the alleged crime.

Tome and the child's mother had been divorced in 1988. A tribal court awarded joint custody of the daughter, A. T., to both parents, but Tome had primary physical custody. In 1989 the mother was unsuccessful in petitioning the tribal court for primary custody of A. T., but was awarded custody for the summer of 1990. On August 27, 1990, the mother contacted Colorado authorities with allegations that Tome had committed sexual abuse against A. T.

The prosecution's theory was that Tome committed sexual assaults upon the child while she was in his custody and that the crime was disclosed when the child was spending vacation time with her mother. The defense argued that the allegations were concocted so the child would not be returned to her father. At trial A. T., then 6 ½ years old, was the Government's first witness. For the most part, her direct testimony consisted of one- and two-word answers to a series of leading questions. Cross-examination took place over two trial days. The defense asked A. T. 348 questions. On the first day A. T. answered all the questions posed to her on general, background subjects.

The next day there was no testimony, and the prosecutor met with A. T. When cross-examination of A. T. resumed, she was questioned about those conversations but was reluctant to discuss them. Defense counsel then began questioning her about the allegations of abuse, and it appears she was reluctant at many points to answer. As the trial judge noted, however, some of the defense questions were imprecise or unclear.

After A. T. testified, the Government produced six witnesses who testified about a total of seven statements made by A. T. describing the alleged sexual assaults: A. T.'s babysitter recited A. T.'s statement to her on August 22, 1990, that she did not want to return to her father because he "gets drunk and he thinks I'm his wife"; the mother recounted what she had heard A. T. tell the babysitter; a social worker recounted details A. T. told her on August 29, 1990, about the assaults; and three pediatricians, Drs. Kuper, Reich, and Spiegel, related A. T.'s statements to them describing how and where she had been touched by Tome.

A. T.'s out-of-court statements, recounted by the six witnesses, were offered by the Government under Rule 801(d)(1)(B). The trial court admitted all of the statements over defense counsel's objection, accepting the Government's argument that they rebutted the implicit charge that A. T.'s testimony was motivated by a desire to live with her mother.

II

The prevailing common-law rule for more than a century before adoption of the Federal Rules of Evidence was that a prior consistent statement introduced to rebut a charge of recent fabrication or improper influence or motive was admissible if the statement had been made before the alleged fabrication, influence, or motive came into being, but it was inadmissible if made afterwards.

Rule 801 provides:

> "(d) Statements which are not hearsay. A statement is not hearsay if
>
> "(1) Prior statement by witness. The declarant testifies at the trial or hearing and is subject to cross-examination concerning the statement, and the statement is . . .
>
> "(B) consistent with the declarant's testimony and is offered to rebut an express or implied charge against the declarant of recent fabrication or improper influence or motive."

Rule 801 defines prior consistent statements as nonhearsay only if they are offered to rebut a charge of "recent fabrication or improper influence or motive." Fed. Rule Evid. 801(d)(1)(B). Noting the "troublesome" logic of treating a witness' prior consistent statements as hearsay at all (because the declarant is present in court and subject to cross-examination), the Advisory Committee decided to treat those consistent statements, once the preconditions of the Rule were satisfied, as nonhearsay and admissible as substantive evidence, not just to rebut an attack on the witness' credibility. See Advisory Committee's Notes on Fed. Rule Evid. 801(d)(1). A consistent statement meeting the requirements of the Rule is thus placed in the same category as a declarant's inconsistent statement made under oath in another proceeding, or prior identification testimony, or admissions by a party opponent. See Fed. Rule Evid. 801.

The Rules do not accord this weighty, nonhearsay status to all prior consistent statements. To the contrary, admissibility under the Rules is confined to those statements offered to rebut a charge of "recent fabrication or improper influence or motive." Prior consistent statements may not be admitted to counter all forms of impeachment or to bolster the witness merely because she has been discredited. In the present context, the question is whether A. T.'s out-of-court statements rebutted the alleged link between her desire to be with her mother and her testimony, not whether they suggested that A. T.'s in-court testimony was true. The Rule speaks of a party rebutting an alleged motive, not bolstering the veracity of the story told.

This limitation is instructive, not only to establish the preconditions of admissibility but also to reinforce the significance of the requirement that the consistent statements must have been made before the alleged influence, or motive to fabricate, arose. That is to say, the forms of impeachment within the Rule's coverage are the ones in which the temporal requirement makes the most sense. Impeachment by charging that the testimony is a recent fabrication or results from an improper influence or motive is, as a general matter, capable of direct and forceful refutation through introduction of out-of-court consistent statements that predate the alleged fabrication, influence, or motive. A consistent statement that predates the motive is a square rebuttal of the charge that the testimony was contrived as a consequence of that motive. By contrast, prior consistent statements carry little rebuttal force when most other types of impeachment are involved.

There may arise instances when out-of-court statements that postdate the alleged fabrication have some probative force in rebutting a charge of fabrication or improper influence or motive, but those statements refute the charged fabrication in a less direct and forceful way. Evidence that a witness made consistent statements after the alleged motive to fabricate arose may suggest in some degree that the in-court testimony is truthful, and thus suggest in some degree that that testimony did not result from some improper influence; but if the drafters of Rule 801(d)(1)(B) intended to countenance rebuttal along that indirect inferential chain, the purpose of confining the types of impeachment that open the door to rebuttal by introducing consistent statements becomes unclear. If consistent statements are admissible without reference to the timeframe we find imbedded in the Rule, there appears no sound reason not to admit consistent statements to rebut other forms of impeachment as well. Whatever objections can be leveled against limiting the Rule to this designated form of impeachment and confining the rebuttal to those statements made before the fabrication or improper influence or motive arose, it is clear to us that the drafters of Rule 801(d)(1)(B) were relying upon the common-law temporal requirement.

The underlying theory of the Government's position is that an out-of-court consistent statement, whenever it was made, tends to bolster the testimony of a witness and so tends also to rebut an express or implied charge that the testimony has been the product of an improper influence. Congress could have adopted that rule with ease, providing, for instance, that "a witness' prior consistent statements are admissible whenever relevant to assess the witness' truthfulness or accuracy." The theory would be that, in a broad sense, any prior statement by a witness concerning the disputed issues at trial would have some relevance in assessing the accuracy or truthfulness of the witness' in-court testimony on the same subject. The narrow Rule enacted by Congress, however, cannot be understood to incorporate the Government's theory.

Our conclusion that Rule 801(d)(1)(B) embodies the common-law premotive requirement is confirmed by an examination of the Advisory Committee's Notes to the Federal Rules of Evidence.

That Rule 801(d)(1)(B) permits prior consistent statements to be used for substantive purposes after the statements are admitted to rebut the existence of an improper influence or motive makes it all the more important to observe the preconditions for admitting the evidence in the first place. The position taken by the Rules reflects a compromise between the views expressed by the "bulk of the case law . . . against allowing prior statements of witnesses to be used generally as substantive evidence" and the views of the majority of "writers . . . [who] had taken the opposite position."

III

Courts must be sensitive to the difficulties attendant upon the prosecution of alleged child abusers. In almost all cases a youth is the prosecution's only eye witness. But "this Court cannot alter evidentiary rules merely because litigants might prefer different rules in a particular class of cases."

Our holding is confined to the requirements for admission under Rule 801(d)(1)(B). The Rule permits the introduction of a declarant's consistent out-of-court statements to rebut a charge of recent fabrication or improper influence or motive only when those statements were made before the charged recent fabrication or improper influence or motive. These conditions of admissibility were not established here.

JUSTICE BREYER, with whom THE CHIEF JUSTICE, JUSTICE O'CONNOR, and JUSTICE THOMAS join, dissenting.

The basic issue in this case concerns not hearsay, but relevance. As the majority points out, the common law permitted a lawyer to rehabilitate a witness (after a charge of improper motive) by pointing to the fact that the witness had said the same thing earlier—but only if the witness made the earlier statement before the motive to lie arose. The reason for the time limitation was that, otherwise, the prior consistent statement had no relevance to rebut the charge that the in-court testimony was the product of the motive to lie.

The majority believes that a hearsay-related rule, Federal Rule of Evidence 801(d)(1)(B), codifies this absolute timing requirement. I do not.

I would hold that the Federal Rules authorize a district court to allow where probative in respect to rehabilitation the use of postmotive prior consistent statements . . . , subject of course to, for example, Rule 403. In most cases, this approach will not yield a different result from a strict adherence to the premotive rule for, in most cases, postmotive statements will not be significantly probative.

In *Tome*, the Supreme Court read FRE 801(d)(1)(B)(i) to incorporate the common-law requirement that a prior consistent statement offered to rebut a charge of recent fabrication or motive to lie must be made *before* the motive to fabricate or lie or the bias arose—if the prior consistent statement is to be admitted for is truth. As *Tome* explained, this timing requirement limits the substantive use of prior consistent statements to the situation in which they are most forceful: "A consistent statement that predates the motive is a square rebuttal of the charge that the testimony was contrived as a consequence of that motive." The following graphic illustrates this timing requirement:

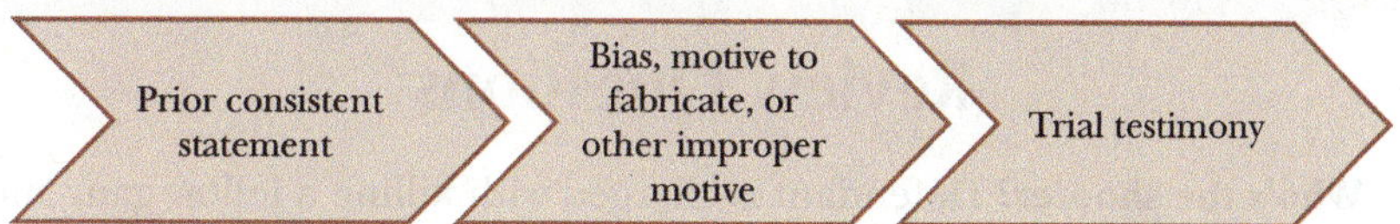

It is still an open question whether this timing requirement applies when the prior consistent statement is admitted solely to rehabilitate the witnesses and *not* as substantive evidence (that is, not for its truth). Consider this example. A witness for plaintiff is asked on cross-examination: "Today, you testified on direct that the light was red for the defendant, but your testimony today comes after her insurance company paid you a tidy settlement for your injuries. Have you *ever* told anyone else, at any point prior to today, that the light was red for the defendant?" Should the witness be able to testify, "Yes, I told your investigator that the light was red for the defendant just a week ago"? This prior consistent statement comes after the witness's alleged bias and motive to lie arose, but is being admitted solely to rehabilitate the witness. Is this statement permissible? Some courts say yes, reasoning that *Tome*'s timing requirement does not apply when a statement is admissible solely for rehabilitation; other courts disagree and would exclude the prior consistent statement—even though it is admitted solely to rehabilitate and not for its truth—because it does not comply with *Tome*'s timing requirement.

(b) When the Prior Consistent Statement Is Offered to Rehabilitate the Witness After the Witness's Credibility Is Attacked on Some Other Ground

In 2014, FRE 801(d)(1)(B) was amended to admit prior consistent statements as substantive evidence when a witness's credibility is attacked on grounds other than a charge of recent bias or motive to lie, such as the claim that the witness has been inconsistent in her remarks or has a faulty memory.[3] In such situations, the rule now allows for prior consistent statements to be substantive evidence regardless of when they were made as long as it tends to rebut the specific kind of attack on the witness's credibility.[4] FRE 801(d)(1)(B)(ii). If a party tries to use prior consistent statements to provide cumulative accounts of an event, the court may exclude them under FRE 403.

---

3. Texas tracks the Federal Rules of Evidence regarding this exception. Tex. R. Evid. 801(d)(1)(B). New York and Florida's exceptions for prior consistent statements only reach those admitted to rebut a charge of recent fabrication or bias. *People v. Ramos*, 70 N.Y.2d 639 (N.Y. 1987); Fl. Stat. § 90.801(2)(b). Illinois has no exception whatsoever allowing for the substantive use of prior consistent statements. Ill. R. Evid. 801(d)(1); *People v. Lambert*, 288 Ill.App.3d 450, 460 (Ill. Ct. App. 1997).

4. Some states retain a timing requirement, even when prior consistent statements are admitted for purposes *other than* rebutting a charge of recent fabrication or bias. California makes a prior consistent statement admissible as substantive evidence to rebut a prior inconsistent statement, but only if the prior consistent statement was made *before* the prior consistent statement. Cal. Evid. Code §§ 1236, 791.

Review Questions

1. **Who's the shooter?** Defendant is charged with killing a fellow gang member. Mary witnessed the murder, but was reluctant to give a statement to the police. However, she did tell her sister, "They've charged Defendant with killing Little Day, but it really was a guy from the rival gang. If you tell anyone, they will kill us next." Defendant calls Mary as a witness at trial. She testifies that Defendant was not the shooter. On cross-examination, Prosecutor asks, "Isn't it true that you are just backing Defendant because you are members of the same gang?" On redirect, Defendant asks Mary, "Isn't it true that right after the shooting, you told your sister that Defendant was not the shooter?" Prosecutor objects. How should the court rule?
2. **Biased witness.** Jerome has sued Ben in a contract dispute. Jerome claims that Ben failed to deliver a new home entertainment center that he had purchased from him. Ben claims that Jerome never paid the full amount for the entertainment center. Jerome calls Manny as a witness. Manny testifies that "Ben said he would set up the center for $20,000, and Jerome paid every cent." On cross-examination, Ben's lawyer asks, "Isn't it true that you never knew the price of the entertainment center and you are only testifying for Jerome because last week he gave you a new iPad?" On redirect, Jerome's lawyer asks, "When I was interviewing you two days ago, didn't you tell me that the price of the entertainment center was $20,000?" Ben objects. How should the court rule?

3. Prior Statements of Identification [FRE 801(d)(1)(C)]

A third category of "not hearsay" statements is a prior identification that a trial witness has made at some point before the trial. It is a relatively straightforward and narrow hearsay exception.

FRE 801(d). Statements That Are Not Hearsay

(d) Statements That Are Not Hearsay. A statement that meets the following conditions is not hearsay:

(1) ***A Declarant-Witness's Prior Statement.*** The declarant testifies and is subject to cross-examination about a prior statement, and the statement:

. . .

(C) identifies a person as someone the declarant perceived earlier.

Hearsay Exception for Prior Identifications

(1) Out-of-court declarant is testifying and subject to cross-examination; *and*
(2) The prior statement identifies a person as someone the witness previously perceived.

The exception requires that the witness be available for cross-examination at trial (thus satisfying the Confrontation Clause), but does not require that the witness make any identification while testifying. Thus, a witness's prior identification can be admitted for its truth even if the witness makes no attempt to identify anyone while testifying in court. The exception does not specify how the prior identification may be proven up, so it may be (1) testified to by the witness *or* (2) established through the testimony of a third party (typically, a law enforcement officer) who witnessed the prior identification.

Examples

1. Defendant is charged with bank robbery. The teller testifies as follows: "The robber stuck a gun in my face and asked for all the money in my drawer. This happened over a year ago. Right after the robbery, I attended a police lineup and identified the person who robbed me." The teller is not asked to make an identification of Defendant in the courtroom, but Prosecutor calls a police officer who testifies that the teller identified Defendant at the lineup. As long as the teller is available for cross-examination regarding the identification (which can be done during her initial testimony or by recalling her to the stand), the prior identification is admissible.
2. Defendant is charged with bank robbery. The teller identifies Defendant in the courtroom as the robber. She is also asked whether she initialed a picture of Defendant in a photo spread when she made an identification in the police station after the robbery. Although the prior identification happened outside the courtroom and therefore would ordinarily be hearsay, FRE 801(d)(1)(C) categorizes it as "not hearsay" because the witness can be asked about it during trial.

So what qualifies as an "identification"? Several types of identifications can occur outside the courtroom, including in-person showups or lineup identifications. A witness may also be asked to make an identification from photographs. One reason that pretrial identifications are more freely admissible is that such identifications may be more accurate than in-court identifications because they occur closer to the time of the offense and in situations that are less suggestive.

In addition to traditional forms of identification, courts may consider whether to admit other types of identifications, such as composite sketches or verbal descriptions of a suspect. Verbal descriptions are more problematic because of the ambiguities in how a person might describe another and the inability of the jury to evaluate how, and under what circumstances, the description was given. However, courts have admitted composite sketches as a pretrial identification. *See State v. Motta*, 659 P.2d 745 (Hawaii 1983).

This category of "not hearsay" reaches only the fact of identification, not the other statements made by the witness at the time of the identification. Thus, if the police conduct a showup of a suspect and the witness says, "Yes, that's the guy who slugged me twice in the back of the head before taking my wallet," this category covers the identification but not the witness's recounting of what happened during the mugging.

United States v. Kaquatosh

242 F. Supp. 2d 562 (E.D. Wis. 2003)

ADELMAN, Judge.

Defendant Kevin Kaquatosh is charged with two counts of assault with intent to kill. Count one alleges that on December 31, 2001, defendant struck Marvin Wayka on the head with a wooden object, causing Wayka to lose consciousness and sustain an open skull fracture. The government moved in limine for an order that law enforcement officers be permitted, pursuant to Fed. R. Evid. 801(d)(1)(C), to testify that two witnesses told them that defendant assaulted Wayka. I orally denied the motion at a pre-trial conference and now issue this opinion to further explain my reasoning.

I.

The government indicated that the officers would testify to statements made by Connie Freeman and Virginia Waupoose regarding the incident alleged in count one of the indictment. On January 7, 2002, Freeman informed one of the officers that on December 31 she observed defendant strike Wayka on the head and face with a piece of wood. Waupoose apparently told a second officer that she also observed defendant hit Wayka on the head with a piece of wood.

Neither Freeman nor Waupoose observed defendant in a line-up, show-up, or photo array and then identified him. Rather, they simply advised the officers that they observed defendant assault Wayka.

II.

Fed. R. Evid. 801(d)(1)(C) provides that a "statement is not hearsay" and thus is admissible as substantive evidence if it was a prior statement by the witness, the "declarant testifies at the trial or hearing and is subject to cross-examination concerning the statement, and the statement is . . . one of identification of a person made after perceiving the person." The Rule was enacted primarily for two reasons.

First, courtroom identifications are thought to be less convincing than prior, out-of-court identifications made when witnesses' memories are fresher and the conditions less suggestive. Therefore, corroboration with the earlier identification should be allowed.

Second, the Rule was designed to address the situation where a witness could not make an in-court identification. Thus, if before trial the witness had identified the defendant but was unable to do so at trial because of memory lapse or recantation, testimony concerning the pre-trial identification would be admissible.

Consistent with the purposes of the Rule, even if the witness is unable to recall or explain the basis of a prior identification, evidence of such identification is admissible so long as the witness is available and subject to cross-examination at trial. *See Owens*, 484 U.S. at 561-64 (allowing witness to testify as to prior identification of assailant where, due to severe head injury and resultant memory loss, he was unable to recall the actual assault). And the out-of-court identification may be introduced through the witness/declarant or through a third party witness to the identification, such as a law enforcement officer.

Because the introduction in a criminal trial of evidence that would otherwise be inadmissible hearsay implicates the defendant's right to confront his accusers, and because such evidence is often of questionable reliability, testimony may be admitted under Rule 801(d)(1)(C) only under certain circumstances. First, the person who made the identification must testify at trial; it not sufficient for only a witness to the identification to testify. This limitation flows not only from the plain language of the Rule but also from the Confrontation Clause of the Sixth Amendment; the defendant must have the opportunity to cross-examine the person who allegedly identified him.

Second, the pre-trial identification which is the subject of the testimony must have been reliable. Generally, "out-of-court identifications are believed to be more reliable than those made under the suggestive conditions prevailing at trial, and the availability of the declarant for cross-examination eliminates the major danger of hearsay testimony." However, otherwise proper testimony concerning prior out-of-court identifications is inadmissible if the initial identification was impermissibly suggestive or obtained in violation of the defendant's right to counsel. This limitation is required to prevent Rule 801(d)(1)(C) from becoming an end run around the constitutional standards governing pre-trial identifications established in cases such as *United States v. Wade* (1967) and *Manson v. Brathwaite* (1977), which were established to ensure the reliability of identifications.

Finally, courts should pay special attention to such testimony from third-parties. If the witness-declarant has not recanted or claimed memory loss, identification testimony from third parties could be cumulative, improperly bolster the declarant, confuse the jury, and waste court time. See Fed. R. Evid. 403.

III.

Based on the plain language and the purposes of Rule 801(d)(1)(C), the testimony proffered by the government must be excluded.

The government's written motion did not explain why it wanted to introduce third-party testimony regarding the out-of-court statements of Freeman and Waupoose. If Freeman and Waupoose testify at trial, as the Rule requires, they could describe what they saw and identify defendant in court. Rule 801(d)(1)(C) is ordinarily invoked when a witness recants or claims amnesia, and the government did not suggest that either would occur here.

More importantly, Rule 801(d)(1)(C) is properly invoked to allow testimony concerning an identification of the defendant by the declarant at a line-up, show-up, in a photo array, or at a prior hearing—in other words, after observing the defendant or his likeness. The Rule itself requires that the identification be made "after perceiving the person." Fed. R. Evid. 801(d)(1)(C).

Although the courts have consistently held that the identification referred to in the Rule need not be a personal identification (it could be of a photograph or sketch), and the statement of identification need not occur "soon" after the initial perception (it may take a while to apprehend the defendant, the victim-declarant may be hospitalized), the purpose of the Rule is to "permit evidence of an identification made after recognizing the assailant on subsequent observation." In the present case, Freeman and Waupoose did not identify defendant after recognizing him on subsequent observation. Rather, they simply told the officers that defendant committed the crime. Their statements were more accusation than identification. The Rule was not intended to allow the introduction as substantive evidence of hearsay statements that "the defendant did it."

Review Questions

1. **Sticky fingers.** Stephanie is accused of shoplifting. The busy teller identifies a picture of Stephanie right after she is apprehended, but by the time of trial, the teller has only a vague memory of how Stephanie looked. At trial, Prosecutor asks the teller to describe what happened, but does not ask the teller to make an identification of Stephanie in the courtroom. Instead, Prosecutor calls the security guard to tell the jury that the security guard selected a picture of Stephanie when the teller was initially asked to make an identification. Is the security guard's testimony admissible?
2. **The better "ID."** Defendant is charged with planting a bomb. At trial, an eyewitness identifies Defendant. Anticipating that defense counsel will argue to the jury that the in-court identification is not very valuable because a courtroom identification is so suggestive, Prosecutor calls an FBI agent to testify that the witness previously identified Defendant in a lineup. Is the FBI agent's testimony admissible?

PART B: HEARSAY EXCEPTIONS FOR ADMISSIONS BY AN OPPOSING PARTY [FRE 801(d)(2)]

The admissions of party opponents are the second category of out-of-court statements that otherwise satisfy the definition of "hearsay" but which the drafters of the Federal Rules of Evidence have designated as "not hearsay." The first category of "not hearsay"—prior statements of witnesses—is considered more reliable by virtue of having the witness on the stand for cross-examination. What justifies this second category?

Rationale for "Not Hearsay" Designation for Opposing Party Admissions

Three reasons have been offered. The first is tradition. Litigation is adversarial such that whatever a party says (in or out of the courtroom) is fair game for use by the party's opponent. The second is procedural. A party whose statement is introduced by their adversary cannot be heard to complain about the inability to cross-examine the statement's declarant because the party can always take the stand and explain that statement. The last is instrumental. It is assumed that a party is unlikely to say something against their own interest unless it was true.

Categories of Opposing Party Admissions

The Federal Rules delineate five categories of adverse party admissions as "not hearsay":

- FRE 801(d)(2)(A): Statements the opposing party has personally made;
- FRE 801(d)(2)(B): Statements made by others, but which the opposing party adopted;
- FRE 801(d)(2)(C): Statements made by persons the opposing party authorized to make statements on his or her behalf;
- FRE 801(d)(2)(D): Statements made by the opposing party's agent or employee; and
- FRE 801(d)(2)(E): Statements made by the opposing party's coconspirators.

Who Decides

By and large, it is up to the trial judge to determine whether statements fall into any of these categories of "not hearsay." FRE 104(a). However, the jury may also need to find some of the prerequisites, such as whether the speaker was authorized to speak on behalf of the adverse party.

1. *Admissions Personally Made by an Adverse Party [FRE 801(d)(2)(A)]*

The simplest type of admission is one made by the opposing party in a personal or representative capacity.

Examples

1. Bernie is suing Terry for hitting his car. Bernie calls Jackie to testify that "Terry told me that he didn't mean to hit Bernie's car." Terry's statement, although made out of court, can be used against Terry.
2. Enron is being sued for fraud. Its CEO tells a reporter, "We are not the only company in America who cheated." Corporations speak through their representatives. Thus, the CEO's statement is an admission.

This category of "not hearsay" is set forth at FRE 801(d)(2)(A).

FRE 801(d). Statements That Are Not Hearsay

(d) Statements That Are Not Hearsay. A statement that meets the following conditions is not hearsay:

. . .

(2) ***An Opposing Party's Statement.*** The statement is offered against an opposing party and:

(A) Was made by the party in an individual or representative capacity[.]

Hearsay Exception for Opposing Party's Admission

(1) The statement was made by the party, whether in an individual or representative capacity, *and*
(2) It is being offered against the party.

(a) Statement Made by Party in Individual or Representative Capacity

Statements falling into this category of "not hearsay" are broad. The prior admissions of party opponents are admissible under this exception:

- *Even if the statement was not based on the party's personal knowledge.* For example, in dog-bite cases, an owner might say, "I really wish that Sparky hadn't jumped on that little kid." Even if the owner did not see the dog's attack, it is still an admission if the owner is sued. The owner then has the opportunity to explain that he was wrong in his assumption. "Trustworthiness" is not a separate requirement for admissibility of an admission. Rather, the admissibility of statements of a party-opponent is grounded on "a kind of estoppel or waiver theory that a party should be entitled to rely on his opponent's statements." *United States v. DiDomenico*, 78 F.3d 294, 303 (7th Cir. 1996).
- *Even if the statement was not against the party's interest at the time it was made.* Thus, when Terry said that he "didn't mean to hit Bernie's car," she might have thought that that was a statement that helped her. However, if the issue in the case is not whether Terry intentionally hit the car but rather whether she was the person driving the car, it still can be used as an admission.
- *Even if the statement is conclusory and based on erroneous assumptions.* Conclusory statements, such as "it was my fault," can also be admissions. If need be, the party can take the stand and try to explain that the statement was based on false assumptions.
- *Even if the party is in a compromised physical condition.* If a party is injured, intoxicated, asleep, or under the influence of narcotics at the time they speak, that party may ask the court to use FRE 403 to exclude their statements. Similarly, although there is no per se rule against allowing statements by minors, the age and condition of the declarant may be factors in the court's FRE 403 analysis.

Thus, this category of "not hearsay" reaches the following:

- *Apologies.* Generally, apologies are admissible as admissions. Thus, if a person says, "I'm sorry" when they are in a car accident, it may be offered as evidence of fault. However, some jurisdictions want to encourage folks to apologize, so such summary apologies are not admissible or are excluded under FRE 403 if they are nothing more than an expression of sympathy to the other side.
- *Guilty pleas, but not "no contest" pleas.* Guilty pleas are the ultimate admissions. When a defendant pleads guilty, the defendant is asked to admit what the defendant did. As such, statements in guilty pleas can be used in a later civil suit against the defendant and often are sufficient to prove the civil case. However, when a defendant pleads nolo contendere ("no contest"), the defendant does not admit their behavior. They simply agree not to contest the prosecution's allegations. As such, such a plea does not become an admission for a later civil case. In some jurisdictions, guilty pleas to minor offenses, like traffic violations, by statute do not constitute admissions and are not admissible later in civil cases.

Because this category of "not hearsay" extends to statements that the party makes in "an individual *or representative* capacity," a party's admissions can also be introduced against the entity or person the party "represents." In determining whether a party is acting in a representative capacity, one may have to turn to other areas of the law, like corporate, agency, or partnership law. Commonly, a trustee, executor, administrator, or guardian may be a party in a representative capacity; thus, that person's statements may be introduced against the trust, the estate, or the person over whom they act as trustee, representative, or guardian.

(b) Statement Is Offered Against That Party

The critical limitation on this category of "not hearsay" is that it may only be used to introduce an *opposing* party's statements. A party cannot introduce their own statements because, while they are statements of a *party*, they are not statements of a *party opponent.* If a case involves multiple plaintiffs, a statement of any plaintiff is "not hearsay" if introduced by a defendant *as to that plaintiff*; to avoid consideration of that plaintiff's statement against the other plaintiffs, a trial judge may give a limiting instruction. The same is true if a plaintiff introduces the statement of one of many defendants in a case, although, as noted below, there are special, constitutional considerations at issue when the case is a criminal case and the prosecution is seeking to admit the statements of one defendant in a multidefendant trial.

(c) Special Concerns When the Party Is a Criminal Defendant

(i) Confessions

A criminal defendant's statements to law enforcement officers are classic examples of admissions that are admissible by the prosecution—as the defendant's "party opponent"—at the defendant's trial. In common parlance, an "admission" is any statement by the defendant that the prosecution seeks to use against a defendant to prove guilt, whereas a "confession" refers to a full admittance of the commission of the charged offense(s). The admissibility of such admissions or confessions turns on more than just the rules of evidence, however. If the defendant makes a statement in the course of "custodial interrogation," the statement may be excluded if the dictates of *Miranda v. Arizona*, 384 U.S. 436 (1966) are not met. Along similar lines, if an undercover cellmate deliberately elicits a statement from a defendant regarding a pending charge, the statement may be excluded under the Sixth Amendment pursuant to *Massiah v. United States*, 377 U.S. 201 (1964). And, if the statement is involuntary, it may be excluded under due process.

(ii) Silence as an admission

Can a criminal defendant's silence constitute an admission that is admissible as substantive evidence of guilt? The answer depends on at what stage of the interaction with police the defendant is silent. If defendant has been arrested and informed, as part of the *Miranda* advisements, that the defendant has the right to remain silent, the defendant's continued silence cannot be used against him or her as substantive evidence of guilt; to do so would be an unfair "bait and switch" that violates due process. *Doyle v. Ohio*, 426 U.S. 610 (1976).

If the defendant has been arrested but has not yet been *Mirandized*, the courts are split over whether the defendant's silence can be used as evidence of consciousness of guilt. *Compare United States v. Velarde-Gomez*, 269 F.3d 1023, 1030 (9th Cir. 2001) (postarrest silence may not be used as substantive evidence of guilt) *with People v. Tom*, 59 Cal. 4th 1210, 1215 (Cal. 2014) (postarrest silence may be used as substantive evidence of guilt). If the defendant has not been arrested, that prearrest silence may be used against the defendant as substantive evidence. For instance, if a defendant testifies that he did not commit the charged murder because he was out boating with a friend at the time of the killing, the defendant's failure to come forward with that alibi after an *America's Most Wanted* episode ran featuring his crime (that is, his silence in the face of that general accusation) can be treated as an admission of his guilt and that there was no alibi.

A similar issue arose in *Salinas v. Texas*, 570 U.S. 178 (2013). There, a person voluntarily spoke with police about what happened at a party he attended the night before, but fidgeted and declined to answer a question posed to him about whether a ballistics test of his rifle would match the bullets found in the victims. A splintered Supreme Court held that the defendant's silence when confronted with that evidence could be used as substantive evidence of the defendant's consciousness of guilt. Although *Salinas* can be viewed as a case dealing with a defendant's silence adopting the truth of a specific question by police, a more generalized silence not in response to a specific question can also sometimes be an admission.

The following table sums up the rules regarding the use of a criminal defendant's silence as an admission:

Timing	Admissibility as Substantive Evidence of Guilt
Prearrest	Admissible
Postarrest, pre-*Miranda* warnings	Depends on the jurisdiction
Postarrest, post-*Miranda* warnings	Inadmissible

(iii) Use of one defendant's admission at a joint trial

In confessing to a crime, a defendant may implicate a codefendant as well as herself. While using that defendant's statements against her is permitted, those portions of the defendant's statement that implicate a codefendant may be a problem. The codefendant has a constitutional right to confront his accuser. If a defendant does not testify and the prosecution seeks to use her statement against both her and a codefendant, the statement is not an "admission" of the codefendant, and the codefendant's constitutional right to confront his accuser is violated. This situation is referred to as a "*Bruton*" problem, after the case *Bruton v. United States,* 391 U.S. 123 (1968) that most definitively addressed this problem. If the prosecution has a *Bruton* problem, it may need to sever the two defendants' cases or redact a defendant's statement that explicitly or implicitly incriminates a codefendant. *See Richardson v. Marsh,* 481 U.S. 200 (1987); *Gray v. Maryland,* 523 U.S. 185 (1998). Although the *Bruton* doctrine is discussed more fully in Chapter Nine, we provide the pertinent excerpts from *Bruton* here.

Bruton v. United States

391 U.S. 123 (1968)

JUSTICE BRENNAN delivered the opinion of the Court.

This case presents the question whether the conviction of a defendant at a joint trial should be set aside although the jury was instructed that a codefendant's confession inculpating the defendant had to be disregarded in determining his guilt or innocence.

A joint trial of petitioner and one Evans resulted in the conviction of both by a jury on a federal charge of armed postal robbery. A postal inspector testified that Evans orally confessed to him that Evans and petitioner committed the armed robbery. We hold that because of the substantial risk that the jury, despite instructions to the contrary, looked to the incriminating extrajudicial statements in determining petitioner's guilt, admission of Evans' confession in this joint trial violated petitioner's right of cross-examination secured by the Confrontation Clause of the Sixth Amendment. We therefore overrule *Delli Paoli* (1957) and reverse.

The basic premise of *Delli Paoli* was that it is "reasonably possible for the jury to follow" sufficiently clear instructions to disregard the confessor's extrajudicial statement that his codefendant participated with him in committing the crime.

Delli Paoli assumed that this encroachment on the right to confrontation could be avoided by the instruction to the jury to disregard the inadmissible hearsay evidence. But, as we have said, that assumption has since been effectively repudiated.

A defendant may be prejudiced by the admission in evidence against a co-defendant of a statement or confession made by that co-defendant. This prejudice cannot be dispelled by cross-examination if the co-defendant does not take the stand. Limiting instructions to the jury may not in fact erase the prejudice.

Despite the concededly clear instructions to the jury to disregard Evans' inadmissible hearsay evidence inculpating petitioner, in the context of a joint trial we cannot accept limiting instructions as an adequate substitute for petitioner's constitutional right of cross-examination. The effect is the same as if there had been no instruction at all.

Reversed.

Review Questions

1. **Prius pilfering.** Daniel is suing Nathan for stealing his car. In his civil lawsuit, Daniel seeks to introduce the following evidence against Nathan. Which would be admissible as an admission?
   a. Testimony from Nathan's roommate that Nathan told him, "I love driving Daniel's car."
   b. An entry in Nathan's journal for the day after Daniel's car disappeared. The entry states, "Got me some cool wheels today, and it didn't cost me a thing."
   c. Testimony from Nathan's friend that Nathan had told him, "I guess it wasn't very nice what I did to Daniel."
   d. Nathan's guilty plea to stealing Daniel's car.
   e. Nathan's comment when he was very drunk that "next to evidence class, stealing cars is my favorite activity."
2. **Possible admission.** Which of the following statements could Daniel introduce as an admission?
   a. Nathan's statement to his roommate that even though he had once thought he would steal Daniel's car, he resisted the urge to do so.
   b. Nathan's journal entry in which he wrote, "So glad I didn't steal Daniel's car."
3. **Parallel criminal case.** In a criminal case, which of the following statements could the prosecution introduce if Nathan is charged with stealing Daniel's car and his roommate, Mark, is charged as an accomplice?
   a. Nathan's statement to the police that "he really, really needed a car."
   b. Mark's statement to the police that "he only helped Nathan because Nathan really, really needed a car."

2. *Adoptive (Tacit) Admissions [FRE 801(d)(2)(B)]*

Another type of admission is when a party tacitly adopts an admission by failing to deny an allegation in a way that "manifest[s] that it adopted or believed [the statement] to be true." FRE 801(d)(2)(B).

Examples

1. Witness testifies: "I heard Keegan say to Olivia, 'Gee, I can't believe you intentionally smashed into Tracy's car.' She just looked at him, smiled and did not reply."
2. Witness testifies: "While we were eating lunch, Nick said right in front of Hannah, 'It was amazing seeing Hannah steal the teacher's purse. I didn't know she had such guts.' Hannah didn't respond at all."

In each of these examples, the proponent will argue that the party adopted what was asserted by the party's actions or failure to object or disavow the assertion. This category of "not hearsay" is set forth at FRE 801(d)(2)(B):

FRE 801(d). Statements That Are Not Hearsay

(d) Statements That Are Not Hearsay. A statement that meets the following conditions is not hearsay:

. . .

(2) ***An Opposing Party's Statement.*** The statement is offered against an opposing party and:

. . .

(B) is one the party manifested that it adopted or believed to be true[.]

Hearsay Exception for Opposing Party's Adoptive Admission

(1) Party manifested that it adopted or believed a statement made by another person; *and*
(2) The statement is offered against that party.

The linchpin element of this category of "not hearsay" is whether the party has adopted the statement as its own. Sometimes, adoption occurs by affirmative comment. For instance, if Lex tells Selina that Harvey killed someone while Harvey is standing there, Harvey's nod and statement, "And he deserved it, too," is an affirmative admission adopting Lex's statement. Other times, however, adoption occurs by a party's silence in response to the statement. Before a party's silence can be said to adopt someone else's statement, the following questions must be answered:

- *Did the party hear the statement?* If the party did not hear or otherwise perceive the statement, they could not have adopted it.

- *Is it the type of statement one could reasonably expect a party to disavow if it were untrue?* If Tom told Jerry that Garfield had killed someone as Garfield is standing there, Garfield's failure to refute that statement may be viewed as an adoption of it.
- *Did the party have an opportunity to reply?* If the party had no opportunity to say, "No, that's wrong," the party's failure to do so does not constitute an adoption of the other person's statement.
- *Did the party fail to respond?*

Mann v. Regan

108 Conn. App. 566 (Conn. Ct. App. 2008)

FLYNN, Chief Judge.

The plaintiff, Mary Anne Mann, brought this action to recover damages for injuries she had sustained to her face when she was bitten by a dog owned by the defendant, Gladys Regan.

On December 17, 2004, the defendant traveled to Connecticut with her dog. The plaintiff and her friend, Barbara Scanlon, met the defendant at the airport. The defendant stayed at the plaintiff's house for a few days before departing on December 20, 2004, to attend a wedding in Wisconsin. Because the parties previously had agreed that the plaintiff would care for the defendant's dog while the defendant traveled out of state, the dog remained at the plaintiff's house.

Approximately six hours after the defendant left for Wisconsin, the plaintiff noticed that the dog was sitting on her couch in the sunroom. The plaintiff decided to place a blanket underneath the dog, and, as she leaned in toward the dog, the dog suddenly bit the plaintiff's right cheek, causing severe puncture wounds. The plaintiff immediately telephoned Scanlon, and Scanlon . . . drove the plaintiff to a medical clinic where the plaintiff received treatment.

On December 22, 2004, the defendant and her daughter went to the plaintiff's house to retrieve the defendant's dog. Upon arriving, the defendant observed the plaintiff's injuries, and a discussion ensued in which, inter alia, the plaintiff explained the incident. Thereafter, the defendant departed. The plaintiff continued to receive medical treatment for her injuries.

The plaintiff subsequently filed this action to recover damages from the defendant, claiming that the defendant was liable on a theory of common-law negligence.

The defendant first claims that the court improperly admitted into evidence the statement of her daughter, Christina Hahn, and the defendant's silence in response to that statement under the tacit admission exception to the hearsay rule.

The plaintiff made an offer of proof, outside of the jury's presence, that the plaintiff's testimony would include a hearsay statement pursuant to the tacit admission exception. During the proffer, the plaintiff testified that when the defendant came to retrieve her dog, the defendant was accompanied by (her daughter) Hahn. The plaintiff's friend, Scanlon, also was present at the plaintiff's house, and the four women were standing in close proximity in the plaintiff's kitchen. Upon observing the plaintiff's bandaged face, the defendant asked the plaintiff what had happened. The plaintiff informed the defendant that the defendant's dog had bitten her. The defendant then stated, "What do you mean Sam bit you? What did you do to him?" The plaintiff told the defendant that she did not do anything to the dog and then explained the dog bite incident. Hahn stated, "Well, mom, you know he bit you." The plaintiff further testified that the defendant, who was standing approximately five feet away, did not respond to Hahn's statement, nor did she deny Hahn's statement. The plaintiff testified that Hahn spoke loud enough for the defendant to hear. On the basis of the foregoing, the court concluded that the evidence qualified under the tacit admission exception. The plaintiff subsequently testified before the jury in a manner consistent with the testimony she gave during the offer of proof.

"The failure of one person to contradict or reply to the statement of another person made in his presence and hearing may amount to an admission by adoption of the other's assertion, providing the person remaining silent actually heard and understood the statement and was not disabled or prevented from replying, and the statement, under the circumstances made, was such as would naturally call for an answer." The plaintiff, as the proponent of the tacit admission, had to establish that (1) the defendant comprehended the statement made, (2) the defendant had the opportunity to speak, (3) the circumstances naturally called for a reply from the defendant and (4) the defendant remained silent.

In support of her claim that the circumstances did not naturally call for a reply, the defendant argues that Hahn's statement was made "in a meeting among long-standing friends who gathered around the holiday season and whose first, concern was not the fault of any person but the injury that the plaintiff incurred."

We cannot conclude that it was unreasonable for the court to determine that the circumstances naturally called for a reply from the defendant. [T]he court reasonably could have determined that under the circumstances of the present case, a dog owner, such as the defendant, either would deny that such an occurrence had occurred or, at the very least, would offer an explanation for the incident so as to distinguish it from the present situation. After reviewing the record, we cannot say that the court abused its discretion in determining that the circumstances surrounding Hahn's statement naturally called for a reply. Accordingly, we conclude that the court did not abuse its discretion in admitting the statement and the defendant's silence under the tacit admission exception to the hearsay rule.

The tacit adoption rule applies to tacit admissions by the defendant in a criminal case as well. In criminal cases, a defendant can make a tacit admission in one of two ways. First, the defendant can tacitly admit something *to the police*. For instance, in the *Salinas* case discussed in Part B.1 above, the defendant declined to answer the specific question posed by the police about whether a ballistics test of his firearm would match the bullets found in the recently murdered victims. The defendant's silence in response to that specific question could be viewed as a tacit admission that there *would* be a match. Because the tacit admission is in response to police questioning, the constitutional concerns outlined above for using silence as an admission apply with equal force here. Second, the defendant can tacitly admit something *to someone else*. Here, the constitutional concerns regarding police questioning are not present. *People v. Colon*, discussed next, falls into this second category.

People v. Colon

117 N.E.3d 278 (Ill. Ct. App. 2018)

GORDON, Justice.

Defendant Pablo Colon was convicted after a jury trial of first degree murder and sentenced to 40 years.

On this appeal, defendant claims that the trial court erred by allowing, as a tacit admission by defendant, the testimony of Wayne Kates recounting statements by Marco Ramirez and Daniel Guerrero that were made during a gang meeting at which defendant was present and that described the murder.

[T]he State's evidence at trial established that on May 29, 2010, at midnight, a group of men, who belonged to the same gang, approached two men on a nearby street because one of the two men was wearing a red shirt, which was the color of a rival gang. One of the two men, Mario Gallegos, was able to escape, and he testified at trial as the State's sole eyewitness. The other man, Alan Oliva, who was wearing the red shirt, was beaten to death. The State's evidence . . . included testimony by fellow gang member Kates, concerning statements made by two of the attackers at a subsequent gang meeting attended by defendant.

Defendant claims that the trial court erred by allowing the testimony of Kates, which described statements made by fellow gang members, Ramirez and Guerrero. The statements by Ramirez and Guerrero were made during a gang meeting at which defendant was also present. The statements included Ramirez's statement that the three men—Ramirez, Guerrero and defendant—exited a vehicle together in order to approach the victim and that "they just kept beating the guy until he stopped moving and then at that point, basically, they took off before the cops would come." Since defendant was present at the gang meeting and did not object to Ramirez's and Guerrero's statements, the trial court admitted the statements as an "admission by silence" by defendant.

THE TACIT ADMISSION RULE

Adopted statements include what the case law calls a "tacit admission" or, as the trial court described it, an "admission by silence." The "tacit admission rule" is well established in our case law. The tacit admission rule provides, "When a statement that is incriminating in nature is made in the presence and hearing of an accused and such statement is not denied, contradicted, or objected to by him, both the statement and the fact of his failure to deny it are admissible in a criminal trial as evidence of the defendant's agreement in its truth."

The necessary elements for admissibility under the tacit admission rule are (1) that the statement incriminates the defendant such that the natural reaction of an innocent person would be to deny it, (2) that the defendant heard the statement, and (3) that the defendant had an opportunity to reply or object and instead remained silent.

The statement need not be made "in an accusatory tone," so long as it is "evident that defendant was being painted or portrayed as a participant in illegal and prohibited activity."

Kates testified that, on August 21, 2010, he went with his brother, Walter Mullenix, to "a gang meeting" at Bernard Monreal's house. The assistant state's attorney (ASA) asked who was at Monreal's house, and Kates identified the people there as (1) himself, (2) Kates's brother, (3) defendant, (4) Ramirez, (5) Guerrero, and (6) Monreal. The topics discussed at the meeting were "the transferring of power from Bernard Monreal to [Kates's] brother," the lack of guns, and the gang's lack of presence on the street. Kates observed that "there wasn't enough people hanging out, outside." With respect to the lack of presence, Kates asked "why there wasn't anyone out there [?]" and Marco Ramirez replied that "the area was hot." There were only 6 people at the meeting and all 6 were present at this point in the conversation.

Kates testified that the meeting occurred in Monreal's living room. The ASA asked, "how close were you to each other during the time you had this discussion?" Kates replied a "couple [of] feet." Kates testified that Ramirez then explained why the area was hot. Ramirez stated that on May 29, 2010, he was driving in a vehicle with defendant, Daniel Guerrero and a man known as "Chucky" when they spotted a man who looked "like a rival gang member or a flake." Ramirez stated that "they pulled into the alley behind a restaurant called a barbecue patio and at that point Marcos Ramirez said that [Ramirez], Daniel Guerrero and [defendant] exited the vehicle." Ramirez stated that they wanted to check if the man had any gang tattoos or gang affiliation. When Ramirez asked the man what gang he belonged to, he responded that he did not belong to a gang and then turned and tried to run away.

Kates testified that Guerrero stated that "he caught up to the guy and he hit him with a baseball bat and he fell down." Then Ramirez stated that "he ran up to him and he started stabbing him while he was on the ground." Ramirez stated that "he was trying to stab him in the head." Ramirez further stated that "they just kept beating the guy until he stopped moving and then at that point, basically, they took off before the cops would come."

On cross, Kates testified that the only two people who talked about the murder at the meeting were Ramirez and Guerrero and that defendant did not make any statements that he stabbed anyone or wielded a baseball bat.

Ramirez's statement that "*they* just kept beating the guy until he stopped moving" implicated defendant in the murder. Ramirez stated that defendant had exited the vehicle with Ramirez and Guerrero; thus, all three of them exited together as one unit to approach the victim. The fact that they continued to move as one unit was evidenced by Ramirez's subsequent statement that "*they* drove off before the cops would come." These statements of "they" included defendant since defendant had arrived at the scene in the same vehicle and exited it with Ramirez and Guerrero. Ramirez's and Guerrero's description of their own acts of stabbing and beating were the initial acts in one course of conduct that ended with their "beating the guy until he stopped moving." Thus, Ramirez's and Guerrero's statements implicated and incriminated defendant.

The natural reaction of an innocent person would have been to deny it or, at least, to deny his own involvement. If defendant was not at fault for this turn of events, one would expect him to protest to the gang leadership—who were demanding an explanation—that he was not one of the people who had beaten an innocent man to death, thereby leading to the extreme police presence on the street. However, defendant remained silent, thereby indicating his assent to Ramirez's and Guerrero's statements, including Ramirez's statement that "*they* just kept beating the guy until he stopped moving."

The second requirement is that the defendant heard the statement. Kates testified that there were only six people at the meeting, that the six of them were meeting in a living room, and that they were only a couple of feet away from each other. Thus, given the small size of the meeting, the physical proximity of the participants to each other, the private and confidential nature of the meeting space, and Kates's testimony about who was present for "this conversation," we cannot find that the trial court erred in concluding that defendant heard Ramirez's and Guerrero's statements.

The third requirement is that the defendant had an opportunity to reply or object and instead remained silent. In Kates's testimony, there was no indication that defendant was prevented at this meeting of only six people from objecting or replying. Thus, all three requirements for admission under the tacit admission rule were satisfied, and we cannot find that the trial court erred by admitting these statements.

Review Question

1. **Smile and nod.** Nathan is being prosecuted for stealing Daniel's car. The prosecution wants to introduce the following evidence. Which would be admissible as an admission?
   a. When Mary said to Nathan, "I can't believe you stole Daniel's car," Nathan just smiled and walked away.
   b. When Nathan was arrested and advised of his *Miranda* rights to remain silent, the arresting officer said to Nathan, "What kind of guy steals his best friend's car?" Nathan did not reply.

3. Authorized Admissions [FRE 801(d)(2)(C)]

A third type of admission that is considered "not hearsay" is a statement that a party authorized someone else to make on its behalf. This type is also referred to as admissions by a "speaking agent."

Examples

1. Ben is Marci's real estate broker. In negotiating the sale, Ben says, "My client dropped the price because it will be so hard to clean out the mold." If the buyer sues over the mold, the buyer can use Ben's statement as an admission by the seller that she knowingly sold a house with mold.
2. LeBrane James hires a sports agent. The agent tells reporters, "James *loves* playing for the Ohio Snowflakes." A month later, James sues the Snowflakes for declaratory relief to get him out of his multiyear contract on

the ground that the Flakes are treating him unfairly. The agent's statements may be used against James.

This category of "not hearsay" is set forth at FRE 801(d)(2)(C).

FRE 801(d). Statements That Are Not Hearsay

(d) Statements That Are Not Hearsay. A statement that meets the following conditions is not hearsay:

. . .

(2) ***An Opposing Party's Statement.*** The statement is offered against an opposing party and:

. . .

(C) was made by a person whom the party authorized to make a statement on the subject.

The statement must be considered but does not by itself establish the declarant's authority under (C).

Hearsay Exception for Opposing Party's Authorized Admission

(1) A statement was made by someone a party authorized to speak on that subject; *and*

(2) The statement is offered against that party.

The linchpin of his category of "not hearsay" is whether the party authorized the person to speak on the particular subject of the statement at issue. As the text of the rule explains, the statement itself can prove *some evidence* of the speaker's authority, but it is insufficient by itself to establish that authority; other independent evidence of the authorization is necessary.

Bonds v. Dautovic

725 F. Supp. 2d 841 (S.D. Iowa 2010)

Pratt, Judge.

On September 13, 2008, Des Moines Police Officers M. Dautovic and J. Mailander ("Officers") pulled over a car carrying Plaintiffs, Erin Evans and Octavius Bonds. During the traffic stop, Evans was forcibly removed from the vehicle by the Officers, and Officer Mailander struck her twice with a steel, tactical baton Officer Dautovic sprayed Bonds in the face with pepper spray, and the Officers repeatedly struck Bonds with their ASP batons. Bonds was later taken to Broadlawns General Hospital where his numerous injuries were treated. Plaintiffs subsequently filed the present action, asserting that the Officers, in both their individual and official capacities, are liable for: (1) assault and (2) violations of Plaintiffs' rights under the Fourth, Eighth and Fourteenth Amendments, pursuant to 42 U.S.C. § 1983. Plaintiffs also assert each of these claims against the City of Des Moines under the theory of respondeat superior.

Plaintiffs now seek a preliminary evidentiary ruling regarding statements made by Des Moines Police Chief Judy Bradshaw, during her July 29, 2009 deposition and in a press conference regarding the use of force employed by the Officers. Plaintiffs have identified the following portions of Chief Bradshaw's deposition testimony [and remarks at a press conference]

"[T]he Officers' use of the ASP [baton], and—during this incident was inappropriate. It did not match the level of resistance that Ms. Evans exhibited that day or Mr. Bonds. And I believe that it was inappropriate."

Plaintiffs move for a preliminary ruling regarding the admissibility of Chief Bradshaw's statements as admissions under Federal Rule of Evidence 801(d)(2) on the basis that Chief Bradshaw was "a person authorized" by the City to speak on the subject matter, and that she is an authorized agent of the City who made the statements within the scope of her employment, and during the existence of her employment relationship. Rule 801(d)(2)(C) and (D).

"A statement by a party's [agent] can be admissible as an admission by a party opponent if it is relevant." Plaintiffs assert that Chief Bradshaw's statements will be relevant to the "reasonableness" inquiry required in a Fourth Amendment excessive force claim. To prove a constitutional violation due to excessive use of force under the Fourth Amendment, Plaintiffs will be required to show that the force used by the Officers was not objectively reasonable given the circumstances of the traffic stop.

The City asserts that the statements should not be admissible at trial because Chief Bradshaw's opinion was affected by her evaluation of the police department policies regarding the excessive use of force, such that it is equivalent to the results of internal departmental investigation.

Opinion statements, such as the statements at issue here, even when made by a person without personal knowledge of the facts, are well are within the ambit of Rule 801(d)(2). *See Mahtlandt v. Wild Canid Survival & Research Ctr., Inc.*, 588 F.2d 626, 630 (8th Cir. 1978) (finding a statement, by a corporate agent, admissible against the corporation even though the agent had no personal knowledge of the alleged incident). As a general matter, a statement by a party, related to behavior or beliefs that, if believed, could satisfy at least one element of a claim against the party, will not only qualify as a party-opponent statement, it will also be relevant.

Here, the majority of the disputed statements present Chief Bradshaw's opinion that the Officers' use of the ASP batons was "inappropriate." As an agent and person authorized to make statements on behalf of the City, which it appears Chief Bradshaw is, her opinion regarding the appropriateness of the use of the ASP batons has substantial probative value with respect to Plaintiffs' excessive use of force claims against the Officers in their official capacity.

[The plaintiff's motion for a preliminary evidentiary ruling admitting the Chief's statements is granted].

Review Questions

1. **Imperfect representation.** Doug Morell is the managing partner of his law firm. A former client, Dr. Brunzell, is suing the firm for malpractice. Morell writes a letter to Brunzell stating, "Our representation may not have been perfect, but that is no reason to sue us." Brunzell seeks to introduce the letter as an admission by the firm. Is it admissible?
2. **Speaking out-of-turn?** Barclay is an expert hired by one of the parties. Without notifying the party that hired him, Barclay makes a series of statements to opposing counsel. Opposing counsel now wants to use Barclay's statements.[5]

4. *Admissions by Employees and Agents [FRE 801(d)(2)(D)]*

One of the most common invoked categories of "not hearsay" is the category that applies to statements made by the employees or agents of a party.[6]

Example

A truck driver making deliveries for Company X hits Jane Doe's car with his truck. He says, "So sorry, I guess I was just in a hurry to make the deliveries for Company X." If Jane Doe sues Company X, she can introduce its truck driver's statement as an admission.

This category of "not hearsay" is set forth at FRE 801(d)(2)(D):

FRE 801(d). Statements That Are Not Hearsay

(d) Statements That Are Not Hearsay. A statement that meets the following conditions is not hearsay:

. . .

(2) ***An Opposing Party's Statement.*** The statement is offered against an opposing party and:

. . .

(D) was made by the party's agent or employee on a matter within the scope of that relationship and while it existed;

The statement must be considered but does not by itself establish . . . the existence or scope of the relationship under (D)[.]

---

5. Hint: Many courts hold that it is problematic to hold that just because someone is hired as an expert witness that person has been authorized to speak for the party that hired him. *See, e.g., Kirk v. Raymark Industries, Inc.*, 61 F.3d 147 (3d Cir. 1995).

6. New York has no such exception. *Lochiavo v. Port Auth. of N.Y. & N.J.*, 58 N.Y.2d 1040, 1041-42 (N.Y. 1983).

Hearsay Exception for Admission by Opposing Party's Employee or Agent

(1) A statement was made by a party's agent or employee;
(2) On a matter within the scope of that relationship;
(3) While that relationship existed; *and*
(4) The statement is offered against that party.

As with admissions by authorized agents, an employee's statement establishing these requirements may be considered, but there also needs to be independent evidence.[7]

This exception operates "one way" only. It permits the agent's or employee's statement to be used against the party who is the principal or employer; it does *not* permit the principal's or employer's statement to be used against the party who is the agent or employee.

(a) Statement by an "Agent" or "Employee"

This category of "not hearsay" reaches only (1) employees[8] and (2) agents of the party. It does *not* cover independent contractors hired by the party. The difference between independent contractors and employees is covered by the laws of the jurisdiction; as a general matter, however, an independent contractor is one who is contracted to do individual services for an entity and over whom the entity does not have the same control as it does over its employees. Although independent contractors are not covered by FRE 801(d)(2)(D), a party may independently adopt their statements, which would render them admissible under FRE 802(d)(2)(B).

Special considerations for agents or employees of the government. Whether a person is an "employee" whose statements are admissible against his or her employer may also turn on whether the party-employer is the government or a public entity (rather than a private company). Given the number of people who work for the government, some courts are reluctant to find that all statements made by government employees can be used in actions against the government. There are several proffered reasons for treating government employees differently: (1) Government

---

7. This principle is not universally followed. In California, for example, the statement itself may not be used at all to establish the agency or employment relationship. *Dooley v. West eAmerican Comm. Ins. Co.*, 133 Cal. App. 58, 62 (Cal. Ct. App. 1933); *People v. Leach*, 15 Cal. 3d 419, 423-24 (Cal. 1975).

8. Some jurisdictions, like California, limit the universe of employees whose statements bind a party-employer to "high-ranking organizational agent[s] who ha[ve the] authority to speak for" the party (rather than *all* employees). *Thompson v. County of Los Angeles*, 142 Cal. App. 4th 154, 169 (Cal. Ct. App. 2006); Cal. Evid. Code § 1222. Like the Federal Rules, Florida, Illinois, and Texas appear to have no such limitation. *Lee v. Department of Health & Rehabilitative Services*, 698 So. 2d 1194, 1200 (Fl. 1997).

employees may not have the same loyalty toward their employer because they do not have the same personal stake in what occurs if there is a judgment against the government; (2) traditionally, the sovereign could not be bound by its agents; (3) there are so many government employees that it is impossible for the government to monitor their statements; and (4) a mistake by a government employee should not impact the outcome of cases beyond those handled by that employee.

(b) Statement Regards a Matter Within the Scope of Agency or Employment

Courts must determine the breadth of an employee's employment or agent's agency. What is within the scope of their duties? Although the employee or agent does not have to be at work when the statement is made and the speaker does not have to have express permission to make the statement, there must be some connection between the subject matter of the employee's or agent's statement and the employee's or agent's duties.

Employee admissions cover statements made both in the workplace and to others outside the workplace. *See, e.g., Sea-Land Service, Inc. v. Lozen International, L.L.C.*, 285 F.3d 808, 820-21 (9th Cir. 2002) (internal company emails constituted employee admissions).

The employee or agent need not have personal knowledge of the matter at hand. The 1972 Advisory Committee Note to FRE 801(d)(2) observed that "[t]he freedom which admissions have enjoyed . . . from the restrictive influences of the opinion rule and the rule requiring firsthand knowledge . . . calls for generous treatment of this avenue to admissibility."

(c) Statement Made While the Employment or Agency Relationship Was in Existence

An employee's admission can only be used against an employer if the employee is still employed at the time the statement is made. Once the employee leaves the employer's employment, the employee admission exception no longer applies. This requirement guards against disgruntled former employees making statements attributable to their former employers.

Mahlandt v. Wild Canid Survival & Research Center, Inc.

588 F.2d 626 (8th Cir. 1978)

SICKLE, Judge.

This is a civil action for damages arising out of an alleged attack by a wolf on a child. The sole issues on appeal are as to the correctness of three rulings which excluded conclusionary statements against interest. Two of them were made by a defendant, who was also an employee of the corporate defendant; and the third was in the form of a statement appearing in the records of a board meeting of the corporate defendant.

On March 23, 1973, Daniel Mahlandt, then 3 years, 10 months, and 8 days old, was sent by his mother to a neighbor's home on an adjoining street to get his older brother, Donald. Daniel's mother watched him cross the street, and then turned into the house to get her car keys. Daniel's path took him along a walkway adjacent to the Poos' residence. Next to the walkway was a five foot chain link fence to which Sophie had been chained with a six foot chain. In other words, Sophie was free to move in a half circle having a six foot radius on the side of the fence opposite from Daniel.

Sophie was a bitch wolf, 11 months and 28 days old, who had been born at the St. Louis Zoo, and kept there until she reached 6 months of age, at which time she was given to the Wild Canid Survival and Research Center, Inc. It was the policy of the Zoo to remove wolves from the Children's Zoo after they reached the age of 5 or 6 months. Sophie was supposed to be kept at the Tyson Research Center, but Kenneth Poos, as Director of Education for the Wild Canid Survival and Research Center, Inc., had been keeping her at his home because he was taking Sophie to schools and institutions where he showed films and gave programs with respect to the nature of wolves. Sophie was known as a very gentle wolf who had proved herself to be good natured and stable during her contacts with thousands of children, while she was in the St. Louis Children's Zoo.

Sophie was chained because the evening before she had jumped the fence and attacked a beagle who was running along the fence and yapping at her.

A neighbor who was ill in bed in the second floor of his home heard a child's screams and went to his window, where he saw a boy lying on his back within the enclosure, with a wolf straddling him. The wolf's face was near Daniel's face, but the distance was so great that he could not see what the wolf was doing, and did not see any biting. Within about 15 seconds the neighbor saw Clarke Poos, about seventeen, run around the house, get the wolf off of the boy, and disappear with the child in his arms to the back of the house. Clarke took the boy in and laid him on the kitchen floor.

Clarke had been returning from his friend's home immediately west when he heard a child's cries and ran around to the enclosure. He found Daniel lying within the enclosure, about three feet from the fence, and Sophie standing back from the boy the length of her chain, and wailing. An expert in the behavior of wolves stated that when a wolf licks a child's face that it is a sign of care, and not a sign of attack; that a wolf's wail is a sign of compassion, and an effort to get attention, not a sign of attack. No witness saw or knew how Daniel was injured. Clarke and his sister ran over to get Daniel's mother. She says that Clarke told her, "a wolf got Danny and he is dying." Clarke denies that statement. The defendant, Mr. Poos, arrived home while Daniel and his mother were in the kitchen. After Daniel was taken in an ambulance, Mr. Poos talked to everyone present, including a neighbor who came in. Within an hour after he arrived home, Mr. Poos went to Washington University to inform Owen Sexton, President of Wild Canid Survival and Research Center, Inc., of the incident. Mr. Sexton was not in his office so Mr. Poos left the following note on his door:

> Owen, would call me at home, 727-5080? Sophie bit a child that came in our back yard. All has been taken care of. I need to convey what happened to you. (Exhibit 11)

Denial of admission of this note is one of the issues on appeal.

Later that day, Mr. Poos found Mr. Sexton at the Tyson Research Center and told him what had happened. Denial of plaintiff's offer to prove that Mr. Poos told Mr. Sexton that, "Sophie had bit a child that day," is the second issue on appeal.

A meeting of the Directors of the Wild Canid Survival and Research Center, Inc., was held on April 4, 1973. Mr. Poos was not present at that meeting. The minutes of that meeting reflect that there was a "great deal of discussion . . . about the legal aspects of the incident of Sophie biting the child." Plaintiff offered an abstract of the minutes containing that reference. Denial of the offer of that abstract is the third issue on appeal.

Daniel had lacerations of the face, left thigh, left calf, and right thigh, and abrasions and bruises of the abdomen and chest. Mr. Mahlandt was permitted to state that Daniel had indicated that he had gone under the fence. Mr. Mahlandt and Mr. Poos, about a month after the incident, examined the fence to determine what caused Daniel's lacerations. Mr. Mahlandt felt that they did not look like animal bites. The parallel scars on Daniel's thigh appeared to match the configuration of the barbs or tines on the fence. The expert as to the behavior of wolves opined that the lacerations were not wolf bites or wounds caused by wolf claws. Wolves have powerful jaws and a wolf bite will result in massive crushing or severing of a limb. He stated that if Sophie had bitten Daniel there would have been clear apposition of teeth and massive crushing of Daniel's hands and arms which were not injured. Also, if Sophie had pulled Daniel under the fence, tooth marks on the foot or leg would have been present, although Sophie possessed enough strength to pull the boy under the fence.

The jury brought in a verdict for the defense.

The trial judge's rationale for excluding the note, the statement, and the corporate minutes, was the same in each case. He reasoned that Mr. Poos did not have any personal knowledge of the facts, and accordingly, the first two admissions were based on hearsay; and the third admission contained in the minutes of the board meeting was subject to the same objection of hearsay, and unreliability because of lack of personal knowledge.

The Federal Rules of Evidence became effective in July 1975 (180 days after passage of the Act). Thus, at this time, there is very little case law to rely upon for resolution of the problems of interpretation.

The relevant rule here is:

> Rule 801. Definitions.
>
> (d) Statements which are not hearsay. A statement is not hearsay if
>
> (2) Admission by party-opponent. The statement is offered against a party and is
>
> (A) his own statement, in either his individual or representative capacity or
>
> (B) a statement of which he has manifested his adoption or belief in its truth, or
>
> (C) a statement by a person authorized by him to make a statement concerning the subject, or
>
> (D) a statement by his agent or servant concerning a matter within the scope of his agency or employment, made during the existence of the relationship. . . .

So the statement in the note pinned on the door is not hearsay, and is admissible against Mr. Poos. It was his own statement, and as such was clearly different from the reported statement of another. Example, "I was told that. . . ." It was also a statement of which he had manifested his adoption or belief in its truth. And the same observations may be made of the statement made later in the day to Mr. Sexton that, "Sophie had bit a child. . . ."

Are these statements admissible against Wild Canid Survival and Research Center, Inc.? They were made by Mr. Poos when he was an agent or servant of the Wild Canid Survival and Research Center, Inc., and they concerned a matter within the scope of his agency, or employment, i. e., his custody of Sophie, and were made during the existence of that relationship.

Defendant argues that Rule 801(d)(2) does not provide for the admission of "in house" statements; that is, it allows only admissions made to third parties.

The notes of the Advisory Committee on the Proposed Rules discuss the problem of "in house" admissions with reference to Rule 801(d)(2)(C) situations. This is not a (C) situation because Mr. Poos was not authorized or directed to make a statement on the matter by anyone. But the rationale developed in that comment does apply to this (D) situation. Mr. Poos had actual physical custody of Sophie. His conclusions, his opinions, were obviously accepted as a basis for action by his principal. See minutes of corporate meeting. As the Advisory Committee points out in its note on (C) situations.

. . . [C]ommunication to an outsider has not generally been thought to be an essential characteristic of an admission. Thus a party's books or records are usable against him, without regard to any intent to disclose to third persons. V Wigmore on Evidence § 1557.

Weinstein's discussion of Rule 801(d)(2)(D) (Weinstein's Evidence § 801(d)(2)(D)(01), p. 801-137), states that:

> Rule 801(d)(2)(D) adopts the approach . . . which, as a general proposition, makes statement made by agents within the scope of their employment admissible. . . . Once agency, and the making of the statement while the relationship continues, are established, the statement is exempt from the hearsay rule so long as it relates to a matter within the scope of the agency.

After reciting a lengthy quotation which justifies the rule as necessary, and suggests that such admissions are trustworthy and reliable, Weinstein states categorically that although an express requirement of personal knowledge on the part of the declarant of the facts underlying his statement is not written into the rule, it should be. He feels that is mandated by Rules 805 and 403.

Rule 805 recites, in effect, that a statement containing hearsay within hearsay is admissible if each part of the statement falls within an exception to the hearsay rule. Rule 805, however, deals only with hearsay exceptions. A statement based on the personal knowledge of the declarant of facts underlying his statement is not the repetition of the statement of another, thus not hearsay. It is merely opinion testimony. Rule 805 cannot mandate the implied condition desired by Judge Weinstein.

Rule 403 provides for the exclusion of relevant evidence if its probative value is substantially outweighed by the danger of unfair prejudice, confusion of the issues, or misleading the jury, or by consideration of undue delay, waste of time, or needless presentation of cumulative evidence. Nor does Rule 403 mandate the implied condition desired by Judge Weinstein.

Thus, while both Rule 805 and Rule 403 provide additional bases for excluding otherwise acceptable evidence, neither rule mandates the introduction into Rule 801(d)(2)(D) of an implied requirement that the declarant have personal knowledge of the facts underlying his statement. So we conclude that the two statements made by Mr. Poos were admissible against Wild Canid Survival and Research Center, Inc.

As to the entry in the records of a corporate meeting, the directors as primary officers of the corporation had the authority to include their conclusions in the record of the meeting. So the evidence would fall within 801(d)(2)(C) as to Wild Canid Survival and Research Center, Inc., and be admissible. The "in house" aspect of this admission has already been discussed, Rule 801(d)(2)(D), Supra.

But there was no servant, or agency, relationship which justified admitting the evidence of the board minutes as against Mr. Poos.

None of the conditions of 801(d)(2) cover the claim that minutes of a corporate board meeting can be used against a non-attending, non-participating employee of that corporation. The evidence was not admissible as against Mr. Poos.

There is left only the question of whether the trial court's rulings which excluded all three items of evidence are justified under Rule 403. He clearly found that the evidence was not reliable, pointing out that none of the statements were based on the personal knowledge of the declarant.

Again, that problem was faced by the Advisory Committee on Proposed Rules. In its discussion of 801(d)(2) exceptions to the hearsay rule, the Committee said:

> The freedom which admissions have enjoyed from technical demands of searching for an assurance of trustworthiness in some against-interest circumstances, and from the restrictive influences of the opinion rule and the rule requiring firsthand knowledge, when taken with the apparently prevalent satisfaction with the results, calls for generous treatment of this avenue to admissibility.

So here, remembering that relevant evidence is usually prejudicial to the cause of the side against which it is presented, and that the prejudice which concerns us is unreasonable prejudice; and applying the spirit of Rule 801(d) (2), we hold that Rule 403 does not warrant the exclusion of the evidence of Mr. Poos' statements as against himself or Wild Canid Survival and Research Center, Inc.

But the limited admissibility of the corporate minutes, coupled with the repetitive nature of the evidence and the low probative value of the minute record, all justify supporting the judgment of the trial court under Rule 403.

The judgment of the District Court is reversed and the matter remanded to the District Court for a new trial consistent with this opinion.

Review Questions

1. **Tired of it.** Leslie is a driver for Uber. She gets into an accident, and Uber is sued by the passenger. When the police took Leslie's statement at the scene, she told them that "Uber has us work so many darn hours that we all get into accidents." Is the statement admissible against Uber?
2. **Prime admissions.** Bryan works at a meatpacking company. His job is to package meat. The plant is audited for false accounting statements. When Bryan sees the auditors, he says, "I bet they cook the books. That is just the kind of folks they are." Is the statement admissible against the meatpacking company?

5. Coconspirator Statements [FRE 801(d)(2)(E)]

The last category of "not hearsay" applies to statements made by an adverse party's coconspirators.

Examples

1. Defendant is charged with being a member of a drug conspiracy. Prosecutor wants to introduce evidence that while Defendant was in the conspiracy, his coconspirator, Trevor, told an undercover agent that Defendant could deliver 5 kilos of cocaine. Prosecutor wants the undercover agent to testify to Trevor's statement.
2. Marlee is being sued for an insider trading scheme. Plaintiffs want Byllie to testify that Marlee's partner, Paul, tried to recruit Byllie to handle some of the trades. While recruiting her, Paul told Byllie: "Don't worry about a thing. Marlee figured this whole scheme out, and we will never get caught."

This category of "not hearsay" is set forth at FRE 801(d)(2)(D).

FRE 801(d). Statements That Are Not Hearsay

(d) Statements That Are Not Hearsay. A statement that meets the following conditions is not hearsay:

. . .

(2) ***An Opposing Party's Statement.*** The statement is offered against an opposing party and:

. . .

(E) was made by the party's coconspirator during and in furtherance of the conspiracy.

The statement must be considered but does not by itself establish . . . the existence of the conspiracy or participation in it under (E).

Hearsay Exception for Admission by Opposing Party's Coconspirator

(1) A statement was made by a party's coconspirator;
(2) The statement was made during the conspiracy;
(3) The statement was made in furtherance of the conspiracy; *and*
(4) The statement is offered against that party.

The rationale for this category of "not hearsay" is that coconspirators are, in effect, agents of one another. As a result, there is no requirement that the party be present when the statement was made, that the party knew the coconspirator, or that the party adopted the statement.

(a) Statement Made by a Party's Coconspirator

The speaker and party must be working together in a conspiracy. The conspiracy may be civil or criminal. There need not be any pending conspiracy charge or conspiracy allegation in a civil complaint for a statement to fall into this category of "not hearsay." The statement itself can be used to establish the existence of the conspiracy, but is not dispositive of the issue.[9] That is a question for the trial judge. The court can either make the determination in a separate hearing outside the presence of the jury before the statement is admitted or allow the statement subject to a proffer that there will be later evidence establishing the requirements. If the trial judge has a hearing to establish that the statement meets the requirements for a coconspirator statement, the hearing is called a *James* hearing. *See United States v. James*, 590 F.2d 575 (5th Cir. 1979) (en banc). Statements made by coconspirators to each other, including undercover agents and informats, are covered by the exception. The exception even covers statements made by individuals who end up becoming government informants. *See United States v. Doe,* 1999 U.S. Dist. LEXIS 5783, *25-*26 (E.D.N.Y. 1999). However, statements by undercover agents posing as informants to other law enforcement are not covered by the exception. *See United States v. Williamson,* 450 F.2d 585, 590-91 (5th Cir. 1971).

(b) Statement Was Made During the Conspiracy

A key requirement of this category of "not hearsay" is that the statement be made during the course of the conspiracy. A statement made *after* the conspiracy

---

9. That is not the universal rule. In California and Florida, for example, the statement itself may *not* be considered at all in determining whether a conspiracy exists; instead, the conspiracy must be proven by wholly independent evidence. *People v. Leach,* 15 Cal. 3d 419, 423-24 (Cal. 1975); Fl. Stat. § 90.803(18)(e).

ends—typically, when the conspirators have been arrested or the declarant has been arrested—usually does not qualify for the exception. A statement made after the party withdraws from the conspiracy by renouncing any involvement does not qualify. A statement made *before* the conspiracy begins is also not covered. However, a statement made *after* the conspiracy begins but *before* the party joins is still covered.

This graphic illustrates the timing requirement for this category of "not hearsay":

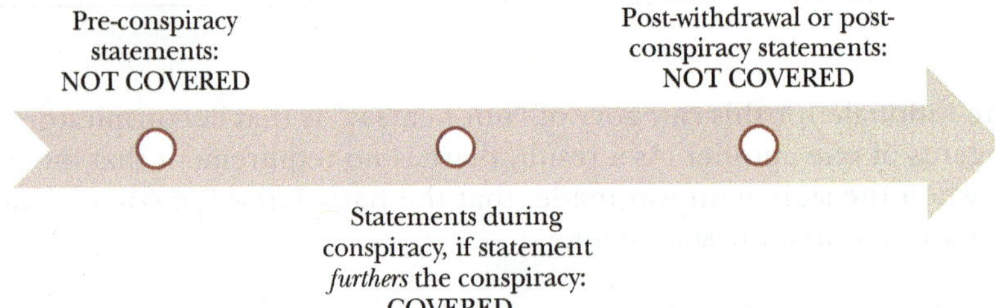
Pre-conspiracy
statements:
NOT COVERED
Post-withdrawal or post-
conspiracy statements:
NOT COVERED
Statements during
conspiracy, if statement
furthers the conspiracy:
COVERED

(c) Statement Is in Furtherance of the Conspiracy

The out-of-court statement must be "in furtherance of a conspiracy." That can refer to a wide variety of statements, from discussions among coconspirators as to how their conspiracy will operate to statements trying to recruit individuals to be part of the conspiracy. The statements may be verbal, written, or electronic. For example, a text message by conspirator A to conspirator B stating that conspirator C will be picking up the drugs can qualify even if conspirator C is not part of the conversation or is unaware that conspirator A will be sending the message.

Bourjaily v. United States

483 U.S. 171 (1987)

CHIEF JUSTICE REHNQUIST delivered the opinion of the Court.

Federal Rule of Evidence 801(d)(2)(E) provides: "A statement is not hearsay if . . . the statement is offered against a party and is . . . a statement by a coconspirator of a party during the course and in furtherance of the conspiracy." We granted certiorari to answer three questions regarding the admission of statements under Rule 801(d)(2)(E): (1) whether the court must determine by independent evidence that the conspiracy existed and that the defendant and the declarant were members of this conspiracy; (2) the quantum of proof on which such determinations must be based; and (3) whether a court must in each case examine the circumstances of such a statement to determine its reliability.

In May 1984, Clarence Greathouse, an informant working for the Federal Bureau of Investigation (FBI), arranged to sell a kilogram of cocaine to Angelo Lonardo. Lonardo agreed that he would find individuals to distribute the drug.

When the sale became imminent, Lonardo stated in a tape-recorded telephone conversation that he had a "gentleman friend" who had some questions to ask about the cocaine. In a subsequent telephone call, Greathouse spoke to the "friend" about the quality of the drug and the price. Greathouse then spoke again with Lonardo, and the two arranged the details of the purchase. They agreed that the sale would take place in a designated hotel parking lot, and Lonardo would transfer the drug from Greathouse's car to the "friend," who would be waiting in the parking lot in his own car. Greathouse proceeded with the transaction as planned, and FBI agents arrested Lonardo and petitioner immediately after Lonardo placed a kilogram of cocaine into petitioner's car in the hotel parking lot. In petitioner's car, the agents found over $20,000 in cash.

Petitioner was charged with conspiring to distribute cocaine, in violation of 21 U. S. C. § 846, and possession of cocaine with intent to distribute, a violation of 21 U. S. C. § 841(a)(1). The Government introduced, over petitioner's objection, Angelo Lonardo's telephone statements regarding the participation of the "friend" in the transaction. The District Court found that, considering the events in the parking lot and Lonardo's statements over the telephone, the Government had established by a preponderance of the evidence that a conspiracy involving Lonardo and petitioner existed, and that Lonardo's statements over the telephone had been made in the course of and in furtherance of the conspiracy. Accordingly, the trial court held that Lonardo's out-of-court statements satisfied Rule 801(d)(2)(E) and were not hearsay. Petitioner was convicted on both counts and sentenced to 15 years. The United States Court of Appeals for the Sixth Circuit affirmed [and] rejected petitioner's contention that because he could not cross-examine Lonardo, the admission of these statements violated his constitutional right to confront the witnesses against him. We affirm.

Before admitting a co-conspirator's statement over an objection that it does not qualify under Rule 801(d)(2)(E), a court must be satisfied that the statement actually falls within the definition of the Rule. There must be evidence that there was a conspiracy involving the declarant and the nonoffering party, and that the statement was made "during the course and in furtherance of the conspiracy." Federal Rule of Evidence 104(a) provides: "Preliminary questions concerning . . . the admissibility of evidence shall be determined by the court." Petitioner and the Government agree that the existence of a conspiracy and petitioner's involvement in it are preliminary questions of fact that, under Rule 104, must be resolved by the court. The Federal Rules, however, nowhere define the standard of proof the court must observe in resolving these questions.

We are therefore guided by our prior decisions regarding admissibility determinations that hinge on preliminary factual questions. We have traditionally required that these matters be established by a preponderance of proof.

Even though petitioner agrees that the courts below applied the proper standard of proof with regard to the preliminary facts relevant to Rule 801(d)(2)(E), he nevertheless challenges the admission of Lonardo's statements. Petitioner argues that in determining whether a conspiracy exists and whether the defendant was a member of it, the court must look only to independent evidence—that is, evidence other than the statements sought to be admitted. Petitioner [argues that using the statement itself to establish the predicate facts is improper "bootstrapping."]

[The cases raising the bootstrapping issue] were decided before Congress enacted the Federal Rules of Evidence in 1975. These Rules now govern the treatment of evidentiary questions in federal courts.

Petitioner concedes that Rule 104, on its face, appears to allow the court to make the preliminary factual determinations relevant to Rule 801(d)(2)(E) by considering any evidence it wishes, unhindered by considerations of admissibility. Congress has decided that courts may consider hearsay in making these factual determinations.

Petitioner starts with the proposition that co-conspirators' out-of-court statements are deemed unreliable and are inadmissible, at least until a conspiracy is shown. Since these statements are unreliable, petitioner contends that they should not form any part of the basis for establishing a conspiracy, the very antecedent that renders them admissible.

Petitioner's theory ignores two simple facts of evidentiary life. First, out-of-court statements are only presumed unreliable. The presumption may be rebutted by appropriate proof. Second, individual pieces of evidence, insufficient in themselves to prove a point, may in cumulation prove it. The sum of an evidentiary presentation may well be greater than its constituent parts. A per se rule barring consideration of these hearsay statements during preliminary factfinding is not therefore required. Even if out-of-court declarations by co-conspirators are presumptively unreliable, trial courts must be permitted to evaluate these statements for their evidentiary worth as revealed by the particular circumstances of the case.

We think that there is little doubt that a co-conspirator's statements could themselves be probative of the existence of a conspiracy and the participation of both the defendant and the declarant in the conspiracy. The out-of-court statements of Lonardo indicated that Lonardo was involved in a conspiracy with a "friend." The statements indicated that the friend had agreed with Lonardo to buy a kilogram of cocaine and to distribute it. The statements also revealed that the friend would be at the hotel parking lot, in his car, and would accept the cocaine from Greathouse's car after Greathouse gave Lonardo the keys. Each one of Lonardo's statements may itself be unreliable, but taken as a whole, the entire conversation between Lonardo and Greathouse was corroborated by independent evidence. The friend, who turned out to be petitioner, showed up at the prearranged spot at the prearranged time. He picked up the cocaine, and a significant sum of money was found in his car. On these facts, the trial court concluded, in our view correctly, that the Government had established the existence of a conspiracy and petitioner's participation in it.

We need not decide in this case whether the courts below could have relied solely upon Lonardo's hearsay statements to determine that a conspiracy had been established by a preponderance of the evidence. It is sufficient for today to hold that a court, in making a preliminary factual determination under Rule 801(d)(2)(E), may examine the hearsay statements sought to be admitted.

We also reject any suggestion that admission of these statements against petitioner violated his rights under the Confrontation Clause of the Sixth Amendment. That Clause provides: "In all criminal prosecutions, the accused shall enjoy the right . . . to be confronted with the witnesses against him." At petitioner's trial, Lonardo exercised his right not to testify. Petitioner argued that Lonardo's unavailability rendered the admission of his out-of-court statements unconstitutional since petitioner had no opportunity to confront Lonardo as to these statements.

While a literal interpretation of the Confrontation Clause could bar the use of any out-of-court statements when the declarant is unavailable, this Court has rejected that view as "unintended and too extreme." We think that the co-conspirator exception to the hearsay rule is firmly enough rooted in our jurisprudence that . . . a court need not independently inquire into the reliability of such statements.[10]

Review Questions

1. **Prison break.** Chuck Manson and Sirhan Sirhan agree to help each other break out of prison. They repeatedly meet to discuss their plans. Manson goes back to his cell and writes down what he plans to do when he gets out. He also tells his cellmate that if the cellmate helps, Sirhan can make sure there is room in the safe house for him. The cellmate tells Manson, "Thanks, but no thanks." The prosecution wants to introduce Manson's notes regarding his plans with Sirhan and what he told his cellmate. Are they admissible?
2. **"Pep" boys.** Manny, Moe, and Jack are reputed drug dealers. In searching Joe's house, the police find a ledger of drug deals with Manny, Moe, and Jack's names next to each entry. Can Prosecutor admit the ledger as a coconspirator statement? Is there sufficient foundation for the ledgers to be admitted?

Test Your Understanding

To test your understanding of the material in this chapter, turn to the Supplement for additional practice problems.

---

10. The Supreme Court subsequently adopted a different test for the Confrontation Clause that focuses on whether the proffered statement was "testimonial." *See Crawford v. Washington*, 541 U.S. 36 (2004). Even under that test, Lonardo's statement to a coconspirator would not be viewed as "testimonial" and therefore would not trigger the right of confrontation. *See* Chapter Nine.

"NOT HEARSAY" SUMMARY CHARTS

Prior Statements by Witnesses [FRE 801(d)(1)]

Prior inconsistent statement	• Declarant is testifying and subject to cross • Prior statement is inconsistent with witness's testimony • Prior statement was "given under penalty of perjury" at a trial, hearing, other proceeding, or deposition

Prior consistent statement	• Declarant is testifying and subject to cross
	• Prior statement is consistent with witness's testimony
	• Prior statement is offered to:
	  • Rebut a charge that witenss has recently fabricated testimony, and statement was made *before* motive arose, OR
	  • Rehabilitate an attack on another ground

Prior identification	• Declarant is testifying and subject to cross • Prior statement identifies someone

Admissions [FRE 801(d)(2)]

Admission by party	• Statement made by party • Offered against that party
Statement by another that party adopts	• Party manifests adoption of statement made by someone else • Offered against that party
Statement by another that party authorizes	• Statement made by someone party authorized to speak on that subject • Offered against that party
Statement by party's employee or agent	• Statement made by party's agent or employee on a matter within scope of agency/employment, and while agency/employment exists • Offered against that party
Statement by party's coconspirator	• Statement made by party's coconspirator in furtherance of the conspiracy and during the conspiracy • Offered against that party

Chapter 7

FRE 803 Hearsay Exceptions Applicable Even When the Declarant Is Available to Testify

In addition to the nonhearsay categories discussed in Chapter Five and the categories of "not hearsay" detailed in Chapter Six, the Federal Rules of Evidence have exceptions to the hearsay rule that the rules label as *bona fide* "exceptions" to the hearsay rule. This chapter discusses the subset of those exceptions, housed in FRE 803, that apply regardless of whether the declarant is available as a witness at the current proceeding. FRE 803 lists 23 hearsay exceptions.

Chapter Eight will then discuss (1) the subset of exceptions, housed in FRE 804, which can only be used when the declarant is unavailable as a witness; and (2) the "residual hearsay exception," housed in FRE 807.

Rationale for FRE 803 Exceptions

Why do the rules of evidence have hearsay exceptions that dispense entirely with the requirement that the declarant be unavailable as a witness at the current proceeding? The availability of the declarant as a witness means that these exceptions are not created out of necessity (that is, due to the absence of the declarant). Instead, these exceptions exist because the out-of-court statements themselves are deemed to be equally, if not more, reliable than anything the declarant would now say on the stand. That is typically because the circumstances under which the out-of-court statement is made make the statement less likely to be contrived or otherwise untrustworthy.

The fact that the hearsay declarant is available to testify may mean that the out-of-court statement is inadmissible under the Confrontation Clause, as discussed more fully in Chapter Nine. Always remember that finding an applicable hearsay exception for an out-of-court statement is only half the battle; the statement must also be admissible under the Confrontation Clause.

A Look at the FRE 803 Exceptions

We will discuss in detail the seven most commonly used exceptions in FRE 803:

Part A will discuss the present sense impression exception.
Part B will discuss the excited utterance exception.
Part C will discuss the exception for then-existing mental, emotional, or physical condition, which is commonly referred to as the "state-of-mind" exception.
Part D will discuss the exception for statements made for medical diagnosis or treatment.
Part E will discuss the exception for past recollection recorded.
Part F will discuss the business records exception as well as the closely related exception for the absence of a business record.
Part G will discuss the public records exception as well as the closely related exception for the absence of a public record.

The final section of this chapter, Part H, will highlight the remaining and less commonly used exceptions under FRE 803.

PART A: PRESENT SENSE IMPRESSION [FRE 803(1)]

Statements made as the declarant is observing an event or experiencing it can be admissible as present sense impressions. The trustworthiness of these statements comes from the fact that the declarant is making the statements either during the event or immediately thereafter. Therefore, there is less a chance of faulty memory and less of an opportunity to reflect (and thus, to distort).

Examples

1. Witness testifies that while she was on the phone with the victim, the victim said, "Hold on. My ex-employee, George, is at the door." The victim never came back to the phone. Prosecutors want to use this statement in the prosecution of George for the victim's murder.
2. Plaintiff is suing his neighbor for trespass. Plaintiff wants to introduce a cell phone video made by his housemate in which the housemate narrates a video of someone entering the yard and says, "Mr. Jones is in our yard again. What a pain."

Specifically, FRE 803(1) provides for the following:

> **FRE 803. Exceptions to the Rule Against Hearsay**
>
> The following are not excluded by the rule against hearsay, regardless of whether the declarant is available as a witness:
>
> **(1) Present Sense Impression.** A statement describing or explaining an event or condition, made while or immediately after the declarant perceived it.

Excerpts from Advisory Committee Notes to FRE 803

- *Participation* by the declarant is not required: a nonparticipant may be moved to described what he perceives, . . .
- Spontaneity is the key factor, . . .

Thus, the hearsay exception for present sense impressions has the following prerequisites:

> **Hearsay Exception for Present Sense Impressions**
>
> (1) Statement describes or explains an event the declarant is perceiving; *and*
> (2) The statement is made while or immediately after the event.

1. *When Does a Statement Describe or Explain an Event the Declarant Is Perceiving?*

Statements of present sense impression may come in various forms. Classically, they may include narrations of an event in which the declarant is involved, such as when a person records statements by text or tweet regarding what they are doing at the moment of that electronic communication. In the Federal Rules of Evidence,[1]

1. Although some states have a present sentence impression exception that parallels the Federal Rules of Evidence, see Tex. R. Evid. 803(1), many states take different approaches to this exception. California limits the present sense impression exception to statements "offered to explain, qualify, or make understandable *the conduct of the declarant*," Cal. Evid. Code § 1241; present sense impressions of what *others* are doing fall outside the exception. Florida and New York do not require that the statement pertain to the declarant, but have a

however, a present sense impression also reaches narrations of events in which the declarant is not involved—but that the declarant is nevertheless perceiving. Thus, a witness may testify that he heard someone on the street say, "That motorcyclist is weaving through traffic. I bet he runs into someone." As a statement describing an event while it is occurring, the declarant's statement could be used to prove that the motorcyclist's reckless conduct led to an accident.

The present sense impression exception is not confined to civil cases. For example, in *Bray v. Commonwealth*, 177 S.W.2d 741 (Ky. 2005), the victim's sister testified that the victim had told her on the phone that the eventual assailant was "sitting at the bottom of the hill" and that she feared for her life. Similarly, in *United States v. Earley*, the victim's statement assisted in identifying her murderer.

United States v. Earley

657 F.2d 195 (8th Cir. 1981)

STEPHENSON, Judge.

Gordon "Butch" Earley, Jr. appeals his conviction of bank larceny of the Grinnell State Bank. The jury found defendant guilty on two counts. In Count I, he was found guilty of killing Dan Kriegel in the course of committing the larceny and in Count III, he was found guilty of killing Dawn Kriegel in the course of committing the larceny.

Earley seeks a new trial on the grounds, inter alia, that certain evidence was erroneously admitted as a present sense impression or as an excited utterance. We affirm the conviction.

Earley was convicted for his participation in the November 1979 larceny from a bank in Grinnell, Iowa, and the killing of Dawn and Dan Kriegel in connection therewith. [Earley claims] that the district court erred in admitting testimony of Barb Whisenand regarding a statement Dawn Kriegel made after she received a phone call while she was with Whisenand. The event occurred on November 10, 1979, approximately two days before her death, when Kriegel received a telephone call while she was at the American Legion Hall in Brooklyn, Iowa. The call apparently upset her. Immediately after hanging up the phone, she said to her mother, while Whisenand stood next to her, "Oh, Mom, what am I going to do? That sounded just like Butch." Earley asserts that this statement is inadmissible hearsay because of its inherent untrustworthiness. Earley argues that it is impossible to determine from the statement whether Dawn meant that Earley was calling or that the caller was saying something that Earley would say.

Earley has not provided us with sufficient reason to hold that the district court's ruling was an abuse of discretion. The spontaneity of the statement in relation to the telephone call attests to its trustworthiness. Any question concerning the meaning of the statement is best left to the judgment of the jury. Therefore, because of the nature of the statement and its proximity to the event, we do not

separate trustworthiness or corroboration requirement. Fl. Stat. § 90.803(1); *People v. Brown*, 80 N.Y.2d 729, 734-37 (N.Y. 1993). Illinois has no such exception at all. See Ill. R. Rule 803(1); *Estate of Parks v. O'Young*, 289 Ill. App. 3d 976, 982 (Ill. Ct. App. 1997) (so noting).

find the district court erred in admitting the evidence under Fed.R.Evid. 803(1) (present sense impression) or Fed.R.Evid. 803(2) (excited utterance).

---

2. *When Is a Statement Made "Immediately" After an Event?*

The rule for present sense impressions covers narrations while an event is occurring and statements "immediately" after the declarant perceived the condition or event. What constitutes "immediately" after an event? The Advisory Committee Note to the original version of this rule—Rule 803(a)—provided that the statement must be "immediately thereafter" an event and that the exception permits only a "slight lapse of time." It is up to the trial judge to make this determination. Generally, the judge will use as a guideline whether the time that has lapsed presented the declarant with an opportunity to consciously misrepresent the events, as the next case demonstrates.

United States v. Lovato

950 F.3d 1337 (10th Cir. 2020)

Carson, Judge.

This action arose out of the district court's admission of a 911 call under the present sense impression exception to the rule against hearsay. Defendant Daniel Lovato ("Defendant") alleges that, in doing so, the district court abused its discretion.

I.

On March 3, 2018, a man called 911 to report that he witnessed two men in a Honda shoot at another car. The caller followed the Honda and dialed 911 within "two to three minutes" of observing the gunfire. During the approximately thirteen-minute 911 call, the caller discussed the shooting, his continuing observations of the Honda and its occupants, and his safety, often in response to the 911 operator's questions.

The caller began the call by stating that occupants of the Honda "just shot at" another car. After providing his location, phone number, and name to the 911 operator, the caller again described his observations of the shooting less than one minute into the call. Specifically, the caller stated that he observed two Hispanic males in the Honda shoot at a white Durango. Less than three minutes into the call, the caller informed the 911 operator that the shooting occurred "five or six minutes ago."

While the caller continued to follow the Honda, he conveyed additional information of his observations of the Honda. The 911 operator returned the conversation to the shooting about five minutes into the call—seven to eight minutes after the shooting occurred. The caller responded that someone in the Honda fired "two shots," and provided the exact location of the shooting. Just over eight minutes into the call, the 911 operator asked for a description of the suspects, which the caller provided. The caller next stated that the passenger of the Honda was the shooter. Finally, the caller observed the Honda run a red light, at which point he lost sight of the Honda. The caller provided his address to the 911 operator and, with the Honda then out of sight, ended the call after about thirteen minutes.

Shortly thereafter, responding police officer Levi Braun ("Officer Braun") located a Honda matching the caller's description. With Officer Braun in pursuit, the Honda slowed down and Defendant jumped out of the passenger's side of the moving car. Officer Braun stopped to detain Defendant, who volunteered that he had a gun on him. At the time of this incident, Defendant had prior felony convictions. The government ultimately charged Defendant with being a felon in possession of a firearm.

At trial, Defendant objected to the admission of the 911 call on hearsay grounds. The district court overruled the objection and admitted the 911 call into evidence under the present sense impression exception to the rule against hearsay.

II.

Defendant contends the district court abused its discretion by admitting the 911 call over his hearsay objection. Specifically, Defendant argues the 911 call does not qualify under the present sense impression exception to the rule against hearsay.

Under Rule 803(1), "[a] statement describing or explaining an event or condition, made while or immediately after the declarant perceived it" is admissible as an exception to the rule against hearsay, regardless of whether the declarant is available as a witness. "In evidence law, we generally credit the proposition that statements about an event and made *soon after* perceiving that event are especially trustworthy because 'substantial contemporaneity of event and statement negate the likelihood of deliberate or conscious misrepresentation." Defendant argues that: (1) the district court abused its discretion by analyzing the 911 call as a whole and (2) the caller's statements were not sufficiently contemporaneous to qualify as present sense impressions.

A.

[First], we conclude that the district court properly analyzed the 911 call as a whole because: (1) no authority requires otherwise in this context, (2) all the statements made within the call pertain to the same temporal event without a substantial change in circumstances, and (3) other relevant factors support the reliability of the statements within the call.

No authority creates a blanket requirement that a court must individually analyze each statement within a broader narrative under the present sense impression exception.

Next, no substantial change in circumstances occurred during the call. When a significant, intervening event or substantial change in circumstances occurs between statements, may require a court to treat a declarant's statements differently. Here, the caller witnessed a shooting, called 911, and followed the Honda during the call with no interruption or police intervention. The caller maintained focus on the Honda and its occupants for the entirety of the discussion. Although the discussion shifts between related topics, the call continually focused on an ongoing stream of observations, which supports the admissibility of the call as a whole.

Finally, the factors relevant to Rule 803(1)'s trustworthiness rationale applied to the call as a whole. "A 911 call has some features that allow for identifying and tracing callers, and thus provide some safeguards against making false reports with immunity." Although the use of the 911 system alone "does not 'suggest that tips in 911 calls are *per se* reliable,'" a caller's use of the system mitigates some concern regarding reliability. Other indicia of reliability are present "when the caller reveals where he is located, jeopardizing his anonymity; does not decline to give any information, especially identifying information; and does not seem in any hurry to make an allegation and hang up."

Those same reliability factors apply here. The caller was not anonymous, but rather provided his full name, phone number, and home address during the call. The circumstances of the call, therefore, created a "disincentive for making false allegations," which increases the reliability of its collective statements. These factors equally support the truthfulness of each statement within the 911 call, which were all admissible as present sense impressions.

B.

Next, we must address whether the caller's statements were sufficiently contemporaneous to qualify as present sense impressions. In addressing this question, we must apply the appropriate level of deference to the district court's consideration of case-specific facts. Defendant contends that Rule 803(1) requires immediate contemporaneity, and, even if it does not, the passage of time between the 911 caller's observations and statements destroyed the necessary contemporaneity. We reject these arguments. To begin with, Rule 803(1) "recognizes that in many, if not most, instances precise contemporaneity is not possible and hence a slight lapse is allowable."

Defendant's position is also belied by the fact that courts addressing the issue have refused to adopt a "*per se* rule indicating what time interval is too long under Rule 803(1)." And that makes sense because "[t]he underlying rationale of the present sense impression exception is that substantial contemporaneity of event and statement minimizes unreliability due to defective recollection or conscious fabrication." Thus, instead of recognizing a bright-line rule for specific time intervals and admissibility, courts have held that "the admissibility of statements under hearsay exceptions depends upon the facts of the particular case."

The 911 call in this case involved statements relaying the caller's contemporaneous observations during his pursuit of the Honda, as well as statements describing what the caller observed minutes earlier. Although the call lasted about thirteen minutes in total, the caller first provided details of the shooting only three or four minutes after observing the event.

The context surrounding the 911 call in this case also supports the reliability of the statements. Although statements about the shooting and suspects are interspersed throughout the call, the 911 caller made the statements in a discrete period without any break, interruption, or intervening event.

Defendant also takes issue with the admission of the 911 call because the caller made several statements in response to the 911 operator's questions. Defendant argues that the 911 operator's questions provided an "opportunity for strategic modification," which "undercuts the reliability that spontaneity insures." The mere fact that the caller made statements in response to questions, however, does not demonstrate that the statements were a product of strategic modification outside the bounds of Rule 803(1). Similarly, the caller's movement from the location of the shooting through his pursuit of the Honda does not eliminate sufficient contemporaneity.

Accordingly, we hold that the 911 caller's statements qualified as present sense impressions. The "timeline of events suggests that the caller reported the [shooting] soon after" he perceived it and his continuing observations of the Honda and its occupants are the "sort of contemporaneous report [that] has long been treated as especially reliable" in evidence law.

BACHRACH, Judge, concurring.

I agree with the majority that the district court did not abuse its discretion in admitting the 911 call. But I respectfully disagree with the majority's conclusions that (1) the court should analyze the 911 call as a whole and (2) we should consider "other indicia of reliability" to determine whether the 911 call is admissible as a present-sense impression under Fed. R. Evid. 803(1).

1. The exception for present-sense impressions applies to individual statements, not conversations.

Under the Federal Rules of Evidence, a present-sense impression is admissible as an exception to the rule against hearsay. Fed. R. Evid. 803. A present-sense impression is "[a] statement describing or explaining an event or condition, made while or immediately after the declarant perceived it."

Under this definition, a 911 call may contain multiple statements. Some statements may qualify as present-sense impressions, and others may not. But to apply these definitions, courts must separately analyze the individual statements.

2. A separate reliability inquiry is not required.

The majority discusses the caller's reliability, considering factors not directly related to contemporaneousness.

In my view, however, the exception for present-sense impressions contains no separate requirement of reliability. The hearsay exceptions themselves are designed to assure reliability. *See* Fed. R. Evid. 803 advisory committee's note to 1972 proposed rules ("The present rule proceeds upon the theory that under appropriate circumstances a hearsay statement may possess circumstantial guarantees of trustworthiness sufficient to justify nonproduction of the declarant in person at the trial even though he may be available."). For example, the exception for present-sense impressions requires temporal proximity, which itself serves as a proxy for reliability.

3. The district court did not abuse its discretion in admitting the statements in the 911 call as present-sense impressions.

Though I respectfully disagree with the majority's approach, I agree with its outcome because the district court reasonably treated the challenged statements as sufficiently contemporaneous to constitute present-sense impressions.

The test [for contemporaneousness] lacks bright-line distinctions. Some statements are so obviously contemporaneous that no one would question whether they constitute present-sense impressions. For example, consider a 911 call in which a witness reports a robbery in progress. This report would obviously be considered contemporaneous. On the other hand, some statements are so clearly separated in time from the incident that no one would regard the statements as present-sense impressions. For example, a 911 call detailing the events of a robbery a week earlier would obviously not qualify as contemporaneous.

For each statement, the district court could reasonably conclude that the caller was

- describing or explaining an event
- while or immediately after the caller saw the event
- sufficiently close in time to the event to qualify as a present-sense impression.

Review Questions

1. **Hallway mayhem.** Defendant is charged with assaulting his neighbor in the interior hallway of the apartment building they share. Prosecutor calls a 911 operator to testify that she received a call from a neighbor while the incident was ongoing. Which of the following statements by the neighbor is admissible as a present sense impression?
   a. The neighbor tells the 911 operator, "I'm looking through my peephole, and I can see [Defendant] punching [victim]."
   b. The neighbor tells the 911 operator, "I can't see anything, but I can hear [victim] screaming, but I'm afraid to go out there."
   c. The neighbor tells the 911 operator, "I can't see anything, but I recognize [Defendant's] and [victim's] voices, and it certainly sounds like [Defendant] is beating the heck out of [victim]."
2. **Deadly parade.** Defendant is charged with multiple counts of murder for driving his car into a crowd watching a Thanksgiving Day parade. Prosecutor seeks to admit a tweet posted at the same time as the incident, which reads, "Some dude with long red hair just drove his Chevy Blazer into a crowd of people! Holy @#$%!" Defendant has long red hair. The tweet is geo-linked to a location along the parade route. Is this tweet a present sense impression?

PART B: EXCITED UTTERANCES [FRE 803(2)]

Statements made when the out-of-court declarant is under the stress of an exciting event, even when that declarant is available to testify, are admissible under the "excited utterance" exception on the theory that the stress of excitement "produces utterances free of conscious fabrication."

Examples

1. "Oh my goodness!! That green car just plowed into the blue car."
2. "Butch just threatened to kill me again!"
3. "That police officer almost killed the guy by putting him in a chokehold!"

Specifically, FRE 803(2) provides the following:

FRE 803. Exceptions to the Rule Against Hearsay

The following are not excluded by the rule against hearsay, regardless of whether the declarant is available as a witness:

. . .

(2) Excited Utterance. A statement relating to a startling event or condition, made while the declarant was under the stress of excitement that it caused.

Excerpts from Advisory Committee Notes to FRE 803

- *Participation* by the declarant is not required: . . . one may be startled by an event in which he is not an actor.
- Spontaneity is the key factor. . . .
- [T]he statement need only "relate" to the startling event, thus affording a broader scope of subject matter coverage [than the present sense impression exception].

Thus, the hearsay exception for excited utterances has the following prerequisites:

Hearsay Exception for Excited Utterances

(1) A startling event or condition occurred;
(2) The statement relates to that startling event or condition; *and*
(3) The statement was made while the declarant was under the stress of excitement caused by the startling event or condition.

As a threshold matter, the excited utterance exception is often considered in conjunction with the present sense impression exception because they are similar and have some overlap. This table illustrates their relationship:

	Present Sense Impression	Excited Utterance
Trigger	None	Startling event or condition
Subject Matter of Statement	An event the declarant is perceiving	The startling event or condition
Timing of Statement	During or immediately after the event	As long as the declarant is under the stress of excitement caused by the startling event or condition

Sometimes, the two exceptions will apply to the same statement. If, for example, a victim screams out what is occurring, such a statement is both a present sense impression *and* an excited utterance. But the two exceptions do not always overlap, because the two exceptions are *not* identical. The excited utterance exception is both narrower and broader than the present sense impression exception: It is narrower because it requires that the event or condition observed by the declarant be "startling" and because the declarant must make the statement while "under the stress of excitement" caused by the event; it is broader because the statement need only be "related" to the startling event rather than "describ[e] or explain" it and because the statement need not be made during or "immediately after" the event—the exception applies as long as the "stress of excitement" persists.

1. *Has a Startling Event or Condition Occurred?*

This prerequisite is satisfied if the event is "'startling enough to produce [a] nervous excitement and render the utterance spontaneous and unreflecting.'" *United States v. Alarcon-Simi*, 300 F.3d 1172, 1176 (9th Cir. 2002). The majority view is that the court may consider the content of the statement in assessing whether the event is sufficiently startling. *See generally* FRE 104(a).

2. *Does the Statement Relate to the Startling Event or Condition?*

A statement can *relate* to the startling event or condition even if it does more than merely "describe or explain" that event. Adv. Comm. Note, FRE 803. As noted above, that is one way in which the excited utterance exception is broader than the present sense impression exception. A statement can sometimes "relate" to a startling event (and thus fall within the excited utterance exception) even if pertains to occurrences that *precede* that event.

3. *Was the Statement Made While the Declarant Was Still Under the Stress of Excitement Caused by the Startling Event or Condition?*

In assessing whether the speaker was still under the stress of excitement caused by the event, courts look to a variety of factors, including:

- How exciting the event was;
- The period of time between the event and the statement. In this regard, a trial judge must be careful to properly define what the "event" is. For instance, the "event" of a horrible accident may not end until the conclusion of the postaccident chaos of trying to find the victims and securing medical care for them. *E.g., Brunsting v. Lutsen Mts. Corp.*, 601 F.3d 813, 818-19 (8th Cir. 2010);
- Whether the statement was in response to a question, or instead entirely spontaneous. If any questions were asked, whether the questions were suggestive;
- The presence or absence of the declarant's self-interest;
- Whether the declarant was a participant in, or instead a bystander to, the event;
- The subject matter of the statement; and
- The characteristics of the declarant, such as age, physical and mental condition.

See, e.g., Chestnut v. Ford Motor Co., 445 F.2d 967 (4th Cir. 1971) (excited utterance occurred 20 hours after the accident when the declarant regained consciousness).

There is no time absolute beyond which a statement is deemed not to be made under the stress of excitement. For instance, if something triggers the declarant's excitement long after the event itself, such that the declarant is under the stress of excitement, the ensuing statement may still qualify as an excited utterance. The next case makes this point.

United States v. Graves

756 F.3d 602 (8th Cir. 2014)

Shepherd, Judge.

A jury convicted Brian Gordon Graves of Assault with a Dangerous Weapon and Domestic Assault by a Habitual Offender. At the trial and over Graves' objections, the district court permitted the government to introduce, as an excited utterance under Federal Rule of Evidence 803(2), statements the alleged victim made to a police officer on the night of the incident. Graves now appeals his conviction, arguing the district court abused its discretion in admitting the statements as an excited utterance because the alleged victim was not under the stress of the incident at the time she made the statements. We affirm.

Graves and his fiancée L.K. were involved in an all-day argument. At some point during the day, Graves left their shared residence. He returned between 10:00 p.m. and 11:00 p.m., kicked in the front door, and confronted L.K. in the back bedroom of the home. During this confrontation, Graves held a loaded shotgun. After

10 to 15 minutes of arguing, Graves left the residence. As he departed, he fired the shotgun five times.

A neighbor called 911 to report the gun shots. Officer Dana Lyons responded. It took Officer Lyons approximately 20 minutes to travel to the residence after being dispatched. When he arrived, he knocked on the front door, and L.K. answered. Officer Lyons observed that L.K. was shaking and appeared to have been crying. Officer Lyons told L.K. that there had been a report of shots being fired and asked, "What's going on here?" L.K. responded by recalling the details of the fight she had with Graves, including the fact that Graves had pointed the shotgun at L.K. and threatened to shoot her in the head.

The sole issue in this appeal is whether the district court abused its discretion in allowing into evidence as an excited utterance L.K.'s statements made to Officer Lyons immediately after Officer Lyons arrived at the residence. "Excited utterances" are excepted from the general rule against hearsay. "The rationale behind this particular exception 'derives from the teaching of experience that the stress of nervous excitement or physical shock stills the reflective faculties, thus removing an impediment to truthfulness.'"

Graves does not contest that L.K. experienced a startling event or that L.K.'s statements related to that incident. Instead, Graves argues that L.K. was no longer "under the stress of excitement" caused by the event or condition, and thus her statements to Officer Lyons are not admissible under the "excited utterance" exception to the hearsay rule. See Fed. R. Evid. 803(2).

To decide the specific question of whether a declarant remains "under the stress of excitement" caused by the event when the declarant makes the statement, courts consider several factors: "[1] the lapse of time between the startling event and the statement, [2] whether the statement was made in response to an inquiry, [3] the age of the declarant, [4] the physical and mental condition of the declarant, [5] the characteristics of the event, and [6] the subject matter of the statement." Courts also consider "whether the declarant's stress or excitement was continuous from the time of the event until the time of the statements." None of these factors is dispositive, and some of the factors may not be relevant in every case.

Outside the presence of the jury, the district court heard testimony from Officer Lyons about his encounter with L.K. After hearing that testimony and arguments from counsel, the district court held that the statements L.K. made to Officer Lyons were not subject to reflection by L.K. because she did not make the call to the police and, thus, was not aware during the approximately 30 minutes from the incident to Officer Lyons' arrival that she was going to be subjected to questioning from a police officer.

In looking at the factors noted above, first the lapse of time in this case—approximately 30 minutes—is seemingly long for the typical application of the excited utterance exception; however, we have previously allowed the inclusion of excited utterances in a similar factual scenario. In *United States v. Phelps*, a victim's boyfriend fired five or six shots in the victim's presence shortly after an argument between the two. A police officer arrived on the scene 15 to 30 minutes after the incident. When the officer made contact with the victim, the victim appeared "very upset," "[h]er hands were shaking," and "she . . . [was] crying."

Second, Officer Lyons testified that L.K. was shaking and appeared to have been crying when she answered the door immediately before giving the statements.

L.K.'s state of distress before she gave her statements supports a finding that L.K.'s statements were "spontaneous, excited or impulsive rather than the product of reflection and deliberation."

Third, L.K. offered her statements to Officer Lyons in response to his general inquiry into what had happened. This question was not the detailed, interrogation-style questioning that might negate the use of the excited utterance exception.

Finally, L.K.'s statements described the argument with Graves, including his placing the gun to her head and threatening to shoot her. The characteristics of such an interaction are the type of event that would cause a reasonable person to experience the type of stress and shock L.K. exhibited.

While Graves may offer alternative explanations for L.K.'s appearance and behavior, those explanations do not undermine the district court's exercise of its discretion in determining that L.K.'s statements bore a "guarantee of trustworthiness" and were not subject to reflection and deliberation. Accordingly, we affirm the district court's admission of the statements as an excited utterance under Federal Rule of Evidence 803(2).

We affirm.

Does the *identity* of the declarant need to be known to determine whether he or she was under the stress of excitement of the event? No, as long as the circumstances of the statement demonstrate that the statement was made while the declarant was actually under the stress of an exciting event.

Mitchell v. Target Corp.

2019 U.S. Dist. LEXIS 181353 (D. Md. 2019)

HOLLANDER, Judge.

In this tort litigation, plaintiffs Ellen and James Mitchell filed suit against Target Corporation. Plaintiffs allege that, due to the negligence of Target, Ms. Mitchell sustained serious injuries on July 31, 2015, when she slipped and fell while shopping at a Target store in Salisbury, Maryland (the "Store").

I. BACKGROUND

On the evening of July 31, 2015, Ms. Mitchell went back-to-school shopping at the Store. She was accompanied by her daughter, Karrsin Mitchell, and her granddaughter, Hanahsin Henry.

While Ms. Mitchell was at the check-out, a cashier told her about a sale that the Store was having on shoes. After purchasing her items, Ms. Mitchell went with Karrsin and Hanahsin to the shoe department, which was located towards the back of the Store. Finding nothing of interest, they decided to leave. They proceeded towards the exit by walking through the baby clothing and baby products aisles.

As the group walked toward the exit, Ms. Mitchell, who was wearing "Flip Flops," stepped on a clear, slick substance on the tile floor. As soon as Ms. Mitchell stepped on the liquid, she "just flew up in the air and went down." She fell hard, hitting her head on the tile floor.

Notably, "within seconds, 30 seconds, when the fall occurred," a couple walked around the corner, because they heard Ms. Mitchell scream. The man asked if plaintiff was "all right" and if she "need[ed] help." Karrsin said that her mother slipped. Karrsin testified that, in response, the man said: "My wife had just slipped in a spot and I had just talked with an associate, or whoever, someone at the front of the store who worked there, that there was something on their floors."

The man squatted down next to Ms. Mitchell, took hold of her arm, and asked if she was okay. According to Ms. Mitchell, the man said to her: "I just went up there and told them my wife nearly slipped here." Ms. Mitchell recalled that the man sounded "a little bit aggravated." The man then asked someone to bring him a pillow for Ms. Mitchell. Although the man stayed with Ms. Mitchell until the paramedics arrived, neither Ms. Mitchell nor Karrsin obtained the man's name or contact information.

Defendant argues strenuously that the Court cannot consider the statements by the unidentified man whom Ms. Mitchell and Karrsin identified as a volunteer fireman because they are "classic hearsay . . . and are thus inadmissible." In response, plaintiffs argue that the unidentified man's statements to Karrsin and Ms. Mitchell are properly before the Court, under the excited utterance exception to the hearsay rule.

One exception to the hearsay rule is the exception for excited utterances. Fed. R. Evid. 803(2). Found in Rule 803(2), this exception permits the admission of any "statement relating to a startling event or condition made while the declarant was under the stress of excitement caused by the event or condition." Such spontaneous declarations are excepted from the hearsay rule because they are thought to be "made in contexts that provide substantial guarantees of their trustworthiness."

In particular, the veracity of excited utterances is premised on the belief "that 'excitement suspends the declarant's powers of reflection and fabrication, consequently minimizing the possibility that the utterance will be influenced by self interest and therefore rendered unreliable.'" Accordingly, for a statement "[t]o qualify under the excited utterance exception, (1) the declarant must have 'experienced a startling event or condition'; (2) she must have related the statement 'while under the stress or excitement of that event or condition, not from reflection'; and (3) the statement or utterance must have 'related[ed] to the startling event or condition.'"

As indicated, Target contends that the statements of the unidentified man are inadmissible hearsay and thus cannot be used to defeat summary judgment. Regarding plaintiff's conversation with the individual, Ms. Mitchell testified, in relevant part:

> "I was in a daze. . . . And then I remember looking up, and this gentleman was—kind of grabbed my arm, and he said—he said are you okay? And I can remember him stating I went up there and told them that my wife like to fell [sic]. And—and he stayed with me the whole time."

The unknown person's statements are quintessential hearsay. Plaintiffs seek to use the man's out-of-court statements "to prove the truth of the matter asserted," *i.e.*, that he alerted a Target employee about the slippery floor before Ms. Mitchell fell. Fed. R. Evid. 801(c).

Here, construing the evidence in the light most favorable to plaintiffs, they have not laid a sufficient foundation to demonstrate by a preponderance of evidence that the unidentified man's statements constituted excited utterances. Ms. Mitchell's fall constituted a startling event—at least to her and her family. It sounded very painful. And she had rolled over to her side in pain in the fetal position. Undoubtedly, hearing a loud thud while shopping and then turning the corner to find a woman on the ground, in pain, could be a startling event. Although there is no evidence that the man witnessed the accident, he arrived at the scene "within . . . 30 seconds [of] the fall[.]" Thus, the record is sufficient to find that the man "experienced 'a startling event or condition[.]'"

But, the record cannot support the conclusion that the man's statements were made "'while under the stress or excitement of that event or condition, not from reflection.'"

As indicated, the statements were made in close temporal proximity to Ms. Mitchell's fall. But, timing is not dispositive. Notably, the description of the man, as provided by Ms. Mitchell and Karrsin, hardly paints a picture of a person "in a state of shock, anger, and confusion." Ms. Mitchell testified that she thought the man sounded "a little angry" when he spoke with her, because he had complained at "the desk" that his wife nearly fell. However, the man told Karrsin that he was a volunteer firefighter and had "been with people . . . in instances where they've been injured[.]" He asked Karrsin if he could render aid before touching Ms. Mitchell. And, after checking to see if Ms. Mitchell was alert, he directed someone to bring him a pillow. The evidence suggests that the man was acting in a calm, reflective, and deliberate fashion when he assisted Ms. Mitchell.

The fact that the declarant is not just unavailable but *unidentified* further militates against admitting the statements as excited utterances. Fed. R. Evid. 803(2) does not categorically exclude statements by unidentified declarants. However, where the declarant is both unavailable and unidentified, the "party seeking to introduce such a statement carries a burden heavier than where the declarant is identified to demonstrate the statement's circumstantial trustworthiness."

The man's statements that his wife almost fell and that he told Target about the slippery floors were heard only by Ms. Mitchell, a party, and her daughter. None of the reports created by Target employees after the incident mention any witnesses, besides Karrsin and Hanahsin.

In sum, because I cannot infer by a preponderance of the evidence that the unidentified man's statements were excited utterances, the statements are inadmissible hearsay. As a result, there is no evidence whatsoever that Target had notice of the slick floors prior to Ms. Mitchell's fall.

Review Questions

1. **Capital rioting.** Defendant is charged with instigating a riot at a government building. Prosecutor seeks to introduce a tweet sent by one of the

elected officials in the building at the time, which reads, "Dude wearing a top hat and face makeup is shouting, 'Shakespeare was right. Let's kill all the law-makers!' I can just barely see him from the desk I'm hiding under." Does the tweet qualify as an excited utterance?

2. **Delayed reaction.** Plaintiff sues Defendant for injuries suffered in an auto accident. Defendant seeks to introduce a statement made by Plaintiff's front-seat passenger. The passenger was knocked unconscious during the accident. When the passenger first regained consciousness three days later, he jolted up in the hospital bed and screamed, "You just ran a red light!" Is this statement an excited utterance?
3. **Bodycam video.** Defendant is charged with domestic violence against his boyfriend. The boyfriend called the police 45 minutes after hitching a ride back to his apartment. When the police arrive, they are wearing body cameras that record audio and video of their interview of the boyfriend. The boyfriend relays that Defendant punched him repeatedly. The bodycam video shows that the boyfriend is bleeding from a head wound; he is also crying and visibly distraught as he relays what happened to him, sometimes in response to questions by police and sometimes on his own. The boyfriend does not show up for trial, and Prosecutor seeks to introduce the bodycam video as an excited utterance. Defendant objects. Is this an excited utterance? Which factors weigh in favor of it fitting into this exception? Which factors weigh against it? How would you balance those competing factors? These questions arise often, as bodycam videos are becoming increasingly commonplace in criminal investigations.

PART C: THE "STATE OF MIND" EXCEPTION [FRE 803(3)]

This hearsay exception applies when the declarant makes a statement about his or her future intentions or plans or how they currently feel physically or emotionally; in other words, it applies to statements relaying the declarant's *then-existing* or *current* state of mind. Because the statement is made while the declarant is experiencing that state of mind, the statement is considered more reliable because there is less time for reflection and possible subterfuge. After all, who would know best how the declarant feels than the declarant herself at the moment she is feeling it?

The key to this exception is that the statement must relate to how the declarant *currently* feels or the declarant's plans for the future. The exception does not apply to a declarant's *backward-looking* statements as to why they did something or how they felt in the past. In such situations, there is a much greater risk that the statement is contrived. The only exception to this rule is that backward-looking statements are admissible if they relate to the validity or terms of the declarant's will.

Examples

1. After an accident, the declarant says: "My leg really hurts." This statement qualifies under this exception because it is a statement of how the declarant's leg is feeling *at that moment*. Had she said, "My leg hurt *last week*," that statement would *not* fall within the exception because it would involve the declarant's state of mind at some prior point in time.
2. To show that Defendant acted in self-defense because he feared the victim, a witness heard Defendant say, "I'm afraid he will kill me one day." This statement qualifies under this exception because it is a statement of Defendant's then-existing emotional condition.
3. To show that the declarant went to meet with the person suspected of kidnapping her ("Buddy"), a witness testifies that the declarant said, "I'm off to meet Buddy." This statement fits within the exception because it is a statement of the declarant's then-existing plan or intent to meet with Buddy.
4. In a will contest, the declarant's son introduces a statement that the declarant said before he died: "I'm leaving all my money to my son, Mikey, who took such good care of me." This statement would normally fall outside of the exception because it deals with a fact the declarant is remembering. But the state-of-mind exception has an exception for cases involving will contests.

Specifically, FRE 803(3) provides the following:

FRE 803. Exceptions to the Rule Against Hearsay

The following are not excluded by the rule against hearsay, regardless of whether the declarant is available as a witness:

...

(3) Then-Existing Mental, Emotional, or Physical Condition. A statement of the declarant's then-existing state of mind (such as motive, intent, or plan) or emotional, sensory, or physical condition (such as mental feeling, pain, or bodily health), but not including a statement of memory or belief to prove the fact remembered or believed unless it relates to the validity or terms of the declarant's will.

Excerpt from Advisory Committee Notes to FRE 803

- The exclusion of "statements of memory or belief to prove the fact remembered or believed" is necessary to avoid the virtual destruction of the hearsay rule which would otherwise result from allowing state of mind, provable by a hearsay statement, to serve as the basis for an inference of the happening of the event which produced the state of mind.

Thus, the hearsay exception for state of mind has the following prerequisites:

Hearsay Exception for State of Mind

(1) The statement regards:
   (a) The declarant's then-existing state of mind (that is, her motive, intent, or plan); *or*
   (b) The declarant's emotional, sensory, or physical condition (that is, her mental or physical health); *and*
(2) The statement does *not* include what the declarant remembers or believes to prove the fact remembered or believed *unless* it relates to the validity or terms of the declarant's will.

Graphically, this so-called state-of-mind exception sets forth the following rules:

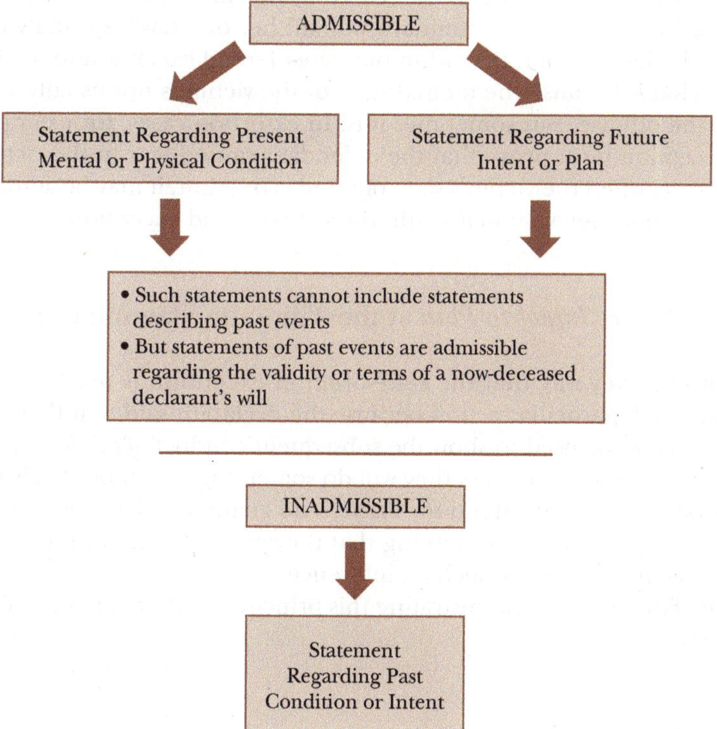

1. *Mental or Physical Condition* at the Time the Statement Is Made

The following are examples of out-of-court statements qualifying as statements of the declarant's physical or mental condition at the time the statement is made.[2]

---

2. Some states, like California and Florida, also require that the statement of then-existing state of mind also be shown to be "trustworthy" before it may be admitted. Cal. Evid. Code §§ 1250, 1252; Fl. Stat. § 90.803(3)(b).

As these examples make clear, whether any such statement is admissible also turns on whether the declarant's state of mind is relevant to any issues in the current proceeding:

- In a case to recover for personal injuries, the declarant's out-of-court statement that his "leg hurt" immediately after an accident would be relevant and admissible under FRE 803(3) because that statement regards the declarant's then-existing physical condition.
- In a sexual harassment/hostile work environment case, how the actions make an employee feel is a key issue in the case. To prove that the employee perceived the environment as hostile, the court may admit the employee's contemporaneous statements that the employee felt humiliated and threatened because those statements constitute statements of the employee's then-existing mental condition.
- In a criminal case, the person whose state of mind is relevant is the defendant. Thus, statements by a defendant that he "fears the victim" could be used to prove self-defense. By contrast, statements by the victim that she is "afraid that the defendant will kill her one day" is usually not relevant, whether or not it fits within the state-of-mind exception to the hearsay rule. That is because the mental state of the victim is not usually an element of the offense. But sometimes it is: In extortion cases, for example, the prosecution must prove that the defendant caused fear in the victim; in such a case, when the victim's state of mind is relevant, it may be admitted because it is both relevant *and* within the state-of-mind exception.

2. *Future Intent to Plan* at the Time the Statement Is Made

Another key way that the state-of-mind exception is used is to infer that a declarant took particular action because the declarant said that they would. These statements may be used to show the subsequent conduct *of the declarant* because we can infer that if someone says they will do something, it is more likely that they carried through with their intention. There is no guarantee that just because someone says they are going to do something that they really did it, but the trier of fact can use the statement to make such an inference.

The famous case demonstrating this principle is *Mutual Life Ins. Co. of New York v. Hillmon.*

Mutual Life Ins. Co. v. Hillmon

145 U.S. 285 (1892)

JUSTICE GRAY delivered the opinion of the court.

On July 13, 1880, Sallie E. Hillmon, a citizen of Kansas, brought an action against the Mutual Life Insurance Company, a corporation of New York, on a policy of insurance, dated December 10, 1878, on the life of her husband, John W. Hillmon, in the sum of $10,000, payable to her within sixty days after notice and proof of his death. On the same day the plaintiff brought two other actions, the one against the New York Life Insurance Company . . . on two similar policies of life insurance for the sum of $5000 each.

In each case, the declaration alleged that Hillmon died on March 17, 1879, during the continuance of the policy, but that the defendant, though duly notified of the fact, had refused to pay the amount of the policy, or any part thereof; and the answer denied the death of Hillmon, and alleged that he, together with John H. Brown and divers[e] other persons, on or before November 30, 1878, conspiring to defraud the defendant, procured the issue of all the policies, and afterwards, in March and April, 1879, falsely pretended and represented that Hillmon was dead, and that a dead body which they had procured was his, whereas in reality he was alive and in hiding.

On February 29, 1888, after two trials at which the jury had disagreed, the three cases came on for trial, under the order of consolidation. . . . At the trial the plaintiff introduced evidence tending to show that on or about March 5, 1879, Hillmon and Brown left Wichita in the State of Kansas, and travelled together through Southern Kansas in search of a site for a cattle ranch; that on the night of March 18, while they were in camp at a place called Crooked Creek, Hillmon was killed by the accidental discharge of a gun; that Brown at once notified persons living in the neighborhood; and that the body was thereupon taken to a neighboring town, where, after an inquest, it was buried.

The defendants introduced evidence tending to show that the body found in the camp at Crooked Creek on the night of March 18 was not the body of Hillmon, but was the body of one Frederick Adolph Walters. Upon the question whose body this was, there was much conflicting evidence, including photographs and descriptions of the corpse, and of the marks and scars upon it, and testimony to its likeness to Hillmon and to Walters.

The matter chiefly contested at the trial was the death of John W. Hillmon, the insured; and that depended upon the question whether the body found at Crooked Creek on the night of March 18, 1879, was his body, or the body of one Walters.

Much conflicting evidence had been introduced as to the identity of the body. The plaintiff had also introduced evidence that Hillmon and one Brown left Wichita in Kansas on or about March 5, 1879, and travelled together through Southern Kansas in search of a site for a cattle ranch, and that on the night of March 18, while they were in camp at Crooked Creek, Hillmon was accidentally killed, and that his body was taken thence and buried. The defendants had introduced evidence, without objection, that Walters left his home and his betrothed in Iowa in March, 1878, and was afterwards in Kansas until March, 1879; that during that time he corresponded regularly with his family and his betrothed; that the last letters received from him were one received by his betrothed on March 3 and postmarked at Wichita March 2, and one received by his sister about March 4 or 5, and dated at Wichita a day or two before; and that he had not been heard from since.

The evidence that Walters was at Wichita on or before March 5, and had not been heard from since, together with the evidence to identify as his the body found at Crooked Creek on March 18, tended to show that he went from Wichita to Crooked Creek between those dates. Evidence that just before March 5 he had the intention of leaving Wichita with Hillmon would tend to corroborate the evidence already admitted, and to show that he went from Wichita to Crooked Creek with Hillmon. Letters from him to his family and his betrothed were the natural, if not the only attainable, evidence of his intention.

The existence of a particular intention in a certain person at a certain time being a material fact to be proved, evidence that he expressed that intention at that time is as direct evidence of the fact, as his own testimony that he then had that intention would be. After his death there can hardly be any other way of proving it; and while he is still alive, his own memory of his state of mind at a former time is no more likely to be clear and true than a bystander's recollection of what he then said, and is less trustworthy than letters written by him at the very time and under circumstances precluding a suspicion of misrepresentation.

The letters in question were competent, not as narratives of facts communicated to the writer by others, nor yet as proof that he actually went away from Wichita, but as evidence that, shortly before the time when other evidence tended to show that he went away, he had the intention of going, and of going with Hillmon, which made it more probable both that he did go and that he went with Hillmon, than if there had been no proof of such intention. In view of the mass of conflicting testimony introduced upon the question whether it was the body of Walters that was found in Hillmon's camp, this evidence might properly influence the jury in determining that question.

Photos of Hillmon

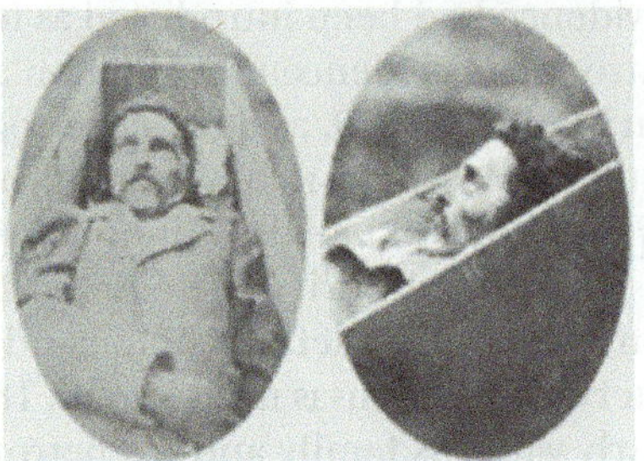
Corpse

Photos of Walters

Postscript: The mystery continues as to who is buried in Hillmon's grave. If it was Hillmon, the insurance carrier unjustly resisted Sallie Hillmon's claim and may have fabricated the alleged letters from Walters. However, if it is Adolph Walters, the insurance company was right to reject the claim and Hillmon was likely responsible for the death of Walters. The photographic evidence that survives today illustrates how tough this question is.

Although it might be appropriate to admit a declarant's statement that the declarant intended to do something to infer that *the declarant* did it, is it appropriate to use such a statement to prove what *someone else* does? For example, if a declarant says, "I'm going to meet with X," can that statement be used to show that X met with the declarant? That was the issue raised in *United States v. Pheaster.*

United States v. Pheaster

544 F.2d 353 (9th Cir. 1976)

RENFREW, Judge.

FACTS:

Appellants Pheaster and Inciso were tried before a jury in the United States District Court for the Central District of California and were convicted on all counts, [including a conspiracy to kidnap and hold Larry Adell for ransom].

This case arises from the disappearance of Larry Adell, the 16-year-old son of Palm Springs multi-millionaire Robert Adell. At approximately 9:30 P.M. on June 1, 1974, Larry Adell left a group of his high school friends in a Palm Springs restaurant known as Sambo's North. He walked into the parking lot of the restaurant with the expressed intention of meeting a man named Angelo who was supposed to deliver a pound of free marijuana. Larry never returned to his friends in the restaurant that evening, and his family never saw him thereafter.

The long, agonizing, and ultimately unsuccessful effort to find Larry began shortly after his disappearance. At about 2:30 A.M. on June 2, 1974, Larry's father was telephoned by a male caller who told him that his son was being held and that further instructions would be left in Larry's car in the parking lot of Sambo's North. Those instructions included a demand for a ransom of $400,000 for the release of Larry. Further instructions regarding the delivery of the ransom were promised within a week. Although the caller had warned Mr. Adell that he would never see Larry again if the police or the F.B.I. were notified, Mr. Adell immediately called the F.B.I., and that agency was actively involved in the investigation of the case from the beginning.

Numerous difficulties were encountered in attempting to deliver the ransom, necessitating a number of communications between the kidnappers and Mr. Adell. The communications from the kidnappers included a mixture of instructions and threats, as well as messages from Larry.

When it appeared that further efforts to communicate with the kidnappers would be futile, the F.B.I. arrested appellants, who had been under surveillance for some time, in a coordinated operation on July 14, 1974.

ISSUES:

[In addition to the evidentiary objections made by the defendants, they also objected to statements taken from them, voice identifications of them during the ransom calls by officers who knew them, handwriting exemplars, and evidence seized with a search warrant].

Admissibility of Hearsay Testimony Concerning Statements of Larry Adell

Appellant Inciso argues that the district court erred in admitting hearsay testimony by two teenaged friends of Larry Adell concerning statements made by Larry on June 1, 1974, the day that he disappeared. Francine Gomes, Larry's date on the evening that he disappeared, testified that when Larry picked her up that evening, he told her that he was going to meet Angelo at Sambo's North at 9:30 P.M. to "pick up a pound of marijuana which Angelo had promised him for free". She also testified that she had been with Larry on another occasion when he met a man named Angelo, and she identified the defendant as that man. Mr. Sendejas also testified that when Larry left the table at Sambo's North to go into the parking lot, Larry stated that "he was going to meet Angelo and he'd be right back."

Inciso's contention that the district court erred in admitting the hearsay testimony of Larry's friends is premised on the view that the statements could not properly be used by the jury to conclude that Larry did in fact meet Inciso in the parking lot of Sambo's North at approximately 9:30 P.M. on June 1, 1974. The correctness of that assumption is, in our view, the key to the analysis of this contention of error. The Government argues that Larry's statements were relevant to two issues in the case. First, the statements are said to be relevant to an issue created by the defense when Inciso's attorney attempted to show that Larry had not been kidnapped but had disappeared voluntarily as part of a simulated kidnapping designed to extort money from his wealthy father from whom he was allegedly estranged. In his brief on appeal, Inciso concedes the relevance and, presumably, the admissibility of the statements to "show that Larry did not voluntarily disappear". However, Inciso argues that for this limited purpose, there was no need to name the person with whom Larry intended to meet, and that the district court's limiting instruction was insufficient to overcome the prejudice to which he was exposed by the testimony.[3] Second, the Government argues that the statements are relevant and admissible to show that, as intended, Larry did meet Inciso in the parking lot at Sambo's North on the evening of June 1, 1974.

The Government's position that Larry Adell's statements can be used to prove that the meeting with Inciso did occur raises a difficult and important question concerning the scope of the so-called "Hillmon doctrine." Under the state of mind exception, hearsay evidence is admissible if it bears on the state of mind of the declarant and if that state of mind is an issue in the case. The exception embodied

---

3. Were this the only theory under which the testimony could come in, we would tend to agree with Inciso. In such a context, the potential prejudice would far outweigh the potential relevance of the testimony, and a limiting instruction would not sufficiently safeguard the defendant.

in the *Hillmon* doctrine is fundamentally different, because it does not require that the state of mind of the declarant be an actual issue in the case. Instead, under the *Hillmon* doctrine the state of mind of the declarant is used inferentially to prove other matters which are in issue. Stated simply, the doctrine provides that when the performance of a particular act by an individual is an issue in a case, his intention (state of mind) to perform that act may be shown. From that intention, the trier of fact may draw the inference that the person carried out his intention and performed the act. Inciso's objection to the doctrine concerns its application in situations in which the declarant has stated his intention to do something with another person, and the issue is whether he did so. There can be no doubt that the theory of the *Hillmon* doctrine is different when the declarant's statement of intention necessarily requires the action of one or more others if it is to be fulfilled.

When hearsay evidence concerns the declarant's statement of his intention to do something with another person, the *Hillmon* doctrine requires that the trier of fact infer from the state of mind of the declarant the probability of a particular act not only by the declarant but also by the other person. Several objections can be raised against a doctrine that would allow such an inference to be made. One such objection is based on the unreliability of the inference but is not, in our view, compelling. A much more significant and troubling objection is based on the inconsistency of such an inference with the state of mind exception. This problem is more easily perceived when one divides what is really a compound statement into its component parts. In the instant case, the statement by Larry Adell, "I am going to meet Angelo in the parking lot to get a pound of grass", is really two statements. The first is the obvious statement of Larry's intention. The second is an implicit statement of Angelo's intention. Surely, if the meeting is to take place in a location which Angelo does not habitually frequent, one must assume that Angelo intended to meet Larry there if one is to make the inference that Angelo was in the parking lot and the meeting occurred. The important point is that the second, implicit statement has nothing to do with Larry's state of mind.

Despite the theoretical awkwardness associated with the application of the *Hillmon* doctrine to facts such as those now before us, the authority in favor of such an application is impressive, beginning with the seminal *Hillmon* decision itself. *Hillmon* was a civil case involving a colorful dispute over certain life insurance claims. The factual issue in the case was whether Hillmon, who had purchased a number of life insurance policies naming his wife as beneficiary, had been killed by the accidental discharge of a gun in a campsite near Crooked Creek, Kansas. If he had been so killed, his wife was entitled to the benefits under the insurance policies. The defendant insurance companies contended, however, that Hillmon was not dead but was in hiding, and that the claims were part of a conspiracy to defraud the companies. While it was undisputed that someone had been killed in the campsite at Crooked Creek, there was complete disagreement as to who the victim was. The defendants in *Hillmon* introduced evidence which tended to show that the body at Crooked Creek was not that of Hillmon, but was that of another man, Frederick Adoph Walters. As part of this attempt to show that it was Walters who was killed at Crooked Creek, the defendants attempted to introduce two letters written by Walters from Wichita, Kansas, shortly before he disappeared, never to be heard from again. In the letters, one written to his sister and the other to his fiancee, Walters stated that he intended to leave Wichita in the near future and to travel with a man named Hillmon. In the letter to his fiancee, Walters explained that Hillmon was making the expedition to search for a suitable site for a sheep ranch, and that Hillmon had promised him employment at the ranch on very favorable terms. Plaintiff's objection to the introduction of the letters on the ground that they were incompetent, irrelevant, and hearsay was sustained by the trial court.

The Supreme Court summarily rejected the argument that the letters were admissible "as memoranda made in the ordinary course of business", but then held that they were admissible as evidence of Walter's intention[.]

Although *Hillmon* was a civil case, the Supreme Court cited with approval a number of criminal cases in support of its decision. "'If it is legitimate to show by a man's own declarations that he left his home to be gone a week, or for a certain destination, which seems incontestable, why may it not be proved in the same way that a designated person was to bear him company?'"

The *Hillmon* doctrine has been applied by the California Supreme Court in *People v. Alcalde*, 24 Cal. 2d 177, 148 P.2d 627 (1944), a criminal case. In *Alcalde* the defendant was tried and convicted of first degree murder for the brutal slaying of a woman whom he had been seeing socially. One of the issues before the California Supreme Court was the asserted error by the trial court in allowing the introduction of certain hearsay testimony concerning statements made by the victim on the day of her murder. As in the instant case, the testimony was highly incriminating, because the victim reportedly said that she was going out with Frank, the defendant, on the evening she was murdered. On appeal, a majority of the California Supreme Court affirmed the defendant's conviction, holding that *Hillmon* was "the leading case on the admissibility of declarations of intent to do an act as proof that the act thereafter was accomplished." Without purporting to "define or summarize all the limitations or restrictions upon the admissibility of" such evidence, the court did mention several prudential considerations . . . the declarant should be dead or otherwise unavailable, and the testimony concerning his statements should be relevant and possess a high degree of trustworthiness. The court also noted that there was other evidence from which the defendant's guilt could be inferred. Applying these standards, the court found no error in the trial court's admission of the disputed hearsay testimony.

Although Rule 803(3) is silent regarding the *Hillmon* doctrine, both the Advisory Committee on the Proposed Rules and the House Committee on the Judiciary specifically addressed the doctrine. After noting that Rule 803(3) would not allow the admission of statements of memory, the Advisory Committee stated broadly that "The rule of *Mutual Life Ins. Co. v. Hillmon* allowing evidence of intention as tending to prove the doing of the act intended, is, of course, left undisturbed."

Although the matter is certainly not free from doubt, we read the note of the Advisory Committee as presuming that the *Hillmon* doctrine would be incorporated in full force. The language suggests that the Advisory Committee presumed that such a broad interpretation was the prevailing common law position.

Although we recognize the force of the objection to the application of the *Hillmon* doctrine in the instant case,[4] we cannot conclude that the district court erred in allowing the testimony concerning Larry Adell's statements to be introduced.

---

3. *Statements Relating to Past Condition or Intent of Declarant*

As the plain text of the state-of-mind exception makes clear, state-of-mind statements must reflect the declarant's *current* intentions or intentions for the future. The rule prohibits statements as to what the declarant "intended" or "meant" to do at some point in time prior to the statement he is making.[5] Accordingly, a defendant could not introduce his own statement made after an altercation that he "never meant to hurt the victim" or "had been afraid" of the victim. Such backward-looking statements pose a greater risk of fabrication because the declarant has had time between the moment at which she *actually* experienced that condition or intent and the moment at which she is expressing it in her out-of-court statement. The gap between those times is time to fabricate.

---

4. Criticism of the *Hillmon* doctrine has come from very distinguished quarters, both judicial and academic. In his opinion for the Court in *Shepard v. United States*, 290 U.S. 96 (1933), Justice Benjamin Cardozo indicated in dicta an apparent hostility to the *Hillmon* doctrine. The Court reviewed the conviction of an army medical officer for the murder of his wife by poison. The asserted error by the trial court was its admission, over defense objection, of certain hearsay testimony by Mrs. Shepard's nurse concerning statements that Mrs. Shepard had made during her final illness. The nurse's testimony was that, after asking whether there was enough whiskey left in the bottle from which she had drunk just prior to her collapse to make a test for poison, Mrs. Shepard stated, "Dr. Shepard has poisoned me." One theory advanced by the Government on appeal was that the testimony was admissible to show that Mrs. Shepard did not have suicidal tendencies and, thus, to refute the defense argument that she took her own life. In rejecting the Government's theory, the Court refused to extend the state of mind exception to statements of memory. In his survey of the state of mind exception, Justice Cardozo appeared to suggest that the *Hillmon* doctrine is limited to "suits upon insurance policies." For a frequently cited academic critique of the *Hillmon* doctrine, see Maguire, *The Hillmon Case—Thirty-Three Years After*, 38 Harv. L. Rev. 709 (1925).

5. Some States, such as California, sometimes allow for the admission of statements of the declarant's state of mind, emotional condition, or physical condition "at a time prior to the statement." In California, for example, such statements may still be admitted if (1) the declarant is unavailable as a witness, (2) the prior state of mind "is itself an issue in the action and the evidence is not offered to prove any [other] fact," and (3) the statement is shown to be trustworthy. Cal. Evid. Code §§ 1251, 1252.

4. *Absolute Prohibition on Statements of Memory or Belief to Prove the Fact Remembered or Believed*

When a person expresses their then-existing mental condition, "I am afraid of the defendant," that condition is almost always the product of some preceding action or event, such as the defendant having previously assaulted the person. However, the state-of-mind exception does not allow the *reasons* for one's condition or intent to be admitted. Along similar lines, and as discussed in footnote 18 of the *Pheaster* case, the United States Supreme Court in *Shepard* ruled that a declarant's statement, "[Defendant] has poisoned me" could not be admitted as proof of her intent not to commit suicide (as suggested by defendant) because her declaration could also be understood as proof of her belief that defendant had, at some point in the past, actually poisoned her. The state-of-mind exception thus generally does not allow for the admission of the declarant's "statement of memory or belief to prove the fact remembered or believed." The exclusion of such statements is "necessary to avoid the virtual destruction of the hearsay rule that would otherwise result from allowing state of mind . . . to serve as the basis for an inference of the happening of an event which produced the state of mind." FRE 803, Adv. Comm. Note. This prohibition has one express, necessity-based exception: Past statements of memory or belief are admissible if they relate to the validity or terms of the declarant's will (because the declarant in this situation is, by definition, dead).[6]

Review Questions

1. **Feigned injury?** Defendant in an accident dispute claims that Plaintiff was not injured in the accident. Plaintiff seeks to call a witness who will testify, "As I approached her car, Plaintiff told me, 'The pain in my neck is the worst I have ever felt.'" Admissible?
2. **Calming Clyde.** Clyde is charged with killing Bonnie. Prosecutor wants to introduce evidence that the day before she was found dead, Bonnie sent an e-mail to her friend Angie stating, "I've got to go meet with Clyde to calm him down." Admissible?
3. **Friendly intentions.** The day before Bonnie is found dead, Clyde tells a friend, "Despite everything, I really like Bonnie. I hope we are friends forever." Clyde wants his friend to testify to the statement. Admissible?
4. **Uncomfortable environment.** Josie claims that she was sexually harassed at work and suffered great emotional distress. She wants to call her friend

6. Although most states have a similarly explicit carve out for wills, not all states do. New York does not, *People v. Reynoso,* 73 N.Y.2d 816, 819 (N.Y. 1988); *People v. Vasquez,* 88 N.Y.2d 561, 580 (N.Y. 1996), but still admits such statements under a *res gestae* (that is, totality of the transaction) theory, *In re Estate of Shlevin,* 157 Misc. 40 (N.Y. Surr. Ct. Richmond Co. 1935). Neither does California, but a decedent's then-existing intent at the time of executing the will would be admissible under California Evidence Code § 1251, which more generally permits statements of past state of mind if the declarant is unavailable (which a decedent necessarily is) and the statement is trustworthy.

Bill, who will testify that Josie said on several occasions, "I'm so depressed. It is hard to work in this environment." Admissible?

5. **The favored "son."** Jaymie is contesting his uncle's will. The will leaves $100,000 "to my favorite nephew, the one who always brought me chocolate." Jaymie claims that he was his uncle's favorite nephew. To prove that his uncle intended for him to get the $100,000, Jaymie wants to introduce evidence that his uncle told others, "Jaymie is a great kid. He is always bringing me chocolate, not like his brother, Brad, who is a real bum. I'll make sure to leave Jaymie a little something when I am gone."

PART D: STATEMENTS OF MEDICAL DIAGNOSIS OR TREATMENT [FRE 803(4)]

If a person goes to her doctor and reports her current medical condition, are those statements barred by the hearsay rule? Generally, the answer is "no" due to the exception for statements made for the purpose of medical diagnosis or treatment.[7]

The rationale for this exception is trustworthiness—namely, a declarant is strongly motivated to be truthful when seeking medical treatment. Although there is no guarantee that this will be true for all patients, especially those who might seek a diagnosis in anticipation of bringing a legal action, there is nevertheless a broad exception for statements to doctors, their assistants, medical personnel, or others who might convey information to a doctor about the patient's medical condition for purposes of diagnosis or treatment.

Examples

1. Andre is hit by a car. He tells the ambulance driver that he crossed the street and that he has a constant ringing in his ears.
2. Andre goes to the doctor's office. His partner tells the doctor's assistant that since the accident, Andre has not been able to eat and appears to be losing weight.

---

7. Not every jurisdiction has such an exception. California does not, making the state-of-mind exception the most applicable exception. However, California's state-of-mind exception covers only statements of *then-existing* medical condition. Nevertheless, California will admit trustworthy statements of *past* medical condition if the condition is at issue and the declarant is unavailable; California also has a special exception admitting trustworthy statements of persons under 12 years old describing "medical history, or past or present symptoms, pain, or sensations, or the inception or general character of the cause or external source thereof" if pertinent to medical diagnosis or treatment and if the statements relate to "child abuse or neglect." Cal. Evid. Code §§ 1251, 1253.

3. Andre's doctor refers him to a specialist. In doing so, the doctor tells the specialist, "My patient suffered a concussion when a car hit him."
4. Quinn goes to the hospital after being assaulted. During her exam, Quinn is asked who her assailant was. She tells the doctor that she was attacked by an older family member. The doctor seeks this information because she is concerned about her patient's psychological welfare.

Each of these statements is admissible under the exception for statements made for medical purposes. Specifically, FRE 803(4) provides the following:

FRE 803. Exceptions to the Rule Against Hearsay

The following are not excluded by the rule against hearsay, regardless of whether the declarant is available as a witness:

. . .

(4) Statement Made for Medical Diagnosis or Treatment. A statement that:

(A) is made for—and is reasonably pertinent to—medical diagnosis or treatment; and

(B) describes medical history; past or present symptoms or sensations; their inception; or their general cause.

Excerpts from Advisory Committee Notes to FRE 803

- Statements as to fault would not ordinarily qualify [under the "general cause" language].
- Under the exception the statement need not have been made to a physician. Statements to hospital attendants, ambulance drivers, or even members of the family might be included.

Thus, the hearsay exception for statements made for medical purposes has the following prerequisites:

Hearsay Exception for Statements Made for Medical Purposes

(1) The statement is made for medical diagnosis or treatment;
(2) The statement describes:
  (a) medical history;
  (b) past or present symptoms or sensations;
  (c) the inception of those symptoms or sensations; *or*
  (d) the general cause of the symptoms or sensations; *and*
(3) The statement is reasonably pertinent to such diagnosis or treatment.

1. *Is the Statement Made for Medical Diagnosis or Treatment?*

To be made for medical diagnosis or treatment, a statement need not be made to the medical professional actually tending to the declarant. Instead, courts have applied the exception to reach statements made to persons other than doctors as long as they are involved in patient intake or care. Thus, the statements and notes of nurses, physician assistants, and intake specialists are covered by the exception. For purposes of this rule, statements made for medical diagnosis or treatment can include statements made to psychologists and psychiatrists, although the federal courts are not uniform in whether the exception extends to statements made to social workers. *See Morgan v. Foretich*, 846 F.2d 941, 948-49 and n.17 (4th Cir. 1988) (psychologists and psychiatrists; within exception); *United States v. Newman*, 965 F.2d 206, 210 (7th Cir. 1992) (same); *United States v. Kappell*, 418 F.3d 550, 556 (6th Cir. 2005) (same); *cf. United States v. Cain*, 603 Fed. Appx. 840, 843-44 (11th Cir. 2015) (clinical social workers; not "clear" whether exception applies).

What if the declarant is someone who is so young that he or she does not understand the significance of speaking with a medical professional (and hence does not have the same incentive to tell the truth that older children and adults understand)? Most courts have held that the exception still applies.

Does the exception reach persons who are speaking on behalf of the victim-patient? For instance, if a person is suffering from food poisoning and is delirious, is the statement by a person's spouse's to an attending EMT that "he ate that deli sandwich and then started to bleed from his gums" a statement made for medical diagnosis or treatment? As a general matter, yes.

Does the exception reach statements from the *doctor* to others? It depends. If one medical professional is communicating with another regarding the patient's condition in order to provide treatment, yes. If the doctor is just telling the patient information not designed in any way to diagnose or treat the patient, the exception would not apply.

2. *Does the Statement Fall into Any of the Categories Covered by the Exception?*

The exception limits itself to statements "describ[ing]" one of four different categories of information:

- The patient's medical history;
- The patient's past or present symptoms or sensations;
- The inception of those symptoms or sensations; or
- The "general cause" of those symptoms or sensations.

These categories can encompass other hearsay. For instance, a patient knows her medical history likely because prior doctors have *told her* what conditions she had.

These categories are both broader and narrower than the state-of-mind exception. As noted above, the state-of-mind exception reaches statements of a person's *then-existing* "physical condition." The state-of-mind exception is broader than the medical diagnosis and treatment exception because it does not require that the statement be "made for . . . medical diagnosis or treatment"; under the state-of-mind exception, any reason will do. The state-of-mind exception is appreciably narrower than the medical diagnosis and treatment exception because it pertains only to the patient's *then-existing* symptoms or sensations—it does not reach *past* symptoms or sensations, their inception, or their cause.

3. *Is the Statement "Reasonably Pertinent" to Medical Diagnosis or Treatment?*

This prerequisite places the greatest limitation on this hearsay exception.[8] The exception encompasses the "inception" and "general cause" of a person's symptoms or conditions and thus ostensibly reaches what led up to those symptoms or conditions, who inflicted them, and whether that person was at fault. But the identity of who inflicted the injuries and who was at fault are not usually reasonably pertinent to medical diagnosis or treatment. A doctor needs to know that the patient's leg is broken; whether the cause of the femur break was the patient's roommate who attacked her without provocation does not help the doctor diagnose or treat the patient. Consequently, that additional information is not covered by the exception and thus is barred by the hearsay rule (unless some other exception applies).

However, there may be some wiggle room. What if the patient is in a position to be harmed again by the person who caused the injury? Isn't knowing the identity of that person relevant to the treatment insofar as it would avoid further infliction of harm? This issue comes up most often in cases where a child is physically or sexually harmed by someone with access to them in the future. That was the case in *United States v. Kootswatewa.*

United States v. Kootswatewa

893 F.3d 1127 (9th Cir. 2018)

WATFORD, Judge.

Theodore Kootswatewa was convicted following a jury trial of sexually abusing K.C., a developmentally delayed 11-year-old girl. On appeal, Kootswatewa challenges two of the district court's evidentiary rulings. Over Kootswatewa's hearsay objections, the court allowed a nurse practitioner and a law enforcement officer to testify about statements K.C. made to them during interviews conducted shortly after the abuse occurred. We conclude that the district court properly exercised its discretion in admitting the testimony of both witnesses.

I

Kootswatewa and K.C., both members of the Hopi Tribe, lived in the same small community on the Hopi Reservation in Arizona. Early one evening, a neighbor saw K.C. follow a man into an abandoned trailer. Soon after, as the neighbor

---

8. Some states, such as Illinois, also exclude from this exception statements made to a health care provider who is consulted solely for purposes of litigation. Ill. R. Evid. 803(4).

approached the trailer to investigate, she saw K.C. emerge looking scared. K.C. told the neighbor that the man had tried to "rape" her. The neighbor identified the man as Kootswatewa when he walked out of the trailer moments later. The neighbor called the police and contacted K.C.'s mother.

The morning after the abuse occurred, K.C.'s mother took her to a part of the outpatient pediatric wing of the Flagstaff Medical Center, called the Safe Child Center. K.C. saw a nurse practitioner there who was certified as a Sexual Assault Nurse Examiner. The nurse practitioner conducted a sexual assault examination of K.C., during which K.C. said that a man who lived in a red house had recently touched her vagina. . . . (Multiple witnesses testified that Kootswatewa lived in a red cinder-block house.) At trial, during the government's case-in-chief, the district court allowed the nurse practitioner to recount K.C.'s statements, again over the defense's hearsay objection. The court ruled that the statements were admissible under the hearsay exception for statements made for purposes of medical diagnosis or treatment. See Fed. R. Evid. 803(4).

The jury convicted Kootswatewa of aggravated sexual abuse of a minor.

II

We first address Kootswatewa's challenge to the admission of the nurse practitioner's testimony under Rule 803(4) of the Federal Rules of Evidence. Under that provision, out-of-court statements made for purposes of medical diagnosis or treatment are admissible as an exception to the hearsay rule, which generally forbids admission of out-of-court statements offered to prove the truth of the matter asserted. A statement is admissible under Rule 803(4) if it: "(A) is made for—and is reasonably pertinent to—medical diagnosis or treatment; and (B) describes medical history; past or present symptoms or sensations; their inception; or their general cause." Fed. R. Evid. 803(4). A statement covered by Rule 803(4) is admissible as substantive evidence, regardless of whether the declarant is available to testify.

Statements covered by Rule 803(4) are admissible because the rationale for excluding hearsay statements does not apply to them. Hearsay statements are inadmissible as a general rule because they typically lack indicia of trustworthiness. Unlike testimony offered in court, hearsay statements are not made under oath and the declarant is not subject to cross-examination, so the accuracy and reliability of the statements cannot be tested. Certain categories of out-of-court statements, however, are excepted from the rule against hearsay because they are made under circumstances in which the declarant would be particularly unlikely to lie. Statements made for purposes of medical diagnosis or treatment comprise one such category. An individual seeking medical care is unlikely to lie about her medical history or symptoms because she knows that "a false statement may cause misdiagnosis or mistreatment." The declarant's selfish interest in obtaining appropriate medical care renders statements made for purposes of diagnosis or treatment inherently trustworthy, such that "adversarial testing [through cross-examination] would add little to their reliability."

The district court properly exercised its discretion in admitting K.C.'s statements to the nurse practitioner because the statements fall comfortably within the scope of Rule 803(4). K.C. spoke to the nurse practitioner as part of a sexual assault examination. As the nurse practitioner testified, one of the purposes of such an examination is to diagnose any physical, psychological, or emotional injuries the victim may have suffered and to prescribe an appropriate course of treatment. To diagnose and treat K.C.'s injuries, the nurse practitioner first had to find out what happened to her, and so she asked K.C., "Did something happen?" K.C.'s statements describing the abuse she suffered were made in response to that question. The statements satisfied both prongs of Rule 803(4): They were made for purposes of medical diagnosis or treatment and were "reasonably pertinent" to that subject; and they described the "inception" or "general cause" of K.C.'s past or present symptoms. In that respect, K.C.'s statements are no different from the statements we have held admissible in past cases involving child sexual abuse.

Kootswatewa contends that the government failed to lay an adequate foundation for admission of K.C.'s statements under Rule 803(4). In particular, he asserts that although the government established that the nurse practitioner elicited the statements for purposes of medical diagnosis or treatment, the government did not establish what K.C. herself was thinking when she made the statements. As Kootswatewa correctly points out. it is the declarant's understanding of the purposes for which the statements were made that matters under Rule 803(4).

Contrary to Kootswatewa's contention, however, the declarant herself need not testify about her subjective thought process at the time she made the statements in question. Indeed, the declarant need not testify at all. An adequate foundation may be laid under Rule 803(4) by introducing objective evidence of the context in which the statements were made. That evidence can include testimony provided by the medical professional who conducted the examination.

Here, the government presented ample evidence supporting the inference that K.C. understood that the nurse practitioner was seeking information for purposes of diagnosis or treatment. Most significantly, K.C. made the statements in response to questions posed by a medical professional during a medical examination conducted at a medical facility. Absent evidence indicating otherwise, the district court could reasonably infer from those circumstances that K.C. understood she was providing information for purposes of diagnosis or treatment. That inference was bolstered by the nurse practitioner's testimony that she conducted K.C.'s examination in an examination room, with her stethoscope on, after measuring K.C.'s height and weight and taking her medical history.

Kootswatewa contends that, even if K.C.'s statements describing the nature of her abuse were admissible under Rule 803(4), her statement identifying the perpetrator was not. Some courts and commentators have held that statements identifying the perpetrator of a crime are not pertinent to medical diagnosis or treatment and therefore fall outside the scope of Rule 803(4) and its state-law counterparts. Our court has squarely rejected that view, at least in cases involving child sexual abuse. We have held that medical providers need to know who abused a child in order to protect her from future abuse at the hands of the same perpetrator, and to assist in diagnosing and treating the psychological and emotional injuries caused by sexual abuse. The nurse practitioner in this case testified that she asks her patients about the identity of their abuser for precisely these reasons.

In short, the government laid an adequate foundation for the admission of K.C.'s statements concerning the nature of the abuse and the identity of her abuser. The district court properly admitted the statements under Rule 803(4).

The FRE 803(4) exception's requirements can be illustrated as follows:

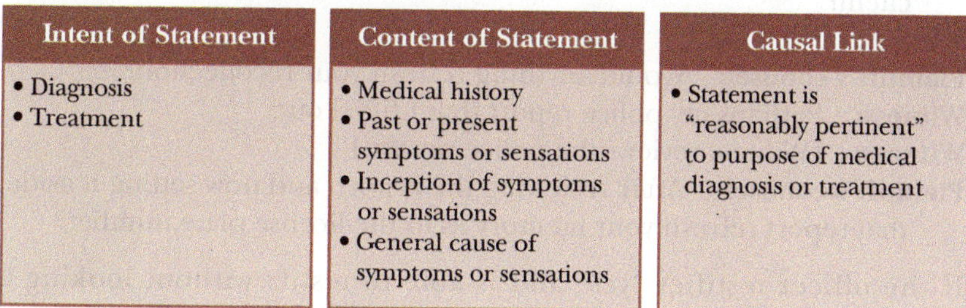

Intent of Statement
• Diagnosis
• Treatment
Content of Statement
• Medical history
• Past or present symptoms or sensations
• Inception of symptoms or sensations
• General cause of symptoms or sensations
Causal Link
• Statement is "reasonably pertinent" to purpose of medical diagnosis or treatment

Review Questions

Elder abuse. Defendant is charged with elder abuse of his 85-year-old great-aunt. Prosecutor seeks to call the aunt's physician to testify that when he examined her, the aunt reported that she had gotten bad stomach pains every time after Defendant came by to fix her macaroni and cheese.

1. May the physician testify to all portions of the aunt's statement?
   a. The nature of her symptoms?
   b. Their timing?
   c. The suspected cause?
2. What if the aunt is available to testify? Does that affect the admissibility of the physician's testimony?

PART E: PAST RECOLLECTION RECORDED [FRE 803(5)]

Consider the scenario in which a witness takes the witness stand but cannot remember some crucial information for their testimony. The first thing the lawyer examining the witness will try to do is refresh the witness's recollection—that is, ask questions or show the witness something to jog the witness's memory. *Anything* can be used to refresh recollection because that thing is not ever admitted into evidence. Thus, if the witness is trying to remember a conversation that happened in a coffee shop, the lawyer can attempt to refresh the witness's recollection by waving a spiced espresso under the witness's nose, assuming that the smell will help the witness remember. The goal is to try to get the witness to be able to testify, "Oh, yes, *now* I remember" and to thereafter testify.

Consider the following scenario:

Plaintiff's counsel: Mr. Witness, did you see a car hit my client on November 4, 2020?

Witness: Yes.

Plaintiff's counsel: Do you remember the license plate of the car that hit my client?
Witness: No.
Plaintiff's counsel: Would anything refresh your recollection?
Witness: Perhaps my police report that I filled out.
Witness: [Witness reviews the police report.]
Plaintiff's counsel: After reviewing the report, and now setting it aside, does that report refresh your memory as to the license plate number?

If the officer testifies "yes" and is able to testify without looking at the report—that is, from her memory *while on the stand*—the problem is solved and the witness is able to testify to the previously forgotten fact.

This strategy is called refreshing a witness's recollection. When refreshing is done by showing the witness a writing, FRE 612 sets forth the special procedures that must be followed when a writing is involved. Those procedures require the party doing the refreshing to provide the adverse party with a copy of the writing, suffer the consequences of having the witness's refreshed testimony stricken, or, worse yet, have a mistrial declared. In light of this obligation to provide the adverse party with a copy of the writing used to refresh, any document shown to a witness—including while preparing the witness to testify prior to trial—may lose its privileged status and become discoverable by the adverse party. *E.g., Adidas Am., Inc. v. TRB Acquisitions, LLC*, 324 F.R.D. 389, 397 (D. Or. 2017). Specifically, FRE 612 provides the following:

FRE 612. Writing Used to Refresh a Witness

(a) Scope. This rule gives an adverse party certain options when a witness uses a writing to refresh memory:

(1) while testifying; or

(2) before testifying, if the court decides that justice requires the party to have those options.

(b) Adverse Party's Options; Deleting Unrelated Matter. Unless 18 U.S.C. § 3500 provides otherwise in a criminal case, an adverse party is entitled to have the writing produced at the hearing, to inspect it, to cross-examine the witness about it, and to introduce in evidence any portion that relates to the witness's testimony. If the producing party claims that the writing includes unrelated matter, the court must examine the writing in camera, delete any unrelated portion, and order that the rest be delivered to the adverse party. Any portion deleted over objection must be preserved for the record.

(c) Failure to Produce or Deliver the Writing. If a writing is not produced or is not delivered as ordered, the court may issue any appropriate order. But if the prosecution does not comply in a criminal case, the court must strike the witness's testimony or—if justice so requires—declare a mistrial.

But what if the testifying witness responds, "No, my memory isn't refreshed"?

If the witness had, at some point in the past, written down or adopted notes of the event that he was unable to remember, the colloquy could continue:

Plaintiff's counsel: At the time of the accident, did you make any notes as to what you saw?

Witness: Yes, I wrote down the license plate number on a card.

Plaintiff's counsel: Were your notes accurate at the time you made them?

Witness: Yes.

Plaintiff's counsel: Your Honor, we would ask the witness to read from his notes the license plate of the car.

Because the prior written notes are the witness's out-of-court statements admitted for their truth, they are hearsay and must fall within a hearsay exception. The pertinent exception is called "past recollection recorded" and is found in FRE 803(5).

Specifically, FRE 803(5) provides the following:

FRE 803. Exceptions to the Rule Against Hearsay

The following are not excluded by the rule against hearsay, regardless of whether the declarant is available as a witness:

. . .

(5) Recorded Recollection. A record that:

(A) is on a matter the witness once knew about but now cannot recall well enough to testify fully and accurately;

(B) was made or adopted by the witness when the matter was fresh in the witness's memory; and

(C) accurately reflects the witness's knowledge.

If admitted, the record may be read into evidence but may be received as an exhibit only if offered by an adverse party.

Thus, the hearsay exception for past recollection recorded has the following prerequisites:

Hearsay Exception for Past Recollection Recorded

(1) The witness cannot recall a matter well enough to testify fully and accurately about it now;

(2) The witness made or adopted a record on that matter;

(3) The record was made or adopted when the matter was fresh in the witness's memory; *and*

(4) The record accurately reflects the witness's knowledge.

1. *Sufficient Lack of Memory*

The exception applies only if the witness lacks insufficient recollection to testify about the matter at issue now. It is up to the trial judge to decide whether a witness once knew the matter and currently lacks a memory of it. To establish a lack of memory, the court may require that counsel try to refresh a witness's memory. The court may also determine whether the witness is feigning a lack of memory. If it appears to the court that a witness is engaging in selective memory loss, the court may disallow use of the exception. *See, e.g., United States v. Williams,* 571 F.2d 344 (6th Cir. 1978). In establishing whether the witness once had firsthand knowledge of a matter, the court may consider all the circumstances of a case.

2. *Witness "Made or Adopted" a Record on the Matter*

The past recollection recorded need not be something authored by the witness. Even if someone else wrote it out, it is enough if the witness adopted it as being accurate.

3. *The Record Was Made When the Matter Was Fresh in the Witness's Memory*

There is no set time limit on when a record must be made or adopted. The closer in time to the events, the more likely the court will accept the record as being made when it was fresh in the witness's mind and the greater likelihood that the record will be seen as accurately reflecting the witness's knowledge. However, there are cases, such as *United States v. Kortright,* in which records made weeks or months after an event are sufficiently fresh to meet the requirement. Other courts disagree, especially when the witness has not specifically reviewed the record made by a third person of their statement.

United States v. Kortright

2011 U.S. Dist. LEXIS 107386 (S.D.N.Y. 2011)

Wood, Judge.

David Kortright ("Defendant") was charged in a one-count indictment, filed on October 12, 2010, with participating in a conspiracy to possess and distribute five grams and more of cocaine base, or "crack" cocaine. [Defendant brought a motion to suppress evidence seized during his arrest.]

A. BACKGROUND

At the Court's May 31, 2011 hearing and oral argument on this suppression motion, Officer Roekthanom testified that he did not have any independent recollection of the events surrounding Defendant's January 12, 2010 arrest. Officer Roekthanom also testified that, even after he reviewed all of the documents related to the arrest, those documents did not refresh his recollection of the events surrounding the arrest. Accordingly, Officer Roekthanom read into the record narrative portions from various documents, pursuant to Federal Rule of Evidence 803(5), the "recorded recollection" exception to the rule against hearsay.

The narrative portions came from: (1) a memo book containing entries he made on January 12, 2010; (2) an arrest report and complaint report that he prepared on January 12, 2010, in relation to Defendant's arrest; (3) an affidavit contained in a criminal complaint prepared by an assistant district attorney on January 13, 2010, based on Officer Roekthanom's sworn statements regarding the January 12, 2010 events; and (4) Officer Roekthanom's grand jury testimony, given on March 5, 2010.

Defendant contends that Officer Roekthanom's grand jury testimony is not admissible under Rule 803(5), and that, even with the testimony, the documentary evidence regarding the events of January 12, 2010 is "scant and contain[s] significant gaps, which cast doubt on the credibility of the officer's claims."

The Government . . . responds that allowing Officer Roekthanom to read portions of the grand jury testimony is permissible under the "recollection recorded" rule.

1. Admissibility

As discussed above, Officer Roekthanom, the only witness called by the Government at the suppression hearing, testified that he has no independent recollection of the events surrounding Defendant's January 12, 2010 arrest. He also testified that, even after he reviewed all of the documents related to that day, those documents did not refresh his recollection. Accordingly, Officer Roekthanom was forced to rely exclusively on descriptions of the January 12, 2010 events that were contained in various memoranda, and he read those descriptions into the record, pursuant to Rule 803(5).

Rule 803(5) is an exception to the rule against hearsay for recorded recollections. To constitute a recorded recollection, a memorandum must "concern[] a matter about which a witness once had knowledge but now has insufficient recollection to enable the witness to testify fully and accurately, [and be] shown to have been made or adopted by the witness when the matter was fresh in the witness memory and to reflect that knowledge correctly." Fed. R. Evid. 803(5). If admitted under Rule 803(5), the memorandum may be read into evidence, but may not itself be received as an exhibit unless offered by an adverse party. Before any document can be read into evidence under Rule 803(5), the proponent of the memorandum must establish that: (i) the witness's "memory of the events detailed in the memorandum was sufficiently impaired"; (ii) the witness had "prepared or adopted the memorandum at or near the time of the events" at issue; and (iii) at the time the witness "prepared or adopted [the memorandum], it correctly reflected his knowledge of the events."

Defendant concedes that the memo book, arrest and complaint reports, and affidavit satisfy the requirements under 803(5). Defendant contends, however, that Officer Roekthanom's grand jury testimony is not admissible under Rule 803(5) because (1) it was removed in time from the January 12, 2010 arrest by nearly two months; and (2) Officer Roekthanom never reviewed or adopted the record of his testimony at a time when he still possessed an independent recollection of the January 12, 2010 events.

With respect to Defendant's argument that the grand jury testimony is not admissible because it was removed in time from the arrest by nearly two months, it is true that, in the principal decisions where courts have admitted evidence under Rule 803(5), the documents were created within days or even hours of the time of the event in question. However, there are also decisions in which the timing between the event in question and the creation of the document is unclear, but, because the witness testified that he made or adopted the document "when the subject was fresh in [his] memory," the document is admitted under Rule 803(5).

Here, although the grand jury testimony was given on March 5, 2010, nearly two months after Defendant's arrest, Officer Roekthanom testified twice that, at the time he gave his grand jury testimony, the events were fresh in his mind. The Court credits this testimony. See *United States v. Patterson*, 678 F.2d 774, 779 (9th Cir. 1982) (admitting grand jury testimony that was at least ten months old, and describing Rule 803(5) as a "flexible rule giving the trial judge discretion to determine freshness on a 'case-by-case basis giving consideration to all pertinent aspects . . . which reasonably and properly bear upon the likelihood of the statement being an accurate recordation of the event to which the memory related'").

Defendant's argument that Officer Roekthanom never reviewed or adopted the record of his grand jury testimony presents a more complex issue. Because Officer Roekthanom did not himself transcribe his grand jury testimony, Rule 803(5) would appear on its face to require that he have reviewed or adopted the testimony at a time when the substance of the testimony was still fresh in his mind. During the suppression hearing, Officer Roekthanom testified that he was not shown a transcript of his grand jury testimony right after he testified; rather, the first time he was shown the transcript was in February 2011, in preparation for this Court's suppression hearing. Defense counsel noted that, had there . . . been a mistake in the transcript, Officer Roekthanom would not have known, because he did not review and verify the transcript.

There does not appear to be any decision in this circuit addressing the precise issue of the admission of grand jury testimony under Rule 803(5). The Court finds that Officer Roekthanom's grand jury testimony is admissible under Rule 803(5). Although Officer Roekthanom did not review the testimony and confirm that it reflected what he had said, his grand jury testimony was taken under oath and was recorded by a court reporter. Further, the grand jury testimony is certified; on the last page of the transcript, the court reporter swore that "the within transcript is a true and accurate record of the testimony given in [Defendant's] case." In addition, Officer Roekthanom has repeatedly stated that, at the time of his grand jury testimony, the events of January 12, 2010 were fresh in his mind.

---

4. *Record Must Accurately Reflect the Witness's Knowledge*

The record need not be a complete report of an event. The issue is whether it accurately reflects the witness's knowledge on the specific point for which it is being offered. A witness can establish the accurate reflection by so testifying. However, if the witness testifies that the prior record does *not* accurately reflect his memory at the time, the exception does not apply. Thus, if a recalcitrant witness shown a copy of his signed confession says, "No, that's not accurate," the confession does not qualify for admission under this exception.

5. *Limitation on Form of Evidence*

It is critical to remember that this exception does not allow the prior record *itself* to be admitted into evidence. Instead, it allows the witness to read the relevant portions of the record into the record. To prevent the record from having too much impact on the jury, the record itself cannot be introduced by the party calling the witness. It is up to the *adverse party* to decide whether to introduce the record itself as an exhibit.[9]

Review Question

1. **Foggy on the date.** Witness is testifying in a murder case. He forgets what date he saw Defendant with the victim. After trying to refresh his recollection, Prosecutor asks the witness to read from the following notations. Is each permissible?
   a. The witness's notation on his electronic diary?
   b. A transcript of a voice message the witness left on his phone?
   c. A report that he gave the detectives when they interviewed him a week later after the victim was found dead?

PART F: BUSINESS RECORDS AND THE ABSENCE OF BUSINESS RECORDS [FRE 803(6), (7)]

Business entities of all shapes and sizes maintain records that enable them to operate. Hospitals maintain records of their patients, their suppliers, and their staff. Commercial businesses maintain records of their suppliers, their customers, their inventory, and their employees. These businesses rely on these records to operate. As a result, business records are generally considered to be more trustworthy because businesses have a built-in incentive to maintain accurate records. Because businesses often do hundreds and thousands—if not hundreds of thousands—of transactions every year, their employees will rarely remember a single transaction, even though a specific transaction may end up being the crux of later litigation. In light of the inherent trustworthiness of business records as well as the practical

9. Not all states have adopted this limit. New York and Illinois have not. *People v. Taylor*, 80 N.Y.2d 1, 8 (N.Y. 1992); Ill. R. Evid. 803(5).

necessity of looking to records when witnesses having specific recollections are unlikely to come forward, every jurisdiction has a hearsay exception for business records.

Examples

1. Defendant is charged with income tax evasion. Prosecutors seek to introduce bank records that show that Defendant had $100,000 cash in his account as well as records from companies that made payments to Defendant.
2. Plaintiff wants to prove that at the time of the accident, Defendant was on her cell phone. Plaintiff introduces the call records from Defendant's cell phone carrier.

In the first example, the businesses are the bank and various payor companies; in the second, the cell phone carrier. In both examples, the businesses maintain voluminous records regarding the transactions in which their customers engage. That they maintain these records electronically (rather than in a hard-copy form) is of no consequence; the records are just as likely to be trustworthy. The requirements of the business records exception are designed to ensure that these are the types of records that are reliable enough to be used by the trier of fact.

Specifically, FRE 803(6) provides the following:

FRE 803. Exceptions to the Rule Against Hearsay

The following are not excluded by the rule against hearsay, regardless of whether the declarant is available as a witness:

. . .

(6) Records of a Regularly Conducted Activity. A record of an act, event, condition, opinion, or diagnosis if:

(A) the record was made at or near the time by—or from information transmitted by—someone with knowledge;

(B) the record was kept in the course of regularly conducted activity of a business, organization, occupation, or calling, whether or not for profit;

(C) making the record was a regular practice of that activity;

(D) all of these conditions are shown by the testimony of the custodian or another qualified witness, or by a certification that complies with [FRE] 902(11) or (12) or with a statute permitting certification; and

(E) the opponent does not show that the possible source of information or the method or circumstances of preparation indicate a lack of trustworthiness.

Excerpts from Advisory Committee Notes to FRE 803

- The element of unusual reliability of business records is said variously to be supplied by systematic checking, by regularity and continuity which produce habits of precision, by actual experience of business in relying upon them, or by a duty to make an accurate record as part of the continuing job or occupation.
- With "ordinary business records," [a]ll participants, including the observer or participant furnishing the information to be recorded, were acting routinely, under a duty of accuracy, with employer reliance on the result, or in short "in the regular course of business." If, however, the supplier of the information does not act in the regular course, an essential link is broken.
- [FRE 803(6)] specifically includes both diagnoses and opinions, in addition to acts, events, and conditions, as proper subjects of admissible entries.

Thus, the hearsay exception for business records has the following prerequisites:

Hearsay Exception for Business Records

(1) The record was made at or near the time of the act, event, condition, opinion, or diagnosis either by (a) by someone with knowledge or (b) from information transmitted by someone with knowledge;

(2) The record was kept in the course of a regularly conducted activity of a business, organization, occupation, or calling, whether or not for profit;

(3) Making the record was a regular practice of the business's regularly conducted activity; *and*

(4) All of these conditions are shown by (a) the testimony of the custodian of records or other qualified witness or (b) by a certification that complies with FRE 902(11) or (12) or with another statute permitting such certification;

UNLESS

The opponent of the evidence shows the source of information or method or circumstances show a lack of trustworthiness.

1. The Record Was Made at or Near the Time of the Act, Event, Condition, Opinion, or Diagnosis Either (a) by Someone with Knowledge or (b) from Information Transmitted by Someone with Knowledge

By requiring that the record be made near or at the time of the event from someone who had access to firsthand information, the rule ensures a greater likelihood of reliability. For example, if the record involves the sale of a good, the record may be the receipt created by the seller or an invoice sent to the buyer. The record could be made by the salesperson or a member of the staff or accounting department who has the responsibility of making such records based on information submitted to them by the salespersons.

By defining a business record to include records made not only by an employee of the business with knowledge, but also to include records made from information transmitted by someone else with knowledge, the business records exception might be read as applying to records that contain information supplied by "outsiders"—that is, people who do not work for or owe any duties to the business. That reading is ostensibly supported by the text of the rule, which does not expressly require that the person with knowledge of the act, event, condition, opinion, or diagnosis be associated with the business. On the other hand, the Advisory Committee Note seems to suggest that the person supplying knowledge be associated with the business. It alludes to the "observer or participant furnishing the information to be recorded" "acting routinely" and "under a duty of accuracy" as an implicit requirement of the record being made "in the regular course of business."

Thus, when the information placed in a business record comes from an "outsider," there are two possible ways to examine whether that information is admissible.

First, one can view the information from the outsider as falling outside the reach of the business records exception, such that it would constitute a separate layer of hearsay that would require a separate hearsay exception be applicable (as is required by FRE 805). *E.g., Petrocelli v. Gallison*, 679 F.2d 286, 291 (1st Cir. 1982). For instance, the patient's statements to his doctor that are part of a hospital's business records would likely fall within the hearsay exception for statements involving medical diagnosis or treatment (under FRE 803(4)) and so, by virtue of that hearsay exception, are deemed to be trustworthy. Along similar lines, if a florist incorporates purchase orders it receives from its customers into its own business records, those purchase orders are likely to fall within the hearsay exception for business records *of the customer* (under FRE 803(6)) and so, by virtue of that hearsay exception, are deemed to be trustworthy. This type of analysis can be represented graphically:

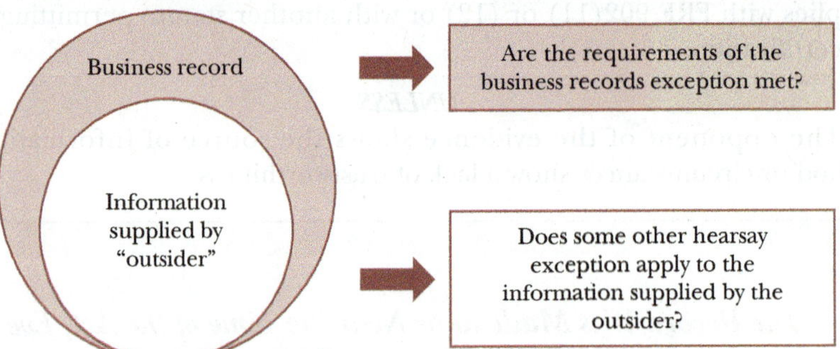

Second, and alternatively, one can view the information from the outsider as falling within the reach of the business records exception. *See generally Rambus, Inc. v. Infineon Tech. AG*, 348 F. Supp. 2d 698, 707-08 (E.D. Va. 2004). However, doing so creates a tension: Part of the reason business records are excepted from the hearsay rule is their inherent trustworthiness, which comes in part from the fact that a business's employees will get into trouble if they do not help the business maintain accurate records. But outsiders do not have that incentive. Is there some danger that the information they supply—and that can be part of a record that qualifies as a business record under this approach—is less likely to be accurate? Yes, there is. However, the business records exception, if viewed as encompassing the outsider's statements, ensures that the records are nevertheless sufficiently reliable through two of the *other* requirements of the business records exception—namely, (1) the record must be part of the business's regularly conducted activity (which assures reliability because it assures that the business is regularly relying on those records), and (2) the record must be trustworthy (which, by definition, assures reliability). Trustworthiness, as noted above, may be satisfied by a showing that the information supplied by the "outsider" falls into a hearsay exception. Thus, if a doctor is deemed to be an "outsider" to the hospital (because she is a visiting physician not employed by the hospital), this approach would ask whether there are reasons to believe that the doctor's entries into the hospital's records are trustworthy. This tension, and resulting accommodation, is illustrated by *Lewis v. Baker.*

Lewis v. Baker

526 F.2d 470 (2d Cir. 1975)

WATERMAN, Judge.

Plaintiff, Clifford J. Lewis, Jr., brought this action pursuant to the Federal Employers' Liability Act, alleging he suffered a disabling injury while employed by the Penn Central Railroad.

On the date of his injury Plaintiff was employed as a freight brakeman or car dropper in the Penn Central railroad freight yard. His work called for him to move freight cars in a railroad yard by riding them down a slope while applying the brake manually. [He claimed his injury occurred when the handbrake on a boxcar he was moving failed to hold.]

At the trial, defendants sought to rebut plaintiff's allegations of a faulty brake with evidence that the brake had functioned properly immediately prior to the accident when the plaintiff tested it, and immediately after the accident when it was checked in connection with the preparation of an accident report. It was the defendants' contention that plaintiff improperly set, or forgot to set, a necessary brake handle, panicked, and then leapt from the car.

In support of their interpretation of the events, defendants offered into evidence a "personal injury report" and an "inspection report." Frank Talbott, a trainmaster, testified that the personal injury report was signed by him and prepared under his supervision. The information had been provided to him by William F. Campbell, the night trainmaster. Talbott confirmed the authenticity of the record and testified that he was required to make out such reports of injuries as part of the regular course of business. At the trial David W. Halderman, an assistant general foreman for the defendants, identified the inspection report which had been prepared by Campbell and by Alfred Zuchero, a gang foreman. This report was based upon an inspection of the car Campbell and Zuchero had conducted less than four hours after the accident. Halderman testified that Zuchero was dead and that Campbell was employed by a railroad in Virginia. The latter was thus beyond the reach of subpoena. Halderman also confirmed that following every accident involving injury to an employee his office was required to complete inspection reports, and that such reports were regularly kept in the course of business. Over objection, the court admitted both reports into evidence.

Determination of the admissibility of these reports under the Federal Business Records Act[10] involves two problems: whether the reports are business records within that statute, and whether the fact that the accident report was prepared by an employee who had neither firsthand knowledge of the accident nor had inspected the purportedly defective car and brake affects admissibility into evidence.

As a preliminary matter, there is little doubt that these reports are each a "writing or record, whether in the form of an entry in a book or otherwise, made as a memorandum or record of any act, transaction, occurrence, or event, . . ." Furthermore, it is beyond dispute that these reports were made pursuant to a regular procedure at the railroad yard, and that Talbott, Campbell and Zuchero made the reports within a reasonable time after the accident. Appellant argues, however, that notwithstanding the presence of those factors which would indicate a full compliance with 28 U.S.C. § 1732, the Supreme Court's decision in *Palmer v. Hoffman*, 318 U.S. 109 (1943), precludes their admission into evidence. There the Court upheld the inadmissibility of an accident report offered by the defendant railroad that had been prepared by one of its locomotive engineers. The Court stated that since the report was not prepared "for the systematic conduct of the business as a business," it was not "made 'in the regular course' of the business" of the railroad. We find significant differences between the report and the circumstances of its making in that case and the facts here, and we uphold the district court's admission of the records below.

In *Palmer v. Hoffman*, the engineer preparing the report had been personally involved in the accident, and, the engineer knew "at the time of making it that he [was] very likely, in a probable lawsuit relating to that accident, to be charged with wrongdoing as a participant in the accident, so that he [was] almost certain, when making the memorandum or report, to be sharply affected by a desire to exculpate himself and to relieve himself or his employer of liability." Here there could have

---

10. 28 U.S.C. § 1732 provides, insofar as is applicable:

Record made in regular course of business * * *

(a) In any court of the United States and in any court established by Act of Congress, any writing or record, whether in the form of an entry in a book or otherwise, made as a memorandum or record of any act, transaction, occurrence, or event, shall be admissible as evidence of such act, transaction, occurrence, or event, if made in regular course of any business, and if it was the regular course of such business to make such memorandum or record at the time of such act, transaction, occurrence, or event or within a reasonable time thereafter.

All other circumstances of the making of such writing or record, including lack of personal knowledge by the entrant or maker, may be shown to affect its weight, but such circumstances shall not affect its admissibility.

The term "business," as used in this section, includes business, profession, occupation, and calling of every kind.

been no similar motivation on the part of Talbott, Campbell or Zuchero, for not one of them was involved in the accident, or could have possibly been the target of a lawsuit by Lewis. In *Palmer v. Hoffman*, "[obviously] the Supreme Court was concerned about a likely untrustworthiness of materials prepared specifically by a prospective litigant for courtroom use." The fact that a report embodies an employee's version of the accident, or happens to work in favor of the entrant's employer, does not, without more, indicate untrustworthiness. In the absence of a motive to fabricate, a motive so clearly spelled out in *Palmer v. Hoffman*, the holding in that case is not controlling. Therefore the trial court must look to those earmarks of reliability which otherwise establish the trustworthiness of the record.

Here the ICC requires the employer to prepare and file monthly reports of all accidents involving railroad employees. Assistant general foreman Halderman testified that following every injury he was required to inspect the equipment involved and to report the results of the inspection on a regular printed form. "[I]t would ill become a court to say that the regular making of reports required by law is not in the regular course of business."

The fact that the trainmaster Talbott completed the personal injury report based on information supplied to him by a third person, Campbell, does not render the report inadmissible.

---

2. *The Record Is Kept in the Course of a Regularly Conducted Activity of a Business, Organization, Occupation, or Calling*

The business records exception is designed to apply to a *very wide* variety of entities. As noted above, this exception rests on a trustworthiness rationale similar to the one that the Federal Rules use to distinguish admissible habit evidence from inadmissible propensity evidence (see Chapter Three)—namely, that regularity breeds consistency and hence greater reliability. Thus, any type of organization that follows regular procedures may maintain records subject to the business records exception. The organization may be a giant corporation or a sole proprietorship; it may be a for-profit or a nonprofit; it may be a lawful enterprise or an illegal one (such as a gambling casino or illicit drug cartel).[11]

Traditionally, the business records exception applied only to records of *acts*, *events*, or *conditions* regularly made and kept by a business; it did *not* apply to records of *opinions* or *diagnoses*. Thus, the medical diagnoses or opinions of psychologists recorded in medical records fell outside the rule. Although some states maintain this distinction,[12] the Federal Rules of Evidence did away with it, and the business records exception in the rules encompasses opinions and diagnoses as well. This approach has allowed the business records exception to encompass a broader array

11. Some states, such as Illinois, declare that the business records exception does not apply to medical records, at least in criminal cases. *See* Ill. R. Evid. 803(6).

12. California is one such state. See Cal. Evid. Code, § 1271(b).

of business records maintained by hospitals and other businesses related to physical and mental health.

A business record need not be in any particular form. It can be written, electronic, photographic, digital, or in another form.

The breadth of the business records exception, including the types of businesses to which it can apply and the form in which those records can be maintained, is illustrated by *Keogh v. Commissioner.*

Keogh v. Commissioner

713 F.2d 496 (9th Cir. 1983)

DUNIWAY, Judge.

In this case we review the tax court's finding of income tax deficiencies against a Las Vegas casino employee. The wife of the employee is a party solely because the two filed a joint return. We affirm.

Appellant husband here, petitioner in the tax court, was employed at the Dunes Hotel & Country Club, in Las Vegas. He worked in the casino, where he dealt blackjack or ran "big wheel" or roulette games and was known as a 21 dealer. The 21 dealers earned regular wages paid semimonthly. In addition, 21 players sometimes gave them tips or "tokes" in the form of coins or casino chips. Players often gave tokes to the dealers directly; at other times, they placed bets for the dealers, with a player determining after a winning bet how much of the winnings was the dealer's to keep.

The Commissioner asserted that the Keoghs had underreported tip income in 1969, 1970, and 1971. He calculated Keogh's toke income through a statistical analysis based on entries in a diary kept by one John Whitlock, Jr., not a party to this action, who worked at the Dunes from March 4, 1967 to May 7, 1970. In the diary, the date of the month and the day of the week were listed on the left side of each page, and separate vertical columns were designated "gross," "net," "tax," and "tips."

The Commissioner's statistical analysis of the tip entries resulted in an average daily toke income per dealer of between $42.04 and $74.24, depending on the year and the day of the week. For days on which Whitlock and Keogh both worked, the Commissioner's estimate for him reflected the diary figure. The appropriate average daily toke entry was used for days worked by Keogh but not by Whitlock. Finally, the Commissioner reduced his total estimated toke income for Keogh by 10 percent to account for variability in statistical projections.

The Whitlock diary, offered in evidence to prove the truth of its contents as they related to tokes received by Dunes 21 dealers, was hearsay and thus inadmissible unless excepted by one or more rules of evidence. In admitting the diary, the tax court cited Rules 803(6).

We hold that the tax court did not abuse its discretion in admitting the diary in evidence.The Keoghs' first argument is that Rule 803(6) does not apply to the diary because it was not a business record. They argue that the diary was Whitlock's personal record, not a record of the business enterprise involved, the Dunes. But

Whitlock's diary, even though personal to him, shows every indication of being kept "in the course of" his own "business activity," "occupation, and calling." Personal records kept for business reasons may be able to qualify. A housekeeper's records kept neatly and accurately for purposes of balancing bank statements, keeping strict budgets and preparing income tax returns could qualify under the statute.

The reliability usually found in records kept by business concerns may be established in personal business records if they are systematically checked and regularly and continually maintained. *See United States v. Hedman* (diary of payoffs by extortion victim); *United States v. McPartlin* (desk calendar-appointment diary, and cases there cited).

Here, Mikle testified that she saw Whitlock and only Whitlock make entries in the diary; that he usually made them after night shifts of work; that when he made no entries for three to four days, he would copy entries for those days from a record kept in his wallet; that he usually made no entries in the diary on his days off; and that she understood the diary to contain a record of tokes he received from his work as a dealer.

The cases that the Keoghs cite for the proposition that Rule 803(6) applies only to commercial business records that are kept by those under a business duty to do so arose in the commercial context, but in fact stress just the sort of timeliness and regularity of entries that are present here.

More to the point is *Sabatino v. Curtiss National Bank of Miami Springs*, reversing a trial court's refusal to admit in evidence a personal check record. The *Sabatino* court said, "A man has a direct financial interest in keeping accurate accounts in his personal business. The cases indicate that private records, if kept regularly and if incidental to some personal business pursuit, are competent evidence." It made no difference whether the check account was used for any specific business. "Moreover, it is settled that the business 'need not be commercial.'"

---

3. *Making the Record Was a Regular Practice of the Business's Regularly Conducted Activity*

A regular activity of that business must be to make and keep the record at issue. This practice is an essential element in ensuring the reliability of records. Different businesses use different records for their business activities. For example, a hospital may keep a "chart" of the patients' vital signs. A florist may keep records of the supplies it receives from growers and the orders it fills for customers. As the *Palmer v. Hoffman* case discussed in *Lewis* illustrates, it may not be the regular practice of a railroad business to maintain records on accidents. 318 U.S. 109 (1943). However, because accidents happen and businesses investigate them, most modern cases (such as *Lewis*) treat *Palmer* as being correct—but on the ground that the accident investigation report in that case was not trustworthy (rather than on the ground that investigating accidents is not part of the regular activity of the business).

4. *The Business Record Is Properly Authenticated*

As discussed in Chapter Thirteen, writings and physical evidence—including records—must be authenticated before they are admitted into evidence. There are two ways such evidence may be authenticated. A "custodian of record" may testify as to the authenticity of the records, even if that person did not create those records. The custodian of record just needs to be familiar with how the business made and kept its records at the time the record was made. Alternatively, FRE 902(11) and (12) make domestic and foreign business records self-authenticating if they are properly certified.

Here is a sample colloquy that lays the foundation for the use of the business record exception by establishing that each of its prerequisites have been met:

Counsel: Ms. Singh, where do you work?
Witness: For Big Widget, Inc.
Counsel: What is your position?
Witness: I am their bookkeeper.
Counsel: As their bookkeeper, what do you do?
Witness: I make and maintain all of the company's invoices and ledgers.
Counsel: What information do you use to do your job?
Witness: The salespersons submit to me the records of sales that they make. I enter those records into our general ledgers and send invoices.
Counsel: Do you recognize Exhibit #1?
Witness: Yes, it is a notebook of invoices and ledgers from our company.
Counsel: Were they made and kept in the regular practice of Big Widget?
Witness: Yes. Some were made by me and some were made by the prior bookkeeper, but the company's billing and bookkeeping practices have remained the same.

For the in-person method, the proponent may call either the business's custodian of records or another "qualified witness." Who falls into this "qualified witness" category? That is discussed in *United States v. Collins.*

United States v. Collins

799 F.3d 554 (6th Cir. 2015)

CLAY, Judge.

Defendants Russell Lee Collins, Eddie Wilburn, and Richard Brosky appeal from final judgments . . . in a methamphetamine manufacturing and distribution conspiracy case.

ADMISSION OF "METHCHECK" RECORDS AS BUSINESS RECORDS

Rule 803(6) of the Federal Rules of Evidence permits records of regularly conducted business activity to be admitted into evidence if the records meet four requirements: 1) they were "created in the course of a regularly conducted business activity," 2) they were "kept in the regular course of that business," 3) they resulted from a "regular practice of the business" to create such documents, and 4) they were "created by a person with knowledge of the transaction or from information transmitted by a person with knowledge." The fulfilment of these conditions must be "shown by the testimony of the custodian or another qualified witness, or by a certification that complies with Rule 902(11) or (12) or with a statute permitting certification." Fed. R. Evid. 803(6)(D).

Brosky argues that the government did not lay the requisite foundation to introduce the pseudoephedrine purchase records created by MethCheck under Rule 803(6) because the officers who first discussed the particular MethCheck records at issue in this case were not "qualified witnesses." On the other hand, the government contends that the records were properly introduced because, consistent with Rule 803(6), "prior to the testimony of [the officers], the custodian of records (Acquisto) provided the general foundational testimony of 'the custodian or another qualified witness.'" We conclude that the district court neither erred nor abused its discretion by admitting pseudoephedrine purchase records as business records under Federal Rule of Evidence 803(6).

MethCheck is a service provided by the NPLEx Project, which is run by Appriss, Inc., a public safety technology company. MethCheck electronically tracks the purchase of precursors for methamphetamine, including Sudafed and other over-the-counter medications, in real time. The government's first witness was James Acquisto, the vice president of government affairs for Appriss. Acquisto testified that Appriss keeps records containing MethCheck entries and that he is the custodian of records for these entries. Acquisto testified at length regarding the process by which MethCheck records are created and stored. In sum, Acquisto explained that when a person goes to a drug store and attempts to purchase a medication that is identified as a methamphetamine precursor, federal and state law require the individual to present the pharmacy employee with government-issued photo identification. The information is then scanned or manually entered into the MethCheck System immediately, and the clerk receives a nearly instantaneous message confirming whether the sale is legal or illegal (based on purchase quantity regulations). This purchase information becomes available to law enforcement in under a minute. Acquisto testified that the entries are automated approximately 75 percent of the time, but that the entries are entered manually in some small independent drug stores. Acquisto further testified that law enforcement officers in Kentucky may apply for access to MethCheck records from the Office of Drug Control Policy. If they are granted access, they receive a secure password and user ID to access the portal through the internet.

Despite obtaining detailed information from Acquisto regarding how MethCheck records are kept, the government did not seek to introduce specific MethCheck records through Acquisto. Instead, the government sought to introduce MethCheck records for specific purchasers through two officers, Detective Farris and Agent O'Neil. These officers testified that they accessed the MethCheck database and retrieved the records for people they suspected of being associated with methamphetamine manufacturing.

When the government sought to introduce specific MethCheck records through the officers, counsel for Brosky objected that the records were not admissible because they had not been authenticated by Acquisto, the custodian of the records. The district court overruled Brosky's objection, concluding that the testimony of the officers, in conjunction with Acquisto's detailed testimony regarding the record keeping process, was sufficient to authenticate the records.

---

5. *The Record Must Not Be Untrustworthy*

Last, FRE 803(6) provides that the exception does not apply if the opponent shows that the source of the information or the method or circumstances of preparation indicate a lack of trustworthiness.[13] The record itself, or the testimony of witnesses, may be used to make this determination.

Untrustworthiness comes up in two common scenarios. First, and as alluded to above, if one construes the business records exception to include information supplied by knowledgeable outsiders, a record may be untrustworthy if the person providing the information to the business is an outsider. In this situation, the best assurance of trustworthiness is that the outsider's statement falls into a hearsay exception. In this regard, other hearsay exceptions are used as proxies for trustworthiness. What if there *is* no applicable hearsay exception to act as a proxy? Courts have in those cases looked to see if the business has taken any efforts to verify the information provided by the outsider; if so, the business record is trustworthy, but if not, it probably is not. *See generally Rambus, Inc. v. Infineon Tech. AG*, 348 F. Supp. 2d 698, 707-708 (E.D. Va. 2004).

Second, a record may be untrustworthy if the business has some ulterior and potentially self-serving motive in preparing the record at issue. *Palmer v. Hoffman* is the prime example. Even if a business does make and keep business records regarding the cause of accidents occurring with its employees, there may be reason to question the trustworthiness of those accident reports if the result of the report or the manner in which it is prepared is aimed at deflecting liability or responsibility for the accident away from the business.

6. *The Absence of a Business Record*

Much as the dog that did not bark, may the *absence* of a business record be admitted to prove that the act, event, condition, opinion, or diagnosis did not happen or exist? The answer is "yes."

---

13. In some states, such as California, the party seeking to introduce the business record (rather than the party opposing its admission) has the duty to prove that the record is trustworthy. Cal. Evid. Code § 1272. Florida's rule could be read as placing the burden on the proponent, Fl. Stat. § 90.803(6), but Florida courts have placed the burden on the opponent to show untrustworthiness. *See Jackson v. Household Fin. Corp. III*, 298 So.3d 531, 544 (Fla. 2020).

FRE 803. Exceptions to the Rule Against Hearsay

The following are not excluded by the rule against hearsay, regardless of whether the declarant is available as a witness:

. . .

(7) Absence of a Record of a Regularly Conducted Activity. Evidence that a matter is not included in a record described in [FRE 803(6)] if:

(A) the evidence is admitted to prove that the matter did not occur or exist;

(B) a record was regularly kept for a matter of that kind; and

(C) the opponent does not show that the possible source of the information or other circumstances indicate a lack of trustworthiness.

Hearsay Exception for the Absence of a Business Record

(1) A record is regularly made and kept for an act, event, condition, opinion, or diagnosis of the kind of matter at issue;

(2) A record of the matter at issue is not included in the business records; *and*

(3) The absence of the record is admitted to prove that the underlying matter did not occur or exist,

UNLESS

The opponent of the evidence shows the source of information or method or circumstances show a lack of trustworthiness.

This exception was applied in *United States v. Gentry.*

United States v. Gentry

925 F.2d 186 (7th Cir. 1991)

EASTERBROOK, Judge.

In the wake of a few maniacs who poisoned foods and medicines, causing not only deaths but also great expense as firms recalled their products, there followed extortion: people threatened to announce that they had poisoned a particular firm's products unless the manufacturer bought them off.

Kevin Mark Gentry is no extortionist, but he made a false report of food tampering. On May 2, 1989, he told fellow employees—plus the security force of the mall where he worked—that he had bit into a pin when he ate M&M candy bought from a vending machine. One of Gentry's fellow employees found some metal embedded in the candy.

Gentry objects to testimony from an employee of the manufacturer that there were no other reports of pins in M&M candy. The testimony was relevant; it implies that the pin came from Gentry rather than the factory (or a tamperer other than Gentry). And Fed. R. Evid. 803(7) allows this use of business records to show the nonoccurrence of an event.

Review Questions

1. **Aftermarket changes.** Plaintiff sues Big Auto Co. ("BAC") for a defective part in his car. BAC argues that the part was installed by someone other than the company after it sold the car. BAC seeks to introduce its records of car sales and the parts used in those sales. Admissible? What foundation would need to be established for their admissibility?
2. **Absence of records.** BAC also wants to introduce its records to show that there are no records in its inventory of the type of part found in the car for the time period in which plaintiff said he purchased the car. Admissible? What foundation is required?
3. **Uniform confusion.** Police receive a tip that a suspect wanted in a robbery was wearing the uniform of Company ABC. Prosecutors seek to introduce the payroll ledgers of Company ABC that show that Defendant worked at the company at the time of the robbery. Admissible? What if the records did not list Defendant's name? Could Defendant seek to introduce those lists? What if the company, after hearing of Defendant's arrest, did its own investigation of his whereabouts on the day of the robbery? Admissible?

PART G: PUBLIC RECORDS AND THE ABSENCE OF PUBLIC RECORDS [FRE 803(8), 803(10)]

If the records of *private business* entities are considered sufficiently trustworthy, as a general matter, to warrant a hearsay exception, should there be a hearsay exception for the records of *public* entities? The answer is "yes," but the exception in the Federal Rules of Evidence is substantively different than the business records exception.

Specifically, FRE 803(8) provides the following:

FRE 803. Exceptions to the Rule Against Hearsay

The following are not excluded by the rule against hearsay, regardless of whether the declarant is available as a witness:

. . .

(8) Public Records. A record or statement of public office if:

(A) it sets out:

(i) the office's activities;

(ii) a matter observed while under a legal duty to report, but not including, in a criminal case, a matter observed by law-enforcement personnel; or

(iii) in a civil case or against the government in a criminal case, factual findings from a legally authorized investigation; and

(B) the opponent does not show that the source of information or other circumstances indicate a lack of trustworthiness.

As its language suggest, the hearsay exception for public records is really three different subexceptions, each for a different type of public record and each of which has its own restrictions on use.[14]

Hearsay Exception for Public Records

(1) The record is a statement or record of a public office; *and*

(2) The record falls into one of the three categories of public records addressed by the exception, and stays within the use restriction for that category of record;

UNLESS

The opponent of the evidence shows the source of information or method or circumstances show a lack of trustworthiness.

The following graphic fleshes out the exception's categories of public records along with their use restrictions:

14. New York has a much narrower exception. *Miriam Osborne Mem. Home Assn. v. Assessor of City of Rye*, 9 Misc. 3d 1019, 1025-26 (N.Y. Sup. Ct. Westchester Co. 2005).

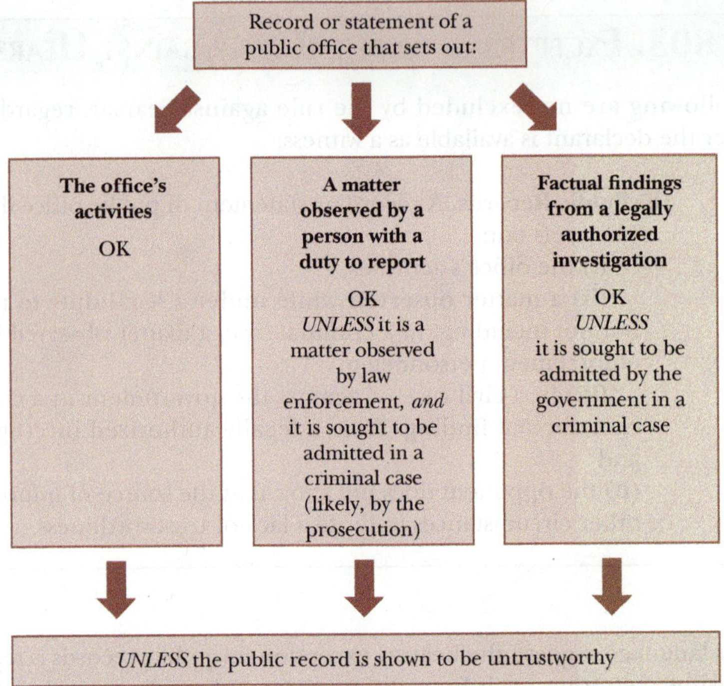

Does the public records exception reach private entities engaged in duties traditionally entrusted to public entities, such as operating prisons and the like? Courts seem to say "yes" when the private company is laboring under the same duties as would apply to a public entity. *See, e.g., United States v. Central Gulf Lines, Inc.*, 747 F.2d 315, 319 (5th Cir. 1984) (applying public records exception to private entity working with Agency for International Development because the entity agreed to follow federal regulations applicable to public agencies); *Roy F. Weston v. Halliburton NUS Environmental Corp.*, 1993 U.S. Dist. LEXIS 13567, *5-*6 (E.D. Pa. 1993) (applying public records exception to waste disposal documents prepared by private entity in compliance with federal regulations); *Bhatt v. State Dept of Health Services*, 133 Cal. App. 4th 923, 929-30 (Cal. Ct. App. 2005) (applying public records exception to private entity implementing public health insurance program when records at issue conformed to federal regulations).

As the prerequisites for the public records exception indicate, this exception to the hearsay rule is both broader and narrower than the business records exception. It is broader because it omits several prerequisites of the business records exception, such as that the act, event, condition, opinion, or diagnosis be recorded at or near the time of its observation and the strict authentication requirement. Why these omissions? Because public employees work under a duty of candor to the public that courts generally presume they follow. The public records exception is also narrower than the business records exception because it is limited to three types of public records and places substantial limits on two of those types.

1. Public Records of the Office's Public Activities

This category of public records includes the routine records of the regular activities of the public office. It includes, for example, how many stamps the post office sold, the number of permits issued by the building authorities, reports of vehicle license plates seen going through a border check, or information provided to immigration officials upon entry to the country. *See United States v. Orozco*, 590 F.2d 789 (9th Cir. 1979); *United States v. Noria*, 945 F.3d 847 (5th Cir. 2019).

Example

Plaintiff sues Defendant for injuries sustained in an auto accident. Plaintiff seeks to introduce a Department of Motor Vehicles record showing that Defendant's driver's license had been revoked. Records reflecting the status of drivers' licenses are routine records of the Department of Motor Vehicles' regular activities and hence admissible under FRE 808(A)(i) unless untrustworthy.

Other than the general trustworthiness consideration, there are no use restrictions on this type of public record: They are regularly admissible in civil and criminal cases, as *United States v. Berry* illustrates.

United States v. Berry

683 F.3d 1015 (9th Cir. 2012)

RAWLINSON, Judge.

Appellant Ethan Berry (Berry) appeals his conviction for social security fraud.

Berry asserts that his conviction should be reversed because the district court erroneously admitted computer records from the SSA under Fed. R. Evid. 803(8), the public records exception to the hearsay rule. Berry specifically contends that his rights under the Confrontation Clause were violated because the SSA application is or potentially could be adversarial in nature. Berry cites to this circuit's decision in *United States v. Orellana-Blanco*, 294 F.3d 1143 (9th Cir. 2002) to support this proposition. In sum, Berry argues that the SSA application is the equivalent of a police report. However, Berry's argument is unpersuasive.

"Business and public records are generally admissible absent confrontation not because they qualify under an exception to the hearsay rules, but because—having been created for the administration of an entity's affairs and not for the purpose of establishing or proving some fact at trial—they are not testimonial." *Melendez-Diaz v. Massachusetts* (2009). "[W]hen the evidence in question is nontestimonial, confrontation is not necessarily required. . . ." Documents or records that are not created in anticipation of litigation, but because of "a routine, objective, cataloging of an unambiguous factual matter" are deemed nontestimonial.

Berry's contention is that, similar to the facts in *Orellana-Blanco*, the SSA application contained adversarial language included in anticipation of litigation. However, SSA employees testified that a SSA interviewer completes the application as part of a routine administrative process. In contrast, the form in *Orellana-Blanco* was signed under oath and completed by law enforcement personnel.

[T]he documents admitted at Berry's trial were routine, administrative documents prepared by the SSA for each and every request for benefits. No affidavit was executed in conjunction with preparation of the documents, and there was no anticipation that the documents would become part of a criminal proceeding.

---

2. *Matters Observed by Persons with a Duty to Report*

This category reaches matters observed by public employees who have a duty to report what they observe. Government personnel are routinely in a situation to make observations that they will document in their reports. This category would include, for example, observations by building or food inspectors. In civil cases, this type of record is admissible into evidence by any and all parties. In a criminal case, however, the prosecution cannot rely on police or other law enforcement personnel reports to make its case against the defendant. It is too likely that these reports will be biased against the defendant, and the defendant also has a separate constitutional right to cross-examine the author of the police report under the right of confrontation. The contours of the confrontation right are spelled out in Chapter Nine.

Example

Defendant is charged with driving under the influence of alcohol. Prosecutor seeks to introduce a police report that Defendant was swerving as she drove. This report is inadmissible because it is a police report being introduced against the defendant in a criminal case. FRE 803(8)(A)(ii).

By definition, this exception—unlike the business records exception—expressly requires that the person making the observation be under a duty to report. Thus, information supplied by "outsiders" (that is, by people not working for a public entity) is not encompassed within the exception. However, one must be careful to ask *who* the outsider is. For example, a police officer taking an accident report may speak with an eyewitness about what happened as well as with a firefighter who responded to the call and helped extract one of the drivers from her car. If the officer includes both statements in his police report, the eyewitness's statement falls outside the public records exception because the eyewitness is under no duty to be truthful, but the firefighter's statement is included because he is a public employee with a duty to be truthful.

The specific exclusion of police reports under FRE 803(8)(A)(ii) raises a question: What if the police report is admissible under *some other* hearsay exception? Is that permissible, or does the exclusion in FRE 803(8)(A)(ii) preclude the admission of police reports against a defendant in criminal cases *no matter what?*

The courts are split on the issue. *United States v. Oates,* excerpted below, holds that FRE 803(8)(A)(ii) erects a categorical bar, such that the failure to meet that rule's requirements bars its admission even if it might qualify for admission under a different hearsay exception. Other courts have come to a contrary conclusion and have looked to the nature of the report to determine whether it falls within the purpose of FRE 803(8)(A)(ii). *E.g., United States v. Quezada,* 754 F.2d 1190, 1193 (5th Cir. 1985) (warrant of deportation, despite being a report of a government enforcement officer, is not barred by FRE 803(8)(A)(ii)).

United States v. Oates

560 F.2d 45 (2d Cir. 1970)

WATERMAN, Judge.

This is an appeal from [defendant's] conviction for possession of heroin with intent to distribute, and of conspiracy to commit that substantive offense.

Appellant claims that the trial court committed error by admitting into evidence at trial two documentary exhibits purporting to be the official report and accompanying worksheet of the United States Customs Service chemist who analyzed the white powdery substance seized from Isaac Daniels. The documents, the crucial nature of which is beyond cavil, concluded that the powder examined was heroin. Appellant contends, first of all, that under the new Federal Rules of Evidence (hereinafter "FRE") the documents should have been excluded as hearsay and, alternatively, that, even if they were not inadmissible on that basis, their exclusion was nonetheless required because their admission into evidence over appellant's objection would have violated and did violate appellant's right under the Sixth Amendment to confront the witnesses against him.

At trial the government had planned upon calling as one of its final witnesses a Mr. Milton Weinberg, a retired United States Customs Service chemist who allegedly had analyzed the white powder seized from Isaac Daniels. It seems that Mr. Weinberg had been present on the day the trial had been scheduled to commence but he was not able to testify then because of a delay occasioned by the unexpected length of the pretrial suppression hearing.

Before the onset of Weinberg's bronchial condition, the prosecutor had planned to call Weinberg for the purpose of eliciting from him testimony that Weinberg had analyzed the powder seized from Daniels and found it to be heroin. When Weinberg became "unavailable," the government decided to call another Customs chemist, Shirley Harrington, who, although she did not know Weinberg personally, was able to testify concerning the regular practices and procedures used by Customs Service chemists in analyzing unknown substances. While principal reliance was placed on the modified "business records" exception found in FRE 803(6), the evidence was also claimed to be admissible under FRE 803(8) as a "public record."

Mrs. Harrington was obviously an experienced chemist, having conducted thousands of tests while working for the Customs Service, including hundreds designed to identify heroin. [However, she never tested defendant's evidence.]

It is eminently clear that the report and worksheet were "written assertions" constituting "statements," FRE 801(a)(1), which were "offered [by the prosecution] in evidence [at trial] to prove the truth of the matters asserted [in them]." FRE 801(c). As such, they were hearsay.

[The government] urges us to find that the challenged evidence falls easily within the scope of what has traditionally been labeled the "business records exception" to the hearsay exclusionary rule, the codification of which in the Federal Rules of Evidence is found in FRE 803(6). Appellant, on the other hand, vigorously asserts that the issue of whether the chemist's report and worksheet were fatal hearsay can be correctly evaluated only by a careful study of the precise wording of FRE 803(8) and the legislative intent underlying the enactment of that rule.

[W]e believe that, on balance, appellant's emphasis on the importance of FRE 803(8) is well-founded. It would certainly seem to be the exception which would logically come to mind if a question arose as to the admissibility of reports of the kind we are considering in this case.

That the chemist's report and worksheet could not satisfy the requirement of the "public records and reports" exception seems evident merely from examining, on its face, the language of FRE 803(8). That rule insulates from the exclusionary effect of the hearsay rule certain:

[FRE 803](8) *Public records and reports.*[15] Records, reports, statements, or data compilations, in any form, of public offices or agencies, setting forth (A) the activities of the office or agency, or (B) matters observed pursuant to duty imposed by law as to which matters there was a duty to report, excluding, however, in criminal cases matters observed by police officers and other law enforcement personnel, or (C) in civil cases and proceedings and against the Government in criminal cases, factual findings resulting from an investigation made pursuant to authority granted by law, unless the sources of information or other circumstances indicate lack of trustworthiness.

It is manifest from the face of item (C) that "factual findings resulting from an investigation made pursuant to authority granted by law" are not shielded from the exclusionary effect of the hearsay rule by "the public records exception" if the government seeks to have those "factual findings" admitted *against* the accused in a *criminal* case. It seems indisputable to us that the chemist's official report and worksheet in the case at bar can be characterized as reports of "factual findings resulting from an investigation made pursuant to authority granted by law." The "factual finding" in each instance, the conclusion of the chemist that the substance analyzed was heroin, obviously is the product of an "investigation."

Though with less confidence, we believe that the chemist's documents might also fail to achieve status as public records under FRE 803(8)(B) because they are records of "matters observed by police officers and other law enforcement personnel." We would . . . construe "other law enforcement personnel" to at least include any officer or employee of a governmental agency which has law enforcement responsibilities. It would therefore seem that if the chemist's report and worksheet here can be deemed to set forth "matters observed," the documents would fail to satisfy the requirements of exception FRE 803(8) for the chemist must be included within the category of "other law enforcement personnel."

As the rules of evidence now stand, police and law enforcement reports are not admissible against defendants in criminal cases. This is made quite clear by the provisions of rule 803(8)(B) and (C). [B]oth the Advisory Committee and the

---

15. The court's opinion reflects the old numbering of FRE 803 and its subsections. (Authors' note).

Congress were preoccupied with "[avoiding] inviting collisions" between the hearsay rule and the confrontation clause. The extent of this concern becomes especially apparent, of course, in FRE 803(8)(B).

Here the hearsay evidence was crucial. We hold that in criminal cases reports of public agencies setting forth matters observed by police officers and other law enforcement personnel and reports of public agencies setting forth factual findings resulting from investigations made pursuant to authority granted by law cannot satisfy the standards of any hearsay exception if those reports are sought to be introduced against the accused. Inasmuch as the chemist's documents here can be characterized as governmental reports which set forth matters observed by law enforcement personnel or which set forth factual findings resulting from an authorized investigation, they were incapable of qualifying under any of the exceptions to the hearsay rule specified in FRE 803 and 804. The documents were crucial to the government's case, they were, of course, hearsay, and, inasmuch as they were ineligible to qualify for any exception to the hearsay rule, their admission at trial against appellant was prejudicial error.

Although the plain terms of FRE 803(8)(A)(ii) seem to indicate that police reports are inadmissible in criminal classes *by either the prosecution or the defense,* the legislative history of the rule makes clear that this restriction was designed to protect defendants from being tried through police reports. Thus, even though the rule states that such reports are not admissible in criminal cases *at all,* courts frequently allow the defense to introduce them notwithstanding the rule's language. *See Bailey v. Lafler,* 209 F. Supp. 3d 955, 976 (W.D. Mich. 2016).

3. Factual Findings from a Legally Authorized Investigation

Government officials may conduct official investigations, such as what occurs when there is an aircraft accident. When the officials make findings, those findings are admissible in civil cases. However, in a criminal case, they are only admissible *against* the government—not *by* the government—because defendants in criminal cases have the right to confront witnesses against them.

So is a "factual finding" only a finding of *fact,* or does it also include legal findings and conclusions? The federal courts were divided for many years until the U.S. Supreme Court decided *Beech Aircraft Corp. v. Rainey,* 488 U.S. 153 (1988), which held that "factual findings" include all final conclusions reached by a public entity.[16]

---

16. Illinois models its public records exception after the Federal Rules of Evidence, but specifically excludes from that exception "findings containing expressions of opinions or the drawing of conclusions." Ill. R. Evid. 803(8).

Examples

1. Plaintiff claims that injuries were caused by safety violations by Defendant. Plaintiff seeks to introduce OSHA's findings regarding the accident. These findings are admissible under FRE 803(8)(A)(iii).
2. Defendant is charged with driving under the influence of alcohol. Prosecutor seeks to introduce a report from the toxicology laboratory that Defendant's blood alcohol content upon arrest was over the legal limit. This lab report is inadmissible under FRE 803(8)(A)(iii) because it is a criminal case and being introduced by the government.

For an example of a case involving the admission of a public agency's factual findings, consider *Crawford v. ITW Food Equipment Group, LLC.*

Crawford v. ITW Food Equipment Group, LLC

977 F.3d 1331 (11th Cir. 2020)

Anderson, Judge.

Danny Crawford sued ITW Food Equipment Group LLC ("FEG") for negligent product design after his arm was amputated when it came into contact with the unguarded blade of one of FEG's commercial meat saws, the Hobart Model 6614. After a jury trial, Crawford and his wife were awarded $4,050,000. FEG now appeals this verdict. We conclude that the district court's evidentiary determinations were within its discretion, and that FEG's other challenges lack merit. Accordingly, we affirm.

INTRODUCTION OF OSHA REPORTS

FEG argues that the district court improperly admitted summaries of OSHA reports of fatalities and catastrophes, a compilation of eight summaries of incident reports of injuries involving meat saws—on two grounds: hearsay and relevance.

A. HEARSAY

The district court acknowledged that the OSHA reports were hearsay, but concluded that they fell under the Federal Rules of Evidence public records exception. Fed. R. Evid. 803(8). To evaluate trustworthiness, courts are to look at a non-exhaustive list of four factors: the timeliness of the investigation, the investigator's skill/experience, whether a hearing was held, and possible bias. *Beech Aircraft Corp. v. Rainey*, 488 U.S. 153, 167 n.11 (1988) (paraphrasing the Advisory Committee's note). The plain language of Rule 803(8)(B), as well as established case law, provides that the burden of demonstrating a lack of trustworthiness is on the party opposing admission.

FEG argues that the OSHA reports fail the Beech Aircraft test because they lack sufficient indicia of trustworthiness. FEG makes several arguments: that the reports do not reveal the investigators' identity, skill, or experience; that they do not note whether a hearing was held in the matter; and that two of the investigations described in the reports were conducted several months after the incidents. FEG also asserts that the reports are "perfunctory."[17]

FEG also argues that the reports contain multiple levels of hearsay. If a statement contains multiple levels of hearsay, each level must satisfy an exception to the hearsay rule. (Fed. R. Evid. 805). While the district court stated that only the parts of the reports that fall under the exceptions to the hearsay rule will be admitted, one of the reports read into the record contained double hearsay.

Crawford argues that the OSHA reports fall squarely within the government records hearsay exception. They are "factual findings from a legally authorized investigation." Rule 803(8)(A)(iii). They are written after OSHA investigations that follow established procedures. Crawford contends that these reports meet three of the Beech Aircraft factors: while there was admittedly no hearing before the reports were prepared, they were all opened less than six months after each incident, and five of the eight were opened within three weeks; they were not prepared in anticipation of litigation; and OSHA requires an "appropriately trained and experienced compliance officer" to oversee the investigations.

We agree with Crawford that the OSHA reports were properly admitted under the public records exception to the general bar on hearsay. The reports are not "mere collection[s] of statements from a witness," but are "factual findings that are based upon the knowledge or observations of the preparer of the report." Indeed, the OSHA reports fall squarely within the public records exception for "factual findings from a legally authorized investigation," Rule 803(8)(A)(iii), a fact not disputed by FEG. Rather, FEG argues only that they should have been excluded as untrustworthy. But FEG has failed to carry its burden of proof that the reports are untrustworthy. There is no evidence of untrustworthiness suggested by the reports themselves. They are timely: only two of the reports were delayed as much as six months after the incidents in question and five of the eight investigations began within three weeks. There is no evidence that the investigators who drafted the reports were unskilled or inexperienced. And there is no evidence of possible bias. The only Beech Aircraft factor that the reports do not meet is that they were not prepared with the aid of a hearing.

In short, FEG has adduced no evidence that the OSHA reports lack trustworthiness. All FEG has done is hypothesize that the investigators might have been biased, unskilled, or inexperienced (notwithstanding OSHA's published assurances that its investigators shall be "appropriately trained or experienced," and notwithstanding the common sense notion that a public official would act with particular care when investigating a fatality or catastrophe). We are unwilling to conclude that mere anonymity—in the absence of any evidence of lack of trustworthiness—is sufficient for a court to infer that OSHA investigators were biased, unskilled, or inexperienced. This is especially true because the burden of proving lack of trustworthiness is on FEG.

---

17. FEG also notes that the investigators who wrote the reports were not available to testify and be cross-examined in the district court. FEG is correct that there is precedent from this Court indicating that the inability to cross-examine the investigators is relevant to Rule 803(8)'s trustworthiness analysis. We emphasize that . . . the inability to cross-examine cannot, by itself, invalidate the report. [A]ll of the Rule 803 exceptions apply notwithstanding the lack of availability of the declarant. And we see nothing special about this situation.

The following table shows the rules applicable to each category of public records in civil and criminal cases.

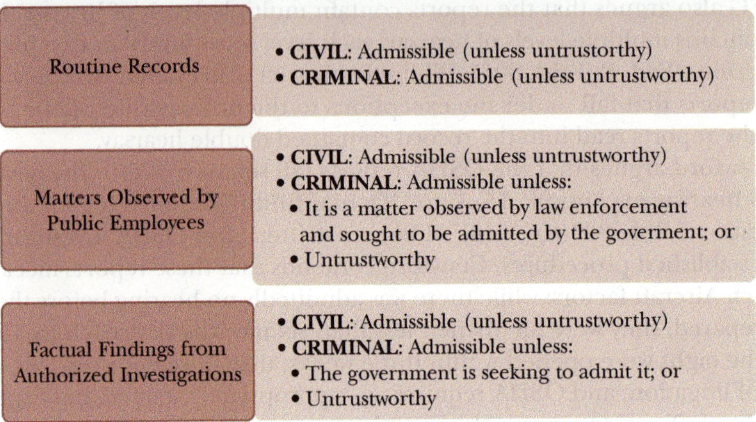

Routine Records
• CIVIL: Admissible (unless untrustorthy)
• CRIMINAL: Admissible (unless untrustworthy)
Matters Observed by Public Employees
• CIVIL: Admissible (unless untrustworthy)
• CRIMINAL: Admissible unless:
• It is a matter observed by law enforcement and sought to be admitted by the goverment; or
• Untrustworthy
Factual Findings from Authorized Investigations
• CIVIL: Admissible (unless untrustworthy)
• CRIMINAL: Admissible unless:
• The government is seeking to admit it; or
• Untrustworthy

4. *Trustworthiness*

Even if a public record satisfies the prerequisites for admission, it may yet be excluded if the opponent shows that it is untrustworthy.[18] The Advisory Committee Note spells out several factors bearing on whether factual findings may be untrustworthy, including (1) the timeliness of the investigation, (2) the special skill or experience of the official, (3) whether a hearing was held and the level at which it was conducted, and (4) possible motivation problems.

5. *The Absence of a Public Record*

Just as the absence of a business record may be admissible under the hearsay exception of FRE 803(7), the absence of a public record—as demonstrated by the fact that a diligent search did not reveal the record—can also be admitted notwithstanding the hearsay rule. This exception applies in civil and criminal cases. In criminal cases, the prosecutor must give notice if this exception will be used.

Examples

1. Defendant is charged with unlawful entry into the United States after deportation. Prosecutor seeks to introduce a certificate that there are no records of Defendant receiving the consent of the secretary of the

18. Again, in some states, such as California, the burden of showing trustworthiness rests on the proponent (rather than the opponent) of the evidence. Cal. Evid. Code § 1280.

Department of Homeland Security to reenter the United States after his deportation. *See United States v. Garcia-Hernandez*, 550 F. Supp. 2d 1228 (S.D. Cal. 2008).

2. Defendant is charged with possession of an unregistered firearm. Prosecutor seeks to introduce evidence that there is no record of Defendant's firearm being registered.

Specifically, FRE 803(10) provides the following:

FRE 803. Exceptions to the Rule Against Hearsay

The following are not excluded by the rule against hearsay, regardless of whether the declarant is available as a witness:

. . .

(10) Absence of a Public Record. Testimony—or a certification under Rule 902—that a diligent search failed to disclose a public record or statement if:

(A) the testimony or certification is admitted to prove that

(i) the record or statement does not exist; or

(ii) a matter did not occur or exist, if a public office regularly kept a record or statement for a matter of that kind; and

(B) in a criminal case, a prosecutor who intends to offer a certification provides written notice of that intent at least 14 days before trial, and the defendant does not object in writing within 7 days of receiving the notice—unless the court sets a different time for the notice or the objection.

Hearsay Exception for the Absence of a Public Record

(1) A record is regularly made and kept for matter of the kind at issue;
(2) There is testimony or certification that diligent search failed to disclose a public record or statement on the matter at issue;
(3) The absence of the record is admitted to prove that the underlying matter did not occur or exist; *and*
(4) In a criminal case, the prosecutor gives advance notice.

Just as with business records, the absence of a public record may be established by testimony or certification in compliance with FRE 902.

The fact that a particular public record (or its absence) satisfies the requirements of this hearsay exception does not guarantee its admissibility. As discussed more fully in Chapter Nine, when the public record is to be admitted in a criminal case against a defendant and to the extent that it is not already excluded by the plain language of FRE 803(8) and 803(10), that record is likely to be "testimonial" within the meaning of the Sixth Amendment's Confrontation Clause; as such, prosecutors must *also* satisfy the dictates of the Confrontation Clause.

Review Questions

1. **Radiation exposure.** Residents near a nuclear power plant sue the plant for illnesses caused by the unlawful discharge of radioactive materials. They seek to introduce the following records:
   a. Number of times that the Nuclear Regulatory Commission ("NRC") has cited the plant for safety violations.
   b. A report by the NRC finding that "the nuclear power plant continues to pose a grave danger to nearby residents."
   c. A finding by the NRC that waste from nuclear power plants can cause radiation illness.
   d. A report by the local sheriff that she saw fluorescent glowing water streaming from the plant.
2. **Illegal dumping.** The owner of the plant is prosecuted for unlawfully discharging nuclear waste into a public waterway, in violation of 42 U.S.C. § 3289(a). During the trial, prosecutors seek to introduce the following records. Which, if any, records would be admissible?
   a. Copies of the defendant's application to operate the plant.
   b. A report by NRC inspectors that the plant had repeated safety violations.
   c. A finding by a congressional subcommittee that the power plant posed a substantial public health hazard.

   The defense then seeks to introduce the following records:

   a. NRC authorizations for the plant to operate.
   b. A Federal Bureau of Investigation report that another company in the area had been seen discharging radioactive industrial waste into the same waterway.
   c. Findings by the Environmental Protection Agency's chief regional director that a government military facility was likely the cause of some of the pollution.
3. **Election fraud.** Candidate for governor Betty Roosevelt sues the secretary of state for election irregularities. She seeks to introduce the following records:
   a. Voter registration rolls.
   b. List of election workers.
   c. County reports on the reliability of punch-ballot machines.
   d. A report by a special state commission finding that antiquated machinery caused "serious flaws" in election results.

4. **Crime lab records.** Defendant is on trial for distributing methamphetamines. Prosecutor seeks to introduce the following reports:
   a. A report by the crime lab that the substance found in Defendant's home was methamphetamines.
   b. A fire department report that there had been previous chemical explosions at Defendant's home.

PART H: OTHER LESS COMMONLY USED HEARSAY EXCEPTIONS UNDER FRE 803

We now turn to the less commonly used hearsay exceptions under FRE 803, which can be grouped into four categories.

1. Certain Private and Public Documents Considered to Be Reliable

Adhering to similar hearsay exceptions under the common law, FRE 803 recognizes a number of hearsay exceptions for private and public records that are, by their very nature and design, meant to be permanent records of important events—and hence are more likely to be reliable. That reliability justifies excepting them from the hearsay rule.

Specifically, FRE 803(9) as well as FRE 803(11) through FRE 803(17) provide the following:

FRE 803. Exceptions to the Rule Against Hearsay

The following are not excluded by the rule against hearsay, regardless of whether the declarant is available as a witness:

. . .

(9) Public Records of Vital Statistics. A record of birth, death, or marriage, if reported to a public office in accordance with a legal duty.

. . .

(11) Records of Religious Organizations Concerning Personal or Family History. A statement of birth, legitimacy, ancestry, marriage, divorce, death, relationship by blood or marriage, or similar facts of personal or family history, contained in a regularly kept record of a religious organization.

(12) Certificates of Marriage, Baptism, and Similar Ceremonies. A statement of fact contained in a certificate:

(A) made by a person who is authorized by a religious organization or by law to perform the act certified;

(B) attesting that the person performed a marriage or similar ceremony or administered a sacrament; and

(C) purporting to have been issued at the time of the act or within a reasonable time after it.

(13) Family Records. A statement of fact about a personal or family history contained in a family record, such as a Bible, genealogy, chart, engraving on a ring, inscription on a portrait, or engraving on an urn or burial marker.

(14) Records of Documents That Affect an Interest in Property. The record of a document that purports to establish or affect and interest in property if:

(A) the record is admitted to prove the content of the original recorded document, along with its signing and its delivery by each person who purports to have signed it;

(B) the record is kept in a public office; and

(C) a statute authorizes recording documents of that kind in that office.

(15) Statements in Documents That Affect an Interest in Property. A statement contained in a document that purports to establish or affect an interest in property if the matter stated was relevant to the document's purpose—unless later dealings with the property are inconsistent with the truth of the statement or the purport of the document.

(16) Statements in Ancient Documents. A statement in a document that was prepared before January 1, 1998, and whose authenticity is established.

(17) Market Reports and Similar Commercial Publications. Market quotations, lists, directories, or other compilations that are generally relied on by the public or by persons in particular occupations.

Although each of these exceptions deals with a different topic, they share the same basic prerequisites or elements—namely, that the documentary record be properly authenticated as a document falling within the pertinent exception.

Hearsay Exception for Public and Private Records Enumerated in FRE 803(9) and FRE 803(11)-(17)

The record is authenticated as a record falling into the pertinent exception.

Examples

1. To prove the age of the decedent, Plaintiff offers her birth certificate, a notation in her church's records of her birth, or an inscription of the date of her birth on a family photo.
2. To show the opening price of a stock on a particular date, Plaintiff suing for misrepresentation regarding a stock purchase offers a market report reciting the stock's price on that date.

With respect to the market reports and other publications, that exception does not necessarily cover credit ratings if those are not simply a recording of statistical information, but instead involve a subjective assessment of the value of a company. *See Phillip Van Heusen, Inc. v. Korn*, 460 P.2d 549 (Kan. 1969) (finding that Dun & Bradstreet credit rating was inadmissible).

2. *Statements in Learned Treatises, Periodicals, or Pamphlets*

As discussed more fully in Chapter Twelve, expert witnesses in forming their opinions may rely on learned treatises and similar publications. The hearsay exception in FRE 803(18) goes one step further and allows for the content of those treatises and publications to be read to the jury, although not introduced as an exhibit.[19] Here, the requirement that the treatise or publication be "established as a reliable authority" by experts or by judicial notice assures that the evidence is sufficiently reliable to justify dispensing with the hearsay rule.

Specifically, FRE 803(18) provides the following:

FRE 803. Exceptions to the Rule Against Hearsay

The following are not excluded by the rule against hearsay, regardless of whether the declarant is available as a witness:

. . .

(18) Statements in Learned Treatises, Periodicals, or Pamphlets. A statement contained in a treatise, periodical, or pamphlet if:

(A) the statement is called to the attention of an expert on cross-examination or relied on by the expert on direct examination; and

(B) the publication is established as a reliable authority by the expert's admission or testimony, by another expert's testimony, or by judicial notice.

If admitted, the statement may be read into evidence but not received as an exhibit.

---

19. Illinois and Florida have no such exception. Ill. R. Evid. 803(18); Fl. Stat. § 90.803.

Hearsay Exception for Learned Treatises and Similar Publications

(1) The treatise or publication is either (a) relied on by an expert witness during direct examination or (b) called to the expert's attention on cross-examination; *and*

(2) The treatise or publication is "established as reliable authority" by:
   (a) The testimony or admission of the expert who relies on the treatise or publication or is confronted with it on cross-examination;
   (b) Another expert's testimony; *or*
   (c) Judicial notice.

The modern exception is broader than the common law exception, which only allowed for the admission of such treatises to impeach, but not for their truth. FRE 803(18) allows the treatises in for their truth, but it attempts to limit their impact by confining their admission to being read to the jury rather than admitting the pertinent portions of the treatise itself into evidence.

Consider the following examples.

Examples

1. Plaintiff is suing Defendant for a slip and fall she suffered in Defendant's store. Defendant's expert claims that Plaintiff's injuries were probably caused long before the fall because Plaintiff did not have any bruising on the day of the fall. Plaintiff can cross-examine Defendant's expert and ask him to read a page of a recognized treatise in the field that states, "Bruising frequently does not occur until two to three days following an injury." It does not matter whether Defendant's expert was not previously familiar with that treatise or did not use it in assessing Plaintiff's condition.
2. Defendant is charged with involuntary manslaughter for accidentally shooting an actor on his movie set. The defense expert claims that the gun discharged because of a manufacturing defect. In support of the expert's testimony, Defendant asks the expert to read from "The 2021 Manual on Gun Manufacturing." The manual's text discusses that there is nearly no way to prevent accidental gun discharges if there is a flaw in the trigger mechanism of the weapon.

3. Reputation Evidence

By its very nature, reputation evidence is a collection of hearsay statements made by others with regard to a person's background, land boundaries, historical events, or a person's character. Accordingly, it is not a surprise that there are several hearsay exceptions for reputation evidence. At times, a judgment can also function as an alternative means of establishing reputation. As stated in the Advisory Committee Notes, "Trustworthiness in reputation evidence is found 'when the topic is such that the facts are likely to have been inquired about and that persons having personal knowledge have disclosed facts which have thus been discussed in the community; and thus the community's conclusion, if any has been formed, is likely to be a trustworthy one.'"

Specifically, FRE 803(19) through FRE 803(21) and FRE 803(23) provide the following:

FRE 803. Exceptions to the Rule Against Hearsay

The following are not excluded by the rule against hearsay, regardless of whether the declarant is available as a witness:

. . .

(19) Reputation Concerning Personal or Family History. A reputation among a person's family by blood, adoption, or marriage—or among a person's associates or in the community—concerning the person's birth, adoption, legitimacy, ancestry, marriage, divorce, death, relationship by blood, adoption, or marriage, or similar facts of personal or family history.

(20) Reputation Concerning Boundaries or General History. A reputation in a community—arising before the controversy—concerning boundaries of land in the community or customs that affect the land, or concerning general historical events important to that community, state, or nation.

(21) Reputation Concerning Character. A reputation among a person's associates or in the community concerning the person's character.

. . .

(23) Judgments Involving Personal, Family, or General History, or a Boundary. A judgment that is admitted to prove a matter of personal, family, or general history, or boundaries, if the matter:

(A) was essential to the judgment; *and*

(B) could be proved by evidence of reputation.

Hearsay Exceptions for Reputation-Related Evidence

(1) The information is commonly known enough to qualify as "reputation" evidence (or, in the case of FRE 803(23), is a judgment); *and*

(2) The reputation evidence pertains to topics enumerated in FRE 803(19), 803(20), 803(21), or 803(23).

Example

Plaintiff brings an action seeking a declaratory judgment that he has been a United States citizen since the time of his birth in order to receive compensation in an action in which money has been set aside for Americans who have lost family members in an international incident. Plaintiff seeks to introduce testimony that Plaintiff's family has lived in the community in the United States for generations.

Character evidence regarding reputation is discussed in greater detail in Chapter Three. As you will recall, to establish that character witnesses have the foundation to provide reputation evidence, those witnesses must demonstrate how they are familiar with the views of the community. In that way, the jury can assess the reliability and weight of the reputation evidence offered.

4. *Judgments of Conviction to Prove an Essential Fact*

As discussed more fully in Chapter Eleven, the credibility of witnesses may be impeached by proof that they have previously suffered a felony conviction. FRE 609 regulates the admission of convictions for such purposes.

FRE 803(22) addresses the admission of prior convictions for an entirely different purpose—namely, when the prior conviction is "admitted to prove any fact essential to the judgment" in a subsequent criminal or civil case. Indeed, FRE 803(22) expressly excludes the use of the rule when the prosecutor in a criminal case is using it for impeachment.

Consider the following examples.

Examples

1. Defendant is charged with not registering under the Sex Offender Registration Notification Act. To prove a violation, it must be proved that Defendant had been convicted of a sex offense. A judgment of conviction showing that Defendant had been convicted of a qualifying sex offense may be admitted under this exception. *See, e.g., United States v. Gilchrist*, 2021 U.S. Dist. LEXIS 39508 (M.D. Pa. 2021).
2. Defendant is charged with robbery. Prosecutor wants to introduce a judgment of conviction showing that the codefendant pled guilty to the robbery. The rule would preclude the use of that judgment of conviction to prove the case against Defendant. *See United States v. Vandetti*, 623 F.2d 1144 (6th Cir. 1980).

Specifically, FRE 803(22) provides the following:

FRE 803. Exceptions to the Rule Against Hearsay

The following are not excluded by the rule against hearsay, regardless of whether the declarant is available as a witness:

. . .

(22) Judgment of a Previous Conviction. Evidence of a final judgment of conviction if:

(A) the judgment was entered after a trial or guilty plea, but not a nolo contendere plea;

(B) the conviction was for a crime punishable by death or by imprisonment for more than one year;

(C) the evidence is admitted to prove any fact essential to the judgment; and

(D) when offered by the prosecutor in a criminal case for a purpose other than impeachment, the judgment was against the defendant.

The pendency of an appeal may be shown but does not affect admissibility.

Hearsay Exception for Previous Conviction to Prove an Essential Fact

(1) There is a prior judgment of conviction for a felony;
(2) The conviction is relevant to prove a fact essential to the judgment (rather than for impeachment); *and*
(3) The conviction is offered:
   (a) In a civil case, against anyone;
   (b) In a criminal case, against the defendant.

The requirement that the conviction in a criminal case be against the defendant precludes prosecutors from using a third party's conviction to prove an essential fact against the defendant. This requirement codifies *Kirby v. United States*, 174 U.S. 47 (1899), which held that a third party's conviction for theft of an item was not admissible to prove that the same item was stolen in the prosecution *against defendant* for receiving that stolen property.

This chapter has addressed the many hearsay exceptions that apply regardless of whether the person who made that statement outside the courtroom is available to call as a witness. Because of the requirements of these rules, the statements are considered trustworthy to admit through another witness or document. By contrast, FRE 804, discussed in Chapter Eight, has exceptions that are only applicable if the declarant is unavailable because those exceptions raise greater concerns regarding reliability and thus are based more on necessity arising from the declarant's unavailability.

Test Your Understanding

To test your understanding of the material in this chapter, turn to the Supplement for additional practice problems.

CHAPTER 8

HEARSAY EXCEPTIONS WHEN THE DECLARANT IS UNAVAILABLE AND THE RESIDUAL HEARSAY EXCEPTION

This chapter rounds out the discussion of hearsay "exceptions" by enumerating the two final categories of hearsay exceptions: (1) the exceptions, housed in FRE 804, that may be invoked only when the declarant is unavailable as a witness at the proceeding at which the statement is to be admitted and (2) the so-called residual hearsay exception, housed in FRE 807, that may be invoked to admit a hearsay statement when there is an exceptional need for the statement and strong indicia of its trustworthiness.

The hearsay exceptions that require the declarant to be unavailable are more necessity-based than the exceptions, housed in FRE 803, that are admissible regardless of the declarant's availability. As the Advisory Committee Note explains, "The rule [against hearsay] expresses preferences: testimony given on the stand in person is preferred over hearsay, and hearsay, if of the specified quality, is preferred over complete loss of the evidence of the declarant." However, the FRE 804 exceptions described in this chapter are not without some assurances of trustworthiness: Some exceptions expressly make trustworthiness an element, whereas others are limited to situations in which the statement is by its very nature more likely to be trustworthy.

In this chapter, Part A discusses the threshold prerequisite for all the hearsay exceptions in FRE 804—namely, that the declarant be unavailable. The Federal Rules of Evidence specifically define the circumstances in which a declarant is "unavailable." Part B then turns to the five hearsay exceptions under FRE 804:

- FRE 804(b)(1): Former testimony
- FRE 804(b)(2): Statement made under the belief of imminent death (a so-called dying declaration)
- FRE 804(b)(3): Declaration against interest

- FRE 804(b)(4): Statement of personal or family history
- FRE 804(b)(6): A statement offered against a party that wrongfully caused the declarant's unavailability[1]

Part C addresses the residual hearsay exception in FRE 807.

PART A: UNAVAILABILITY FOR PURPOSES OF THE HEARSAY EXCEPTIONS IN FRE 804 [FRE 804(a)]

Whether a witness is "unavailable" to testify is relevant both to the applicability of the hearsay exceptions listed in FRE 804 as well as the Confrontation Clause analysis set forth in Chapter Nine. Here, we are discussing solely the definition of "unavailability" that is a prerequisite to the applicability of the hearsay exceptions listed in FRE 804(b) (although, as Chapter Nine notes, courts sometimes look to this rule-based definition as a bellwether for the Confrontation Clause analysis).

FRE 804(a) defines "unavailability" as follows:

FRE 804. Hearsay Exceptions; Declarant Unavailable

(a) Criteria for Being Unavailable. A declarant is considered to be unavailable as a witness if the declarant:

(1) is exempted from testifying about the subject matter of the declarant's statement because the court rules that a privilege applies;

(2) refuses to testify about the subject matter despite a court order to do so;

(3) testifies to not remembering the subject matter;

(4) cannot be present or testify at the trial or hearing because of death or a then-existing infirmity, physical illness, or mental illness; or

(5) is absent from the trial or hearing and the statement's proponent has not been able, by process or other reasonable means, to procure:

(A) the declarant's attendance, in the hearsay exception under [FRE] 804(b)(1) or (6); or

(B) the declarant's attendance or testimony, in the case of a hearsay exception under [FRE] 804(b)(2), (3), or (4).

But this subdivision (a) does not apply if the statement's proponent procured or wrongfully caused the declarant's unavailability as a witness in order to prevent the declarant from attending or testifying.

---

1. There is no longer a hearsay exception housed at FRE 804(b)(5).

Graphically, the definition of unavailability may be represented as follows:

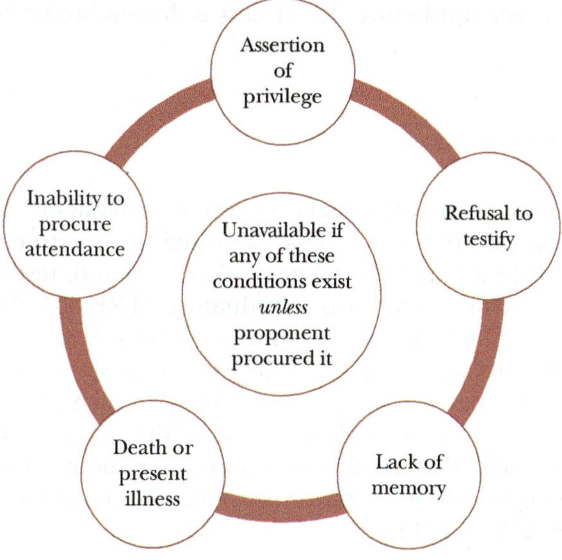

1. *Assertion of Privilege*

Under FRE 804(a)(1), a witness is unavailable if she invokes a privilege and "the court *rules*" that the privilege applies. In other words, the declarant must actually go through the motions of invoking the privilege and the trial judge must then rule on it. There are many privileges a witness might invoke, including the (a) attorney-client privilege, (b) marital communication privilege, (c) clergy-penitent privilege, and (d) psychotherapist-patient privilege. *See* Chapter Fifteen. Because these privileges generally put only the privileged portions of a witness's testimony off-limits from consideration by the trier of fact, these witnesses can be "unavailable" even if they are physically present in the courtroom and available to testify about other, nonprivileged matters. The privilege against self-incrimination is treated a little differently. It is not invoked in front of the jury. For this privilege, it is enough if the defendant indicates an intention to invoke that privilege. *See United States v. Gossett*, 877 F.2d 901, 907 (11th Cir. 1989).

2. *Refusal to Testify*

A witness may refuse to testify even without asserting a privilege. To invoke this definition of unavailability, the declarant must actually go through the steps of refusing to testify—that is, (1) be called to the stand, (2) refuse to testify, and (3) be ordered by the trial judge to provide testimony. A judge can then hold a witness in contempt and even order the witness to jail if the witness does not cooperate,[2] although the Federal Rules of Evidence do not specify that the judge must hold the witness in contempt before the witness is deemed to be "unavailable" under FRE 804(a).[3]

3. *Lack of Memory*

A lack of memory may also make a declarant unavailable. Because FRE 804(a) requires that the lack of memory be established by the witness's "testimony," this definition is satisfied only if the witness takes the stand, testifies that she cannot remember, and is subject to cross-examination.[4] FRE 804, Adv. Comm. Note. A witness is unavailable if she cannot remember the *subject matter* of her testimony, although she is still deemed to be subject to cross-examination (for purposes of the hearsay exceptions, noted in Chapter Six, that turn on still being "subject to cross-examination"). *See United States v. Owens*, 484 U.S. 554, 561-62 (1988). However, a "lack of memory" is not shown by a witness's failure to remember *making the out-of-court statement. Gilmore v. Palestinian Interim Self-Government Auth.*, 53 F. Supp. 3d 191, 207-08 (D.D.C. 2014).

4. *Death, Illness, or Infirmity*

A witness is (obviously) unavailable to testify if she is dead. A witness may also be unavailable if the witness is suffering from an infirmity, physical illness, or mental illness. Not every infirmity or illness will suffice. Instead, trial judges examine whether the infirmity or illness "preclude the witness from testifying" during the duration of the proceeding. In making this examination, trial judges look to the nature of the illness, the symptoms the witness suffers from, the remoteness of the last physical or mental examination of the witness, the witness's prognosis, the expected time of recovery, and any other relevant factor.

Mental illness, anguish, and trauma can render a witness unavailable, but mere discomfort, embarrassment, or apprehension about testifying do not. Rather, the trial judge can allow the witness to have some form of support during her testimony (such as a "support person" nearby) or can consider using the residual exception (FRE 807) to the hearsay rule.

---

2. When federal prosecutors indicted professional baseball player Barry Bonds for perjury and for obstructing justice by lying to a grand jury, Bonds' trainer Greg Anderson refused to testify against Bonds before the grand jury and at Bonds' trial. Anderson was held in contempt and jailed for more than a year as a means of inducing him to testify; Anderson never did.

3. The rule is not the same in every jurisdiction. California, for example, deems a witness unavailable to testify due to her refusal to testify only if the witness is "persistent in refusing to testify . . . *despite having been found in contempt for refusal to testify.*" Cal. Evid. Code § 240(a)(6) (emphasis added).

4. In Florida, the witness need not testify to a lack of memory. Fl. Stat. § 90.804(1)(c).

Examples

1. During trial, a party indicates that a witness is in the hospital recovering from a heart attack. On these facts, the witness is unavailable.
2. During trial, a witness is in the first trimester of a high-risk pregnancy, and a physician attests that having to travel to court and testify may have adverse effects on the witness and her fetus. On these facts, the witness is unavailable.
3. During trial, a 92-year-old witness has a physical disability that prevents him from traveling to testify. This witness is unavailable.
4. During trial, two doctors opine that a witness has amnesia due to post-traumatic stress disorder. On these facts, the witness is unavailable.
5. During trial, a witness's mother says that the witness will become very upset if forced to testify. On these facts, the witness is not unavailable.

5. Inability, by Process or Other Means, to Procure the Witness's Attendance or Testimony

By the plain language of FRE 804(a)(5), a witness is unavailable if (1) the witness is beyond the court's process to subpoena *and* (2) there are no other reasonable means to procure the witness's attendance at the hearing or at a deposition.[5]

The subpoena power in federal court is broad. In criminal cases, it is nationwide. Fed. R. Crim. P. 17(e). In civil cases, it reaches to the boundaries of the state where the witness "resides, is employed, or regularly transacts business in person," *or* within 100 miles of the courthouse (even if that bubble with a 100-mile radius crosses state lines). Fed. R. Civ. P. 45(c)(1). If the witness is in a foreign country, the party seeking to call the witness may have to establish that service through 28 U.S.C. § 1783 was not fruitful.

The person seeking to establish that the witness is unavailable under FRE 804(a)(5) *also* has to establish that there are no "reasonable means" to procure the witness's attendance. This mandate seems to require more than a showing that the witness is merely beyond the court's process, particularly in criminal cases. Thus, a proponent may also have to show that she made efforts to locate the witness and to bring her before the court that were ultimately unsuccessful or that a deposition under Federal Rule of Criminal Procedure 15 or Letters Rogatory were sought but unsuccessful.

What is more, for the exception for dying declarations, declarations against interest, and statements of personal or family history, the proponent also has to

---

5. California splits up these two requirements into separate exceptions—one for being beyond the reach of process and another for not being present despite a party exercising "reasonable diligence" in attempting to procure the witness's attendance. Cal. Evid. Code § 240(a)(4), (a)(5).

show that the witness is unavailable for a deposition *and* for testimony at the proceeding itself. Given the burden that this definition imposes, a proponent who waits until the last minute to seek a subpoena is unlikely to be able to establish unavailability on the ground that there are no "reasonable means" to procure the witness's attendance.

United States v. Yida

498 F.3d 945 (9th Cir. 2007)

GOULD, Judge.

The United States government appeals the district court's order excluding the former trial testimony of witness David Reziniano in the retrial of defendant Yacov Yida. In 1999 and 2000, Yida, Reziniano, and other coconspirators allegedly participated in an ecstasy smuggling operation. Reziniano pleaded guilty in 2004 to conspiring to import ecstasy and was sentenced to a term of sixty-three months. On November 25, 2005, Reziniano, a native and citizen of Israel, was released into the custody of the Department of Homeland Security ("DHS") for deportation proceedings. Reziniano did not contest the proceedings and on December 7, 2005, an immigration judge ordered his deportation.

Special Agent Catherine Miller of Immigration and Customs Enforcement obtained a material witness warrant for Reziniano on December 8, 2005, as he was scheduled to testify at Yida's upcoming trial. Reziniano remained in custody pursuant to the material witness warrant for about five months before and during Yida's April 2006 trial. During his incarceration, Reziniano complained that his medical and dietary needs were not being adequately addressed, and that he wished to be released from custody and deported.

On April 4, 2006, Reziniano testified that he had conspired with Yida to import ecstasy into the United States via Europe on multiple occasions. According to the government, "Reziniano proved to be a critical witness at trial." The jury reached an impasse in its deliberations, and the district court declared a mistrial on April 13, 2006.

After the district court declared a mistrial, Reziniano's attorney, Randy Sue Pollock, contacted the government in an attempt to resume her client's deportation proceedings. The government explored whether it would be possible to release Reziniano and arrange for his return in the event of a retrial. The government did not, however, notify the district court or Yida's defense counsel about these conversations or about Reziniano's subsequent release and deportation. After receiving assurances from both Reziniano and Pollock that Reziniano would return to testify if asked, and receiving advance approval from DHS to have him paroled back into the United States, the government agreed to Reziniano's deportation. The government also agreed to pay for Reziniano's airfare, hotel, food, and incidental expenses if it called upon him to testify at the retrial. After the government released Reziniano's material witness warrant, he was returned to DHS custody and deported to Israel.

On June 12, 2006, Reziniano called Pollock and said that he would not return to the United States to testify because "he needed to obtain medical treatment and . . . he had not been well since his return to Israel." Pollock and another former attorney for Reziniano were unable to convince Reziniano to return to testify.

Both [the prosecutor] and Special Agent Miller tried to convince Rezinaino to fulfill his promise to return and testify. Reziniano told the government that he was having medical problems. He estimated that it would be months until he would be able to travel internationally.

On July 5, 2006, the government filed a motion in limine seeking to admit Reziniano's testimony from Yida's first trial pursuant to Federal Rule of Evidence 804(b)(1), arguing that Reziniano was unavailable under 804(a)(5) and 804(a)(4).

Although the district court found that the government had acted in good faith when it allowed Reziniano to be deported, it did not conclude that the government had acted reasonably. Accordingly, the district court held that Reziniano's testimony could not be admitted under either Rule 804(a)(4) or 804(a)(5)'s hearsay exceptions because he was not an "unavailable" witness.

Federal Rule of Evidence 804(a)(5) provides that a declarant is unavailable as a witness if he "is absent from the hearing and the proponent of a statement has been unable to procure the declarant's attendance . . . by process or other reasonable means." Fed. R. Evid. 804(a)(5) (emphasis added). These reasonable means must be "genuine and bona fide." Prosecutors must not only act in good faith but also operate in a competent manner; a prosecutor cannot claim that a witness is unavailable because the prosecutor has acted in an "empty-head pure-heart" way.

We have considered the application of Rule 804(a)(5) to deported witnesses on two previous occasions and the government argues that those cases are dispositive. However, both of these cases involved illegal immigration prosecutions in which material witnesses were removed from the country before trial and were not present to testify.

Neither [case] is controlling here, as the district court correctly concluded, because neither case considered or addressed Rule 804's unavailability requirement and the government's obligation to use "reasonable means" to "procure the declarant's testimony" in the context of the government's affirmative role in a witness's deportation. The percipient witnesses in the prior case were deported without the prosecutor's knowledge or involvement; indeed, they were deported before any criminal charges were filed . . . whatsoever. Under these circumstances, the court was not presented with an occasion to assess the reasonableness of the government's actions before the witnesses were deported.

We agree . . . that "[i]mplicit . . . in the duty to use reasonable means to procure the presence of an absent witness is the duty to use reasonable means to prevent a present witness from becoming absent." Here, it is clear that the appropriate time-frame should not be limited to the government's efforts to procure Reziniano's testimony after it let him be deported, but should instead include an assessment of the government's affirmative conduct which allowed Reziniano to be deported to Israel in the first instance.

The government's reliance on Reziniano's cooperation before and during Yida's first trial, is similarly misplaced and unavailing. As the district court emphasized: "the Government apparently fails to recognize the likelihood that Reziniano cooperated with the Government because he remained in custody for that sole purpose." Again, Reziniano's testimony at Yida's first trial supports this conclusion because he repeatedly indicated that he did not want to be in the United States and had wished to return to Israel since completing his prison sentence in late November 2005. Reziniano's cooperation was a condition of his plea agreement and his testimony could have been compelled by contempt proceedings if necessary. The district court concluded, and we agree, that any cooperation from Reziniano was "coerced in some fashion by the fact that he remained in federal custody" and that "such involuntary cooperation was insufficient to indicate to the Government that he would return to testify once he was deported to Israel."

We agree with the district court and conclude that the government's decision to deport Reziniano without informing either the court or Yida's counsel, without taking a video deposition, and without having any means of compelling his return, was not reasonable. . . . Finally, while the government did offer to pay Reziniano's travel expenses, the district court was "not convinced" that this was sufficient under the circumstances. . . . A witness who poses a risk of flight, who has spent nearly five years in prison serving his sentence for a felony conviction, who has stated that he did not wish to testify in the first trial, and who has expressed his desire to return to his native county [sic], is unlikely to be swayed to return to the United States by the Government's offer to pay his expenses.

We also reject the government's argument that Reziniano is unavailable by reason of medical necessity pursuant to Federal Rule of Evidence 804(a)(4). We conclude that the district court did not err when it found that the government had failed to establish Reziniano's unavailability due to medical necessity. As Yida points out, "[n]othing about the district court's ruling supports the government's contention that the district court failed to consider the medical-necessity argument." In its written decision, the district court explicitly referred to its conclusions that there was nothing in the record to suggest that Reziniano's health precluded him from "traveling for a short period of time."

Accordingly, we affirm the district court's exclusion of Reziniano's prior testimony in Yida's retrial because the government has not established that the witness is unavailable under Federal Rule of Evidence 804(a).

---

6. *Finding of "Availability" If the Proponent Is Responsible for the Witness's Unavailability*

Even if the proponent seeking to show that a witness is unavailable establishes that one of the five definitions of "unavailability" is met, the witness will not be deemed to be unavailable if the proponent is the one who *caused* the witness to be unavailable. Thus, a party who shoots a witness dead cannot show up to court and say, "Well, he's unavailable, so please admit his declarations against interest."

The issues can get more complex in criminal cases. The mere fact that the prosecution refuses to give immunity to a witness who is asserting a Fifth Amendment privilege is ordinarily not enough to claim that the government "procured" the unavailability of the witness. By contrast, if the government in a criminal case allows a witness to leave the jurisdiction without first securing the witness's testimony, it may be barred from claiming that the witness is unavailable under FRE 804(a)(5).

Review Questions

1. **Former testimony.** Plaintiff seeks to introduce the former testimony of a witness. In which of the following situations would the witness be "unavailable" pursuant to FRE 804(a)?
   a. The witness is on a long trip and is not expected to return for three months.
   b. A week before trial, Plaintiff attempted to serve a subpoena on the witness, but the witness would not open her door.
   c. The witness has suffered a stroke and will be in the hospital for the foreseeable future.
   d. The witness has invoked the Fifth Amendment privilege not to testify.
   e. The elderly witness has only a spotty memory of the events at issue in the case.
   f. Plaintiff paid for the witness to go on a lengthy cruise at the time of trial.
   g. Plaintiff declined to take the witness's deposition before trial.

PART B: HEARSAY EXCEPTIONS APPLICABLE WHEN THE DECLARANT IS UNAVAILABLE AS A WITNESS

1. Former Testimony Exception [FRE 804(b)(1)]

The former testimony exception sometimes allows testimony from a former proceeding—which is hearsay because it was not adduced in *this* proceeding—to be admitted if the witness is not available to testify in the current proceeding. When former testimony is admitted, the court may allow the parties to read the prior testimony to the jury or, if the testimony was videotaped (such as in a deposition), to play the appropriate portions of the testimony for the trier of fact.

The following graphic illustrates how the former testimony exception typically arises:

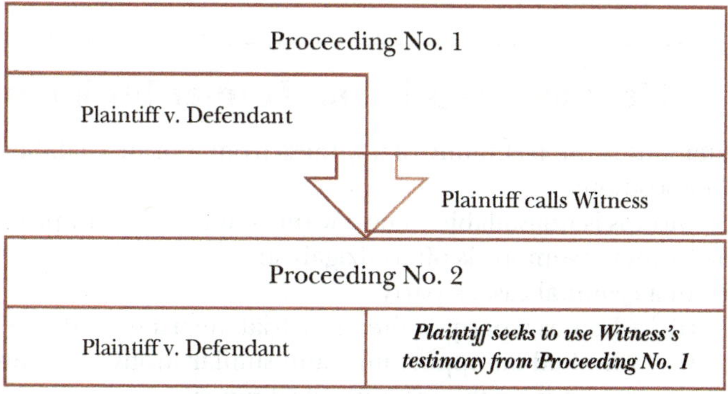
Proceeding No. 1
Plaintiff v. Defendant
Plaintiff calls Witness
Proceeding No. 2
Plaintiff v. Defendant
Plaintiff seeks to use Witness's testimony from Proceeding No. 1

Here are a few concrete examples.

Examples

1. Defendant was charged with narcotics possession. The first trial results in a mistrial. Before the retrial, a witness dies. Prosecutor or Defendant seeks to introduce the witness's testimony from the first trial.
2. Plaintiff sues his employer for injuries suffered at work. The defense calls an expert at the first trial. Plaintiff wins the case, but the judgment is reversed on appeal. By this time, the defense expert is unavailable to testify. The defense will seek to introduce its expert's testimony from the first trial.

The exception is set forth in FRE 804(b)(1):

FRE 804. Hearsay Exceptions; Declarant Unavailable

(b) The Exceptions. The following are not excluded by the rule against hearsay if the declarant is unavailable as a witness:

(1) ***Former Testimony.*** Testimony that:

(A) was given as a witness at trial, hearing, or lawful deposition, whether given during the current proceeding or a different one; and

(B) is now offered against a party who had—or, in a civil case, whose predecessor in interest had—an opportunity and similar motive to develop it by direct, cross-, or redirect examination.

Thus, the hearsay exception for former testimony has the following requirements:

Hearsay Exception for Former Testimony

(1) Statement is the testimony of a witness from a prior trial, hearing, or lawful deposition;
(2) The witness is unavailable to be a witness in the present proceeding; *and*
(3) The former testimony is offered against:
  (A) In a criminal case, a party
    (i) who was a party in the prior trial, hearing, or deposition; and
    (ii) who had an opportunity and similar motive to examine the witness during the prior proceeding; *or*
  (B) In a civil case, a party

(i) who was a party or whose predecessor in interest was a party in the prior trial, hearing, or deposition; and
(ii) who (or whose predecessor in interest) had an opportunity and similar motive to examine the witness during the prior proceeding.

As these requirements indicate, the former testimony exception is grounded in both necessity and trustworthiness. It is based on necessity insofar as it applies only if the witness is now unavailable to testify. It is based on the trustworthiness of the prior testimony as it applies only if the witness's testimony—during the prior proceeding—was subjected to testing by a party (or, in a civil case, by the party's predecessor in interest).

In addition to the unavailability of the witness, the applicability of the former testimony exception turns on three further questions:

- From what *types of proceedings* may the prior testimony come, and who must have been a party to those prior proceedings?
- When does a party to a prior proceeding (or, in a civil case, the party's predecessor in interest) have an *opportunity and similar motive to examine* the witness?
- *Against whom* may former testimony be introduced?

(a) From What Types of Proceedings May the Prior Testimony Come, and Who Must Have Been a Party to Those Proceedings?

To qualify as a "prior proceeding" from which former testimony may be drawn, the prior proceeding must be the type that would have given the party against whom it is offered now (or, in a civil case, the party's predecessor in interest) an opportunity to cross-examine that witness in a meaningful fashion. In civil cases, the prior proceeding does not have to be from the same case, but it has to have been from a parallel case in which the same issues were raised and therefore the witness's testimony would relate to the issues in the current lawsuit.

In a civil case, the former testimony exception may apply even when the party to the prior proceeding is a current party's predecessor-in-interest. The question, of course, is who does the rule consider to be a "predecessor in interest"?[6] Unfortunately, FRE 804(b)(1) does not define this term. If construed narrowly, a predecessor in interest could take on the formal, legal meaning as persons who have joint

6. Some states, such as California and Texas, sidestep this question by allowing former testimony to be introduced in a civil case against a party as long as the witness's testimony was presented or tested by a party to the prior proceeding "with an interest and motive similar to that which the party against whom the testimony is offered has." Cal. Evid. Code § 1292; Tex. R. Evid. 804(b)(1)(A)(ii) (asking whether the nonparty had a "similar interest"). California also allows former testimony to be used against a party if the party's predecessor in interest *introduced* that testimony at the prior proceeding. Cal. Evid Code § 1292.

or successive legal rights, such that the successor must stand in their shoes in the eyes of the law. This definition would include the successor to a corporation, the heirs to a decedent, a successor property owner, and the like. If construed broadly, a predecessor in interest could mean anyone who had the same motives and incentives to examine the witness in the prior proceeding as the party in the current proceeding would have had. Construing the term so broadly might effectively write the predecessor-in-interest requirement out of the exception because the requirement would become entirely duplicative of the "similar motive" requirement that is already in the exception.

Which definition have the federal courts chosen? Most have adopted the broader definition. *See Lloyd v. American Export Lines*, 580 F.2d 1179 (3d Cir. 1978); *Dykes v. Raymark Industries, Inc.*, 801 F.2d 810, 816 (6th Cir. 1986). A more recent case adopting the broader definition is *Corcoran v. CVS Pharmacies, Inc.*

Corcoran v. CVS Pharm., Inc.

2021 U.S. Dist. LEXIS 104422 (N.D. Cal. 2021)

Gonzalez Rogers, Judge.

[CVS Pharmacy was sued for systematically overcharging people who bought certain generic drugs using insurance rather than cash. CVS had been engaged in prior litigation regarding its billing practices.]

Plaintiffs' Motion to Exclude Deposition Testimony Obtained by CVS in Other Litigation

[P]laintiffs filed a motion seeking an order excluding deposition testimony of Joseph Zavalishin obtained by CVS in *Sheet Metal Worker Local No. 20 v. CVS Pharmacy, Inc.* ("*Sheet Metal*"). Plaintiffs contend that the designated excerpts from such testimony taken in April 2019 are inadmissible hearsay that do not qualify as an exception under Federal Rule of Evidence ("FRE") 804(b)(1).

CVS contends that the Sheet Metal plaintiffs are "predecessors in interest" of plaintiffs here in light of the subject matter of the two cases and their shared motives in cross-examining the witness. The Court agrees.

Under the FRE 804(b)(1), "predecessor in interest" is meant to be read generously where a former action involved a party with similar motives to cross-examine as the present party on similar issues.

The Sheet Metal action was filed by third-party payors alleging that CVS and five pharmacy benefit mangers ("PBMs"), including OptumRx, engaged in a scheme to overcharge the third-party payors in violation of the Racketeer Influenced and Corrupt Organizations Act and various state laws. Specifically, the Sheet Metal plaintiffs alleged that CVS defrauded and overcharged the health plans in failing to treat its Health Savings Pass membership prices as its Usual and Customary prices when reporting U&C prices to the PBMs. Accordingly, plaintiffs' contention that "the Sheet Metal plaintiffs have different legal theories and motives in questioning the PBMs" does not persuade.

Indeed, at the conference, plaintiffs' counsel appeared to concede that counsel for the Sheet Metal plaintiffs, who are members of a national well-respected plaintiffs firm, conducted a meaningful cross-examination of another PBM but for whatever reason "limited their cross examination [of Zavalishin] to a handful of questions that are not relevant to Plaintiffs' claims here." The standard is not whether plaintiffs believe counsel for the Sheet Metal plaintiffs could have more effectively cross-examined Mr. Zavalishin. Rather, the relevant question is whether the Sheet Metal plaintiffs "had an opportunity and similar motive to develop the testimony" in their case. The Court finds that they did and thereby concludes that Mr. Zavalishin's deposition testimony in the Sheet Metal case qualifies as a hearsay exception under FRE 804(b)(1). Accordingly, plaintiffs' motion to exclude this testimony is DENIED.

FRE 804(b)(1)(A) provides that former testimony may be given at a "trial, hearing, or lawful deposition." In criminal cases, the prior proceedings must have been prior proceedings against that defendant where the defendant would have had an opportunity to examine or cross-examine the witness. Here are some of the most common prior proceedings and a discussion of whether they satisfy this statutory definition:

- *Prior trial.* In either a civil or criminal case, a witness's testimony at a prior trial can qualify under the former testimony exception. "Trial" is expressly listed as a permissible type of former proceeding and it is an adversarial proceeding.
- *Grand jury proceedings.* The grand jury is a body drawn from members of the community who evaluate the evidence presented to them by the prosecutor and, in a secret vote, decide whether the prosecutor has presented sufficient evidence to find probable cause to believe a person has committed the crimes the prosecution charges; as to those crimes, the grand jury returns an indictment. Grand jury proceedings are *not* adversarial; the defendant is not present (unless called as a witness), and no judge presides.
  - *Against the defendant.* Prosecutors cannot use a witness's grand jury testimony against a criminal defendant at a later proceeding because (1) the former testimony exception requires that the same party be a party in the prior proceeding and (2) the criminal defendant was not a party to the grand jury proceeding.
  - *Against the prosecution.* It is less clear whether defendants can use a witness's grand jury testimony against the prosecution at a later proceeding. There is no absolute bar on such use because the prosecution was a party to both proceedings. As discussed below, what is less clear is whether the prosecution has a sufficiently similar motive to examine a grand jury witness.
- *Preliminary hearings.* A preliminary hearing is an adversarial proceeding at which the prosecution presents evidence to convince a trial judge that there is probable cause to believe that the individual has committed the crimes that the prosecutor alleges. A preliminary hearing serves the same function as the grand jury except that the defendant is present and represented at the hearing. Preliminary hearings are rare in federal court

(because they are used only if the defendant waives the constitutional right to indictment by grand jury), but are commonplace in state criminal proceedings. Because a preliminary hearing is a prior "hearing" and involves the same parties as the later criminal trial, preliminary hearing testimony can qualify as former testimony. Indeed, the potential availability of this hearsay exception is why prosecutors will often call a witness who they fear may flee or recant as a witness at the preliminary hearing, thus preserving the possibility of qualifying that testimony as "former testimony." The key determinant is whether the parties had the same incentive to examine the witnesses at a preliminary hearing as they do at trial.

- *Suppression hearings.* At a suppression hearing, a criminal defendant invokes constitutional or statutory rights to suppress a prior confession or other incriminating physical evidence. This adversarial proceeding involves the same parties as the subsequent trial. As such, testimony from a suppression hearing can qualify as former testimony; the determinative issue is whether the parties had the same motive to examine witnesses at the suppression hearing as they do at the trial.[7]
- *Depositions.* Depositions occur upon the parties' demand in civil cases and with court permission in criminal cases when there are "exceptional circumstances" and the "interest of justice" so require. Fed. R. Civ. Pro. 30; Fed. R. Crim. P. 15. However, a witness's testimony during a deposition can qualify as former testimony because depositions are listed in the exception and because they involve the same parties.
- *Internal hearings.* A non-judicial hearing may qualify, but not if it was too informal and did not provide opportunities to examine or cross-examine a witness similar to those opportunities at trial. For example, if an employee sues an employer for sexual harassment, the fact that the harasser's boss held an informal hearing before firing the harasser does not necessarily qualify as testimony from a hearing that can be introduced in the employee's sexual harassment lawsuit under the former testimony exception.

Importantly, it does not matter whether the testimony was offered *by* the party (that is, if the party called the witness and examined him on direct or redirect) in the prior proceeding or offered *against* that party (that is, if the party cross-examined the witness who was called by someone else). The former testimony exception covers both.

(b) When Does a Party to a Prior Proceeding (or, in a Civil Case, the Party's Predecessor in Interest) Have an Opportunity and Similar Motive to Examine the Witness?

This prerequisite is often the linchpin of applying the former testimony exception. It is aimed at assuring the trustworthiness of the former testimony: If the party to the prior proceeding had the same incentives to root out falsehoods in a witness's

7. Even if a criminal defendant's testimony at a suppression hearing satisfies the former testimony hearsay exception (or the opposing party hearsay exception), the prosecution will still not be able to admit that testimony in its case-in-chief at trial; this special rule rests on policy considerations wholly apart from the rules of evidence. *See Simmons v. United States*, 390 U.S. 377, 394 (1968).

testimony in that proceeding, that prior testimony is trustworthy enough to be admitted in the current proceeding without the opportunity for further adversarial testing.

Whether the party (or, in a civil case, the party's predecessor in interest) had an *opportunity* to examine the witness in a prior proceeding was discussed in the last section. However, there are two additional points. First, even if a party had the opportunity *in theory* to examine a witness in the prior proceeding, if the judge presiding over that proceeding unnecessarily curtailed that opportunity, the former testimony exception may not apply. For instance, if the trial judge presiding over a preliminary hearing allowed the defendant to cross-examine a witness for five minutes and no longer and cut off defense counsel at that five-minute mark, the defendant may have a good argument that he was denied the opportunity to examine that witness (even though, in general, defendants have the opportunity to examine witnesses at preliminary hearings). Second, all that is required is the *opportunity*. If a defendant elects not to question a witness during a preliminary hearing, he still had the opportunity to do so.

Whether the party (or, in a civil case, the party's predecessor in interest) had a *similar motive* to examine the witness in the prior proceeding is usually the harder question. In determining whether the prior party had a similar motive to examine the witness at a prior proceeding, courts will consider whether the circumstances and issues in the prior case were so different that it would not be appropriate to allow the testimony to be used against a party. However, arguments that the subsequent party would have been better at doing the examination or had different resources to attack the witness's testimony may not be sufficient to challenge the admission of the former testimony.

(i) Prior trial

Does a defendant have the similar motive to examine the same witness in a first trial as he has in a second trial? That was the question at issue in *United States v. Ausby*.

United States v. Ausby

436 F. Supp. 3d 134 (D.D.C. 2019)

HOWELL, Judge.

The defendant, John Milton Ausby, faces retrial on one count of felony murder, for the murder of Deborah Noel on December 14, 1971, after the defendant's 1972 conviction on the same charge was vacated pursuant to [a motion to vacate his conviction]. As retrial approaches, the parties now dispute whether the trial transcripts from the defendant's original trial in 1972 should be admitted as evidence. The government moves to admit the trial transcripts for twelve unavailable witnesses pursuant to Federal Rule of Evidence 804(b)(1). Conversely, the defendant seeks to exclude these and any other transcripts.

I. BACKGROUND

On December 14, 1971, Deborah Noel was raped and murdered in her apartment in Northwest Washington, D.C. In 1972, the defendant was tried and convicted by a jury of one count of felony murder and one count of rape while armed, for the rape and murder of Noel. He was sentenced to life in prison for the felony murder conviction and 10 to 30 years. At a separate trial, in 1973, the defendant was also convicted of murdering two other women, Sharon Tapp and Sherry Frahm. The defendant has been incarcerated for 47 years.

While the defendant was still incarcerated on the felony murder conviction, in 2015, following review of the defendant's case by the Department of Justice and the Federal Bureau of Investigation ("FBI"), the government concluded that "microscopic hair comparison analysis" used in the defendant's original trial "contained erroneous statements" and "exceeded the limits of science."

In 2016, the defendant filed a Motion to Vacate Conviction, arguing that "the government's knowing presentation of false and misleading expert hair examination testimony" violated the Due Process Clause of the Fifth Amendment and required vacatur of the defendant's conviction. Apart from the hair matching testimony, this evidence included: a fingerprint found in Noel's apartment, matched to a known fingerprint of the defendant by a government expert, testimony from a forensic firearms expert concluding that the bullet used to kill Noel was compatible with the gun seized from the defendant upon his arrest in New York City three days after the murder, testimony from a neighbor who said she saw the defendant on the third floor of Noel's apartment building, near Noel's apartment, and testimony from an importer and seller of scented oils, who said he sold to the defendant two vials of the same oil later found at the crime scene.

Now, on remand, the government seeks to proceed with a new trial. Aside from the forensic hair examiner, twenty-two witnesses testified for the government, including neighbors and employees in the building where Noel lived, the police officers who examined the crime scene and undertook forensic analysis of the evidence, and the medical examiner who performed the autopsy on Noel. In addition, the government relied on physical evidence, which included: the bullet used to kill Noel, a fingerprint found in her apartment, later matched to a known fingerprint of the defendant; vials of scented oil found in the apartment and similar vials from the same source in the possession of the defendant at the time of his arrest.

Forty-seven years later, much of this original trial evidence is no longer available. Of the twenty-two witnesses . . . originally presented by the government, nine are no longer alive, and the whereabouts of two others are unknown. The memories of the remaining ten government witnesses, meanwhile, "have faded or are gone completely." The government's fifty original trial exhibits, including all of the physical evidence in the case, have been lost or destroyed. Thus, the primary evidence that remains, and that the government intends to introduce, is the transcripts of the 1972 trial.

The government contends that the prior testimony of twelve government witnesses who testified at the defendant's original trial in 1972 is admissible under Federal Rule of Evidence 804(b)(1) because each of the witnesses is either deceased or "unavailable" and the defendant "had an opportunity to cross-examine" each witness during the original trial.

Admissibility of Prior Trial Testimony Under Fed. R. Evid. 804(b)(1)

The defendant argues that the trial transcripts are inadmissible under Federal Rule of Evidence 804(b)(1). Here, eleven of the witnesses whose transcripts the government seeks to admit have died, are believed to have died, or cannot be located. One additional witness, the fingerprint analyst Joseph Mullinax, has a medical condition preventing him from traveling or testifying.

To be sure, the record in this case does not show that the government "procured" or "wrongfully caused" the unavailability of its witnesses. Under the defense theory of unavailability, the government intentionally cloaked the flaws in the forensic hair testimony presented in the defendant's case, resulting in the almost fifty-year delay in the retrial. [T]he record does not support the contention that the government purposefully delayed revealing the evidence in the defendant's case, or that the government has failed to demonstrate "good-faith, reasonable efforts" to procure its witnesses for trial. Accordingly, the witnesses are "unavailable" within the meaning of Rule 804.

The defendant further contends that the defense did not have an "opportunity and similar motive" to develop the government's witness testimony at the original trial. Focusing in particular on the government's expert witnesses, the defendant first argues that he lacked an "opportunity" to cross-examine the now unavailable witnesses because at the time of the original trial, "relevant information, particular technical standards, and widespread availability of independent testing did not yet exist." Put another way, the defendant believes his opportunity to cross-examine would be more fulsome with today's forensic and scientific knowledge than was possible in 1972.

Second, the defendant argues that he lacked a "similar motive" during the original trial because prior defense counsel pursued a relatively narrow defense theory, while current counsel plans to pursue a broader trial strategy. According to the defendant, prior defense counsel chose not to contest government evidence suggesting that the defendant had been in the building and even in the Noel's apartment prior to the murder, but proffered a defense theory that the defendant had not been present on the day of the crime. Current defense counsel, by contrast, will develop a broader defense theory in two ways. First, current counsel intends to challenge the scientific validity of the government's expert testimony and to question the reliability of the eyewitness testimony used to establish the defendant's presence in the building prior to the crime.

[The court finds] the defendant undoubtedly had a similar motive to cross-examine the government's witnesses during the original trial as now. In both circumstances, the defendant's ultimate interest and "fundamental objective" was to contest the government's evidence as much as possible, so as to disprove the felony-murder charge against him.

[However,] the defendant [also argues that] the use of Rule 804(b)(1) to admit prior testimony in bulk, has greater force [because] admitting so much prior testimony . . . would "freez[e]" the new trial, leaving the defendant with a "trial by transcript" and a mere "replay of 1972." Any evidence admissible under Rule 804(b) must also pass muster under Federal Rule of Evidence 403. Where, as here, a party seeks the admission of "entire transcripts" into evidence, the "required analysis [under Rule 403] is context-specific and must be made on a case-by-case basis." [So much of the prior witness's testimony relies on exhibits that are no longer available, the prejudice of admitting the prior testimony outweighs its probative value. There is also no way to test the memory of the witness at the time and how they would have been affected by new information obtained regarding the case.] Accordingly, [the court will allow the former testimony of some of the government's witnesses, but will preclude the testimony of others who are no longer available.]

(ii) Prior grand jury proceeding

As noted above, a witness's testimony before a grand jury is never admissible as former testimony against the criminal defendant because the defendant was not a party to the grand jury proceeding. But the prosecution was. When can a witness's testimony before a grand jury be deemed former testimony admissible *against the prosecution*? The answer turns on whether the prosecution had a similar motive to examine the witness before the grand jury as it does at the trial. Such was the issue in *United States v. DiNapoli.*

United States v. DiNapoli

8 F.3d 909 (2d Cir. 1993)

NEWMAN, Chief Judge.

On this criminal appeal . . . the issue concerns Rule 804(b)(1) of the Federal Rules of Evidence, which provides that testimony given by a currently unavailable witness at a prior hearing is not excluded by the hearsay rule if "the party against whom the testimony is now offered . . . had an opportunity and *similar motive to develop the testimony* by direct, cross, or redirect examination." Our precise issue is whether the prosecution had a "similar motive to develop" the testimony of two grand jury witnesses compared to its motive at a subsequent criminal trial at which the witnesses were unavailable.

BACKGROUND

Briefly, the case concerns conspiracy and substantive charges under the Racketeer Influenced and Corrupt Organizations Act ("RICO") . . . against several defendants accused of participating in a bid-rigging scheme in the concrete construction industry in Manhattan. The trial evidence indicated the existence of a "Club" of six concrete construction companies that during 1980-1985 rigged the bids for concrete superstructure work on nearly every high-rise construction project in Manhattan involving more than $ 2 million of concrete work.

The grand jury investigating the matter returned its first indictment. . . . That indictment alleged the essential aspects of the criminal activity and named all of the appellants as defendants. The grand jury continued its investigation in an effort to identify additional participants and additional construction projects that might have been victimized by the bid-rigging scheme. In this subsequent phase of the inquiry, the grand jury called Frederick DeMatteis and Pasquale Bruno as witnesses.

They had been principals in Cedar Park Concrete Construction Corporation ("Cedar Park") [and] both testifying under grants of immunity, denied awareness of a bid-rigging scheme.

DeMatteis testified in the grand jury on three occasions . . . At his third appearance, the prosecutor pointedly asked whether DeMatteis had been instructed not to bid on the Javits Convention Center project and whether he was aware of an arrangement whereby the successful bidder paid two percent of the bid price to organized crime figures. DeMatteis denied both the instruction not to bid and awareness of the two percent arrangement. The prosecutor, obviously skeptical of the denials, pressed DeMatteis with a few questions in the nature of cross-examination. However, in order not to reveal the identity of then undisclosed cooperating witnesses or the existence of then undisclosed wiretapped conversations that refuted DeMatteis's denials, the prosecutor refrained from confronting him with the substance of such evidence. Instead, the prosecutor called to DeMatteis's attention the substance of only the one relevant wiretapped conversation that had already become public. . . .

Bruno testified at the grand jury. . . . Like DeMatteis, Bruno was asked about and denied knowledge of the "Club" and the two percent arrangement for successful bidders. And, like DeMatteis, he was briefly cross-examined and confronted with the contents of the publicly disclosed tape . . . but not with any of the information from undisclosed witnesses or wiretaps.

A thirteen-month trial on a superseding indictment . . . commenced against eleven defendants, with the convictions of nine defendants, including the six appellants. During the trial, the defendants endeavored to call DeMatteis and Bruno as witnesses. Both invoked the privilege against self-incrimination. The defendants then offered the testimony DeMatteis and Bruno had given to the grand jury. After examining sealed affidavits presented by the prosecution, the District Court refused to admit the grand jury testimony as prior testimony under Rule 804(b)(1). Judge Lowe . . . ruled generally that the "motive of a prosecutor . . . in the investigatory stages of a case is far different from the motive of a prosecutor in conducting the trial" and hence the "similar motive" requirement of Rule 804(b)(1) was not satisfied.

[T]he Supreme Court reversed the panel's reversal of the convictions. The Supreme Court ruled that all of the requirements of Rule 804(b)(1) must be met, including the "similar motive" requirement. The Court declined to decide whether the "similar motive" requirement was satisfied in this case, believing it "prudent to remand the case for further consideration" of that issue.

DISCUSSION

Our initial task is to determine how similarity of motive at two proceedings will be determined for purposes of Rule 804(b)(1). In resolving this matter, we do not accept the position, apparently urged by the appellants, that the test of similar motive is simply whether at the two proceedings the questioner takes the same side of the same issue. The test must turn not only on whether the questioner is on the same side of the same issue at both proceedings, but also on whether the questioner had a substantially similar interest in asserting that side of the issue.

If a fact is critical to a cause of action at a second proceeding but the same fact was only peripherally related to a different cause of action at a first proceeding, no one would claim that the questioner had a similar motive at both proceedings to show that the fact had been established (or disproved).

Whether the degree of interest in prevailing on an issue is substantially similar at two proceedings will sometimes be affected by the nature of the proceedings. Where both proceedings are trials and the same matter is seriously disputed at both trials, it will normally be the case that the side opposing the version of a witness at the first trial had a motive to develop that witness's testimony similar to the motive at the second trial.

The situation is not necessarily the same where the two proceedings are different in significant respects, such as their purposes or the applicable burden of proof. The grand jury context, with which we are concerned in this case, well illustrates the point. If a prosecutor is using the grand jury to investigate possible crimes and identify possible criminals, it may be quite unrealistic to characterize the prosecutor as the "opponent" of a witness's version.

Even in cases like the pending one, where the grand jury proceeding has progressed far beyond the stage of a general inquiry, the motive to develop grand jury testimony that disputes a position already taken by the prosecutor is not necessarily the same as the motive the prosecutor would have if that same testimony was presented at trial. Once the prosecutor has decided to seek an indictment against identified suspects, that prosecutor may fairly be characterized as "opposed" to any testimony that tends to exonerate one of the suspects. But, because of the low burden of proof at the grand jury stage, even the prosecutor's status as an "opponent" of the testimony does not necessarily create a motive to challenge the testimony that is *similar* to the motive at trial.

The proper approach, therefore, in assessing similarity of motive under Rule 804(b)(1) must consider whether the party resisting the offered testimony at a pending proceeding had at a prior proceeding an interest of substantially similar intensity to prove (or disprove) the same side of a substantially similar issue. The nature of the two proceedings—both what is at stake and the applicable burden of proof—and, to a lesser extent, the cross-examination at the prior proceeding—both what was undertaken and what was available but forgone—will be relevant though not conclusive on the ultimate issue of similarity of motive.

Since the grand jury as fact-finder had already resolved the issue of the Club's existence in the prosecutor's favor and had announced disbelief of the witnesses' contrary statements, dissimilarity of motive is beyond dispute. The District Court's exclusion of the witnesses' grand jury testimony was therefore entirely correct, and this ground for reversal of the convictions is rejected.

DiNapoli is not the only word on this issue. Other courts have found that the prosecution has the same motive to elicit testimony before the grand jury as it does at trial. *United States v. Foster,* 128 F.3d 949, 955-56 (6th Cir. 1997) (collecting cases). Still other courts take a more fact-specific approach by asking whether the prosecution had a similar motive to develop "the specific portion of the testimony at issue" (rather than looking to the witness's testimony as a whole). *See United States v. Omar*, 104 F.3d 519, 523 (1st Cir. 1997).

(iii) Prior preliminary hearing

The courts are split over whether a criminal defendant has a sufficiently similar motive to examine a witness at a preliminary hearing as she does at trial. On the one hand, the same general question is at issue at both trials—namely, did the defendant do it? On the other hand, the burden of proof at a preliminary hearing is much lower (probable cause rather than beyond a reasonable doubt), so defendants often use preliminary hearing questioning as a discovery tool and otherwise do not press a witness too much because (1) it is very difficult to get a charge dismissed on the basis of insufficient evidence at the preliminary hearing stage and (2) too much questioning might reveal the defense strategy for trial.

The courts are also split over whether the prosecution has a sufficiently similar motive to examine witnesses at the preliminary hearing as they do at trial. Although the ultimate issue (of guilt) is the same, prosecutors do not have much of a reason to *attack* the witnesses they call at a preliminary hearing, where the sole purpose is only to establish probable cause.

(iv) Suppression hearings

Whether the prosecution or defense has a sufficiently similar motive in examining witnesses at a suppression hearing as they do at trial likely turns on the subject matter of the witness's testimony. If the issue at trial is the voluntariness or circumstances of the defendant's confession challenged at the suppression hearing, both parties likely have a strong incentive to probe the witness on that topic, and the unavailable witness's testimony on that topic may be admissible as former testimony. But if the issue is something unrelated to the subject of the suppression motion, the fact that the witness was previously on the stand at the suppression hearing is unlikely to be enough to qualify the prior testimony as former testimony.

(v) Depositions

The prior deposition testimony of a witness in a proceeding between the parties on the same issue is likely to qualify as former testimony because the parties likely had a sufficiently similar motive in the deposition as they do at the subsequent trial.

(c) Against Whom May Former Testimony Be Introduced?

As touched on above, when it comes to the party *against whom* former testimony may be admitted, the answer turns first and foremost on whether the current proceeding is a criminal proceeding or a civil proceeding. Specifically, FRE 804(b)(1) sets up the following rules:

Nature of Current Proceeding	Rule
Criminal	Against party who was a party to the prior proceeding
Civil	Against party who was a party to the prior proceeding; *or*
	Against party whose predecessor in interest was a party to the prior proceeding

(i) Criminal proceedings

By its plain text, FRE 804(b)(1) allows former testimony to be admitted in a criminal case only against an entity or person who was a party to the prior proceeding. FRE 804(b)(1)(A). This limitation dovetails with the criminal defendant's Sixth Amendment right to confront and cross-examine witnesses. *See* Chapter Nine. If the prosecutor could introduce witness testimony from a prior trial against *someone else,* the defendant would never have had the opportunity to examine that witness.

Thus, if the prosecution is going to use former testimony against a defendant, the most likely scenario is as follows:

Trial #1: Defendant was charged with offense. Witness X testifies.
Trial #2: Defendant still charged with same offense. Witness X is now unavailable. Witness's X's testimony from first trial is admitted.

(ii) Civil proceedings

The Federal Rules of Evidence are more flexible in civil cases.

Examples

1. Plaintiff sued Defendant for injuries in an accident. Witness A testified that Defendant's vehicle hit Plaintiff's vehicle. The verdict was overturned on appeal. By the time of the retrial, Witness A has died. Plaintiff seeks to introduce a transcript of Witness A's testimony from the first trial.
2. Plaintiff 1 sued defendant Pharmaceutical Co. because of problems with its medications. During the trial, Pharmaceutical Co. calls an expert to testify that the company's product was safe. The jury returns a defense verdict. Plaintiff 2 then proceeds with its case against defendant Pharmaceutical Co. The defense expert is now unavailable. Pharmaceutical Co. wants to introduce the expert's testimony from Plaintiff 1's trial. The key issue is again whether the product was safe. Plaintiff 2 never had a chance to cross-examine the expert in a deposition or other hearing.

In such cases, the former testimony of a witness may be admitted against a party if that party (as in Example 1) *or* a predecessor in interest to that party had a prior opportunity to examine that witness (as possibly in Example 2). As described above, the majority of federal courts have ruled that a predecessor in interest is anyone who had the same motives and incentives to examine the witness in the prior proceeding as the party would have had.

Review Questions

1. **No teller on the stand.** Ani and Fabi are arrested for bank robbery. They are tried separately. In Ani's trial, the teller testifies that Ani and Fabi robbed the bank. Ani is convicted. Before Fabi's trial, the teller dies. Prosecutor wants to introduce the teller's testimony from Ani's trial in its trial of Fabi. Admissible?
2. **Eyewitness expert.** In her defense, Ani calls an eyewitness expert to testify that bank tellers are notoriously inaccurate in their identifications because of the trauma of a robbery. The expert becomes unavailable before Fabi's trial. Fabi wants to use the expert's testimony from Ani's trial in her trial. Admissible?
3. **Unsafe apartment.** Toni Tenant sues her landlord, Sam Slumlord, after she is mugged in the entrance of her apartment building. Six months earlier, another tenant, Linda Lessee, had sued Sam Slumlord for the same type of incident. Toni Tenant wants to introduce testimony from Linda Lessee's trial from a witness who is no longer available. Admissible?
4. **Change in management.** Now, assume that Larry Landlord had purchased the building from Sam Slumlord and he owned it at the time that Linda Lessee was mugged. Linda Lessee wants to introduce witness testimony from Toni Tenant's case against Sam Slumlord. Admissible?
5. **Safety procedures.** Larry Landlord wants to introduce evidence from Toni Tenant's case that the safety procedures at the apartment met all appropriate safety standards. Admissible?

2. *Dying Declaration Exception [FRE 804(b)(2)]*

Dying declarations are one of the oldest exceptions to the hearsay rule. At common law, the exception was limited to a person's last words before death. The exception adopted by the Federal Rules of Evidence is slightly broader because it applies as long as the person *believes* they are facing imminent death, even if they do not actually die.

Consider the following examples.

Examples

1. Defendants are charged with killing a federal prison guard. As the guard is dying, he tells a fellow guard, "Johnny always had it out for me. He tried to shank me last week, but he missed. This time, he and his buddy, Joe, got the job done."
2. Kate is on the *Titanic* as it is sinking. She tells a fellow passenger, "The cruise line owner told me that the only way this boat could sink was if the captain didn't do his job right." Kate didn't die in the sinking, but she is in a coma and is unavailable to testify. Her family has sued the cruise company and wants to call the passenger to testify.

Specifically, FRE 804(b)(2) provides the following:

FRE 804. Hearsay Exceptions; Declarant Unavailable

(b) The Exceptions. The following are not excluded by the rule against hearsay if the declarant is unavailable as a witness:

(2) ***Statement Under the Belief of Imminent Death.*** In a prosecution for homicide or in a civil case, a statement that the declarant, while believing the declarant's death to be imminent, made about its cause or circumstances.

Thus, the hearsay exception for dying declarations has the following prerequisites:

Hearsay Exception for Dying Declarations

(1) The declarant is unavailable to be a witness in the present proceeding;
(2) The statement is being admitted in a criminal homicide case or a civil case;
(3) The declarant believed death was imminent; *and*
(4) The statement is about the cause or circumstances of what the declarant believed to be their impending death.

The dying declaration exception is partly based on necessity and partly based on implicit trustworthiness. It is based on necessity because it requires that the declarant be unavailable now—either because they died or for some other reason (they are in a coma or even currently beyond the court's jurisdiction). It is based on trustworthiness because the common belief is that people will make what they think are their last words on Earth count. In addition to the prerequisites that the declarant be unavailable as a witness and the limitation that the exception applies only in civil cases and in criminal cases for homicide (but not other crimes),[8] the dying declaration's two further elements warrant extended discussion.

(a) Belief That Death Is Imminent

Although the declarant's subsequent death is not a prerequisite to the admission of a dying declaration under the Federal Rules of Evidence,[9] the statement must be made while the declarant believes that he or she is *about to die.* As Justice Benjamin Cardozo eloquently put it, the exception applies only when "death is near at hand, and what is said [was] spoke in the hush of its impending presence." *Shepard v. United States,* 290 U.S. 96, 100 (1933). In deciding whether the declarant was in this frame of mind, courts look to (1) the declarant's physical condition, (2) the nature and seriousness of the victim's wounds or condition, (3) the victim's conduct, and (4) the victim's statements as well as knowledge of his or her condition. A few examples illustrate how the courts have applied these conditions regarding this prerequisite.

In *Shepard,* Dr. Charles Shepard was on trial for allegedly poisoning his wife. Weeks before her death, the wife declared that she believed that her husband was poisoning her. In *Shepard,* the Supreme Court held that the dying declaration exception did not apply. Although the wife may have feared that she would die, her condition at the time of the statement was not so dire as to suggest that she believed that death was imminent.

But there is no absolute time limit between the time of the statement and the time of death. If it appears that death is imminent, such as when a victim has been shot but manages to linger for weeks before succumbing to their wounds, a trial judge may find that the exception applies.

Suicide notes can also qualify as dying declarations if they demonstrate that the deceased believed that death was imminent. In evaluating whether the deceased believed that death was imminent, the trial judge may use the note itself to determine the declarant's belief.

Nadeau v. Shipman

2020 U.S. Dist. LEXIS 247846 (D.N.D. 2020)

Traynor, Judge.

This Matter comes before the Court on numerous Motions in Limine:

I. JOHN NADEAU'S RECORDED JAIL PHONE CALLS

Plaintiff Diana Nadeau, individually and on behalf of the next-of-kin of John Nadeau, moves for a preliminary ruling on the admissibility of seven recorded phone calls made by John Nadeau [from prison].

---

8. New York and Illinois limit it even further—just to homicide prosecutions. *People v. Becker,* 215 N.Y. 126, 145 (N.Y. 1915); Ill. R. Evid. 804(b)(2). By contrast, Texas, California and Florida impose no case-type limitations on the use of dying declarations. Tex. R. Evid. 804(b)(2); Cal. Evid. Code § 1242; Fl. Stat. § 90.804(2)(b).

9. Other jurisdiction still follow the common-law rule and make the declarant's post-statement death a prerequisite of this exception. California and New York fall into this category. Cal. Evid. Code § 1242; *People v. Nieves,* 67 N.Y.2d 125, 131-34 (N.Y. 1986).

This case is about a suicide in the jail and the contents of the phone call either deal with John Nadeau's suicidal ideations [or] mental health treatment, both of which relate to the claims in this case.

The calls Plaintiff seeks to admit are from one month or closer to the date of John Nadeau's suicide. They speak to his mental health struggles while in custody at MCCC and his suicidal ideations. The Court concludes the jail calls Plaintiff seeks to admit are not too remote to require exclusion.

II. SUICIDE NOTES

Plaintiff [also] moves for admission of John Nadeau's suicide notes on the same grounds as the jail calls.

This Court concludes the suicide note is a dying declaration under Rule 804(b)(2). To qualify as a dying declaration, the note must have been made by John Nadeau "while believing the [his] death to be imminent, made about its causes or circumstances." Fed. R. Evid. 804(b)(2). Two things are required to be admissible under Rule 804(b)(2): (1) John Nadeau wrote the letters while believing his death to be imminent and (2) the notes must be about the causes or circumstances surrounding his death.

The suicide note was found in his jail cell after John Nadeau committed suicide. The Court has reviewed the suicide note and concludes it is reasonable to believe John Nadeau wrote it believing his death was imminent because it included information pertaining to John Nadeau taking his own life. John Nadeau had been suffering with mental health concerns for months without appropriate attention from Dr. Addy, despite his retained position with the Morton County jail. In that way, the suicide notes describe the causes or circumstances surrounding Nadeau's death. Accordingly, the suicide notes are admissible as dying declarations. *See Pittman v. County of Madison* (2015) (concluding suicide notes in a deliberate indifference case involving a near-successful suicide are admissible as a dying declaration pursuant to Rule 804(b)(2) of the Federal Rules of Evidence).

Plaintiff's in Limine for the admission of a suicide note to John Nadeau's mother is GRANTED.

(b) Statement Regards Cause or Circumstances of Death

Because it aims to guarantee the trustworthiness of the statement, the requirement that the statement be about the cause and circumstances of the declarant's perceived impending death is limited in two ways.

First, it is explicitly limited to statements *about* the impending death. Statements about prior events fall outside the exception. Thus, in Example 1 above, the final portion of the declarant's statement (that Johnny and Joe "got the job done") is a dying declaration, the second portion (that "Johnny always had it out for me") may be a dying declaration to the extent it is evidence of Johnny's motive that circumstantially establishes the cause or circumstance of the declarant's death, and the first portion (that Johnny "tried to shank me last week, but he missed") is not a dying declaration, because the first portion does not deal with the cause or circumstances of the declarant's death but instead a prior incident.

Second, and like most (but not all) statements admissible under hearsay exceptions, a dying declaration must be based on personal knowledge. Thus, the declaration, "Bob just told me that Fidel shot me from behind the grassy knoll" does not qualify because it is not based on the declarant's personal knowledge but rather on what Bob told him. Similarly, the statement in Example 2 about the cause of the *Titanic* sinking is not based on personal knowledge. The personal knowledge requirement ensures that dying declarations are not speculative.

The requirements of the dying declaration exception under the Federal Rules are summed up in the following table:

Nature of Statement	(1) Based on personal knowledge (2) Made while speaker believed death was imminent; *and* (3) Regarding the cause or circumstances of the impending death
Status of Speaker	Unavailable (but not necessarily due to death)
Nature of Pending Case	(1) Homicide case; *or* (2) Any civil case

Review Questions

1. **Final subterfuge.** John is charged with attempted murder. He calls Jane Doe to testify that as the victim was dying, the victim said that her college roommate, Sally, had stabbed her but that Sally was going to pin it on John. Is this a dying declaration?
2. **Typo or ID?** John is charged with murder of A, and police find the word "John" typed on A's computer screen, next to his body. Is this a dying declaration?
3. **Tapped out.** Joe Victim is left paralyzed and incapable of communicating after a terrible car accident. His family has sued Big Motor Company. To prove that the accident was caused by faulty brakes, Joe's family wants to introduce the testimony of a passerby who heard Joe calmly say shortly after the accident, "I tried everything I could to stop, but the brakes have never worked." Is this a dying declaration?

3. Declaration Against Interest Exception [FRE 804(b)(3)]

As its name suggests, the hearsay exception for declarations against interest allows for the admission of statements that are harmful to the speaker himself—by subjecting the speaker to either penal or civil liability.

Examples

1. Plaintiff is suing his boss for wrongful termination. The boss fired Plaintiff when his department repeatedly sent the wrong product for orders. Plaintiff calls a witness to testify that another coworker had confided in him that "I keep messing up with the orders. I'm in big trouble if they figure out it is my fault, not [Plaintiff's]."
2. Defendant is charged with murdering Smith. He wants to call a fellow inmate who will testify that he heard another guy in the jail—who has since been released and cannot be found—say that "I hated Smith and was happy to get rid of him."

Specifically, FRE 804(b)(3) provides the following:

FRE 804. Hearsay Exceptions; Declarant Unavailable

(b) The Exceptions. The following are not excluded by the rule against hearsay if the declarant is unavailable as a witness:

(3) ***Statements Against Interest.*** A statement that:

(A) a reasonable person in the declarant's position would have made only if the person believed it to be true because, when made, it was so contrary to the declarant's proprietary or pecuniary interest or had so great a tendency to invalidate the declarant's claim against someone else or to expose the declarant to civil or criminal liability; and

(B) is supported by corroborating circumstances that clearly indicate its trustworthiness, if it is offered in a criminal case as one that tends to expose the declarant to criminal liability.

Thus, the hearsay exception for declarations against interest has the following prerequisites:

Hearsay Exception for Declarations Against Interest

(1) The declarant is unavailable to be a witness in the present proceeding;

(2) The statement was against the declarant's interest because it:

(A) was contrary to the declarant's proprietary or pecuniary interest;

(B) had a tendency to invalidate the declarant's claim against someone else; *or*

(C) had a tendency to expose the declarant to civil or criminal liability; *and*

(3) if offered in a criminal case and the statement subjects the declarant to criminal liability, the statement is supported by corroborating circumstances that clearly indicate the statement is trustworthy.

The declaration against interest exception is grounded in both necessity *and* trustworthiness. It is necessity-based to the extent that it requires the declarant currently be unavailable to testify.[10] It is trustworthiness-based in two ways. The exception has an implicit trustworthiness requirement because a declaration against interest is defined as a statement a reasonable person would not make unless it were true. Why admit, "Yeah, I shot Winifred" or "I totally made up the story about Tina harassing me at work" (thereby tanking a pending lawsuit) unless it were true? This implicit trustworthiness requirement rests on the notion that people are inherently self-interested. In criminal cases, the exception has a second *express* trustworthiness requirement—namely, it requires that the statement be backed up by corroborating circumstances.

(a) When Is a Statement Against the Declarant's Interest

In assessing whether a statement is against the declarant's interest, there are two subissues to consider: (1) what types of interests must be negatively impacted, and (2) when is the statement truly *against* one of those interests?

(i) What interests must be negatively impacted?

At common law, the declaration against interest exception applied only to pecuniary or proprietary interests. FRE 804(b)(3) is much broader and reaches statements that are harmful because they:

- Harm the declarant's ownership interests in property (that is, the declarant's proprietary interests);
- Cost the declarant money (that is, the declarant's pecuniary interests);
- Undermine a potential claim the declarant has against another;
- Render him civilly liable for his conduct; or
- Render him criminally liable for his conduct.

Some jurisdictions go ever further, reaching statements that are against the declarant's *social* interest by "creat[ing] a risk of making [the declarant] the object of hatred, ridicule, or social disgrace in the community." Cal. Evid. Code § 1230. FRE 804(b)(3) does not reach that far.

(ii) When is a statement *against* the declarant's interest?

In assessing whether a statement is against interest, two considerations are key.

First, context matters. The statement "Sure, I was at the bank at noon on Thursday" is not against one's interest in the abstract. However, if the bank was being robbed at noon on Thursday, admitting to being at the scene *can* be against one's interest. Along similar lines, a person's admission that he owes Darius $10,000 would seem to be against his pecuniary interest. However, if Darius is suing the person for $100,000, the admission to owing just a fraction of that amount may be more *in* the person's interest rather than *against* it.

This point is particularly important in the criminal context. Some statements that may seem to be against a person's penal interest may not be if they are designed

---

10. Texas does not require the unavailability of the witness. Tex. R. Evid. 803(24).

to curry favor with investigators or prosecutors. Admitting to a small role in a larger crime may be designed to put the declarant in the good graces of prosecutors to the declarant's advantage; such a statement is not against the declarant's interest. Some statements that may seem to be against a person's penal interest may not be if they shift the blame to someone else in the hopes of currying favor or of making the declarant's role seem small by comparison. Blame-shifting statements are likely not admissible under the exception because, as discussed next, the portion of those statements casting blame elsewhere are not inculpatory *as to the declarant*.

Contextual factors relevant to determining whether a statement is genuinely against a person's interest include:

- The content of the statement itself (for example, is the declarant shifting blame?);
- The circumstances under which the statement was made (for example, to the police (where there is a greater incentive to curry favor or shift blame) or instead to a close friend or relative (where there is no such incentive)?);
- The declarant's possible motivation(s);
- The declarant's relationship to the defendant; and
- Any corroboration of the statement by independent evidence.

Second, each statement, on its own, is to be evaluated for its possible adverse impact on the declarant. Put differently, the fact that the sum total of the declarant's statements has a "net inculpatory effect" is beside the point because *each statement* must be against the declarant's interest in order to be admissible. If a declarant makes four statements in a single conversation, the fact that one of them is genuinely inculpatory does not justify the admission of the other three statements that are not. Those other statements are considered "collateral."

The Supreme Court confronted these concerns in *Williamson v. United States.*

Williamson v. United States

512 U.S. 594 (1994)

JUSTICE O'CONNOR delivered the opinion of the Court, except as to Part II-C.

In this case we clarify the scope of the hearsay exception for statements against penal interest. Fed. Rule Evid. 804(b)(3).

A deputy sheriff stopped the rental car driven by Reginald Harris for weaving on the highway. Harris consented to a search of the car, which revealed 19 kilograms of cocaine in two suitcases in the trunk. Harris was promptly arrested. Shortly after Harris' arrest, Special Agent Donald Walton of the Drug Enforcement Administration (DEA) interviewed him by telephone. During that conversation, Harris said that he got the cocaine from an unidentified Cuban in Fort Lauderdale; that the cocaine belonged to petitioner Williamson; and that it was to be delivered that night to a particular dumpster. Williamson was also connected to Harris by physical evidence: Several hours later, Agent Walton spoke to Harris in person. During that interview, Harris said he had rented the car a few days earlier and had driven it to Fort Lauderdale to meet Williamson. According to Harris, he had gotten the cocaine from a Cuban who was Williamson's acquaintance, and the

Cuban had put the cocaine in the car with a note telling Harris how to deliver the drugs. Harris repeated that he had been instructed to leave the drugs in a certain dumpster, to return to his car, and to leave without waiting for anyone to pick up the drugs.

Agent Walton then took steps to arrange a controlled delivery of the cocaine. But as Walton was preparing to leave the interview room, Harris told Walton he had lied about the Cuban, the note, and the dumpster. The real story, Harris said, was that he was transporting the cocaine to Atlanta for Williamson, and that Williamson was traveling in front of him in another rental car. Harris added that after his car was stopped, Williamson turned around and drove past the location of the stop, where he could see Harris' car with its trunk open.

Harris told Walton that he had lied about the source of the drugs because he was afraid of Williamson. Though Harris freely implicated himself, he did not want his story to be recorded, and he refused to sign a written version of the statement. Walton testified that he had promised to report any cooperation by Harris to the Assistant United States Attorney.

Williamson was eventually convicted of possessing cocaine with intent to distribute, conspiring to possess cocaine with intent to distribute, and traveling interstate to promote the distribution of cocaine. When called to testify at Williamson's trial, Harris refused, even though the prosecution gave him use immunity and the court ordered him to testify and eventually held him in contempt. The District Court then ruled that, under Rule 804(b)(3), Agent Walton could relate what Harris had said to him.

Williamson appealed his conviction, claiming that the admission of Harris' statements violated Rule 804(b)(3) and the Confrontation Clause of the Sixth Amendment. Rule 804(b)(3) is founded on the commonsense notion that reasonable people, even reasonable people who are not especially honest, tend not to make self-inculpatory statements unless they believe them to be true. The fact that a person is making a broadly self-inculpatory confession does not make more credible the confession's non-self-inculpatory parts. One of the most effective ways to lie is to mix falsehood with truth, especially truth that seems particularly persuasive because of its self-inculpatory nature.

In this respect, it is telling that the non-self-inculpatory things Harris said in his first statement actually proved to be false, as Harris himself admitted during the second interrogation. And when part of the confession is actually self-exculpatory, the generalization on which Rule 804(b)(3) is founded becomes even less applicable.

Justice Kennedy suggests that the Advisory Committee's Notes to Rule 804(b)(3) should be read as endorsing the position we reject—that an entire narrative, including non-self-inculpatory parts (but excluding the clearly self-serving parts), may be admissible if it is in the aggregate self-inculpatory.

Whether a statement is in fact against interest must be determined from the circumstances of each case. Thus a statement admitting guilt and implicating another person, made while in custody, may well be motivated by a desire to curry favor with the authorities and hence fail to qualify as against interest. . . . On the other hand, the same words spoken under different circumstances, e. g., to an acquaintance, would have no difficulty in qualifying. . . .

Moreover, whether a statement is self-inculpatory or not can only be determined by viewing it in context. Even statements that are on their face neutral may actually be against the declarant's interest. "I hid the gun in Joe's apartment" may not be a confession of a crime; but if it is likely to help the police find the murder weapon, then it is certainly self-inculpatory. "Sam and I went to Joe's house" might be against the declarant's interest if a reasonable person in the declarant's shoes would realize that being linked to Joe and Sam would implicate the declarant in Joe and Sam's conspiracy. And other statements that give the police significant details about the crime may also, depending on the situation, be against the declarant's interest. The question under Rule 804(b)(3) is always whether the statement was sufficiently against the declarant's penal interest "that a reasonable person in the declarant's position would not have made the statement unless believing it to be true," and this question can only be answered in light of all the surrounding circumstances.

In this case, however, we cannot conclude that all that Harris said was properly admitted. Some of Harris' confession would clearly have been admissible under Rule 804(b)(3); for instance, when he said he knew there was cocaine in the suitcase, he essentially forfeited his only possible defense to a charge of cocaine possession, lack of knowledge. But other parts of his confession, especially the parts that implicated Williamson, did little to subject Harris himself to criminal liability. A reasonable person in Harris' position might even think that implicating someone else would decrease his practical exposure to criminal liability, at least so far as sentencing goes. Small fish in a big conspiracy often get shorter sentences than people who are running the whole show.

Nothing in the record shows that the District Court or the Court of Appeals inquired whether each of the statements in Harris' confession was truly self-inculpatory. As we explained above, this can be a fact-intensive inquiry, which would require careful examination of all the circumstances surrounding the criminal activity involved; we therefore remand to the Court of Appeals to conduct this inquiry in the first instance.

In light of this disposition, we need not address Williamson's claim that the statements were also made inadmissible by the Confrontation Clause.

Justice Kennedy, with whom The Chief Justice and Justice Thomas join, concurring in the judgment.

Because the text of Rule 804(b)(3) expresses no position regarding the admissibility of collateral statements, we must determine whether there are other authoritative guides on the question. In my view, three sources demonstrate that Rule 804(b)(3) allows the admission of some collateral statements: the Advisory Committee's Note, the common law of the hearsay exception for statements against interest, and the general presumption that Congress does not enact statutes that have almost no effect.

Though I would conclude that Rule 804(b)(3) allows admission of statements collateral to the precise words against interest, that conclusion of course does not answer the remaining question whether all collateral statements related to the statement against interest are admissible; and if not, what limiting principles should apply.

In the criminal context, a self-serving statement is one that tends to reduce the charges or mitigate the punishment for which the declarant might be liable. For example, if two masked gunmen robbed a bank and one of them shot and killed the bank teller, a statement by one robber that the other robber was the triggerman may be the kind of self-serving statement that should be inadmissible. By contrast, when two or more people are capable of committing a crime and the declarant simply names the involved parties, that statement often is considered neutral, not self-serving.

In sum, I would adhere to the following approach with respect to statements against penal interest that inculpate the accused. A court first should determine whether the declarant made a statement that contained a fact against penal interest. If so, the court should admit all statements related to the precise statement against penal interest, subject to two limits. Consistent with the Advisory Committee's Note, the court should exclude a collateral statement that is so self-serving as to render it unreliable (if, for example, it shifts blame to someone else for a crime the defendant could have committed). In addition, in cases where the statement was made under circumstances where it is likely that the declarant had a significant motivation to obtain favorable treatment, as when the government made an explicit offer of leniency in exchange for the declarant's admission of guilt, the entire statement should be inadmissible.

(b) What Type of Corroboration Is Required When a Statement That Subjects the Declarant to Criminal Liability Is to Be Admitted in a Criminal Case?

FRE 804(b)(3)(B)'s corroboration requirement applies in two scenarios. First, it applies when a defendant in a criminal case seeks to call a witness who will say that she heard a third party confess to the crime. This statement is a declaration that would subject that third party to criminal liability and is sought to be admitted in a criminal case, so the corroboration requirement applies. Second, the requirement applies when the prosecution seeks to use statements of third parties that also inculpate the defendant in a criminal case. (The *defendant's* inculpatory statements are likely to be admissible as adverse party admissions, eliminating any need to decide whether they are also declarations against interest.)

Corroboration can be any evidence—direct or circumstantial—that demonstrates that the unavailable declarant believed that it was against their penal interest to make the statement at the time it was made.

(c) Confrontation Clause Overlay

As discussed more fully in Chapter Nine, a criminal defendant has a Sixth Amendment right to confront witnesses against him, and this right includes the right to exclude out-of-court "testimonial" statements admitted for their truth unless the declarant is unavailable as a witness and the defendant has had a prior opportunity to cross-examine the declarant. *Crawford v. Washington*, 541 U.S. 36 (2004). These requirements make it nearly impossible to admit declarations against interest made by third parties to police because (1) statements to police are almost always testimonial (although statements made to private parties would not be), and (2) the same unavailability of a witness to testify at the hearing that renders a statement potentially admissible as a declaration against interest also means that the statement is inadmissible under *Crawford* (unless the declarant had the opportunity to cross-examine the declarant at an earlier hearing in the same case, such as during a preliminary hearing or prior trial).

The requirements for the declaration against interest exception can be graphically illustrated like this:

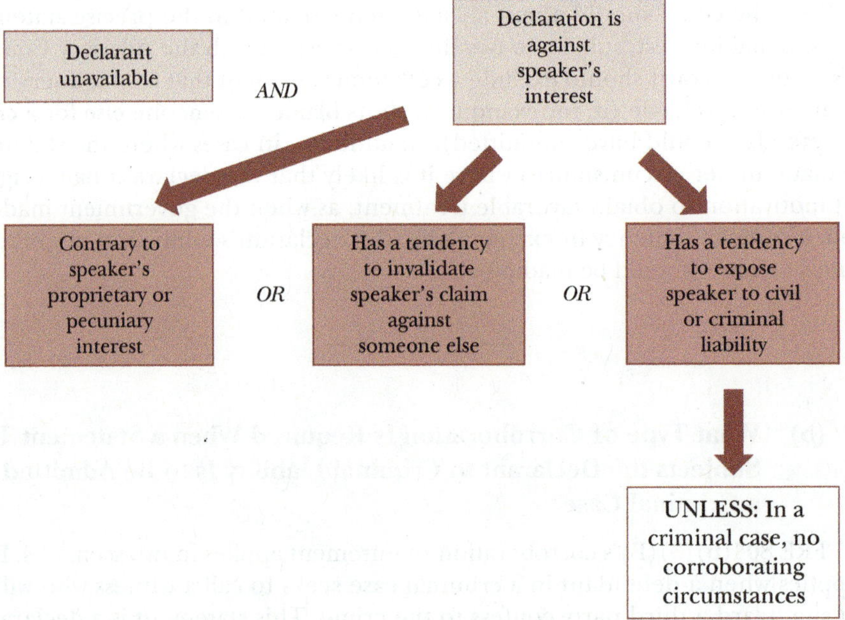

Review Questions

1. **Et tu, Travis?** Travis is charged with murder. Prosecutors contend that Travis killed his business partner when he caught the partner stealing from the company. Prosecutors want to call a witness who heard the partner say, "Don't tell Travis, but I have been skimming from this business for years. He'd kill me if he knew." The witness noted that the partner was buying a fancy new car at the time he made the remark.
2. **Laundering drug money.** Travis wants to call his own witness who will testify that he heard Travis's neighbor say, "Travis and I have been using his business to launder money I bring in from selling cocaine. I hope he keeps his mouth shut. If Travis's business partner ever finds out, I will do what is necessary to keep him quiet." The neighbor has disappeared, but his account shows several large deposits of cash before he disappeared.

4. *Statements of Personal or Family History Exception [FRE 804(b)(4)]*

The hearsay exception for statements of personal or family history is a practicality-based exception recognizing that families often pass down information about their members without any way to verify it, but which—by its very nature—is unlikely to be untrue.

Example

Anna Nicole Jones died and left behind an enormous estate. People have been popping out of the woodwork to claim a portion of the estate. Billy Bob files a claim. He wants to introduce testimony from Jones's ex-boyfriend who will testify that he was at a family reunion and heard Jones's cousin saying, "I'm wondering if Anna Nicole has met her other distant cousin, Billy Bob."

Specifically, FRE 804(b)(4) provides the following:

FRE 804. Hearsay Exceptions; Declarant Unavailable

(b) The Exceptions. The following are not excluded by the rule against hearsay if the declarant is unavailable as a witness:

(4) ***Statement of Personal or Family History.*** A statement about:

(A) the declarant's own birth, adoption, legitimacy, ancestry, marriage, divorce, relationship by blood, adoption, or marriage, or similar facts of personal or family history, even though the declarant had no way of acquiring personal knowledge about that fact; or

(B) another person concerning any of these facts, as well as death, if the declarant was related to the person by blood, adoption, or marriage or was so intimately associated with the person's family that the declarant's information is likely to be accurate.

Thus, the hearsay exception for personal or family history has the following prerequisites:

Hearsay Exception for Personal or Family History

(1) The declarant is unavailable to be a witness in the present proceeding; *and*

(2) The statement concerns *either*:

(A) *the declarant's* own personal or family history (including birth, adoption, legitimacy, ancestry, marriage, divorce, relationship by blood, adoption, or marriage or "similar facts"), even if the declarant lacks personal knowledge; *or*

(B) *someone else's* personal or family history (plus that person's death), but only if the declarant was (i) related to the person by blood, adoption, or marriage, *or* (ii) "so intimately associated" with the person's family that the declarant's information is likely to be accurate.[11]

The rationale underlying FRE 804(b)(4) is necessity and, to a lesser extent, trustworthiness. FRE 804(b)(4) is necessary because most of us do not have direct knowledge of our personal or family history. How do we know where we were born or who we are related to? We ordinarily know this kind of information because we have been told by someone else. If that person is no longer available, a statement about a person's personal or family background can be used as long as it is likely to be accurate. These statements are unlikely to be inaccurate because the family lore is passed from generation to generation, and families typically want only accurate information to be passed down in this fashion.

Courts are nevertheless reluctant to use this exception in circumstances when a statement of family history is made simply to assist a relative in pending litigation. *Bermea v. Limon* illustrates this point.

Bermea v. Limon

2018 U.S. Dist. LEXIS 218543 (S.D. Tex. 2018)

HANEN, Judge.

Plaintiff Arturo Pacheco Bermea, who was born in Mexico, brought this lawsuit . . . seeking to establish his citizenship in the United States. He claims to have derived citizenship from his mother and seeks a declaratory judgment from this Court to that effect. The Court held a bench trial, at which time evidence was presented and testimony heard. After reviewing the evidence presented at trial and considering the arguments of counsel, the Court hereby denies Plaintiff's claim.

A. BACKGROUND

Pursuant to [federal immigration law], a person may derive citizenship from his or her United States citizen parent if the parent was physically present in the United States for ten years before the person's birth, five of which must have been after the parent's fourteenth birthday. The Plaintiff claims that he qualifies for this provision because his mother, a United States citizen, meets this test. The parties agreed that this issue was the pivotal factor in this case. If Bermea could prove this, he would prevail on his derivative citizenship claim. If his proof fails, his claim to citizenship fails as well.

11. Some states do not extend this exception to persons *other* than the declarant. Fl. Stat. § 90.805(2)(d).

To prove his mother lived in the United States for five years after the age of fourteen, the Plaintiff provides a sworn statement, made by his mother to his lawyer in 2010 when he first applied for citizenship. The Plaintiff alleges that his mother spent five years in this area between 1954 and 1961. Her affidavit, however, is the only evidence available on this point because the Plaintiff's mother has since become incapacitated, and the parties agree she is unavailable to testify.

B. THE AFFIDAVIT IS INADMISSIBLE

Rule 804(b)(4) excepts from the rule against the admissibility of hearsay statements those statements that are "about the declarant's own birth, adoption, legitimacy, ancestry, marriage, divorce, relationship by blood, adoption, or marriage, or similar facts of personal or family history, even though the declarant had no way of acquiring personal knowledge about that fact." Fed. R. Evid. 804(b)(4).

Other courts adjudicating immigration cases have held similar statements to be inadmissible under this rule because physical relocation does not fall into the category of familial matters anticipated by Rule 804(b)(4). *See Vega-Alvarado v. Holder* (2011) (finding statements that the Plaintiff's father had lived and worked in the United States as a child inadmissible because "statements concerning his time and work in the United States do not constitute 'personal or family history' within the meaning of the exception" because they "do not concern matters of pedigree, such as the fact or date of a birth, marriage or death, nor do they relate to the existence of a ceremony or family relationship.").[4] The Court holds that the affidavit in this case is not admissible under Rule 804(b)(4) because the statement made by the Plaintiff's mother is not of the kind that falls within the ambit of the rule.

Even if it fell within the ambit of the exception, this Court would still find this particular statement to be problematic. This Court understands that the advisory notes to Rule 804 suggest that the common law requirement of "ante litem motam," or lack of motive to tell the truth, is no longer a requirement to qualify for this exception, and that those notes suggest motive should go to weight given the testimony, not the admissibility. Nevertheless, while not crucial to the Court's holding, this Court notes that this statement does not contain the same indicia of reliability as do statements concerning births, marriages, deaths, and other important family events. Those types of events are categorically different: they are "marked item[s] in the ordinary family history and so interesting to the family in common

---

4. Although these cases appear to state the majority rule, there is some disagreement. *See* 30B Charles Alan Wright & Arthur R. Miller, Federal Practice and Procedure § 7013 (2018 ed.) ("The inquiry demanded by the rule is . . . whether the approximate date of a family move from one country to another is a fact that is similar in nature to a person's birth, marriage or divorce. In that light, a family's move from one nation to another appears to qualify comfortably for admission under the rule."); *see also Leal Santos v. Gonzales*, 495 F. Supp. 2d 180, 185 (D. Mass. 2007) (admitting under 804(b)(4)—without analysis—a secondhand statement concerning international travel in the context of an immigration matter).

that statements about them in the family would be likely to be based on fairly accurate knowledge and to be sincerely uttered."

Central to the Court's above observation are the circumstances under which this affidavit was made. The statement was not made to denote important family events; instead it was done for litigation purposes. The Plaintiff's mother provided her statement to her son's lawyer for the express purpose of assisting her son in obtaining United States citizenship. Ordinarily, a person has little motivation to be untruthful about family events. Here, however, the affiant had a strong incentive to help her son. Thus, the statement is not "inherently reliable," in the same manner that is contemplated by other hearsay exceptions within the Federal Rules of Evidence.

The Court holds that the Plaintiff has failed to submit sufficient evidence to support his claim of derived citizenship.

---

5. *Forfeiture by Wrongdoing Exception [FRE 804(b)(6)]*

The last exception under FRE 804(b) is when a party has intentionally caused a witness to be unavailable.[12] This exception is commonly known as "forfeiture by wrongdoing." The rationale for this exception is that a party should not be able to intentionally cause a witness to be unavailable in order to prevent that witness from testifying against that party.

Specifically, FRE 804(b)(6) provides the following:

> **FRE 804. Hearsay Exceptions; Declarant Unavailable**
>
> **(b) The Exceptions.** The following are not excluded by the rule against hearsay if the declarant is unavailable as a witness:
>
> **(6)** ***Statement Offered Against a Party That Wrongfully Caused the Declarant's Unavailability.*** A statement offered against a party that wrongfully caused — or acquiesced in wrongfully causing — the declarant's unavailability as a witness, and did so intending that result.

Thus, the hearsay exception for forfeiture by wrongdoing has the following prerequisites:

12. It is not clear whether this exception exists in Texas. It is not set forth in the Texas Rules of Evidence, and the courts have declined to take a position on its existence. *E.g.*, *McGee v. State*, 2019 Tex. App. LEXIS 3701, *23-*24 (Tex. Ap. Ct. 2019).

Hearsay Exception for Forfeiture by Wrongdoing

(1) The declarant is unavailable to be a witness in the present proceeding;
(2) The party against whom the statement is offered wrongfully caused—or acquiesced in someone else wrongfully causing—the declarant's unavailability; *and*
(3) The party did so intending to cause the declarant's unavailability.

(a) Party Against Whom Statement Is to Be Admitted Wrongfully Caused or Acquiesced in Someone Else Wrongfully Causing the Declarant's Unavailability

Understanding this prerequisite requires an understanding of (1) what conduct by a party qualifies and (2) by what standard of proof that conduct must be proven.

As the text of the exception makes clear, a party need not *personally* wrongfully cause the declarant's unavailability. It is sufficient if the party "acquiesces" in someone else's causing the declarant's unavailability. Thus, this exception will apply to admit a declarant's statement against a party if that party joins a conspiracy to kill the declarant, even if the party is not the one who pulls the trigger. *United States v. Cherry*, 217 F.3d 811, 818 (10th Cir. 2000).[13]

The conduct itself can include everything from interference to intimidation to homicide.

Examples

1. Defendant is charged with drug offenses. Prosecutors want to call the case agent to testify to what he was told by their key witness before that witness refused to testify and was held in contempt. Evidently, the witness clammed up when he found a dead fish on his windshield with a note written by Defendant that said, "There is a price to be paid by stool pigeons."
2. Whistleblower Willie reported his employer to the Environmental Protection Agency for dumping toxic waste into the river. By the time of trial, the employer has shipped Willie to the North Pole, and he cannot be located for the civil case against the employer. The Environmental Protection Agency wants to use Willie's whistleblowing reports as evidence in a civil proceeding against the employer.

---

13. New York requires proof of this wrongdoing by clear and convincing evidence. *People v. Cotto*, 92 N.Y.2d 68, 76 (N.Y. 1998).

What if the witness-declarant is also the victim of the charged crime? Say, for example, that a defendant is charged with killing his wife and the prosecution wishes to introduce the wife's statement to the police, taken after she has reported his domestic violence against her. To prove the defendant's *guilt* of the killing, the prosecution must prove guilt beyond a reasonable doubt. Does that same standard of proof apply to the admissibility of the wife's statement? No. The admissibility of this statement is for the trial judge pursuant to FRE 104(a), and the judge is to apply the preponderance of the evidence standard. (Because FRE 104(a) applies, the judge may also consider the content of the hearsay statement in applying the exception.)[14] Admittedly, there is some tension in having a judge determine by a preponderance of the evidence whether the defendant committed the same killing that the jury has yet to find him guilty of beyond a reasonable about. As *United States v. Johnson* illustrates, however, the courts have stuck with the FRE 104(a) standard of proof.

United States v. Johnson

767 F.3d 815 (9th Cir. 2014)

Schroeder, Judge.

The appellants are Antoine Johnson and Michael Williams, who appeal their convictions for armed robbery and murder. They each raise a number of issues from their joint trial for the robbery of an armored truck and murder of a guard, for which each received a life sentence.

On March 1, 2004, four assailants ambushed an armored truck as it was making a cash delivery to a Bank of America in South Central Los Angeles. One of the assailants was wearing a Rastafarian wig and at least one was wearing gloves. During the robbery, one of the armored truck security guards was shot and killed. On June 19, 2007, appellants Antoine Johnson and Michael Williams, both of whom had affiliations with a group known as the Hoover Street Gang, were indicted by a grand jury for their involvement in the robbery and murder. The charges carried a maximum possible penalty of death.

At trial, the Government introduced several out-of-court statements made by an informant, Veronica Burgess. Burgess had come forward to police in 2004, claiming that, while eating lunch at a restaurant in Watts, she had overheard several Hoover gang members planning an armored truck heist. She identified Johnson from a photo spread as one of the participants, and later testified to this effect before the grand jury. Burgess also picked Williams out of a photo-lineup on one occasion. Burgess was to be an important witness at trial, but shortly before trial the Government was unable to locate her, even after checking her public records and conducting extensive surveillance of her known residences.

The district court in this case permitted the Government, after a pretrial hearing, to introduce her statements against Johnson under the forfeiture exception to the hearsay rule. To support admissibility, the Government contended that Johnson

14. The rule is not the same in all states. In California, the trial judge's finding of wrongdoing may not be based *solely* on the content of the statement at issue. Cal. Pen. Code § 1390.

had threatened Burgess in order to prevent her from testifying. In the pretrial hearing, the Government presented evidence that Burgess had received death threats from members of the Hoover gang. Her live-in boyfriend, Patrick Smith, told police that the Hoovers had placed a "hit" on Burgess for "snitching on a boy fighting death."

A defendant may forfeit confrontation rights and render hearsay rules inapplicable if the defendant is responsible for the witness's unavailability, i.e., if the defendant "engaged or acquiesced in wrongdoing that was intended to, and did, procure the unavailability of the declarant as a witness." *Giles [v. California]*, 554 U.S. [353,] 367 [(2008)] (quoting Fed. R. Evid. 804(b)(6)).

The district court found that the government in this case had proven forfeiture by a preponderance of the evidence, referring to the applicable Rule of Evidence, 804(b)(6). Johnson contends that the court should have applied the more demanding clear and convincing standard. Our research tells us that while the history of the exception began on his side, it did not stay there.

In 1997, the Federal Rules of Evidence were amended to include the forfeiture by wrongdoing exception. Fed. R. Evid. 804(b)(6). The Advisory Committee adopted the preponderance standard in order to deter defendants from trying to prevent witnesses from testifying, noting that this was the majority rule among the circuits.

The Court's subsequent opinions interpreting the scope of the forfeiture exception also strongly suggest, if not squarely hold, that the preponderance standard applies.

The district court applied the preponderance standard here. The court did not err in concluding that the Government produced sufficient evidence to demonstrate that Johnson had intentionally prevented Burgess from testifying. There is no serious dispute that the government wanted Burgess to testify and was unable to locate her. The district court concluded that, based on Johnson's actions and the timing of Burgess's disappearance, it could reasonably be inferred that Johnson had informed other Hoover gang members of Burgess's identity so that they could threaten her against testifying. As the district court noted, Burgess began receiving threats one day after the defense attorneys were permitted to disclose the witness lists to their clients. Johnson's attorney visited him on that same day, and Johnson had previously expressed interest in receiving the witness list.

In short, the evidence tended to show that Johnson alone had the means, motive, and opportunity to threaten Burgess, and did not show anyone else did. This was sufficient to satisfy the preponderance standard.

(b) Party Intended to Cause the Declarant's Unavailability

As the Supreme Court clarified in *Giles v. California*, 554 U.S. 353 (2008), this exception parallels the Confrontation Clause's similar "forfeiture by wrongdoing" exception, which is discussed more fully in Chapter Nine. In *Giles*, the Supreme

Court held that a defendant forfeits his ability to object that his Confrontation Clause rights have been violated when the reason he cannot cross-examine a hearsay declarant is because he killed the declarant *with the specific intent to prevent her from testifying*. The same test applies here: If a party wrongfully causes a declarant's unavailability with the specific intent to prevent that witness's testimony, that declarant's out-of-court statements are admissible under FRE 804(b)(6).

Review Questions

1. **Around-the-world absence.** Nikki is charged with bribing a police officer. The prosecution's key witness is the officer's partner. When interviewed by internal affairs, the partner said that the officer had been on the take for years. However, shortly after the interview, the officer paid for his partner to go on a lengthy cruise around the world. The partner has not been seen since.
2. **Killer business deal?** ABC Corporation has brought a copyright action against its competitor, XYZ Corporation. ABC had planned on having a recent employee of XYZ testify, but the employee was found dead in her apartment. Her spouse says that she had tried to hide from her former employer ever since he sent some thugs to try to convince her not to testify.

PART C: THE RESIDUAL HEARSAY EXCEPTION [FRE 807]

The residual or "catch-all" exception, now housed in FRE 807, is a safety valve that gives trial judges limited discretion to admit a hearsay statement for its truth even if that statement does not satisfy the requirements of any of the specific hearsay exceptions set forth in the Federal Rules of Evidence. Although having a residual exception makes it more difficult for the parties to know, in advance, whether a particular hearsay statement will be admitted, the drafters of the Federal Rules of Evidence figured that this uncertainty did not outweigh the benefit of giving trial judges the ability to recognize that the specific exceptions in the rules "may not encompass every situation in which reliability and appropriateness of a particular piece of hearsay make clear that it should be heard and considered by a trier of fact."[15] Advisory Committee Note and Report of Senate Committee on the Judiciary on Rules 803(24) and 804(b)(5), which were the predecessor rules to FRE 807.

15. Not all jurisdictions have come to the same conclusion. Florida, Texas, Illinois, and New York, for example, have no residual hearsay exception; if an item of hearsay does not fit within an enumerated hearsay exception, it is barred by the rule against hearsay. *E.g.*, *Blandenburg v. State*, 890 So. 2d 267, 271 (Fla. Dist. Ct. App. 2004); *Bee v. State*, 974 S.W.2d 184, 188 n.3 (Tex. Ct. App. 1998); *People v. Neal*, 2020 Ill. App. 4th 170869 (Ill. Ct. App. 2020); *People v. Brown*, 166 Misc. 2d 539, 543 (N.Y. Sup. Ct. Kings Co. 1995). California has no exception in its Evidence Code, but California courts have the power to create new exceptions as a matter of decisional law, though are counseled against doing so. *People v. Ayala*, 23 Cal. 4th 225, 268 (Cal. 2000).

Consider the following example.

Example

Defendant is charged with murder because a child she was babysitting suffered a seizure and died. Prosecutor argued that the child's injuries were consistent with shaken baby syndrome. Defendant wants to present statements made by five women several weeks before the child died that the mother had told them that the child had accidentally fallen and had hit her head. *See State v. Weaver*, 554 N.W.2d 240 (Iowa 1996) (trustworthiness established by the fact that the women did not know each other and that each reported injury of child before the event involving Defendant).

In the above example, if the mother is not available as a witness, the statements of the five women would seem to have some guarantees of trustworthiness, and there is certainly a necessity. The evidence is critical to the defense that someone else was responsible for the child's death, and there is no specifically applicable hearsay exception. This example presents a good candidate for use of the residual exception. But using the residual exception could come as an unfair surprise to the prosecution because it falls outside any specific exception.

To accommodate the concerns of certainty and the primacy of the specific hearsay exceptions, the residual exception in FRE 807 is very narrow and premised on the giving of advance notice.

Specifically, FRE 807 provides the following:

FRE 807. Residual Exception

(a) In General. Under the following conditions, a hearsay statement is not excluded by the rule against hearsay even if the statement is not admissible under a hearsay exception in Rule 803 or 804:

(1) the statement is supported by sufficient guarantees of trustworthiness—after considering the totality of circumstances of which it is made and evidence, if any, corroborating the statement; and

(2) it is more probative on the point for which it is offered than any other evidence that the proponent can obtain through reasonable efforts.

(b) Notice. The statement is admissible only if the proponent gives an adverse party reasonable notice of the intent to offer the statement—including its substance and the declarant's name—so that the party has a fair opportunity to meet it. The notice must be provided in writing before the trial or hearing—or in any form during the trial or hearing if the court, for good cause, excuses a lack of earlier notice.

Thus, the residual hearsay exception has the following prerequisites:

Residual Hearsay Exception

(1) The statement is supported by sufficient guarantees of trustworthiness, after considering:
  (A) the totality of the circumstances in which the statement is made; *and*
  (B) any corroboration of the statement;
(2) The statement is more probative than any other evidence the proponent can find with reasonable efforts; *and*
(3) The proponent gives advance written notice unless the matter arises during trial and the trial judge allows oral notice to suffice.

Not surprisingly, these elements track the two considerations underlying the hearsay rule: (1) trustworthiness and (2) necessity. The first element is, quite literally, a trustworthiness requirement. By requiring that no more probative evidence be readily available, the second element functions as a necessity requirement.

In terms of how the residual exception operates, *Dallas County v. Commercial Union Assurance Company* is a great example. This case predates the Federal Rules of Evidence and bears more than a passing resemblance to the critical scene in *Back to the Future.* Ultimately, the court admitted a newspaper clipping regarding the cause of the collapse of a wooden clock tower above the courthouse in Selma, Alabama. The opinion was written by the legendary Judge Minor Wisdom. It sets forth the rationale for allowing a residual exception to the hearsay rule.

Dallas County v. Commercial Union Assurance Co.

286 F.2d 388 (5th Cir. 1961)

Wisdom, Judge.

[In this case, the clock tower of the Dallas County Courthouse in Selma, Alabama, collapsed on a Sunday morning, July 7, 1957. No one was injured, but there was over $100,000 in damage. The State Toxicologist reported that char in the timers was evidence that lightning struck the courthouse five days sooner, on July 2, 1957. On this evidence, Dallas County concluded that a lightning bolt was the cause of the tower's collapse. The insurance company did not want to pay because it claimed that the charred timbers came from a fire that had happened while the tower was under construction many years earlier. Thus, the key issue in the case was whether lighting caused the collapse of the clock tower.]

[The insurance company sought to introduce a copy of a newspaper article in the Morning Times of Selma for June 9, 1901. The article reported a fire in the courthouse dome while it was under construction.]

In the Anglo-American adversary system of law, courts usually will not admit evidence unless its accuracy and trustworthiness may be tested by cross-examination. Here, therefore, the plaintiff argues that the newspaper should not be admitted: "You cannot cross-examine a newspaper." Of course, a newspaper article is hearsay, and in almost all circumstances is inadmissible. However, the law governing hearsay is somewhat less than pellucid. And, as with most rules, the hearsay rule is not absolute; it is replete with exceptions. Witnesses die, documents are lost, deeds are destroyed, memories fade.

If they are worth their salt, evidentiary rules are to aid the search for truth. Rule 4.3(a), notwithstanding its shortcomings, carries out that purpose by enabling federal courts to apply a liberal, flexible rule for the admissibility of evidence, unencumbered by common law archaisms.

The fire referred to in the newspaper account occurred fifty-eight years before the trial of this case. Any witness who saw that fire with sufficient understanding to observe it and describe it accurately, would have been older than a young child at the time of the fire. We may reasonably assume that at the time of the trial he was either dead or his faculties were dimmed by the passage of fifty-eight years.

The principle of necessity, not requiring absolute impossibility or total inaccessibility of first-hand knowledge, is satisfied by the practicalities of the situation before us.

The second requisite for admission of hearsay evidence is trustworthiness. There is no procedural canon against the exercise of common sense in deciding the admissibility of hearsay evidence. In 1901 Selma, Alabama, was a small town. Taking a common sense view of this case, it is inconceivable to us that a newspaper reporter in a small town would report that there was a fire in the dome of the new courthouse—if there had been no fire. He is without motive to falsify, and a false report would have subjected the newspaper and him to embarrassment in the community. The usual dangers inherent in hearsay evidence, such as lack of memory, faulty narration, intent to influence the court proceedings, and plain lack of truthfulness are not present here. To our minds, the article published in the Selma Morning-Times on the day of the fire is more reliable, more trustworthy, more competent evidence than the testimony of a witness called to the stand fifty-eight years later.

We do not characterize this newspaper as a "business record," nor as an "ancient document,"[16] nor as any other readily identifiable and happily tagged species of hearsay evidence. It is admissible because it is necessary and trustworthy, relevant and material, and its admission is within the trial judge's exercise of discretion. . . .

Is there a fourth prerequisite to the residual exception? Some courts have held that, to be admissible under FRE 807, a hearsay statement must not only meet the requirements of FRE 807 but also not be too close to any specific hearsay exception. In other words, these courts hold that FRE 807 does not apply if the hearsay statement at issues falls just outside of a specific hearsay exception. "Near misses" are not admissible because admitting such statements, these courts reason, erodes the boundaries of the nearby specific hearsay exceptions. Most federal courts, however, have declined to engraft a "no near miss" requirement onto FRE 807, reasoning that doing so would unduly limit the use of the residual exception and "put[] the federal evidence rules back into the straightjacket from which the residual exception [was intended to free them]." *In re Japanese Electronic Products Antitrust Litig.*, 723 F.2d 238 (3d Cir. 1983).

Harris v. City of Chicago

327 F.R.D. 199 (N.D. Ill. 2018)

FEINERMAN, Judge.

Andre Lepinay brought this 42 U.S.C. § 1983 suit against the City of Chicago and nine Chicago police officers, alleging that they violated the Fourth Amendment by using excessive force against him when executing a search warrant at his apartment. After Lepinay died, the court appointed his niece, Sharon Harris, as the

16. Today, FRE 803(16)'s hearsay exception for ancient documents might apply.

special administrator of his estate for the purpose of continuing the suit. Although Lepinay was not deposed before he died, he did give a sworn interview to an investigator with the City's Independent Police Review Authority ("IPRA").

The alleged excessive force took place on October 21, 2016. One week later, on October 28, Lepinay gave his sworn interview to the IPRA investigator. Lepinay told the investigator that he was sitting in the living room when the officers entered, that three officers immediately "bum rushed" him, with one jabbing him in the stomach with a rifle, and that the officers then took him to the floor, with one kneeing him in the back. Lepinay also stated that he had recently been diagnosed with advanced liver cancer and had "c[o]me home to die." After the interview, Lepinay signed an affidavit in which he "sw[ore] or affirm[ed], under penalties provided by law, that the information contained in . . . [his] electronically recorded statement, [was] true and accurate." He filed this suit some three weeks later, on November 17, 2016, and died in April 2017.

Harris contends that the recording of Lepinay's IPRA interview is admissible under Federal Rule of Evidence 807, the residual exception to the hearsay rule. "A proponent of hearsay evidence must establish five elements in order to satisfy Rule 807: (1) circumstantial guarantees of trustworthiness; (2) materiality; (3) probative value; (4) the interests of justice; and (5) notice." Defendants do not contest the second and fifth elements, materiality and notice. [They defer to the court on whether admission of the statement is in the interests of justice.]

Review Questions

Should the court admit Plaintiff's interview by the investigator of the city's Independent Police Review Authority under the FRE 807 residual exception? Here are the facts for determining whether the statement is sufficiently trustworthy and probative to meet the exception:

1. Lepinay admitted in the interview that he possessed illegal drugs the day of the incident.
2. The statement was given voluntarily, under oath, subject to cross-examination and penalty of perjury.
3. The interview took place in a car outside Lepinay's residence, rather than a more formal setting like a courtroom. Therefore, the statement would not qualify under the exception for former testimony. FRE 804(b)(1).
4. Lepinay gave a sworn statement under penalty of perjury and responded to many clarifying questions from someone whose job it was to investigate allegations of police misconduct.
5. At the time of Lepinay's interview, no one had ever been prosecuted for making false statements to IPRA and Lepinay knew he had a terminal illness, although his statement does not qualify as a dying declaration.

6. It is highly unlikely that, as a layperson, Lepinay realized that his interview could provide a basis for a family member to pursue his claim after his death.
7. The only person in the living room when the officers arrived was Lepinay, and none of the witnesses who were in other apartments nearby can be located.

Test Your Understanding

To test your understanding of the material in this chapter, turn to the Supplement for additional practice problems.

Chapter 9

The Constitutional Overlay

So far, we have focused chiefly on the Federal Rules of Evidence and what they require before evidence will be admitted. But are those rules the *sole* source of law for determining whether evidence is admissible or inadmissible? The answer is "no." That is because the Sixth Amendment's Confrontation Clause gives criminal defendants the right to confront witnesses against them. Since 2004, however, the Clause has placed additional requirements on the admissibility of out-of-court statements admitted for their truth and used against a defendant in a criminal case—over and above the requirements of the rules of evidence—that must be satisfied before such statements may be admitted.

This chapter discusses the three provisions of the United States Constitution that have been found, in certain circumstances, to override the rules of evidence: the Sixth Amendment's Confrontation Clause, the Sixth Amendment's Compulsory Process Clause, and the Due Process Clause applicable to the federal government through the Fifth Amendment and to the states through the Fourteenth Amendment.[1]

Part A discusses the history of how hearsay exceptions were treated by the Supreme Court and how the Court has shifted from a constitutional standard based on reliability to one more focused on the right of confrontation. The Confrontation Clause sometimes imposes additional requirements on the admission of out-of-court statements sought to be introduced as evidence against a criminal defendant. Part B discusses how the Confrontation Clause operates during joint trials when the confession of one defendant is admitted. Part C discusses how the Confrontation Clause generally mandates a *physical* (that is, face-to-face) confrontation. Part D discusses the Compulsory Process Clause and how it can require the admission of evidence in support of a criminal defendant's case, even when the rules of evidence would exclude that evidence. Part E discusses the limitations that the Due Process Clause imposes on the power of the States to exclude evidence that might aid a defendant in a criminal case.

---

1. The first two of these provisions also supersedes state rules of evidence as well, because each has been deemed to be incorporated as an element of due process under the Fourteenth Amendment that is directly applicable to the states. *Pointer v. Texas*, 380 U.S. 400, 406 (1965) (Confrontation Clause); *Washington v. Texas*, 388 U.S. 14, 18 (1967) (Compulsory Process Clause).

PART A: CONSTITUTIONAL LIMITATIONS ON THE USE OF OUT-OF-COURT STATEMENTS

Under the Sixth Amendment, all defendants in a criminal case have the right to confront the witnesses against them.

Sixth Amendment, U.S. Constitution

In all criminal prosecutions, the accused shall enjoy the right . . . to be confronted with the witnesses against him. . . .

This language constitutes the Confrontation Clause. As with many provisions of the U.S. Constitution, few words are used, and, accordingly, much is left undefined. The Amendment itself does not explain how the right of confrontation applies and how it is intended to interact with the hearsay exceptions. By its terms, there are only three fundamental outer boundaries on *when* the Clause applies.

First, the Clause only applies *in criminal cases* and when the government is seeking to introduce evidence *against the defendant.* It does not grant any rights to the prosecution and does not apply at all in civil cases; rather, the plain language of the Clause grants only "the accused" the "right" to "confront[]" "[i]n . . . criminal prosecutions."

Second, the Clause only applies when the prosecution is trying to introduce an out-of-court statement *for its truth.* If it introduces the statement for some other purpose, the Clause does not apply. That is because confrontation is designed to ferret out the truth or falsity; if a statement is not being introduced for its truth, this concern is simply not implicated. *Crawford v. Washington*, 541 U.S. 36, 59 n.9 (2004).

Consider the following examples.

Examples

1. The People charge Defendant with murder. Prosecutor calls a witness to the stand, and the witness testifies that, on the day before the murder, he was present when the victim told Defendant, "I'm having an affair with your wife." Because this statement is being introduced to prove Defendant's motive for the killing, it does not matter whether it is true; what matters is that Defendant heard it.
2. The People charge Defendant with importation of cocaine. Defendant claims that she thought she was importing teddy bears, not cocaine. Prosecutor calls a witness who testifies that he was present when the kingpin of the organization told everyone present, including Defendant, that he was stuffing cocaine into teddy bears and shipping the teddy bears to the United States.

Third, although the Clause applies in "criminal prosecutions," its chief purpose is to protect the criminal defendant *at trial.* As the U.S. Supreme Court has said time and again, "The right to confrontation is basically a trial right." *Barber v. Page,* 390 U.S. 719, 725 (1968). Thus, the Clause does *not* typically apply in other phases of a criminal prosecution, such as the following:

- *Grand jury. Giles v. California,* 554 U.S. 353, 371 (2008).
- *Preliminary hearings (in states where charges need not be initiated by grand jury). E.g., People v. Gonzales,* 54 Cal.4th 1234, 1267 (Cal. 2012).
- *Sentencing proceedings, except capital sentencing.* The Supreme Court has held that the Confrontation Clause does not apply at sentencing hearings. *Williams v. New York,* 337 U.S. 241, 246-47 (1949).[2]
- *Probation and parole hearings.* There is no Confrontation Clause–based right of confrontation during probation and parole hearings, but there is a *due process*–based right to cross-examine. *Gagnon v. Scarpelli,* 411 U.S. 778, 786 (1973); *Morrissey v. Brewer,* 408 U.S. 471, 480-89 (1972). The scope of confrontation under these different provisions may not be identical.

These outer boundaries are the easier part. The more difficult question is defining precisely when, within those boundaries, the Clause applies to out-of-court statements admitted for their truth. The Supreme Court has taken various approaches and adopted its most recent approach in 2004 in *Crawford v. Washington,* 541 U.S. 36 (2004). However, to better understand how *Crawford* changed the Confrontation Clause landscape, it is important to touch on the approach used by the Supreme Court prior to *Crawford.*

1. *The Law Before* Crawford

For the quarter century leading up to *Crawford,* the key case defining the Confrontation Clause was *Ohio v. Roberts,* 448 U.S. 56 (1980). In *Roberts,* the defendant was ultimately charged with forgery and receiving stolen property for his possession and use of checks and credit cards belonging to Bernard and Anita Isaacs. At the preliminary hearing, the defendant called the Isaacs's adult daughter Anita as a witness, and she testified that she allowed the defendant to stay in her apartment for a few days, but denied giving him permission to take her parents' checks or credit cards. At trial, the defendant testified that Anita gave him the checks and credit cards. Anita could not be located, so the prosecutor sought to introduce her preliminary hearing testimony to contradict the defendant's testimony. The defendant objected that introduction of this testimony violated the Confrontation Clause.

2. The lower federal courts have followed this rule by holding that *Crawford* does not apply at noncapital sentencing proceedings (that is, where the sentence is less than death). *United States v. Chau,* 426 F.3d 1318, 1323 (11th Cir. 2005). However, they are split on whether *Crawford* applies in capital proceedings. *Compare, e.g., United States v. Umana,* 750 F.3d 320, 348 (4th Cir. 2014) (*Crawford* does not apply) *with e.g., United States v. Fields,* 483 F.3d 313, 332 (5th Cir. 2007) (*Crawford* does apply).

Roberts recognized that the Clause's language, if read "literally," would require confrontation before *any* out-of-court statement could be admitted and hence "would abrogate virtually every hearsay exception." 448 U.S. at 63. This reading, *Roberts* held, was "unintended and too extreme." *Id.* Under *Roberts,* the Clause's guarantee of confrontation "reflect[ed] a *preference* for face-to-face confrontation at trial," but one that had to be reconciled with "competing interests." *Id.* at 63-64. To accommodate these competing interests, *Roberts* held that the Clause will not bar the admission of an out-of-court statement admitted for its truth, even if the declarant was not subject to cross-examination, as long as (1) the declarant was shown to be "unavailable" for cross-examination and (2) the statement itself "bears adequate 'indicia of reliability,'" which can be established by proof that the statement (a) falls within a "firmly rooted hearsay exception" or (b) otherwise bears "particularized guarantees of trustworthiness." *Id.* at 66.

In sum, *Roberts* held:

- The Confrontation Clause potentially applies to *all* out-of-court statements admitted for their truth.
- The Clause is concerned with the *reliability* of those statements, and the Court will accordingly allow for the admission of out-of-court statements as long as the declarant is unavailable and the statements fall within a "firmly rooted hearsay exception" or otherwise bear "particularized guarantees of trustworthiness."

2. Crawford

In 2004, a key decision written by Justice Antonin Scalia led to a different approach to the Confrontation Clause. Rather than focusing on the reliability of the statements, the Court in *Crawford v. Washington* shifted its focus to the separate right of actually confronting one's accuser.

Crawford grew out of an attempted murder prosecution. Michael Crawford, the defendant, was charged with stabbing a neighbor. The police interrogated Crawford's wife regarding the stabbing, which she witnessed. The wife's account was different than Crawford's; Crawford said the neighbor had a knife in his hand, whereas the wife told the police she saw nothing in the neighbor's hand. When the wife invoked the marital privilege at trial, the prosecutor introduced her statement to police under a hearsay exception for statements against interest (FRE 804(b)(3)). Crawford was convicted.

Using the old *Ohio v. Roberts* approach, courts had been regularly admitting statements against interest because the hearsay exception for declarations against interest was a firmly rooted hearsay exception and because there was otherwise sufficient indicia that such statements were reliable.

The Supreme Court held that the trial court erred in admitting the wife's statement. Although all nine Justices in *Crawford* agreed with this evidentiary ruling, Justice Scalia used the opinion to set forth a different approach to addressing whether evidence admitted under a hearsay exception meets the constitutional standard of the Confrontation Clause.

Crawford v. Washington

541 U.S. 36 (2004)

JUSTICE SCALIA delivered the opinion of the Court.

Petitioner Michael Crawford stabbed a man who allegedly tried to rape his wife, Sylvia. At his trial, the State played for the jury Sylvia's tape-recorded statement to the police describing the stabbing, even though he had no opportunity for cross-examination. The Washington Supreme Court upheld petitioner's conviction after determining that Sylvia's statement was reliable. The question presented is whether this procedure complied with the Sixth Amendment's guarantee that, "[i]n all criminal prosecutions, the accused shall enjoy the right . . . to be confronted with the witnesses against him."

I

On August 5, 1999, Kenneth Lee was stabbed at his apartment. Police arrested petitioner later that night. After giving petitioner and his wife *Miranda* warnings, detectives interrogated each of them twice. Petitioner eventually confessed that he and Sylvia had gone in search of Lee because he was upset over an earlier incident in which Lee had tried to rape her. The two had found Lee at his apartment, and a fight ensued in which Lee was stabbed in the torso and petitioner's hand was cut.

Petitioner gave the following account of the fight:

"**Q.** Okay. Did you ever see anything in [Lee's] hands?
"**A.** I think so, but I'm not positive.
"**Q.** Okay, when you think so, what do you mean by that?
"**A.** I coulda swore I seen him goin' for somethin' before, right before everything happened. He was like reachin', fiddlin' around down here and stuff . . . and I just . . . I don't know, I think, this is just a possibility, but I think, I think that he pulled somethin' out and I grabbed for it and that's how I got cut . . . but I'm not positive. I, I, my mind goes blank when things like this happen. I mean, I just, I remember things wrong, I remember things that just doesn't, don't make sense to me later."

Sylvia generally corroborated petitioner's story about the events leading up to the fight, but her account of the fight itself was arguably different—particularly with respect to whether Lee had drawn a weapon before petitioner assaulted him:

"**Q.** Did Kenny do anything to fight back from this assault?
"**A.** (pausing) I know he reached into his pocket . . . or somethin' . . . I don't know what.
"**Q.** After he was stabbed?
"**A.** He saw Michael coming up. He lifted his hand . . . his chest open, he might [have] went to go strike his hand out or something and then (inaudible).
"**Q.** Okay, you, you gotta speak up.
"**A.** Okay, he lifted his hand over his head maybe to strike Michael's hand down or something and then he put his hands in his . . . put his right

hand in his right pocket . . . took a step back . . . Michael proceeded to stab him . . . then his hands were like . . . how do you explain this . . . open arms . . . with his hands open and he fell down . . . and we ran (describing subject holding hands open, palms toward assailant).

"Q. Okay, when he's standing there with his open hands, you're talking about Kenny, correct?

"A. Yeah, after, after the fact, yes.

"Q. Did you see anything in his hands at that point?

"A. (pausing) um um (no)."

The State charged petitioner with assault and attempted murder. At trial, he claimed self-defense. Sylvia did not testify because of the state marital privilege, which generally bars a spouse from testifying without the other spouse's consent . . . so the State sought to introduce Sylvia's tape-recorded statements to the police as evidence that the stabbing was not in self-defense. Noting that Sylvia had admitted she led petitioner to Lee's apartment and thus had facilitated the assault, the State invoked the hearsay exception for statements against penal interest,

Petitioner countered that . . . admitting the evidence would violate his federal constitutional right to be "confronted with the witnesses against him." According to our description of that right in *Ohio v. Roberts* (1980), it does not bar admission of an unavailable witness's statement against a criminal defendant if the statement bears "adequate 'indicia of reliability.'" To meet that test, evidence must either fall within a "firmly rooted hearsay exception" or bear "particularized guarantees of trustworthiness." The trial court here admitted the statement on the latter ground, offering several reasons why it was trustworthy: Sylvia was not shifting blame but rather corroborating her husband's story that he acted in self-defense or "justified reprisal"; she had direct knowledge as an eyewitness; she was describing recent events; and she was being questioned by a "neutral" law enforcement officer. The prosecution played the tape for the jury and relied on it in closing, arguing that it was "damning evidence" that "completely refutes [petitioner's] claim of self-defense." The jury convicted petitioner of assault.

We granted certiorari to determine whether the State's use of Sylvia's statement violated the Confrontation Clause.

II

The Sixth Amendment's Confrontation Clause provides that,"[i]n all criminal prosecutions, the accused shall enjoy the right . . . to be confronted with the witnesses against him." We have held that this bedrock procedural guarantee applies to both federal and state prosecutions. As noted above, *Roberts* says that an unavailable witness's out-of-court statement may be admitted so long as it has adequate indicia of reliability—*i.e.*, falls within a "firmly rooted hearsay exception" or bears "particularized guarantees of trustworthiness." Petitioner argues that this test strays from the original meaning of the Confrontation Clause and urges us to reconsider it.

A

The Constitution's text does not alone resolve this case. One could plausibly read "witnesses against" a defendant to mean those who actually testify at trial, those whose statements are offered at trial, or something in-between. We must therefore turn to the historical background of the Clause to understand its meaning.

Pretrial examinations became routine under two statutes passed during the reign of Queen Mary in the 16th century. These Marian bail and committal statutes required justices of the peace to examine suspects and witnesses in felony cases and to certify the results to the court. It is doubtful that the original purpose of the examinations was to produce evidence admissible at trial. Whatever the original purpose, however, they came to be used as evidence in some cases, resulting in an adoption of continental procedure.

The most notorious instances of civil-law examination occurred in the great political trials of the 16th and 17th centuries. One such was the 1603 trial of Sir Walter Raleigh for treason. Lord Cobham, Raleigh's alleged accomplice, had implicated him in an examination before the Privy Council and in a letter. At Raleigh's trial, these were read to the jury. Raleigh argued that Cobham had lied to save himself: "Cobham is absolutely in the King's mercy; to excuse me cannot avail him; by accusing me he may hope for favour." Suspecting that Cobham would recant, Raleigh demanded that the judges call him to appear, arguing . . . "let Cobham be here, let him speak it. Call my accuser before my face. . . ." The judges refused, and, despite Raleigh's protestations that he was being tried "by the Spanish Inquisition," the jury convicted, and Raleigh was sentenced to death.

One of Raleigh's trial judges later lamented that "'the justice of England has never been so degraded and injured as by the condemnation of Sir Walter Raleigh.'" Through a series of statutory and judicial reforms, English law developed a right of confrontation that limited these abuses.

One recurring question was whether the admissibility of an unavailable witness's pretrial examination depended on whether the defendant had had an opportunity to cross-examine him. In 1696, the Court of King's Bench answered this question in the affirmative. The court ruled that, even though a witness was dead, his examination was not admissible where "the defendant not being present when [it was] taken before the mayor . . . had lost the benefit of a cross-examination."

Controversial examination practices were also used in the Colonies.

III

This history supports two inferences about the meaning of the Sixth Amendment.

A

First, the principal evil at which the Confrontation Clause was directed was the civil-law mode of criminal procedure, and particularly its use of *ex parte* examinations as evidence against the accused. It was these practices that the Crown deployed in notorious treason cases like Raleigh's; that the Marian statutes invited; that English law's assertion of a right to confrontation was meant to prohibit; and that the founding-era rhetoric decried. The Sixth Amendment must be interpreted with this focus in mind.

This focus also suggests that not all hearsay implicates the Sixth Amendment's core concerns. An off-hand, overheard remark might be unreliable evidence and thus a good candidate for exclusion under hearsay rules, but it bears little resemblance to the civil-law abuses the Confrontation Clause targeted. On the other hand, ex parte examinations might sometimes be admissible under modern hearsay rules, but the Framers certainly would not have condoned them.

The text of the Confrontation Clause reflects this focus. It applies to "witnesses" against the accused—in other words, those who "bear testimony." "Testimony," in turn, is typically "[a] solemn declaration or affirmation made for the purpose of establishing or proving some fact." An accuser who makes a formal statement to government officers bears testimony in a sense that a person who makes a casual remark to an acquaintance does not. The constitutional text, like the history underlying the common-law right of confrontation, thus reflects an especially acute concern with a specific type of out-of-court statement.

Various formulations of this core class of "testimonial" statements exist: "ex parte in-court testimony or its functional equivalent—that is, material such as affidavits, custodial examinations, prior testimony that the defendant was unable to cross-examine, or similar pretrial statements that declarants would reasonably expect to be used prosecutorially."

Statements taken by police officers in the course of interrogations are also testimonial under even a narrow standard. Police interrogations bear a striking resemblance to examinations by justices of the peace in England. The statements are not sworn testimony, but the absence of oath was not dispositive. . . .

In sum, even if the Sixth Amendment is not solely concerned with testimonial hearsay, that is its primary object, and interrogations by law enforcement officers fall squarely within that class.

B

The historical record also supports a second proposition: that the Framers would not have allowed admission of testimonial statements of a witness who did not appear at trial unless he was unavailable to testify, and the defendant had had a prior opportunity for cross-examination. The text of the Sixth Amendment does not suggest any open-ended exceptions from the confrontation requirement to be developed by the courts. Rather, the "right . . . to be confronted with the witnesses against him," is most naturally read as a reference to the right of confrontation at common law, admitting only those exceptions established at the time of the founding. As the English authorities above reveal, the common law in 1791 conditioned admissibility of an absent witness's examination on unavailability and a prior opportunity to cross-examine. The Sixth Amendment therefore incorporates those limitations.

We do not read the historical sources to say that a prior opportunity to cross-examine was merely a sufficient, rather than a necessary, condition for admissibility of testimonial statements. They suggest that this requirement was dispositive, and not merely one of several ways to establish reliability. This is not to deny that "[t]here were always exceptions to the general rule of exclusion" of hearsay evidence. Several had become well established by 1791. But there is scant evidence that exceptions were invoked to admit *testimonial* statements against the accused in a *criminal* case.[6] Most of the hearsay exceptions covered statements that by their nature were not testimonial—for example, business records or statements in furtherance of a conspiracy. We do not infer from these that the Framers thought exceptions would apply even to prior testimony. Cf. *Lilly v. Virginia* (1999) (plurality opinion) ("[A]ccomplices' confessions that inculpate a criminal defendant are not within a firmly rooted exception to the hearsay rule").

Roberts conditions the admissibility of all hearsay evidence on whether it falls under a "firmly rooted hearsay exception" or bears "particularized guarantees of trustworthiness." This test departs from the historical principles identified above in two respects. First, it is too broad: It applies the same mode of analysis whether or not the hearsay consists of ex parte testimony. This often results in close constitutional scrutiny in cases that are far removed from the core concerns of the Clause. At the same time, however, the test is too narrow: It admits statements that do consist of ex parte testimony upon a mere finding of reliability. This malleable standard often fails to protect against paradigmatic confrontation violations.

Where testimonial statements are involved, we do not think the Framers meant to leave the Sixth Amendment's protection to the vagaries of the rules of evidence, much less to amorphous notions of "reliability." Certainly none of the authorities discussed above acknowledges any general reliability exception to the common-law rule. Admitting statements deemed reliable by a judge is fundamentally at odds with the right of confrontation. To be sure, the Clause's ultimate goal is to ensure reliability of evidence, but it is a procedural rather than a substantive guarantee. It commands, not that evidence be reliable, but that reliability be assessed in a particular manner: by testing in the crucible of cross-examination. The Clause thus reflects a judgment, not only about the desirability of reliable evidence, but about how reliability can best be determined.

The *Roberts* test allows a jury to hear evidence, untested by the adversary process, based on a mere judicial determination of reliability. It thus replaces the constitutionally prescribed method of assessing reliability with a wholly foreign one. In this respect, it is very different from exceptions to the Confrontation Clause that make no claim to be a surrogate means of assessing reliability.

V

B

The legacy of *Roberts* in other courts vindicates the Framers' wisdom in rejecting a general reliability exception. The framework is so unpredictable that it fails to provide meaningful protection from even core confrontation violations.

Reliability is an amorphous, if not entirely subjective, concept. There are countless factors bearing on whether a statement is reliable. Whether a statement is deemed reliable depends heavily on which factors the judge considers and how much weight he accords each of them. Some courts wind up attaching the same

---

6. The one deviation we have found involves dying declarations. The existence of that exception as a general rule of criminal hearsay law cannot be disputed. We need not decide in this case whether the Sixth Amendment incorporates an exception for testimonial dying declarations. If this exception must be accepted on historical grounds, it is *sui generis*.

significance to opposite facts. For example, the Colorado Supreme Court held a statement more reliable because its inculpation of the defendant was "detailed," while the Fourth Circuit found a statement more reliable because the portion implicating another was "fleeting." The Virginia Court of Appeals found a statement more reliable because the witness was in custody and charged with a crime (thus making the statement more obviously against her penal interest), while the Wisconsin Court of Appeals found a statement more reliable because the witness was *not* in custody and *not* a suspect. Finally, the Colorado Supreme Court in one case found a statement more reliable because it was given "immediately after" the events at issue, while that same court, in another case, found a statement more reliable because two years had elapsed.

The unpardonable vice of the *Roberts* test, however, is not its unpredictability, but its demonstrated capacity to admit core testimonial statements that the Confrontation Clause plainly meant to exclude. Despite the plurality's speculation in *Lilly*, that it was "highly unlikely" that accomplice confessions implicating the accused could survive *Roberts*, courts continue routinely to admit them.

Where testimonial evidence is at issue, however, the Sixth Amendment demands what the common law required: unavailability and a prior opportunity for cross-examination. We leave for another day any effort to spell out a comprehensive definition of "testimonial." Whatever else the term covers, it applies at a minimum to prior testimony at a preliminary hearing, before a grand jury, or at a former trial; and to police interrogations. These are the modern practices with closest kinship to the abuses at which the Confrontation Clause was directed.

In this case, the State admitted Sylvia's testimonial statement against petitioner, despite the fact that he had no opportunity to cross-examine her. That alone is sufficient to make out a violation of the Sixth Amendment. *Roberts* notwithstanding, we decline to mine the record in search of indicia of reliability. Where testimonial statements are at issue, the only indicium of reliability sufficient to satisfy constitutional demands is the one the Constitution actually prescribes: confrontation.

Crawford moved away from *Roberts* in two significant ways. Under *Crawford*:

- The Confrontation Clause applies only to out-of-court "testimonial" statements, not *all* out-of-court statements. Although *Crawford* itself said that testimonial statements were the Clause's "core" concern, the Court in later cases clarified that testimonial statements are its *sole* concern—and that the Clause does not apply *at all* to nontestimonial statements. *Whorton v. Bockting*, 549 U.S. 406, 420 (2007).
- The primary concern of the Clause is not whether a particular out-of-court statement is *reliable*. Instead, the Clause is meant to guarantee *confrontation*. Indeed, the U.S. Supreme Court has subsequently acknowledged that "[i]t is . . . unclear whether *Crawford*, on the whole, decreased or increased the number of unreliable out of court statements that may be admitted in criminal trials." *Whorton*, 549 U.S. at 420.

The way in which the Confrontation Clause's scope changed between *Roberts* and *Crawford* is illustrated by this graphic:

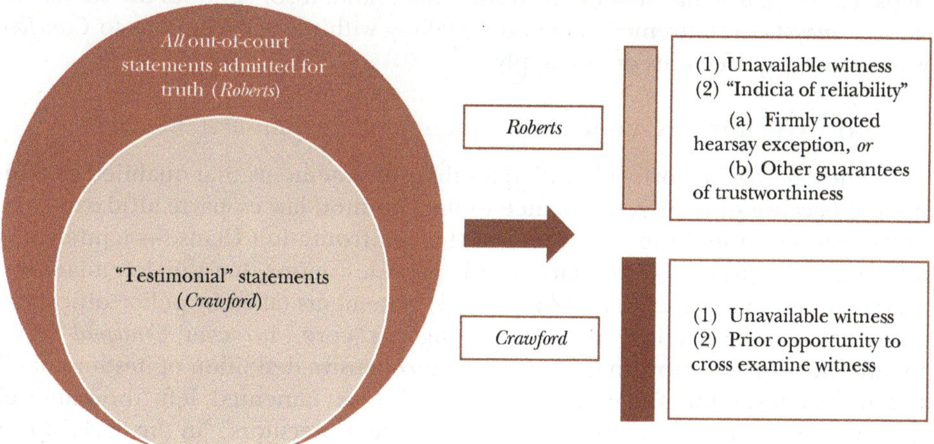

What, then, is the practical impact of this shift in the Confrontation Clause's test? As it turns out, it is potentially quite significant.

Examples

1. The People charge Defendant with a cold case murder committed in 1993. A coroner performed the autopsy on the victim and recovered a bullet from the victim's body that could be matched with the gun found in Defendant's possession when he was arrested. The coroner has since died. The coroner's observations and conclusions are out-of-court statements being admitted for their truth. If they are "testimonial" under *Crawford*, they must be excluded and Defendant would likely be acquitted.
2. The People charge Defendant with domestic violence. The victim is her boyfriend. Right after the incident, the boyfriend told the police that Defendant pushed him down the stairs. He has since recanted and claims that he tripped on a toy and fell down the stairs. His statements are out-of-court statements admitted for their truth. If they are "testimonial" under *Crawford*, they must be excluded—even if they otherwise qualify as an excited utterance and even if they are the key evidence tying Defendant to the crime.

In other words, *Crawford*'s strict rule comes with a price. The tension between *Crawford*'s rule and the cost of that rule is evident in the cases that define *Crawford*'s contours. We discuss them next.

3. *Interpreting* Crawford*: Testimonial Versus Nontestimonial Statements*

Because *Crawford* makes the Confrontation Clause applicable only when an out-of-court statement is "testimonial," applying *Crawford* breaks down into two steps: (1) Is a particular statement "testimonial," and, if so, (2) does the statement satisfy *Crawford*'s requirements, including falling within any exceptions to *Crawford* when those requirements do not apply?

(a) When Is an Out-of-Court Statement "Testimonial"?

The *Crawford* majority identified a subset of statements that qualified as testimonial because of their resemblance to the common law ex parte affidavits that, in its view, motivated the enactment of the Confrontation Clause—namely, (1) affidavits, (2) custodial examinations, (3) prior testimony that the defendant was unable to test by cross-examination, and (4) statements taken by police officers in the course of investigation. Beyond defining this "core," however, *Crawford* "le[ft] for another day any effort to spell out a comprehensive definition of 'testimonial.'" Leaving the term undefined, the concurring Justices lamented, left "thousands of federal prosecutors and tens of thousands of state prosecutors" "in the dark." *Crawford*, 541 U.S. at 75-76 (Rehnquist, C.J., concurring).

The Court has spent the ensuing years defining when a statement is "testimonial" for purposes of the Confrontation Clause.

(i) "Testimonial" versus "nontestimonial" in the context of police interviews

In two companion cases, decided a year after *Crawford*, the Supreme Court grappled with when a statement was "testimonial" in the context of a domestic violence case. In the lead case *Davis v. Washington*, 547 U.S. 813 (2005), the prosecutor sought to introduce a 911 call from a domestic violence victim to the 911 dispatcher, made while the defendant was still in the house and reporting that the defendant was "jumpin' on [her] again" and "usin' his fists." In *Hammon v. Illinois*, the companion case, the prosecutor sought to introduce testimony from a police officer relaying what a victim of domestic violence told him during an interview about the incident; the interview occurred in the living room of the couple's home, while the defendant was speaking with a different officer in the kitchen. The victims in both cases recanted and did not show up at trial.

Davis v. Washington

547 U.S. 813 (2005)

Justice Scalia delivered the opinion of the Court.

These cases require us to determine when statements made to law enforcement personnel during a 911 call or at a crime scene are "testimonial" and thus subject to the requirements of the Sixth Amendment's Confrontation Clause.

I.

A.

The relevant statements in *Davis v. Washington* were made to a 911 emergency operator on February 1, 2001. When the operator answered the initial call, the connection terminated before anyone spoke. She reversed the call, and Michelle

McCottry answered. In the ensuing conversation, the operator ascertained that McCottry was involved in a domestic disturbance with her former boyfriend Adrian Davis, the petitioner in this case:

"911 Operator: Hello.
"Complainant: Hello.
"911 Operator: What's going on?
"Complainant: He's here jumpin' on me again.
"911 Operator: Okay. Listen to me carefully. Are you in a house or an apartment?
"Complainant: I'm in a house.
"911 Operator: Are there any weapons?
"Complainant: No. He's usin' his fists.
"911 Operator: Okay. Has he been drinking?
"Complainant: No.
"911 Operator: Okay, sweetie. I've got help started. Stay on the line with me, okay?
"Complainant: I'm on the line.
"911 Operator: Listen to me carefully. Do you know his last name?
"Complainant: It's Davis.
"911 Operator: Davis? Okay, what's his first name?
"Complainant: Adran
"911 Operator: What is it?
"Complainant: Adrian.
"911 Operator: Adrian?
"Complainant: Yeah.
"911 Operator: Okay. What's his middle initial?
"Complainant: Martell. He's runnin' now."

As the conversation continued, the operator learned that Davis had "just r[un] out the door" after hitting McCottry, and that he was leaving in a car with someone else. McCottry started talking, but the operator cut her off, saying, "Stop talking and answer my questions." She then gathered more information about Davis (including his birthday), and learned that Davis had told McCottry that his purpose in coming to the house was "to get his stuff," since McCottry was moving. McCottry described the context of the assault, after which the operator told her that the police were on their way. "They're gonna check the area for him first," the operator said, "and then they're gonna come talk to you."

The police arrived within four minutes of the 911 call and observed McCottry's shaken state, the "fresh injuries on her forearm and her face," and her "frantic efforts to gather her belongings and her children so that they could leave the residence."

The State charged Davis with felony violation of a domestic no-contact order. "The State's only witnesses were the two police officers who responded to the 911 call. Both officers testified that McCottry exhibited injuries that appeared to be recent, but neither officer could testify as to the cause of the injuries." McCottry presumably could have testified as to whether Davis was her assailant, but she did not appear.

B.

In *Hammon* v. *Indiana*, police responded late on the night of February 26, 2003, to a "reported domestic disturbance" at the home of Hershel and Amy Hammon. They found Amy alone on the front porch, appearing "'somewhat frightened,'" but she told them that "'nothing was the matter,'" She gave them permission to enter the house, where an officer saw "a gas heating unit in the corner of the living room" that had "flames coming out of the . . . partial glass front. There were pieces of glass on the ground in front of it and there was flame emitting from the front of the heating unit."

Hershel, meanwhile, was in the kitchen. He told the police "that he and his wife had 'been in an argument' but 'everything was fine now' and the argument 'never became physical.'" By this point Amy had come back inside. One of the officers remained with Hershel; the other went to the living room to talk with Amy, and "again asked [her] what had occurred." Hershel made several attempts to participate in Amy's conversation with the police, but was rebuffed. After hearing Amy's account, the officer "had her fill out and sign a battery affidavit." Amy handwrote the following: "Broke our Furnace & shoved me down on the floor into the broken glass. Hit me in the chest and threw me down. Broke our lamps & phone. Tore up my van where I couldn't leave the house. Attacked my daughter."

The State charged Hershel with domestic battery and with violating his probation. Amy was subpoenaed, but she did not appear at his subsequent bench trial. The State called the officer who had questioned Amy, and asked him to recount what Amy told him and to authenticate the affidavit.

II

Our opinion in *Crawford* set forth "[v]arious formulations" of the core class of "'testimonial'" statements, but found it unnecessary to endorse any of them, because "some statements qualify under any definition." Among those, we said, were "[s]tatements taken by police officers in the course of interrogations." The questioning that generated the deponent's statement in *Crawford*—which was made and recorded while she was in police custody, after having been given Miranda warnings as a possible suspect herself—"qualifies under any conceivable definition" of an "'interrogation.'" We therefore did not define that term, except to say that "[w]e use [it] . . . in its colloquial, rather than any technical legal, sense," and that "one can imagine various definitions . . . , and we need not select among them in this case." The character of the statements in the present cases is not as clear, and these cases require us to determine more precisely which police interrogations produce testimony.

Without attempting to produce an exhaustive classification of all conceivable statements—or even all conceivable statements in response to police interrogation—as either testimonial or nontestimonial, it suffices to decide the present cases to hold as follows: Statements are nontestimonial when made in the course of police interrogation under circumstances objectively indicating that the primary purpose of the interrogation is to enable police assistance to meet an ongoing emergency. They are testimonial when the circumstances objectively indicate that there is no such ongoing emergency, and that the primary purpose of the interrogation is to establish or prove past events potentially relevant to later criminal prosecution.

The question before us in *Davis*, then, is whether, objectively considered, the interrogation that took place in the course of the 911 call produced testimonial statements. When we said in *Crawford*, that "interrogations by law enforcement officers fall squarely within [the] class" of testimonial hearsay, we had immediately in mind (for that was the case before us) interrogations solely directed at establishing the facts of a past crime, in order to identify (or provide evidence to convict) the perpetrator. The product of such interrogation, whether reduced to a writing signed by the declarant or embedded in the memory (and perhaps notes) of the interrogating officer, is testimonial. It is, in the terms of the 1828 American dictionary quoted in *Crawford*, "'[a] solemn declaration or affirmation made for the purpose of establishing or proving some fact.'" A 911 call, on the other hand, and at least the initial interrogation conducted in connection with a 911 call, is ordinarily not designed primarily to "establis[h] or prov[e]" some past fact, but to describe current circumstances requiring police assistance.

The difference between the interrogation in *Davis* and the one in *Crawford* is apparent on the face of things. In *Davis*, McCottry was speaking about events as they were actually happening, rather than "describ[ing] past events." Sylvia Crawford's interrogation, on the other hand, took place hours after the events she described had occurred. Moreover, any reasonable listener would recognize that McCottry (unlike Sylvia Crawford) was facing an ongoing emergency. Although one might call 911 to provide a narrative report of a crime absent any imminent danger, McCottry's call was plainly a call for help against a bona fide physical threat. Third, the nature of what was asked and answered in *Davis*, again viewed objectively, was such that the elicited statements were necessary to be able to resolve the present emergency, rather than simply to learn (as in *Crawford*) what had happened in the past. That is true even of the operator's effort to establish the identity of the assailant, so that the dispatched officers might know whether they would be encountering a violent felon. And finally, the difference in the level of formality between the two interviews is striking. Crawford was responding calmly, at the station house, to a series of questions, with the officer-interrogator taping and making notes of her answers; McCottry's frantic answers were provided over the phone, in an environment that was not tranquil, or even (as far as any reasonable 911 operator could make out) safe.

We conclude from all this that the circumstances of McCottry's interrogation objectively indicate its primary purpose was to enable police assistance to meet an ongoing emergency. She simply was not acting as a witness; she was not testifying.

Determining the testimonial or nontestimonial character of the statements that were the product of the interrogation in *Hammon* is a much easier task, since they were not much different from the statements we found to be testimonial in *Crawford*. It is entirely clear from the circumstances that the interrogation was part of an investigation into possibly criminal past conduct—as, indeed, the testifying officer expressly acknowledged. There was no emergency in progress; the interrogating officer testified that he had heard no arguments or crashing and saw no one throw or break anything. When the officers first arrived, Amy told them that things were fine, and there was no immediate threat to her person. When the officer questioned Amy for the second time, and elicited the challenged statements, he was not seeking to determine (as in *Davis*) "what is happening," but rather "what happened." Objectively viewed, the primary, if not indeed the sole, purpose of the interrogation was to investigate a possible crime—which is, of course, precisely what the officer *should* have done.

It is true that the *Crawford* interrogation was more formal. It followed a *Miranda* warning, was tape-recorded, and took place at the station house. While these features certainly strengthened the statements' testimonial aspect—made it more objectively apparent, that is, that the purpose of the exercise was to nail down the truth about past criminal events—none was essential to the point. It was formal enough that Amy's interrogation was conducted in a separate room, away from her husband (who tried to intervene), with the officer receiving her replies for use in his "investigat[ion]." What we called the "striking resemblance" of the *Crawford* statement to civil-law ex parte examinations is shared by Amy's statement here. Both declarants were actively separated from the defendant—officers forcibly prevented Hershel from participating in the interrogation. Both statements deliberately recounted, in response to police questioning, how potentially criminal past events began and progressed. And both took place some time after the events described were over. Such statements under official interrogation are an obvious substitute for live testimony, because they do precisely what a witness does on direct examination; they are inherently testimonial.

Tellingly, the *Davis* court declined to create a "domestic violence" exception to *Crawford* that would have declared *any* statements vis-à-vis domestic violence to be nontestimonial.

The Supreme Court confronted a different type of emergency situation in *Michigan v. Bryant*, 562 U.S. 344 (2011). There, the police responded to a radio dispatch call reporting a man being shot and found the victim lying in the parking lot of a gas station at 3:25 a.m. The victim had a gunshot wound to the abdomen. The police asked him what happened, who had shot him, and where the shooting occurred. The victim reported that "Rick" (the defendant) had shot him around 3 a.m. at the defendant's home, before the victim drove to the gas station. *Bryant* addressed whether the victim's statements to police were "testimonial."

Michigan v. Bryant

562 U.S. 344 (2011)

JUSTICE SOTOMAYOR delivered the opinion of the Court.

At respondent Richard Bryant's trial, the court admitted statements that the victim, Anthony Covington, made to police officers who discovered him mortally wounded in a gas station parking lot. A jury convicted Bryant of, second-degree murder. On appeal, the Supreme Court of Michigan held that the Sixth Amendment's Confrontation Clause, as explained in our decisions in *Crawford v. Washington* and *Davis v. Washington* rendered Covington's statements inadmissible testimonial hearsay, and the court reversed Bryant's conviction. We hold that the circumstances of the interaction between Covington and the police objectively indicate that the "primary purpose of the interrogation" was "to enable police assistance to meet an ongoing emergency." Therefore, Covington's identification and description of the shooter and the location of the shooting were not testimonial statements, and their admission at Bryant's trial did not violate the Confrontation Clause. We vacate the judgment of the Supreme Court of Michigan and remand.

Davis and *Hammon* were both domestic violence cases. [However], there may be *other* circumstances, aside from ongoing emergencies, when a statement is not procured with a primary purpose of creating an out-of-court substitute for trial testimony. We now face a new context: a nondomestic dispute, involving a victim found in a public location, suffering from a fatal gunshot wound, and a perpetrator whose location was unknown at the time the police located the victim. Thus, we confront for the first time circumstances in which the "ongoing emergency" discussed in *Davis* extends beyond an initial victim to a potential threat to the responding police and the public at large. This new context requires us to provide additional clarification with regard to what *Davis* meant by "the primary purpose of the interrogation is to enable police assistance to meet an ongoing emergency."

III

To determine whether the "primary purpose" of an interrogation is "to enable police assistance to meet an ongoing emergency," which would render the resulting statements nontestimonial, we objectively evaluate the circumstances in which the encounter occurs and the statements and actions of the parties.

An objective analysis of the circumstances of an encounter and the statements and actions of the parties to it provides the most accurate assessment of the "primary purpose of the interrogation." The circumstances in which an encounter occurs—*e.g.*, at or near the scene of the crime versus at a police station, during an ongoing emergency or afterwards—are clearly matters of objective fact. The statements and actions of the parties must also be objectively evaluated. That is, the relevant inquiry is not the subjective or actual purpose of the individuals involved in a particular encounter, but rather the purpose that reasonable participants would have had, as ascertained from the individuals' statements and actions and the circumstances in which the encounter occurred.

As our recent Confrontation Clause cases have explained, the existence of an "ongoing emergency" at the time of an encounter between an individual and the police is among the most important circumstances informing the "primary purpose" of an interrogation. The existence of an ongoing emergency is relevant to determining the primary purpose of the interrogation because an emergency focuses the participants on something other than "prov[ing] past events potentially relevant to later criminal prosecution." Rather, it focuses them on "end[ing] a threatening situation." Implicit in *Davis* is the idea that because the prospect of fabrication in statements given for the primary purpose of resolving that emergency is presumably significantly diminished, the Confrontation Clause does not require such statements to be subject to the crucible of cross-examination.

This logic is not unlike that justifying the excited utterance exception in hearsay law. Statements "relating to a startling event or condition made while the declarant was under the stress of excitement caused by the event or condition," Fed. Rule Evid. 803(2); see also Mich. Rule Evid. 803(2) (2010), are considered reliable because the declarant, in the excitement, presumably cannot form a falsehood.

As *Davis* made clear, whether an ongoing emergency exists is simply one factor—albeit an important factor—that informs the ultimate inquiry regarding the "primary purpose" of an interrogation. Another factor the Michigan Supreme Court did not sufficiently account for is the importance of *informality* in an encounter between a victim and police. Formality is not the sole touchstone of our primary purpose inquiry because, although formality suggests the absence of an emergency and therefore an increased likelihood that the purpose of the interrogation is to "establish or prove past events potentially relevant to later criminal prosecution," informality does not necessarily indicate the presence of an emergency or the lack of testimonial intent. *Cf. Davis*, 126 S. Ct. 2266 (explaining that Confrontation Clause requirements cannot "readily be evaded" by the parties deliberately keeping the written product of an interrogation informal "instead of having the declarant sign a deposition").

As we suggested in *Davis*, when a court must determine whether the Confrontation Clause bars the admission of a statement at trial, it should determine the "primary purpose of the interrogation" by objectively evaluating the statements and actions of the parties to the encounter, in light of the circumstances in which the interrogation occurs. The existence of an emergency or the parties' perception that an emergency is ongoing is among the most important circumstances that courts must take into account in determining whether an interrogation is testimonial because statements made to assist police in addressing an ongoing emergency presumably lack the testimonial purpose that would subject them to the requirement of confrontation. As the context of this case brings into sharp relief, the existence and duration of an emergency depend on the type and scope of danger posed to the victim, the police, and the public.

The majority in *Bryant* held that the statements were not "testimonial" because (1) there was an ongoing emergency at the time the police questioned the victim because the police did not know anything about the shooter's motive or whereabouts; (2) the assailant had a gun, so remained a threat to the public; (3) the victim was in pain and dying; and (4) the encounter was more informal, "similar" to the "harried" 911 call in *Davis*. The majority in *Bryant* also indicated that the primary purpose of the statement was to be assessed by looking to the purposes of the speaker *and* the questioner and by examining their purposes "objectively"—that is, by asking what the primary purpose of reasonable people in the speaker's and questioner's situations would have been (rather than what *this* speaker and *this* questioner *subjectively* believed their purposes were).

(ii) "Testimonial" versus "nontestimonial" in the context of laboratory reports

Apart from determining the relevance of "emergencies" to whether a statement is "testimonial," the Supreme Court has also examined whether forensic reports used in a criminal prosecution are testimonial. Prosecutors regularly rely on forensic laboratories to, for example, examine blood samples for alcohol in driving while intoxicated cases, to examine the chemical composition of substances seized to confirm that they are illegal narcotics, and to generate DNA profiles from blood and other bodily fluids. Prior to *Crawford,* these laboratories would prepare certified reports attesting to their findings, which prosecutors could move into evidence without the need to call a live witness. In *Melendez-Diaz v. Massachusetts,* 557 U.S. 305 (2009), the prosecution sought to introduce a sworn and notarized laboratory report finding that the drugs seized from the defendant contained cocaine, a controlled substance.

Melendez-Diaz v. Massachusetts

557 U.S. 305 (2009)

JUSTICE SCALIA delivered the opinion of the Court.

The Massachusetts courts in this case admitted into evidence affidavits reporting the results of forensic analysis which showed that material seized by the police and connected to the defendant was cocaine. The question presented is whether those affidavits are "testimonial," rendering the affiants "witnesses" subject to the defendant's right of confrontation under the Sixth Amendment.

There is little doubt that the documents at issue in this case fall within the "core class of testimonial statements" thus described. Our description of that category mentions affidavits twice. The documents at issue here, while denominated by Massachusetts law "certificates," are quite plainly affidavits: "declaration[s] of facts written down and sworn to by the declarant before an officer authorized to administer oaths." The fact in question is that the substance found in the possession of Melendez-Diaz and his codefendants was, as the prosecution claimed, cocaine—the precise testimony the analysts would be expected to provide if called at trial. The "certificates" are functionally identical to live, in-court testimony, doing "precisely what a witness does on direct examination."

[N]ot only were the affidavits "'made under circumstances which would lead an objective witness reasonably to believe that the statement would be available for use at a later trial,'" but under Massachusetts law the *sole purpose* of the affidavits was to provide "prima facie evidence of the composition, quality, and the net weight" of the analyzed substance.

Respondent first argues that the analysts are not subject to confrontation because they are not "accusatory" witnesses, in that they do not directly accuse petitioner of wrongdoing; rather, their testimony is inculpatory only when taken together with other evidence linking petitioner to the contraband. This finds no support in the text of the Sixth Amendment or in our case law. It is often, indeed perhaps usually, the case that an adverse witness's testimony, taken alone, will not suffice to convict. Yet respondent fails to cite a single case in which such testimony was admitted absent a defendant's opportunity to cross-examine.

Respondent and the dissent argue that the analysts should not be subject to confrontation because they are not "conventional" (or "typical" or "ordinary") witnesses of the sort whose *ex parte* testimony was most notoriously used at the trial of Sir Walter Raleigh. It is true, as the Court recognized in *Crawford,* that *ex parte* examinations of the sort used at Raleigh's trial have "long been thought a paradigmatic confrontation violation." But the paradigmatic case identifies the core of the right to confrontation, not its limits. Forensic evidence is not uniquely immune from the risk of manipulation.

A forensic analyst responding to a request from a law enforcement official may feel pressure—or have an incentive—to alter the evidence in a manner favorable to the prosecution. Confrontation is one means of ensuring accurate forensic analysis. Confrontation is designed to weed out not only the fraudulent analyst, but the incompetent one as well. Serious deficiencies have been found in the forensic evidence used in criminal trials. Like expert witnesses generally, an analyst's lack of proper training or deficiency in judgment may be disclosed in cross-examination.

Respondent argues that the analysts' affidavits are admissible without confrontation because they are "akin to the types of official and business records admissible at common law." But the affidavits do not qualify as traditional official or business records, and even if they did, their authors would be subject to confrontation nonetheless.

Documents kept in the regular course of business may ordinarily be admitted at trial despite their hearsay status. See Fed. Rule Evid. 803(6). But that is not the case if the regularly conducted business activity is the production of evidence for use at trial. The analysts' certificates—like police reports generated by law enforcement officials—do not qualify as business or public records for precisely the same reason. See Rule 803(8) (defining public records as "excluding, however, in criminal cases matters observed by police officers and other law enforcement personnel").

Finally, respondent asks us to relax the requirements of the Confrontation Clause to accommodate the "'necessities of trial and the adversary process.'" The Confrontation Clause may make the prosecution of criminals more burdensome, but that is equally true of the right to trial by jury and the privilege against self-incrimination. The Confrontation Clause—like those other constitutional provisions—is binding, and we may not disregard it at our convenience.

We also doubt the accuracy of respondent's and the dissent's dire predictions. The dissent, respondent, and its *amici* highlight the substantial total number of controlled-substance analyses performed by state and federal laboratories in recent years. But only some of those tests are implicated in prosecutions, and only a small fraction of those cases actually proceed to trial.

Perhaps the best indication that the sky will not fall after today's decision is that it has not done so already. Many States have already adopted the constitutional rule we announce today, while many others permit the defendant to assert (or forfeit by silence) his Confrontation Clause right after receiving notice of the prosecution's intent to use a forensic analyst's report. Despite these widespread practices, there is no evidence that the criminal justice system has ground to a halt in the States that, one way or another, empower a defendant to insist upon the analyst's appearance at trial.

[It is not surprising that defense] attorneys and their clients will often stipulate to the nature of the substance in the ordinary drug case. It is unlikely that defense counsel will insist on live testimony whose effect will be merely to highlight rather than cast doubt upon the forensic analysis. Nor will defense attorneys want to antagonize the judge or jury by wasting their time with the appearance of a witness whose testimony defense counsel does not intend to rebut in any fashion.

Generally, defendants do not object to the admission of drug certificates most likely because there is no benefit to a defendant from such testimony." Given these strategic considerations, and in light of the experience in those States that already provide the same or similar protections to defendants, there is little reason to believe that our decision today will commence the parade of horribles respondent and the dissent predict.

This case involves little more than the application of our holding in *Crawford v. Washington.* The Sixth Amendment does not permit the prosecution to prove its case via *ex parte* out-of-court affidavits, and the admission of such evidence against *Melendez-Diaz* was error.

In light of *Melendez-Diaz's* holding that certified and notarized laboratory reports are "testimonial" statements subject to *Crawford*'s rule of exclusion unless a declarant is subject to cross-examination, the next question the Supreme Court considered is *who* that witness must be before a laboratory report can be admitted. Must the witness be the actual declarant who prepared the report at issue, or is it sufficient that the witness is someone likely to be as knowledgeable as the declarant? That was the issue in *Bullcoming v. New Mexico,* 564 U.S. 647 (2011). In *Bullcoming,* the defendant was charged with driving while under the influence of alcohol, and the prosecution sought to rely on a certified but unsworn forensic laboratory report of the defendant's blood alcohol content. The laboratory analyst who performed the test on the defendant's sample was unavailable, so the prosecutor called another analyst for the same laboratory to testify about the laboratory's procedures. Did the use of this "surrogate" witness satisfy *Crawford*'s mandate?

Bullcoming v. New Mexico

564 U.S. 647 (2011)

JUSTICE GINSBURG delivered the opinion of the Court [as to all but certain portions]:

The question presented is whether the Confrontation Clause permits the prosecution to introduce a forensic laboratory report containing a testimonial certification—made for the purpose of proving a particular fact—through the in-court testimony of a scientist who did not sign the certification or perform or observe the test reported in the certification. We hold that surrogate testimony of that order does not meet the constitutional requirement. The accused's right is to be confronted with the analyst who made the certification, unless that analyst is unavailable at trial, and the accused had an opportunity, pretrial, to cross-examine that particular scientist.

More fundamentally, as this Court stressed in *Crawford,* "[t]he text of the Sixth Amendment does not suggest any open-ended exceptions from the confrontation requirement to be developed by the courts." 541 U.S. at 54. Nor is it "the role of courts to extrapolate from the words of the [Confrontation Clause] to the values behind it, and then to enforce its guarantees only to the extent they serve (in the courts' views) those underlying values." *Giles v. California*, 554 U.S. 353, 375 (2008) (plurality). Accordingly, the Clause does not tolerate dispensing with confrontation simply because the court believes that questioning one witness about another's testimonial statements provides a fair enough opportunity for cross-examination.

Justice Sotomayor, concurring in part.

This is not a case in which the person testifying is a supervisor, reviewer, or someone else with a personal, albeit limited, connection to the scientific test at issue. Razatos [(who was the proffered substitute witness)] conceded on cross-examination that he played no role in producing the BAC report and did not observe any portion of Curtis Caylor's conduct of the testing. The court below also recognized Razatos' total lack of connection to the test at issue. It would be a different case if, for example, a supervisor who observed an analyst conducting a test testified about the results or a report about such results. We need not address what degree of involvement is sufficient because here Razatos had no involvement whatsoever in the relevant test and report.

Consider *People v. Ogaz*, 53 Cal. App. 5th 280 (Cal. Ct. App. 2020). There, the defendant was prosecuted for possessing heroin and methamphetamine. The prosecutor introduced a signed laboratory report attesting that the drugs seized from the defendant were, chemically, heroin and methamphetamine. However, the lab technician who did the analysis did not testify; instead, her supervisor did. *Ogaz* held that this was an error under *Crawford.* The court concluded that the lab report was "testimonial" because it was a signed attestation to the chemical analysis, and that its primary purpose was for use at trial (not, as the prosecutor argued, as a business record of the laboratory). Citing *Bullcoming,* the court went on to hold that making the supervisor available for cross-examination (rather than the lab technician) was insufficient to satisfy *Crawford*'s cross-examination requirement because the supervisor "was not personally involved in the test [the technician] conducted" and because the supervisor did not "formulate[] his own independent opinions based on the data [the technician] produced during the testing process."

Until this point, most of the Supreme Court's post-*Crawford* decisions had been 5-4 decisions, but they had at least commanded a majority opinion with a holding regarding the meaning of "testimonial." That changed with *Williams v. Illinois,* 567 U.S. 50 (2012). Williams was on trial for rape. The prosecutor called a DNA expert who testified to a match between the defendant's known DNA profile (as collected by the police) and the DNA profile recovered from the victim's body (which was extracted from the samples analyzed by an outside laboratory called Cellmark). The expert testified that she relied on Cellmark's analysis and report in coming to her conclusion. *Williams* raised the question: Was Cellmark's report a "testimonial" statement? The Court in *Williams* split 4-1-4 on the answer, with five of the justices concluding that it was not testimonial. The rationales of the three factions of justices varied widely.

Williams v. Illinois

567 U.S. 50 (2012)

JUSTICE ALITO announced the judgement of the Court and delivered an opinion, joined by THE CHIEF JUSTICE, JUSTICE KENNEDY, and JUSTICE BREYER.

On February 10, 2000, in Chicago, Illinois, a young woman, L. J., was abducted while she was walking home from work. The perpetrator forced her into his car and raped her, then robbed her of her money and other personal items and pushed her out into the street. An ambulance took L. J. to the hospital, where doctors treated her wounds and took a blood sample and vaginal swabs for a sexual-assault kit. A Chicago Police detective collected the kit, labeled it with an inventory number, and sent it under seal to the Illinois State Police (ISP) lab.

At the ISP lab, a forensic scientist received the sealed kit. He conducted a chemical test that confirmed the presence of semen on the vaginal swabs, and he then resealed the kit and placed it in a secure evidence freezer.

During the period in question, the ISP lab often sent biological samples to Cellmark Diagnostics Laboratory in Germantown, Maryland, for DNA testing. There was evidence that the ISP lab sent L. J.'s vaginal swabs to Cellmark for testing and that Cellmark sent back a report containing a male DNA profile produced from semen taken from those swabs. At this time, petitioner was not under suspicion for L. J.'s rape.

Sandra Lambatos, a forensic specialist at the ISP lab, conducted a computer search to see if the Cellmark profile matched any of the entries in the state DNA database. The computer showed a match to a profile produced by the lab from a sample of petitioner's blood that had been taken after he was arrested on unrelated charges on August 3, 2000.

On April 17, 2001, the police conducted a lineup at which L. J. identified petitioner as her assailant. Petitioner was then indicted for aggravated criminal sexual assault, aggravated kidnaping, and aggravated robbery. In lieu of a jury trial, petitioner chose to be tried before a state judge.

We now conclude that this form of expert testimony does not violate the Confrontation Clause because that provision has no application to out-of-court statements that are not offered to prove the truth of the matter asserted. When an expert testifies for the prosecution in a criminal case, the defendant has the opportunity to cross-examine the expert about any statements that are offered for their truth. Out-of-court statements that are related by the expert solely for the purpose of explaining the assumptions on which that opinion rests are not offered for their truth and thus fall outside the scope of the Confrontation Clause. Applying this rule to the present case, we conclude that the expert's testimony did not violate the Sixth Amendment.

As a second, independent basis for our decision, we also conclude that even if the report produced by Cellmark had been admitted into evidence, there would have been no Confrontation Clause violation. The Cellmark report is very different from the sort of extrajudicial statements, such as affidavits, depositions, prior testimony, and confessions, that the Confrontation Clause was originally understood to reach. The report was produced before any suspect was identified. The report was sought not for the purpose of obtaining evidence to be used against petitioner, who was not even under suspicion at the time, but for the purpose of finding a rapist who was on the loose.

The abuses that the Court has identified as prompting the adoption of the Confrontation Clause shared the following two characteristics: (1) They involved out-of-court statements having the primary purpose of accusing a targeted individual of engaging in criminal conduct and (2) they involved formalized statements such as affidavits, depositions, prior testimony, or confessions. In all but one of the post-*Crawford* cases in which a Confrontation Clause violation has been found, both of these characteristics were present.

The Cellmark report is very different. It plainly was not prepared for the primary purpose of accusing a targeted individual. In identifying the primary purpose of an out-of-court statement, we apply an objective test.

Here, the primary purpose of the Cellmark report, viewed objectively, was not to accuse petitioner or to create evidence for use at trial. When the ISP lab sent the sample to Cellmark, its primary purpose was to catch a dangerous rapist who was still at large, not to obtain evidence for use against petitioner, who was neither in custody nor under suspicion at that time. Similarly, no one at Cellmark could have possibly known that the profile that it produced would turn out to inculpate petitioner—or for that matter, anyone else whose DNA profile was in a law enforcement database. Under these circumstances, there was no "prospect of fabrication" and no incentive to produce anything other than a scientifically sound and reliable profile.

Justice Thomas, concurring in the judgment.

I agree with the plurality that the disclosure of Cellmark's out-of-court statements through the expert testimony of Sandra Lambatos did not violate the Confrontation Clause. I reach this conclusion, however, solely because Cellmark's statements lacked the requisite "formality and solemnity" to be considered "'testimonial'" for purposes of the Confrontation Clause.

The Cellmark report is distinguishable from the laboratory reports that we determined were testimonial in *Melendez-Diaz* and in *Bullcoming v. New Mexico.* In *Melendez-Diaz,* the reports in question were "sworn to before a notary public by [the] analysts" who tested a substance for cocaine. In *Bullcoming,* the report, though unsworn, included a "Certificate of Analyst" signed by the forensic analyst who tested the defendant's blood sample.

Justice Kagan, joined by Justices Scalia, Ginsburg and Sotomayor, dissenting.

Under our Confrontation Clause precedents, this is an open-and-shut case. The State of Illinois prosecuted Sandy Williams for rape based in part on a DNA profile created in Cellmark's laboratory. Yet the State did not give Williams a chance to question the analyst who produced that evidence. Instead, the prosecution introduced the results of Cellmark's testing through an expert witness who had no idea how they were generated. That approach—no less (perhaps more) than the confrontation-free methods of presenting forensic evidence we have formerly banned—deprived Williams of his Sixth Amendment right to "confron[t] . . . the witnesses against him."

The Court today disagrees, though it cannot settle on a reason why. Justice Alito, joined by three other Justices, advances two theories—that the expert's summary of the Cellmark report was not offered for its truth, and that the report is not the kind of statement triggering the Confrontation Clause's protection. Justices specifically reject every aspect of its reasoning and every paragraph of its explication. Justice Thomas, for his part, contends that the Cellmark report is nontestimonial on a different rationale. But no other Justice joins his opinion or subscribes to the test he offers.

That creates five votes to approve the admission of the Cellmark report, but not a single good explanation. Because defendants like Williams have a constitutional right to confront the witnesses against them, I respectfully dissent from the Court's fractured decision.

As its first stab, the plurality states that the Cellmark report was "not prepared for the primary purpose of accusing a targeted individual." Where that test comes from is anyone's guess. . . . And it has no basis in our precedents. We have previously asked whether a statement was made for the primary purpose of establishing "past events potentially relevant to later criminal prosecution"—in other words, for the purpose of providing evidence. None of our cases has ever suggested that, in addition, the statement must be meant to accuse a previously identified individual; indeed, in *Melendez-Diaz,* we rejected a related argument that laboratory "analysts are not subject to confrontation because they are not 'accusatory' witnesses."

Justice Thomas's unique method of defining testimonial statements fares no better. On his view, the Confrontation Clause "regulates only the use of statements bearing 'indicia of solemnity.'" And Cellmark's report, he concludes, does not qualify because it is "neither a sworn nor a certified declaration of fact." But Justice Thomas's approach grants constitutional significance to minutia, in a way that can only undermine the Confrontation Clause's protections.

Before today's decision, a prosecutor wishing to admit the results of forensic testing had to produce the technician responsible for the analysis. That was the result of not one, but two decisions this Court issued in the last three years. But that clear rule is clear no longer. The five Justices who control the outcome of today's case agree on very little. Among them, though, they can boast of two accomplishments. First, they have approved the introduction of testimony at Williams's trial that the Confrontation Clause, rightly understood, clearly prohibits. Second, they have left significant confusion in their wake.

The better course in this case would have been simply to follow *Melendez-Diaz* and *Bullcoming.* And until a majority of this Court reverses or confines those decisions, I would understand them as continuing to govern, in every particular, the admission of forensic evidence.

I respectfully dissent.

As the dissent pointed out, five Justices—Justice Thomas and the dissenters—concluded that the Cellmark laboratory report was being admitted for its truth and not simply as a basis for evaluating the expert's opinion, which is a nonhearsay purpose. But a different five Justices—Justice Thomas and the plurality—concluded that the laboratory report was not "testimonial," albeit for two different reasons: Justice Thomas did not think that the report was "formal" enough to be testimonial, while the plurality concluded that the report did not meet the definition of its redefined "primary purpose" test, which required that the out-of-court statement be targeting a known individual before it can be considered "testimonial."

(iii) "Testimonial" versus "nontestimonial" in the context of statements to private persons

An issue left open in *Crawford* was whether statements to private persons, as opposed to police or government officials, would be considered "testimonial" and thus trigger the right of confrontation. In *Ohio v. Clark*, 576 U.S. 237 (2015), the Supreme Court addressed whether a young child's report of child abuse to his teacher constitutes "testimonial" hearsay. In *Clark*, a three-year-old child (L.P.) showed up at preschool with bloodshot eyes. When the teacher asked why he was crying, the toddler first said he "fell," then disclosed that "Dee Dee" did it and said that "Dee Dee" was "big." When the teacher's supervisor lifted the toddler's shirt, she found more injuries. The teacher and supervisor were both "mandatory reporters" obligated to report any child abuse they see to law enforcement. The defendant—who was identified as "Dee Dee"—was charged with child abuse and, after the trial judge found the toddler not competent to testify, the prosecutor sought to have the teacher testify to what the toddler said. Was the toddler's statement to his teacher "testimonial"?

Ohio v. Clark

576 U.S. 237 (2015)

JUSTICE ALITO delivered the opinion of the Court.

A grand jury indicted Clark on five counts of felonious assault (four related to A. T. and one related to L. P.), two counts of endangering children (one for each child), and two counts of domestic violence (one for each child). At trial, the State introduced L. P.'s statements to his teachers as evidence of Clark's guilt, but L. P. did not testify. Under Ohio law, children younger than 10 years old are incompetent to testify if they "appear incapable of receiving just impressions of the facts and transactions respecting which they are examined, or of relating them truly." Ohio Rule Evid. 601(A). After conducting a hearing, the trial court concluded that L. P. was not competent to testify. But under Ohio Rule of Evidence 807, which allows the admission of reliable hearsay by child abuse victims, the court ruled that L. P.'s statements to his teachers bore sufficient guarantees of trustworthiness to be admitted as evidence.

Clark moved to exclude testimony about L. P.'s out-of-court statements under the Confrontation Clause. The trial court denied the motion, ruling that L. P.'s responses were not testimonial statements covered by the Sixth Amendment.

II.

In *Michigan v. Bryant* (2011), we . . . expounded on the primary purpose test. The inquiry [into primary purpose], we emphasized, must consider "all of the relevant circumstances." And we reiterated our view in *Davis* [*v. Washington* (2005)] that, when "the primary purpose of an interrogation is to respond to an 'ongoing emergency,' its purpose is not to create a record for trial and thus is not within the scope of the [Confrontation] Clause." At the same time, we noted that "there may be other circumstances, aside from ongoing emergencies, when a statement is not procured with a primary purpose of creating an out-of-court substitute for trial testimony."

[We also noted that] [o]ne additional factor is "the informality of the situation and the interrogation." A "formal station-house interrogation," like the questioning in *Crawford* [*v. Washington* (2004)], is more likely to provoke testimonial statements, while less formal questioning is less likely to reflect a primary purpose aimed at obtaining testimonial evidence against the accused. In the end, the question is whether, in light of all the circumstances, viewed objectively, the "primary purpose" of the conversation was to "creat[e] an out-of-court substitute for trial testimony."

In this case, we consider statements made to preschool teachers, not the police. We are therefore presented with the question we have repeatedly reserved: whether statements to persons other than law enforcement officers are subject to the Confrontation Clause. Because at least some statements to individuals who are not law enforcement officers could conceivably raise confrontation concerns, we decline to adopt a categorical rule excluding them from the Sixth Amendment's reach. Nevertheless, such statements are much less likely to be testimonial than statements to law enforcement officers. And considering all the relevant circumstances here, L. P.'s statements clearly were not made with the primary purpose of creating evidence for Clark's prosecution. Thus, their introduction at trial did not violate the Confrontation Clause.

L. P.'s statements occurred in the context of an ongoing emergency involving suspected child abuse. When L. P.'s teachers noticed his injuries, they rightly became worried that the 3-year-old was the victim of serious violence. Because the teachers needed to know whether it was safe to release L. P. to his guardian at the end of the day, they needed to determine who might be abusing the child. Thus, the immediate concern was to protect a vulnerable child who needed help.

There is no indication that the primary purpose of the conversation was to gather evidence for Clark's prosecution. On the contrary, it is clear that the first objective was to protect L. P. At no point did the teachers inform L. P. that his answers would be used to arrest or punish his abuser. L. P. never hinted that he intended his statements to be used by the police or prosecutors. And the conversation between L. P. and his teachers was informal and spontaneous. The teachers asked L. P. about his injuries immediately upon discovering them, in the informal setting of a preschool lunchroom and classroom, and they did so precisely as any concerned citizen would talk to a child who might be the victim of abuse. This was nothing like the formalized station-house questioning in *Crawford* or the police interrogation and battery affidavit in *Hammon* [*v. Indiana* (2005)].

L. P.'s age fortifies our conclusion that the statements in question were not testimonial. Statements by very young children will rarely, if ever, implicate the Confrontation Clause. Few preschool students understand the details of our criminal justice system. Thus, it is extremely unlikely that a 3-year-old child in L. P.'s position would intend his statements to be a substitute for trial testimony. On the contrary, a young child in these circumstances would simply want the abuse to end, would want to protect other victims, or would have no discernible purpose at all.

As a historical matter, moreover, there is strong evidence that statements made in circumstances similar to those facing L. P. and his teachers were admissible.

Finally, although we decline to adopt a rule that statements to individuals who are not law enforcement officers are categorically outside the Sixth Amendment, the fact that L. P. was speaking to his teachers remains highly relevant. Courts must evaluate challenged statements in context, and part of that context is the questioner's identity. Statements made to someone who is not principally charged with uncovering and prosecuting criminal behavior are significantly less likely to be testimonial than statements given to law enforcement officers. It is common sense that the relationship between a student and his teacher is very different from that between a citizen and the police. We do not ignore that reality. In light of these circumstances, the Sixth Amendment did not prohibit the State from introducing L. P.'s statements at trial.

As this series of cases demonstrates, the current test for evaluating whether an out-of-court statement is "testimonial" is the product of more than a decade of precedent bobbing and weaving as shifting majorities of the Supreme Court sought to define and delimit the scope of the Confrontation Clause.

Taken together, these cases provide the following definition of "testimonial":

An out-of-court statement is "testimonial" if its "primary purpose" is "to establish or prove past events potentially relevant to later criminal prosecution." "Primary purpose" looks to the objective purpose of both the speaker (in making the statement) and the questioner (in eliciting the statement). The actual, subjective purposes of the speaker and questioner are irrelevant. If the speaker or questioner had more than one purpose, the *primary* purpose controls. In assessing purpose, courts are to examine "all" the relevant circumstances surrounding the making of the statement. These circumstances include:

(1) *What are the general circumstances surrounding the making of the statement?*
   (a) *Was the statement made in the midst of an ongoing emergency?* Statements made in the midst of an ongoing emergency are more likely to be testimonial.
      - *Does there still remain a danger to (i) the speaker, (ii) the questioner, or (iii) the public at large?*
   (b) *Where was the statement made?* Statements made at a police station or other environment controlled by law enforcement are more likely to be "testimonial." The converse is also true.
   (c) *How formal or informal was the exchange?* Statements made during a formal interrogation where there is a back and forth question-and-answer format are more likely to be "testimonial." Written statements that are signed, sworn or notarized are more likely to be "testimonial." Statements made in less formal settings or circumstances are less likely to be testimonial.

(2) *Who was the speaker, and to whom was he or she speaking?*
   (a) *What are the ages of the speaker or questioner?* Children, especially young children, are less likely to be making statements for "testimonial" purposes.

(b) *Is the questioner associated with law enforcement, and if so, does the speaker know it?* Statements made to law enforcement officers or persons whom the speaker knows to be law enforcement officers are more likely to be "testimonial."

Review Questions

1. **Dead coroner's notes.** Defendant is charged with a murder committed in 1995. The coroner who performed the autopsy on the victim has died. Prosecutor seeks to admit the coroner's notes of his observations of the body. Are the coroner's notes "testimonial"?
2. **Dead coroner's conclusions.** Defendant is charged with a murder committed in 1995. The coroner who performed the autopsy on the victim has died. Prosecutor seeks to admit the coroner's conclusions regarding the cause of death. Are the coroner's conclusions "testimonial"? How does your analysis differ, if at all, from Question 1?
3. **Overheard conversation.** A police officer overhears a woman and her neighbor talking, and the woman says, "I saw my son walk into the room just seconds before I heard the gunshot." The son is charged with murder, and Prosecutor seeks to admit the woman's statement, as she now suffers from dementia. Is the woman's statement "testimonial"?
4. **Cellmate chat.** Kenny is a gang member arrested for putting graffiti on City Hall. At the time of his arrest, Kenny is placed in a jail cell with a fellow inmate, and states that he and Defendant together robbed a hardware store for spray paint a few hours before they were caught tagging a rival gang's headquarters. In a prosecution of Defendant for that robbery, Kenny is unavailable to testify. Are Kenny's statements "testimonial"?
5. **Cellmate chat, redux.** Following on the facts of Question 4, what if the police place an undercover officer in the cell posing as a gang member, and Kenny relays the facts of the assault to the undercover officer. Is Kenny's statement "testimonial"? How does your analysis differ, if at all, from Question 4?

(b) When Does a "Testimonial" Statement Satisfy *Crawford's* Requirements?

Determining that an out-of-court statement is "testimonial" is the threshold question. If it so qualifies, it is inadmissible unless it satisfies *Crawford*'s requirement of unavailability and the opportunity to cross-examine or it falls into some other exception to *Crawford*.

(i) *Crawford's* Stated Exception

Crawford itself provides that an out-of-court, testimonial statement may be admitted if (1) the declarant is "unavailable" to testify at the trial and (2) the defendant had a prior opportunity to cross-examine the declarant.

When is a witness "unavailable" for purposes of *Crawford*? *Crawford* and its progeny have not defined that term. However, and as discussed in Chapter Eight, FRE 804(a) provides a definition of unavailability. Most federal courts have used the FRE's definition for purposes of *Crawford*.

The witness who must be subject to cross-examination at trial or whom the defendant must have had the opportunity to cross-examine prior to trial must be the declarant of the out-of-court statement. As we saw in *Bullcoming v. New Mexico*, it is insufficient to have another witness testify as to test results if that surrogate was not involved in the actual testing procedure.

Assuming the prosecution has the correct declarant to cross-examine, what matters is the *opportunity* for cross-examination, not whether the defendant took advantage of that opportunity. For example, if the prosecution seeks to admit the preliminary hearing testimony of a witness who is unavailable for trial, the fact that the defendant's lawyer had the opportunity to cross-examine that witness is sufficient—even if the attorney asked few questions at that prior hearing. By contrast, the defendant is not a party to a grand jury proceeding, so the fact that a witness previously testified before the grand jury does not satisfy *Crawford*'s exception because the defendant never had an opportunity to cross-examine that witness.

(ii) Forfeiture of Rights Under *Crawford*

Are there situations in which a defendant—by his or her conduct prior to or during trial—can forfeit the right to insist that the prosecutor meet all of *Crawford's* requirements?

Let us start with a defendant's conduct *prior to trial.* Consider the following. The defendant is charged with murdering his girlfriend. Three days before her death, the girlfriend filed a report with police reporting that the defendant had been regularly beating her. When the prosecutor seeks to admit the statements in her report, the defendant objects under *Crawford* because the statements are "testimonial" and the girlfriend is not available for cross-examination. The prosecutor responds, "The only reason she is unavailable is because the defendant killed her!" Should the defendant's conduct in rendering the out-of-court declarant unavailable deprive him of the opportunity to object on the ground that the declarant is unavailable? Does answering this question require a court to prejudge the defendant's guilt?

The Supreme Court addressed this issue in *Giles v. California*, 554 U.S. 353 (2008). In *Giles*, the defendant was charged with murdering his ex-girlfriend by shooting her six times. The prosecutor sought to admit statements that the ex-girlfriend had made to the police approximately three weeks before her death, when she tearfully recounted that the defendant accused her of cheating, started to choke her, punched her in the face, pulled a knife on her, and threatened to kill her if he found her cheating on him. The prosecutor argued that the ex-girlfriend's unavailability was due to her death at the defendant's hands, so the defendant cannot be heard to complain that his confrontation rights were not fully honored. Relying on the common law doctrine of "forfeiture by wrongdoing," *Giles* held that a defendant forfeits his right to insist on cross-examination under *Crawford* if he "engage[s] in conduct *designed* to prevent the witness from testifying." *Id.* at 359. Looking to cases and treatises from the late eighteenth and early nineteenth centuries, the *Giles* majority ruled that there is a forfeiture by wrongdoing only if the defendant renders the declarant unavailable with the "specific intent" to prevent her testimony. *Id.* at 373.

People v. Merchant

40 Cal. App. 5th 1179 (Cal. Ct. App. 2019)

DATO, Justice.

A jury convicted Jecarr Franswa Merchant of kidnapping, battery, and dissuading a witness after he careened down the freeway refusing girlfriend Lisa R.'s pleas to stop or let her out, pulled Lisa's hair, and flung her cell phone out the window as she tried to call 911. Lisa did not appear at trial.

Merchant exited the highway and drove over a center island. Lisa tried to open the door to escape. Law enforcement caught up just as Lisa managed to shift the gear into park. Merchant's vehicle was low on gas and would not restart. A California Highway Patrol officer interviewed Lisa at the scene. She described what happened in detail and estimated Merchant drove for 10 or 12 minutes as she begged to be let out.

With Lisa unavailable, her hearsay statements to the responding highway patrol officer were central to the prosecution's case. In addition, the prosecution relied on law enforcement witnesses to describe Lisa's past domestic violence reports. This evidence was admitted under the forfeiture-by-wrongdoing exception to Merchant's Sixth Amendment right to confrontation.

A criminal defendant has a Sixth Amendment right "to be confronted with the witnesses against him." A court may not admit a witness's testimonial hearsay statements against a defendant unless the witness is unavailable and the defendant had a prior opportunity for cross-examination. (*Crawford v. Washington* (2004) 541 U.S. 36, 53–54.) Nonetheless, in narrow circumstances a defendant may forfeit his right to confrontation by his own wrongdoing. "[W]hen defendants seek to undermine the judicial process by procuring or coercing silence from witnesses and victims, the Sixth Amendment does not require courts to acquiesce. While defendants have no duty to assist the State in proving their guilt, they *do* have the duty to refrain from acting in ways that destroy the integrity of the criminal-trial system." For the forfeiture-by-wrongdoing exception to apply, a defendant must have engaged in wrongful conduct *designed* to prevent a witness from testifying. (*Giles v. California* (2008) 554 U.S. 353, 359–361.) Said differently, a defendant must "engag[e] in wrongdoing that renders the declarant unavailable with an intent to prevent that declarant's in-court testimony."

"[W]rongdoing" need not rise to the level of murder. "The common-law forfeiture rule was aimed at removing the otherwise powerful incentive for defendants to intimidate, bribe, and kill the witnesses against them—in other words, it is grounded in 'the ability of courts to protect the integrity of their proceedings.'"

Thus in *Jones,* the defendant forfeited his right to confrontation when during phone calls from jail he dissuaded his ex-girlfriend from testifying by implying he had friends on the outside available to do "'whatever [was] necessary.'"

Nevertheless, reviewing Merchant's recorded jail calls, it determined he intentionally secured Lisa's unavailability at trial and thereby forfeited his confrontation right. The judge acknowledged the case was "a lot weaker" than the usual forfeiture-by-wrongdoing case because Lisa was not killed or expressly threatened with harm to make her stay away. Merchant instead engaged in "more of a passive coercion." Yet there was enough evidence from the jail calls and Merchant's pattern of abuse to find by a preponderance that his actions intended to and succeeded in keeping Lisa away.

Sufficient evidence supports the trial court's finding. A criminal protective order was entered two days after the offense on December 24, 2014, precluding Merchant from any contact with Lisa. On January 6, Merchant called his friends "Groove," "Buck," and "Snake." Groove said the D.A. was in the area searching for Lisa. Buck told Merchant, "As long as she don't come in to court you could be all right." Merchant asked Groove or Snake to check in on Lisa and "keep her away for six months." Groove agreed.

On January 7, Merchant called Lisa. He told her the D.A. had offered him 15 years, but if he proceeded to trial he faced 28. He claimed his counsel recommended that Lisa "stay away for six months." Merchant said he was "scared to fuckin' go to trial 'cause if you pop up, I'm gone, like no ifs, ands, and buts—my life is gone." He told her he had asked Buck to "[g]o over there and tell my girl what's up." Although Buck had purportedly told him that Lisa would not show up, Merchant said he needed to hear it from her directly. He pressed Lisa, "[Y]ou know I didn't kidnap[] you babe. You know what I'm sayin'? You know that, babe. You hear me?" and told her how stressed he was that someone could find her. Merchant told Lisa not to write him letters because she might be located. Finally, Lisa acquiesced: "Okay. I'm not." [¶] . . . [¶] "I'm not goin' over, babe. I'm with you." "Don't worry about it," she assured him, "I'm [sticking] by your side." Merchant expressed relief and thanked her. He asked, "[S]o you want me to go through with the trial?" Lisa replied, "Yeah. 'Cause I'm not going to babe." The couple exchanged "I love you['s]" and ended the call.

Merchant called later that day to remind Lisa to stay under the radar. He told her he knew she would be there for him and reconfirmed whether he should "[g]o all the way to trial with this?" Lisa again assured him that she was not going anywhere. Merchant seemed satisfied. The call ended shortly after with an exchange of "I love you['s]."

In all, Merchant called Lisa 167 times between January and May 2015. Although he made no direct threat to harm her, Lisa's friend told the D.A.'s office weeks before trial that Lisa remained terrified of what might happen to her if she came to court. Sufficient evidence supports the court's finding that Merchant engaged in wrongdoing designed to prevent Lisa from testifying. Through obsessive, repeated calls, he begged Lisa to lay low, stay at home, and not invite company, venture out, or write correspondence. He told her charges would be dismissed if she evaded detection, whereas his life would be over if she came forward. Lisa was made aware that though he was incarcerated, Merchant had friends on the outside watching her. When she equivocated that she was *trying* to stick by him, Merchant immediately responded, "You better. What the fuck you mean, you're trying to? You better." Gratitude and expressions of love followed each time Lisa promised not to appear. In the context of an abusive relationship with its dynamics of control, the trial court could reasonably find that Merchant intended to, and did, secure Lisa's nonappearance.

Review Questions

1. **Vile uncle.** Defendant is charged with murdering his niece. Days before the killing, the niece spoke with police and reported that Defendant had touched her inappropriately and without her consent. A witness to the killing testifies that, as Defendant pulled out a gun, he told the niece, "I won't let you testify at that hearing next week." He then pulled the trigger.
2. **Parting words.** Same as Question 1, except Defendant, just before pulling the trigger, told his niece, "I heard you talked to the cops. That stops now."
3. **Silent killing.** Same as Question 1, except Defendant said nothing at the time of the shooting. However, he had been served with his niece's paperwork seeking a restraining order against him.
4. **Burst of hate.** Same as Question 1, but Defendant, just before pulling the trigger, told his niece, "I hate your f@#$ing guts."

Can a defendant's introduction of evidence *at trial* forfeit the right to rely on *Crawford*? In *Hemphill v. New York*, 142 S. Ct. 681 (2022), the United States Supreme Court held that the answer is "no" when the sole theory is that the defendant's introduction of evidence *opened the door* to responsive evidence. In *Hemphill*, the defendant was charged with murdering a child who was a passenger in a nearby car stuck by a 9-millimeter bullet. The defendant's primary defense was that a man named Morris was the actual shooter. In support of that defense, the defendant introduced evidence that shells from a 9-millimeter gun were found on Morris's nightstand. In response, the prosecutor sought to introduce evidence that (1) shells from a .357 firearm were also found on Morris's nightstand, and (2) Morris, during the colloquy to his plea to possessing the .357 firearm, stated that he had *only* possessed a .357 revolver. The defendant objected that Morris's statements during the plea colloquy constituted a "testimonial" statement admitted in violation of *Crawford*. In *Hemphill*, the Supreme Court sided with the defendant. Specifically, the Court ruled that trial judges did *not* have discretion to admit statements that would be barred by *Crawford* merely because the judge thought that doing so was "reasonably necessary to correct" a "misleading impression" created by evidence offered by a criminal defendant. *Hemphill* also rejected the prosecutor's argument that the defendant's introduction of the evidence regarding the ammunition found on Morris's nightstand somehow "opened the door" to admitting evidence in violation of *Crawford*. But *Hemphill* explicitly left open one possible avenue for admissibility: If a defendant introduces one portion of a person's statement, may other portions of that person's statement be introduced under the rule of completeness (FRE 106)—even if admission of those portions would otherwise violate *Crawford*? (That issue was not presented in *Hemphill* because the defendant had not introduced any misleading portion of Morris's plea colloquy.)

(iii) Categorical/Common Law Exceptions to *Crawford*

Crawford itself acknowledged that at least one category of statements are admissible even if they are testimonial and even if there is no opportunity for cross-examination—namely, dying declarations. *Crawford*, 541 U.S. at 56 n.6. Dying declarations are seen as "*sui generis*" because they have always been admissible, even under common law.

Here is a summary of *Crawford* and its progeny, in chronological order:

Case	Year	Holding
Crawford v. Washington	2004	The Confrontation Clause, at its core, prohibits prosecutors from introducing out-of-court "testimonial" statements unless the declarant is unavailable as a witness *and* the defendant has had a prior opportunity to cross-examine the declarant.
Davis v. Washington/ Hammon v. Indiana	2005	In determining whether an out-of-court statement is "testimonial," courts should examine the "primary purpose" of the statement: If it is "to establish or prove past events potentially relevant to later criminal prosecution," it is "testimonial"; if it is to meet an ongoing emergency, it is not.
Giles v. California	2008	The defendant forfeits his ability to object to the introduction of out-of-court "testimonial" statements if he renders the declarant unavailable with the specific intent to prevent her testimony.
Melendez-Diaz v. Massachusetts	2009	A certified lab report to be used in lieu of testimony at trial is "testimonial."
Michigan v. Bryant	2011	In assessing the "primary purpose" of an out-of-court declaration, a court should examine the objective statements and actions of the parties, including the circumstances under which the declaration was made and how formal (or informal) the statement was; the primary purpose of police questioning of a victim of gun violence was *not* to gather evidence when police could also be gathering information to halt an ongoing emergency.

Case	Year	Holding
Bullcoming v. New Mexico	2011	A certified lab report to be used in lieu of testimony at trial is "testimonial," and the availability of lab personnel other than the lab technician who performed the analysis does not cure the lack of cross-examination.
Williams v. Illinois	2012	In a 4-1-4 opinion, a DNA expert was permitted to testify that one part of a DNA match came from the crime scene based on a lab report. The four-Justice plurality held that the lab report was not "testimonial" because the primary purpose of the lab report was not to accuse a "targeted individual of engaging in criminal conduct," whereas the fifth Justice concurred that the lab report was not "testimonial" because it was too informal.
Ohio v. Clark	2015	A statement from a toddler to a preschool teacher regarding possible physical abuse by a parent is not "testimonial," in part because the teacher—despite being required to report any abuse—was not a law enforcement officer.

As this discussion indicates, *Crawford* chiefly regulates the admission of out-of-court statements for their truth. *Crawford*'s requirements are distinct from—*and in addition to*—the hearsay rule discussed in Chapter Five and its many exceptions discussed in Chapters Six through Eight. Thus, the fact that a statement fits within a hearsay exception is no guarantee that it satisfies *Crawford*'s dictates. However, the statements admitted under various hearsay exceptions fall along a spectrum from statements more likely to raise *Crawford* problems to statements less likely to raise *Crawford* problems.

It is critical to keep in mind that the placement of a particular *category* of statements along this spectrum is no guarantee of *Crawford*'s applicability. Under *Crawford*, whether the Sixth Amendment's Confrontation Clause is violated turns on nuanced and case-specific considerations; however, the spectrum constructed below may be helpful in assessing what initial level of alertness to give a particular out-of-court statement (and the reason(s) why). It focuses on the hearsay exceptions used most frequently.

Highly Unlikely to Raise *Crawford* Issue	**May, but Unlikely to, Raise *Crawford* Issue**	**Likely to Raise *Crawford* Issue**
Dying declarations **Historical exception noted in* Crawford	**Business and official records of non-law enforcement agencies** * *Unlikely because primary purpose is typically to maintain records*	**Declaration against interest** * *Likely because often made to law enforcement*

Highly Unlikely to Raise *Crawford* Issue	**May, but Unlikely to, Raise *Crawford* Issue**	**Likely to Raise *Crawford* Issue**
Opposing party's admissions * *Highly unlikely because opposing party can always take the stand and be subject to cross-examination*	**Present sense impression** * *Unlikely to be "testimonial," unless said in response to official's questioning*	**Official records of law enforcement agencies** * *Likely because primary purpose is to document investigations and prosecutions*
Coconspirator statements * *Highly unlikely to be "testimonial" because statements made during conspiracy to coconspirators (and not to law enforcement)*	**Excited utterance** * *Unlikely to be "testimonial," unless said in response to official's questioning*	**Catch-all exception (FRE 807)** * *Likely, at least, if statement made in response to questioning, especially by law enforcement*
Prior inconsistent and consistent statements * *Highly unlikely because witness is present to be cross-examined about prior statement*	**Statements made for medical diagnoses** * *Unlikely to be "testimonial," unless made to forensic medical personnel*	
Public records of vital statistics * *Unlikely to be "testimonial" because not gathered for prosecutorial purposes*	**Statements in ancient documents** * *Unlikely to be "testimonial," unless they are ancient law enforcement documents*	
Former testimony * *Highly unlikely because exception only applies in criminal case when there was a prior opportunity to cross-examine*		

PART B: LIMITATIONS ON THE ADMISSION OF EVIDENCE DURING JOINT CRIMINAL TRIALS (BRUTON *ISSUES*)

Does the Confrontation Clause provide additional limitations on the admissibility of out-of-court statements over-and-above *Crawford*?

Consider the following. The prosecutor charges two people—Defendant A and Defendant B—with murder. During a *Mirandized* interview, Defendant A tells police that he and Defendant B drove into rival gang territory with the intent to shoot rival gang members and that Defendant B opened fire when they saw a group hanging out on a street corner. Defendant A and Defendant B are tried jointly—that is, at the same time and before the same jury. Neither defendant testifies. The prosecutor seeks to introduce Defendant A's confession, but *only* against Defendant A; the prosecutor asks for—and the trial judge gives—a limiting instruction that tells the jury, "Only consider Defendant A's confession against Defendant A; you are *not* to consider it as evidence against Defendant B."

Is this instruction sufficient to protect Defendant B's constitutional right of confrontation? Courts generally presume that juries are capable of following limiting instructions. If the jury follows the limiting instruction in this case, there would not seem to be a Confrontation Clause problem. That is because Defendant A cannot be heard to complain about the introduction of his own confession against him and because the limiting instruction makes clear that the confession is not admissible *against Defendant B* (so Defendant A is not, in the words of the Confrontation Clause, a "witness[] against" Defendant B).

In *Bruton v. United States*, 391 U.S. 123 (1968), however, the Supreme Court held that confessions like Defendant A's are so "powerfully" incendiary that "the risk that the jury will not, or cannot, follow [a limiting] instruction is so great, and the consequences of failure so vital" that the confession should be treated as if it is being admitted against Defendant B as well. *Id.* at 135.

This so-called *Bruton* issue only arises if the confession of the first defendant sufficiently implicates the second defendant in the crime. When the first defendant's confession "expressly implicates" the second defendant, *Bruton* applies. That is true even if the second defendant's confession is also admitted into evidence and corroborates what is in the first defendant's confession. *Cruz v. New York*, 481 U.S. 186 (1987). However, where the first defendant's confession is "not incriminating on its face" against the second defendant and becomes "so only when linked with evidence introduced later at trial," there is no *Bruton* problem. *Richardson v. Marsh*, 481 U.S. 200, 208 (1987).

Are there ways to avoid this spillover effect? The Supreme Court has suggested a few:

- *Redaction.* It may be possible to redact the first defendant's confession to eliminate references to the second, nontestifying defendant. *Richardson*, 481 U.S. at 203-05. This must be done carefully. On the one hand, simply replacing the second defendant's name with a blank space or an asterisk will not suffice because the jury will likely connect the dots that the name deleted belongs to the person sitting next to the first defendant at the trial. *Gray v. Maryland*, 523 U.S. 185, 192-95 (1998). On the other hand, the redaction must not be done in a way that overinflates the first defendant's role in the crime and thus ends up being inaccurately and hence unfairly incriminating to the first defendant.
- *Severance of trials.* If Defendant A is tried separately from Defendant B, the admission of Defendant A's confession at Defendant A's trial will have no effect on Defendant B if Defendant B is tried separately. This option solves the problem, but it can be expensive (because now there are two trials instead of one) and goes against the general grain of most states' criminal procedure rules that prefer joint trials.
- *Separate juries.* Sometimes, courts have the ability to seat two juries at once—one for each defendant. Although both juries would sit through most of the trial together, when Defendant A's confession is introduced, only Defendant A's jury would be in the courtroom; Defendant B's jury

would not hear the confession. This option entails greater expense (because twice as many jurors are needed), greater time (to select two juries rather than one), and larger courtrooms (as most courtrooms are large enough to accommodate only one jury, not multiple juries).

- *Exclusion of Defendant's A confession.* Excluding the confession solves any *Bruton* problem, but also results in the loss of reliable evidence and thereby undermines the accuracy of the jury verdict.

Review Questions

Who's on the stand? Abbott and Costello are jointly charged with murdering Vaudeville. In a postarrest interview, Abbott confesses that he and Costello snuck up behind Vaudeville and stabbed him in the back. The case against Abbott and Costello proceeds to a joint trial. Prior to trial, Prosecutor seeks to admit Abbott's confession at the trial but with a limiting instruction telling the jury to consider the confession only as evidence against Abbott. Costello objects.

a. Is Abbott's confession problematic under *Bruton*? Does the limiting instruction cure any problem?
b. Prosecutor offers to redact Abbott's confession to read, "Me and ***** snuck up behind Vaudeville and stabbed him in the back." Does this redaction cure any *Bruton* problem?
c. What if Prosecutor redacts Abbott's confession to read, "I snuck up behind Vaudeville and stabbed him in the back." Does this redaction cure any *Bruton* problem? Does it overinflate Abbott's role in the killing?
d. What other options does Prosecutor have if she wants to admit Abbott's confession against Abbott?

PART C: FACE-TO-FACE CONFRONTATION AND THE CONFRONTATION CLAUSE

When watching courtroom dramas unfold—whether fictional or nonfictional—the high point of drama is when the victim of a crime takes the stand and identifies the defendant and recounts what the defendant did. The drama is most intense because that is the moment when the defendant and victim once again meet eye-to-eye. Tracing all the way back to Roman times, the right of a defendant to meet accusers face to face has been a longstanding fixture of trial proceedings.

Why do we insist on this right? Face-to-face confrontation ensures that the witness, while under oath, is in the defendant's presence, all of which impresses on the witness "'the seriousness of the matter and guard[s] against the lie by the possibility of a penalty for perjury.'" *Maryland v. Craig,* 497 U.S. 836, 845-46 (1990). This assurance is critical when what the witness says can be what deprives the defendant of his liberty and, in some instances, his life. Face-to-face confrontation also "'permits the jury to decide the defendant's fate to observe the demeanor of the witness in making his statement." *Ibid.*

In *Coy v. Iowa*, 487 U.S. 1012 (1987), the Supreme Court reaffirmed that the Confrontation Clause "guarantees the defendant a face-to-face meeting with witnesses appearing before the trier of fact." *Id.* at 1016.

Does face-to-face mean eye-to-eye? May a witness look elsewhere other than at the defendant while testifying? Although the Supreme Court has yet to squarely confront the question, many lower courts have held that the Confrontation Clause does not entitle a defendant to "stare down" a testifying witness. *People v. Bharth*, 68 Cal. App. 5th 801 (Cal. Ct. App. 2021).

Is the right to face-to-face (but not eye-to-eye) confrontation absolute? Or are there circumstances in which it is still constitutional to have something less than a full face-to-face confrontation?

Examples

1. Defendant is charged with child molestation. The state legislature passes a law that allows child victims of sexual crimes to testify via a closed-circuit TV or with a screen to block their view of a defendant.
2. Defendant is charged with child molestation. Prosecutor puts on evidence, at an *in camera* hearing, that the child victim would suffer trauma if forced to testify in front of Defendant; that evidence includes the testimony of a psychologist who interviewed the child. The trial judge allows Prosecutor to put up a screen that blocks the witness's view of Defendant, but still allows the jury and defense attorney to see the witness's face.
3. Defendant is charged with murdering a four-year-old. The victim's seven-year-old sister, who witnessed much of the physical abuse that led up to the killing, is to testify. Prosecutor introduces evidence, at an *in camera* hearing, that the sister would be traumatized if forced to confront Defendant in trial; that evidence includes the testimony of a psychologist who interviewed the sister. The trial judge allows Prosecutor to have the child testify in front of the jury, with Defendant watching via closed-circuit television.
4. Defendant is charged with child molestation. Since the time of the crime, the victim has turned 18. She shows up to court in tears. Prosecutor asks that the victim be permitted to testify from behind a screen. The trial judge allows it.

The Supreme Court has acknowledged that there are some circumstances in which the Clause's guarantee of face-to-face confrontation may be overcome by a showing that "denial of such confrontation is necessary to further an important public policy and only where the reliability of the testimony is otherwise assured." *Craig*, 497 U.S. at 850. One such important public policy is the "protection of minor victims of sex crimes from further trauma and embarrassment." To dispense with face-to-face confrontation in order to avoid trauma, the showing of trauma must be "case specific" (that is, *individual* to this child witness); a legislature's across-the-board determination that an entire category of witnesses will be traumatized is insufficient. *Coy*, 487 U.S. at 1020-21. This policy extends not only to the victim of the charged crimes, but also to other children who were traumatized by witnessing the charged crimes and who are shown to be traumatized by having to testify. It does not extend to adults or to persons who are emotionally fragile for reasons *other than* being traumatized by having to confront this defendant again. More recently, the lower federal courts have upheld mask mandates against a Confrontation Clause challenge—at least during the height of the COVID-19 pandemic—even though masks necessarily cover the lower portion of a witness's face, reasoning that such mandates are necessary to further the important public interest in protecting public health. *E.g., United States v. Crittenden*, 2020 U.S. Dist. LEXIS 151950 (M.D. Ga. 2020).

PART D: COMPULSORY PROCESS

One reason the *Crawford* majority cited for rejecting the *Roberts* test is its concern that looking to the existence of hearsay exceptions under state rules of evidence would tie the meaning of the Constitution to the "vagaries of the rules of evidence." Although the general rules of evidence are generally consistent from state to state, they do sometimes vary. What happens when a state rule of evidence prevents a defendant from introducing evidence that is helpful to the defense? Will the Constitution supersede the state rule of evidence?

Consider the following examples.

Examples

1. Defendant is charged with participating in a gang beating. He seeks to call one of his fellow gang members to testify that Defendant did not land any blows. Because this witness was involved in the beating, he is an accomplice. State law bars testimony from accomplices. Can this state law prohibit Defendant from calling a witness who could potentially exonerate him?
2. Defendant is charged with rape. Defendant seeks to testify in his own defense, but state law precludes the testimony of any witness whose testimony has been hypnotically refreshed, and Defendant had undergone hypnosis. Can this state law prohibit Defendant from taking the stand in his own defense?

The constitutional provision that may provide some support to the defendants in these examples is the Compulsory Process Clause.

Sixth Amendment, U.S. Constitution

In all criminal prosecutions, the accused shall enjoy the right . . . to have compulsory process for obtaining witnesses in his favor. . . .

The Supreme Court confronted Example 1 in *Washington v. Texas,* 388 U.S. 14, 23 (1967). The Court held that the Compulsory Process Clause invalidated the state law, which it viewed as "an arbitrary rule[] that prevent[s] whole categories of defense witnesses from testifying on the basis of *a priori* categories that presume them unworthy of belief." The *Washington* court highlighted the arbitrariness of the state rule because the same rule allowed the prosecution to call the very same witness that the defense could not.

The Supreme Court confronted Example 2 in *Rock v. Arkansas,* 483 U.S. 44, 52-53 (1987). The Court held that the Compulsory Process Clause invalidated the state law *as applied to a defendant seeking to testify on his own behalf. Id.* at 55-56. The Court found that the bar went too far because it was a "*per se* rule" that applied even when the defendant's testimony "may be reliable in an individual case." *Id.* at 56, 61. *Rock* did not purport to invalidate state laws prohibiting testimony from hypnotically refreshed witnesses *other than the defendant. Id.* at 58.

Despite *Washington* and *Rock,* however, there have been no other Supreme Court cases invalidating state rules of evidence under the Compulsory Process Clause. As a general matter, the rules of evidence take an item-by-item approach to the evaluation of evidence—and thus do not offend the Compulsory Process Clause like the arbitrary and "per se" rules struck down in *Washington* and *Rock.*

PART E: DUE PROCESS

Are there other instances in which the rules of evidence can deny a criminal defendant a "fair trial" and, in so doing, violate due process? As a general matter, the answer is "no." That is because one of the main purposes underlying the rules of evidence—discussed in Chapter One—is to assure the reliability of evidence—and hence the accuracy of the resulting verdicts. However, the Supreme Court has on occasion struck down rules of evidence that *interfere* with a defendant's right to present relevant and reliable evidence and, in so doing, deny the defendant a fair trial.

The constitutional guarantee of due process appears in two places in the Constitution—namely, (1) the Fifth Amendment, which applies directly to the federal government, and (2) the Fourteenth Amendment, which applies directly to the states.

Fifth Amendment, U.S. Constitution

No person shall . . . be deprived of life, liberty, or property, without due process of law. . . .

Fourteenth Amendment, Clause 1, U.S. Constitution

[N]or shall any State deprive any person of life, liberty, or property, without due process of law. . . .

In *Chambers v. Mississippi*, 410 U.S. 284 (1973), the Supreme Court struck down two of Mississippi's rules of evidence that are no longer very common today. Chambers was charged with killing a police officer during a melee on the streets. Another man, McDonald, had confessed to the killing but later recanted his confession. Chambers sought to persuade the jury that he was innocent because McDonald was the actual killer, and he tried to do so by (1) calling McDonald as a witness and impeaching him with his prior confession to the killing and (2) calling three witnesses in whom McDonald had confided that he was the killer. The trial judge did not allow either category of evidence. Specifically, the judge held that Mississippi's "voucher rule"—which prevents a party from impeaching any witness it calls to the stand—did not allow Chambers to impeach McDonald with his prior confession. And the judge held that McDonald's confessions to the three other witnesses was hearsay and that Mississippi had no exception for declarations against penal interest. The Supreme Court held that these rules denied Chambers his constitutional right to put on a defense and thereby denied him a fair trial. *Id.* at 302-03.

In *Crane v. Kentucky*, 476 U.S. 683 (1986), the Supreme Court struck down a Kentucky rule that precluded admitting the circumstances surrounding a defendant's confession once the trial judge found, in a pretrial hearing, that the confession was voluntary. Crane was charged with murder for a killing in the course of a liquor store robbery. The Court found that the circumstances surrounding his confession, even if that confession was voluntary, was "highly relevant to [the] reliability and credibility" of the confession. Categorically denying the defendant the right to present that relevant evidence denied him "'a meaningful opportunity to present a complete defense'" and thus offended due process or compulsory process.

And in *Holmes v. South Carolina*, 547 U.S. 319 (2006), the Supreme Court struck down a South Carolina rule that prevented a defendant from introducing evidence that a third party committed the charged crime if there was otherwise "strong evidence of [the defendant']s guilt," such that the "proffered evidence about the third party's alleged guilt does not raise a reasonable inference as to the [defendant's] own innocence." The Court reasoned that the rule was arbitrary because it focused on the strength of the prosecution's case rather than the relevance of the defendant's proffered evidence of third party guilt.

Test Your Understanding

To test your understanding of the material in this chapter, turn to the Supplement for additional practice problems

Chapter 10

Competency of Witnesses

At common law, there were strict restrictions on who could testify as a witness. Wholesale categories of individuals were deemed legally incompetent to serve as witnesses. However, the modern approach has shifted to presuming individuals will be allowed to testify. As long as the witnesses meet basic requirements for reliability, they will be allowed to testify.

As detailed in this chapter, a witness is competent to testify if:

- The witness is *sincere*—that is, honest—in his or her testimony;
- The witness *perceived* the subject of his or her testimony and, with the exception of experts, has personal knowledge of the matters about which he or she testifies;
- The witness has sufficient *recollection* of what he or she perceived; and
- The witness is able to *narrate*—that is, to relate to the trier of fact what he or she perceived and now recollects.

Each of these attributes—sincerity, perception, recollection, and narration—is essential for a witness's testimony to be reliable. If there is not some base assurance that the witness is being sincere, nothing she says is reliable. If there is not some base assurance that the witness had the ability to perceive and recollect the subject of her testimony, those perceptions and recollections are not reliable. And if there is not some base assurance that the witness is able to accurately convey what she knows, her testimony is not reliable.

Consider the following examples, which illustrate how each of these attributes is implicated in a witness's testimony.

Examples

1. In a lawsuit for injuries sustained in an auto accident, Plaintiff calls an eyewitness to testify about what he saw. The eyewitness refuses to take the oath administered by the judge, insisting instead that he will only make an oath to C'thulhu, who will take his "eternal soul" if he shall utter a falsehood. The concern here is the witness's sincerity.

2. Defendant is on trial for making a criminal threat. The victim is called as a witness. When the victim takes the stand and starts to recount what happened, she admits that she was high on LSD at the time Defendant allegedly made the threat. LSD affects one's perception. The concern here is the witness's ability to perceive.
3. Defendant is charged with child molestation occurring in 1991. The trial is in 2021. The victim testifies that she remembered the molestation only after undergoing hypnosis, which enabled her to recall what happened. The concern here is the witness's ability to recollect.
4. Plaintiff sues Defendant for injuries she suffered while riding a bicycle and was struck by Defendant's car. Plaintiff is now a quadriplegic and can only move her eyes. Plaintiff seeks to testify, and to have her sister explain to the jury what Plaintiff's eye movements mean. The concern here is the witness's ability to narrate.

The rules regarding witness competency are a filter meant to exclude witnesses who entirely lack any of the key four attributes. For example, and as discussed more fully below, a witness is sufficiently "sincere" to testify as long as the witness takes an oath or makes an affirmation to the tell the truth. The trial judge does not have to be *sure* that the witness will tell the truth; the witness's sworn or attested promise to do so is enough. Along similar lines, defects in a witness's perception, recollection, or ability to narrate are not a basis to deem the witness incompetent to testify unless those abilities are wholly absent; as long as the witness has established personal knowledge, an ability to remember, and an ability to share what he or she remembers with the trier of fact, any shortcomings are merely grist for the mill of impeachment rather than a basis for excluding the witness's testimony entirely.

Because the testimony of a witness who does not meet these minimum requirements for competency is, by definition, not reliable, the trial judge is tasked with deciding whether a witness meets those requirements. FRE 104(a). This way, a jury is not exposed to unreliable evidence that may taint its verdict.

Part A of this chapter sets forth the modern test for evaluating the competency of witnesses. Part B explains how the test is implemented by the Federal Rules of Evidence and details the procedural mechanisms for evaluating competency. Part C examines the special rules that apply to the competency of lawyers, judges, jurors, and those who seek to challenge a will.

PART A: THE GENERAL PRESUMPTION IN FAVOR OF COMPETENCY

1. The Common Law Approach

At common law, courts used the doctrine of witness competency to keep a wide swath of witnesses off the stand. More specifically, the common law deemed incompetent anyone who fell within the "five I's" (which are as insensitive as they are archaic):

- *Infancy.* The common law categorically prohibited witnesses younger than a specific age.
- *Insanity.* The common law categorically prohibited witnesses deemed to be mentally incompetent.
- *Interest.* The common law categorically prohibited witnesses deemed to be biased in favor of the party calling them, such as coconspirators, accomplices, and spouses.
- *Infamy.* The common law categorically prohibited witnesses who had suffered criminal convictions.
- *Idolatry.* The common law categorically prohibited witnesses who adhered to certain, disfavored religions.

Until as late as the conclusion of the Civil War, many states also had laws that declared African Americans to be incompetent to testify.

2. *The Four-Pillared Modern Approach to Competency*

The modern approach to the competency of witnesses rejects the common law's strict, categorical exclusionary approach in favor of a permissive one that presumes witnesses to be competent. *Briggs & Riley Travelware, LLC v. Paragon Luggage, Inc.*, 324 F. Supp. 2d 395, 400 (S.D.N.Y. 2003). The modern competency rule is set forth in FRE 601.

FRE 601. Competency to Testify in General

Every person is competent to be a witness unless these rules provide otherwise. But in a civil case, state law governs the witness's competency regarding a claim or defense for which state law supplies the rule of decision.

Under FRE 601, no class of witness is categorically prohibited from testifying. A person's age, mental competency, bias or motive to testify, and prior criminal history are grounds for impeaching a witness rather than for keeping the witness off the stand entirely.[1] A person's religious beliefs are, except in rare and unusual circumstance, neither a basis for barring a witness entirely nor for impeachment. *See* FRE 610. With the exception of religious beliefs, the modern view is to allow the jury to hear about—and thus to assess for itself—the effect of circumstances that bear upon the witness's credibility or ability to perceive, recall, or narrate.

1. For more on the rules governing the impeachment of witnesses on these grounds, see Chapter Eleven.

PART B: ASSURING THE COMPETENCY OF WITNESSES

As explained above, witness competency is a function of four attributes: sincerity, perception, recollection, and narration. Each of them is an essential pillar of competency:

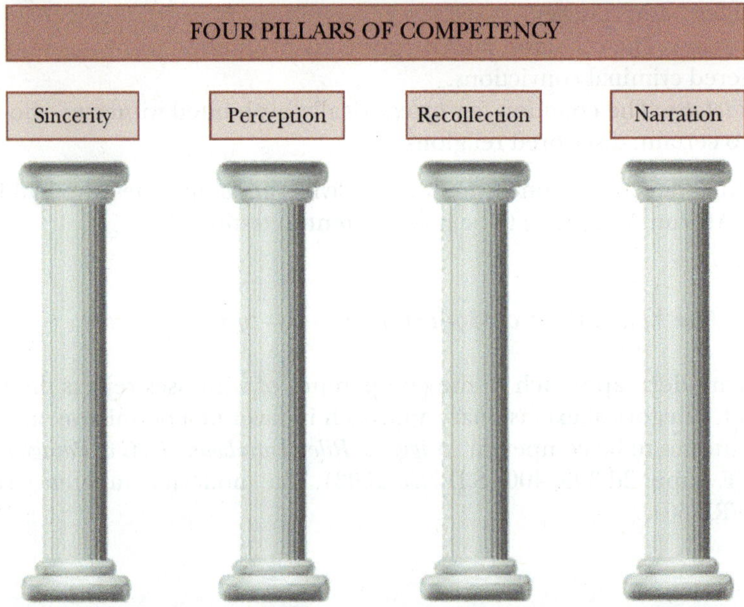

1. How the Federal Rules of Evidence Implement the Four Pillars

The Federal Rules of Evidence implement the four pillars of witness competency by specifying two express requirements (that is, an oath and personal knowledge) and by otherwise leaving it up to trial judges to assess competency.

(a) Sincerity

To assure that a witness is sincere, FRE 603 requires an oath or affirmation. Both require that a witness commit to telling the truth, but an affirmation does not refer to "swearing" or a divine power.

FRE 603. Oath or Affirmation to Testify Truthfully

Before testifying, a witness must give an oath or affirmation to testify truthfully. It must be in a form designed to impress that duty on the witness's conscience.

There are no "magic words" for the oath or affirmation; as the Advisory Committee Notes explain, "[N]o special verbal formula is required." Thus, although most trial judges require witnesses to swear to tell "the truth, the whole truth, and nothing but he truth," it is enough if a witness promises to "speak with fully integrated Honesty." *United States v. Ward*, 989 F.2d 1015, 1017-20 (9th Cir. 1992). Unlike what is popularly portrayed in movies or television shows, there is no requirement that the witness raise her hand or swear on a bible. Witnesses can commit to telling the truth in a variety of ways, including by swearing on the Koran, participating in a drum ceremony, or using another type of cultural ritual that commits the witness to telling the truth. *See United States v. Looper*, 419 F.2d 1405, 1407 n.4 (4th Cir. 1969) (English courts "have permitted Chinese to break a saucer, a Mohammedan to bow before the Koran and touch it to his head and a Parsee to tie a rope around his waist to qualify them to tell the truth"). A proposed oath to tell the truth is inadequate only if it is a "cleverly worded oath that creates loopholes for falsehood or attempts to create a safe harbor for perjury." *Ward*, 989 F.2d at 1020.

If a witness testifies with the use of an interpreter, does the interpreter also have to be under oath? FRE 604 says "yes."

FRE 604. Interpreter

An interpreter must be qualified and must give an oath or affirmation to make a true translation.

(b) Perception

To ensure that a witness reliably perceived the subject of her testimony, FRE 602 requires that the witness's testimony be based on personal knowledge. Specifically, FRE 602 provides the following:

FRE 602. Need for Personal Knowledge

A witness may testify to a matter only if evidence is introduced sufficient to support a finding that the witness has personal knowledge of the matter. Evidence to prove personal knowledge may consist of the witness's own testimony. This rule does not apply to a witness's expert testimony under [FRE] 703.

Examples

1. Defendant is charged with murdering his stepson in the garage of the family home. Prosecutor seeks to call Defendant's nephew to testify that Defendant had been hostile to the stepson in the past. On direct examination, the nephew testifies that he has not personally witnessed any hostility but has heard about it from other family members. Defendant moves to strike the nephew's testimony for lack of personal knowledge. That motion should be granted.
2. In a will contest, a niece seeks to invalidate an updated will that alters the prior will and leaves her nothing on the ground that the decedent was mentally unsound when he executed the updated will. A nephew (who inherits everything under the updated will) seeks to call two witnesses to testify that the decedent was of "sound mind." One had spoken to the decedent the day before the decedent signed the updated will; the other had not spoken with the decedent for three years. The niece objects that the second proposed witness is not competent to testify because she has no personal knowledge of the decedent's mental state at the pertinent time. That objection should be sustained.
3. Plaintiff sues Defendant in a business dispute. Defendant seeks to introduce the business records of a third-party company by calling someone who worked as a summer intern for the company to authenticate the business records. Plaintiff objects that the intern lacks personal knowledge as to how the business records are created and maintained and thus is incompetent to testify on this point. The objection should be sustained.

Under FRE 602, personal knowledge (of a witness who is not an expert witness) is *necessary* to establish that witness's reliable perception, but it is not always *sufficient* to do so; other considerations, such as drug use or mental illness, might interfere with that perception and justify a ruling that the presumption in favor of competency has been rebutted.

(c) Recollection and Narration

Because the Federal Rules of Evidence do not have any further explicit requirements regarding recollection and narration, those rules leave it to the trial judge to assess whether the presumption of competency has been rebutted by a showing that a witness lacks the ability of accurate recall or is unable to coherently relate his or her recollections to the trier of fact.

2. *Situations in Which Competency Issues Arise with Frequency*

Competency issues come up most often in situations involving child witnesses, witnesses with mental illness, witnesses who are under the influence of drugs or alcohol at the time of testimony, and witnesses who have previously been hypnotized.

(a) Child Witnesses

Not only does FRE 601 reject the common law, across-the-board disqualification of witnesses on the basis of their infancy, but federal law elsewhere specifically decrees that "[a] child is presumed to be competent" as a witness. 18 U.S.C. § 3509(c)(2).

The same federal statute that lays out the presumption in favor of a child's competency also spells out the procedures to be followed in assessing whether that presumption has been rebutted in a criminal case—namely, that the trial judge conduct a hearing on the issue of competency outside the jury's presence, but only after a preliminary showing that a "compelling reason" exists to question the child's competency. 18 U.S.C. § 3509(c)(4)-(c)(9).

The critical concerns are whether the child has the ability to distinguish fantasy from reality in what they perceive and recall and to understand the duty to tell the truth. When it comes to the oath, "the trial [judge] may fashion an oath or affirmation that is meaningful to the [child] witness." *Spigarolo v. Meachum*, 934 F.2d 19, 24 (2d Cir. 1991). Courts are accorded enormous flexibility in fashioning an oath or affirmation and in assessing the child's ability to perceive, recollect, and narrate, as *Tate v. Board of Education* and *United States v. Stops* illustrate.

Tate v. Board of Education

346 F. Supp. 2d 536 (S.D.N.Y. 2004)

ROBINSON, Judge.

Michael M. Tate, a minor, by guardian ad litem Monique Y. Tate ("Michael M."), Monique Y. Tate, and Michael F. Tate (collectively the "Plaintiffs") brought this action against the Board of Education of the City School District of Peekskill, various individuals associated with the Board, Westchester Exceptional Children, Inc. ("WEC"), and various individuals associated with WEC (collectively the "Defendants") for subjecting Michael M. to physical abuse, and for permitting, condoning, failing to investigate and failing to stop abuse of students with disabilities at their facilities.

Michael M. is a six-year old boy who has been classified as "multiply disabled" by the Peekskill Committee on Special Education. At the time of the acts at issue in this case, he had been attending kindergarten at WEC. By order dated August 27, 2004, this court found reasonable cause to hold a hearing to determine whether Michael M. is competent to testify at a deposition and at trial in this matter.

Whether a witness is competent to testify depends on the individual's ability to observe, to remember, to communicate, and to understand that the oath imposes a duty to tell the truth.

Based on Michael M's responses to the court's questions during the competency hearing, the court finds that he is competent to testify in this case. Despite being questioned on a wide array of topics, the vast majority of Michael M.'s answers were responsive to the questions asked. His responses and demeanor were not inconsistent with the behavior one would expect of other children his age and, although his statements may not always have been consistent with each other, he demonstrated an understanding of the questions he was being asked, attempted to answer them, and articulated responses that were easily decipherable to the court, counsel and the court reporter. Michael M. evidenced an ability to communicate his recollection of the events that form the subject matter of this litigation and corrected himself when, upon reflection, he determined that a previous response was not accurate. Moreover, with respect to the duty to tell the truth, he indicated that he had a basic understanding of the concept of truthfulness and appreciation for the obligation to be truthful when he stated that telling the truth was both "saying something that is real" and "right."

United States v. Stops

2020 U.S. Dist. LEXIS 133153 (D. Mt. 2020)

WATTERS, Judge.

Before the Court is Defendant Joshua Stops' motion contesting witness competency under Fed. R. Evid. 601. The Government intends to have Stops' five-year-old daughter, Jane Doe, testify at trial about what she witnessed the night of the alleged assault. Stops argues that the child witness is not competent to provide that testimony under Fed. R. Evid. 601 due to her age and the possible influence of her mother's, the alleged victim, recitation of the night's events to law enforcement. Stops requests a hearing to establish the child witness' competency. The Government responds that Stops is conflating competency with reliability and, while the child's responses during her forensic interview were sparse in detail, the answers demonstrated that Jane Doe can understand simple questions and distinguish truth from lies. For the following reasons, Stops' motion and request for a hearing are DENIED.

I. FACTUAL BACKGROUND

On September 9, 2018, law enforcement responded to the home of Joshua Stops after his then-wife called 911 to report an assault. Stops had left the scene before law enforcement arrived, but the child stayed with the mother through the night. The mother informed law enforcement that Stops had physically assaulted her earlier that evening by hitting and strangling her. The child heard the mother repeat her version of what transpired multiple times and interjected at one point, stating "choked you," when the mother was discussing the events to an officer. Stops arrived back at the house a short time after departing to find law enforcement on the scene. Officers promptly placed Stops in a patrol car and arrested him.

Three days later, on September 12, 2018, a forensic interviewer questioned Jane Doe about what she witnessed the night of September 9. Jane Doe told the interviewer, through short statements and gestures, that she saw her father put his hand on her mother's face and hit her arm multiple times in Jane Doe's bedroom and the living room. Throughout the conversation, the interviewer also conducted several exercises with Jane Doe to test her recollection and ability to distinguish truth from lies. These exercises included asking Jane Doe about what she did the morning before the interview, who dressed her for the day, and showing her flashcards correctly and falsely identifying an animal or item and asking Jane Doe which card was telling the truth. Jane Doe did not appear to have any trouble recalling the events of her morning and correctly distinguished between the truthful cards and the false cards.

II. DISCUSSION

Fed. R. Evid. 601 provides, "[e]very person is competent to be a witness unless these rules provide otherwise." This presumption extends to child witnesses. A party wishing to challenge this presumption must submit a written motion and offer proof of a compelling reason the child witness is incompetent. 18 U.S.C. § 3509(c)(3)-(4). Age alone is not a compelling reason. 18 U.S.C. § 3509(c)(4).

To support his motion, Stops submitted a report from a developmental psychologist specializing in child forensic memory and suggestibility. The report identifies three issues with Jane Doe's forensic interview and witness competency. First, the report identifies Jane Doe's exposure to the mother's formal report provided to law enforcement. This exposure creates concern, according to the psychologist, that Jane Doe's own memories of the events will be affected or possibly changed to mirror those of the mother's recollection. Second, Jane Doe's forensic interview contains very few substantive answers. Although the child answered every question, the answers were often two or three words in length or simply gestures. The report states the lack of detailed responses creates doubt about the child's ability to adequately recall or express her memories. The third concern is similar to the first—by witnessing the mother provide multiple statements, Jane Doe might mix those statements with her own memories of the events and fail to properly distinguish the difference. While these concerns may speak to the reliability of Jane Doe's testimony, they fail to address her competency to provide that testimony.

As Congress and the Ninth Circuit have determined, "when a court examines the competence of a minor to testify, it may assess only 'the child's ability to understand and answer simple questions.'" A child witness is competent if they can understand and answer simple questions, understand the difference between veracity and falsity, and appreciate the importance of telling the truth. Whether the child witness satisfies those requirements is within the trial court's discretion.

The Government points to the various exercises conducted by the forensic interviewer as proof that Jane Doe is competent to answer simple questions and understands the difference between truth and lies. As noted above, the interviewer tested Jane Doe's ability to distinguish falsehoods by showing her flashcards depicting a pizza and other cards with an individual stating the pizza was pizza and an individual stating the pizza was ice cream. The interviewer asked Jane Doe which individual was telling the truth. She successfully identified the one stating the pizza was pizza. The interviewer repeated the exercise twice more with flashcards showing a bear and an apple. Jane Doe successfully identified the lie all three times.

The interviewer also discussed the importance of telling the truth with Jane Doe and the need to correct people when they are incorrect. Jane Doe practiced this by successfully correcting the interviewer when he intentionally mispronounced her name and asked her to clarify several of her answers. The child's answers were usually short and sparse on details, but they nonetheless demonstrated her ability to answer questions and distinguish true and false statements. Concerns about the mother's influence on the child witness's reliability aside, the Court sees no concerns with the child's competency to provide testimony.

IT IS HEREBY ORDERED that the Defendant's motion contesting the competency of the child witness under Fed. R. Evid. 601 and request for a hearing are DENIED.

(b) Witnesses with Mental Illness

What type of mental illness renders a witness incompetent to testify? The answer is that only those mental illnesses that preclude the witness from understanding the duty to tell the truth or interfere with the ability to perceive, recollect, or narrate qualify. It is not enough that the witness be diagnosed with a mental illness or that a witness be found incompetent to stand trial. *United States v. Lightly* is a good example.

United States v. Lightly

677 F.2d 1027 (4th Cir. 1982)

ERVIN, Judge.

On December 19, 1979, Terrance McKinley, an inmate at Lorton Reformatory in northern Virginia, sustained serious stab wounds from an assault in his cell. Two of McKinley's fellow inmates, Randy Lightly and Clifton McDuffie, were investigated, but only Lightly was formally charged. McDuffie was not indicted by the grand jury because a court appointed psychiatrist found him incompetent to stand trial and criminally insane at the time of the offense. He is presently confined in a mental hospital.

On May 22, 1980, Lightly was convicted of assault with intent to commit murder. The government's case included testimony from the victim, Terrance McKinley, inmates Harvey Boyd and Robert Thomas, and McKinley's treating physician, Dr. Lance Weaver, which indicated that McDuffie and Lightly cornered McKinley in his cell and repeatedly stabbed him with half pairs of scissors. Lightly received a severe cut on his hand in the assault. Lightly's account of the stabbing was that he was walking along cell block three when he saw McDuffie and McKinley fighting in McKinley's cell. Lightly said he went into the cell to stop the fight and while he was pulling McDuffie off of McKinley, McDuffie turned around and cut him. His testimony was corroborated by three other inmates.

The defense also attempted to have McDuffie testify. McDuffie would have testified that only he and not Lightly had assaulted McKinley. The court ruled McDuffie incompetent to testify because he had been found to be criminally insane and incompetent to stand trial, and was subject to hallucinations. [Specifically, McDuffie believed that "Star Child" told him to kill McKinley because McKinley and Hodge, who apparently was a prison administrator, were going to kill him.] We believe this was error and that Lightly is entitled to a new trial.

Every witness is presumed competent to testify, Fed.R.Evid. 601, unless it can be shown that the witness does not have personal knowledge of the matters about which he is to testify, that he does not have the capacity to recall, or that he does not understand the duty to testify truthfully. This rule applies to persons considered to be insane to the same extent that it applies to other persons. In this case, the testimony of McDuffie's treating physician indicated that McDuffie had a sufficient memory, that he understood the oath, and that he could communicate what he saw. The district judge chose not to conduct an in camera examination of McDuffie. On this record, it was clearly improper for the court to disqualify McDuffie from testifying.

Trial judges have the authority to require a witness to submit to a psychiatric examination before determining that they are competent, but that power is to be used "sparingly." *United States v. Raineri,* 670 F.2d 702, 709 (7th Cir. 1982).

(c) Witnesses Under the Influence of Drugs or Alcohol

As a general matter, a witness's intoxication on drugs or alcohol is not a basis for concluding that he or she is not competent, at least not permanently. In the usual case, intoxication or addiction is a basis for impeachment, not a finding of incompetence. *United States v. Roach,* 590 F.2d 181, 185-86 (5th Cir. 1979). However, when a witness is intoxicated during his testimony and to a degree that it may interfere with the ability to recall or narrate (or to understand the duty to tell the truth), the trial judge may pause proceedings, investigate the temporary incompetence, and postpone the witness's testimony until the effects wear off. *United States v. Hyson,* 721 F.2d 856, 863-64 (1st Cir. 1983). *United States v. Barbee* addressed such an issue.

United States v. Barbee

524 Fed. Appx. 15 (4th Cir. 2013)

PER CURIAM.

In these consolidated appeals, Antonio Barbee and David Ricardo Stewart challenge their convictions on one count each of attempted interference with commerce by robbery, and carrying, using or brandishing a firearm during and in relation to a crime of violence.

Stewart . . . argues that the district court erred when it allowed a Government witness to testify at trial because she was medicated at the time of her testimony due to a head injury she sustained the day before. A witness is presumed to be competent unless it is shown that she does not have personal knowledge of the matter about which she testifies, does not have the ability to recall, or does not understand the oath. "[A] district judge has great latitude in the procedure he may follow in determining the competency of a witness to testify."

In this case, the district court sua sponte conducted a thorough voir dire outside of the jury's presence to determine whether the Government's witness was competent to testify, despite her medicated state. Although the witness expressed a desire not to testify and, after inquiry by the district court, stated that the medication she was taking could "cause inconsistency," we have found nothing in her testimony to indicate that she did not have personal knowledge of the matters at hand, that she did not have the ability to recall the events, or that she did not understand the oath under which she was testifying. Given the absence of evidence in the record supporting Stewart's summary assertion to the contrary, and in light of the district court's instruction to the jury that the witness was medicated at the time of her testimony and that the medication could have an effect on her recollection and ability to understand what was taking place, we conclude that the district court did not clearly err in finding that witness was competent to testify.

(d) Hypnotized Witnesses

When a witness is hypnotized prior to testifying, there is a danger that the witness's recollection may have been tainted by statements suggested to the witness while under hypnosis. Courts have taken a variety of approaches to hypnotized witnesses: Some courts deem such persons incompetent to testify *at all* or to testify about anything that happened prior to the hypnosis; other courts take a more case-by-case approach that measures the effect of the hypnosis on the witness's memory. *United States v. Kimberlin*, 805 F.2d 210, 218-19 (7th Cir. 1986). Some of the courts that take the case-by-case approach often allow only the admission of posthypnosis events and only if they are corroborated; even then, the fact of prior hypnosis is a proper topic for impeachment. *United States v Valdez*, 722 F.2d 1196, 1200-04 (5th Cir. 1984); *Brown v. State*, 426 So. 2d 76, 90-93 (Fla. Dist. Ct. App. 1983); *People v. Smrekar*, 68 Ill. App. 3d 379, 388 (Ill. Ct. App. 1979); *People v. Boudin*, 118 Misc. 2d 230, 239-42 (N.Y. Sup. Ct. Rockland. Co. 1983); *State v. Medrano*, 127 S.W. 3d 781 (Tex. Ct. App. 2004).[2]

The Constitution nevertheless provides a backstop. As a matter of compulsory process, a criminal defendant cannot be categorically precluded from testifying just because the defendant was previously hypnotized. *See Rock v. Arkansas*, 483 U.S. 44, 52-53 (1987).

3. *Procedures for Assessing a Witness's Competency to Testify*

Although witnesses are presumed to be competent, that presumption is rebuttable. Typically, issues of witness competence are procedurally addressed in one of two ways. First, in situations in which the parties anticipate a competency issue, the trial judge or the parties may ask the witness questions (or *voir dire*) bearing on

---

2. Some jurisdictions have erected a categorical bar to testimony from hypnotized witnesses. California is one such state, *People v. Shirley*, 31 Cal. 3d 18, 66-67 (Cal. 1982), although a witness may still testify about prehypnosis matters if the prehypnosis statement was "preserved in a writing, audio recording, or video recording," Cal. Evid. Code § 795.

competency outside the presence of the jury. The judge then makes a ruling as to whether the witness is competent to testify. Second, if the issue of lack of competency arises in the midst of testimony, the parties can ask the judge for a midtrial hearing outside the jury's presence and, at that point, *voir dire* the witness. *See United States v. Gutman*, 725 F.2d 417, 420 (7th Cir. 1984).

PART C: SPECIAL RULES OF COMPETENCY

There are special rules that govern the competency of certain categories of witnesses—namely, lawyers, judges, jurors, and those who wish to challenge a will after the will's maker has died.

1. Lawyers as Advocates and Witnesses

Example

In a lawsuit for breach of contract, Plaintiff seeks to call Defendant's lawyer to testify that before the lawsuit was filed, Defendant's lawyer said in a phone call, "I know my client didn't fulfill the contract, but he had a good reason—he thinks [Plaintiff] is a jerk who doesn't deserve his business." Can Plaintiff call Defendant's *lawyer who is representing Defendant in that case?*

The rules of evidence do not pose a bar for a lawyer who is called as a witness in the same case in which she represents a party: The lawyer can take an oath and may have no issues with her perception, recollection, or narration. However, the rules of ethics generally prohibit a lawyer from being an advocate *and* a witness in the same case. The ABA Model Rules on Professional Responsibility provide that a lawyer "shall not act as an advocate" unless (1) the lawyer's anticipated testimony "relates to an uncontested issue"; (2) that testimony "relates to" a collateral matter, such as "the nature and value of the legal services rendered in a case"; or (3) "disqualification of the lawyer would work substantial hardship on the client." ABA Model Rules, Rule 3.7(a). The "substantial hardship" exception requires the trial judge to "balance the interests of the parties." *Anderson v. Reliance Standard Life Ins. Co.*, 1988 U.S. Dist. LEXIS 7914, *5 (E.D. Pa. 1988).

The reasons for this presumptive bar are simple: (1) A lawyer is a less effective witness because she is more easily impeached based on her bias; (2) opposing counsel may be reluctant to challenge the credibility of a lawyer who is also an advocate; (3) the lawyer-witness may be called on to argue her own credibility; and (4) the roles of a witness and advocate are incompatible—the former's job is to objectively relate facts, while the latter's job is to advance her client's interest. *FDIC v. United States Fire Ins. Co.*, 50 F.3d 1304, 1311 (5th Cir. 1995).

The solution, however, is generally not to bar the lawyer from testifying as a witness. Instead, in cases where a lawyer may not also serve as a witness, the default solution is to permit the lawyer to testify but to disqualify the lawyer from serving as counsel in that case. *Net 2 Press, Inc. v. 58 Dix Ave. Corp.*, 212 F.R.D. 37, 39 (D. Me. 2002). That way, the jury will not be deprived of facts—even if the client is deprived of their counsel of choice.

The situation is more nuanced in criminal cases. What if a criminal defendant seeks to call his own attorney as a witness? The right of a criminal defendant to his counsel of choice is grounded in the Sixth Amendment, *see United States v. Gonzalez-Lopez*, 548 U.S. 140 (2006), such that disqualification of the lawyer presents a potential constitutional violation. Thus, in this situation, trial judges must "balance the defendant's constitutional right [to be represented by his counsel of choice] against the need to preserve the highest ethical standards of professional responsibility." *United States v. Cunningham*, 672 F.2d 1064, 1070 (2d Cir. 1982). What if a criminal defendant seeks to call the prosecutor as a witness? Does such a request obligate the prosecutor to disqualify herself from the case? The answer is "it depends," particularly on whether there are other witnesses who have the same knowledge as the prosecutor; in such a case, the defendant will not be permitted to call the prosecutor as a witness. *United States v. Rodella*, 59 F. Supp. 3d 1331, 1363 (D.N.M. 2014). Otherwise, a prosecutor may testify as a witness in a trial where she is an advocate only if there is a "compelling need." *United States v. Lorenzo*, 995 F.2d 1448, 1452 (9th Cir. 1993).

These considerations do not apply to pro se litigants—that is, litigants who represent themselves and also testify. *United States v. Wilson*, 979 F.3d 889, 914, n.13 (11th Cir. 2020).

2. *Judges*

May a judge be called as a witness in the matter over which she is presiding? FRE 605 says that the answer is "no" and adopts a "broad rule of incompetency." FRE 605, Adv. Comm. Note.

> **FRE 605. Judge's Competency as a Witness**
>
> The presiding judge may not testify as a witness at the trial. A party need not object to preserve the issue.

As the rule indicates, this prohibition is so strong that a party need not object to preserve the issue.[3] FRE 605 expressly prevents a trial judge from being formally

3. California permits the judge to testify if there is no objection. Cal. Evid. Code § 703(d). In California, judges also may not be called as a witness in *subsequent cases* regarding any "statement, conduct, decision or ruling" they made in a prior case unless it (1) can give rise to contempt, (2) constitutes a crime, (3) is the subject of a State Bar or judicial discipline investigation, or (4) is the basis for disqualifying the judge. Cal. Evid. Code § 703.5.

called as a witness. *Terrell v. United States*, 6 F.2d 498, 499 (4th Cir. 1925) ("If a judge has in his possession evidence of a defendant's guilt or innocence they can be adduced for or against him only by examination and cross-examination of the judge on the witness stand at a trial presided over by another judge."). But FRE 605 reaches even further. Although FRE 614 allows trial judges to question witnesses, judges cannot make comments to the jury that present information to the jury not introduced into evidence, cannot testify in the form of questions, and cannot otherwise ask questions in a manner that suggests that they are actually conveying to the jury, as witnesses would, their opinions on a case. *United States v. Nickl*, 427 F.3d 1286, 1293 (10th Cir. 2005). If a trial judge transgresses these limits, the judge may be deemed to be a "witness," although the extent of judicial questioning or commentary necessary to render a judge a "witness" is high. *Ouachita National Bank v. Tosco Corp.*, 686 F.2d 1291, 1301 (8th Cir. 1982) (allegation that judge "pursued a course of conduct during the trial that overstepped the line of permissible liberties" is insufficient to state a violation of FRE 605).

3. Jurors

When is it permissible for a party to call a *sitting juror* as a witness in a case? Are those jurors competent to be witnesses? Consider the following examples:

Examples

1. Defendant is charged with, and on trial for, making a criminal threat. Prosecutor seeks to call one of the jurors in the case to testify that, during a break in the proceedings, the juror overheard Defendant telling his lawyer, "Next time, I'll make damned sure I carry through with my threat."
2. Defendant is convicted of murder. In a post-trial motion for new trial, Defendant seeks to call one of the 12 jurors on his case to testify that three of the jurors were high on marijuana during the deliberations.
3. Plaintiff sues Defendant for injuries sustained in an auto accident. After a verdict in the amount of $800,000 for Plaintiff was returned, Defendant filed a post-trial motion for a new trial and seeks to call three of the six jurors from his case to testify that the jury reached the $800,000 amount by having each juror submit an amount on a piece of paper and then by averaging the amounts.
4. Defendant is convicted of sexual assault. In a post-trial motion for a new trial, Defendant seeks to call two of the 12 jurors on his case to testify that the verdict is tainted because one of those jurors said, "I think he did it because he's Mexican, and Mexican men take whatever they want" and "Nine times out of ten, Mexican men were guilty of being aggressive toward women and young girls." (These are the facts from a U.S. Supreme Court case.)

(a) During the Trial

The first example addresses the situation in which a party calls a sitting juror to testify during the trial (and hence in front of the other jurors). For obvious reasons, this situation calls on a juror to sit as the judge of his own credibility, while at the same time calling on the other jurors to evaluate their fellow juror's credibility during deliberations when that juror is present and participating. Not surprisingly, the Federal Rules of Evidence generally prohibit putting jurors in this difficult, if not impossible, position.[4]

Specifically, FRE 606(a) provides the following:

> **FRE 606. Juror's Competency as a Witness**
>
> **(a) At the Trial.** A juror may not testify as a witness before the other jurors at the trial. If the juror is called to testify, the court must give a party an opportunity to object outside the jury's presence.

(b) Using Jurors' Testimony to Impeach Their Verdict

Is the dynamic any different once a verdict has been rendered and the party dissatisfied with that verdict seeks to elicit testimony from jurors to show some irregularity in the deliberations that might provide a basis for overturning that verdict? This situation is presented in the remaining examples set forth above.

FRE 606(b) addresses the competency of jurors to impeach their verdict:

> **FRE 606. Juror's Competency as a Witness**
>
> **(b) During an Inquiry into the Validity of a Verdict or Indictment.**
>
> **(1)** ***Prohibited Testimony or Other Evidence.*** During an inquiry into the validity of a verdict or indictment, a juror may not testify about any statement made or incident that occurred during the jury's deliberations; the effect of anything on that juror's or another juror's vote; or any juror's mental processes concerning the verdict or indictment. The court may not receive a juror's affidavit or evidence of a juror's statement on these matters.
>
> **(2)** ***Exceptions.*** A juror may testify about whether:
>
> **(A)** extraneous prejudicial information was improperly brought to the jury's attention;

4. California allows sitting jurors to be called if there is no objection. Cal. Evid. Code § 704(d).

> **(B)** an outside influence was improperly brought to bear on any juror; or
>
> **(C)** a mistake was made in entering the verdict on the verdict form.

FRE 606(b) largely follows the common law rule and sets up the following scheme:

Jurors are *incompetent* to testify about:
- Statements made during deliberations
- Incidents that occurred during deliberations
- The effect of anything on that juror's vote
- Any juror's mental processes concerning the verdict

BUT MAY TESTIFY ABOUT:

Outside influence improperly brought to bear on any juror	Extraneous prejudicial information brought to jury's attention	Mistakes in filling out verdict form

Examples

1. Plaintiff sues Defendant for battery for placing 18 tablets of ground-up Extra Strength Tylenol in her water. The jury returns a verdict for Defendant. Plaintiff moves for a new trial on the ground of juror misconduct. In support of her motion, Plaintiff submits a declaration from Juror No. 9, who relates that one of the other jurors said that when he went home the night before and ground up 18 tablets of Extra Strength Tylenol and placed them in a cup of water, the water looked obviously contaminated, which in his view undermined Plaintiff's claim that she drank the water completely unaware of what was in it. Juror No. 9's experiment constitutes "extraneous prejudicial information" brought to the jury's attention and thus is something upon which a juror is competent to testify.
2. Plaintiff sues Defendant for injuries suffered in an auto accident. The jury returns a verdict for Defendant. Plaintiff moves for a new trial on the ground of juror misconduct. In support of her motion, Plaintiff submits declarations from three jurors; all declare that Juror No. 4 spent most of the deliberations looking at her family pictures and not participating in the deliberations. Those juror declarations are not to be considered because they deal with incidents that occurred during deliberations and possibly with the jury's mental processes; Juror No. 4's inattentiveness does not fall into any of the exceptions in FRE 606(b).

3. Plaintiff sues Defendant for breach of contract. The jury returns a verdict for Defendant. Plaintiff moves for a new trial on the ground of juror misconduct. In support of the motion, Plaintiff submits declarations from two jurors; those jurors declare that Juror No. 10 disclosed that he had been approached by Plaintiff's father outside the courtroom and the father offered that juror money if he ruled in Plaintiff's favor and also that Juror No. 10 was so offended by the incident that he believed that Plaintiff's lawsuit had no merit. This conduct is an outside influence that would be properly admitted, although the *effect* of the incident on Juror No. 10's vote is likely inadmissible as dealing with the juror's mental processes.

Why such a broad rule of incompetency with such narrow exceptions?[5] The reasons are many—namely, limiting the competency of jurors (1) reduces the harassment of jurors by parties looking for a way to overturn a verdict they dislike, (2) enhances the privacy of deliberations by making it harder to breach that privacy, (3) makes it harder for jurors disgruntled with how the deliberations turned out to undermine that verdict, and (4) enhances the finality of verdicts by making them harder to overturn.

Does FRE 606(b)'s prohibition on juror incompetence go too far by categorically excluding witnesses whose testimony cast substantial doubt on the integrity of the jury's deliberations and verdict? Consider *Tanner v. United States.*

Tanner v. United States

483 U.S. 107 (1987)

JUSTICE O'CONNOR delivered the opinion of the Court.

Petitioners William Conover and Anthony Tanner were convicted of conspiring to defraud the United States, and of committing mail fraud. The United

5. Some states adhere to the federal rule. See Ill. R. Evid. 606(b).

As discussed more fully below, some states follow a narrower rule of disqualification known as the Iowa rule. California is one such jurisdiction. In California, a juror is deemed to be generally competent to testify. Cal. Evid. Code § 1150(b). Further, a juror may offer evidence about "statements made or conduct, conditions or events" "of such a character as is likely to have influenced the jury improperly" no matter where they occurred, but is only prohibited from offering evidence "to show the effect of such statement, conduct, condition or event upon a juror in influencing him to assent to or dissent from the verdict or concerning the mental processes by which it was determined." Cal. Evid. Code § 1150(a).

Other states follow a *broader* rule of incompetence than the Federal Rule of Evidence. Florida declares a juror incompetent "to testify as to any matter which essentially inheres in the verdict . . ." Fl. Stat. § 90.607(b). Texas only allows a juror to testify about (1) whether "an outside influence was improperly brought to bear on any juror" or (2) "to rebut a claim that the juror was not qualified to serve." Tex. R. Evid. 606(b)(2).

States Court of Appeals for the Eleventh Circuit affirmed the convictions. Petitioners argue that the District Court erred in refusing to admit juror testimony at a post-verdict hearing on juror intoxication during the trial; and that the conspiracy count of the indictment failed to charge a crime against the United States. We affirm in part and remand.

The day before petitioners were scheduled to be sentenced, Tanner filed a motion, in which Conover subsequently joined, seeking continuance of the sentencing date, permission to interview jurors, an evidentiary hearing, and a new trial. According to an affidavit accompanying the motion, Tanner's attorney had received an unsolicited telephone call from one of the trial jurors, Vera Asbul. Juror Asbul informed Tanner's attorney that several of the jurors consumed alcohol during the lunch breaks at various times throughout the trial, causing them to sleep through the afternoons.

[P]etitioners filed another new trial motion based on additional evidence of jury misconduct. In another affidavit, Tanner's attorney stated that he received an unsolicited visit at his residence from a second juror, Daniel Hardy. Despite the fact that the District Court had denied petitioners' motion for leave to interview jurors, two days after Hardy's visit Tanner's attorney arranged for Hardy to be interviewed by two private investigators. The interview was transcribed, sworn to by the juror, and attached to the new trial motion. In the interview Hardy stated that he "felt like . . . the jury was on one big party." Hardy indicated that seven of the jurors drank alcohol during the noon recess. Four jurors, including Hardy, consumed between them "a pitcher to three pitchers" of beer during various recesses. Of the three other jurors who were alleged to have consumed alcohol, Hardy stated that on several occasions he observed two jurors having one or two mixed drinks during the lunch recess, and one other juror, who was also the foreperson, having a liter of wine on each of three occasions. Juror Hardy also stated that he and three other jurors smoked marijuana quite regularly during the trial. Moreover, Hardy stated that during the trial he observed one juror ingest cocaine five times and another juror ingest cocaine two or three times. One juror sold a quarter pound of marijuana to another juror during the trial, and took marijuana, cocaine, and drug paraphernalia into the courthouse. Hardy noted that some of the jurors were falling asleep during the trial, and that one of the jurors described himself to Hardy as "flying." Hardy stated that before he visited Tanner's attorney at his residence, no one had contacted him concerning the jury's conduct, and Hardy had not been offered anything in return for his statement. Hardy said that he came forward "to clear my conscience" and "because I felt . . . that the people on the jury didn't have no business being on the jury. I felt . . . that Mr. Tanner should have a better opportunity to get somebody that would review the facts right."

[The district court denied the defendants' motions, and the Eleventh Circuit affirmed.]

Petitioners argue that the District Court erred in not ordering an additional evidentiary hearing at which jurors would testify concerning drug and alcohol use during the trial. Petitioners assert that . . . juror testimony on ingestion of drugs or alcohol during the trial is not barred by Federal Rule of Evidence 606(b). Moreover, petitioners argue that whether or not authorized by Rule 606(b), an evidentiary hearing including juror testimony on drug and alcohol use is compelled by their Sixth Amendment right to trial by a competent jury.

By the beginning of this century, if not earlier, the near-universal and firmly established common-law rule in the United States flatly prohibited the admission of juror testimony to impeach a jury verdict.

Exceptions to the common-law rule were recognized only in situations in which an "extraneous influence," *Mattox* v. *United States*, 146 U.S. 140, 149 (1892), was alleged to have affected the jury. In *Mattox*, this Court held admissible the testimony of jurors describing how they heard and read prejudicial information not admitted into evidence. The Court allowed juror testimony on influence by outsiders in *Parker* v. *Gladden*, 385 U.S. 363, 365 (1966) (bailiff's comments on defendant), and *Remmer* v. *United States*, 347 U.S. 227, 228-230 (1954) (bribe offered to juror). See also *Smith* v. *Phillips*, 455 U.S. 209 (1982) (juror in criminal trial had submitted an application for employment at the District Attorney's office). In situations that did not fall into this exception for external influence, however, the Court adhered to the common-law rule against admitting juror testimony to impeach a verdict.

Lower courts used this external/internal distinction to identify those instances in which juror testimony impeaching a verdict would be admissible. The distinction was not based on whether the juror was literally inside or outside the jury room when the alleged irregularity took place; rather, the distinction was based on the nature of the allegation. Clearly a rigid distinction based only on whether the event took place inside or outside the jury room would have been quite unhelpful. For example, under a distinction based on location a juror could not testify concerning a newspaper read inside the jury room. Instead, of course, this has been considered an external influence about which juror testimony is admissible. Similarly, under a rigid locational distinction jurors could be regularly required to testify after the verdict as to whether they heard and comprehended the judge's instructions, since the charge to the jury takes place outside the jury room. Courts wisely have treated allegations of a juror's inability to hear or comprehend at trial as an internal matter. Most significant for the present case, however, is the fact that lower federal courts treated allegations of the physical or mental incompetence of a juror as "internal" rather than "external" matters.

The Court of Appeals concluded that when faced with allegations that a juror was mentally incompetent, "courts have refused to set aside a verdict, or even to make further inquiry, unless there be proof of an adjudication of insanity or mental incompetence closely in advance . . . of jury service," or proof of "a closely contemporaneous and independent post-trial adjudication of incompetency." See also *Sullivan* v. *Fogg*, 613 F.2d 465, 467 (CA2 1980) (allegation of juror insanity is internal consideration); *United States* v. *Allen*, 588 F.2d 1100, 1106, n. 12 (CA5 1979) (noting "specific reluctance to probe the minds of jurors once they have deliberated their verdict"); *United States* v. *Pellegrini*, 441 F. Supp. 1367 (ED Pa. 1977), aff'd, 586 F.2d 836 (CA3) (whether juror sufficiently understood English language was not a question of "extraneous influence"). This line of federal decisions was reviewed in *Government of the Virgin Islands* v. *Nicholas, supra*, in which the Court of Appeals concluded that a juror's allegation that a hearing impairment interfered with his understanding of the evidence at trial was not a matter of "external influence."

Substantial policy considerations support the common-law rule against the admission of jury testimony to impeach a verdict. As early as 1915 this Court explained the necessity of shielding jury deliberations from public scrutiny:

> "Let it once be established that verdicts solemnly made and publicly returned into court can be attacked and set aside on the testimony of those who took part in their publication and all verdicts could be, and many would be, followed by an inquiry in the hope of discovering something which might invalidate the finding. Jurors would be harassed and beset by the defeated party in an effort to secure from them evidence of facts which might establish misconduct sufficient to set aside a verdict. If evidence thus secured could be thus used, the result would be to make what was intended to be a private deliberation, the constant subject of public investigation — to the destruction of all frankness and freedom of discussion and conference."

The Court's statement in *Remmer* that "the integrity of jury proceedings must not be jeopardized by unauthorized invasions," could also be applied to the inquiry petitioners seek to make into the internal processes of the jury.

There is little doubt that postverdict investigation into juror misconduct would in some instances lead to the invalidation of verdicts reached after irresponsible or improper juror behavior. It is not at all clear, however, that the jury system could survive such efforts to perfect it. Allegations of juror misconduct, incompetency, or inattentiveness, raised for the first time days, weeks, or months after the verdict, seriously disrupt the finality of the process. Moreover, full and frank discussion in the jury room, jurors' willingness to return an unpopular verdict, and the community's trust in a system that relies on the decisions of laypeople would all be undermined by a barrage of postverdict scrutiny of juror conduct.

Federal Rule of Evidence 606(b) is grounded in the common-law rule against admission of jury testimony to impeach a verdict and the exception for juror testimony relating to extraneous influences. See *Government of the Virgin Islands* v. *Gereau*, 523 F.2d 140, 149, n. 22 (CA3 1975); S. Rep. No. 93-1277, p. 13 (1974) (observing that Rule 606(b) "embodied long-accepted Federal law").

Thus, the legislative history demonstrates with uncommon clarity that Congress specifically understood, considered, and rejected a version of Rule 606(b) that would have allowed jurors to testify on juror conduct during deliberations, including juror intoxication. This legislative history provides strong support for the most reasonable reading of the language of Rule 606(b) — that juror intoxication is not an "outside influence" about which jurors may testify to impeach their verdict.

Finally, even if Rule 606(b) is interpreted to retain the common-law exception allowing postverdict inquiry of juror incompetence in cases of "substantial if not wholly conclusive evidence of incompetency," the showing made by petitioners falls far short of this standard. The affidavits and testimony presented in support of the first new trial motion suggested, at worst, that several of the jurors fell asleep at times during the afternoons. The District Court Judge appropriately considered the fact that he had "an unobstructed view" of the jury, and did not see any juror sleeping. Hardy's allegations of *incompetence* are meager. Hardy stated that the alcohol consumption he engaged in with three other jurors did not leave any of them intoxicated. App. to Pet. for Cert. 47 ("I told [the prosecutor] that we would just go out and get us a pitcher of beer and drink it, but as far as us being drunk, no we wasn't"). The only allegations concerning the jurors' ability to properly consider the evidence were Hardy's observations that some jurors were "falling asleep all the time during the trial," and that his own reasoning ability was affected on one day of the trial. These allegations would not suffice to bring this case under the common-law exception allowing postverdict inquiry when an extremely strong showing of incompetency has been made.

Petitioners also argue that the refusal to hold an additional evidentiary hearing at which jurors would testify as to their conduct "violates the sixth amendment's guarantee to a fair trial before an impartial and *competent* jury." This Court has recognized that a defendant has a right to "a tribunal both impartial and mentally competent to afford a hearing." *Jordan v. Massachusetts,* 225 U.S. 167, 176 (1912). In this case the District Court held an evidentiary hearing in response to petitioners' first new trial motion at which the judge invited petitioners to introduce any admissible evidence in support of their allegations. At issue in this case is whether the Constitution compelled the District Court to hold an additional evidentiary hearing including one particular kind of evidence inadmissible under the Federal Rules.

As described above, long-recognized and very substantial concerns support the protection of jury deliberations from intrusive inquiry. Petitioners' Sixth Amendment interests in an unimpaired jury, on the other hand, are protected by several aspects of the trial process. The suitability of an individual for the responsibility of jury service, of course, is examined during *voir dire.* Moreover, during the trial the jury is observable by the court, by counsel, and by court personnel. Moreover, jurors are observable by each other, and may report inappropriate juror behavior to the court *before* they render a verdict. Finally, after the trial a party may seek to impeach the verdict by nonjuror evidence of misconduct. See *United States v. Taliaferro,* 558 F.2d 724, 725-726 (CA4 1977) (court considered records of club where jurors dined, and testimony of marshal who accompanied jurors, to determine whether jurors were intoxicated during deliberations). Indeed, in this case the District Court held an evidentiary hearing giving petitioners ample opportunity to produce nonjuror evidence supporting their allegations.

In light of these other sources of protection of petitioners' right to a competent jury, we conclude that the District Court did not err in deciding, based on the inadmissibility of juror testimony and the clear insufficiency of the nonjuror evidence offered by petitioners, that an additional postverdict evidentiary hearing was unnecessary.

Tanner establishes that juror misconduct may go uncorrected, at least if it does not fall into the three exceptions to FRE 606(b) for extraneous information brought to the jury's attention, an outside influence, or a mistake in entering the verdict on the verdict form. But *Tanner* suggests that post-verdict testimony from jurors is not always necessary to root out such misconduct because other mechanisms exist to do so, including (1) *voir dire,* which enables the parties and the trial judge to ensure that jurors are impartial; (2) the parties' and trial judge's observations of the jurors during trial; and (3) the ability of other jurors to report misconduct as the trial is proceeding.

But what if the juror misconduct amounts to a *constitutional* violation? Are jurors competent to testify to such misconduct? That was the issue confronted in *Pena-Rodriguez v. Colorado.*

Peña-Rodriguez v. Colorado

137 S. Ct. 855 (2017)

JUSTICE KENNEDY delivered the opinion of the Court.

The jury is a central foundation of our justice system and our democracy. Whatever its imperfections in a particular case, the jury is a necessary check on governmental power. The jury, over the centuries, has been an inspired, trusted, and effective instrument for resolving factual disputes and determining ultimate questions of guilt or innocence in criminal cases. Over the long course its judgments find acceptance in the community, an acceptance essential to respect for the rule of law. The jury is a tangible implementation of the principle that the law comes from the people.

Like all human institutions, the jury system has its flaws, yet experience shows that fair and impartial verdicts can be reached if the jury follows the court's instructions and undertakes deliberations that are honest, candid, robust, and based on common sense. A general rule has evolved to give substantial protection to verdict finality and to assure jurors that, once their verdict has been entered, it will not later be called into question based on the comments or conclusions they expressed during deliberations. This principle, itself centuries old, is often referred to as the no-impeachment rule. The instant case presents the question whether there is an exception to the no-impeachment rule when, after the jury is discharged, a juror comes forward with compelling evidence that another juror made clear and explicit statements indicating that racial animus was a significant motivating factor in his or her vote to convict.

I

State prosecutors in Colorado brought criminal charges against petitioner, Miguel Angel Peña-Rodriguez, based on the following allegations. In 2007, in the bathroom of a Colorado horse-racing facility, a man sexually assaulted two teenage sisters. The girls told their father and identified the man as an employee of the racetrack. The police located and arrested petitioner. Each girl separately identified petitioner as the man who had assaulted her.

The State charged petitioner with harassment, unlawful sexual contact, and attempted sexual assault on a child. Before the jury was empaneled, members of the venire were repeatedly asked whether they believed that they could be fair and impartial in the case. A written questionnaire asked if there was "anything about you that you feel would make it difficult for you to be a fair juror." The court repeated the question to the panel of prospective jurors and encouraged jurors to speak in private with the court if they had any concerns about their impartiality. Defense counsel likewise asked whether anyone felt that "this is simply not a good case" for them to be a fair juror. None of the empaneled jurors expressed any reservations based on racial or any other bias. And none asked to speak with the trial judge.

After a 3-day trial, the jury found petitioner guilty of unlawful sexual contact and harassment, but it failed to reach a verdict on the attempted sexual assault charge.

Following the discharge of the jury, petitioner's counsel entered the jury room to discuss the trial with the jurors. As the room was emptying, two jurors remained to speak with counsel in private. They stated that, during deliberations, another juror had expressed anti-Hispanic bias toward petitioner and petitioner's alibi witness. Petitioner's counsel reported this to the court and, with the court's supervision, obtained sworn affidavits from the two jurors.

The affidavits by the two jurors described a number of biased statements made by another juror, identified as Juror H. C. According to the two jurors, H. C. told the other jurors that he "believed the defendant was guilty because, in [H. C.'s] experience as an ex-law enforcement officer, Mexican men had a bravado that caused them to believe they could do whatever they wanted with women." The jurors reported that H. C. stated his belief that Mexican men are physically controlling of women because of their sense of entitlement, and further stated, "'I think he did it because he's Mexican and Mexican men take whatever they want.'" According to the jurors, H. C. further explained that, in his experience, "nine times out of ten Mexican men were guilty of being aggressive toward women and young girls." Finally, the jurors recounted that Juror H. C. said that he did not find petitioner's alibi witness credible because, among other things, the witness was "'an illegal.'" (In fact, the witness testified during trial that he was a legal resident of the United States.)

After reviewing the affidavits, the trial court acknowledged H. C.'s apparent bias. But the court denied petitioner's motion for a new trial, noting that "[t]he actual deliberations that occur among the jurors are protected from inquiry under [Colorado Rule of Evidence] 606(b)." Like its federal counterpart, Colorado's Rule 606(b) generally prohibits a juror from testifying as to any statement made during deliberations in a proceeding inquiring into the validity of the verdict. See Fed. Rule Evid. 606(b).

II

A

At common law jurors were forbidden to impeach their verdict, either by affidavit or live testimony. This rule originated in *Vaise* v. *Delaval*, 1 T. R. 11, 99 Eng. Rep. 944 (K. B. 1785). There, Lord Mansfield excluded juror testimony that the jury had decided the case through a game of chance. The Mansfield rule, as it came to be known, prohibited jurors, after the verdict was entered, from testifying either about their subjective mental processes or about objective events that occurred during deliberations.

American courts adopted the Mansfield rule as a matter of common law, though not in every detail. Some jurisdictions adopted a different, more flexible version of the no-impeachment bar known as the "Iowa rule." Under that rule, jurors were prevented only from testifying about their own subjective beliefs, thoughts, or motives during deliberations. See *Wright* v. *Illinois & Miss. Tel. Co.*,

20 Iowa 195 (1866). Jurors could, however, testify about objective facts and events occurring during deliberations, in part because other jurors could corroborate that testimony.

An alternative approach, later referred to as the federal approach, stayed closer to the original Mansfield rule. See *Warger*, 135 S. Ct. 521. Under this version of the rule, the no-impeachment bar permitted an exception only for testimony about events extraneous to the deliberative process, such as reliance on outside evidence—newspapers, dictionaries, and the like—or personal investigation of the facts.

This Court's early decisions did not establish a clear preference for a particular version of the no-impeachment rule.

In a following case the Court required the admission of juror affidavits stating that the jury consulted information that was not in evidence, including a prejudicial newspaper article. *Mattox* v. *United States*, 146 U. S. 140, 151 (1892). The Court suggested, furthermore, that the admission of juror testimony might be governed by a more flexible rule, one permitting jury testimony even where it did not involve consultation of prejudicial extraneous information

Later, however, the Court rejected the more lenient Iowa rule. In *McDonald* v. *Pless*, 238 U. S. 264 (1915), the Court affirmed the exclusion of juror testimony about objective events in the jury room. There, the jury allegedly had calculated a damages award by averaging the numerical submissions of each member. As the Court explained, admitting that evidence would have "dangerous consequences": "no verdict would be safe" and the practice would "open the door to the most pernicious arts and tampering with jurors." Yet the Court reiterated its admonition from *Reid*, again cautioning that the no-impeachment rule might recognize exceptions "in the gravest and most important cases" where exclusion of juror affidavits might well violate "the plainest principles of justice."

The common-law development of the no-impeachment rule reached a milestone in 1975, when Congress adopted the Federal Rules of Evidence, including Rule 606(b). Congress, like the *McDonald* Court, rejected the Iowa rule. Instead it endorsed a broad no-impeachment rule, with only limited exceptions.

B

Some version of the no-impeachment rule is followed in every State and the District of Columbia. Variations make classification imprecise, but, as a general matter, it appears that 42 jurisdictions follow the Federal Rule, while 9 follow the Iowa Rule. Within both classifications there is a diversity of approaches.

C

In addressing the scope of the common-law no-impeachment rule before Rule 606(b)'s adoption, the *Reid* and *McDonald* Courts noted the possibility of an exception to the rule in the "gravest and most important cases." Yet since the enactment of Rule 606(b), the Court has addressed the precise question whether the Constitution mandates an exception to it in just two instances.

In its first case, *Tanner*, 483 U. S. 107, the Court rejected a Sixth Amendment exception for evidence that some jurors were under the influence of drugs and alcohol during the trial. Central to the Court's reasoning were the "long-recognized and very substantial concerns" supporting "the protection of jury deliberations from intrusive inquiry." The *Tanner* Court echoed *McDonald*'s concern that, if attorneys could use juror testimony to attack verdicts, jurors would be "harassed and beset by the defeated party," thus destroying "all frankness and freedom of discussion and conference." The Court was concerned, moreover, that attempts to impeach a verdict would "disrupt the finality of the process" and undermine both "jurors' willingness to return an unpopular verdict" and "the community's trust in a system that relies on the decisions of laypeople."

The *Tanner* Court outlined existing, significant safeguards for the defendant's right to an impartial and competent jury beyond post-trial juror testimony. At the outset of the trial process, *voir dire* provides an opportunity for the court and counsel to examine members of the venire for impartiality. As a trial proceeds, the court, counsel, and court personnel have some opportunity to learn of any juror misconduct. And, before the verdict, jurors themselves can report misconduct to the court. These procedures do not undermine the stability of a verdict once rendered. Even after the trial, evidence of misconduct other than juror testimony can be used to attempt to impeach the verdict. Balancing these interests and safeguards against the defendant's Sixth Amendment interest in that case, the Court affirmed the exclusion of affidavits pertaining to the jury's inebriated state.

The second case to consider the general issue presented here was *Warger*, 135 S. Ct. 521. The Court again rejected the argument that, in the circumstances there, the jury trial right required an exception to the no-impeachment rule. *Warger* involved a civil case where, after the verdict was entered, the losing party sought to proffer evidence that the jury forewoman had failed to disclose prodefendant bias during *voir dire*. As in *Tanner*, the Court put substantial reliance on existing safeguards for a fair trial. The Court stated: "Even if jurors lie in *voir dire* in a way that conceals bias, juror impartiality is adequately assured by the parties' ability to bring to the court's attention any evidence of bias before the verdict is rendered, and to employ nonjuror evidence even after the verdict is rendered."

In *Warger*, however, the Court did reiterate that the no-impeachment rule may admit exceptions. As in *Reid* and *McDonald*, the Court warned of "juror bias so extreme that, almost by definition, the jury trial right has been abridged." "If and when such a case arises," the Court indicated it would "consider whether the usual safeguards are or are not sufficient to protect the integrity of the process."

III

It must become the heritage of our Nation to rise above racial classifications that are so inconsistent with our commitment to the equal dignity of all persons. This imperative to purge racial prejudice from the administration of justice was given new force and direction by the ratification of the Civil War Amendments.

"[T]he central purpose of the Fourteenth Amendment was to eliminate racial discrimination emanating from official sources in the States." In the years before and after the ratification of the Fourteenth Amendment, it became clear that racial discrimination in the jury system posed a particular threat both to the promise of the Amendment and to the integrity of the jury trial. "Almost immediately after the Civil War, the South began a practice that would continue for many decades: All-white juries punished black defendants particularly harshly, while simultaneously refusing to punish violence by whites, including Ku Klux Klan members, against blacks and Republicans." To take one example, just in the years 1865 and 1866, all-white juries in Texas decided a total of 500 prosecutions of white defendants charged with killing African-Americans. All 500 were acquitted. The stark and unapologetic nature of race-motivated outcomes challenged the American belief that "the jury was a bulwark of liberty," and prompted Congress to pass legislation to integrate the jury system and to bar persons from eligibility for jury service if they had conspired to deny the civil rights of African-Americans. Members of Congress stressed that the legislation was necessary to preserve the right to a fair trial and to guarantee the equal protection of the laws.

The duty to confront racial animus in the justice system is not the legislature's alone. Time and again, this Court has been called upon to enforce the Constitution's guarantee against state-sponsored racial discrimination in the jury system. Beginning in 1880, the Court interpreted the Fourteenth Amendment to prohibit the exclusion of jurors on the basis of race. *Strauder* v. *West Virginia,* 100 U. S. 303, 305-309 (1880). The Court has repeatedly struck down laws and practices that systematically exclude racial minorities from juries. To guard against discrimination in jury selection, the Court has ruled that no litigant may exclude a prospective juror on the basis of race. *Batson* v. *Kentucky,* 476 U. S. 79 (1986); *Edmonson* v. *Leesville Concrete Co.,* 500 U. S. 614 (1991); *Georgia* v. *McCollum,* 505 U. S. 42 (1992). In an effort to ensure that individuals who sit on juries are free of racial bias, the Court has held that the Constitution at times demands that defendants be permitted to ask questions about racial bias during *voir dire.* The unmistakable principle underlying these precedents is that discrimination on the basis of race, "odious in all aspects, is especially pernicious in the administration of justice." The jury is to be "a criminal defendant's fundamental 'protection of life and liberty against race or color prejudice.'" Permitting racial prejudice in the jury system damages "both the fact and the perception" of the jury's role as "a vital check against the wrongful exercise of power by the State."

IV

A

This case lies at the intersection of the Court's decisions endorsing the no-impeachment rule and its decisions seeking to eliminate racial bias in the jury system. The two lines of precedent, however, need not conflict.

Racial bias of the kind alleged in this case differs in critical ways from the compromise verdict in *McDonald,* the drug and alcohol abuse in *Tanner,* or the pro-defendant bias in *Warger.* The behavior in those cases is troubling and unacceptable, but each involved anomalous behavior from a single jury—or juror—gone off course. Jurors are presumed to follow their oath, and neither history nor common experience show that the jury system is rife with mischief of these or similar kinds. To attempt to rid the jury of every irregularity of this sort would be to expose it to unrelenting scrutiny. "It is not at all clear . . . that the jury system could survive such efforts to perfect it."

The same cannot be said about racial bias, a familiar and recurring evil that, if left unaddressed, would risk systemic injury to the administration of justice. This Court's decisions demonstrate that racial bias implicates unique historical, constitutional, and institutional concerns. An effort to address the most grave and serious statements of racial bias is not an effort to perfect the jury but to ensure that our legal system remains capable of coming ever closer to the promise of equal treatment under the law that is so central to a functioning democracy.

Racial bias is distinct in a pragmatic sense as well. In past cases this Court has relied on other safeguards to protect the right to an impartial jury. Some of those safeguards, to be sure, can disclose racial bias. *Voir dire* at the outset of trial, observation of juror demeanor and conduct during trial, juror reports before the verdict, and nonjuror evidence after trial are important mechanisms for discovering bias. Yet their operation may be compromised, or they may prove insufficient. For instance, this Court has noted the dilemma faced by trial court judges and counsel in deciding whether to explore potential racial bias at *voir dire.* Generic questions about juror impartiality may not expose specific attitudes or biases that can poison jury deliberations. Yet more pointed questions "could well exacerbate whatever prejudice might exist without substantially aiding in exposing it."

The stigma that attends racial bias may make it difficult for a juror to report inappropriate statements during the course of juror deliberations. It is one thing to accuse a fellow juror of having a personal experience that improperly influences her consideration of the case, as would have been required in *Warger.* It is quite another to call her a bigot.

The recognition that certain of the *Tanner* safeguards may be less effective in rooting out racial bias than other kinds of bias is not dispositive. All forms of improper bias pose challenges to the trial process. But there is a sound basis to treat racial bias with added precaution. A constitutional rule that racial bias in the justice system must be addressed—including, in some instances, after the verdict has been entered—is necessary to prevent a systemic loss of confidence in jury verdicts, a confidence that is a central premise of the Sixth Amendment trial right.

B

For the reasons explained above, the Court now holds that where a juror makes a clear statement that indicates he or she relied on racial stereotypes or animus to convict a criminal defendant, the Sixth Amendment requires that the no-impeachment rule give way in order to permit the trial court to consider the evidence of the juror's statement and any resulting denial of the jury trial guarantee.

Not every offhand comment indicating racial bias or hostility will justify setting aside the no-impeachment bar to allow further judicial inquiry. For the inquiry to proceed, there must be a showing that one or more jurors made statements exhibiting overt racial bias that cast serious doubt on the fairness and impartiality of the jury's deliberations and resulting verdict. To qualify, the statement must tend to show that racial animus was a significant motivating factor in the juror's vote to convict. Whether that threshold showing has been satisfied is a matter committed to the substantial discretion of the trial court in light of all the circumstances, including the content and timing of the alleged statements and the reliability of the proffered evidence.

Pena-Rodriguez limits its holding to juror misconduct based on racial prejudice. But what about other types of prejudice protected by equal protection, such as prejudice based on sex? What about other categories that have been deemed protected in other jurisdictions, such as sexual orientation or religion? And what about violations of due process? Due process prohibits arbitrary action. What if a jury decided a defendant's guilt by the flip of a coin? That obviously goes to their mental processes (or lack thereof) and would thus be barred by FRE 606(b), but would the exception recognized in *Pena-Rodriguez* reach such a situation and thereby allow jurors to be deemed competent witnesses to testify to such randomness? As of yet, these are unanswered questions.

In light of *Pena-Rodriguez*, the analysis under FRE 606(b) now looks like the following:

Jurors are incompetent to testify about:
- Statements made during deliberations
- Incidents that occurred during deliberations
- The effect of anything on that juror's vote
- Any juror's mental processes concerning the verdict

BUT MAY TESTIFY ABOUT:

Extraneous prejudicial information brought to jury's attention	Outside influence improperly brought to bear on any juror	Mistakes in filling out verdict form	Evidence of racial bias by deliberating jurors

4. *Persons Challenging a Decedent's Will*

Many States have so-called Dead Man's Statutes on their books. *E.g.*, Tex. R. Evid. 601(b); *Matter of Zalk*, 10 N.Y.3d 699, 678-79 (N.Y. 2008); *Hoem v. Zia*, 159 Ill.2d 193, 200 (Ill. 1994); 735 Ill. Comp. Stat. 5/8-201. These statutes declare a witness incompetent if his or her goal is to contradict the wishes of a now-deceased person under that person's will (on the theory that the deceased is no longer around to offer conflicting testimony). The rationale is that the decedent cannot respond, so it is better to preclude testimony from witnesses who challenge the decedent's wishes. Many states, such as California, have repealed their Dead Man's Statutes in favor of allowing the jury to hear the testimony of the witness as well as the decedent's statements, which are in many states now exempted from the hearsay rule. *See, e.g.*, Cal. Evid. Code §§ 1250, 1261; Fl. Stat. § 90.602 (repealed). Where such statutes exist, the Federal Rules of Evidence defer to the jurisdiction's specialized competency rule on the ground that it is a substantive rule of decision that is most appropriately entrusted to state law under *Erie Railroad Co. v. Tompkins*, 304 U.S. 64 (1938).

Review Questions

1. **Child witness.** In a child molestation case, the victim was three years old at the time of the alleged molestation and is four years old at the time of trial. Will the child witness be able to testify if:
   a. The child witness agrees that she will tell the truth because Santa Claus "won't come" if she tells a lie?
   b. The child witness is examined about her ability to distinguish fantasy from reality outside the jury's presence?
   c. The child witness is permitted to testify from a remote room on a two-way monitor after a child psychologist who interviewed her opined that in-court testimony would traumatize her? *See* Chapter Nine.
2. **Truth mojo.** In a lawsuit arising from a slip-and-fall accident occurring near a "free love" colony, one of the witnesses—who answers only to the name "The Baron Ness"—refuses to take the traditional oath. However, he agrees to swear on his "mojo of love" to tell only the truth. Is this witness competent to testify?
3. **Hypnotized witness.** Defendant is charged with attempted murder.
   a. Prosecutor seeks to call the victim as a witness. The victim's memory has been hypnotically refreshed after she awoke from a coma. Is this witness competent to testify?
   b. Defendant wishes to testify, even though he was placed under hypnosis during a therapy session. Is he competent to testify?
4. **Dual roles.** Plaintiff sues Defendant for injuries suffered when Plaintiff was injured in the parking lot of a shopping mall owned by Defendant.
   a. After Defendant takes the stand and testifies that he does not own the mall, Plaintiff wishes to call Defendant's attorney as a witness to testify that during a brief conversation in the courthouse hallway between Defendant, Defendant's attorney, and Plaintiff's attorney, Defendant said, "Yeah, my family's owned the mall ever since it had a Sam Goody, back in the '80's." May she?
   b. Defendant's attorney wishes to take the stand and testify about a conversation she had with Plaintiff's attorney, during a friendly lunch, about the strength of the evidence in this case. There were never any settlement negotiations in this case. May she?
   c. Plaintiff seeks to call a witness who is exhibiting signs of intoxication upon taking the stand. What may the trial judge do?
5. **Attempted sporking.** Plaintiff sues Defendant, her ex-husband, for injuries suffered when Defendant allegedly stabbed Plaintiff in the back with a plastic cake-cutting knife. The jury returned a verdict for Defendant. Plaintiff files a motion for a new trial on the basis of juror misconduct.
   a. To her new trial motion, Plaintiff attaches an affidavit of Juror No. 10, who testifies that the jury decided to award Plaintiff no damages because they disliked her immensely. Is Juror No. 10 competent to offer this testimony?

b. To her new trial motion, Plaintiff attaches an affidavit of Juror No. 9, who testifies that Juror No. 8 looked up Plaintiff and Defendant on the Internet, found Plaintiff's Facebook page, and found photos of Plaintiff partying with her friends the day after the alleged incident. Is Juror No. 9 competent to offer this testimony?

c. To her new trial motion, Plaintiff attaches an affidavit of Juror No. 12, who testifies that Juror No. 1 went out and bought a plastic knife like the one Plaintiff testified was used to stab her, that Juror No. 1 tried to stab himself with the knife, and that Juror No. 1 found that the knife was too flimsy to break anyone's skin. Is Juror No. 12 competent to offer this testimony?

d. To her new trial motion, Plaintiff attaches an affidavit of Juror No. 4, who testifies that Juror No. 5 stated, during deliberations, that "Plaintiff was nagging Defendant to death. You know how women are. Even if she was stabbed, it was totally justified." Plaintiff argues that gender bias infected the verdict. Is Juror No. 4 competent to offer this testimony?

6. **Challenging the dead.** Plaintiff challenges the decedent's will on the ground that it did not accurately reflect what the decedent told Plaintiff she would receive. Plaintiff filed her lawsuit in a state that has a Dead Man's Statute. Is Plaintiff competent to testify about what the decedent told her prior to the decedent's death?

Test Your Understanding

To test your understanding of the material in this chapter, turn to the Supplement for additional practice problems.

Chapter 11

Impeachment of Witnesses

The party with the burden of proof—whether it be the plaintiff in a civil case or the prosecutor in a criminal case—calls its "star witness." This person may be a witness who overheard the defendant admit that he had no intent to fulfill the contract or an eyewitness who has identified the defendant as the bank robber. The star witness testifies, and her testimony appears to be damning. But is it?

Then comes cross-examination. Does the witness already know the defendant and have a grudge against him? Was the witness under the influence of alcohol at the time she overheard the conversation or saw the defendant? Does the witness have a reputation for lying? Is the witness fidgeting or avoiding eye contact during her testimony? Has the witness previously told others something inconsistent with her testimony at trial? Is there other evidence that contradicts the witness's testimony, such as an e-mail from the defendant to the witness expressing a desire to fulfill the contract or surveillance camera footage that shows the robber looking nothing like the defendant?

If true, any of these matters is likely to substantially undercut the believability of the witness's testimony. In other words, it would *impeach* the witness.

As discussed in Chapter Two, impeachment is *always* relevant because the credibility of a witness is always relevant.

However, only a person who is a *witness* may be impeached. If a defendant in a civil or criminal case does not testify, impeachment is not relevant because the defendant's credibility has not been put in issue. (As discussed in Chapter Three, a nonwitness's other acts—including those showing him to be an untrustworthy person in general—might be admitted for some purpose other than impeachment under FRE 404(b), such as to show his knowledge, motive, or intent, but those other acts are not being admitted *to impeach* because that person is not a witness.) For purposes of impeachment, a witness means (1) a person who takes the witness stand and offers testimony during the trial *or* (2) a person whose out-of-court statement is admitted for its truth (that is, a hearsay declarant). FRE 806 permits impeachment of hearsay declarants and describes how the rules governing impeachment apply to such declarants.

FRE 806. Attacking and Supporting the Declarant's Credibility

When a hearsay statement—or a statement described in Rule 801(d)(2)(C), (D), or (E)—has been admitted in evidence, the declarant's credibility may be attacked, and then supported, by any evidence that would be admissible for those purposes if the declarant had testified as a witness. The court may admit evidence of the declarant's inconsistent statement or conduct, regardless of when it occurred or whether the declarant had an opportunity to explain or deny it. If the party against whom the statement was admitted calls the declarant as a witness, the party may examine the declarant on the statement as if on cross-examination.

There are several permissible ways to impeach a witness. They include the following:

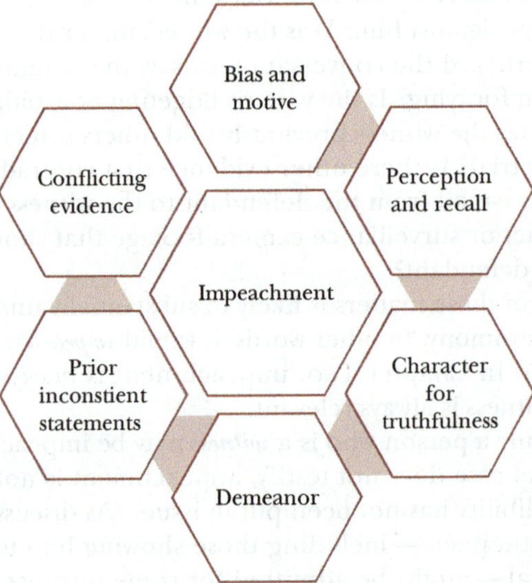

Impeachment through these means typically occurs through one of two mechanisms. First, a witness may be impeached by the questions she is asked on cross-examination. Second, a witness may be impeached by calling another witness or introducing documents or other physical evidence in an effort to show that the witness should not be believed. Because this second mechanism involves the introduction of evidence beyond the witness's answers to questions while being examined, it is called *extrinsic evidence*. The rules of evidence place limits on the use of extrinsic evidence for certain types of impeachment. Even if an item of extrinsic evidence stays within those limits, it is admissible only if it otherwise satisfies the rules of evidence (that is, hearsay, authentication, and the like).

Once a witness is impeached, the party who called her may try to convince the trier of fact that the witness should still be believed. Trying to repair a witness's credibility is called *rehabilitating* a witness.

Part A of this chapter discusses the four general methods of impeaching a witness—namely, by showing that the witness (1) has a bias or motive to shade her testimony, (2) did not accurately perceive or remember the subject of her testimony, (3) is known to be the type of person who lies, or (4) looks or acts untrustworthy while testifying. Part B discusses two further methods of impeaching a witness that are specific to her testimony in that particular case—namely, by showing that the witness (1) has previously said something inconsistent with her testimony or (2) is testifying to matters that are contradicted by other evidence in the case. Part C discusses the methods and means of rehabilitating a witness, including through a witness's prior consistent statements that corroborate her trial testimony or evidence showing her propensity to tell the truth. Part D discusses the types of evidence that are generally off-limits for impeachment, such as the witness's religious beliefs. We will also discuss some limited circumstances when those types of evidence may still be used to impeach.

For each type of impeachment evidence, we must ask the following questions:

(1) How does the proffered impeachment evidence undercut the credibility of the witness's testimony?
(2) What are the prerequisites, if any, to using the impeachment evidence?
(3) In what form, and at what point, is the impeachment evidence admissible?
(4) For those types of impeachment evidence that can also be introduced for purposes *other than* impeachment, does the possibility of this dual purpose warrant a limiting instruction or exclusion for all purposes under FRE 403?

Examples

A witness is on the stand for Plaintiff in an auto accident case.

1. On cross-examination of the witness, Defendant asks, "You and [Plaintiff] were good friends growing up, weren't you?" This question is impeachment by showing bias or motive and through the mechanism of asking questions on cross-examination.
2. After the witness testifies, Defendant calls an old friend of Plaintiff's to testify that the witness, Plaintiff, and the old friend grew up in the same neighborhood and that Plaintiff and the witness continue to be close friends. This testimony is impeachment by showing bias or motive and through the mechanism of extrinsic evidence (that is, by calling a separate witness).
3. On cross-examination of the witness, Defendant asks, "You need your glasses to see more than 10 feet away, right? You weren't wearing your glasses at the time you witnessed the collision, were you?" This is impeachment by showing lack of perception and through the mechanism of asking questions on cross-examination.

4. After the witness testifies, Defendant calls a coworker of the witness who has known the witness for five years to testify, and the coworker opines that the witness is an untruthful person. This testimony is impeachment by character evidence for untruthfulness and through the mechanism of extrinsic evidence (that is, by calling the coworker to offer an opinion on the witness's character for untruthfulness).
5. During the closing argument, Defendant argues to the jury, "Did you see how the witness was sweating and fidgeting while she testified? Did you notice how she was all sunshine and rainbows with Plaintiff's counsel, but short and abrupt with me?" This argument is an attempt to impeach through evidence of witness demeanor.
6. During cross-examination of the witness, Defendant asks, "Today you testified that the light was green for Plaintiff. But you told the police at the scene that the light was red for Plaintiff, didn't you?" After the witness denies the prior statement, Defendant calls the police officer who spoke with the witness to testify that the witness said that the light was red for Plaintiff. This testimony is impeachment by a prior inconsistent statement and through both cross-examination *and* extrinsic evidence.
7. During cross-examination of the witness, Defendant asks, "Today you testified that the light was green for Plaintiff, right?" Defendant then calls another bystander who testifies that the light was red for Plaintiff. This testimony is impeachment by contradictory evidence and through extrinsic evidence.

PART A: GENERAL IMPEACHMENT

Most of the time, the party seeking to impeach a witness is *not* the party who called the witness. That is because, most of the time, the party calling a witness wants the jury to believe what the witness is saying. At common law, this practical reality was an absolute rule known as the "voucher rule": At common law, a party was deemed to *vouch* for the credibility of the witnesses it called and was prohibited from impeaching them. This rule created problems, however, when witnesses did not say what the party who called them to the stand anticipated they would say or when the witness was the only eyewitness to the event and the party who called them had no choice but to call them. FRE 607 does away with the voucher rule.[1] However, a party may not call a witness *solely* to impeach the witness with evidence that would otherwise be inadmissible. *E.g., United States v. Morlang*, 531 F.2d 183, 188-90 (4th Cir. 1975) (so holding, when prosecutors called a witness who had consistently maintained that defendant *did not* commit the crime, in order to impeach the witness with his prior inconsistent statement that defendant *did* commit the crime).

1. New York still follows the voucher rule, but still allows the party to present a witness's prior inconsistent statements or to "front" information that the opposing party is likely to produce to undermine the witness's credibility. *See People v. Fitzpatrick*, 40 N.Y.2d 44, 49-53 (N.Y. 1976); *People v. Minsky*, 227 N.Y. 94, 98 (N.Y. 1919).

FRE 607. Who May Impeach a Witness

Any party, including the party that called the witness, may attack the witness's credibility.

Of the four types of general impeachment evidence, the Federal Rules of Evidence specifically address only one—namely, evidence of character for untruthfulness. The rules governing the other three types of general impeachment evidence are governed by the common law.

1. *Bias and Motive*

Most people would agree that the best witness for a party is one who "has no dog in the fight"—that is, a witness who is completely neutral because the witness has no connection to either party and has no stake in the outcome of the case. Why is that? The answer is that a witness with a connection or stake may be biased or may otherwise have a motive to sway the outcome of the proceeding one way or the other.

Examples

1. A witness is on the stand for Plaintiff. On cross-examination, Defendant asks the witness, "Plaintiff is your boyfriend, isn't he? You love him?" If the witness answers "Yes," the answer is evidence of her bias or motive to shade her testimony to help out the person the witness loves.
2. A witness is on the stand for the prosecution. On cross-examination, Defendant asks the witness, "You were convicted last month of carjacking, weren't you? Your sentencing hearing has been postponed a few times, hasn't it, awaiting your testimony in *this* trial, correct?" If the witness answers "Yes," this answer is evidence of bias or motive for the witness to shade his testimony in a manner that helps the prosecution in the hopes of getting a lower sentencing recommendation from the prosecutor.
3. A witness is on the stand for Defendant corporation in a case by Plaintiff to adversely possess a slice of Defendant's very valuable beachfront land. Plaintiff introduces evidence that the witness is a stockholder in Defendant's corporation. This information is evidence of bias or motive for the witness to shade the witness's testimony so that Defendant prevails and the witness's stock value does not take a hit from the loss of part of the corporation's valuable asset.

As these examples illustrate, bias and motive can be established due to the following reasons:

- *Witness's reasons to favor one party.* A witness's relationship with a party may give that witness a reason to shade his or her testimony to favor that party. For example, the fact that an expert witness is being compensated by a party is a bias; so is the fact that the expert is retained by plaintiffs the vast majority of the time.
- *Witness's reasons to disfavor another party.* A witness's dislike or enmity toward the opposing party (or someone aligned with the opposing party) may give that witness a reason to shade his or her testimony against the opposing party.
- *Witness's receipt of threats or promises of leniency.* If someone aligned with one of the parties has threatened the witness or promised the witness something of value, that threat or promise may give the witness a reason to shade his or her testimony to avoid the threat or obtain the thing of value.
- *Witness's unilateral hope of a benefit.* If a witness believes that the content of his testimony might provide him a benefit, even if no promises have been made, that belief might give the witness a reason to shade his testimony in a way that gets him that benefit.
- *Witness's stake in the outcome.* If a witness has a financial, reputational, or other stake in the outcome of the proceeding, the witness may have a reason to shade his or her testimony to favor that stake.

There is no federal rule of evidence specifically governing the use of bias and motive evidence to impeach. The Supreme Court confronted what that meant in *United States v. Abel*, 469 U.S. 45 (1984).

United States v. Abel

469 U.S. 45 (1984)

JUSTICE REHNQUIST delivered the opinion of the Court.

Respondent John Abel and two cohorts were indicted for robbing a savings and loan in Bellflower, Cal., in violation of 18 U. S. C. §§ 2113(a) and (d). The cohorts elected to plead guilty, but respondent went to trial. One of the cohorts, Kurt Ehle, agreed to testify against respondent and identify him as a participant in the robbery.

Respondent informed the District Court at a pretrial conference that he would seek to counter Ehle's testimony with that of Robert Mills. Mills was not a participant in the robbery but was friendly with respondent and with Ehle, and had spent time with both in prison. Mills planned to testify that after the robbery Ehle had admitted to Mills that Ehle intended to implicate respondent falsely, in order to receive favorable treatment from the Government. The prosecutor in turn disclosed that he intended to discredit Mills' testimony by calling Ehle back to the stand and eliciting from Ehle the fact that respondent, Mills, and Ehle were all members of the "Aryan Brotherhood," a secret prison gang that required its members always to deny the existence of the organization and to commit perjury, theft, and murder on each member's behalf.

We hold that the evidence showing Mills' and respondent's membership in the prison gang was sufficiently probative of Mills' possible bias towards respondent to warrant its admission into evidence.[2]

Both parties correctly assume, as did the District Court and the Court of Appeals, that the question is governed by the Federal Rules of Evidence. But the Rules do not by their terms deal with impeachment for "bias."

Before the present Rules were promulgated, the admissibility of evidence in the federal courts was governed in part by statutes or Rules, and in part by case law. This Court had held in *Alford* v. *United States*, 282 U.S. 687 (1931), that a trial court must allow some cross-examination of a witness to show bias. This holding was in accord with the overwhelming weight of authority in the state courts as reflected in Wigmore's classic treatise on the law of evidence. Our decision in *Davis* v. *Alaska*, 415 U.S. 308 (1974), holds that the Confrontation Clause of the Sixth Amendment requires a defendant to have some opportunity to show bias on the part of a prosecution witness.

We think this conclusion is obviously correct. Rule 401 defines as "relevant evidence" evidence having any tendency to make the existence of any fact that is of consequence to the determination of the action more probable or less probable than it would be without the evidence. Rule 402 provides that all relevant evidence is admissible. A successful showing of bias on the part of a witness would have a tendency to make the facts to which he testified less probable in the eyes of the jury than it would be without such testimony.

The correctness of the conclusion that the Rules contemplate impeachment by showing of bias is confirmed by the references to bias in the Advisory Committee Notes to Rules 608 and 610, and by the provisions allowing any party to attack credibility in Rule 607, and allowing cross-examination on "matters affecting the credibility of the witness" in Rule 611(b).

The Courts of Appeals have upheld use of extrinsic evidence to show bias both before and after the adoption of the Federal Rules of Evidence.

We think the lesson to be drawn from all of this is that it is permissible to impeach witness by showing his bias under the Federal Rules of Evidence just as it was permissible to do so before their adoption.

Respondent argues that even if the evidence of membership in the prison gang were relevant to show bias, the District Court erred in permitting a full description of the gang and its odious tenets. Respondent contends that the District Court abused its discretion under Federal Rule of Evidence 403, because the prejudicial effect of the contested evidence outweighed its probative value. In other words, testimony about the gang inflamed the jury against respondent, and the chance that he would be convicted by his mere association with the organization outweighed any probative value the testimony may have had on Mills' bias.

Respondent specifically contends that the District Court should not have permitted Ehle's precise description of the gang as a lying and murderous group.

---

2. Author's note: Mills was no ordinary member of the Aryan Brotherhood. Instead, he rose to a leadership role in the gang from his initial incarceration in 1969 until his death in prison in 2018. While in prison, he orchestrated attempted murders, drug trafficking, and racketeering both inside and outside the prison system.

Respondent suggests that the District Court should have cut off the testimony after the prosecutor had elicited that Mills knew respondent and both may have belonged to an organization together. This argument ignores the fact that the *type* of organization in which a witness and a party share membership may be relevant to show bias. If the organization is a loosely knit group having nothing to do with the subject matter of the litigation, the inference of bias arising from common membership may be small or nonexistent. If the prosecutor had elicited that both respondent and Mills belonged to the Book of the Month Club, the jury probably would not have inferred bias even if the District Court had admitted the testimony. The attributes of the Aryan Brotherhood—a secret prison sect sworn to perjury and self-protection—bore directly not only on the *fact* of bias but also on the *source* and *strength* of Mills' bias. The tenets of this group showed that Mills had a powerful motive to slant his testimony towards respondent, or even commit perjury outright.

A district court is accorded a wide discretion in determining the admissibility of evidence under the Federal Rules. Assessing the probative value of common membership in any particular group, and weighing any factors counseling against admissibility is a matter first for the district court's sound judgment under Rules 401 and 403 and ultimately, if the evidence is admitted, for the trier of fact.

Before admitting Ehle's rebuttal testimony, the District Court gave heed to the extensive arguments of counsel, both in chambers and at the bench. In an attempt to avoid undue prejudice to respondent the court ordered that the name "Aryan Brotherhood" not be used. The court also offered to give a limiting instruction concerning the testimony, and it sustained defense objections to the prosecutor's questions concerning the punishment meted out to unfaithful members. These precautions did not prevent *all* prejudice to respondent from Ehle's testimony, but they did, in our opinion, ensure that the admission of this highly probative evidence did not *unduly* prejudice respondent. We hold there was no abuse of discretion under Rule 403 in admitting Ehle's testimony as to membership and tenets.

As *Abel* makes clear, there are few prerequisites to the use of evidence of bias or motive to impeach. Bias and motive are always relevant. Indeed, it is *so* relevant that the Supreme Court has held that the importance of eliciting a witness's bias—at least when a criminal defendant is invoking his Sixth and Fourteenth Amendment rights—can sometimes trump other rules of evidence.[3]

---

3. In *Davis v. Alaska,* 415 U.S. 308 (1974), the Supreme Court held that a state privilege protecting the identity of juvenile offenders had to yield to the defendant's right to cross-examine a witness against him regarding the fact that the witness was, at the time of the testimony, on probation for a juvenile adjudication. The trial judge allowed the defendant to ask the witness whether he was "biased" against the defendant, but did not permit any inquiry into the pending probation. *Davis* held this was error: "The State's policy interest in protecting the confidentiality of a juvenile offender's record cannot require yielding so vital a constitutional right as the effective cross-examination for bias of an adverse witness."

In *Olden v. Kentucky,* 488 U.S. 227 (1988), the Supreme Court held that the fact that the key witness accusing the defendant of raping her was having an extramarital affair with the defendant's half-brother constituted a motive to lie and that the trial court erred in excluding that evidence even though it involved the witness's sexual conduct with someone other

As far as proof goes, evidence of motive and bias may be proven (1) by cross-examination of the witness being impeached or (2) through the introduction of extrinsic evidence. Although, as discussed below, extrinsic evidence of certain types of impeachment evidence is prohibited if it is deemed "collateral" (that is, too far afield to warrant admission into evidence), "bias is never classified as a collateral matter." *United States v. Keys*, 899 F.2d 983, 986 n.2 (10th Cir. 1990). Bias and motive are most commonly established through testimony regarding the specific instances of prior conduct from which the bias or motive arises.

The chief limitations on the type of evidence are FRE 403 and FRE 611(a). FRE 403, as discussed in Chapter Two, gives the trial judge discretion to reject or limit evidence when its probative value is substantially outweighed by its prejudicial effect. For example, assume that the plaintiff is suing the defendant for fraud and the plaintiff calls a witness to testify to the allegedly false statements the defendant made. The defendant impeaches the witness with the witness's prior felony conviction for financial elder abuse. The defendant then seeks to introduce evidence that the witness has a propensity to defraud elderly victims, on the theory that the witness is shading his testimony to get in the plaintiff's good graces so as to have access to the plaintiff's elderly grandmother. On these facts, a trial judge may well decide that the probative value of this bias evidence is weak and is substantially outweighed by the very real danger of prejudicing the jury against the plaintiff (because it implies that the plaintiff would let her grandmother be duped). FRE 611 also gives the judge the power to control the courtroom, including examinations that are designed to harass or embarrass a witness. For example, in a case where the plaintiff seeks to impeach a defense witness through questioning regarding the witness's on-again, off-again sexual liaisons with the defendant, a trial judge may preclude the plaintiff from asking questions about the details of each and every liaison and instead require a more generalized level of questioning.

FRE 611. Mode and Order of Examining Witnesses and Presenting Evidence

(a) Control by the Court; Purposes. The court should exercise reasonable control over the mode and order of examining witnesses and presenting evidence so as to:

(1) make those procedures effective for determining the truth;

(2) avoid wasting time; and

(3) protect witnesses from harassment or undue embarrassment.

---

than the defendant. Indeed, *Olden* was the justification to include the exception to the rape shield law (FRE 412) for "evidence whose exclusion would violate the defendant's constitutional rights." FRE 412(b)(1)(C); Adv. Comm. Note, 1994 Amendment. *See* Chapter Three.

For these purposes, the fact that evidence of bias may also reflect on the witness's character for truth-telling does not matter; it is still admissible to show bias. *Abel*, 469 U.S. at 56.

2. *Defects in Perception and Recollection*

In the movie *My Cousin Vinny*, the titular lawyer conducts an incisive but polite cross-examination of two eyewitnesses who claimed to see his clients leaving the scene of the crime. With the first, the lawyer elicits that the witness is nearly blind without her glasses and, critically, she was not wearing her glasses at the time she saw the perpetrators leave the scene. With the second, the lawyer elicits that the witness's view of the perpetrators was effectively obstructed by trees, bushes, and a dirty, "crud-covered" screen. Both cross-examinations got at the same point: The witnesses had defects in their perception of the events, even assuming that they were earnestly trying to be truthful when testifying. Obviously, a witness who could not see or hear—or, based on the same logic, cannot recall—what they testify to is a witness whose testimony is less deserving of being believed.

A defect in perception or recollection can arise from the following:

- The witness's use of substances (drugs, alcohol and the like);
- The witness's mental illness, defect, or disability;
- The witness's physical shortcomings, such as bad eyesight;
- External factors affecting the witness's ability to perceive, such as the witness's distance from the event or whether the witness's view was blocked or sound was muffled.

As with evidence of bias or motive used to impeach, evidence of defects in perception and recollection are not specifically addressed by the Federal Rules of Evidence and thus are left to the decisions of trial and appellate courts, as well FRE 611(a) and FRE 403.

There are few prerequisites to the use of evidence of defective perception or recollection to impeach. Such evidence is always relevant.

As far as proof goes, evidence of a defect in perception or recollection may be proven (1) by cross-examination of the witness being impeached or (2) through the introduction of extrinsic evidence. When proof is by extrinsic evidence, courts are likely to limit the introduction of extrinsic evidence to defects in perception or recollection that interfere with the witness's ability to perceive or remember only the events at issue in the case. For example, a trial judge is unlikely to admit evidence that the witness could not remember her niece's birthday simply to prove that the witness has a bad memory; on those facts, the witness's lack of recollection will likely be deemed "collateral" and excluded. But if the witness testified that she saw the defendant leaving the bank that was robbed on the way back from her niece's birthday party on a specific day that other evidence showed to be incorrect, the witness's lack of recollection of the niece's birthday may be a central issue in the case and hence not "collateral." What is collateral depends on the context.

3. *Character for Untruthfulness*

When trying to attack a witness's credibility, the fact that the witness has lied in the past might be useful in trying to persuade a jury not to believe the witness's testimony now. What if the witness has lied twice? Five times? Ten? What if the witness has lied so many times that people who know the witness have formed the opinion that this person is a liar? What if the witness's reputation as a liar precedes him? Can such a history of lying show that the witness has a propensity for lying and thus is more likely to be lying right now?

We discussed propensity evidence in Chapter Three and learned that propensity evidence regarding a person's character in general or particular trait of character is excluded except in certain circumstances carefully delineated by the rules of evidence. Here, however, we are dealing with a witness's character for truthfulness or untruthfulness (sometimes called character for truth and veracity) as it bears on whether the witness is likely to be telling the truth while testifying. Is that type of propensity evidence allowed under the FRE?

It is.

> **FRE 404. Character Evidence; Other Crimes, Wrongs, or Acts**
>
> **(a) Character Evidence.**
>
> **(3)** ***Exceptions for a Witness.*** Evidence of a witness's character may be admitted under Rules 607, 608, and 609.

Why do the Federal Rules of Evidence allow parties to introduce evidence of a witness's propensity for lying or telling the truth? There appear to be two reasons. First and foremost, there is widespread support for the notion, in pop culture slang, that "liars gonna lie." In other words, a person's willingness to bend the truth in one context is probative of his or her willingness to do so again, and this propensity is useful in assessing whether to believe that person as a witness. Second, and relatedly, there is a widespread view that jurors are capable of distinguishing between the propensity to lie or tell the truth (which people encounter every day in dealing with each other) on the one hand, and the propensity to engage in other types of conduct, such as propensity for violence (which people are less likely to encounter regularly), on the other.

Together, FRE 404(a)(3), FRE 607, FRE 608, and FRE 609 set forth the prerequisites for the use of evidence of character to prove truthfulness as well as the permissible methods for proving such character.

(a) Prerequisites

Consider the following examples.

Examples

1. Defendant is charged with animal mistreatment. Prosecutor calls one of Defendant's coworkers, and the coworker testifies that, in his opinion, Defendant is a liar. Defendant does not testify at trial. This is inadmissible because Defendant's character for truthfulness is not an issue in the case given that Defendant is not a witness, and the crime at issue has nothing to do with honesty or lack thereof.
2. Plaintiff sues Defendant in a probate dispute over what the testator meant in her will. Plaintiff testifies to what the testator said. Then Plaintiff calls four witnesses to testify that, in their opinion, Plaintiff has a character for telling the truth. These four witnesses' testimony is inadmissible because Plaintiff's character for truthfulness has not yet been attacked.

These examples highlight the two main prerequisites to the introduction of character evidence for truthfulness.

First and foremost, this type of character evidence is relevant only as to a person who is a *witness.* For these purposes, as with other forms of impeachment evidence, a person is a witness if (1) she testifies at trial or (2) her out-of-court statement is introduced for its truth. FRE 806. If a person is not a witness, her character for truthfulness is simply not relevant to the issue of *credibility.*

Second, and just as important, the Federal Rules of Evidence insist that a witness's *character for truthfulness* be *attacked* before it may be rehabilitated. Under this rule, known as the "bad before good" rule,[4] it is not enough that the witness is impeached; the impeachment must be through an attack on the witness's character for truthfulness. The purpose of the rule is efficiency: Without it, parties would be tempted to lard their cases with character testimony extolling the truthfulness of their witnesses as part of their cases-in-chief. This rule is codified in FRE 608:

FRE 608. A Witness's Character for Truthfulness or Untruthfulness

(a) Reputation or Opinion Evidence. A witness's credibility may be attacked or supported by testimony about the witness's reputation for having a character for truthfulness or untruthfulness, or by testimony in the form of an opinion about that character. But evidence of truthful character is admissible only after the witness's character for truthfulness has been attacked.

4. California's Evidence Code has the same "good before bad" rule for evidence of a witness's character for truth and veracity. Cal. Evid. Code § 790. However, the California Constitution overrides that provision in criminal cases. Cal. Const., art. I, § 28(f)(2); *People v. Harris,* 47 Cal. 3d 1047, 1081 (N.Y. 1989).

Because we are discussing impeachment, and only character evidence for *untruthfulness* is impeaching, the "bad before good" rule places no limits on *impeachment.* However, it places significant limits on *rehabilitation* and begs the question: When is a witness's character for truthfulness attacked in a way that allows for rehabilitation with positive character evidence? We will discuss that topic in the section on rehabilitation.

(b) How Is Character for Untruthfulness to Be Proven?

As discussed more fully in Chapter Three, there are three ways that a person's character or pertinent trait of character may be proven: (1) reputation evidence, (2) opinion evidence, and (3) specific instances.

(i) Reputation evidence

As FRE 608(a) states, a party may impeach a witness by introducing evidence of that witness's reputation in the community for untruthfulness. Impeachment by reputation is almost always done with extrinsic evidence—namely, through the testimony of someone who can attest to the witness's reputation for untruthfulness. The chief prerequisite for such reputation testimony is the witness's familiarity with the community.

Example

Defendant is charged with fraud. Prosecutor calls one of the victims to the stand to testify about the representations that Defendant made about the art investment program that Prosecutor is alleging was fraudulent. Defendant calls as a witness one of the victim's neighbors, who testifies that the victim has a reputation in the neighborhood for lying. This testimony is impeachment through the introduction of evidence of the witness's bad reputation evidence for lying.

(ii) Opinion evidence

As FRE 608(a) also states, a party may impeach a witness by introducing evidence of the personal opinions of others that the witness is an untruthful person.[5] Impeachment by opinion is generally done through extrinsic evidence—namely, by calling those other individuals to offer their opinions on the witness's lack of candor. The foundation for opinion testimony is discussed more fully in Chapter Twelve. As applied to character witnesses, the primary foundation is establishing the character witness's familiarity with the witness that would provide a basis for his or her opinion.

5. Some states, like Florida and New York, do not permit opinion evidence. *See* Fl. Stat. § 90.609; *People v. Hanley*, 5 N.Y.3d 108, 112 (N.Y. 2005).

Example

Defendant is charged with fraud. Prosecutor calls one of the victims to the stand to testify about the representations that Defendant made about the art investment program that Prosecutor is alleging was fraudulent. Defendant calls as a witness one of the victim's neighbors, who testifies that, based on knowing the victim for three years, it is her opinion that the victim has the character for untruthfulness. This testimony is impeachment through the introduction of opinion evidence of character.

(iii) Evidence of specific instances of untruthfulness

FRE 608(b) addresses when a witness's character may be impeached by inquiring into specific instances in which the witness has previously exhibited their character for untruthfulness.

FRE 608. A Witness's Character for Truthfulness or Untruthfulness

(b) Specific Instances of Conduct. Except for a criminal conviction under Rule 609, extrinsic evidence is not admissible to prove specific instances of a witness's conduct in order to attack or support the witness's character for truthfulness. But the court may, on cross-examination, allow them to be inquired into if they are probative of the character for truthfulness or untruthfulness of:

(1) the witness; or

(2) another witness whose character the witness being cross-examined has testified about.

By testifying on another matter, a witness does not waive any privilege against self-incrimination that relates only to the witness's character for truthfulness.

As FRE 608(b) makes clear, the general rule is that a party seeking to impeach a witness by demonstrating the witness's character for untruthfulness cannot do so by presenting evidence of the specific instances in the past where the witness has been untruthful.[6] Why does the general rule prohibit specific instance evidence?

6. In California, the Truth-In-Evidence provision of the California Constitution allows parties to a criminal prosecution to introduce specific instances notwithstanding California's "no specific instances" rule set forth in California Evidence Code section 787. Cal. Const., art. I, § 28(f)(2); *People v. Dalton*, 7 Cal. 5th 166, 214 (Cal. 2019). New York also allows for impeachment with specific instances of prior conduct bearing on credibility. *People v. Smith*, 27 N.Y.3d 652, 660, 662 (N.Y. 2016).

The answer is because it is time consuming. Not only might there be *a lot* of prior specific instances of lying for some people, but also the time needed to prove each one is likely to be substantial because it includes the time necessary to prove what the witness said as well as to prove why that statement was untrue. There are two exceptions to this general rule, discussed next.

(A) Eliciting specific instances on cross-examination

(I) Regarding the witness being impeached

During the cross-examination of the witness to be impeached, a party may ask that witness about specific instances of the witness's conduct that demonstrate the witness's character for untruthfulness.

Example

Plaintiff sues Defendant for breach of contract. Defendant testifies that he delivered the appliances as required by the contract and says he has no idea why Plaintiff does not have those appliances in its inventory. On cross-examination of Defendant, Plaintiff asks, "Didn't you tell the same 'I delivered it' story the last time you were sued and found liable for breach of contract?"

Because a character witness is also a witness whose credibility is at issue, a party may also ask a character witness about specific instances of the character witness's conduct to demonstrate that the character witness has a character for untruthfulness and is not to be believed.

Example

Defendant is charged with car theft. Prosecutor calls Witness A as an eyewitness. The defense, in response, calls Witness B. Witness B testifies that (1) he has known Witness A for five years, and his opinion is that Witness A is a habitual liar; and (2) Witness A has the reputation in the community for being a habitual liar. On cross-examination of Witness B, Prosecutor asks, "Didn't you lie to your child that you weren't her father for the first 10 years of her life?"

Critically, however, the party asking that question is stuck with whatever answer the witness gives in response. That is because the party cannot introduce extrinsic evidence to prove that the witness's answer was incorrect because such evidence would violate FRE 608(b)'s general prohibition of extrinsic evidence.

(II) Regarding another witness

During cross-examination of the character witness called to offer reputation or opinion evidence about some other witness, a party may ask the character witness about specific instances of the *other witness's* conduct that demonstrate that (1) the character witness's opinion of the other witness's character for truthfulness is flawed or (2) the character witness's knowledge of the other witness's reputation for truthfulness is lacking.

Example

Plaintiff sues Defendant for the dangerous condition of his property, where Plaintiff fell and was injured. Plaintiff calls an eyewitness to the incident, and the eyewitness testifies that Plaintiff fell into a deep recess that was definitely located on Defendant's side of the property line. After Defendant calls the eyewitness's former spouse to testify to her opinion that the eyewitness has a character for being untruthful, Plaintiff then calls the eyewitness's best friend to testify to his opinion that the eyewitness has the character for truthfulness and that he has a good reputation for truthfulness in the community. On cross-examination of the best friend, Defendant might ask the best friend, "Were you aware of [the eyewitness's] prior conviction for perjury?" Or Defendant might ask the best friend, "Didn't you move away from Defendant's community five years ago?" The first question is aimed at impeaching the best friend's opinion that the eyewitness is a truthful person, the second at impeaching the best friend's testimony that he was well acquainted with the eyewitness's reputation in the local community. Are these questions allowed?

Michelson v. United States, 335 U.S. 469 (1948), explains the scope of such questioning. Michelson was on trial for bribing a federal revenue agent. Michelson testified that he had passed money to the agent, but claimed he was entrapped. After Michelson's character was attacked during his cross-examination, he called five character witnesses to testify that he had a good reputation for being truthful.

Michelson v. United States

335 U.S. 469 (1948)

JUSTICE JACKSON delivered the opinion of the Court.

On cross-examination, four of the witnesses were asked, in substance, this question: "Did you ever hear that Mr. Michelson on March 4, 1927, was convicted of a violation of the trademark law in New York City in regard to watches?" This referred to the twenty-year-old conviction about which defendant himself had testified on direct examination. Two of them had heard of it and two had not.

To four of these witnesses the prosecution also addressed the question the allowance of which, over defendant's objection, is claimed to be reversible error:

> "Did you ever hear that on October 11, 1920, the defendant, Solomon Michelson, was arrested for receiving stolen goods?"

None of the witnesses appears to have heard of this.

When the defendant elects to initiate a character inquiry, another anomalous rule comes into play. Not only is he permitted to call witnesses to testify from hearsay, but indeed such a witness is not allowed to base his testimony on anything but hearsay. What commonly is called "character evidence" is only such when "character" is employed as a synonym for "reputation." The witness may not testify about defendant's specific acts or courses of conduct or his possession of a particular disposition or of benign mental and moral traits; nor can he testify that his own acquaintance, observation, and knowledge of defendant leads to his own independent opinion that defendant possesses a good general or specific character, inconsistent with commission of acts charged. The witness is, however, allowed to summarize what he has heard in the community, although much of it may have been said by persons less qualified to judge than himself. The evidence which the law permits is not as to the personality of defendant but only as to the shadow his daily life has cast in his neighborhood. This has been well described in a different connection as "the slow growth of months and years, the resultant picture of forgotten incidents, passing events, habitual and daily conduct, presumably honest because disinterested, and safer to be trusted because prone to suspect. . . . It is for that reason that such general repute is permitted to be proven. It sums up a multitude of trivial details. It compacts into the brief phrase of a verdict the teaching of many incidents and the conduct of years. It is the average intelligence drawing its conclusion." Finch, J., in *Badger* v. *Badger*, 88 N. Y. 546, 552.

However, the witness must qualify to give an opinion by showing such acquaintance with the defendant, the community in which he has lived and the circles in which he has moved, as to speak with authority of the terms in which generally he is regarded. To require affirmative knowledge of the reputation may seem inconsistent with the latitude given to the witness to testify when all he can say of the reputation is that he has "heard nothing against defendant." This is permitted upon assumption that, if no ill is reported of one, his reputation must be good. But this answer is accepted only from a witness whose knowledge of defendant's habitat and surroundings is intimate enough so that his failure to hear of any relevant ill repute is an assurance that no ugly rumors were about.

Thus the law extends helpful but illogical options to a defendant. Experience taught a necessity that they be counterweighted with equally illogical conditions to keep the advantage from becoming an unfair and unreasonable one. The price a defendant must pay for attempting to prove his good name is to throw open the entire subject which the law has kept closed for his benefit and to make himself vulnerable where the law otherwise shields him. The prosecution may pursue the inquiry with contradictory witnesses to show that damaging rumors, whether or not well-grounded, were afloat—for it is not the man that he is, but the name that he has which is put in issue. Another hazard is that his own witness is subject to cross-examination as to the contents and extent of the hearsay on which he bases his conclusions, and he may be required to disclose rumors and reports that are current even if they do not affect his own conclusion. It may test the sufficiency of his knowledge by asking what stories were circulating concerning events, such as one's arrest, about which people normally comment and speculate. Thus, while the law gives defendant the option to show as a fact that his reputation reflects a life and habit incompatible with commission of the offense charged, it subjects his proof to tests of credibility designed to prevent him from profiting by a mere parade of partisans.

The *form* of cross-examination by specific instances depends on the type of character evidence offered:

- When a character witness testifies to his or her *opinion* of the other witness's character for truthfulness, the validity of that opinion can be tested on cross-examination by the question, "Did you know about [the specific instance that undermines the opinion]?" *E.g., United States v. Hough,* 803 F.3d 1181, 1191 (11th Cir. 2015).
- When a character witness testifies to the other witness's *reputation* for truthfulness, the validity of that reputation can be tested on cross-examination by the question, "Have you heard about [the specific instance that undermines the opinion]?" *E.g., Michelson.*

Before these questions may be asked, the questioner must have a "good faith" basis for believing that the specific instance at issue is, in fact, true. *E.g., United States v. Guay,* 108 F.3d 545, 552 (4th Cir. 1997). For example, before a party can on cross-examination ask a character witness "Did you know that the defendant perjured himself 20 times?" the party must have a good faith basis for believing that fact to be true. Otherwise, a questioner could do untold damage by suggesting misconduct by the person whose character is at issue that is entirely untrue.

Once again, the questioner is stuck with whatever answer the character witness gives; the questioner cannot introduce extrinsic evidence to prove that the answer is wrong. As it turns out, however, that is unlikely to matter, as the following example illustrates.

Example

Defendant is charged with making a criminal threat. Defendant testifies and denies making the threat. After Defendant's character is impeached by a prior perjury conviction, Defendant calls three character witnesses who testify to their opinions that Defendant is a truthful person. On cross-examination of each of those witnesses, Prosecutor asks, "Did you know that Defendant has cheated on his taxes for the last 10 years?" Prosecutor does not really care how they answer. If they answer "no," it shows that their opinion is not a well-informed one. If they answer "yes" Prosecutor will then ask: "Would it change your opinion if you knew [the specific instance that undermines the opinion]?" If they answer "No" and still maintain that Defendant has a good reputation for truth, the jury is likely to infer that the witnesses' opinions of "truthfulness" are not worth much. Indeed, the significant impact of being able to ask such questions reaffirms why it is critical that the questioner have a good faith basis to believe that Defendant did, in fact, cheat on his taxes for 10 years before being permitted to ask that question.[7]

The rules governing when specific instances can be used on cross-examination provide the following:

Type of Impeachment	Allowed?
Cross-examining a witness (including a character witness)	Can ask about prior falsehoods by that witness (FRE 608(b))
Cross-examining character witness called regarding opinion of other witness's truthfulness	Can ask about whether character witness would have same opinion if they knew of prior falsehood (FRE 608(b))
Cross-examining character witness called regarding reputation of other witness for truthfulness	Can ask about familiarity of specific instances of falsehood by other witness to establish problems with reputation evidence (FRE 608(b))
Proving up specific instance of lying if witness denies falsehood during cross-examination	No (FRE 608(b))
Note: There must be a good faith basis for asking about prior instances.	

(B) Introducing extrinsic evidence of felony convictions

As FRE 608(b) indicates, specific instances of conduct bearing on character for truthfulness or untruthfulness may not be proven by extrinsic evidence with one exception—namely, "criminal conviction[s] under [FRE] 609."

The exception allowing for the use of felony convictions to impeach exists for two reasons. The first is historical. The common law allowed for such use, although the common law courts were not of one mind as to whether it applied to convictions for *every* felony or just the subset of felonies reflecting a lack of truthfulness (such as perjury, fraud, and the like). The second is logical. A person who has been convicted of a crime is less likely to be law-abiding overall and hence less likely to put much stock in being under oath while testifying. The split among the

7. This example deals with how to impeach a witness relevant to a witness *character for truthfulness*. As discussed in Chapter Three, character witnesses may also be called to testify about character traits other than truthfulness; on cross-examination, those witnesses may be asked about specific instances under FRE 405(b).

common law approach spawned a vigorous debate in Congress regarding which felony convictions could be used to impeach. Unlike many states that have adopted approaches that vest trial judges with a vast amount of discretion to use in deciding whether to allow felony convictions for impeachment on a case-by-case basis,[8] Congress with FRE 609 opted to instead prescribe specific rules for trial judges to use in deciding whether to allow felony convictions for impeachment in several explicitly enumerated factual scenarios.

FRE 609. Impeachment by Evidence of a Criminal Conviction

(a) In General. The following rules apply to attacking a witness's character for truthfulness by evidence of a criminal conviction:

(1) for a crime that, in the convicting jurisdiction, was punishable by death or by imprisonment for more than one year, the evidence:

(A) must be admitted, subject to Rule 403, in a civil case or in a criminal case in which the witness is not a defendant; and

(B) must be admitted in a criminal case in which the witness is a defendant, if the probative value of the evidence outweighs its prejudicial effect to that defendant; and

(2) for any crime regardless of the punishment, the evidence must be admitted if the court can readily determine that establishing the elements of the crime required proving—or the witness's admitting—a dishonest act or false statement.

---

8. For instance, in civil cases, California allows extrinsic evidence of prior felony convictions to impeach a witness if the felony involved a crime of moral turpitude (that is, a "readiness to do evil" rather than a regulatory crime), *People v. Anderson*, 5 Cal. 5th 372, 407 (Cal. 2018); and in criminal cases, California allows extrinsic evidence of prior felony convictions or misdemeanor conduct to impeach a witness if the conviction rests on a crime involving moral turpitude or the conduct involves moral turpitude. In all instances, admission of a qualifying conviction or conduct is still subject to a FRE 403–like balancing that looks to how directly the underlying crime or conduct speaks to honesty and veracity, the age of the prior conviction or conduct, its similarity to the charged crime, and whether admitting the prior conviction or conduct would discourage a criminal defendant from testifying. Cal. Evid. Code § 788; *People v. Castro*, 38 Cal. 3d 301, 306 (Cal. 1985); *People v. Beagle*, 6 Cal. 3d 441, 453 (Cal. 1972).

Other states also take a more flexible approach. Florida admits any felony conviction and any conviction for a crime "involv[ing] dishonesty or a false statement" unless the conviction is "so remote in time as to have no bearing on the present character of the witness." Fl. Stat. § 90.610(1). Texas and Illinois allow for admission of any felony conviction or any conviction for a crime "involv[ing] moral turpitude" but only if it is less than 10 years old and if its probative value outweighs its prejudicial effect. Tex. R. Evid. 609(a), (b); Ill. R. Evid. 609. New York also grants a trial judge discretion as to which prior convictions to admit for impeachment purposes. *People v. Sandoval*, 34 N.Y.2d 371, 376-78 (N.Y. 1974).

(b) Limit on Using the Evidence After 10 Years. This subdivision (b) applies if more than 10 years have passed since the witness's conviction or release from confinement for it, whichever is later. Evidence of the conviction is admissible only if:

(1) its probative value, supported by specific facts and circumstances, substantially outweighs its prejudicial effect; and

(2) the proponent gives an adverse party reasonable written notice of the intent to use it so that the party has a fair opportunity to contest its use.

(c) Effect of a Pardon, Annulment, or Certificate of Rehabilitation. Evidence of a conviction is not admissible if:

(1) the conviction has been the subject of a pardon, annulment, certificate of rehabilitation, or other equivalent procedure based on a finding that the person has been rehabilitated, and the person has not been convicted of a later crime punishable by death or by imprisonment for more than one year; or

(2) the conviction has been the subject of a pardon, annulment, or other equivalent procedure based on a finding of innocence.

(d) Juvenile Adjudications. Evidence of a juvenile adjudication is admissible under this rule only if:

(1) it is offered in a criminal case;

(2) the adjudication was of a witness other than the defendant;

(3) an adult's conviction for that offense would be admissible to attack the adult's credibility; and

(4) admitting the evidence is necessary to fairly determine guilt or innocence.

(e) Pendency of an Appeal. A conviction that satisfies this rule is admissible even if an appeal is pending. Evidence of the pendency is also admissible.

As the text of FRE 609 makes clear, the standard to apply in deciding whether to admit a conviction for impeachment purposes is a function of various criteria:

- The nature of the prior conviction, including:
  - The severity of the conviction (that is, whether it is a felony or a misdemeanor); and
  - The nature of the crime (that is, whether the elements of that crime require proof of a dishonest act or false statement);
- Who is to be impeached with the conviction (that is, whether it is the defendant in a criminal case or someone else);
- The age of the prior conviction; and
- Whether the "conviction" is a criminal conviction (either after a jury trial ending in a verdict of guilt or after a plea) entered against an adult or whether it is an adjudication of guilt against a minor in the juvenile courts.

Rather than try to explain what FRE 609's various standards are *all at once*, it may be helpful to start with the most relevant criteria—the nature of the prior conviction and the identity of the person being impeached. Although the identity of the person being impeached is fairly straightforward (is it the defendant or is it some other witness?), the nature of the prior conviction warrants further discussion. As noted above, the nature of the prior conviction is a function of two considerations: (1) the severity of the conviction (felony versus misdemeanor) and (2) the nature of the underlying crime.

- *The nature of the conviction — severity.* FRE 609(a)(1) looks to whether the conviction was for a crime that "was punishable by death or by imprisonment for more than one year." Note that the key here is the *maximum punishment* for the crime (that is, what was "punishable by") rather than the punishment *actually imposed.* Under federal law and most state laws, a crime punishable by more than one year in custody is classified as a "felony." 18 U.S.C. § 3559(a)(5). Crimes punishable by one year or less are considered "misdemeanors." *Id.* § 3559(a)(6).
- *The nature of the conviction — nature of the crime.* FRE 609(a)(2) looks to whether the elements of the crime of conviction "require" proof of "a dishonest act or false statement." Under this definition, it is not enough that the crime in some way *involved* dishonesty or a false statement; to qualify, a dishonest act or false statement must be *an element* of that crime. The elements underlying a particular crime of conviction can be found by looking at the elements set forth in the statute defining that crime. Certain crimes by definition require proof of these elements, including perjury, subordination of perjury, making a false statement, criminal fraud, embezzlement, and obtaining property by false pretenses. Yet there are other crimes that can be committed in two or more ways, only some of which require proof of a dishonest act or false statement.[9] For such crimes, it is important to ascertain whether the crime underlying the witness's conviction has these elements. It may be necessary to look at the elements of proof required in the witness's specific case by examining (1) the elements set forth in the charging document (indictment or information) in the defendant's case, (2) the jury instructions used to define the elements in the defendant's case, (3) any pertinent recitation in the judgment of conviction, or, as to a plea, (4) the factual basis for that plea or the recitation of elements given during the plea colloquy.

Taking just these two considerations into account, FRE 609 requires a trial judge to apply the varying standards set forth below:

9. For example, if a defendant's prior conviction is for "theft" and the statute defining theft lists three types of theft — (1) by exerting unauthorized control over property, (2) by obtaining property by deception, or (3) by obtaining property by threat — only the second type involves a dishonest act or false statement, so whether this prior conviction requires proof of a dishonest act or false statement depends on the precise variant of theft of which the defendant was convicted.

Nature of Crime	To Impeach Any Witness Who Is Not a Criminal Defendant	To Impeach a Criminal Defendant
Crime requiring "proof" of "dishonest act or false statement"—felony *or* misdemeanor	Always admissible (no FRE 403 balancing allowed)	Always admissible (no FRE 403 balancing allowed)
Any crime designated as a *felony* that does *not* require proof of a "dishonest act or false statement"	Admissible unless party opposing impeachment shows, under FRE 403, that probative value is substantially outweighed by prejudicial effect	Inadmissible unless prosecutor shows probative value outweighs prejudicial effect
Any crime designated as a *misdemeanor* that does *not* require proof of a "dishonest act or false statement"	Inadmissible	Inadmissible

The next criterion that must be accounted for is the age of the prior conviction. FRE 609(b) looks to whether "more than 10 years have passed since the witness's conviction or release from confinement for it, whichever is later." Applying this criteria requires the trial judge to know two things: (1) when does the 10-year clock *start* ticking and (2) when does that clock *stop* ticking? The rule itself largely answers the first question: The clock starts ticking on the "later" of the date of conviction or the "release from confinement" on that conviction. What if a defendant is released, placed on parole or probation, and subsequently ordered back into custody for violating that parole or probation? Here, there are arguably two dates of "release from confinement." Which is the start date? The general rule is that the clock starts ticking on the date of the *latest* release. *E.g., United States v. McClintock,* 748 F.2d 1278, 1289 (9th Cir. 1984).

The second question as to when the clock stops ticking is *not* answered by the rule. There could be several different stopping points: when the defendant is formally charged by indictment or information (or when the civil plaintiff files his or her complaint), when the trial begins, when the witness to be impeached takes the stand, or when that witness's impeachment begins. The majority rule appears to be the date that trial begins, *United States v. Rogers,* 542 F.3d 197, 201 (7th Cir. 2008); *United States v. Hans,* 738 F.2d 88, 93 (3d Cir. 1984), although some courts look to when the witness takes the stand, *United States v. Pettiford,* 238 F.R.D. 33, 37 (D.D.C. 2006). When a conviction is subject to the more stringent test that applies when "more than 10 years have passed" since the date of conviction or latest release, a trial judge is required to apply that test no matter what the nature of the conviction and no matter whether it was suffered by a criminal defendant or some other witness.

Adding the age-of-conviction consideration to the mix yields the following chart:

<table>
<tr><th>Nature of Crime</th><th>To Impeach Any Witness Who Is Not a Criminal Defendant</th><th>To Impeach a Criminal Defendant</th></tr>
<tr><td>Crime requiring “proof” of “dishonest act or false statement”—felony or misdemeanor</td><td>Always admissible (no FRE 403 balancing allowed)</td><td>Always admissible (no FRE 403 balancing allowed)</td></tr>
<tr><td>Any crime designated as a felony that does not require proof of a “dishonest act or false statement”</td><td>Admissible unless party opposing impeachment shows, under FRE 403, that probative value is substantially outweighed by prejudicial effect</td><td>Inadmissible unless prosecutor shows probative value outweighs prejudicial effect</td></tr>
<tr><td colspan="3">EXCEPT:
(1) If conviction is more than 10 years old, inadmissible unless opponent shows probative value substantially outweighs prejudicial effect, no matter who the witness is.</td></tr>
<tr><td>Any crime designated as a misdemeanor that does not require proof of a “dishonest act or false statement”</td><td>Inadmissible</td><td>Inadmissible</td></tr>
</table>

The final factor to consider is whether the prior conviction is one sustained when the witness was an adult or instead one sustained when the witness was a juvenile; for juveniles, such “convictions” are called “adjudications” to reflect the more rehabilitative focus of the juvenile justice courts. This consideration trumps all the others.

Weaving in this final consideration yields the following table that accounts for *all* of FRE 609's criteria:

Nature of Crime	To Impeach a Witness Who Is Not a Criminal Defendant	To Impeach a Criminal Defendant
Crime requiring “proof” of “dishonest act or false statement”—felony *or* misdemeanor	Always admissible (no FRE 403 balancing allowed)	Always admissible (no FRE 403 balancing allowed)
Any crime designated as a *felony* that does *not* require proof of a “dishonest act or false statement”	Admissible unless party opposing impeachment shows, under FRE 403, that probative value is substantially outweighed by prejudicial effect	Inadmissible unless prosecutor shows probative value outweighs prejudicial effect

<table>
<tr><th>Nature of Crime</th><th>To Impeach a Witness Who Is Not a Criminal Defendant</th><th>To Impeach a Criminal Defendant</th></tr>
<tr><td colspan="3">EXCEPT:
(1) If conviction is more than 10 years old, inadmissible unless opponent of the evidence shows probative value substantially outweighs prejudicial effect, no matter who the witness is.
(2) If conviction is a "juvenile adjudication":</td></tr>
<tr><td></td><td>Inadmissible unless necessary to fairly determine innocence or guilt</td><td>Inadmissible</td></tr>
<tr><td>Any crime designated as a misdemeanor that does not require proof of a "dishonest act or false statement"</td><td>Inadmissible</td><td>Inadmissible</td></tr>
</table>

Most of these standards call on the trial court to balance the probative value of the conviction against its prejudicial effect. Where they vary is in how they strike the balance. But how is the probative value of a conviction used for impeachment to be assessed? The criteria used by FRE 609 give us a hint. Even for convictions that are less than 10 years old, a conviction that is just one year old is more probative than a conviction that is eight years old because people can change, and more recent behavior is likely more probative of the witness's current character. Along similar lines, a felony not requiring proof of a dishonest act or false statement that nevertheless involves conduct that is deceitful is more likely to be probative of the witness's truthfulness than a felony involving the use of brute force. And how is the prejudicial effect of a conviction used for impeachment to be assessed? The general worry here is the spillover effect. If a defendant is charged with bank robbery in the current case and the prior conviction used to impeach is also for bank robbery, a jury's temptation to use the prior conviction as evidence of the defendant's propensity to commit bank robberies (rather than his propensity to lie) is much greater than if the prior conviction were for making a criminal threat. Along similar lines, if a defendant is charged with battery but the prior conviction is for sexual assault, the relatively greater severity of the prior conviction might eclipse the relatively minor nature of the current charge and prompt a jury to convict the defendant merely because he is a "really bad guy" rather than based on the evidence presented.

FRE 609 calls on courts to balance these considerations differently, depending on the criteria outlined above. The following table lists the different balances in order from "always inadmissible" to "always admissible."

Conditions	Applicable Test	Net Effect
Juvenile adjudication of testifying defendant in a criminal case	NOT ADMISSIBLE	Mandates exclusion
Adult misdemeanor conviction, when the elements of the crime do not require proof of a dishonest act or false statement	NOT ADMISSIBLE	Mandates exclusion
Juvenile adjudication of any witness other than testifying defendant in a criminal case	Admissible only if adjudication "is necessary to fairly determine guilt or innocence"	Very strongly favors exclusion
Adult conviction with more than 10 years between last date of release and date of trial/testimony	Admissible only if "probative value" of conviction "substantially outweighs its prejudicial effect" and if proper notice is given (reverse FRE 403 test)	Strongly favors exclusion
Adult felony conviction in last 10 years of testifying defendant in a criminal case, when the elements of the crime do not require proof of a dishonest act or false statement	Admissible only if "probative value" of conviction "outweighs its prejudicial effect" and if proper notice is given (diluted reverse FRE 403 test)	Slightly favors exclusion
Adult felony conviction in last 10 years of any witness other than testifying defendant in a criminal case, when the elements of the crime do not require proof of a dishonest act or false statement	Admissible unless "probative value" of conviction is "substantially outweighed" by the danger of unfair prejudice (regular FRE 403 test)	Strongly favors admission
Adult conviction (felony or misdemeanor) in last 10 years of any witness when the elements of the crime require proof of dishonest act or false statement	MUST BE ADMITTED (without any FRE 403 balancing)	Mandates admission

So if a party is allowed to introduce a witness's conviction for impeachment, what facts are admitted? In almost every case, courts allow the admission of (1) the date of the prior conviction and (2) whether the conviction is for a felony or a misdemeanor. Whether to also admit the nature of the crime (for example, burglary, murder, perjury) is a function of balancing the probative value of that additional information against its prejudicial effect under FRE 403. *E.g., United States v. Howell*, 285 F.3d 1263, 1270 (10th Cir. 2002). If, for instance, the prior conviction is for the same crime as the crime charged, there is a greater danger that the jury might impermissibly treat the prior conviction as propensity evidence, which weighs against admitting that information. The process of editing out the nature of the crime is sometimes called "sanitizing" the conviction.

United States v. Gomez

772 F. Supp. 2d 1185 (C.D. Cal. 2011)

SNYDER, Judge.

For the purpose of attacking the credibility of a witness, Rule 609(a)(1) permits the introduction of "evidence that an accused has been convicted of [a crime punishable by death or imprisonment in excess of one year] . . . if the court determines that the probative value of admitting this evidence outweighs its prejudicial effect to the accused." Fed. R. Evid. 609(a)(1). Rule 609(b) places a presumptive time limit on the admissibility of the prior conviction if "a period of more than ten years has elapsed since the date of the conviction or of the release of the witness from the confinement imposed for that conviction, whichever is the later date." Fed. R. Evid. 609(b).

Here, defendant's conviction for conspiracy to distribute methamphetamine was a felony punishable by imprisonment in excess of one year. In addition, it appears that defendant was released from confinement on December 4, 2004, within ten years of the instant case. Accordingly, the prior conviction is not presumptively remote pursuant to Fed. R. Evid. 609(b). The Court finds, however, that in light of defendant's two more recent 2006 convictions for methamphetamine possession consistent with personal use, the impeachment value of the 1997 felony conviction for conspiracy to possess with intent to distribute is slight. Furthermore, given the nature of the 1997 felony, which bears an identical name to the charged offense in this case, the risk of prejudice to defendant is high. The Court recognizes, however, that if defendant testifies his credibility will be in issue and the 1997 conviction has some impeachment value. Accordingly, if defendant testifies, the Court is inclined to permit the government to cross-examine defendant about his 1997 felony conviction. To mitigate the risk of prejudice to defendant, the Court will "sanitize" the conviction and not allow the government to introduce evidence regarding the nature of the felony for which defendant was convicted—conspiracy to possess with intent to distribute methamphetamine.

Courts almost never admit the criminal conduct underlying the prior conviction. The fact that the conviction is in the midst of being challenged on appeal may be admitted, but it does not preclude use of that conviction to impeach. FRE 609(e).

The ability to use a prior conviction as impeachment evidence does not necessarily last forever. Presidents and governors have the power to issue pardons or to annul convictions, and many states allow convicted persons to apply for certificates of rehabilitation that, if granted, relieve many of the burdens of having a prior conviction on one's record. If a person has received any of these forms of executive clemency, the conviction at issue cannot be used to impeach that person as a witness (1) if the clemency was "based on a finding of innocence" or, (2) if the clemency was based on some other ground, the person has not subsequently been convicted of a felony. FRE 609(c).

Challenging a trial court's ruling to allow a conviction to be used to impeach a witness can be tricky, particularly when the witness to be impeached is the defendant in a criminal case. In *Luce v. United States,* 469 U.S. 38 (1984), the Supreme Court held that a criminal defendant could not challenge a trial court's pretrial ruling to permit impeachment with some of the defendant's prior convictions unless the defendant actually took the stand; if the defendant did not testify, he could not complain about the pretrial ruling—even if that ruling quite understandably influenced his decision not to testify. In *Ohler v. United States,* 529 U.S. 753 (2000), the Supreme Court held that a defendant who elected to testify despite a pretrial ruling permitting impeachment with his prior convictions lost the ability to challenge that ruling if he admitted to those convictions during his direct examination in order to "take the sting" out of them being elicited for the first time during cross-examination.[10]

4. *Demeanor*

When a witness testifies, the witness may through words and appearance come across to the trier of fact as more or less believable. May the jury or judge consider the witness's demeanor while testifying to impeach him or consider evidence of a declarant's demeanor at the time a declarant made an out-of-court statement admitted for its truth? The answer is "yes, it can." *E.g., Edmunds v. Deppisch,* 313 F.3d 997, 999 (7th Cir. 2002) ("Evidence concerning witnesses' demeanor, whether on or off the stand, is routinely admitted to establish that a witness is lying . . ."); *United States v. Salim,* 664 F. Supp. 682, 692 (E.D.N.Y. 1987) (same). But demeanor evidence is not *inevitably* admissible, and courts often question the probative value of a person's affect while speaking. In *Edmunds,* for example, a nanny charged with murdering the seven-month-old baby in her care sought to introduce evidence that the baby's parents seemed unexpectedly calm upon hearing that the baby had been violently shaken, which the nanny wanted to use to prove that the parents may have been responsible for the baby's death. The nanny also testified in her defense. Thus, *Edmunds* examined the impact of demeanor evidence for out-of-court declarants as well as a testifying witness.

---

10. Not all states follow *Ohler.* In California, a defendant's decision to "front" his conviction during his direct examination does not forfeit the issue on appeal. *People v. Turner,* 50 Cal. 3d 668, 704-05 (Cal. 1990).

Edmunds v. Deppisch

313 F.3d 997 (7th Cir. 2002)

POSNER, Judge.

The excluded evidence was evidence that would have been given by three witnesses: (1) the helicopter pilot who brought Natalie to the hospital, who saw the parents a few minutes after he arrived walking normally in the parking lot of the hospital, appearing neither distraught nor emotional, and later speaking with an "odd" lack of panic in their voices; (2) a police officer who talked to the parents toward evening, and observed that the father seemed "nervous" and "fidgety"; and (3) a chaplain who met with the parents twice during the afternoon, and who thought they displayed "a guarded demeanor, showing very limited expression of grief," which was not what he would have expected in the circumstances; he also thought that the father had seemed afraid to enter Natalie's hospital room, and he observed that in the hospital room the father stood a few feet behind his wife with his hands in his pockets and then left the room while his wife remained. The trial judge excluded all this evidence on the ground that "absent someone who has the expertise to interpret reactions, I don't think the observations have any probative value."

The validity of the inferences drawn from demeanor evidence in these settings has been questioned. As Olin Guy Wellborn III, "Demeanor," 76 *Cornell L. Rev.* 1075 (1991), bluntly puts it, summarizing empirical studies: "According to the empirical evidence, ordinary people cannot make effective use of demeanor in deciding whether to believe a witness." Yet it would be an unreasonable curtailment of a criminal defendant's constitutional right to put on a defense for a judge to forbid the defendant's lawyer to draw attention to aspects of demeanor that the lawyer thought undermined an adverse witness's testimony. We cannot find a case on the point, but perhaps only because the suggestion is too outre to have been litigated. The demeanor evidence at issue in this case, however, is of a different character. It presupposes a benchmark consisting of "normal" behavior in the face of a shocking incident. Is it true that a "normal" (and innocent) father in the situation of Natalie's father would have strode unhesitatingly into Natalie's hospital room? Would not have kept his hands in his pocket? Would have walked at an abnormal pace in the parking lot? Would have had panic in his voice yet would have been neither nervous nor fidgety? Maybe so; but these propositions, and the others necessary to show that one or both parents manifested lack of grief and consciousness of guilt, are not so obvious that a judge who like Olin Wellborn thought them devoid of probative value could be thought unreasonable, though again we cannot find a case on the point, let alone a U.S. Supreme Court case—which cannot however help Edmunds.

The trial judge's assessment of Edmunds' demeanor under cross-examination had a somewhat solider basis in common experience: "The cross-examination of the defendant [Edmunds] was devastating to the defense. The transition from a confident, comfortable, organized witness on direct examination to a halting, uncomfortable, insecure witness on cross-examination was remarkable. The tone of voice, the body language (i.e. looking pleadingly toward her counsel before answering questions), the pace of the answers changed dramatically from the presumably well-prepared direct to the not totally predictable cross by a very skilled prosecutor." Indeed the cross-examination brought out significant contradictions between Edmunds' trial testimony and the statement she had given the police a few days after Natalie's death. For example, she had told the police (according to one of the officers who had interviewed her) that on the fatal morning, until shortly before Natalie's collapse, Natalie had been "tracking" Edmunds—that is, had been making eye contact with her, as babies instinctively do. This would have been unlikely behavior for a severely neurologically damaged baby, and at trial Edmunds denied that Natalie had been tracking. Her testimony was further undermined by such implausible statements as that she had loved Natalie as much as she loved her own children, even though Natalie was a fussy and difficult baby who had been in Edmunds' care for only 17 days before the child's death.

Although this book discusses these four types of general impeachment separately in order to explain their differing contours, it is critical to remember that—in the real world—the same prior act may constitute more than one form of impeachment evidence and may also be admissible as substantive evidence. In such cases, one must examine the admissibility of the evidence under each doctrine and, at the same time, be cognizant that admitting the evidence under one doctrine may have a prejudicial effect on its admission overall.

Example: "The Trifecta"

Defendant was previously convicted of fraud. The fraud related to specific misrepresentations that Defendant made regarding the value of securities traded on the stock exchange. Defendant is now charged with fraud for making misrepresentations about the value of a different type of securities. Defendant testifies in her defense. At trial, Prosecutor seeks (1) to admit Defendant's prior fraud conviction, (2) to ask Defendant, on cross-examination, about the specific misrepresentations she made as part of the prior fraud scheme, and (3) to introduce evidence regarding the prior fraud scheme as a whole. These different items of evidence are likely admissible under three different evidence rules. FRE 609 governs the admission of Defendant's prior fraud conviction as a prior conviction involving a "dishonest act or false statement" bearing on Defendant's character for untruthfulness. FRE 608(b) governs the right of Prosecutor to ask Defendant, on cross-examination, about specific instances showing her character for untruthfulness. And FRE 404(b) governs the right of Prosecutor to introduce the details of the prior scheme to prove Defendant's common scheme or plan, her intent, or her absence of mistake.

This example illustrates the importance of examining a single piece of evidence through the prism of the various purposes for which it might be admitted and the applicable rules for each purpose.

Review Questions

1. **Gang motives.** Defendant is charged with a gang-related shooting. Prosecutor calls an eyewitness. On cross-examination, Defendant asks the eyewitness if her cousin had been killed by members of the same gang to which Defendant belongs.
   a. What type of impeachment evidence does this question attempt to elicit? Is it a permissible question?
   b. If the eyewitness answers "no," can Defendant introduce extrinsic evidence by calling the eyewitness's mother to explain that the cousin had been killed by members of Defendant's gang?
2. **Drugged up.** Defendant is charged with carjacking. Prosecutor calls the victim to identify Defendant. During cross-examination of the victim, Defendant asks, "Were you on opioids when you saw Defendant?"
   a. What type of impeachment evidence does this question attempt to elicit? Is it a permissible question?
   b. If the victim answers "no," can Defendant call the police officer who recovered the carjacked car to testify that it contained several empty bottles of prescription opioids with the victim's name on them?
3. **Testifying felon.** Defendant is charged with fraud. In her case-in-chief, Prosecutor seeks to introduce evidence of Defendant's prior conviction for perjury. Is this evidence permissible?
4. **Jilted lovers.** Defendant is charged with bank robbery. Prosecutor calls a bank teller to identify Defendant as one of the robbers. On cross-examination, Defendant asks the teller, "Isn't Defendant your ex-boyfriend?"
   a. What type of impeachment evidence does this question attempt to elicit? Is it a permissible question?
   b. After the teller answers, "Yes, but we broke up on good terms," Prosecutor seeks to call character witnesses to opine on the teller's character for truthfulness. Is this testimony allowed?
5. **Honest witness?** Plaintiff sues Defendant for breach of an oral contract. After Plaintiff testifies to the promises Defendant made, Defendant introduces Plaintiff's prior conviction for embezzlement.
   a. What type of impeachment does this evidence attempt to establish? Is it permissible?
   b. Assume that the trial judge admits the conviction. Plaintiff then calls his spouse to testify to her opinion that Plaintiff is a truthful person. Is this testimony permissible?
6. **Thieving officer.** Plaintiff sues Defendant for breach of fiduciary duty for embezzling money while acting as an officer of Plaintiff's business. Defendant testifies that all the transactions underlying the alleged embezzlement were approved by Plaintiff in advance. Plaintiff seeks to introduce Defendant's prior conviction for driving while under the influence. What standard applies in evaluating whether to admit this conviction in each of the following situations?

a. The conviction is actually a juvenile adjudication Defendant suffered when he was 17.
b. The trial is in 2022, the conviction was entered in 2008, and Defendant was released from custody in 2013.
c. The trial is in 2022, and the conviction was entered in 2017.

7. **Chat room confession.** Defendant is charged with child molestation. Prosecutor introduces evidence of Defendant's admission in a dark-web chat room that he molested a family member. Defendant seeks to introduce evidence that he was joking when he was in the chat room. Is this evidence permissible?
8. **Childhood friends.** A witness is on the stand for Plaintiff. On cross-examination, Defendant asks the witness, "Plaintiff is your cousin, right? And you two grew up together, spent summers together?" Is this questioning permissible?
9. **Parental pressure.** A witness is on the stand for the prosecution. On cross-examination, Defendant asks the witness, "Now you've testified that my client was the person who threatened you. But you didn't identify him the first time you spoke with police. In fact, you didn't come forward with his identity until the child welfare services department told you that you might lose custody of your kids, isn't that true?" Is this questioning permissible?
10. **Convicted pals.** A witness is on the stand for Defendant in a criminal case. On cross-examination, Prosecutor asks, "You've known defendant for years now, haven't you? In fact, you two were both convicted of carjacking in 2012, weren't you?" Is this questioning permissible?
11. **Paroled witness.** A witness is on the stand for the prosecution. On cross-examination, Defendant asks, "You're currently on parole, aren't you?" Is this questioning permissible?
12. **Motive to lie?** A witness is on the stand for Defendant in a criminal case. On cross-examination, Prosecutor asks, "You know this case was investigated by the Los Angeles Police Department, right? Didn't you sue the same department for violating your civil rights?" Is this questioning permissible?
13. **Financial motive?** A witness is on the stand for Plaintiff in a theft of trade secrets case. On cross-examination, Defendant asks, "You have a 20 percent interest in plaintiff's company, don't you?" Is this questioning permissible?

PART B: SPECIFIC IMPEACHMENT

Aside from general attacks about the witness himself—including the witness's credibility stemming from his bias or motive to testify, his ability to perceive or recall, his character for untruthfulness, or his demeanor while speaking—a party can also level more specific attacks on the content of a witness's testimony regarding the case by showing that (1) the witness has previously said something *inconsistent* with his testimony or (2) other evidence contradicts the witness's testimony.

1. *Prior Inconsistent Statements*

The witness who has made internally inconsistent statements is less believable than one who has been consistent in her story all along. A bystander testifies that the light was red for the defendant. Is that bystander's testimony more likely—or less likely—to be believed if the bystander told the police officer who responded to the accident that the light was green for the defendant? The bystander is less likely to be believable because we presume that the truth is a constant that does not change over time. Thus, introduction of the bystander's prior inconsistent statement is admissible to impeach her subsequent testimony.

As discussed in Chapter Six, a witness's prior inconsistent statement is admissible *for its truth* if the prior statement meets the requirements to fit within the hearsay exception. However, a prior inconsistent statement is separately admissible *to impeach*—that is, whether or not it fits within the hearsay exception. Impeachment is meant to show that the witness is not telling the truth; showing that the witness has said inconsistent things about the same fact makes her less believable no matter which of the two inconsistent statements is true. A witness confronted with inconsistent statements might be asked, "Were you lying then, or are you lying now?" For purposes of assessing her credibility, it does not matter *which* was the lie.

There are three (and possibly four) main prerequisites for introducing the prior inconsistent statement of a witness:

1. The witness's prior statement must be inconsistent.
2. The inconsistency must be relevant to something beyond merely showing a contradiction; in other words, the subject of the inconsistent statement cannot be *collateral.*
3. Admission of the prior inconsistent statement is not barred by some other doctrine or policy, within or without the Federal Rules of Evidence.
4. *If the witness is testifying (rather than a hearsay declarant whose statement is being admitted at trial),* the witness must be given an opportunity to explain or deny the prior inconsistent statement.

(a) Inconsistency

The inconsistency of a prior statement is easy to ascertain when the prior statement is an *affirmative* statement. For instance, if the witness testifies at trial that "the light was green for plaintiff," a prior statement that "the light was red for plaintiff" is obviously inconsistent.

Inconsistency is more difficult to assess when:

- *The prior statement was an omission.* If the witness, in the prior statement, did not include a fact that her testimony now includes, is the prior omission of that fact inconsistent? The answer is "yes," at least if, under the circumstances, the omitted fact would have likely been included in the prior statement if it had been true. For example, if the plaintiff in an auto accident case calls a bystander who testifies at trial that she saw the defendant get out of his car swaying and stumbling in a way that indicated that he was intoxicated, the bystander's failure to include those observations in her statement to the responding police officers at the scene would likely be deemed a prior inconsistent statement because most people would expect a bystander to tell the police officers about the intoxication of one of the two people involved in a car crash.

Treating silence as a prior inconsistent statement is potentially more problematic when the witness is a criminal defendant who was silent at the time of his arrest. The Supreme Court has held that a suspect's silence prior to arrest as well as silence after arrest but before receiving *Miranda* warnings can be used to impeach the suspect if he later testifies as a defendant at the trial and testifies to facts that he might have reasonably been expected to tell police officers at the time prior to arrest or after arrest but prior to receiving *Miranda* warnings. *Jenkins v. Anderson*, 447 U.S. 231 (1980) (prearrest silence may be used to impeach); *Fletcher v. Weir*, 455 U.S. 603 (1982) (postarrest, pre-*Miranda* silence). However, once a suspect has been advised of his *Miranda* rights, his post-*Miranda* silence cannot be used to impeach him. *Doyle v. Ohio*, 426 U.S. 610 (1976). The *Doyle* rule is based on the Due Process Clause's concern with fairness: Once a suspect is told he has a right to remain silent, it is unfair to later use that silence to impeach him. These rules regarding the use of silence as a prior inconsistent statement *when used to impeach* are different from the rules, discussed in Chapter Six, regarding the use of silence as a prior inconsistent statement *when used as substantive evidence of guilt.*

- *The witness's testimony is that she does not remember.* If the witness made a prior statement to others regarding what a party said or did, but when called as a witness at trial says he cannot remember what happened, is the witness's prior statement inconsistent with his testimony? This issues arises most often with victims of domestic violence or witnesses fearing retaliation from neighborhood gangs. The Supreme Court has suggested that a failure to remember is inconsistent with a prior statement evincing the witness's knowledge and ability to remember. *California v. Green*, 399 U.S. 149, 164 (1970); *see also United States v. Owens*, 484 U.S. 554, 561-62 (1988) (applying this rule in the context of a prior identification).[11]

Example

Defendant is charged with a gang-related shooting in the home territory of Defendant's gang. Prosecutor calls one of the neighborhood's residents, who told the police who responded to the shooting that he saw a red Camaro with

11. Some jurisdictions, such as Illinois, follow the federal approach. *People v. Leonard*, 391 Ill. App. 3d 926, 933 (Ill. Ct. App. 2009); *People v. Flores*, 128 Ill. 2d 66, 87-88 (Ill. 1989). Other jurisdictions, such as California, Florida, and Texas, will not treat a witness's testimony that he cannot remember as inconsistent unless the lack of memory is feigned and constitutes a "deliberate evasion" of the witness's duty to testify truthfully. *People v. Green*, 3 Cal. 3d 981, 988-89 (Cal. 1971); *James v. State*, 765 So. 2d 763, 766 (Fla. 2000); *Sanchez v. State*, 2005 Tex. App. LEXIS 2176, *8 (Tex. Ct. App. 2005).

a skull and crossbones painted on the hood speed away immediately after the victim collapsed on the sidewalk. (Defendant owns just such a car.) During the direct examination of the resident, the resident testifies that he cannot remember the color or markings on the car that left the scene, that he was in his backyard at the time, and that he only caught a momentary glimpse through his fence. Prosecutor asks the resident if he is afraid of Defendant's gang, and the resident answers, "Who wouldn't be?" On this showing, the trial judge would likely be within her discretion to find that the resident's lack of memory was feigned and therefore admit his prior inconsistent statement for impeachment purposes.

(b) Not "Collateral"

To qualify as a prior inconsistent statement admissible to impeach, the subject matter of the inconsistency must pertain to some fact at issue in the controversy.

Examples

1. Plaintiff sues Defendant for injuries sustained in an auto accident. Plaintiff calls a bystander as a witness, who testifies, "Defendant ran the red light." Defendant can introduce evidence that the bystander told a responding police officer, "Plaintiff ran the red light" because which party entered the intersection unlawfully is central to the lawsuit (and hence is not "collateral").
2. Plaintiff sues Defendant for injuries sustained in an auto accident. Plaintiff calls a bystander as a witness, who testifies that Defendant was at fault and that it was at least 80°F at the time of the accident. Defendant cannot introduce evidence that the bystander previously told the responding officer that it was a "chilly 65°F" at the time of the accident. That is because although the bystander made inconsistent statements about the weather, that inconsistency has no bearing on what happened or who was at fault.
3. Plaintiff sues Defendant for injuries sustained in an auto accident. Plaintiff calls a bystander as a witness, who testifies that the light was green for Plaintiff and that Plaintiff was wearing a green dress. Defendant seeks to introduce evidence that the bystander told a responding officer that Plaintiff was wearing a red dress, arguing that it shows Plaintiff's red-green color blindness. Although the color of Plaintiff's clothing is collateral, the inconsistency—if tied to color blindness—might impeach the bystander's ability to perceive colors properly, which could impeach the bystander's testimony about the color of the traffic light.

The "collateral" requirement is an outgrowth of FRE 403: Inconsistencies have minimal probative value and also consume a lot of time when they are not pertinent to issues that affect the events being adjudicated at trial.

(c) Not Barred by Another Policy

Some prior statements are inadmissible for *any* purpose, including when admitted only as a prior inconsistent statement for impeachment purposes. Such statements include the following:

- *Statements obtained under a grant of immunity.* When a witness is granted immunity and compelled to answer questions pursuant to that grant, the resulting statements are compelled within the meaning of the Fifth Amendment's privilege against self-incrimination and cannot be used to impeach the witness. *New Jersey v. Portash*, 440 U.S. 450, 459-60 (1979).
- *Statements found to be involuntary.* When a witness's statement or confession is found to be "involuntary" within the meaning of the Due Process Clause, that statement cannot be used to impeach the witness. *Mincey v. Arizona*, 437 U.S. 385, 398-401 (1978). For example, if a trial court finds that a defendant's confession to a murder is involuntary because the police threatened to shoot the defendant in the head if he did not confess, it would be manifestly unfair to treat such an untrustworthy statement as inconsistent with that defendant's subsequent testimony denying any involvement with the killing.
- *Statements rendered inadmissible by the special rules of relevance. See* Chapter Four.

(d) If the Witness Is Testifying at Trial, the Opportunity to Explain or Deny the Prior Inconsistent Statement

As noted above, the "witnesses" who may be impeached—and hence whose prior inconsistent statements may be used for impeachment—include (1) persons who testify at trial and (2) persons whose out-of-court statements are admitted for their truth. FRE 613 sets forth the procedural requirements for admitting prior inconsistent statements to impeach.

FRE 613. Witness's Prior Statement

(a) Showing or Disclosing the Statement During Examination. When examining a witness about the witness's prior statement, a party need not show it or disclose its contents to the witness. But the party must, on request, show it or disclose its contents to an adverse party's attorney.

(b) Extrinsic Evidence of a Prior Inconsistent Statement. Extrinsic evidence of a witness's prior inconsistent statement is admissible only if the witness is given an opportunity to explain or deny the statement and an adverse party is given an opportunity to examine the witness about it, or if justice so requires. This subdivision (b) does not apply to an opposing party's statement under Rule 801(d)(2).

FRE 613 provides that, when the witness to be impeached with a prior inconsistent statement is testifying at the hearing:

- The party impeaching the witness must show or disclose the contents of the statement to the adverse party's attorney, if that attorney requests.
- The witness must be given an opportunity to explain or deny the statement, and the adverse party must be given an opportunity to examine the witness regarding the statement. This requirement is satisfied if (1) the extrinsic evidence is admitted *before* the witness testified or (2) the witness is subject to being recalled as a witness. This requirement does not apply when the witness impeached is the adverse party. Also, the trial judge retains the authority to dispense with this requirement "if justice so requires."
- The *witness* need not be shown the statement before being questioned about it.[12] (This requirement is designed to prevent the witness from having time in advance to think about how to reconcile her testimony with her prior inconsistent statement.)

These requirements do not apply to witnesses whose out-of-court statements are admitted for their truth. In pertinent part, FRE 806 provides that "[t]he court may admit evidence of the declarant's inconsistent statement or conduct, regardless of when it occurred or whether the declarant had an opportunity to explain or deny it."

As these requirements indicate, a prior inconsistent statement may be proven by (1) asking the witness about the statement while the witness is testifying or (2) admitting extrinsic evidence of that statement (by introducing a prior written statement or by calling a witness who can testify to what the witness previously stated). This rule is different than the rule regarding the admission of character evidence for truthfulness, for which specific instances are inadmissible except for prior convictions. See FRE 608(b). As this next case illustrates, sometimes the line between a prior inconsistent statement and character evidence can be a hazy one.

United States v. McGee

408 F.3d 966 (7th Cir. 2005)

BAUER, Judge.

[While in jail on this case prior to trial, defendant Smith called his employer and explained that he would not be at work because "a relative from out of state had been murdered and that [he] had to retrieve the [relative's] children." Smith subsequently bragged to his wife about his elaborate lie. During cross-examination at trial, Smith was asked, "do you [tell stories] to get out of a jam, to get out of a bind"? and responded that he did not. The prosecutor then played the jailhouse recording where he bragged to his wife about his lie.]

---

12. New York does not follow this rule and requires a party to show the statement or disclose its contents to the witness before examining her about it unless the witness is also a party. *Larkin v. Nassau Elec R.R. Co.*, 205 N.Y. 267, 269 (N.Y. 1912); *Blossom v. Barrett*, 37 N.Y. 434, 438 (N.Y. 1868). Florida empowers the adverse party to ask that the witness be shown a copy of the prior inconsistent statement. Fl. Stat. § 90.614(1).

Citing Rule 608(b) of the Federal Rules of Evidence, Smith asserts that the MCC tape was inadmissible extrinsic evidence of a specific instance of conduct bearing on his character for truthfulness. Smith argues that playing the tape devastated his credibility, and that the only remedy was a mistrial because Smith's defense rested on his credibility. In response, the government maintains that the tape was admissible extrinsic evidence of a prior inconsistent statement under Fed. R. Evid. 613. The government also notes that even if the tape was inadmissible extrinsic evidence, Rule 608(b) does not bar questioning about the conduct, and Smith eventually admitted that he told this story to his employer.

Although Rule 608(b) bars extrinsic evidence of specific instances of conduct bearing on a witness' character for truthfulness, the extrinsic evidence may still be admissible for another reason, such as impeachment for bias, contradiction, or prior inconsistent statement. *United States v. Abel* (1984). The government argues that the tape was admissible because it was extrinsic evidence of a prior inconsistent statement. Under Rule 613(b), extrinsic evidence of a witness' prior inconsistent statement is admissible as long as the witness is given an opportunity to explain the statement and opposing counsel is afforded an opportunity to question the witness about it.

In some instances, it is difficult to distinguish between Rule 608(b) evidence and Rule 613(b) evidence. In this case, however, the government's attempt to characterize the MCC tape as Rule 613(b) evidence is unconvincing and would amount to an end-run around Rule 608(b)'s bar on extrinsic evidence. The First Circuit's discussion in *United States v. Winchenbach*, 197 F.3d 548 (1st Cir. 1999) helps clarify the distinction between these rules and illustrates why the government's position is without merit:

> In our view, Rule 613(b) applies when two statements, one made at trial and one made previously, are irreconcilably at odds. In such an event, the cross-examiner is permitted to show the discrepancy by extrinsic evidence if necessary—not to demonstrate which of the two is true but, rather, to show that the two do not jibe (thus calling the declarant's credibility into question). In short, comparison and contradiction are the hallmarks of Rule 613(b). . . . In contrast, Rule 608(b) addresses situations in which a witness' prior activity, whether exemplified by conduct or by a statement, in and of itself casts significant doubt upon his veracity. . . . So viewed, Rule 608(b) applies to a statement, as long as the statement in and of itself stands as an independent means of impeachment without any need to compare it to contradictory trial testimony.

The force of the MCC phone call recording was not due to a comparison of Smith's statements on the tape and his equivocations at trial. Rather, Smith's elaborate lie to his supervisor, in and of itself, cast significant doubt on Smith's character for truthfulness. For this reason, the MCC tape falls squarely within the ambit of Rule 608(b), and it was error for the district court to allow the government to play the tape.

---

2. *Contradiction by Other Evidence*

A witness's believability is also harmed if her testimony or out-of-court statement is contradicted by other evidence. If, for instance, a witness's out-of-court statement (during her preliminary hearing testimony) is that the defendant charged with reckless driving sped through a red light at more than 100 miles per hour, video footage from a storefront camera that recorded the defendant's car traveling much more slowly when the light was green would call into question the witness's credibility.

The Federal Rules of Evidence do not speak directly to the admission of other evidence for purposes of contradicting and thereby impeaching a witness. There are, however, two main prerequisites for introducing other evidence to contradict a witness's testimony:

1. The other evidence must be relevant to something beyond merely showing a contradiction; in other words, the other evidence cannot be dealing with a subject that is *collateral.*
2. Admission of the contradictory evidence is not barred by some other doctrine or policy, within or without the Federal Rules of Evidence.

(a) Not "Collateral"

The primary prerequisite to the admission of other evidence to contradict a witness's testimony is that the fact to be contradicted not be collateral. Other evidence is collateral if it impeaches the witness on a point that "'itself is not relevant in the litigation to establish a fact of consequence, i.e., not relevant for a purpose other than mere contradiction of the in-court testimony of the witness.'" *United States v. Catalan-Roman,* 585 F.3d 453, 468-69 (1st Cir. 2009). The requirement that the impeachment not be collateral is grounded in FRE 403, on the theory that allowing a party to introduce evidence to impeach a witness on matters that do not go to the substance of the case takes up valuable time but does not help resolve the key issues in the case. *Id.*

Examples

1. Pam sues Jeremy in family court for dissolution of marriage. Pam testifies that the couple's lakefront home in Vermont is her separate property. Jeremy seeks to introduce the deed of trust for the home, which indicates that the couple own the home as "joint tenants and as community property." Here, the deed is evidence that contradicts Pam's testimony and is also not collateral because it is a central issue in the case. (The deed is also likely admissible as substantive evidence of how the home is owned.)
2. Pam sues Jeremy in family court for dissolution of marriage. Pam testifies that the couple's lakefront home in Vermont has six bedrooms and is her separate property. The value of the home is undisputed. Jeremy seeks to introduce the floor plans showing that the house has eight bedrooms. Here, the floor plans are evidence that contradicts Pam's testimony, but they are collateral because the layout of the house is relevant at most to valuation, which is not disputed in the case.

(b) Not Barred by Another Policy

At times, evidence that might contradict a witness's testimony or out-of-court statement is not admissible to impeach; other times, that evidence might be admissible to impeach, but not as part of the other party's case-in-chief.

Examples

1. Defendant is charged with a gang-related drive-by shooting. Defendant takes the stand and denies any affiliation with other members of the street gang at issue, which is an element of the gang enhancement in that case. Prosecutor seeks to introduce the statement of another gang member indicating that he and Defendant used to hang out all the time with other gang members. Another court found that the other gang member's statement was made involuntarily. Because that statement was involuntary, it cannot be used at all—even to impeach Defendant.
2. Defendant is charged with a gang-related drive-by shooting. Defendant takes the stand and denies ever possessing the gun used to shoot the victim. Prosecutor calls the police officer who executed a search warrant at Defendant's house to testify that he recovered the semiautomatic firearm that matched the bullet removed from the victim's body. The trial judge had previously suppressed the fruits of the search as obtained in violation of the Fourth Amendment. Although the items recovered in the search could not be used in Prosecutor's case-in-chief, it may be used to impeach Defendant.

Policies that prohibit evidence to be introduced for purposes of impeachment include the following:

- *Involuntary statements.* Statements determined to be involuntary under the Due Process Clause, as well as the fruits obtained from such statements, may not be used to contradict a witness's testimony.
- *Fourth Amendment violations.* Items seized in a search found to violate the Fourth Amendment may be used to contradict a defendant's testimony in a case, *Walder v. United States*, 347 U.S. 62, 65 (1954), but not to contradict *other defense witnesses, James v. Illinois*, 493 U.S. 307, 309 (1990). The distinction exists to preclude prosecutors from trying to put illegally seized evidence before the jury during the cross-examination of any and all defense witnesses.
- *Fifth and Sixth Amendment violations.* Items seized as fruits of statements obtained in violation of *Miranda v. Arizona*, 384 U.S. 436 (1963) (under the Fifth Amendment) and in violation of *Massiah v. United States*, 377 U.S. 201 (1964) (under the Sixth Amendment) may be used to impeach witnesses. *Harris v. New York*, 401 U.S. 222, 225 (1971) (statements obtained in violation of *Miranda*).

By definition, evidence introduced to contradict a witness is extrinsic evidence.

Review Questions

1. **Forgetful victim.** Defendant is charged with kidnapping. Prosecutor calls the victim, and the victim testifies that he does not remember what happened. Prosecutor seeks to call the police officer who interviewed the victim immediately after he was rescued, to relay what the victim had told him about the details of the kidnapping. Is the officer's testimony a proper form of impeachment?
2. **GTA.** Defendant is charged with grand theft auto. Prosecutor calls the victim, who testifies that he saw a person with a purple fedora get into his car and drive off and that, 20 minutes later, he later saw a person of the same height and stature wearing a purple fedora—whom he recognized as Defendant—walking back from the direction his car had been driven.
   a. Defendant seeks to introduce the victim's statement to police immediately after he reported the crime that the thief was wearing a grey fedora with a feather. May this statement be used to impeach the victim?
   b. Defendant seeks to introduce a photograph of himself taken immediately after his arrest, at which time Defendant was wearing a cowboy hat. Is this evidence admissible to impeach the victim?

PART C: REHABILITATING CREDIBILITY

Rehabilitating credibility refers to introducing evidence aimed at persuading the jury to find that a witness's testimony or out-of-court statement is worthy of belief. Just as a person is "rehabilitated" only after he is injured, evidence aimed at convincing the trier of fact to believe a witness is admissible only if the witness's credibility is attacked. The rule that rehabilitation follow impeachment is known as the "no bolstering" or "bad before good" rule. There are also prerequisites to specific types of rehabilitative evidence.

1. The "No Bolstering" or "Bad Before Good" Rule

We have discussed six different ways to attack a witness's credibility. Must a party wait for its witnesses to be attacked before trying to elicit evidence as to why those witnesses should be believed? The Federal Rules of Evidence only speak to that question with regard to character evidence: FRE 608(a), as noted above, provides that "evidence of truthful character is admissible only after the witness's charter for truthfulness has been attacked." But what about the other five types of impeachment evidence? Are they subject to the same "bad before good" rule?

The answer is "yes," and this answer is derived from the common law. Evidence that "enhance[s] a witness's credibility before that credibility is attacked . . . is inadmissible because it 'has the potential for extending the length of trials enormously, . . . asks the jury to take the witness's testimony on faith, . . . and may . . . reduce the care with which jurors listen for inconsistencies and other signs of falsehood or inaccuracy.'" *United States v. Lindemann*, 85 F.3d 1232, 1242 (7th Cir. 1996).

2. *Rehabilitating with Specific Types of Evidence*

(a) Prior Consistent Statements

A witness's prior consistent statements can be admitted for one of two purposes. First, and as discussed in Chapter Six, the prior consistent statement can be admitted *for its truth*—that is, as additional evidence that substantively corroborates the witness's in-court testimony or other out-of-court statement admitted for its truth. When admitted for the truth, the prior consistent statement must meet the requirements of FRE 801(d)(1)(B). Second, the prior consistent statement can be admitted solely to rehabilitate the witness's credibility and *not* as substantive evidence.[13]

When admitted solely for rehabilitation, the sole requirement is that the prior consistent statement (1) be responsive to the prior inconsistent statement previously admitted or (2) be aimed at negating an express or implied accusation that the witness has recently fabricated the testimony or acted from an improper influence or motive in testifying. When admitted solely to rehabilitate, courts generally believe there is no further timing requirement (that is, the prior consistent statement need not be made before the prior inconsistent statement or before the motive to fabricate arose).

A prior consistent statement may be proven (1) by a witness's testimony during redirect or (2) by extrinsic evidence.

(b) Character for Truthfulness

Evidence showing that a witness has a character for truthfulness may be admitted to rehabilitate the witness, but its admission is carefully regulated.

(i) Prerequisites

Separate from the general requirement that a witness's character be attacked before any rehabilitative evidence is admissible, FRE 608(a) conditions the admission of "evidence of truthful character" on whether "the witness's *character for truthfulness* has been attacked." This raises the question: Accusing a witness of having a bias is an attack on her character, but is that an "attack" on "the witness's character for truthfulness"? What about other attacks on credibility—such as attacking the

---

13. Some jurisdictions, such as California, have more stringent prerequisites to the admission of prior consistent statements—even when solely for purposes of rehabilitation. In California, a prior consistent statement is admissible to impeach only if it (1) was made *prior to* the prior inconsistent statement or (2) was made *prior to* when the witness is alleged to have developed a bias, motive to fabricate, or other improper motive. Cal. Evid. Code § 791.

witness's perception and recollection, confronting her with a prior inconsistent statement, or introducing conflicting evidence? Do *those* attacks constitute an attack on the witness's character? As the next case explains, the answer is generally "no."

United States v. Martinez

923 F.3d 806 (10th Cir. 2019)

HARTZ, Judge.

An advisory committee note clarifies what constitutes an attack on character for truthfulness:

> Opinion or reputation that the witness is untruthful specifically qualifies as an attack under the rule, and evidence of misconduct, including conviction of crime, and of corruption also fall within this category. Evidence of bias or interest does not. Whether evidence in the form of contradiction is an attack upon the character of the witness must depend upon the circumstances.

Fed. R. Evid. 608(a) Advisory Committee Notes to 1972 proposed rules. No firm line can be drawn regarding whether cross-examination of a witness amounts to an attack on the witness's character for truthfulness. But a useful test employed by the courts is whether the questioning attacks the veracity of the witness's account of the facts in the specific case before the court or attacks the witness's veracity in general. The Ninth Circuit expressed the point as follows:

> The purpose of Rule [608(a)] is to encourage direct attacks on a witness's veracity in the instant case and to discourage peripheral attacks on a witness's general character for truthfulness. To this end, the Rule prohibits rehabilitation by character evidence of truthfulness after direct attacks on a witness's veracity in the instant case. However, the Rule permits rehabilitation after indirect attacks on a witness's general character for truthfulness.

Some circumstances are easy to characterize. For example, impeachment of the witness through evidence of a prior felony conviction or prior fraudulent activity is not specific to the case being tried and amounts to an attack on character. In contrast, a cross-examination that focuses on the witness's memory or perception does not implicate character. Also, evidence of bias generally is not an attack on character. The fact that the witness is a party's mother may lessen her credibility in this case, but it does not mean that she is usually an untruthful person. And "most courts do not view contradiction of one witness's testimony by other witnesses as an attack on character."

Perhaps the most difficult questions arise when a witness has been vigorously cross-examined. "[A] slashing cross-examination can carry strong accusations of misconduct and bad character, which even the witness's forceful denial will not remove from the jury's mind." Those are situations in which our standard of review properly affords substantial discretion to the trial judge.

As *Martinez* explains, evidence of a person's character for truthfulness is only admissible if (1) the person is a witness and (2) that witness's *character for truthfulness* has been attacked.

(ii) How is character for truthfulness to be proven?

The rules governing the types of proof for a witness's character for truthfulness are the same as the rules applicable to a witness's character for untruthfulness: Character may be proven through extrinsic reputation or opinion evidence. FRE 608(b). (Although character for untruthfulness can also be proven by extrinsic evidence in the form of prior felony convictions, pursuant to FRE 609, convictions by their nature *impeach* credibility rather than *rehabilitate* it; thus, the types of permissible proof of character for truthfulness are not identical to the types of permissible proof of character for untruthfulness.)

(c) Other Types of Rehabilitative Evidence

What if a witness is attacked with an accusation of bias or motive to shade her testimony, her perception or recall is attacked, her demeanor is attacked, or other evidence is introduced to contradict her testimony? What can the opposing party do to rehabilitate that witness? Because "[t]he admissibility of [such] evidence . . . is not specifically addressed by the Rules, . . . [its] admissibility is limited only by the relevance standard" and the related considerations under FRE 403. *United States v. Lindemann*, 85 F.3d 1232, 1243 (7th Cir. 1996). Because such evidence is, by definition, responsive to impeachment evidence that has already been determined to be relevant and not collateral, the "no collateral evidence" rule is necessarily satisfied. And because these types of attacks may be proven by questioning on cross-examination or through extrinsic evidence, evidence aimed at rebutting a witness's bias, correcting the jury's assessment of her perception or recall, correcting the jury's perception of her demeanor, or undermining the other evidence that contradicted her testimony may also consist of questioning on redirect examination or extrinsic evidence.

Review Questions

1. **Swamp land in Florida.** Defendant is charged with fraud for operating a Ponzi scheme. Prosecutor calls one of Defendant's employees, who testifies that Defendant was aware that the "investment" that Defendant was selling was a sham. On cross-examination, Defendant asks the employee whether he is getting a plea deal for his testimony. Prosecutor's next witness is the employee's spouse.
   a. The spouse testifies that the employee had told her about Defendant's awareness of the fraudulent nature of the scheme the week before trial. Is this testimony admissible?
   b. The spouse testifies that, in her opinion, the employee has a good character for truthfulness. Is this testimony admissible?

   c. The spouse testifies to three separate occasions when the employee had the opportunity to keep money left in an abandoned wallet, but each time returned the wallet to its true owner. Is this testimony admissible?

2. **Bystander's integrity.** Defendant is charged with a carjacking. Prosecutor calls a bystander witness to the carjacking. On cross-examination, Defendant questions the bystander about his prior conviction for selling drugs, and the bystander admits the prior conviction.
   a. Prosecutor calls the bystander's college professor to testify that the bystander has a reputation around campus for being truthful. Is this testimony admissible?
   b. Prosecutor calls the bystander's college professor to testify about three instances when the bystander reported others cheating on their final exam. Is this testimony admissible?

PART D: FORBIDDEN ATTACKS

There are a few topics that are deemed off-limits as a basis for impeachment, except in very narrow circumstances. The Federal Rules of Evidence only expressly set forth one such basis explicitly, but other bases may be subject to exclusion under FRE 403. Also, state evidence codes may contain other verboten topics as well.

1. Religious Beliefs or Opinions

As a general matter, a witness's religious beliefs or opinions do not provide a basis for impeachment or rehabilitation.

FRE 610. Religious Beliefs or Opinions

Evidence of a witness's religious beliefs or opinions is not admissible to attack or support the witness's credibility.

The reason for making religion off-limits is straight-forward: One's religious beliefs should not have any effect on whether a person is telling the truth—or on whether the person is *viewed* as telling the truth. There are, however, situations in which one's religion may still be relevant:

- *Bias.* If a witness works for a particular religious institution that is a party to the litigation, that fact may be elicited to show bias.
- *Explaining the witness's behavior.* For instance, if a witness is responding to accusations that she is untruthful because she did not resist the defendant, who was an authority figure, the witness may be able to explain her passivity

by testifying that she adheres to a religion that teaches the need to defer to authority figures. *People v. King,* 183 Cal. App. 4th 1281, 1311-12 (Cal. Ct. App. 2010).

2. *Other Forbidden Topics*

In many jurisdictions, a witness's immigration status alone is not a basis for impeachment. *State v. Sanchez-Medina,* 231 N.J. 452, 461 (N.J. 2018); *Mischalski v. Ford Motor Co.,* 935 F. Supp. 203, 207-08 (E.D.N.Y. 1999) (immigration status "is not admissible for impeachment purposes"). Despite this general prohibition, however, there are still instances in which immigration status is relevant and hence admissible, such as to prove that a defendant's fear of deportation due to his immigration status was his motive for opening fire on officers pulling him over for a traffic violation. *E.g., People v. Casillas,* 65 Cal. App. 5th 135, 151-52 (Cal. Ct. App. 2021).

Test Your Understanding

To test your understanding of the material in this chapter, turn to the Supplement for additional practice problems.

CHAPTER 12

LAY AND EXPERT TESTIMONY

Not all witnesses provide the same type of testimony.

Factual Testimony

Some witnesses testify to fundamental facts. A police officer who responds to an auto accident may testify that the skid marks extended 35 feet back from the point of impact. A person suing for breach of contract may testify that, over a cup of coffee at Starbucks, the person he is suing agreed to sell him his mint condition copy of *Spiderman Issue 1*. Each of these witnesses is testifying to raw facts—that is, to what it is that they saw or heard or smelled or otherwise sensed, without any commentary or further explication. These witnesses are offering *factual testimony.*

Lay Opinion Testimony

Other witnesses provide testimony that goes beyond fundamental facts and encompasses the inferences that they draw from those facts. An eyewitness to an auto accident could testify that he saw the driver of the red car get out of the car, stumble three steps, sway back and forth five times, and then grab onto the roof of the car; or, the eyewitness can testify that the driver of that car "appeared to be drunk." A person who witnessed someone being beaten in an alleyway and identifies the defendant as the assailant could testify to the exact time of the beating, and a separate witness can testify to the time of sunset that date; or, the person can testify that the beating occurred "at twilight." Each of these witnesses is adding an inference over and above the building-block facts they observed. Critically, they did not use any specialized knowledge to draw those inferences. Any of us could have drawn the same inferences. These witnesses are offering *lay opinion testimony.*

Expert Testimony

Still other witnesses provide testimony that is based on their specialized knowledge that lies beyond the common experience of most people. A person who graduated from medical school and is licensed to practice medicine may testify about what protocols are typically followed by surgeons, that the surgery the defendant performed on the plaintiff did not adhere to those protocols, and that the partial paralysis that the plaintiff suffered is a highly likely consequence of the improperly performed surgical procedure. A police officer who has served for decades on a police force and trains others in the proper use of force may testify that the defendant officer's use of force was excessive. A forensic scientist may testify that the DNA recovered from the crime scene matches the defendant's DNA, as was the case in the criminal trial of O.J. Simpson, pictured here. These witnesses are testifying to matters grounded in their expertise and can testify to (1) the specialized knowledge they have and (2) how it specifically applies to the facts of this case (as adduced by other witnesses, documents, and physical evidence). These witnesses are offering *expert testimony.*

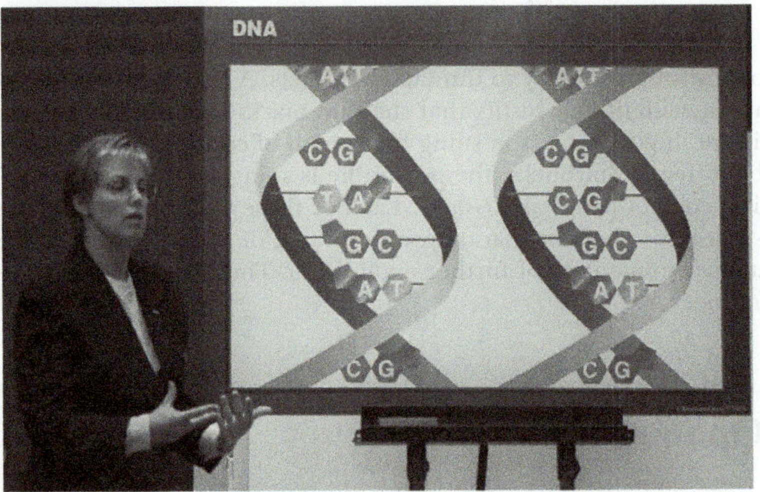

Thus, there are three types of witness testimony: factual testimony, lay opinion testimony, and expert testimony. However, for any given witness, their testimony may encompass one or more of these types:

Although judges and lawyers often refer to a particular witness as an "expert witness" or a "lay witness," a witness who offers opinion testimony can also be a fact witness. For instance, a plaintiff who sues a grocery store after she fell in the store might call a witness who testifies that he obtained a sample of the vinyl flooring from the defendant's store, performed tests on that flooring, calculated the coefficient of friction for that flooring when it is dry and when it is wet, and opines that the coefficient when the floor is wet does not meet federal safety standards. When this witness testifies to the testing he personally performed and observed, he is offering factual testimony and, if he draws inferences from what he observed, possibly lay opinion testimony. But when that witness testifies to the coefficient of friction he calculated, explains what a coefficient of friction is, and offers an opinion that the coefficient he calculated does not meet federal safety standards, he is offering expert testimony.

That the same witness can offer factual testimony as well as expert opinion testimony in the same trial is not without a downside. Jurors are often tempted to give the opinions of expert witnesses special weight due to their expertise, so there is a danger that jurors may also give that witness's *factual* testimony special weight even though it may be wholly unrelated to their expertise, which could skew the jury's weighing of competing factual testimony.

As the Advisory Committee Note to FRE 701 indicates, the rules "do[] not distinguish between expert and lay *witnesses*, but rather between expert and lay *testimony.*" As a result, when determining whether testimony meets the requirements of the rules of evidence, it is important to focus on each pertinent part of the witness's testimony rather than trying to fit the witness, as a whole, into a particular category.

Importantly, the Federal Rules of Evidence place special requirements on the admission of lay opinion testimony and expert testimony. What is more, those requirements are different. Thus, it is critical to ask the following questions:

(1) What is the nature of the nonfactual witness testimony that is being offered?
(2) Depending on whether it is lay opinion testimony or expert testimony, are the particular requirements for that type of testimony satisfied?

Importance of Accurately Evaluating Forensic Evidence

In learning about opinion evidence, especially expert forensic evidence, it is important to keep in mind the enormous impact such evidence can have on jurors. The misapplication of forensic science has contributed to 52 percent of wrongful convictions in Innocence Project cases in the United States.[1] Forensic evidence ranges from hair comparisons to arson analysis and bullet comparisons. As you will learn, the Federal Rules of Evidence attempt to provide a framework that allows for the use of new types of expertise, but that framework still requires that the expertise offered has some assurance of reliability before a trial judge will allow it to be considered by the trier of fact. Because jurors often place special weight on the opinions of experts as a result of their expertise, it is critical that the Federal Rules of Evidence be used in a manner that keeps unreliable expert methodologies—such as those underlying many of the wrongful convictions—out of a trial; doing so helps effectuate one of the fundamental purposes of the rules to "ascertain[] the truth and secur[e] a just determination" of guilt or innocence. FRE 102.

Lay Opinion Versus Expert Opinion

Part A of this chapter examines the prerequisites to lay opinion testimony—namely, that it must be based on the witness's personal knowledge, that it must be helpful to the jury, and that it must *not* be based on any specialized knowledge. These requirements are set forth in FRE 701 and FRE 602. Part B examines the special rules that apply to expert testimony, which encompass not only the background information regarding their expertise but also any opinions they offer on the basis of that expertise. These rules break down into three categories. First, the topic must be appropriate for expert testimony. Second, and even if it is a proper topic for expert testimony, this particular expert must be qualified to testify as an expert on the topic. Last, and even if the topic is proper and the expert is qualified, the substance of the expert's testimony must be grounded in a sufficient factual basis and a rational and applicable methodology. These requirements for expert testimony are set forth in FRE 702 through FRE 706.

PART A: LAY OPINION TESTIMONY [FRE 701 AND FRE 602]

When and why is it appropriate to allow percipient witnesses to testify to more than the facts that they see, hear, and otherwise observe? Assume, for instance, that a prosecutor calls a witness to say that the defendant was "angry" and "agitated" when talking with the witness about a dispute the defendant was having with his neighbor the day before that neighbor was viciously assaulted. The witness's observation that the defendant was "angry" and "agitated" is obviously an inference that the witness has drawn from observing the sum total of the defendant's tone of voice, the volume of his voice, his manner of speaking, his facial expression, and whether his skin tone was flush. Is it better to limit the witness's testimony just to

1. *See Overturning Wrongful Convictions Involving Misapplied Forensics,* https://innocenceproject.org/overturning-wrongful-convictions-involving-flawed-forensics (2021).

those specific observations, or is there some benefit to allowing the witness to share his overall perception with the jury (subject to having that perception explored during direct or cross-examination)?

At common law, witnesses were largely prohibited from offering their lay opinions on the theory that it was best for the jury to get the "raw data" unfiltered by the witness's observations. The Federal Rules of Evidence moved away from this common law rule, preferring instead to grant far greater leeway to the admission of such lay opinion testimony. The reason is simple: A witness's firsthand observations—even if based on the inferences drawn from more fundamental facts—can be very helpful to the trier of fact in its evaluation of the evidence. But the Federal Rules of Evidence did not give carte blanche permission to admit *all* such inferences. Instead, FRE 701—and, to a lesser extent, FRE 602—define the requirements for admitting lay opinion testimony.

FRE 701. Opinion Testimony by Lay Witnesses

If a witness is not testifying as an expert, testimony in the form of an opinion is limited to one that is:

(a) rationally based on the witness's perception;

(b) helpful to clearly understanding the witness's testimony or to determining a fact in issue; and

(c) not based on scientific, technical, or other specialized knowledge within the scope of Rule 702.

Each of FRE 701's three requirements is discussed separately.

1. Personal Knowledge

The requirement in FRE 701 that a lay opinion be "rationally based on the witness's perception" is a particularized application of the general rule set forth in FRE 602 requiring all witnesses—except expert witnesses—to have "personal knowledge of the matter."[2]

When there is a jury, the judge's job is to assess whether there is "sufficient" "evidence" "to support" a finding of personal knowledge; if there is, it is up to the jury to decide whether the witness *actually had* that personal knowledge. FRE 104(b). This requirement of personal knowledge is one of the main requirements that distinguishes lay opinion testimony from expert testimony.

---

2. FRE 602, Need for Personal Knowledge, provides: "A witness may testify to a matter only if evidence is introduced sufficient to support a finding that the witness has personal knowledge of the matter. Evidence to prove personal knowledge may consist of the witness's own testimony. This rule does not apply to a witness's expert testimony under [FRE] 703."

2. *Helpful to Understanding the Lay Witness's Testimony*

The line between purely factual observations and lay opinion based on inferences can be a fuzzy one, as the following examples illustrate.

Examples

1. Defendant is charged with the murder of his wife. Prosecutor calls a witness to testify that, moments before the witness heard a gunshot, he heard—through the apartment's walls—Defendant shouting, "I just wish you'd die!" As a purely factual matter, the volume at which a person is speaking is measured by decibels. The testimony that Defendant was "shouting" is a characterization of that volume, an inference that the witness has drawn. Is that testimony permissible? Yes, because it is helpful to give the jury context.
2. Defendant is charged with reckless driving. A pedestrian bystander testifies that Defendant's car "was going *way* faster than the posted 35 mph speed limit." Is this testimony permissible? Although the bystander did not have a radar gun, as long as he was familiar with how cars appear while traveling at the posted speed limit, this testimony is helpful to explain Defendant's speed, particularly if the witness is the sole unbiased witness on that issue.
3. Plaintiff sues Defendant for breach of contract. Plaintiff calls Defendant's former girlfriend, who testifies that Defendant told her about Plaintiff's pending lawsuit and denied any wrongdoing, but she had dated him long enough that she knew Defendant's telltale signs of lying and opines that he was lying when he denied any wrongdoing. Although a witness advising the jury whom to believe might appear helpful to the jury at first blush, most courts have for many years held that jurors are just as adept as any witness at assessing whether someone is to be believed, so such witness testimony is not generally deemed to be "helpful."

What the first two examples illustrate is that there are instances when the inferences a witness draws from his or her direct observations can be helpful. The third example illustrates that there are instances when, in the eyes of the law, it is *not* helpful.

As a general matter, the instances when a lay witness's opinion testimony is "helpful to clearly understand the witness's testimony or to determine a fact in issue" arise in two situations:

(1) When the lay opinion relates to facts that resist reduction down to their fundamental facts. Lay opinions falling into this category include:
- Relative size and weight (for example, "The robber was a tall guy" or "a big guy")
- Age (for example, "She looked like she was in her early teens")

- Distance (for example, "I'd say it was about a football field away from the accident")
- Color (for example, "She was wearing a light brown jacket")
- Similarity between two objects (for example, "The car that drove away from the bank looked like that 'Family Truckster' station wagon from the *Vacation* movies—you know, green with brown wood paneling")
- Relative light or darkness (for example, "It was just after the sun went down, so there was still a good amount of light")
- Odors (for example, "The room smelled like day-old chicken had been sitting on the counter")

(2) When the lay opinion relates to facts that *can* be reduced, but where the witness's inference adds value. Lay opinions falling into this category include:

- Emotional state (for example, "When I spoke with defendant that day, he seemed meek, remorseful")
- Overall impression (for example, "Oh, yeah, when he got out of his car, he was drunk, stumbling all over the place")

Conversely, a lay opinion is generally *not* helpful when ""the witness is no better suited than the jury"'" to opine on the issue, such that the opinion does little more than ""tell the jury what result to reach."'" *E.g., United States v. Meises,* 645 F.3d 5, 16 (1st Cir. 2011). A lay opinion is *not* helpful when it offers:

- An opinion on credibility (for example, "I've known the defendant for years, and when he told me about X, I knew that he was telling the truth"). *E.g., United States v. Beierle,* 810 F.3d 1193, 1204 n.2 (10th Cir. 2016); *United States v. Forrester,* 60 F.3d 62, 63 (2d Cir. 1995). However, some federal courts allow some lay witnesses to opine on the credibility of someone they know well if their opinion is based on more than "conclusory observation." *United States v. Cortez,* 935 F.2d 135, 139 (8th Cir. 1991)
- An opinion about someone else's state of mind (for example, "Based on what I assume that the defendant had heard, the defendant knew that the investment was destined to fail"). Such opinions are not helpful because they are necessarily speculative: How can Witness X really know what Witness Y was thinking? *E.g., United States v. Heine,* 2017 U.S. Dist. LEXIS 165367, *26-*27 (D. Or. 2017)

3. *Not "Based on Scientific, Technical, or Other Specialized Knowledge"*

The final requirement is that the lay opinion be the opinion of a *layperson*—not an expert. As discussed in Part B, expert opinion testimony is subjected to additional scrutiny under the Federal Rules. As a result, it is critical that testimony that is truly expert testimony not be erroneously admitted as lay opinion testimony. The subject matter of lay testimony should not be outside the "ken" of average people. As the Advisory Committee Notes explain, "lay [opinion] testimony 'results from a process of reasoning familiar in everyday life,' while expert testimony 'results from a process of reasoning which can be mastered only by specialists in the field.'"

The following examples illustrate this distinction.

Examples

1. Defendant is charged with fraud. Prosecutor calls a police officer who executed the search warrant at Defendant's house to testify.
   a. The officer testifies that she found hard copies of earlier drafts of the allegedly fraudulent documents and further states: "So I compared these earlier drafts to the final brochures and noticed that the brochures removed the language indicating the risk of the investment."
   b. The officer testifies that she found a computer at Defendant's house, imaged the hard drive, examined the "slack space" of the hard drive, and was able to reconstruct deleted files by matching the header data with the file data. She then compared the retrieved drafts with the brochure and found the same discrepancies.

   Example 1(a) is permissible lay opinion testimony because comparing one hard copy to another does not require any scientific, technical, or other specialized knowledge. However, Example 1(b) is not lay opinion testimony because the expertise it takes to reconstitute slack space on a computer is one that requires technical or specialized knowledge.

2. Defendant is charged with drug trafficking. Prosecutor calls the investigating officer on the case to testify.
   a. The officer testifies that he seized Defendant's diary, but it was written in an ink that could be viewed only when wearing a certain type of eyeglasses, and a pair of those eyeglasses was sitting atop the diary.
   b. The officer testifies that he seized Defendant's diary, but it was in code. However, he was able to apply an algorithm he learned in a few cryptography courses and decipher it.

   Example 2(a) is permissible lay opinion because it requires no specialized knowledge over and above simple codebreaking anyone could do. Example 2(b), however, relies on the officer's specialized knowledge.

3. In a will contest, the question is whether the will's drafter (the testator) was competent to change the will on December 25.
   a. The testator's niece, who is seeking to invalidate the will that leaves her nothing, testifies that she has known her uncle for 30 years, that she has visited him regularly over the years, and that the last time she saw him, on December 24, he seemed "out of it" (that is, "unaware of his surroundings" and "unaware of to whom he was talking").
   b. The testator's son, who stands to inherit everything under the new will, calls a psychologist who explains the telltale signs of competency

and that the testator exhibited each of those signs in the weeks leading up to signing the new will.

Example 3(a) is a permissible lay opinion because it rests on the niece's personal knowledge of how her uncle usually is and how he appeared to her on December 24. Example 3(b), however, relies on the witness's experience and specialized knowledge.

4. In a martial dissolution action, one major question is the value of the wife's business and the couple's residence.
   a. The wife testifies to the value of her business as well as to the value of the residence.
   b. The husband calls an economist, who testifies to the value of the wife's business and the value of the residence.

   Example 4(a) is permissible because the wife has personal knowledge of the value of her business and residence, and such opinions are historically permissible lay opinions. See Adv. Comm. Note to 2000 Amendment to FRE 701. Example 4(b) requires an expert.

5. Defendant is charged with drug trafficking. The long-time narcotics officer who arrested Defendant testifies.
   a. The officer testifies that, when she arrested Defendant, she recovered a baggie that contained several off-white, rock-like substances that appeared to be rock cocaine.
   b. The officer testifies regarding how rock cocaine is typically manufactured.

   Example 5(a) is permissible lay opinion because the officer has personal knowledge, based on her many years as a narcotics officer, identifying what drugs look like and the process of matching what she knows with what she saw (at least in terms of "off-white, rock-like" substances being rock cocaine); her testimony requires no specialized knowledge. Example 5(b) rests on the officer's specialized knowledge of chemistry; as such, she is in that respect offering expert testimony.

6. Plaintiff sues Defendant for medical malpractice.
   a. Defendant introduces Plaintiff's statement to Plaintiff's best friend, "I have had a herniated disc for the last five years."
   b. Defendant calls a doctor who reviews Plaintiff's medical records to testify that Plaintiff has a herniated disc.

   Example 6(a) is permissible lay opinion because people are knowledgeable about their own medical conditions, even though they were usually told about those conditions by someone else (typically, their physician). Example 6(b) is an expert opinion because it rests on the doctor's specialized medical knowledge.

7. Defendant is charged with murder, along with an allegation that the crime was committed for the benefit of a criminal street gang.

a. Prosecutor calls a narcotics detective to opine that, based on Defendant's prior admissions to the expert, Defendant is a member of the All Saints gang.

b. Prosecutor asks the same detective to opine that the All Saints gang meets the definition of a "criminal street gang" and that the murder in this case benefited the gang by resulting in the death of a rival gang member who was seeking to sell drugs in All Saints' territory.

Example 7(a) is a permissible lay opinion because it is based on the detective's personal knowledge of Defendant's admissions and rests on what Defendant said without the need to resort to any specialized knowledge. Example 7(b) rests on the detective's specialized knowledge about gang culture; in this respect, the detective is offering permissible expert testimony.

In part (a) of each example above, the witness's testimony was the product of a "process of reasoning familiar in everyday life" as applied to facts within the witness's personal knowledge. No "scientific, technical, or other specialized knowledge" was necessary to compare the words of one document to another; to put on a pair of glasses; to assess whether someone you know very well is not mentally sound; to value assets with which you are very familiar; to recognize that the off-white, rock-like substance you have seen several times before appeared to be rock cocaine; to relay your own medical conditions; or to repeat a party's self-admission of gang affiliation.

Review Questions

1. **Inebriation.** Defendant is charged with driving while under the influence. The arresting officer testifies that (a) Defendant's breath smelled of alcohol, (b) Defendant swayed when she got out of the car, (c) Defendant could not walk in a straight line when asked to do so, (d) Defendant could not recite the alphabet backwards, and (e) based on these observations, Defendant appeared to be under the influence. Which of these observations qualifies as lay opinion testimony? Which qualifies as factual testimony? Which qualifies as expert testimony?
2. **Mood opinion.** Plaintiff sues Defendant, a doctor, for negligent infliction of emotional distress, in misdiagnosing Plaintiff's mother. Defendant calls Plaintiff's roommate as a witness, and the roommate testifies that she spoke with Plaintiff right after Defendant is alleged to have wrongly told Plaintiff that Plaintiff's mother had inoperable cancer and that Plaintiff was in good spirits and taking the news in stride. Is this testimony a permissible lay opinion?

3. **Gait recognition.** Defendant is charged with felony murder for a shooting in the course of the robbery of a convenience store. Prosecutor calls Defendant's ex-girlfriend as a witness. The ex-girlfriend reviews the somewhat grainy surveillance video from the store and testifies, "Yeah, that's [Defendant]. It looks like him, and [Defendant] walks the same way." Is this testimony a permissible lay opinion?
4. **Age of a child victim.** Defendant is charged with committing lewd acts on a person under the age of 14:
   a. The officer who interviewed the victim testifies, "She looked to be 10 or 11."
   b. A pediatric nurse examines photographs of the victim and testifies, "Based on her stage of anatomical development, she was under the age of 12."

   Are these opinions regarding the victim's age admissible? As lay opinion testimony or as expert testimony?

PART B: EXPERT TESTIMONY [FRE 702 THROUGH FRE 706]

Expert witnesses are critical to our legal system. For example, if a person injured by a physician's negligent performance of a surgery sues the physician and goes to trial, he will in nearly every case need to call a physician in the pertinent medical discipline to testify about how the surgery should have been performed and why the defendant-physician's surgery did not meet that standard.

Experts are also commonplace in criminal cases:

- Medical experts, such as coroners, provide expert testimony on the cause of death.
- DNA experts provide expert testimony on DNA matches linking a defendant to DNA found at the scene of the crime.
- Fingerprint experts provide expert testimony on fingerprint matches.
- Experts on excessive force provide expert testimony on whether law enforcement's use of force exceeded what was necessary and lawful.
- Ballistics experts provide expert testimony matching bullets fired from one gun to bullets found at the scene of the crime.
- Chemists provide expert testimony on the composition of drugs and on the alcohol level found in a person's blood.
- Psychologists provide expert testimony about the difficulties and pitfalls of eyewitness identification.
- Psychologists and therapists provide expert testimony on the trauma that people sometimes experience following a crime, including intimate partner battering syndrome and child sexual abuse accommodation syndrome.
- Gang experts testify about gang culture.

Indeed, expert testimony can sometimes be the difference between a sentence of life in prison or an acquittal. Consider this scenario. A defendant is walking down the sidewalk as a car with a blue bandana sticking out the passenger side pulls up alongside him. The passenger rolls down the window and asks, "Where are you from?" Immediately thereafter, the defendant pulls a gun from his waistband and opens fire into the car, killing the passenger. The defendant is charged with murder. The defense is self-defense—namely, "I shot first because I was about to be shot at." To support this defense, a gang expert is critical. The gang expert could testify that the defendant belongs to one gang; that the defendant was walking down the sidewalk in his own gang's territory; that the blue bandana is a symbol of a rival gang; that the car was "on a mission" into its rival gang's territory; and that the question, "Where are you from?" is a gang challenge that, once answered, is typically followed by immediate violence. Based on the expert's testimony, the defendant could argue that he was actually and reasonably in fear of death or serious bodily injury and thus acted in self-defense by firing first.

Unlike lay witnesses, who as noted above apply a "process of reasoning familiar in everyday life" to facts in their personal knowledge, experts apply their specialized knowledge to the facts presented to them—even if those facts are outside their personal knowledge. Because jurors often have a tendency to place greater weight on what "the experts" say and, because, as we discuss below, expert witnesses are given more leeway in how they may testify, the rules of evidence are more stringent about what requirements must be met before testimony is deemed worthy of wearing the mantle of "expert testimony."

These next examples explore some of the issues that arise with expert testimony.

Examples

1. Plaintiff sues Defendant for injuries suffered in an auto accident. After plaintiff testifies, Defendant calls a psychologist to testify that, based on her observation of Plaintiff while testifying, her opinion is that Plaintiff was not telling the truth. Although the psychologist may be a qualified psychologist, it is not appropriate for expert witnesses to opine on whom a jury should believe.
2. Plaintiff sues Defendant for injuries suffered in an auto accident. To explain his injuries, Plaintiff calls a "human factors" expert to testify about the biomechanics of how the physics of the auto accident translated into the injuries Plaintiff sustained. In response, Defendant calls a physicist to refute the opinion of Plaintiff's expert about the causal link between the accident and Plaintiff's injuries. Although the physicist may be qualified to opine about basic principles of physics, this expert is not qualified to link those principles to the medical injuries that Plaintiff may have suffered.
3. Plaintiff sues Defendant for injuries suffered in an auto accident. To provide the mechanics of the accident, Plaintiff calls an accident reconstruction expert. The expert opines that the front of Defendant's car slammed into the side of Plaintiff's car at a certain speed and with a certain

quantum of force. In explaining how he came to these conclusions, the expert testifies that he set up a miniature model of the intersection with Hot Wheels cars, measured how fast *they* moved, and then "scaled up" the speeds and weights to come to his calculation. Here, this expert's opinion rests on an insufficiently reliable methodology.

What are the requirements before an expert may testify? The main rules delineating them are FRE 702 and FRE 703.

The federal courts designated trial judges as "gatekeepers" in regulating the admission of expert testimony and, for testimony based on the sciences, for many years set a high bar for admission—namely, a requirement that the scientific methodology at issue be "generally accepted" in the pertinent field. *See Frye v. United States*, 293 F. 1013 (D.C. Cir. 1923). In the 1970s, FRE 702 was promulgated to regulate expert testimony. As discussed in more detail below, the Supreme Court in *Daubert v. Merrell Dow Pharmaceuticals, Inc.*, 509 U.S. 579 (1993) interpreted the then-existing version of FRE 702—which required that expert testimony be "scientific" and "help the trier of fact"—as departing from *Frye* and requiring that scientific expert testimony meet a "standard of evidentiary reliability" (which, in turn, required that the expert's "reasoning or methodology" be "scientifically valid") and that the reasoning or methodology be "properly applied to the facts in issue." FRE 702 was subsequently amended to incorporate *Daubert's* guidance.

FRE 702. Testimony by Expert Witnesses

A witness who is qualified as an expert by knowledge, skill, experience, training, or education may testify in the form of an opinion or otherwise if:

(a) the expert's scientific, technical, or other specialized knowledge will help the trier of fact to understand the evidence or to determine a fact in issue;

(b) the testimony is based on sufficient facts or data;

(c) the testimony is the product of reliable principles and methods; and

(d) the expert has reliably applied the principles and methods to the facts of the case.

Excerpts from Advisory Committee Notes to FRE 702

- The trial judge in all cases of proffered expert testimony must find that it is properly grounded, well-reasoned, and not speculative before it can be admitted.
- The trial court's gatekeeping function requires more than simply "taking the expert's word for it."

FRE 703. BASES OF AN EXPERT'S OPINION TESTIMONY

An expert may base an opinion on facts or data in the case that the expert has been made aware of or personally observed. If experts in the particular field would reasonably rely on those kinds of facts or data in forming an opinion on the subject, they need not be admissible for the opinion to be admitted. But if the facts or data would otherwise be inadmissible, the proponent of the opinion may disclose them to the jury only if their probative value in helping the jury evaluate the opinion substantially outweighs their prejudicial effect.

Excerpts from Advisory Committee Notes to FRE 703

- [T]he underlying information is not admissible simply because the opinion . . . is admitted.
- Nothing in [FRE 703] restricts the presentation of underlying expert facts or data when offered by an adverse party.

Read together, these rules impose three distinct prerequisites to the admission of expert testimony. Whether these requirements have been met is a question for the judge under FRE 104(a) and not for the jury. A proposed 2022 amendment to FRE 702, if adopted, would clarify that these requirements must be "demonstrated by a preponderance of the evidence."

First, the subject itself must be one that is appropriate for expert testimony. Second, the specific expert witness must be qualified to offer the testimony he or she seeks to offer. Last, there must be a proper and sufficient basis—in fact *and* in methodology—for the expert's testimony.

1. *Proper Subject for Expert Testimony*

The fundamental rule regarding the proper subject for expert testimony is in FRE 702(a):

(1) As stated, the expert testimony must be based on "scientific, technical, or other specialized knowledge," FRE 702(a); and

(2) The expert testimony must "help the trier of fact to understand the evidence or to determine a fact in issue," FRE 702(a). Even if the opinion relates to an ultimate issue the jury must decide, the court will generally allow opinion testimony unless, in a criminal case, the expert is asked to opine on "whether the defendant did or did not have a mental state or condition that constitutes an element of the crime charged or of a defense." FRE 704(b).

In offering expert testimony, it is important to identify which issues the expert will help the trier of fact decide and why such an expertise would be helpful. This step is a necessary part of pretrial discovery. In civil cases, for instance, parties are required to make a pretrial disclosure of the identity of their expert witnesses as well as to provide "a complete statement of all opinions the witness will express and the basis for them." Fed. R. Civ. P. 26(a)(2). This information is also critical to address any pretrial motions aimed at excluding the expert testimony disclosed in discovery. For example, if a plaintiff is suing the defendant for construction defects with his home after it collapsed during a mild earthquake, the plaintiff will know that her construction expert will be testifying about safe construction practices in earthquake-prone zones as well as whether those practices were followed here. Without more, this expert would probably *not* be qualified to opine about how earthquakes move the earth beneath a home. Thinking through these issues in advance ensures that a party will not inadvertently "overdesignate" the expert witness in discovery, which may avoid unnecessary pretrial litigation regarding the permissible scope of expert testimony.

(a) Based on Scientific, Technical, or Other Specialized Knowledge

The first requirement is that the expert's testimony be based on scientific, technical, or other specialized knowledge. It is the flip side of the requirement discussed above that lay opinion testimony *not* be based on such knowledge. Although an expert must have some "specialized" knowledge, the rule is not limited to scientific or academic experts. There are many ways that individuals may obtain specialized knowledge. For example, an elevator repair person may never have obtained a specialized degree, but that person may be a specialist on the construction and operation of elevators.

There are many different areas in which expert testimony has been admitted. They include the following:

- *Topics based on scientific knowledge,* such as chemistry, physics, biology, and the like.
- *Topics based on technical knowledge,* such as engineering.
- *Topics based on other specialized knowledge,* such as (1) psychology or other disciplines that do not have a scientific or technical underpinning, (2) economics, (3) financial markets, and, as the next case illustrates, (4) industry custom.

United States v. Hoang

891 F. Supp. 2d 1355 (M.D. Ga. 2012)

ROYAL, Judge.

The Government has indicted Defendant Thanh Quoc Hoang for eleven counts of bank fraud. The superseding indictment accuses Hoang of using a scheme to defraud credit card companies by opening credit card accounts and then illegally obtaining goods, services, and cash from credit card companies. To carry out the scheme, he wrote worthless checks. The indictment alleges that from April 1, 2004, until May 31, 2004, Hoang defrauded financial institutions out of $349,071.33. Simply stated, Hoang allegedly scammed credit card companies out of huge sums of money.

[Defendant seeks to call J.P. Gingras as an expert witness.]

Gingras is a forensic accountant. He has four opinions based on his review of Hoang's financial records, credit card applications, and banking records. These are common financial records, the likes of which millions of Americans routinely receive and read, and the jury will have them in evidence. Based on these records, he opines that:

Opinion 1: Defendant's bank account and credit card statements are "not determinative" that Defendant is responsible for the fraud.

Opinion 2: The pattern of activity during the Indictment Period, when compared to pre-indictment activity, is "unusual," "out of the ordinary," and "unique."

Opinion 3: The actual amount of the alleged total fraud ("Adjusted Amount") is "less significant" than the amount presented in the Indictment.

Opinion 4: The size and magnitude of the Adjusted Amount is consistent with "the possibility" that Defendant was a victim of identity theft.

The Court will first consider whether the three excluded opinions assist the trier of fact. To assist a jury, the expert's opinions must cover matters beyond the ken of jurors—something beyond the average citizen's experience. The Court can address this issue with several questions. First, the Court can ask "whether the expert testimony improperly addresses matters within the understanding of the average juror." The answer is yes. Next, the Court can ask if the issues are highly technical and complicated. The answer is no. Next, the Court can ask if the factual and legal issues in the case involve specialized knowledge. Again, the answer is no. This case involves matters of common knowledge.

Credit card scams are common, everyday schemes to cheat banks out of money. Such scams are the well-travelled, dark alleys to easy cash. As outlined above, jurors hearing this case will have ample experience with banks, checking accounts, and credit cards to decide this case. The case involves common knowledge, common experience, and common crimes.

As such, in a matter that is obviously within the juror's common knowledge, expert testimony "almost by definition, can be of no assistance" and "[t]rouble is encountered only when the evaluation of the commonplace by an expert witness might supplant a jury's independent exercise of common sense." Writing checks and charging with credit cards are routine life activities. Likewise, there is nothing esoteric about defrauding banks by writing bad checks or scamming banks with credit card schemes. Yet, an expert must do more than repeat common knowledge and common sense. The court believes that the jury can understand this case without an expert's specialized knowledge. Consequently, the expert must offer more than what the witnesses can say and what the evidence shows, and Gingras fails to do that in this case with opinions 1, 2, and 4. Regarding his third opinion, it may or may not assist the jury.

Next, an expert's opinions must offer the jury more than what a lawyer can say in closing argument. Indeed, "the trial judge ought to insist that a proffered expert bring to the jury more than the lawyers can offer in argument." A witness cannot merely deliver a jury argument from the witness stand. Opinions 1, 2 and 4 are all nothing more than jury arguments.

In contrast to *Hoang*, in which the proffered expert opinion testimony rested on common knowledge held by most jurors, at times specialized testimony can sometimes be so important that a party's failure to call an expert witness is considered fatal to their claim. For instance, a plaintiff suing for medical malpractice is usually required to call an expert medical witness to testify about what the physician-defendant did wrong. What if the physician-defendant's negligence is so obvious that the fact of negligence is within the "common knowledge" of the average juror? For instance, what if the surgeon-defendant left a sponge in the plaintiff-patient's abdominal cavity before sewing her back up? In such cases, the plaintiff *can* call an expert but will not be required to do so. *E.g., In re Lipitor (Atorvastatin Calcium) Marketing, Sales Practices & Products Liability Litigation*, 227 F. Supp. 3d 452, 469-70 (D.S.C. 2017) (collecting cases).

(b) Helpful to the Trier of Fact

In addition to being based on some species of specialized knowledge, expert testimony must also be helpful to the trier of fact.

Litigators typically take one of two approaches to expert testimony. Those approaches are illustrated by the following examples.

Examples

1. Defendant is charged with a drive-by shooting as well as a gang enhancement. Through various witnesses, Prosecutor establishes that Defendant was the member of the We Kings Rule street gang, that he and two of his fellow gang members drove into the territory controlled by their rival gang (Pawns Will Rise), and that Defendant opened fire on two people they saw sitting at a bus stop. Prosecutor calls an expert witness to testify about gang culture and specifically how gangs will drive into a rival gang's territory on a "mission" to shoot at rival gang members to instill fear and enhance the gang's reputation. In closing, Prosecutor argues that Defendant's conduct in driving into rival gang territory and opening fire benefited his gang when he shot the two victims.
2. Same as Example 1, except the expert also offers the opinion, in response to a hypothetical question based on the facts of the case, that the killings in this case benefited the gang.
3. Plaintiff sues a pharmaceutical company for adverse side effects from taking one of its drugs. Plaintiff calls a pharmacologist to explain that the chemical compounds that make up the drug at issue affect human physiology; specifically, the expert testifies that the drug is known to cause a rare form of blood disease. In closing argument, Plaintiff's lawyer argues the company's drug caused Plaintiff's ailment.
4. Same as Example 3, except the expert also offers an opinion, in response to a hypothetical question based on the facts of the case, that Plaintiff's current blood disease was, to a reasonable degree of medical certainty, caused by Plaintiff's ingestion of the company's drug.

In Examples 1 and 3, the expert witnesses provided the jury with additional information based on their specialized knowledge of gang culture and pharmacology, respectively. However, the experts did not opine on how their knowledge applied to the facts of the case. Instead, the *prosecutor* and *plaintiff's counsel*, respectively, connected those dots during argument. In Examples 2 and 4, the expert witnesses provided the jury with additional information *and* offered an opinion about how that information applied to this case. The experts connected those dots as part of their expert testimony.

2. *Qualifications of the Expert*

A person may testify as an expert witness only if she is qualified to do so. A person may be "qualified as an expert" by her (1) knowledge, (2) skill, (3) experience, (4) training, or (5) education. FRE 702.

Consider the following examples.

Examples

1. In a negligence case involving injuries arising out of acupuncture, Plaintiff calls a person who has read extensively on the subjects of acupuncture and the nervous system. This person may qualify as an expert on the basis of her *knowledge.*
2. In a negligence case involving injuries arising out of acupuncture, Plaintiff calls a person who has performed acupuncture for more than five years. This person may qualify as an expert on the basis of her *skill* or *experience.*
3. In a negligence case involving injuries arising out of acupuncture, Plaintiff calls a person who trained as an apprentice acupuncturist for three years but never actually practiced herself. This person may qualify as an expert on the basis of her *training.*
4. In a negligence action involving injuries arising out of acupuncture, Plaintiff calls a Harvard-educated physician with a specialty in musculature and the nervous system. This person may qualify as an expert on the basis of her *education.*
5. In a negligence action involving a malfunctioning elevator manufactured by Up, Up and Away Elevator Company that plummeted several floors and caused injuries, the injured Plaintiff-passengers call Eliza Otis, who is the CEO of Otis Elevator (and a descendent of its original founder, Elisha Otis), to testify about how the malfunction was caused by improper maintenance rather than a design flaw. This person may qualify as an expert on the basis of her *knowledge* and *experience.*

There is no fixed, minimum threshold for determining whether a witness has the requisite knowledge, skill, experience, training, or education to qualify as an expert witness. Thus, a person can still qualify as an expert even if:

- The person has never previously testified as an expert. Every expert witness was, at some point, qualified as an expert "for the first time"; what matters is their expertise, even if it is the first time they have provided testimony.
- The person has not himself or herself performed precisely the same procedure(s) involved in the underlying case. Thus, an orthopedic surgeon may testify as an expert on a case involving a botched rotator cuff surgery even if the surgeon has never performed such a surgery. (However, if the opposing party calls an expert who *has* performed such surgeries, that party may argue that the expert who has not done so is less qualified and that her opinion should be disregarded. But the lack of directly on point experience does not render the expert *unqualified.*)
- Other experts disagree with the person's proffered opinion. Indeed, so-called battles of the experts—where each party calls an expert witness who offers an opinion diametrically opposed to the other party's expert—are quite common.

Whether a witness is qualified to testify as an expert is a question for the judge, not the jury. FRE 104(a).

There is no single process for qualifying an expert witness. The qualification of an expert is typically handled via one of the following procedures:

(1) The party opposing the testimony of a proposed expert witness requests a pretrial hearing at which the proffered expert can be examined—outside the presence of the jury—regarding his or her qualifications.

(2) The party opposing the testimony of a proposed expert witness will wait for the party who called the witness to question the witness about her qualifications before the jury. At that point, and thus still in the middle of the expert's direct examination, the party will ask the court for permission to "voir dire the expert"—that is, to question the proffered expert regarding her qualifications. If the expert's answers suggest a basis to challenge the expert on her lack of qualifications, the party can then request a hearing (commonly called a *Daubert* hearing, after the *Daubert* case discussed below) out of the jury's presence to argue that the expert is not qualified. If the judge determines that the expert is not qualified, no further testimony from the witness is permitted. If no further challenge is made or if the judge determines that the expert is qualified, the direct examination of the expert resumes.

(3) The party opposing the testimony of a proposed expert witness will allow the expert to testify and will cross-examine the witness about her qualifications. If the expert's answers suggest a basis to challenge the expert on her lack of qualifications, the further procedures set forth in procedure 2 will be followed.

Because parties are required by the rules of civil and criminal discovery to exchange information regarding the qualifications and likely substance of their proposed expert prior to trial, parties will typically make a pretrial motion in those cases in which there is a genuine likelihood that the expert is not qualified. The practice of conducting a voir dire examination of the expert and cross-examining the expert regarding qualifications are typically used when the party anticipates that the expert is qualified, but wishes to plumb specific aspects of those qualifications as grist for attacking the expert's opinion (rather than as a basis for excluding the expert's testimony in its entirety).

Although it was common at common law for a party, after going through the proffered expert's testimony, to "tender" the witness "as an expert" to the trial judge and then to have the trial judge "accept" the witness as an "expert," this step is no longer required, and many trial judges decline to do so on the ground that jurors might view the practice as giving the imprimatur of the court to whatever the expert thereafter says.

3. *Proper Basis for Expert Opinion Testimony*

Even if the subject is appropriate for expert testimony, and even if the expert is qualified, an expert witness may offer an opinion only if the opinion has a proper and sufficient (1) factual basis and (2) methodological basis. Whether these bases exist are questions for the judge, not the jury. FRE 104(a).

(a) Factual Basis for the Expert's Opinion

The Federal Rules of Evidence authorize the admission of an expert witness's opinion only if it is "based on sufficient facts and data." FRE 702(b). This rule raises two separate questions:

(1) Which "facts and data" may an expert *rely* on in formulating his or her expert opinion?

(2) Which "facts and data" may an expert *relay* to the trier of fact when explaining his or her expert opinion?

(i) Which "facts and data" may an expert witness *rely* on?

Whether an expert witness may rely on specific "facts and data" to support his or her expert opinion is a function of (1) whether those "facts and data" are relevant under the expert's proffered methodology and (2) whether those "facts and data" are derived from sources that the expert is allowed to consider under the rules of evidence.

Regarding the first question, an expert may rely on any "facts or data" as long as "experts in the particular field would reasonably rely on those kinds of facts or data in forming an opinion on the subject." FRE 703. Whether experts in a particular field would reasonably rely on certain facts or data is a function of the methodology the expert is using and whether that methodology is reliable, as discussed in the "methodological basis" section below. If the methodology is reliable, however, any facts or data that experts following that methodology would "reasonably rely on" may permissibly constitute the factual basis for the proffered opinion, whether or not the facts or data are inadmissible into evidence. FRE 703. If others would reasonably rely on them, an expert can also rely on the opinions of other experts in formulating his or her expert opinion.

Regarding the second question, the rules of evidence allow an expert to obtain the facts and data relied on from three different sources:

- *Personal observation.* FRE 703 provides that "[a]n expert may base an opinion on facts or data in the case that the expert has . . . personally observed." Thus, a plaintiff may call her personal physician as an expert witness, and that expert's opinion can be based in part on the observations that the expert personally made regarding the plaintiff's body.
- *Facts presented at trial.* FRE 703 provides that "[a]n expert may base an opinion on facts or data in the case that the expert has been made aware of." Thus, an expert may rely on facts (1) offered by other witnesses at the trial, which either the expert heard while observing the trial or an attorney tells the expert were elicited at trial, or (2) offered as the basis for a hypothetical question posed to the expert, as long as the factual premises of the hypothetical question have been admitted into evidence or will at some point be admitted into evidence. Accordingly, it is not unusual for an expert to sit in during a trial to listen to the other side's witnesses or read a transcript of their testimony.
- *Facts acquired prior to trial.* The "facts or data in the case that the expert has been made aware of" includes not only the facts presented at trial, but facts presented to the expert prior to trial. FRE 703. They include (1) the facts and data specific to the case at issue and (2) the facts and data underlying the expert witness's general specialized knowledge. Thus, an expert witness can rely on (1) facts and data about the patient-plaintiff's physical condition told to him or her by the patient-plaintiff's relatives, other doctors, and the like; and (2) facts and data contained in literature in his or her field of expertise, as part of the expert's background knowledge. This knowledge may come from treatises or even from websites that are commonly used as reference tools by experts and others in a field. Accordingly, an expert may testify that the drugs seized from the defendant's possession were Xanax on the ground that those pills matched the size, shape, and color of Xanax as identified on a website known as Ident-A-Drug. The ability of the expert to rely on background knowledge is a "matter of practicality"; without it, experts would be required to have *personal* experience with all the tenets of their discipline in order to base an opinion on generally accepted knowledge in that discipline. This background knowledge is necessarily hearsay, but may form the basis for the expert's opinion under the Federal Rules of Evidence.

(ii) Which "facts and data" may an expert witness *relay* to the trier of fact?

Although the common law required expert witnesses to detail the facts and data underlying their opinions before testifying to the opinion itself, the Federal Rules of Evidence have done away with that requirement. Thus, most experts are first asked to state their opinion and are then asked to explain the basis for that opinion; skilled advocates will typically conclude by asking the expert to restate their opinion, thereby emphasizing that opinion to the jury.

FRE 705. Disclosing the Facts or Data Underlying an Expert's Opinion

Unless the court orders otherwise, an expert may state an opinion—and give the reasons for it—without first testifying to the underlying facts or data. But the expert may be required to disclose those facts or data on cross-examination.

Example

Defendant is charged with importing cocaine into the United States. Prosecutor calls the chemist who analyzed the substances seized from Defendant's van. After establishing the chemist's expertise in drug analysis, the following colloquy ensues:

Prosecutor: So did you have the opportunity examine Exhibit 104, which Officer Lee previously testified was a sample of the substance taken from Defendant's van?

Chemist: Yes, I did.

Prosecutor: What is your opinion as to the composition of that substance?

Chemist: In my opinion, it is cocaine.

Prosecutor: What is the basis for that opinion?

Chemist: After checking the sample out from the evidence locker, I took it to the lab and performed three separate chemical litmus tests on a fragment of the sample. Each test confirmed that the substance was cocaine.

Prosecutor: So what is your opinion to a reasonable degree of scientific certainty regarding the composition of the substance?

Chemist: It is cocaine.

FRE 705 leaves it up to the trial judge whether to require the chemist to provide greater explanation of the testing she did and how it supports her opinion. If the judge does not impose that requirement, it is up to Defendant to cross-examine the chemist about the specific facts and data underlying her opinion.

What if the party calling the expert on direct examination—or the party cross-examining the expert witness—wants to have the expert witness relay the "underlying facts or data" to the trier of fact. Are there any impediments to doing so? If the underlying facts and data have already been admitted into evidence, or if they have not previously been admitted into evidence but can be or will be at some point during the proceeding, the expert may relay those facts and data during her testimony.

But what if the underlying facts or data are *not* admissible into evidence? In federal court, a party calling an expert witness can have the expert witness relay inadmissible facts or data to a jury only if:

(1) "the probative value [of the underlying facts and data] in helping the jury evaluate the [expert's] opinion substantially outweighs their prejudicial effect," FRE 703. This provision is a "reverse FRE 403" test that heavily disfavors admission of this information because admission is allowed only if the probative value substantially outweighs its prejudicial effect (whereas FRE 403, as noted in Chapter Two, heavily favors admission by allowing for exclusion only if the probative value is substantially outweighed by the prejudicial effect);[3] *and*

(2) in a criminal case where the prosecution is calling the expert witness, the underlying facts and data are not "testimonial" statements rendered inadmissible under the Confrontation Clause as interpreted by *Crawford v. Washington*, 541 U.S. 36 (2004) and *Williams v. Illinois*, 567 U.S. 50 (2012) (concluding that unsworn DNA report was not "testimonial"); *see generally* Chapter Nine.

Example

Defendant is charged with a gang-related drive-by shooting. Prosecutor calls a long-time police officer as a gang expert. During the expert's direct testimony, the expert opines that the crime was gang-related, even though it occurred in the home territory of Defendant's own gang and the victims were not gang members. In response to further questions from Prosecutor, the expert explains that his opinion rests on information he learned from talking to another police officer, who spoke with the person who was driving the car from which Defendant fired his gun, during an interview at the police

3. California takes a different approach to the admission of expert testimony. First, as discussed more fully below, California retains the *Frye* test as the standard for admitting scientific expert testimony. Second, California does not follow FRE 703's approach to when an expert—scientific or not—may relay inadmissible hearsay in explaining the basis for the expert's opinion. Specifically, California law provides that expert witnesses may relay "background information and knowledge in the area of [their] expertise," even if it is inadmissible, but they may *not* relay "case-specific facts about which the [expert] has no personal" or "independent" knowledge if those case-specific facts are inadmissible. *People v. Sanchez*, 63 Cal. 4th 665, 676 (Cal. 2016). For these purposes, a "case-specific fact" is a fact "relating to the particular events and participants alleged to have been involved in the case being tried." Thus, in *Sanchez*, a gang expert opining that the defendant belonged to a certain street gang was not permitted to relay to the jury the specific hearsay statements he relied upon in forming his opinion, in which specific persons indicated that the defendant belonged to that gang. However, experts may "tell the jury *in general terms*" that they relied upon inadmissible hearsay by describing no more than the "type or source of the matter relied upon." *Id.* at 685-86.

station after the driver was arrested on other charges. The driver said that the victims were cousins of a rival gang member and that the goal was to retaliate against the rival gang.

Before the trial judge will allow the expert to testify about what the driver said—if that evidence has not been admitted during the trial—the judge has to find that (1) "the probative value" of the driver's statement in helping to understand the expert's opinion substantially outweighs its prejudicial effect and (2) the driver's statement is not testimonial under *Crawford*. The driver's statement probably does not satisfy either of these requirements. Because the driver's statement would be very prejudicial to Defendant if considered for its truth (that is, to prove that Defendant shot the cousins to get back at the rival gang member), its prejudicial effect is probably not substantially outweighed by its probative value in helping the jury evaluate the gang expert's opinion. Further, the driver's statement is testimonial because it is a statement he made during a police interview at the station after arrest. If that statement is admitted for its truth, it would violate *Crawford* absent proof that the driver was a witness at trial or is unavailable for trial and was subject to cross-examination at some point in the past.

If the party calling the expert witness *is* allowed to have the expert witness testify to the otherwise inadmissible facts or data, the other party is entitled, upon request, to a limiting instruction telling the jury only to consider the evidence while evaluating the basis of the expert witness's opinion—and *not* for its truth. FRE 703, Adv. Comm. Note for 2000 Amendment.

The party opposing and cross-examining the witness is allowed to elicit facts and data underlying the expert's opinion, even if it is inadmissible (although if the prosecution is cross-examining the defendant's expert in a criminal case, the Confrontation Clause may be implicated to the extent the basis consists of testimonial statements that are being admitted against the defendant). That is because the party that *elicits* the inadmissible evidence while trying to impeach the expert's opinion on cross-examination can hardly be heard to complain about the inadmissible answers to questions that it posed to the expert. These facts may include facts and data contained in treatises upon which the expert relied, or which contradict the expert's opinion.[4] However, if *new* facts or data not relied upon by the expert are put before the expert witness (and hence the jury) in order to impeach or test an expert's opinion on cross-examination, those new facts or data may not be admissible if they fail to satisfy the same test for information relayed on direct examination.

---

4. California also takes a different approach in regulating the materials with which an expert witness may be cross-examined. Specifically, California limits the use of treatises to cross-examine expert witnesses to treatises that (1) the expert witness "referred to, considered, or relied upon" in forming his or her opinion, (2) have been admitted into evidence, or (3) "have been established as a reliable authority by the testimony or admission of the witness or by other expert testimony or by judicial notice." Cal. Evid. Code § 721(b).

Examples

1. Defendant is charged with a gang-related drive-by shooting. Prosecutor calls a gang expert to opine that the crime was gang-related, even though it occurred in the home territory of Defendant's own gang and the victims were not gang members. On cross-examination of the gang expert, Defendant asks, "So why did you think it was gang-related if no rival gang members were harmed and the shooting occurred in the territory of the gang you say that Defendant belongs to?" The expert responds, "Because the driver of the car that Defendant fired from said that Defendant was targeting the cousins of Diablo, a rival gang member." This testimony is permissible because Defendant is the one who is eliciting this evidence and cannot be heard to complain if he elicits facts that are inadmissible or testimonial under *Crawford.*
2. Defendant is charged with a gang-related drive-by shooting. After Prosecutor calls a gang expert who opines that the crime was gang-related, Defendant calls a gang expert who opines it was not. On cross-examination of Defendant's gang expert, Prosecutor asks, "In coming to your conclusion that the shooting was not gang-related, did you consider the statement of the driver of the car that Defendant was shooting at a rival gang member's cousins in order to retaliate against that rival gang?" Under FRE 703, the trial judge has the discretion to allow the question for its effect on the expert's opinion and not for the truth, but only after the judge has determined that the probative value in helping the jury evaluate the expert's opinion substantially outweighs the prejudicial effect of the driver's statement and only if the judge gives a limiting instruction informing the jury not to consider the statement for its truth. To the extent that the trial judge is asked to admit the driver's statement for its truth, the admission of the statement may raise *Crawford* issues because it is a testimonial statement being admitted against Defendant.

(b) Methodological Basis for the Expert's Opinion

Before an expert may testify about his specialized knowledge or his opinions premised on it, that testimony must be "the product of reliable principles" and the resulting opinion must "reliably appl[y] the principles and methods to the facts of the case."[5] FRE 702(c),(d). Why is this requirement important? Consider the following example. A prosecutor who is prosecuting the defendant for murder calls a witness who has spent years studying the Ouija board to testify that he asked the Spirits of Great Beyond whether the defendant was guilty, and the Spirits used the Ouija board to answer, "Yes." This "expert" would get nowhere near a courtroom

5. A proposed 2022 amendment to FRE 702, if adopted, would modify the second requirement to clarify that the "expert's opinion reflects a reliable application of the principles and methods to the facts of the case."

because his opinion of the defendant's guilt (aside from being inadmissible as *the* ultimate issue in the case) is not "the product of reliable principles."

The Supreme Court has designated trial judges as the "gatekeepers" of the reliability of expert methodologies. *Kumho Tire Co., Ltd. v. Carmichael*, 526 U.S. 137 (1999); *GE v. Joinder*, 522 U.S. 136, 142 (1997). How are judges expected to carry out this function—and, more importantly, what standards must litigants meet in order to establish the reliability of their experts' methodologies?

For many years, the answer to this question in the federal courts depended on whether or not the expert testimony was scientific in nature or instead rested on a nonscientific discipline. In many states, such as California, the answer still turns on this distinction. *People v. Kelly*, 17 Cal. 3d 24, 30 (Cal. 1976); *People v. Leahy*, 8 Cal. 4th 587, 611-12 (Cal. 1994).

(i) Expert testimony based on scientific knowledge

Until 1993, the leading federal case on how to assess the reliability of scientific expert testimony was *Frye v. United States*, 293 F. 1013 (D.C. Cir. 1923). At issue in *Frye* was whether a defense expert could opine that the defendant in a criminal case was telling the truth based on a "systolic blood pressure deception test" because the defendant's blood pressure did not rise when he recounted his innocence.

Frye v. United States

293 F. 1013 (D.C. Cir. 1923)

Van Orsdel, Justice.

"The rule is that the opinions of experts or skilled witnesses are admissible in evidence in those cases in which the matter of inquiry is such that inexperienced persons are unlikely to prove capable of forming a correct judgment upon it, for the reason that the subject-matter so far partakes of a science, art, or trade as to require a previous habit or experience or study in it, in order to acquire a knowledge of it. When the question involved does not lie within the range of common experience or common knowledge, but requires special experience or special knowledge, then the opinions of witnesses skilled in that particular science, art, or trade to which the question relates are admissible in evidence."

Numerous cases are cited in support of this rule. Just when a scientific principle or discovery crosses the line between the experimental and demonstrable stages is difficult to define. Somewhere in this twilight zone the evidential force of the principle must be recognized, and while courts will go a long way in admitting expert testimony deduced from a well-recognized scientific principle or discovery, the thing from which the deduction is made must be sufficiently established to have gained general acceptance in the particular field in which it belongs.

We think the systolic blood pressure deception test has not yet gained such standing and scientific recognition among physiological and psychological authorities as would justify the courts in admitting expert testimony deduced from the discovery, development, and experiments thus far made.

Following *Frye*, federal courts for many years would allow an expert to offer expert testimony only if the underlying methodology had "gained general acceptance in the particular field in which it belongs." Applying *Frye*, federal courts excluded the following types of expert testimony:

- Use of unique "voiceprints" to identify individuals;
- Use of dogs to "identify" individuals in a "scent lineup" using gauze pads, some of which contain the suspect's scent and some of which come from evidence that police believe the suspect has touched;
- Use of certain drugs to retrieve repressed memories;
- Use of "truth serum."

The next case, *United States v. Fishman*, more fully examines how the federal courts previously applied the so-called *Frye* test before the *Daubert* test was adopted.

United States v. Fishman

743 F. Supp. 713 (N.D. Cal. 1990)

JENSEN, Judge.

The United States indicted Steven Fishman on eleven counts of mail fraud, in violation of 18 U.S.C. § 1341, on September 23, 1988. The indictment charges that Mr. Fishman defrauded various federal district courts, including those in the Northern District of California, by fraudulently obtaining settlement monies and securities in connection with shareholder class action lawsuits. This fraud allegedly occurred over a lengthy period of time—from September 1983 to May 1988.

Two months after his indictment, defendant notified this Court of his intent to rely on an insanity defense, pursuant to Rule 12.2 of the Federal Rules of Criminal Procedure. Within the context of his insanity defense, defendant seeks to present evidence that influence techniques, or brainwashing, practiced upon him by the Church of Scientology ("the Church") was a cause of his state of mind at the time of the charged offenses. Defendant contends that he has been a member of the Church since 1979. In furtherance of the brainwashing aspect of his defense, Mr. Fishman seeks to call two expert witnesses, Dr. Margaret Singer and Dr. Richard Ofshe. Presently before the Court is the government's motion to exclude the testimony of these witnesses.

Dr. Margaret Singer is a well known and highly regarded forensic psychologist. She evaluated Stephen Fishman's mental state shortly after his indictment. Having formed certain psychological opinions and preliminary conclusions from this evaluation, Dr. Singer is expected to testify that defendant's delusional view of the world at the time he committed the alleged fraud supports her opinion that he was legally insane.

Based on her training in psychology, Dr. Singer is expected to testify that defendant is incredibly suggestible, compulsive and obsessive. She further believes that this suggestibleness is long-standing, as is his peculiar behavior and bizarre reasoning. Dr. Singer thus characterizes the defendant as a strange and eccentric person *before* he came into contact with the Church of Scientology. Dr. Singer is also expected to testify that upon joining the Church of Scientology, defendant was subjected to intense suggestion procedures as well as other social and behavioral influence processes. In the opinion of Dr. Singer, the conjoining of the Church's influence techniques and Mr. Fishman's previous psychological condition permitted his mental state to evolve to a point of extremely clouded reasoning and judgment. Defendant created an alternative reality, and then lived in this mental state for at least five years. Dr. Singer concludes that while the defendant is bright, obsessive, and capable in many ways, his entire view of reality during this period was delusional.

Dr. Richard Ofshe is a social psychologist who holds a Ph.D. degree in sociology. Defendant concedes that Dr. Ofshe is not a mental health professional, and therefore cannot testify as to the defendant's mental state at the time of the charged offenses. Rather, defendant presents Dr. Ofshe as a person whose expertise enables him to describe the coordinated program of coercive influence and behavioral control that defendant was subjected to by members of the Church of Scientology. Dr. Ofshe would testify to his opinion that, by controlling certain social influence variables, Scientology can induce a person to believe that he or she has acquired and can currently utilize superhuman powers. Dr. Ofshe's proffered opinion is that the Church's influence process regularly leads people to believe that they have the power to control mental matter, energy, space and time.

With reference to defendant's case in particular, Dr. Ofshe is of the belief that defendant was made the target of a prolonged, organized program of influence, which was designed to lead Mr. Fishman to believe that participation in Scientology's fraud scheme was not a reprehensible act.

III. ACCEPTANCE WITHIN THE SCIENTIFIC COMMUNITY

In this case Dr. Margaret Singer and Dr. Richard Ofshe seek to testify regarding thought reform theories, particularly with respect to religious cults.

Thought reform theory is not new; it derives from studies of American prisoners of war during the Korean conflict in the 1950s.

Dr. Robert Lifton and Dr. Edgar Schein produced the foundational scientific scholarship on thought reform theory. Relying as Hunter did on the experiences of American POW's in China, Dr. Lifton and Dr. Schein concluded that brainwashing, or "coercive persuasion," exists and is remarkably effective.

The application of the concept of coercive persuasion to religious cults by persons such as Dr. Singer and Dr. Ofshe is a relatively recent development. This extension of Lifton and Schein's theories has met resistance from members of the scientific community who believe that legitimate thought reform theory is necessarily limited to persuasion accompanied by physical restraint or mistreatment.

A more significant barometer of prevailing views within the scientific community is provided by professional organizations such as the American Psychological Association ("APA") and American Sociological Association ("ASA"). The evidence before the Court, which is detailed below, shows that neither the APA nor the ASA has endorsed the views of Dr. Singer and Dr. Ofshe on thought reform.

As chronicled above, the record in this case establishes that the scientific community has resisted the Singer-Ofshe thesis applying coercive persuasion to religious cults. The thesis that these cults overcome the free will of their members is controversial. But in determining the admissibility of expert testimony, the Court recognizes that the general acceptance standard enunciated in *Frye* allows for some controversy. *Frye* holds that "while courts will go a long way in admitting expert testimony deduced from a well recognized scientific principle or discovery, the thing from which the deduction is made must be sufficiently established to have gained general acceptance in the particular field in which it belongs." *Frye v. United States.*

The issue of whether or not the proffered testimony in this case satisfies the *Frye* test is not one of first impression among the federal courts. In *Kropinski v. World Plan Executive Council-U.S.* (D.C. Cir. 1988), the Court of Appeals unanimously reversed the trial court for permitting Dr. Singer to testify on coercive persuasion.

There is little dispute in this case that the relevant field for purposes of the *Frye* analysis encompasses the American Psychological Association and the American Sociological Association. Based on the expansive record in this case, the Court finds that there is no consensus or general acceptance within these associations regarding the thought reform theories of Dr. Singer and Dr. Ofshe. The proffered testimony in this case has been challenged by the scientific community on grounds of both scientific merit and methodological rigor.

Accordingly, the Court finds that defendant has not met its burden under *Frye* of showing that Dr. Singer's and Dr. Ofshe's theories of thought reform are generally accepted within their fields. Not only has Dr. Lifton expressed reservations regarding these theories, but more importantly the Singer-Ofshe thesis lacks the imprimatur of the APA and ASA. Thought reform is a complex and controversial subject within the scientific community, and defendant bears the burden of establishing the scientific basis, reliability, and general acceptance of his proffered expert testimony. At best, the evidence establishes that psychiatrists, psychologists, and sociologists disagree as to whether or not there is agreement regarding the Singer-Ofshe thesis. The Court therefore excludes defendant's proffered testimony.

As *Fishman* illustrates, a party proffering a methodology under the *Frye* test must establish that the methodology has gained an "imprimatur" of legitimacy within the pertinent field. Because it takes time for a new methodology to gain such legitimacy, the *Frye* test had the effect of limiting expert testimony to only those methodologies that had been around for a while, even though newer methodologies might be equally if not more reliable.

Frye's "general acceptance" test was relegated to the status of being one of several relevant considerations bearing on the validity of an expert's methodology when the Supreme Court decided *Daubert v. Merrell Dow Pharmaceuticals, Inc.*, 509 U.S. 579 (1993).[6] *Daubert* was brought on behalf of two children born with serious birth defects after their mothers ingested Bendectin, a prescription antinausea drug marketed by Merrell Dow. Merrell Dow had moved for summary judgment

6. Many jurisdictions, such as Florida and Texas, follow *Daubert. In re Amendments to the Fla. Evidence Code*, 278 So. 3d 551, 551-52 (Fla. 2019); Fla. Stat. §§ 90.702, 90.704; *E.I. du Pont Nemours & Co. v. Robinson*, 923 S.W.2d 549, 555 (Tex. 1995). Some jurisdictions continue to follow the *Frye* test for scientific methodologies. *See People v. Leahy*, 8 Cal. 4th 587, 591-92 (Cal. 1994); *People v. McKown*, 226 Ill. 2d 245, 257 (Ill. 2007); Ill. R. Evid. 702; *People v. Bullard-Daniel*, 54 Misc. 3d 177, 185 (N.Y. Sup. Ct. Niagara Co. 2016); *Parker v. Mobile Oil Corp.*, 7 N.Y.3d 434, 446-47 & n.3 (N.Y. 2006).

on the ground that Bendectin did not cause birth defects as a matter of law; for support, Merrell Dow submitted the affidavit of an epidemiologist who opined that "all the literature on Bendectin and human birth defects" concluded that Bendectin was not a "substance capable of causing malformations in [human] fetuses." The *Daubert* plaintiffs opposed the summary judgment motion with affidavits from scientists who opined that there *was* a link between Bendectin and birth defects based on "animal-cell studies, live-animal studies," and the "similarities between the [chemical] structure of [Bendectin] and that of other substances known to cause birth defects." The trial judge—and the circuit court of appeal—excluded the *Daubert* plaintiffs' experts' testimony because the studies they relied on had not, under *Frye*, gained general acceptance in the particular field. The Supreme Court in *Daubert* considered the continued propriety of using the so-called *Frye* test.

Daubert v. Merrell Dow Pharmaceuticals, Inc.

509 U.S. 579 (1993)

JUSTICE BLACKMUN delivered the opinion of the Court.

In the 70 years since its formulation in the *Frye* case, the "general acceptance" test has been the dominant standard for determining the admissibility of novel scientific evidence at trial. See E. Green & C. Nesson, Problems, Cases, and Materials on Evidence 649 (1983). Although under increasing attack of late, the rule continues to be followed by a majority of courts, including the Ninth Circuit.

The merits of the *Frye* test have been much debated, and scholarship on its proper scope and application is legion. Petitioners' primary attack, however, is not on the content but on the continuing authority of the rule. They contend that the *Frye* test was superseded by the adoption of the Federal Rules of Evidence. We agree.

Here there is a specific Rule that speaks to the contested issue. Rule 702, governing expert testimony, [at the time of *Daubert*] provides:

> "If scientific, technical, or other specialized knowledge will assist the trier of fact to understand the evidence or to determine a fact in issue, a witness qualified as an expert by knowledge, skill, experience, training, or education, may testify thereto in the form of an opinion or otherwise."

Nothing in the text of this Rule establishes "general acceptance" as an absolute prerequisite to admissibility. Nor does respondent present any clear indication that Rule 702 or the Rules as a whole were intended to incorporate a "general acceptance" standard.

That the *Frye* test was displaced by the Rules of Evidence does not mean, however, that the Rules themselves place no limits on the admissibility of purportedly scientific evidence. Nor is the trial judge disabled from screening such evidence. To the contrary, under the Rules the trial judge must ensure that any and all scientific testimony or evidence admitted is not only relevant, but reliable.

The primary locus of this obligation is Rule 702, which clearly contemplates some degree of regulation of the subjects and theories about which an expert may testify. "*If scientific,* technical, or other specialized *knowledge will assist the trier of fact* to understand the evidence or to determine a fact in issue" an expert "may testify *thereto.*" (Emphasis added.) The subject of an expert's testimony must be "scientific . . . knowledge." The adjective "scientific" implies a grounding in the methods and procedures of science. Similarly, the word "knowledge" connotes more than subjective belief or unsupported speculation. The term "applies to any body of known facts or to any body of ideas inferred from such facts or accepted as truths on good grounds." Of course, it would be unreasonable to conclude that the subject of scientific testimony must be "known" to a certainty; arguably, there are no certainties in science. . . . But, in order to qualify as "scientific knowledge," an inference or assertion must be derived by the scientific method. Proposed testimony must be supported by appropriate validation—*i.e.*, "good grounds," based on what is known. In short, the requirement that an expert's testimony pertain to "scientific knowledge" establishes a standard of evidentiary reliability.

Rule 702 further requires that the evidence or testimony "assist the trier of fact to understand the evidence or to determine a fact in issue." This condition goes primarily to relevance. "Expert testimony which does not relate to any issue in the case is not relevant and, ergo, non-helpful." . . . The consideration has been aptly described by Judge Becker as one of "fit." "Fit" is not always obvious, and scientific validity for one purpose is not necessarily scientific validity for other, unrelated purposes. The study of the phases of the moon, for example, may provide valid scientific "knowledge" about whether a certain night was dark, and if darkness is a fact in issue, the knowledge will assist the trier of fact. However (absent creditable grounds supporting such a link), evidence that the moon was full on a certain night will not assist the trier of fact in determining whether an individual was unusually likely to have behaved irrationally on that night. Rule 702's "helpfulness" standard requires a valid scientific connection to the pertinent inquiry as a precondition to admissibility.

That these requirements are embodied in Rule 702 is not surprising. Unlike an ordinary witness, see Rule 701, an expert is permitted wide latitude to offer opinions, including those that are not based on firsthand knowledge or observation. See Rules 702 and 703. Presumably, this relaxation of the usual requirement of firsthand knowledge—a rule which represents "a 'most pervasive manifestation' of the common law insistence upon 'the most reliable sources of information,'" Advisory Committee's Notes on Fed. Rule Evid. 602, 28 U.S.C. App., p. 755 (citation omitted)—is premised on an assumption that the expert's opinion will have a reliable basis in the knowledge and experience of his discipline.

Faced with a proffer of expert scientific testimony, then, the trial judge must determine at the outset, pursuant to Rule 104(a), whether the expert is proposing to testify to (1) scientific knowledge that (2) will assist the trier of fact to understand or determine a fact in issue. This entails a preliminary assessment of whether the reasoning or methodology underlying the testimony is scientifically valid and of whether that reasoning or methodology properly can be applied to the facts in issue. We are confident that federal judges possess the capacity to undertake this review. Many factors will bear on the inquiry, and we do not presume to set out a definitive checklist or test. But some general observations are appropriate.

Ordinarily, a key question to be answered in determining whether a theory or technique is scientific knowledge that will assist the trier of fact will be whether it can be (and has been) tested. "Scientific methodology today is based on generating hypotheses and testing them to see if they can be falsified; indeed, this methodology is what distinguishes science from other fields of human inquiry."

Another pertinent consideration is whether the theory or technique has been subjected to peer review and publication. . . . But submission to the scrutiny of the scientific community is a component of "good science," in part because it increases the likelihood that substantive flaws in methodology will be detected. The fact of publication (or lack thereof) in a peer reviewed journal thus will be a relevant, though not dispositive, consideration in assessing the scientific validity of a particular technique or methodology on which an opinion is premised.

Additionally, in the case of a particular scientific technique, the court ordinarily should consider the known or potential rate of error. . . .

Finally, "general acceptance" can yet have a bearing on the inquiry. A "reliability assessment does not require, although it does permit, explicit identification of a relevant scientific community and an express determination of a particular degree of acceptance within that community." Widespread acceptance can be an important factor in ruling particular evidence admissible, and "a known technique which has been able to attract only minimal support within the community," may properly be viewed with skepticism.

The inquiry envisioned by Rule 702 is, we emphasize, a flexible one. Its overarching subject is the scientific validity—and thus the evidentiary relevance and reliability—of the principles that underlie a proposed submission. The focus, of course, must be solely on principles and methodology, not on the conclusions that they generate.

To summarize: "General acceptance" is not a necessary precondition to the admissibility of scientific evidence under the Federal Rules of Evidence, but the Rules of Evidence—especially Rule 702—do assign to the trial judge the task of ensuring that an expert's testimony both rests on a reliable foundation and is relevant to the task at hand. Pertinent evidence based on scientifically valid principles will satisfy those demands.

After the Supreme Court remanded *Daubert* back to the Ninth Circuit, the Ninth Circuit applied the newly minted *Daubert* test to exclude the plaintiffs' experts' testimony as a matter of law. *Daubert v. Merrell Dow Pharmaceuticals*, 43 F.3d 1311 (9th Cir. 1995). The Ninth Circuit found that plaintiffs might be able to produce more evidence to support a finding that their experts' methodology was reliable, but found that the experts' opinion did not assist the trier of fact because those experts' opinions established—at best—that Bendectin *possibly* caused the plaintiffs' birth defects (rather than having *actually* caused them) and thus was too speculative to assist the jury.

In 1997, the Supreme Court refined the *Daubert* test in *GE v. Joiner*, 522 U.S. 136 (1997). Joiner had contracted small cell lung cancer after many years working for a local utility company where he was exposed to various chemicals—specifically, polychlorinated biphenyls (PCBs) and their derivatives, polychlorinated dibenzofurans (furans), and polychlorinated dibenzodioxins (dioxins). In opposing a motion for summary judgment, Joiner submitted an expert's opinion that Joiner's exposure to the chemicals contributed to his lung cancer. However, the trial judge excluded the expert's opinion after finding that the opinion was based on "isolated studies of laboratory animals" exposed to far greater quantities of these chemicals than Joiner's extent of exposure, as well as studies showing that workers exposed to these chemicals faced only a statistically insignificant increased risk of contracting cancer. In concluding that the trial judge did not abuse its discretion in excluding the expert's opinion, the Supreme Court noted that trial judges are to examine the expert's methodology as well as conclusions, reasoning that "conclusions and methodology are not entirely distinct from one another." Further, the court held that "nothing in *Daubert* or the Federal Rules . . . requires a [trial judge] to admit opinion evidence that is connected to existing data only by the *ipse dixit* of the expert. A court may conclude that there is simply too great an analytical gap between the data and the opinion proffered." *Id.* at 146.

To sum up, *Daubert* held:

(1) FRE 702 (as it read in 1993) displaced the *Frye* test as to scientific experts;
(2) FRE 702's requirement that expert testimony be "scientific" requires that the expert's testimony meet a "standard of evidentiary reliability" and that the expert's "reasoning or methodology" be "scientifically valid;"
(3) FRE 702's requirement that expert testimony "help the trier of fact" requires that the expert's reasoning or methodology "fit" the facts of this case because they can "properly be applied to the facts in issue;" *and*
(4) the inquiries into scientific validity and fit (in holdings (2) and (3)) must account for a variety of factors, including but not limited to:
   (a) Whether the methodology can be—or has been—tested;
   (b) Whether the methodology has been subject to peer review;
   (c) The known or potential error rate of the methodology;
   (d) Whether standards exist to control the methodology's operation; and
   (e) Whether the methodology has been "generally accepted" in the pertinent field.

Subsequent cases have examined additional factors:

(f) Whether the methodology predates the litigation in which it is being invoked (or whether it was developed specifically for this litigation), *Smelser v. Norfolk Southern Railway Co.*, 105 F.3d 299, 303 (6th Cir. 1997). For example, if a plaintiff sues a drug company for designing a defective drug, testimony from the drug company's chemist that he developed a new methodology after the plaintiff brought suit in this case and that the methodology shows that the drug could not have caused the plaintiff's complained-of injury is less likely to be considered a valid methodology given that it sprung from the very litigation at issue;
(g) Whether there is "simply too great an analytical gap between the data and the opinion proffered," *GE v. Joiner*, 522 U.S. at 146. This factor includes such considerations as:
   (i) Whether the expert's extrapolation from an accepted premise to his conclusion was justifiable, Adv. Comm. Note to FRE 702;

(ii) Whether the expert has sufficiently accounted for obvious alternative explanations, Adv. Comm. Note to FRE 702; *Claar v. Burlington Northern R.R.*, 29 F.3d 499, 502 (9th Cir. 1994); *and*

(h) Whether the field of expertise claimed by the expert is known to reach reliable results for the type of opinion the expert would give, Adv. Comm. Note to FRE 702; *Kumho Tire Co. v. Carmichael*, 526 U.S. 137, 151 (1999).

For example, assume that a winery sues for just compensation when the state takes its land to widen a highway and seeks to establish that it was going to use the condemned land to grow its "premium" wine. If the winery's expert calculates the value of this never-before-grown grape and never-before-vinted wine by estimating that it will yield $10 more per bottle than competing varietals, this expert testimony is likely to be excluded because there is really no data to support the expert's estimation of success of the nascent premium wine and hence too great an analytical gap between the facts and the opinion regarding value for the nonexistent wine. Also, the expert's methodology was created specifically for this litigation.

Gray v. LG&M Holdings, LLC, 2020 U.S. Dist. LEXIS 188376 (D. Ariz. 2020) examines how *Daubert* applies to the expertise in administering consumer surveys.

Gray v. LG&M Holdings, LLC

2020 U.S. Dist. LEXIS 188376 (D. Az. 2020)

Bolton, Judge.

Plaintiffs Tiffany Toth Gray, Melanie Iglesias, Ana Cheri, Mariana Davalos, Jaime Edmondson Longoria, and Dessie Mitcheson ("Plaintiffs") are professional models, actresses, and social media personalities whose photos have appeared in magazines such as *Playboy, Maxim, Esquire, Sport Truck, Muscle and Fitness, Imagen, Para Hombre, Spiritual Jeans*, and *Seventeen*; who have modeled for brands such as Rockstar Energy Drinks, Monster Energy Drinks, Palms Hotel, the Hard Rock Hotel, Shredz Supplements, Nacar Cosmetics, the MGM Grand Las Vegas, Crest Toothpaste, and Tecate; and who have appeared in television shows, movies, music videos, and commercials. Plaintiffs allege that Defendant misappropriated, altered, and used without permission seven images ("Images") of Plaintiffs to promote its strip club ("Xplicit") on social media. Defendant's promotions consisted of digital flyers containing information about food and drink specials or special events alongside a pasted Image of a Plaintiff (hereinafter "Advertisements"). Plaintiffs allege that Defendant's Advertisements created the false impression that Plaintiffs were strippers who worked at or endorsed Xplicit. Plaintiffs bring one claim for misappropriation of likeness under Arizona law (Count 1); two claims for violation of the Lanham Act, 15 U.S.C. § 1125(a) (Count 2); and one claim for false light invasion of privacy under Arizona law (Count 3).

Plaintiffs retained Martin Buncher ("Mr. Buncher") to conduct a survey measuring the likelihood of consumer confusion resulting from Defendant's use of the Images.

Plaintiffs retained Mr. Buncher to conduct a marketing research survey "designed to measure the degree of confusion which may have been created by the use of eight [*sic*] women . . . in the Internet advertising of the [X]plicit

Gentleman's Club relative to their acting as spokespeople representing the brand, endorsing the brand, and participating in the activities at the Clubs and/or the life style represented in the advertisements, and/or being otherwise affiliated or associated with the brand." Potential respondents were solicited through email or the internet; 606 individuals completed the survey. These individuals were men and women from metropolitan areas surrounding Xplicit who are over 21 and who in the past two years participated in social activities with paid admittance and entertainment—specifically, live music concerts, jazz or comedy night clubs, or "bikini bars/gentleman's clubs/strip clubs."

Each survey contained photos of three Advertisements. Each Advertisement contained one Image. The survey asked respondents to indicate, *inter alia*: what they believed the photos were trying to communicate to them; whether they believed the women pictured had any affiliation with Xplicit; whether they believed the women agreed to sponsor, endorse, or promote Xplicit; whether they agreed that the women in the photos "enjoy a lifestyle" like that reflected in the advertisement; whether they agreed the women in the photos "participate in the events or activities" that take place in Xplicit; whether they agreed the women were paid to appear in the photos; and whether they recognized the women in the photos.

Mr. Buncher proposes to testify about the survey's results. His report recounts that: 16% of respondents recognized the Plaintiffs featured in the three Advertisements; 63% agreed that Plaintiffs "probably do participate in the events and activities which take place in [Xplicit]"; and an "overwhelming majority" "felt [Plaintiffs] had been paid for their appearance." Based on these results, Mr. Buncher concludes that the respondents "mostly tend[ed] to see [Defendant]" as "using [Plaintiffs] to make them think they are the kind of women they would expect to see inside the Explicit [*sic*] Club," and that the use of Plaintiffs' Images "contribute[d] in a major way to [causing respondents to] consider patronizing [Xplicit]."

In the Ninth Circuit, "survey evidence should be admitted 'as long as [the survey is] conducted according to accepted principles and [is] relevant.'" The Ninth Circuit has explained that

> [t]reatment of surveys is a two-step process. First, is the survey admissible? That is, is there a proper foundation for admissibility, and is it relevant and conducted according to accepted principles? This threshold question may be determined by the judge. Once the survey is admitted, however, follow-on issues of methodology, survey design, reliability, the experience and reputation of the expert, critique of conclusions, and the like go to the weight of the survey rather than its admissibility. These are issues for a jury or, in a bench trial, the judge.

In designing the survey, Mr. Buncher relied on his knowledge, education, and experience, which includes the previous administration of thousands of surveys. He drew on "generally accepted standards and procedures in the fielding of surveys set forth by the American Marketing Association, Marketing Research Association, CASRO and ESOMAR." He designed the survey "to meet the criteria for survey trustworthiness detailed in the Federal Judicial Center's Manual for Complex Litigation." His report contains detailed explanations of his methodology and how his methods conform with principles draws from these sources. Mr. Buncher's demonstrated reliance on credible sources establishes that he designed and conducted the survey "according to accepted principles."

As in *Townsend v. Monster Beverage Corp.*, Defendant's arguments are an attempt to "lob a number of criticisms against the methodology" used by Mr. Buncher. As the *Townsend* court recognized, criticisms related to the sample surveyed, use of a control group, design, and question selection "all concern . . . methodology." In the Ninth Circuit, this means that Defendant's challenges are properly directed at the weight, not admissibility, of the survey evidence. Defendant may, of course, critique Mr. Buncher's methodology during cross-examination. Because Mr. Buncher designed and conducted the survey according to accepted principles, the survey evidence is reliable.

RELIABILITY OF TESTIMONY

Defendant next argues that Mr. Buncher's report inaccurately recounts the survey's results. Specifically, Defendant argues that "[Mr.] Buncher seems confused about the facts of the case and what he did[,]" highlights numerous typos in Mr. Buncher's report, and challenges the wordings of specific questions. Tellingly, Defendant does not dispute that the figures recounted in the report—and thus the figures that will be testified to—accurately reflect the raw numbers generated by the survey responses. As Defendant itself acknowledges, typographical and grammatical errors bear on "the professionalism of the expert"—not on the admissibility of his testimony. To the extent Defendant's critiques of the report are simply repackaged critiques of the survey, they are rejected.

Because the *Daubert* test demoted a methodology's "general acceptance" from being the dispositive factor to being one of several relevant factors to consider in assessing whether a methodology is sufficiently reliable, the *Daubert* test *as articulated* is necessarily more liberal when it comes to admitting expert testimony. *Accord Joiner*, 522 U.S. at 142 ("the Federal Rules of Evidence allow district courts to admit a somewhat broader range of scientific testimony than would have been admissible under *Frye* . . . "). But has it proven to be more liberal *in application*? Many commentators contend that *Daubert* has made trial judges more reluctant to admit expert testimony based on methodologies that they—as judges—cannot fully comprehend.[7]

(ii) Expert testimony based on nonscientific knowledge (that is, based on technical or other specialized knowledge)

Expert witnesses often testify on matters that do not rest solely on scientific principles; their testimony may rest partly on scientific principles or rest not at all

---

7. *See* G. Michael Fenner, *The Daubert Handbook: The Case, Its Essential Dilemma, and Its Progeny*, 29 Creighton L. Rev. 939, 953 (1996) (arguing that *Daubert* "is at the same time both more restrictive of expert evidence and less restrictive of expert evidence" because "general acceptance" is no longer a strict requirement but is also not a guarantee of admissibility); David L. Faigman, *Admissibility Regimes: The "Opinion Rule" and Other Oddities and Exceptions to Scientific Evidence, the Scientific Revolution, and Common Sense*, 36 Sw. U. L. Rev. 699, 718 (2008) ("there are assorted hints that federal courts use a *Daubert*-permissive admissibility scheme for prosecution-based expert opinion, while in the civil arena they use a *Daubert*-restrictive test").

on those principles. Just to name a few, experts can acquire specialized knowledge and offer opinions on the following:

- Psychological diagnoses, including trauma and various conditions and syndromes (for example, intimate partner battering syndrome, child sexual abuse accommodation syndrome, posttraumatic stress disorder); *see, e.g.*, *People v. Munch*, 52 Cal. App. 5th 464 (Ca. Ct. App. 2020);
- Handwriting analysis;
- Fingerprint analysis;
- Ballistics analysis;
- Economic analysis;
- Forensic analysis of bookkeeper records;
- Accident reconstruction analysis;
- Human factors analysis (which looks at the biomedical movement of bodies upon impact);
- Damages calculations, including lost profits, lost wages, and earning potential;
- Standards of care for nonscientific professions (such as legal malpractice);
- Expertise on the culture of criminal street gangs.

Is the more admission-friendly *Daubert* test limited to expert testimony based on scientific principles, or does it apply to *all* expert testimony? That was the issue before the Supreme Court in *Kumho Tire Co., Ltd. v. Carmichael*, 526 U.S. 137 (1999). In *Kumho Tire*, the plaintiffs were injured when one of the tires on their minivan had a blowout, causing an accident that resulted in the death of one of the minivan's occupants. The plaintiffs sued Kumho Tire Co., the tire's manufacturer, for manufacturing a defective product. In support of their theory of a product defect, the plaintiffs sough to admit the testimony of an expert in "tire failure analysis." As pertinent here, the expert opined that the blowout was due to a tire defect because (1) blowouts *not* caused by a misuse of tires, called "overdeflection," are "ordinarily" due to a defect in the tire; (2) there are four "physical signs" of overdeflection; (3) a tire that does not have "at least two of the four physical signs" of overdeflection suffered a blowout due to a defect in the tire; and (4) based solely on his visual and tactile inspection of the tire that blew out in this case, the tire on the plaintiff's minivan did not have "at least two of the four overdeflection symptoms." *Id.* at 144-45. Here is an illustration of the composition of the radial tire at issue in *Kumho Tire*.

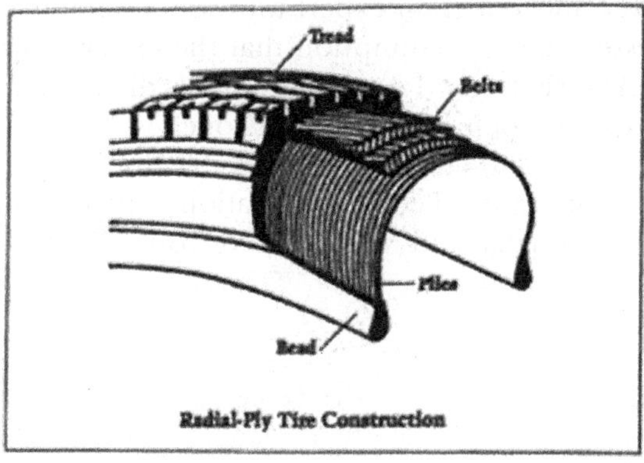

Radial-Ply Tire Construction

Kumho Tire Co., Ltd. v. Carmichael

526 U.S. 137 (1999)

JUSTICE BREYER delivered the opinion of the Court.

This case requires us to decide how *Daubert* applies to the testimony of engineers and other experts who are not scientists. We conclude *Daubert*'s general holding—setting forth the trial judge's general "gatekeeping" obligation—applies not only to testimony based on "scientific" knowledge, but also to testimony based on "technical" and "other specialized" knowledge. See Fed. Rule Evid. 702. We also conclude that a trial court *may* consider one or more of the more specific factors that *Daubert* mentioned when doing so will help determine that testimony's reliability. But, as the Court stated in *Daubert*, the test of reliability is "flexible," and *Daubert*'s list of specific factors neither necessarily nor exclusively applies to all experts or in every case. Rather, the law grants a district court the same broad latitude when it decides *how* to determine reliability as it enjoys in respect to its ultimate reliability determination.

In *Daubert*, this Court held that Federal Rule of Evidence 702 imposes a special obligation upon a trial judge to "ensure that any and all scientific testimony . . . is not only relevant, but reliable." The initial question before us is whether this basic gatekeeping obligation applies only to "scientific" testimony or to all expert testimony. We, like the parties, believe that it applies to all expert testimony. . . .

For one thing, Rule 702 itself says:

> "If scientific, technical, or other specialized knowledge will assist the trier of fact to understand the evidence or to determine a fact in issue, a witness qualified as an expert by knowledge, skill, experience, training, or education, may testify thereto in the form of an opinion or otherwise."

This language makes no relevant distinction between "scientific" knowledge and "technical" or "other specialized" knowledge. It makes clear that any such knowledge might become the subject of expert testimony. In *Daubert*, the Court specified that it is the Rule's word "knowledge," not the words (like "scientific") that modify that word, that "establishes a standard of evidentiary reliability." Hence, as a matter of language, the Rule applies its reliability standard to all "scientific," "technical," or "other specialized" matters within its scope.

Neither is the evidentiary rationale that underlay the Court's basic *Daubert* "gatekeeping" determination limited to "scientific" knowledge. *Daubert* pointed out that Federal Rules 702 and 703 grant expert witnesses testimonial latitude unavailable to other witnesses on the "assumption that the expert's opinion will have a reliable basis in the knowledge and experience of his discipline." The Rules grant that latitude to all experts, not just to "scientific" ones.

Finally, it would prove difficult, if not impossible, for judges to administer evidentiary rules under which a gatekeeping obligation depended upon a distinction between "scientific" knowledge and "technical" or "other specialized" knowledge.

There is no clear line that divides the one from the others. Disciplines such as engineering rest upon scientific knowledge. Pure scientific theory itself may depend for its development upon observation and properly engineered machinery. And conceptual efforts to distinguish the two are unlikely to produce clear legal lines capable of application in particular cases.

Neither is there a convincing need to make such distinctions. Experts of all kinds tie observations to conclusions through the use of what Judge Learned Hand called "general truths derived from . . . specialized experience." And whether the specific expert testimony focuses upon specialized observations, the specialized translation of those observations into theory, a specialized theory itself, or the application of such a theory in a particular case, the expert's testimony often will rest "upon an experience confessedly foreign in kind to [the jury's] own." The trial judge's effort to assure that the specialized testimony is reliable and relevant can help the jury evaluate that foreign experience, whether the testimony reflects scientific, technical, or other specialized knowledge.

We conclude that *Daubert*'s general principles apply to the expert matters described in Rule 702. The Rule, in respect to all such matters, "establishes a standard of evidentiary reliability." It "requires a valid . . . connection to the pertinent inquiry as a precondition to admissibility." And where such testimony's factual basis, data, principles, methods, or their application are called sufficiently into question, see Part III, *infra*, the trial judge must determine whether the testimony has "a reliable basis in the knowledge and experience of [the relevant] discipline."

Our emphasis on the word "may" thus reflects *Daubert*'s description of the Rule 702 inquiry as "a flexible one." *Daubert* makes clear that the factors it mentions do *not* constitute a "definitive checklist or test." And *Daubert* adds that the gatekeeping inquiry must be "'tied to the facts'" of a particular "case." We agree with the Solicitor General that "the factors identified in *Daubert* may or may not be pertinent in assessing reliability, depending on the nature of the issue, the expert's particular expertise, and the subject of his testimony."

To say this is not to deny the importance of *Daubert*'s gatekeeping requirement. The objective of that requirement is to ensure the reliability and relevancy of expert testimony. It is to make certain that an expert, whether basing testimony upon professional studies or personal experience, employs in the courtroom the same level of intellectual rigor that characterizes the practice of an expert in the relevant field. Nor do we deny that, as stated in *Daubert*, the particular questions that it mentioned will often be appropriate for use in determining the reliability of challenged expert testimony. Rather, we conclude that the trial judge must have considerable leeway in deciding in a particular case how to go about determining whether particular expert testimony is reliable. That is to say, a trial court should consider the specific factors identified in *Daubert* where they are reasonable measures of the reliability of expert testimony.

The particular issue in this case concerned the use of Carlson's [(that is, the plaintiffs' expert witness's)] two-factor test and his related use of visual/tactile inspection to draw conclusions on the basis of what seemed small observational differences. We have found no indication in the record that other experts in the industry use Carlson's two-factor test or that tire experts such as Carlson normally make the very fine distinctions about, say, the symmetry of comparatively greater shoulder tread wear that were necessary, on Carlson's own theory, to support his conclusions. Nor, despite the prevalence of tire testing, does anyone refer to any articles or papers that validate Carlson's approach. Indeed, no one has argued that Carlson himself, were he still working for Michelin, would have concluded in a report to his employer that a similar tire was similarly defective on grounds identical to those upon which he rested his conclusion here. Of course, Carlson himself claimed that his method was accurate, but, as we pointed out in *Joiner*, "nothing in either *Daubert* or the Federal Rules of Evidence requires a district court to admit opinion evidence that is connected to existing data only by the *ipse dixit* of the expert."

After *Kumho Tire*, FRE 702 was amended to incorporate *Daubert*'s "reliability" and "fit" requirements into the Federal Rules of Evidence. Those requirements are now codified in FRE 702(c) and FRE 702(d) and apply to all experts regardless of the scientific or nonscientific underpinnings of their expert testimony.[8]

Examples

1. Plaintiff sues Defendant for wrongful death of his spouse. Plaintiff calls an expert to opine that Plaintiff is entitled to $50 million in damages based on "hedonics." Rather than value a person by the value of her labor (and hence to look to her earning potential), hedonics looks to the value that each individual attaches to being alive and looks to the sum total of what a person is willing to pay to stay alive. Defendant objects, saying that hedonics is an invalid methodology. This methodology is nonscientific. Looking to the *Daubert* factors, the methodology may have standards regulating how to try to assess what a person would pay to stay alive, but it is unknown whether the methodology has been peer-reviewed, and the

---

8. Even though California still uses the *Frye* test to evaluate the methodological basis for scientific expert testimony, it has adopted an approach similar to *Daubert* in evaluating the basis for nonscientific expert testimony. Specifically, California trial judges assess the reliability of nonscientific expert testimony by assuring that the testimony is (1) based on facts and data on which experts may reasonably rely, (2) based on reasons supported by the material on which the expert relies (and hence does not have any "analytical gaps" that render the expert's methodology invalid as a matter of logic, other studies in the field, or other information cited by other experts), and (3) not speculative. *Sargon Enterprises, Inc. v. University of Southern California*, 55 Cal. 4th 747, 771-72 (Cal. 2012).

methodology has not been tested and its error rate is impossible to know. Many courts have found hedonics-based valuations to be inadmissible.

2. Defendant is charged with willfully failing to pay his federal income taxes. Prosecutor calls an accounting and tax expert to testify that Defendant must have acted willfully (that is, with a motive to defraud the government) because the tax returns at issue were glaringly inconsistent with the Internal Revenue Code. This expert opinion is likely inadmissible because it rests on nothing but speculation regarding Defendant's motive.
3. Defendant is charged with possessing child pornography. Police used a computer program that sends out search queries to databases suspected of exchanging images depicting child pornography and then compares the "hash value" of any files sent in response to the queries against the "hash values" of known images of child pornography; if the hash values match, it is likely that the file is a copy of the known image of child pornography. Expert opinion explaining this computer program and that it led to the images found on Defendant's computer is admissible because it is sufficiently reliable under *Daubert*.

(iii) New frontiers in expert testimony

Just as the sciences (whether they be hard sciences or the social sciences) are not static, the vanguard of the law regarding expert testimony is always shifting. Here are a few areas where the law on expert witnesses continues to change as the science changes.

(A) *Eyewitness identification experts*

In criminal cases, defendants often proffer expert testimony on the dangers and pitfalls of eyewitness identifications. This expert testimony is grounded in the study of psychology and examines how people perceive other people, how memory works (or does not work), and how the conditions under which identifications are made or exposure to other information can influence and even warp one's memory. These experts often opine on the unreliability of cross-racial identifications (that is, that members of one race are not adept at distinguishing between members of an ethnicity other than their own) or the dangers of "unconscious transference" where a witness who sees a person in one location will mistakenly recall that he saw the person at the scene of the crime. Although the federal courts were initially quite hostile to such testimony on the ground that it took the issue of witness credibility away from the jury and risked confusing the jury with a battle of the experts, *United States v. Langan*, 263 F.3d 613, 621 (6th Cir. 2001) (collecting cases), courts have more recently concluded that such testimony satisfies the *Daubert* standard and that excluding it can even be error. *E.g., United States v. Smith*, 621 F. Supp. 2d 1207, 1214-15 (M.D. Ala. 2009) (so holding).

(B) *Brain scan experts*

For years, scientists have tried to find a surefire way to determine if a person is telling the truth or lying. In the mid-twentieth century, the lie detector *du jour* was the polygraph test, which uses a galvanic skin response (GSR) test that measures fluctuations in a person's skin moisture as a proxy for whether she was under additional stress due to having to fabricate what she was saying. These days, most courts do not admit such evidence. *United States v. Scheffer*, 523 U.S. 303, 310-11 (1998) (cataloguing general rule). But the frontier for lie detection has moved on. Now, scientists are trying to determine if changes in brain chemistry are a telltale sign for whether a person is lying. A few technologies have been developed to do so. Functional magnetic resonance imaging (or fMRI) uses brain scans captured every few seconds to measure brain activity with the aim of recognizing different activity levels depending on whether the subject is lying or telling the truth. A second technology uses electroencephalography (EEG) to record the emission of P300 waves that are thought to register brain activity *for recognition* on the theory that when a person is confronted with something (or someone) that he claims not to recognize, the portion of his brain recognizing that object or person will become active, despite his denial of any such recognition. Obviously, if adequately supported by the science, a foolproof lie detector test would make a jury's job of assessing who is lying considerably easier. But the science is not yet there, as various studies indicate that people can "fool" the brain scans by employing countermeasures.

The advancement of knowledge and expertise in these areas is not purely academic; it really matters. In recent years, advancements in science have revealed that forensic practices historically thought to be reliable are, in reality, not scientifically valid and thus do not provide a reliable means of identifying the perpetrator of a crime. On the basis of these advancements, many criminal defendants have sought—and some have obtained—reversals of their convictions based on this now-debunked science. The fallibility and discrediting of some of these now-debunked forensic technologies reinforce the critical role that trial judges play as gatekeepers tasked with keeping expert opinions based on unreliable science out of trials, especially criminal trials.

4. *Additional Rules Governing Experts*

Thus far, we have covered the three main requirements for expert opinion testimony: the proper subject for expert testimony, the proper qualifications of the testifying expert, and the proper basis for the expert opinion. The Federal Rules of Evidence provide additional details regarding the introduction of expert opinion testimony. We cover two of them now, namely, the rules governing how far an expert opinion may go (which is governed by FRE 704) and who may call an expert (which is governed by FRE 706).

(a) Opinions on Ultimate Issues

FRE 702 requires that an expert opinion must "help the trier of fact to understand the evidence or to determine a fact in issue." FRE 702(a). What are the limits of a "helpful" opinion? May the expert go as far as to offer an opinion on the "ultimate issues" in a case (such as whether the defendant killed the victim, whether the defendant intended to kill the victim, or whether the defendant did so to benefit a gang and therefore his conviction warrants a longer sentence)? FRE 704 addresses this question. Specifically, FRE 704 provides the following:

FRE 704. Opinion on an Ultimate Issue

(a) In General—Not Automatically Objectionable. An opinion is not objectionable just because it embraces an ultimate issue.

(b) Exception. In a criminal case, an expert witness must not state an opinion about whether the defendant did or did not have a mental state or condition that constitutes an element of the crime charged or of a defense. Those matters are for the trier of fact.

The common law did not permit an expert to opine on ultimate issues, so FRE 704(a) departs from the common law rule by generally permitting such opinions. For example, depending on the case, the "ultimate issue" may include the following:

- Whether the defendant's conduct was the cause of the plaintiff's injury;
- Whether a person had the required mental state to sign a will or contract;
- Whether the defendant took unauthorized deductions on his income tax returns;
- Whether two companies are alter egos of one another;
- Whether a competing claim infringed a patent.

The latitude that the rules of evidence grant expert testimony to embrace ultimate issues is not a blank check, however. There are two limits.

The first is set forth in FRE 704 itself. FRE 704(b) explicitly requires the exclusion in a criminal case of an expert opinion "about whether the defendant did or did not have a mental state or condition that constitutes an element of the crime charged or of a defense." FRE 704 provides that "[t]hose matters are for the trier of fact alone."

Despite this limit under FRE 704(b), the rule does not prohibit an expert in a criminal case from providing background information that stops just short of offering an opinion on the defendant's mental state.

Consider the following examples.

Examples

1. Defendant is charged with possessing cocaine with intent to distribute. Prosecutor calls a narcotics detective to testify about which quantities of cocaine are consistent with personal use of the drug and which quantities

of cocaine are consistent with possession of the drug for distribution to others. Using this information, Prosecutor could argue to the jury that Defendant possessed the cocaine with the intent to distribute it. What the expert *cannot* do is offer an opinion that Defendant acted with the intent to distribute.

2. In a will contest between a brother and a sister, the sister calls an expert to opine that their mother—the decedent—did not have a proper understanding of her surroundings and her health at the time that she executed her will. This testimony is admissible because FRE 704(b)'s exception does not apply in this civil case.
3. Defendant is charged with murdering his roommate. Defendant raises the defense of not guilty by reason of insanity. In federal court, insanity is a defense to the crime of murder, so an expert may not opine that Defendant was "sane" or "insane."[9] However, the expert may testify about the hallmarks of a lack of sanity, such as Defendant did not seem to understand or appreciate the nature of his acts, which the defense attorney may use to argue to the jury that Defendant was not sane at the time that he committed the crime.[10]
4. Defendant is charged with murder. Defendant argues that she acted in self-defense because the murder victim—her husband—had physically and verbally abused her for many years leading up to the charged crime. Defendant calls a psychologist to testify about intimate partner battering syndrome and the effects it can have on those who are battered. The psychologist may also testify about the typical behaviors that indicate whether a person is suffering from this syndrome. This testimony is all admissible because it can help explain Defendant's behavior. However, the psychologist may *not* take the further step of testifying that, as a result of the syndrome, Defendant subjectively believed that the use of deadly force was necessary to avoid imminent harm to herself. This testimony would run afoul of FRE 704(b)'s bar.
5. Defendant is charged with murder. Defendant raises a defense of "diminished capacity," which requires proof that Defendant suffers from a mental disorder that prevents him from formulating the specific intent to kill that is an element of murder. Defendant calls a psychologist to opine that (1) Defendant suffers from bipolar disorder and schizophrenia and (2) Defendant's mental disorders prevent him from forming the intent to kill. The expert's first opinion is not barred by FRE 704(b); the second opinion is barred. *See United States v. Cohen*, 510 F.3d 1114 (9th Cir. 2007).

---

9. California has a similar exclusion, which calls for the exclusion of expert opinions on sanity during the guilt phase (when "not guilty by reason of insanity" is a defense) but allows for such opinions in the "sanity" phase of the trial. See Cal. Pen. Code § 29; *People v. Kelly*, 1 Cal. 4th 495, 539 fn. 10 (Cal. 1992); *People v. Wilson*, 25 Cal. 2d 341, 349 (Cal. 1944).

10. These prohibitions on mental state do not reach expert opinions on whether a defendant is competent to stand trial, which is a question separate and apart from the defendant's guilt.

The second limit on opinion testimony on an ultimate issue grows out of FRE 702's general requirement that an expert opinion be helpful to the jury. This limit provides that an expert opinion is *not* helpful if it encroaches on matters entrusted to the jurors or the trial judge. Topics that invade the so-called province of the jury include whether a criminal defendant is "guilty" of the charged crime(s) or whether the defendant was "at fault" in a civil case, as well as whether a witness was telling the truth. *E.g., United States v. Scop*, 846 F.2d 135, 142 (2d Cir. 1988) ("expert witnesses may not offer opinions . . . the credibility of another witness's testimony"). Topics that invade the trial judge's role include opinions on the meaning of the law, because it is the trial judge's job to interpret and define the law for the jury. *Jiminez v. City of Chicago*, 732 F.3d 710, 720 (7th Cir. 2013) ("experts should not provide legal opinions").

Consider the following examples.

Examples

1. Defendant is charged with murder. Prosecutor calls the lead investigative officer to testify as the final witness in her case-in-chief. She asks, "Now that you have heard all the evidence and in light of your experience investigating hundreds of murder cases, do you believe that the evidence presented in this case establishes Defendant's guilt of this murder beyond a reasonable doubt?" This question asks for an impermissible opinion regarding the ultimate determination of fault, which in a criminal case is "guilt."
2. Plaintiff sues Defendant for injuries sustained in a car-bicycle collision. Defendant calls an accident reconstruction expert and asks, "Who is at fault for this accident?" This question asks for an impermissible opinion regarding the ultimate determination of fault.
3. A grandchild sues to invalidate a will in a probate action. The will in effect at the time of death left everything to the deceased's estranged son. The grandchild testifies that the deceased—the grandmother—told her, just days before her death, that she wanted to leave everything to the grandchild and nothing to the son. The son calls an expert witness who observed the grandchild's testimony and asks the expert witness, "Based on your observations and your experience in studying the link between demeanor and truth-telling, do you think that [grandchild] was telling the truth or lying during her testimony?" This question asks for an impermissible opinion regarding a witness's believability.
4. A former criminal defendant sues the police department for violating his civil rights in searching his car without probable cause. The former defendant calls an expert on Fourth Amendment law and asks, "Did the police conduct in this case constitute a 'search' within the meaning of the Fourth Amendment?" This question asks for an impermissible legal opinion.
5. In a will contest proceeding, one of the parties calls an expert witness and asks, "Did [the deceased] have the capacity to make a will at the time that the last will was executed in this case?" This "ultimate question" is

permissible in theory, but is impermissible in practice because it uses a shorthand for the proper standard—"capacity"—rather than the actual legal standard for assessing capacity. The Advisory Committee Notes refer to this question as being an ultimate opinion "phrased in terms of inadequately explored legal criteria."

Given this limitation on expert opinions, as well as the basic requirement that expert opinion testimony be "helpful" and that an expert opinion is only helpful if it is based on expertise beyond the juror's common knowledge, courts do not allow expert opinion that invades the jury's special role in evaluating credibility and making the final determination of guilt or liability in a case.

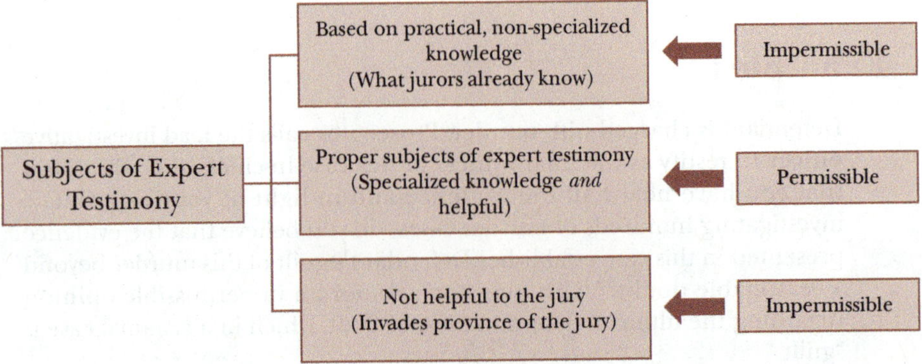

(b) Court-Appointed Experts

Expert witnesses are typically called by the parties to a case. Can the trial judge appoint and call as a witness an expert? The answer is "yes," if the judge believes that she or the jury needs the assistance of an expert to resolve a case.

Specifically, FRE 706 provides the following:

FRE 706. Court-Appointed Expert Witnesses

(a) Appointment Process. On a party's motion or on its own, the court may order the parties to show cause why expert witnesses should not be appointed and may ask the parties to submit nominations. The court may appoint any expert that the parties agree on and any of its own choosing. But the court may only appoint someone who consents to act.

(b) Expert's Role. The court must inform the expert of the expert's duties. The court may do so in writing and have a copy filed with the clerk or may do so orally at a conference in which the parties have an opportunity participate. The expert:

(1) must advise the parties of any findings the expert makes;

(2) may be deposed by any party;

(3) may be called to testify by the court or any party; and

(4) may be cross-examined by any party, including the party that called the expert.

(c) Compensation. The expert is entitled to a reasonable compensation, as set by the court. The compensation is payable as follows:

(1) in a criminal case or in a civil case involving just compensation under the Fifth Amendment, from any funds that are provided by law; and

(2) in any other civil case, by the parties in the proportion and at the time that the court directs—and the compensation is then charged like other costs.

(d) Disclosing the Appointment to the Jury. The court may authorize disclosure to the jury that the court appointed the expert.

(e) Parties Choice of Their Own Experts. This rule does not limit a party in calling its own experts.

Walker v. American Home Shield Long Term Disability Plan

180 F.3d 1065 (9th Cir. 1999)

McKeown, Judge.

As an account executive for American Home Shield, Pamela Walker sold home warranty insurance to home buyers through real estate agents. Each day her job required her to drive to at least 12 different real estate offices throughout the Los Angeles area, make multiple telephone calls to customers and attend various meetings. In April 1990, Walker stopped working and applied for long-term disability benefits due to extreme pain, fatigue and stress arising from her job.

Virtually all of the seven doctors who examined Walker or her file agreed that Walker had fibromyalgia, but the doctors disputed the extent to which Walker's fibromyalgia affected her ability to work. Fibromyalgia is a form of rheumatic disease with no known cause or cure. The principal symptoms, which are entirely subjective, are pain and tenderness in muscles, joints and ligaments, but the disease is frequently accompanied by fatigue, sleep disturbances, anxiety, dizziness, irritable bowels and tension headaches. Stress is both a symptom of fibromyalgia and an exacerbating factor. Because proving the disease is difficult and no objective test exists, fibromyalgia presents a conundrum for insurers and courts evaluating disability claims[.]

Walker was eligible for disability benefits under a UNUM disability policy that provides for disability benefits upon "proof that an insured is disabled due to sickness or injury and requires the regular attendance of a physician." Eligibility for disability requires proof that "the insured cannot perform each of the material duties of his regular occupation." To receive ongoing benefits, the insured must provide "proof of continued disability."

UNUM subsequently terminated Walker's continuing disability benefits, stating in the termination letter that Walker was not disabled because (1) she was physically capable of performing her job, (2) even if she were disabled, she failed to provide objective medical evidence of a disability, and (3) even if she were disabled due to stress, she was not receiving treatment for stress.

Walker appealed the termination of her benefits and UNUM referred Walker to another examining physician and appointed yet another doctor to review her file. Each of these physicians concluded that Walker could work full-time but with certain restrictions.

Based on UNUM's decision not to reinstate her benefits, Walker filed suit under ERISA for wrongful termination of disability benefits. The parties filed cross-motions for summary judgment. The district court determined that . . . the appropriate standard of review of the plan administrator's decision was *de novo.* Because of the difficulty of reviewing the administrator's decision *de novo* where the medical evidence was not "particularly clear," the district court appointed an independent expert, Dr. Daniel Wallace, the Clinical Chief of Rheumatology at Cedars-Sinai Medical Center in Los Angeles, a Clinical Professor at UCLA School of Medicine, former Chairman of the Fibromyalgia Subcommittee of the Arthritis Foundation and an author of numerous publications on fibromyalgia.

Dr. Wallace examined Walker and concluded that she had fibromyalgia and was totally disabled from performing her job. Based upon the entire record, including Dr. Wallace's report, the district court granted Walker's motion for summary judgment. UNUM appeals from this judgment.

The district court did not abuse its discretion in appointing an independent medical expert to help evaluate medical evidence. We have previously held that the district court has discretion to consider evidence beyond the record where "additional evidence is necessary to conduct an adequate de novo review of the benefit decision." Armed with the authority to consider additional evidence in its de novo review, the district court also has the discretion to appoint an expert *sua sponte* under Federal Rule of Evidence 706(a):

> The court may on its own motion . . . enter an order to show cause why expert witnesses should not be appointed. . . . The court . . . may appoint witnesses of its own selection.

The district court followed the dictates of Rule 706(a) by issuing an order to show cause why an expert should not be appointed, ordering briefing, holding a hearing and then appointing an expert of its own selection. Both the consideration of additional evidence and the appointment of an expert under Rule 706 are reviewed for abuse of discretion.

UNUM argues that additional evidence is not "necessary" because the record was sufficiently developed and the plan administrator made no error of law, unlike the plan administrator in *Mongeluzo.* UNUM mistakenly characterizes the district court as viewing the evidence in equipoise. Instead, the district court's statement that the medical testimony was not "particularly clear" suggests that the court found the evidence concerning fibromyalgia to be confusing and conflicting. This case presented the district court an appropriate occasion to appoint an independent expert to assist the court in evaluating contradictory evidence about an elusive disease of unknown cause.

Review Questions

1. **Accident reconstruction.** Plaintiff sues Defendant for injuries sustained in a pedestrian-automobile collision. Plaintiff calls an accident reconstruction expert, who opines on how the accident happened based on forensic evidence (such as almost nonexistent skid marks) and based on how eyewitnesses described what happened. The expert also opines that Defendant was at fault. Defendant calls an expert who opines that the accident happened a completely different way.
   a. Is Plaintiff's accident reconstruction expert permitted, under the rules of evidence, to opine on (i) how the accident happened and (ii) who was most at fault?
   b. Do the expert's opinion(s) have a sufficient factual basis?
   c. If the expert testifies before the eyewitnesses upon whose testimony he partly relies, may he relay the content of their testimony to the jury?
   d. Does the fact that Defendant's expert offers a contrary opinion undermine the methodological reliability of Plaintiff's expert's testimony?
2. **Certainty of identification.** Defendant is charged with bank robbery. Prosecutor calls a bank teller, who identified Defendant with "70 percent certainty" in a lineup conducted immediately after the robbery, but testifies that she is "100 percent certain" Defendant was the man who held a gun to her face. Defendant seeks to call an expert witness to testify about the flaws in eyewitness testimony, including the lack of correlation between accuracy and certainty as well as the added difficulties of cross-racial identification.
   a, What type of testimony is this expert witness offering: scientific, technical, or other specialized knowledge?
   b. Does the admissibility of this testimony turn at all on whether the bank teller and Defendant are of the same race, or are of different races?
3. **Excessive force.** When police officers are trying to arrest Defendant, he resists. The police officers used force to detain him. Defendant is prosecuted for resisting arrest and alleges excessive force as a defense. Defendant also sues the officers for damages in a civil lawsuit based on the violations of his civil rights due to the officers' use of excessive force. In each case, Defendant calls an expert who testifies to what less forceful options the police officers had when dealing with a person in Defendant's situation and his opinion that the officers used excessive force.
   a. Are both portions of the expert's opinion admissible?
   b. Does the admissibility of the expert's opinion regarding the ultimate issue of the use of excessive force depend on whether this case is a criminal or a civil case?

SUMMARY OF ADMISSIBILITY REQUIREMENTS FOR OPINION TESTIMONY

	Lay Opinion	Expert Opinion
Subject Matter	*Not* based on scientific, technical, or other specialized knowledge	Based on scientific, technical, or other scientific knowledge
Qualification of witness	Personal knowledge	Expertise based on knowledge, skill, experience, training, or education
Opinion prerequisites	Opinion is helpful to trier of fact	(1) Opinion is helpful to trier of fact (2) Opinion has a sufficient and reliable factual basis (3) Opinion is based on a sufficient and reliable methodology (4) The opinion's methodology can reliably be applied to the facts of this case

TEST YOUR UNDERSTANDING

To test your understanding of the material in this chapter, turn to the Supplement for additional practice problems.

Chapter 13

Authentication, the Best Evidence Rule, and Demonstrative Evidence

After focusing on the Federal Rules of Evidence applicable specifically to the testimony of witnesses (in Chapters Ten through Twelve), we now turn to the rules of evidence applicable specifically to the other main categories of evidence—namely, documents and nondocumentary physical evidence (firearms, drugs, and the like). In addition to satisfying the rules regarding relevance and, if applicable, hearsay, documents and physical evidence may also need to satisfy further evidentiary requirements as a prerequisite to admissibility:

- Documentary evidence (1) must be *authenticated* and (2) may need to satisfy the *best evidence rule*; and
- Physical evidence must be authenticated.

Part A of this chapter discusses the authentication of evidence. *Authentication* requires the party seeking to admit the document or physical item into evidence to establish that the document or physical item "is what the proponent claims it is." FRE 901(a). It is often referred to as "laying the foundation" for the evidence. Part B discusses the *best evidence rule*, which establishes a preference that the party seeking to prove the content of a writing (or a recording or photograph) do so by introducing the original of the writing (or recording or photograph) rather than a duplicate or testimony about that writing (or recording or photograph). The best evidence rule is more of a preference than a requirement because it has a number of exceptions that allow for liberal use of duplicates (rather than the original) and that allow for the use of testimony when the original or a duplicate is not readily available. Part C examines the use of demonstrative evidence. Demonstrative evidence can make a courtroom come to life. It includes charts, demonstrations, illustrations, and simulations that will be useful to witnesses and the lawyers in presenting the case to the jury.

PART A: AUTHENTICATION

1. General Principles

The authentication requirement is set forth in FRE 901. It provides the following:

FRE 901. Authenticating or Identifying Evidence

(a) In General. To satisfy the requirement of authenticating or identifying an item of evidence, the proponent must produce evidence sufficient to support a finding that the item is what the proponent claims it is.

(b) Examples. The following are examples only—not a complete list—of evidence that satisfies the requirement:

(1) ***Testimony of a Witness with Knowledge.*** Testimony that an item is what it is claimed to be.

(2) ***Nonexpert Opinion About Handwriting.*** A nonexpert's opinion that handwriting is genuine, based on a familiarity with it that was not acquired for the current litigation.

(3) ***Comparison by an Expert Witness or the Trier of Fact.*** A comparison with an authenticated specimen by an expert witness or the trier of fact.

(4) ***Distinctive Characteristics and the Like.*** The appearance, contents, substance, internal patterns, or other distinctive characteristics of the item, taken together with all the circumstances.

(5) ***Opinion About a Voice.*** An opinion identifying a person's voice—whether heard firsthand or through mechanical or electronic transmission or recording—based on hearing the voice at any time under circumstances that connect it with the alleged speaker.

(6) ***Evidence About a Telephone Conversation.*** For a telephone conversation, evidence that a call was made to the number assigned at the time to:

(A) a particular person, if circumstances, including self-identification, show that the person answering was the one called; or

(B) a particular business, if the call was made to a business and the call related to business reasonably transacted over the telephone.

(7) ***Evidence About Public Records.*** Evidence that:

(A) a document was recorded or filed in a public office as authorized by law; or

(B) a purported public record or statement is from the office where items of this kind are kept.

(8) ***Evidence About Ancient Documents or Data Compilations.*** For a document or data compilation, evidence that it:

(A) is in a condition that creates no suspicion about its authenticity;

(B) was in a place where, if authentic, it would likely be; and

(C) is at least 20 years old when offered.

(9) ***Evidence About a Process or System.*** Evidence describing a process or system and showing that it produces an accurate result.

(10) ***Methods Provided by a Statute or Rule.*** Any method of authentication or identification allowed by a federal statute or a rule prescribed by the Supreme Court.

Excerpt from Advisory Committee Notes to FRE 901

- The examples [set forth in FRE 901(b)] are not intended as an exclusive enumeration of allowable methods but are meant to guide and suggest, leaving room for growth and development in this area of the law.

As its language suggests and the Advisory Committee Note confirms, FRE 901(a) takes an extremely flexible approach to the authentication of evidence. The rule further emphasizes its flexibility by laying out "Examples" in 901(b) rather than by specifying mandates that must always be followed in authenticating evidence. Some of these examples pertain to authenticating documents; others pertain to authenticating physical evidence.

Consider the following examples.

Examples

1. Plaintiff sues her landlord for not maintaining the safety of the complex's premises after she was mugged while walking up a stairwell to her apartment. Plaintiff seeks to introduce a photograph of the stairwell to show how dark it was at the time of the mugging. To authenticate the photograph for this purpose, Plaintiff could testify that the photograph depicts the stairwell where she was mugged and is a fair and accurate representation of how dark it was at the time of the mugging.
2. Plaintiff sues Defendant for breach of contract. Plaintiff seeks to introduce the contract that she alleges was breached. To authenticate the contract as the actual contract at issue, Plaintiff can testify that (1) she was present when it was signed and witnessed its signing or (2) she recognizes the contract by its content (that is, by its terms).
3. Defendant is charged with making criminal threats to the victim. The victim testifies that Defendant called her and, while on the phone, stated, "I will tear you limb from limb." To authenticate that it was Defendant's voice on the other end of the phone, the victim can testify that (1) she has known Defendant for years and recognizes his voice or (2) Defendant, before making the threat, referred to an earlier conversation that the victim had with Defendant (and only Defendant). If it is established

that the call was made by Defendant, this finding will also lay the foundation for admitting the call as an opposing party's "admission" under FRE 801(d)(2).

4. Defendant is charged with drug trafficking. Prosecutor wants to establish that the baggie of drugs seized from Defendant's pocket were the same drugs that the state chemist tested and determined to be methamphetamine. To authenticate that the baggie of drugs tested by the chemist was the same baggie seized from Defendant, Prosecutor seeks to establish the "chain of custody" to show that the same baggie was passed from the seizing officer to the evidence custodian at the police station to the chemist who retrieved the baggie from the custodian.
5. Prosecutor seeks to introduce a letter against Defendant in which Defendant purportedly threatens the victim. The victim can authenticate the letter by her recognition of Defendant's handwriting, by recognizing Defendant's signature, or the fact that an exact copy of the letter was found in Defendant's desk drawer. If it is established that the letter was sent by Defendant, this finding will also lay the foundation for admitting the statement as an opposing party's "admission" under FRE 801(d)(2).
6. Plaintiff sues Defendant for an accidental shooting on a movie set. Plaintiff seeks to introduce the gun that was used in the shooting by having a stagehand testify that the gun he is being shown at the trial has the same appearance as a gun that Defendant used, the gun has Defendant's initials on it, and in a picture taken on the set, Defendant is depicted holding a gun that appears to be identical. In this situation, no further foundation is necessary because the gun is physical evidence, its relevance is clear, and no hearsay issues are raised.

As these examples make clear, there is often more than one way to authenticate a document or a physical item of evidence. What is more, authentication can serve multiple purposes at the same time. In Examples 3 and 5 above, for instance, the victim's identification of the defendant on the other end of the line or as the sender of the letter not only authenticates the call and the letter themselves, but also establishes that the hearsay exception for adverse party admissions applies.

As these examples also make clear, authentication is a *relevance*-based doctrine because it establishes that the document or physical item being introduced into evidence is that one that matters to this case. If the photograph in Example 1 does not accurately reflect the lighting in the stairwell, it is not relevant to show the conditions of the landlord's property. If the contract in Example 2 is not the contract the defendant signed, it is not relevant to a case seeking to establish breach of contract by the defendant. If the person on the other end of the phone in Example 3 is not the defendant, the speaker's words are irrelevant. If the baggie of drugs tested by the chemist in Example 4 is not the baggie seized from the defendant, its chemical composition is irrelevant to proving the defendant's guilt for drug trafficking. If the letter in Example 5 did not come from the defendant, it is irrelevant to the charges against the defendant. And if the gun in Example 6 is not the gun fired on the movie set, the gun has no relevance to the accidental shooting that occurred.

The key question in determining whether a document or an item of physical evidence is properly authenticated is, "What is this document or item of physical evidence being admitted to prove?" Consider the following examples.

Examples

Defendant is being charged with the crime of stalking his ex-girlfriend. The charge is based on a text message the ex-girlfriend received, which read, "Just saw *Scream V.* You should check to make sure I'm not in *your* house at night."

1. One element of the crime of stalking is that the victim was placed in fear. If Prosecutor is introducing the text message to prove the ex-girlfriend's fear, the text message is authenticated *for that purpose* if the ex-girlfriend testifies that she received the text message. (She would go on to testify that it made her afraid.) For this purpose, the ex-girlfriend need not testify that Defendant was the person who sent the text message. (Prosecutor would need to prove that in some other way.)
2. Another element of the crime of stalking is that Defendant was the person who committed the crime—or, in this case, the person who sent the text message. To prove that the text message was sent by Defendant, Prosecutor could (a) call the ex-girlfriend to say it appeared in response to her last text message to Defendant or that it contained information that only Defendant knew or (b) call the cell phone company to testify that the company's records showed a message going from Defendant's phone to the ex-girlfriend's phone at the same date and time that the ex-girlfriend received the text message.

In each example, the questions asked to authenticate the text message turned on what the text message was being introduced to prove—either to prove the victim's fear or instead the defendant's identity as the perpetrator.

Despite the variety of different methods used to authenticate evidence, the mechanics or procedure for authenticating evidence are fairly standardized. They are illustrated by the following graphic.

Mark item as (P's or D's) Exhibit No. X → Lay foundation for Exhibit No. X → Move to admit Exhibit No. X

Here is a typical line of questioning to authenticate a piece of evidence:

Lawyer: I hand you what has been marked as Exhibit 7. Do you recognize it?
Witness: Yes.
Lawyer: How do you recognize it?
Witness: It is the hatchet I found at Defendant's home.
Lawyer: How can you tell it is the same hatchet?
Witness: It had a black blade with initials, "BH," etched on it.
Lawyer: The prosecution moves Exhibit 7 into evidence.

If the relevance of the evidence has been established or will be established by other witnesses who will tie the hatchet to the victim's killing, the witness's testimony is sufficient to establish authenticity.

The task of deciding whether a document or other physical item of evidence is authenticated is divided between the trial judge and the jury. The judge makes the threshold, preliminary determination that there is sufficient evidence for a jury to find that the evidence is what it purports to be, but it is up the jury to make the ultimate finding of authenticity. If it does not, the jury may disregard the evidence. The trial judge has the flexibility to admit an item of evidence conditionally—that is, before it is fully authenticated—with the understanding that the party introducing that evidence will authenticate it later (and, if the party does not, that the evidence will be excluded and testimony relating to it stricken from the record). FRE 104(b).

2. *Authenticating Documentary Evidence*

The Federal Rules of Evidence offer two ways to authenticate documents. Some documents are presumptively authenticated (and the rules refer to them as "self-authenticating"), and all other documents must be authenticated by the introduction of evidence.

(a) Self-Authenticating Documents

In recognition of the likelihood that certain documents are going to be authentic and to save time, FRE 902 delineates 14 categories of "self-authenticating" documents. Documents falling into those categories are generally public documents, business records, and even electronic records that have been "certified" by their authors as being authentic. They are deemed to be authentic without the need for any further proof on that point.

Examples

1. A party seeks to introduce a certified copy of a birth certificate. If the birth certificate bears a seal of certification, there is no need to call a witness from the county records office to authenticate it.

2. Defendant seeks to introduce ABC Corporation's business records. The company's custodian of records attaches an affidavit that the records satisfy the requirements of the business records exception. The records are "self-authenticating," unless the opposing party, who must be given notice, seeks in a timely manner to challenge them.

A document's status as "self-authenticating" does not conclusively establish its authentication because the opposing party may still dispute its authenticity. FRE 902, Adv. Comm. Note.

Specifically, FRE 902 provides the following:

FRE 902. Evidence That Is Self-Authenticating

The following items of evidence are self-authenticating; they require no extrinsic evidence of authenticity in order to be admitted:

(1) ***Domestic Public Documents That Are Sealed and Signed.*** A document that bears:

(A) a seal purporting to be that of the United States; any state, district, commonwealth, territory, or insular possession of the United States; the former Panama Canal Zone; the Trust Territory of the Pacific Islands; a political subdivision of any of these entities; or a department, agency, or officer of any entity named above; and

(B) a signature purporting to be an execution or attestation.

(2) ***Domestic Public Documents That Are Not Sealed but Are Signed and Certified.*** A document that bears no seal if:

(A) it bears the signature of an officer or employee of an entity named in Rule 902(1)(A); and

(B) another public officer who has a seal and official duties within that same entity certifies under seal—or its equivalent—that the signer has the official capacity and that the signature is genuine.

(3) ***Foreign Public Documents.*** A document that purports to be signed or attested by a person who is authorized by a foreign country's law to do so. The document must be accompanied by a final certification that certifies the genuineness of the signature and official position of the signer or attester—or of any foreign official whose certificate of genuineness relates to the signature or attestation or is in a chain of certificates of genuineness relating to the signature or attestation. The certification may be made by a secretary of a United States embassy or legation; by a consul general, vice consul, or consular agent of the United States; or by a diplomatic or consular official of the foreign country assigned or accredited to the United States. If all parties have been given a reasonable opportunity to investigate the document's authenticity and accuracy, the court may, for good cause, either:

(A) order that it be treated as presumptively authentic without final certification; or

(B) allow it to be evidenced by an attested summary with or without final certification.

(4) ***Certified Copies of Public Records.*** A copy of an official record—or a copy of a document that was recorded or filed in a public office as authorized by law—if the copy is certified as correct by:

(A) the custodian or another person authorized to make the certification; or

(B) a certificate that complies with Rule 902(1), (2), or (3), a federal statute, or a rule prescribed by the Supreme Court.

(5) ***Official Publications.*** A book, pamphlet, or other publication purporting to be issued by a public authority.

(6) ***Newspapers and Periodicals.*** Printed material purporting to be a newspaper or periodical.

(7) ***Trade Inscriptions and the Like.*** An inscription, sign, tag, or label purporting to have been affixed in the course of business and indicating origin, ownership, or control.

(8) ***Acknowledged Documents.*** A document accompanied by a certificate of acknowledgment that is lawfully executed by a notary public or another officer who is authorized to take acknowledgments.

(9) ***Commercial Paper and Related Documents.*** Commercial paper, a signature on it, and related documents, to the extent allowed by general commercial law.

(10) ***Presumptions Under a Federal Statute.*** A signature, document, or anything else that a federal statute declares to be presumptively or prima facie genuine or authentic.

(11) ***Certified Domestic Records of a Regularly Conducted Activity.*** The original or a copy of a domestic record that meets the requirements of Rule 803(6)(A)-(C), as shown by a certification of the custodian or another qualified person that complies with a federal statute or a rule prescribed by the Supreme Court. Before the trial or hearing, the proponent must give an adverse party reasonable written notice of the intent to offer the record—and must make the record and certification available for inspection—so that the party has a fair opportunity to challenge them.

(12) ***Certified Foreign Records of a Regularly Conducted Activity.*** In a civil case, the original or a copy of a foreign record that meets the requirements of Rule 902(11), modified as follows: the certification, rather than complying with a federal statute or Supreme Court rule, must be signed in a manner that, if falsely made, would subject the maker to a criminal penalty in the country where the certification is signed. The proponent must also meet the notice requirements of Rule 902(11).

(13) ***Certified Records Generated by an Electronic Process or System.*** A record generated by an electronic process or system that produces an accurate result, as shown by a certification of a qualified person that complies with the certification requirements of Rule 902(11) or (12). The proponent must also meet the notice requirements of Rule 902(11).

(14) ***Certified Data Copied from an Electronic Device, Storage Medium, or File.*** Data copied from an electronic device, storage medium, or file, if authenticated by a process of digital identification, as shown by a certification of a qualified person that complies with the certification requirements of Rule 902(11) or (12). The proponent also must meet the notice requirements of Rule 902(11).

(b) Authenticating Documents with Proof

When a document is not self-authenticating, the party seeking to admit the document has to introduce evidence to authenticate the document. As FRE 901(b) illustrates, there are several ways to do so.

(i) Testimony by someone who is familiar with the document

A document can be authenticated by a person who is familiar with the document. That familiarity can come from the document's "distinctive characteristics," such as its appearance or content. FRE 901(b)(1), (b)(4). The person need not witness the document being created or signed in order to authenticate it. The person also need not be the signatory of the document unless a specific statute so requires. This latter rule is set forth in FRE 903.

FRE 903. Subscribing Witness

A subscribing witness's testimony is necessary to authenticate a writing only if required by the law of the jurisdiction that governs its validity.

Example

Defendant is charged with murder. Defendant calls a witness to cast doubt on his identity as the perpetrator. Prosecutor cross-examines the witness about text messages between the witness and his girlfriend. Defendant objects, "Lack of foundation" because the girlfriend did not testify that *she* sent the messages to the witness, and thus the messages purporting to be from her might have been sent by someone else. If the witness testifies to the general content of the text message conversation or that the content of the messages purporting to be from the girlfriend is something that only the girlfriend would know, that is sufficient to lay the foundation; the testimony of both text message authors is not necessary.

(ii) Circumstantial evidence of authenticity

A document can also be authenticated circumstantially. For instance, evidence that a will was found in the decedent's home, in a file called "Will," is circumstantial evidence of its authenticity. Along similar lines, evidence that a letter has a letterhead from the author or was found in an envelope with the author's return address is circumstantial evidence that the letter came from the author. In the same vein, if an e-mail comes in response to an earlier e-mail in a chain, that fact is circumstantial evidence that the e-mail originated from the person who received the earlier response. Evidence that a contract between two businesses is authentic can be established by showing that the party denying the contract's existence nevertheless engaged in conduct consistent with the specific terms of the contract.

(iii) Handwriting match

A document can be authenticated as coming from a particular person by the handwriting on the document. A handwriting match can be established by (1) the lay opinion of anyone familiar with the author's handwriting as long as their familiarity "was not acquired for the current litigation",[1] (2) an expert opinion comparing the handwriting on the document to a known sample of the author's handwriting, or (3) a comparison of the handwriting on the document to a known sample of the author's handwriting by the jury or, if it is a bench trial, the judge. FRE 901(b)(2), (b)(3).

(iv) Ancient documents

A document that is "ancient"—that is, one that is at least 20 years old—can be authenticated by proof of its age; that it was found in a place "where, if authentic," it would likely be; and that its condition does not raise any suspicion.[2] FRE 901(b)(8).

(v) Public records

If a public record does not meet the qualifications to be self-authenticating, a public record can still be authenticated by proof that (1) it is a document recorded or filed in a public office as authorized by law or (2) it is a public record or statement from the public office where items of that kind are kept. FRE 901(b)(7).

---

1. New York, Texas, and Illinois follow the federal requirement that a lay witness's familiarity with handwriting not be acquired for the purpose of litigation. *People v. Molineux*, 168 N.Y. 264, 320-21 (N.Y. 1901); Tex. R. Evid. 901(b)(2); Ill. R. Evid. 901(b)(2). Florida's authentication statute does not specify the particular method of authentication, Fl. Stat. § 90.901, but its case law follows the Federal Rules of Evidence on this point. *Proctor v. State*, 97 So. 3d 313, 315 (Fla. Dist. Ct. App. 2012). In California, a lay witness who gained familiarity with a person's handwriting in anticipation of litigation may still testify. Cal. Evid. Code § 1416.

2. In California, a document must be 30 years old to qualify as "ancient." Cal. Evid. Code § 1419.

(vi) Documents produced by a system or process

If a document is a readout from a machine, it can be authenticated by proof that the machine is operating properly and that it "produces an accurate result." FRE 901(b)(9). Thus, if a police officer testifies that his radar gun clocked the defendant driving 93 miles per hour down a residential street, that writing is admissible only if the officer or another witness establishes that the radar gun was operating properly that day (and that the officer was operating the radar gun properly). If it was not, the reading is meaningless and irrelevant. Similarly, if a lab chemist testifies that the gas chromatography machine registered that the sample placed into its testing chamber came back with a 0.25 blood alcohol content, that writing is admissible only if there is proof that the machine was working properly (and that the lab chemist was operating it properly).

(vii) Other statutes or rules authorizing authentication

If a federal statute or other rule promulgated by the Supreme Court authorizes a different way to authenticate an item of evidence, that method will also suffice. FRE 901(b)(10). For instance, Federal Rule of Civil Procedure 30(f) details how to authenticate a deposition in a civil case (namely, by certifying and sealing the deposition transcript and sending it to the attorney who ordered the deposition for safekeeping).

(viii) Electronically stored documents

When a hard copy of a document is stored in a physical file, access to the document is limited to those with physical access to the file and tampering is more likely to be detectable visually. But what if a document is stored electronically? With most computers connected to the Internet, the data stored on those computers is potentially accessible to a skilled hacker. Also, electronically stored documents can be altered in a way that is more difficult to detect. However, many software programs and computer systems use "metadata" (or keep track of data using hash values) that go along with the electronically stored records; that metadata or those hash values, which are not always easily accessible, can reveal whether documents have been altered. Expert witnesses are frequently called upon to examine the electronic characteristics of such evidence to determine whether it has been altered or to establish the source of the data.

But does the mere possibility that an electronically stored document can be more easily altered preclude its authentication? *United States v. Safavian* answers, "No."

United States v. Safavian

435 F. Supp. 2d 36 (D.C.D.C. 2006)

FRIEDMAN, Judge.

[Defendant is charged with making a false statement with regard to a government investigation. The government made a motion in limine to introduce a series of e-mails as admissions or adoptive admissions by the defendant. To do so, the government needed to establish the authenticity of the e-mails and their source.]

A. AUTHENTICATION OF E-MAILS

The requirement of authentication or identification as a condition precedent to admissibility is satisfied by evidence sufficient to support a finding that the matter in question is what its proponent claims." FED. R. EVID. 901(a). The threshold for the Court's determination of authenticity is not high. The question for the Court under Rule 901 is whether the proponent of the evidence has "offered a foundation from which the jury could reasonably find that the evidence is what the proponent says it is." The Court need not find that the evidence is necessarily what the proponent claims, but only that there is sufficient evidence that the jury ultimately might do so.

1. Rule 902(11)

Rule 902 of the Federal Rules of Evidence lists those documents that are self-authenticating—that is, those that do not require extrinsic evidence of authenticity as a condition precedent to admissibility. Rule 902(11) is intended to set forth "a procedure by which parties can authenticate certain records of regularly conducted activity, other than through the testimony of a foundation witness." Pursuant to Rule 902(11), the government submitted a certification from Jay Nogle, the official custodian of records for Greenberg Traurig, LLP, the law firm that once employed Jack Abramoff. Mr. Nogle stated that in his capacity as official custodian he could certify that 467,747 e-mails had been produced by Greenberg Traurig to the United States and that those e-mails comport with the requirements of Rule 902(11), in part because the e-mails "would be admissible under Fed. R. Evid. 803(6) if accompanied by a written declaration of [their] custodian or other qualified person." The government does not, however, seek to admit these e-mails pursuant to the business records exception to the hearsay rule in Rule 803(6), but offers other hearsay exceptions and non-hearsay arguments (discussed later in this Opinion) as bases for admission. The defendant objects to the authentication of the Greenberg Traurig e-mails pursuant to Mr. Nogle's Rule 902(11) certification.[1] Because Rule 902(11) was intended as a means of authenticating only that evidence which is being offered under the business records exception to the hearsay rule, the Court will not accept the proffered Rule 902(11) certification of Mr. Nogle with reference to the Greenberg Traurig e-mail exhibits.

2. Rule 901

Because it is not appropriate for these e-mails to be admitted as self-authenticating under Rule 902 of the Federal Rules of Evidence, the Court turns to the authentication requirements set forth in Rule 901. The question under Rule 901 is whether there is sufficient evidence "to support a finding that the matter in question is what its proponent claims"—in this case, e-mails between Mr. Safavian, Mr. Abramoff, and other individuals.

---

1. The government has submitted 902(11) certifications for other documents, but the defendant at a hearing before the Court on the motions conceded that the other ones were appropriate, leaving its only remaining objection to Mr. Nogle's certification of the Greenberg Traurig e-mails.

One method of authentication identified under Rule 901 is to examine the evidence's "distinctive characteristics and the like," including "[a]ppearance, contents, substance, internal patterns, or other distinctive characteristics, taken in conjunction with circumstances." Most of the proffered exhibits can be authenticated in this manner. The e-mails in question have many distinctive characteristics, including the actual e-mail addresses containing the "@" symbol, widely known to be part of an e-mail address, and certainly a distinctive mark that identifies the document in question as an e-mail. In addition, most of the e-mail addresses themselves contain the name of the person connected to the address, such as "abramoffj@gtlaw.com," "David.Safavian@mail.house.gov," or "david.safavian@gsa.gov." Frequently these e-mails contain the name of the sender or recipient in the bodies of the e-mail, in the signature blocks at the end of the e-mail, in the "To:" and "From:" headings, and by signature of the sender. The contents of the e-mails also authenticate them as being from the purported sender and to the purported recipient, containing as they do discussions of various identifiable matters, such as Mr. Safavian's work at the General Services Administration ("GSA"), Mr. Abramoff's work as a lobbyist, Mr. Abramoff's restaurant, Signatures, and various other personal and professional matters.

Those e-mails that are not clearly identifiable on their own can be authenticated under Rule 901(b)(3), which states that such evidence may be authenticated by comparison by the trier of fact (the jury) with "specimens which have been [otherwise] authenticated"—in this case, those e-mails that already have been independently authenticated under Rule 901(b)(4). For instance, certain e-mails contain the address "MerrittDC@aol.com" with no further indication of what person uses that e-mail address either through the contents or in the e-mail heading itself. When these e-mails are examined alongside [other exhibits], it becomes clear that MerrittDC@aol.com was an address used by the defendant. The comparison of those e-mails containing MerrittDC@aol.com with [other exhibits], can provide the jury with a sufficient basis to find that these two exhibits are what they purport to be—that is, e-mails to or from Mr. Safavian.

The defendant argues that the trustworthiness of these e-mails cannot be demonstrated, particularly those e-mails that are embedded within e-mails as having been forwarded to or by others or as the previous e-mail to which a reply was sent. The Court rejects this as an argument against authentication of the e-mails. The defendant's argument is more appropriately directed to the weight the jury should give the evidence, not to its authenticity. While the defendant is correct that earlier e-mails that are included in a chain—either as ones that have been forwarded or to which another has replied—may be altered, this trait is not specific to e-mail evidence. It can be true of any piece of documentary evidence, such as a letter, a contract or an invoice. Indeed, fraud trials frequently center on altered paper documentation, which, through the use of techniques such as photocopies, white-out, or wholesale forgery, easily can be altered. The possibility of alteration does not and cannot be the basis for excluding e-mails as unidentified or unauthenticated as a matter of course, any more than it can be the rationale for excluding paper documents (and copies of those documents). We live in an age of technology and computer use where e-mail communication now is a normal and frequent fact for the majority of this nation's population, and is of particular importance in the professional world. The defendant is free to raise this issue with the jury and put on evidence that e-mails are capable of being altered before they are passed on. Absent specific evidence showing alteration, however, the Court will not exclude any embedded e-mails because of the mere possibility that it can be done.

(ix) Documents pulled from the Internet

There are special issues that arise when it comes to authenticating information pulled from the Internet.

Example

Defendant is charged with assault with a deadly weapon with a gang allegation. Prosecutor seeks to introduce evidence from a Facebook page for "Diablo" that shows Defendant and others throwing gang signs and that says, "Imma Crip killa" in one of the posts. Defendant objects, "Lack of foundation."

The photograph and posting in the above example are relevant to prove the gang allegation only if (1) the photo is an authentic photo of the defendant and (2) the defendant is responsible for posting "Imma Crip killa" on the website (thereby showing his motive and intent to kill his gang's rivals). However, the data posted on a Facebook page—like the data posted on any website—changes over time and can be hacked. How can the prosecutor prove that the web-postings are attributable to the defendant and not someone else?

The courts have not yet settled on the answer. Some courts will authenticate a webpage found on the Internet only if the witness testifying to authenticate the webpage has personal knowledge capable of verifying the source of the information, *e.g.*, *Weinhoffer v. David Shoring, Inc.*, 2022 U.S. App. LEXIS 1774, *2-*6 (5th Cir. 2022); *Nightlight Sys. v. Nitelites Franchise Sys.*, 2007 U.S. Dist. LEXIS 95538, *15-*17 (N.D. Ga. 2007). Where a witness seeks to testify that the webpage is attributable to a particular person, courts have required proof that the person created or controlled the webpage (to obviate the possibility that someone else created the webpage in their name). *E.g.*, *United States v. Vayner*, 769 F.3d 125, 129-33 (2d Cir. 2014). And other courts have admitted webpages that looked identical to the pages that witnesses had previously seen and knew to be authentic, at least in the absence of proof that the webpages were altered in any material respect. *E.g.*, *Live Face On Web, LLC v. Integrity Solutions Group, Inc.*, 421 F. Supp. 3d 1051, 1068-70 (D. Colo. 2019). One expert has recommended a panoply of options for authenticating information found on a website:

> In assessing the authenticity of website data, important evidence is normally available from the personnel managing the website ("webmaster" personnel). A webmaster can establish that a particular file, or identifiable content, was placed on the website at a specific time. This may be

> done through direct testimony or through documentation, which may be generated automatically by the software of the web server. . . . [Sometimes, a] second witness (or set of documentation) may be necessary to reasonably ensure that the content which appeared on the site is the same as that proffered[.]

Gregory P. Joseph, Esq., "Internet and Email Evidence," *The Practical Lawyer*, at p. 21 (Feb. 2012).

3. *Authenticating Evidence (Other Than Documents)*

There is no self-authentication provision for nondocumentary evidence. However, the manner by which nondocumentary evidence can be authenticated is open-ended and broad. As detailed below, the most common forms of authentication typically depend on the type of evidence to be authenticated.

(a) Physical Evidence (That Is, Objects)

Physical (or real) evidence consists of items themselves — the drugs seized from a defendant's car, a particular piece of fenced jewelry, the gun fished from the river, the bullet shells collected from the murder scene. There are two main methods for authenticating physical evidence.

First, when the item is *unique* in some way due to having a nonfungible appearance, a serial number, or other imperfection that distinguishes it from others of its kind, the item can be authenticated by the testimony of the person who recognizes the item due to its unique features.

Second, when the item is more generic and cannot be tracked due to anything unique about it, the item can be authenticated by establishing the chain of custody of the item that shows how it got from the place it was most relevant (for example, the crime scene) to the place it was tested and, in some cases, also to the courtroom. "Chain of custody" refers to the different individuals who might have handled the evidence. Calling these persons as witnesses shows that the evidence was not tampered with during its handling. However, it is not required that *every* link in the chain of custody be called as a witness. The ultimate question is whether the authentication was sufficiently complete to convince the court that it is unlikely that the evidence was exchanged or tampered with during its handling. When there is a sufficient chain of custody, a break in the chain is said to go more to the weight of the evidence than the admissibility. Even though the evidence is admitted, the opposing party may still argue to the jury that the evidence has been altered. *United States v. Howard-Arias* illustrates this point.

United States v. Howard-Arias

679 F.2d 363 (4th Cir. 1982)

SPROUSE, Judge.

[A]ppellant, Edmundo Howard-Arias was convicted after a jury trial of possession of marijuana on the high seas with intent to distribute it and of possession with intent to import it into the United States. [Approximately 240 bales of marijuana were discovered on defendant's ship, the "Don Frank." It was turned over to the Coast Guard and Drug Enforcement Administration (DEA) investigators.]

The appellant's claims regarding the admission of certain evidence need not long detain us. His first argument is that the government failed to establish a continuous "chain of custody" for the marijuana from the time of its seizure on the seas off the Virginia coast until introduction at trial. It is conceded that one of the DEA agents involved in the transfer and testing of the bales and samples drawn from them did not testify at trial. The Coast Guard officer who seized and tested the marijuana, the officer to whom he surrendered it, the DEA custodian at Norfolk, and the DEA chemist all appeared as witnesses. The special agent who received the marijuana from the Coast Guard for transit to the DEA in Norfolk did not.

The "chain of custody" rule is but a variation of the principle that real evidence must be authenticated prior to its admission into evidence. See Fed.R.Evid. 901. The purpose of this threshold requirement is to establish that the item to be introduced, i.e., marijuana, is what it purports to be, i.e., marijuana seized from the "Don Frank." Therefore, the ultimate question is whether the authentication testimony was sufficiently complete so as to convince the court that it is improbable that the original item had been exchanged with another or otherwise tampered with. Contrary to the appellant's assertion, precision in developing the "chain of custody" is not an iron-clad requirement, and the fact of a "missing link does not prevent the admission of real evidence, so long as there is sufficient proof that the evidence is what it purports to be and has not been altered in any material aspect." Resolution of this question rests with the sound discretion of the trial judge, and we cannot say that he abused that discretion in this case.

Some courts will refer to a "presumption of official regularity" when there are official records or testimony establishing that the physical evidence was handled in accordance with "normal police procedures." *See, e.g., United States v. Collado*, 957 F.2d 38 (1st Cir. 1992). That may aid in authenticating items that have been in official custody. Moreover, in civil cases, Federal Rule of Civil Procedure 26(a)(1) requires that each party provide copies of their tangible evidence to the other side before trial, and if an objection is not made in a timely matter, authentication is waived.

(b) Mechanical/Computer/System Processes

As noted above, sometimes mechanical and computer processes produce a writing documenting their output. Other times, such as when a drug-trained dog alerts, the process produces something other than a writing. In either situation, the result of the mechanical or system process is admissible only if its output is accurate and that accuracy is established by showing that the process is operating properly and was properly used in that case. FRE 901(b)(9). Thus, a prosecutor seeking to use a drug dog's positive alert has to establish that the dog at issue was properly trained and that its track record of positive hits was sufficiently strong that a reasonable jury could surmise that the dog's result was accurate in this case. Similarly, a landlord could show that his tenant suing him for injuries was drunk at the time that he was injured by seeking to introduce surveillance video of the apartment complex showing the plaintiff staggering moments before he injured himself; to authenticate that video, the landlord would have to show that the recording equipment was properly working and that the date and time stamp were accurate.

(c) Telephone Calls and Other Voice Identifications

Establishing who is on the other end of a voice communication can be relevant for multiple purposes. A person's testimony that it was the defendant's voice on the other end of the line can prove (1) that the defendant was the one who made the charged threat over the phone or (2) the admissibility of the call under the opposing party admission exception to the hearsay rule.

The possible methods to authenticate a voice include the following:

(1) For either outgoing or incoming calls, a witness can testify that he or she recognizes the person's voice based on past familiarity with it. FRE 901(b)(5).

(2) When it comes to outgoing calls, a witness can also testify that (a) he called a specific person or business at the number assigned to it and a person answering the phone was the person or business assigned and identified himself as such, FRE 901(b)(6), or (b) the person who answered knew information that only the person he is identified as being would know.

(3) When it comes to incoming calls, a witness can also testify that she recognizes the caller based on what the caller knows.

(4) An expert witness can make a "voiceprint" identification between the person on the call and the defendant's voice. FRE 901(b)(3).

Courts are wary when the only evidence offered to authenticate a conversation is that a caller used a certain nickname. Although there might be other evidence, such as the number called and who is the known user of that number, a caller out of the blue who self-identifies with a particular name may be insufficient. *United States v. Pool* illustrates this point.

United States v. Pool

660 F.2d 547 (5th Cir. 1981)

HILL, Judge.

A jury found beyond a reasonable doubt that the eight appellants participated in a scheme to import approximately 225,000 pounds of marijuana worth $ 60,000,000 into the United States.

This case is a testament to the excellent and resourceful work of the Drug Enforcement Administration (DEA). Through skillful undercover infiltration, several DEA agents were able to monitor the appellants' constantly changing plans to import marijuana into this country. Ultimately, the appellants were arrested while attempting to import $ 60,000,000 of marijuana. We set out the facts in some detail to accurately portray each appellant's role in the scheme.

On August 5, 1978, at 10:40 a.m. DEA Agent Starratt received a call from a person who identified himself as "Chip," a nickname used by appellant Loye throughout the investigation. The caller told the agent that Petrulla wanted DEA Agent Story to obtain another boat. Based on this conversation Agent Starratt identified Loye as the telephone participant charged with the § 843(b) violation in Count 9. The conversation was not recorded. Starratt never met Chip and he never made any voice comparison with Loye. The only way Starratt could identify the caller was through the caller's self-identification. Under these circumstances, Loye argues that Starratt's testimony identifying him is inadmissible because it was not authenticated.

We have previously remarked that "a telephone call out of the blue from one who identifies himself as X may not be, in itself, sufficient authentication of the call as in fact coming from X." We agree with the government that the standard of admissibility of voice identification testimony is prima facie. We also agree that circumstantial evidence may be used in meeting this standard. However, there is not sufficient evidence to support the conclusion that Agent Starratt actually heard Loye's voice. As noted, Starratt had never met Loye and no voice comparisons were made. Under these circumstances, Loye's use of the nickname "Chip" does not make out a prima facie case that he was the caller. The possibility that someone else was using his nickname in this clandestine operation is too great to properly admit Agent Starratt's identification. This identification was essential to Loye's § 843(b) conviction. Accordingly, we reverse Loye's conviction for Count 9.

(d) Photographs and Sketches

A photograph or sketch may be authenticated as accurately depicting what is shown in the photograph or what is sketched in a number of ways.

First, either may be authenticated by the person who took the photograph or drew the sketch. That person can explain how the photo or sketch accurately depicts what they saw at the time the photo was taken or the sketch was created.

Second, anyone who recognizes the content of the photo or in the sketch can testify that the photo or sketch is a fair and accurate representation of what the person observed at the pertinent time. For example, a teller may describe a bank robber to a police artist who makes a sketch. At trial, the teller can identify the sketch as the one made from the teller's description. In analyzing whether there is sufficient foundation to authenticate the evidence, it is important that the photograph not just represent the scene in general, but represent the conditions that are relevant to the case. For example:

Lawyer: Were you at the scene when the plaintiff slipped?
Witness: Yes, I was standing right on the sidewalk.
Lawyer: Looking at Exhibit A, is that how the sidewalk appeared that evening?
Witness: Yes, but the lighting was not as bright.

In this scenario, an opponent of the evidence might contest the photograph because it does not accurately represent the lighting at the scene at the time of the accident. The trial judge has broad discretion to determine whether all the circumstances in the case, as presented by one or several witnesses, establish sufficient authenticity for a photograph or drawing. There is no absolute requirement that the photograph be taken at the exact same time, as long as what is depicted fairly and accurately reflects what the witness saw firsthand.

United States v. Taylor

530 F.2d 639 (5th Cir. 1976)

TUTTLE, Judge.

Appellants James Crawford Hicks and Freddie Lee Taylor were convicted by a jury . . . for armed robbery of a federally-insured state bank. Briefly stated: at approximately 9 a.m. on February 10, 1975, the Havana State Bank in Havana, Florida, was robbed of about $6,700 at gunpoint by two men wearing masks. The robbers took the money, ordered everyone present into the bank vault, and locked them inside. A bank camera, tripped after the bank personnel were locked in the vault, took pictures of the robbers. A local grocer saw two men pass his storefront window immediately after the robbery, and saw one of the men's faces. Approximately one hour later, appellants Hicks and Taylor were stopped, questioned, and their car searched by consent in Bainbridge, Georgia by a county sheriff. Two bank tellers present during the robbery then went to Bainbridge but were unable to identify appellants as the perpetrators of the robbery when confronted face to face with them. Appellants were thereupon released, but were arrested the following day in Tallahassee, Florida, by F.B.I. agents, on the strength of some of the bank photographs taken during the robbery.

Hicks . . . argues that the district court erred in admitting into evidence contact prints made from the film taken by the bank camera after the tellers and a bank official, Henry Slappey, were locked in the bank vault. Appellant contends that the government failed to lay the proper foundation for admission of these photographs since none of the eyewitnesses to the robbery testified that the pictures accurately represented the bank interior and the events that transpired.

In the case before us it was, of course, impossible for any of the tellers to testify that the film accurately depicted the events as witnessed by them, since the camera was activated only after the bank personnel were locked in the vault. The only testimony offered as foundation for the introduction of the photographs was by government witnesses who were not present during the actual robbery. These witnesses, however, testified as to the manner in which the film was installed in the camera, how the camera was activated, the fact that the film was removed immediately after the robbery, the chain of its possession, and the fact that it was properly developed and contact prints made from it. Under the circumstances of this case, we find that such testimony furnished sufficient authentication for the admission of the contact prints into evidence. Admission of this type of photographic evidence is a matter largely within the discretion of the court. [I]n certain instances photographs may be admissible as probative evidence in themselves, rather than solely as illustrative evidence to support a witness's testimony, provided that sufficient foundation evidence is adduced to show the circumstances under which it was taken and the reliability of the reproduction process.

(e) Transcripts

When recordings are admitted into evidence, transcripts are frequently used to assist the jury in following along with the recording. However, the transcripts themselves are not evidence; rather, they are a tool that jurors can use to follow along with the recording. When recordings are not in English, an interpreter may be called to provide the foundation for a translated transcript. That interpreter can then be cross-examined as to the accuracy of the translated transcript. When a transcript is in English, either a stipulation or testimony from a person who compared the tape to the transcript and who can testify that the transcript is accurate will suffice to allow the use of that transcript as an aid.

Review Questions

1. **X-rays.** Plaintiff sues Defendant for injuries suffered in an automobile accident. To support his claim for damages, Plaintiff introduces an x-ray of his spine. What will suffice to authenticate the x-ray?
   a. Plaintiff's testimony regarding what his spine looks like?
   b. Testimony from Plaintiff's physician describing the injuries depicted in the x-ray?
   c. Testimony from the radiologist about how x-rays are taken, how the machine that takes them is calibrated, whether the machine that produced this x-ray was properly calibrated, whether the x-ray machine was properly used on the day that it produced Plaintiff's x-ray, and how x-ray images are properly developed?
2. **1-800-BOOKIES.** Defendant is charged with running a gambling operation over the phone. Prosecutor seeks to introduce evidence of (a) a telephone call someone made to Defendant and (b) a telephone call Defendant's phone made to a well-known "bookie" in Las Vegas. What must Prosecutor do to authenticate these calls?
3. **Flight records.** Defendant is charged with interstate transportation of narcotics. She was arrested with heroin after a plane flight when she landed in Salt Lake City, Utah. Prosecutor seeks to introduce records from "Flying High" airlines to prove that the flight originated in San Francisco, California. How would Prosecutor authenticate the records?
4. **Flyover photos.** Defendant is charged with illegally cultivating marijuana. Prosecutor seeks to introduce photographs taken by a drone that flew over Defendant's backyard. What must Prosecutor do to authenticate those photos?

PART B: THE BEST EVIDENCE RULE

If a party to a civil or criminal case wishes to admit a document into evidence to prove its contents, the options for doing so include the following:

- Introduce the original of the document;
- Introduce a copy of the original; or
- Introduce no document, but have someone testify about what the document says.

Should the Federal Rules of Evidence prefer one type of proof over another? Consider the following examples.

Examples

1. Plaintiff sues Defendant for breach of contract in not delivering the widgets that Plaintiff ordered. Defendant seeks to introduce its original shipping records showing that the widgets were shipped.
2. Same as Example 1, but Defendant seeks to introduce a copy of those records rather than the originals.
3. Same as Example 1, but Defendant testifies about the shipping records without introducing them into evidence.

For purposes of proving what the shipping records say, the original shipping records (from Example 1) are the most reliable (and hence "best") evidence. That is because the original records are less likely to be tampered with and are being directly received into evidence rather than transmitted secondhand or thirdhand. Proof via a copy (from Example 2) is the next most reliable (and hence next "best") evidence; copies are not as good as the originals, but are still better than secondhand recollections of what the document says. And proof via testimony without any records at all (from Example 3) is the least reliable (and hence least "best") form of evidence because there is a very real risk that the testimony might be mistaken or, worse yet, intentionally inaccurate.

The *best evidence rule* reflects these two preferences when it comes to proving what a document says—a preference for the original over copies and a preference for *any* original or copy over testimonial evidence of what the document says.

Despite what its name might connote, however, the best evidence rule is limited to the above purpose. It is not a free-floating requirement that parties always present the "best evidence" of a point.[3] Thus, if a defendant is on trial for suborning perjury, the prosecutor does not run afoul of the best evidence rule by calling a person who attended the hearing where the alleged perjury took place to testify about what the lying witness said. Although the official reporter's transcript from

---

3. That is likely why California changed the name of its best evidence rule to the "secondary evidence rule."

that hearing would undoubtedly be the best evidence of what the witness said, the best evidence rule does not apply here because the prosecutor is not trying to introduce *what the transcript says*; instead, she is trying to introduce evidence of what the witness said in court, and the fact that the testimony was later transcribed into a document is of no moment. (If the transcript is available, the trial judge may exclude the testimony under FRE 403, but that exclusion would not be due to noncompliance with the best evidence rule.)

For these reasons, the best evidence rule is better thought of as the "original writings" rule.

For the most part, and consistent with most other rules aimed at assuring the reliability of evidence, whether evidence proffered by a party satisfies the best evidence rule is a question for the trial judge. FRE 1008 provides the following:

FRE 1008. Functions of the Court and Jury

Ordinarily, the court determines whether the proponent has fulfilled the factual conditions for admitting other evidence of the content of a writing, recording, or photograph under Rule 1004 or 1005. But in a jury trial, the jury determines—in accordance with Rule 104(b)—any issue about whether:

(a) an asserted writing, recording, or photograph ever existed;
(b) another one produced at the trial or hearing is the original; or
(c) other evidence of content accurately reflects the content.

FRE 1008 reserves the three above-enumerated issues for a jury because those issues "go beyond the mere administration of the rule preferring the original and into the merits of the controversy." FRE 1008, Adv. Comm. Note.

It is important to keep in mind that the best evidence rule is separate and distinct from the requirement that a document be authenticated. Indeed, the best evidence rule may require a party to authenticate a document *as the original* or *as a copy (or duplicate) of the original* in order to figure out how the best evidence rule applies.

1. *The Rule Itself*

FRE 1002 sets forth the best evidence rule:

FRE 1002. Requirement of the Original

An original writing, recording, or photograph is required in order to prove its content unless these rules or a federal statute provides otherwise.

The best evidence rule can be illustrated as follows:

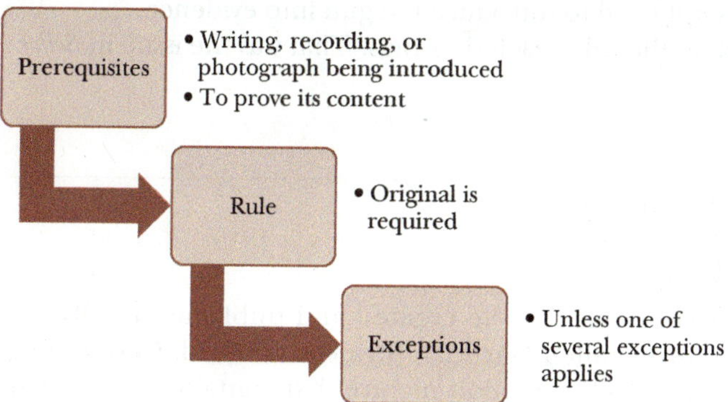

(a) Prerequisites

The best evidence rule only applies if the party is (1) seeking to prove the content (2) of a "writing," "recording," or "photograph."

Taking the second prerequisite first, the Federal Rules of Evidence define each of those terms.

FRE 1001. Definitions That Apply to This Article

In this article:

(a) A "writing" consists of letters, words, numbers, or their equivalent set down in any form.

(b) A "recording" consists of letters, words, numbers, or their equivalent recorded in any manner.

(c) A "photograph" means a photographic image or its equivalent stored in any form.

These definitions also include electronically stored writings, recordings, and photographs. Specifically, FRE 101 provides the following:

FRE 101. Scope; Definitions

(b) Definitions. In these rules:

(6) a reference to any kind of written material or any other medium includes electronically stored information.

These definitions do *not* apply to physical evidence that is not documentary in nature. Thus, if a prosecutor wishes to introduce testimony about a gun, the prosecutor does not need to introduce the gun into evidence.

But does the rule reach drawings? That was the issue in *Seiler v. Lucasfilm, Ltd.*

Seiler v. Lucasfilm, Ltd.

808 F.2d 1316 (9th Cir. 1987)

Farris, Judge.

Seiler contends that he created and published in 1976 and 1977 science fiction creatures called Garthian Striders. In 1980, George Lucas released The Empire Strikes Back, a motion picture that contains a battle sequence depicting giant machines called Imperial Walkers. In 1981 Seiler obtained a copyright on his Striders, depositing with the Copyright Office "reconstructions" of the originals as they had appeared in 1976 and 1977.

Seiler contends that Lucas' Walkers were copied from Seiler's Striders which were allegedly published in 1976 and 1977. Lucas responds that Seiler did not obtain his copyright until one year after the release of The Empire Strikes Back and that Seiler can produce no documents that antedate The Empire Strikes Back.

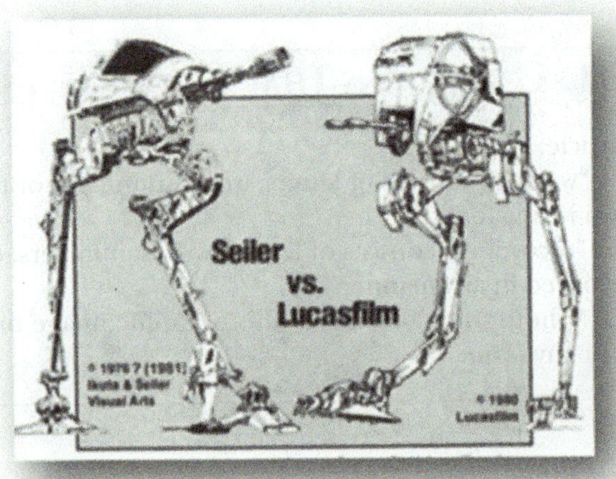

Because Seiler proposed to exhibit his Striders in a blow-up comparison to Lucas' Walkers at opening statement, the district judge held an evidentiary hearing on the admissibility of the "reconstructions" of Seiler's Striders. Applying the "best evidence rule," Fed. R. Evid. 1001-1008, the district court found at the end of a seven-day hearing that Seiler lost or destroyed the originals in bad faith under Rule 1004(1) and that consequently no secondary evidence, such as the post-Empire Strikes Back reconstructions, was admissible. In its opinion the court found specifically that Seiler testified falsely, purposefully destroyed or withheld in bad faith the originals, and fabricated and misrepresented the nature of his reconstructions. The district court granted summary judgment to Lucas after the evidentiary hearing.

DISCUSSION

The best evidence rule embodied in Rules 1001-1008 represented a codification of longstanding common law doctrine. Dating back to 1700, the rule requires not, as its common name implies, the best evidence in every case but rather the production of an original document instead of a copy. Many commentators refer to the rule not as the best evidence rule but as the original document rule.

Rule 1002 states: "To prove the content of a writing, recording, or photograph, the original writing, recording, or photograph is required, except as otherwise provided in these rules or by Act of Congress." Writings and recordings are defined in Rule 1001 as "letters, words, or numbers, or their equivalent, set down by handwriting, typewriting, printing, photostating, photographing, magnetic impulse, mechanical or electronic recording, or other form of data compilation."

The Advisory Committee Note supplies the following gloss:

> Traditionally the rule requiring the original centered upon accumulations of data and expressions affecting legal relations set forth in words and figures. This meant that the rule was one essentially related to writings. Present day techniques have expanded methods of storing data, yet the essential form which the information ultimately assumes for usable purposes is words and figures. Hence the considerations underlying the rule dictate its expansion to include computers, photographic systems, and other modern developments.

Some treatises, whose approach seems more historical than rigorously analytic, opine without support from any cases that the rule is limited to words and figures.

We hold that Seiler's drawings were "writings" within the meaning of Rule 1001(1); they consist not of "letters, words, or numbers" but of "their equivalent." To hold otherwise would frustrate the policies underlying the rule and introduce undesirable inconsistencies into the application of the rule.

In the days before liberal rules of discovery and modern techniques of electronic copying, the rule guarded against incomplete or fraudulent proof. By requiring the possessor of the original to produce it, the rule prevented the introduction of altered copies and the withholding of originals. The purpose of the rule was thus long thought to be one of fraud prevention, but Wigmore pointed out that the rule operated even in cases where fraud was not at issue, such as where secondary evidence is not admitted even though its proponent acts in utmost good faith. Wigmore also noted that if prevention of fraud were the foundation of the rule, it should apply to objects as well as writings, which it does not.

The modern justification for the rule has expanded from prevention of fraud to a recognition that writings occupy a central position in the law. When the contents of a writing are at issue, oral testimony as to the terms of the writing is subject to a greater risk of error than oral testimony as to events or other situations. The human memory is not often capable of reciting the precise terms of a writing, and when the terms are in dispute only the writing itself, or a true copy, provides reliable evidence. To summarize then, we observe that the importance of the precise terms of writings in the world of legal relations, the fallibility of the human memory as reliable evidence of the terms, and the hazards of inaccurate or incomplete duplication are the concerns addressed by the best evidence rule.

Viewing the dispute in the context of the concerns underlying the best evidence rule, we conclude that the rule applies. McCormick summarizes the rule as follows:

> In proving the terms of a writing, where the terms are material, the original writing must be produced unless it is shown to be unavailable for some reason other than the serious fault of the proponent.

The contents of Seiler's work are at issue. There can be no proof of "substantial similarity" and thus of copyright infringement unless Seiler's works are juxtaposed with Lucas' and their contents compared. Since the contents are material and must be proved, Seiler must either produce the original or show that it is unavailable through no fault of his own. Rule 1004(1). This he could not do.

The facts of this case implicate the very concerns that justify the best evidence rule. Seiler alleges infringement by The Empire Strikes Back, but he can produce no documentary evidence of any originals existing before the release of the movie. His secondary evidence does not consist of true copies or exact duplicates but of "reconstructions" made after The Empire Strikes Back. In short, Seiler claims that the movie infringed his originals, yet he has no proof of those originals.

The dangers of fraud in this situation are clear. The rule would ensure that proof of the infringement claim consists of the works alleged to be infringed. Otherwise, "reconstructions" which might have no resemblance to the purported original would suffice as proof for infringement of the original. Furthermore, application of the rule here defers to the rule's special concern for the contents of writings. Seiler's claim depends on the content of the originals, and the rule would exclude reconstituted proof of the originals' content. Under the circumstances here, no "reconstruction" can substitute for the original.

Seiler argues that the best evidence rule does not apply to his work, in that it is artwork rather than "writings, recordings, or photographs." He contends that the rule both historically and currently embraces only words or numbers. Neither party has cited us to cases which discuss the applicability of the rule to drawings.

To recognize Seiler's works as writings does not, as Seiler argues, run counter to the rule's preoccupation with the centrality of the written word in the world of legal relations. Just as a contract objectively manifests the subjective intent of the makers, so Seiler's drawings are objective manifestations of the creative mind. The copyright laws give legal protection to the objective manifestations of an artist's ideas, just as the law of contract protects through its multifarious principles the meeting of minds evidenced in the contract. Comparing Seiler's drawings with Lucas' drawings is no different in principle than evaluating a contract and the intent behind it. Seiler's "reconstructions" are "writings" that affect legal relations; their copyrightability attests to that.

A creative literary work, which is artwork, and a photograph whose contents are sought to be proved, as in copyright, defamation, or invasion of privacy, are both covered by the best evidence rule. We would be inconsistent to apply the rule to artwork which is literary or photographic but not to artwork of other forms. Furthermore, blueprints, engineering drawings, architectural designs may all lack words or numbers yet still be capable of copyright and susceptible to fraudulent alteration. In short, Seiler's argument would have us restrict the definitions of Rule

1001(1) to "words" and "numbers" but ignore "or their equivalent." We will not do so in the circumstances of this case.

Our holding is also supported by the policy served by the best evidence rule in protecting against faulty memory. Seiler's reconstructions were made four to seven years after the alleged originals; his memory as to specifications and dimensions may have dimmed significantly. Furthermore, reconstructions made after the release of the Empire Strikes Back may be tainted, even if unintentionally, by exposure to the movie. Our holding guards against these problems.

A witness's mention or reference to a writing, recording, or photograph is not enough to trigger the best evidence rule; as the first prerequisite indicates, the best evidence rule applies only if a party is trying to *prove the content* of such a writing, recording, or photograph.

Consider the following examples.

Examples

1. Defendant is charged with the armed robbery of a convenience store. Prosecutor calls the store clerk to testify about what Defendant did and said during the robbery. Defendant objects, "Best evidence rule. There was a surveillance video of the store." This objection would be overruled because the store clerk is not testifying about the content of the video; rather, he is testifying about what he witnessed. The fact that it was recorded by a tape does not matter.
2. Same as Example 1, but Prosecutor calls a police officer to testify that he watched the surveillance video minutes after the robbery, and he goes on to describe what he saw on the video. Defendant objects, "Best evidence rule." Absent an applicable exception, this objection would be sustained because the officer is relaying the content of the video, as he has no independent knowledge of the robbery.
3. Plaintiff sues Defendant for breach of contract for failing to ship 100,000 Batman action figures as ordered. Plaintiff testifies that the contract was for 100,000 action figures, but does not introduce the contract. Defendant objects, "Best evidence rule." Absent an applicable exception, this objection should be sustained because Plaintiff is using her testimony to relay the content of the contract.
4. Plaintiff sues Defendant for breach of contract. Defendant testifies, "We've entered into contracts before." Plaintiff objects, "Best evidence rule." This objection should be overruled. The fact that a party mentions a contract does not mean that she is trying to prove the content of that contract.
5. Plaintiff sues Defendant for breach of contract, and one of the alleged breaches is a failure to use expedited delivery. Defendant testifies, "We

entered into a similar contract last year, and it didn't have an expedited delivery term in it." Plaintiff objects, "Best evidence rule." This objection would be overruled because Defendant's testimony is being introduced to show what is *not* in the document, not what *is* in the document.

As the above examples illustrate, the best evidence rule has limited application and does not apply *at all* if a party is not trying to prove the *content* of documentary evidence.

(b) The Original Is Required

If the prerequisites to applying the best evidence rule are met, the party seeking to introduce the evidence must introduce an "original" of the writing, recording, or photograph. This begs the question, What is an "original"? FRE 1001(d) defines the term.

FRE 1001. Definitions That Apply to This Article

In this article:

(d) An "original" of a writing or recording means the writing or recording itself or any counterpart intended to have the same effect by the person who executed or issued it. For electronically stored information, "original" means any printout—or other output readable by sight—if it accurately reflects the information. An "original" of a photograph includes the negative or a print from it.

Under this definition, what is an original can turn on the following points:

- *What the party introducing the evidence regarding the document is trying to prove.* For instance, if a party is attempting to prove what she *sent* from her e-mail, the "original" is the e-mail located in the party's "outbox." However, if a party is attempting to prove what e-mail he *received* from someone else, the "original" is the e-mail located in the party's "inbox."
- *The nature of the underlying transaction.* At times, there can be *more than one* original. Sometimes a transaction creates multiple identical documents; all those documents are "originals." Thus, if a party makes multiple impressions from the same credit card, they are *all* originals.
- *The medium on which the document is stored.* As FRE 1001(d) itself indicates, an "original" of electronically stored information consists of a printout or other readable output. Along similar lines, the "original" of a photograph includes the negative or any print from it.

Also, when it comes to recordings, the "original" is the recording, not a transcript created from the recording. At what point does the act of altering an original recording render it no longer an "original"? That was the issue in *United States v. Seifert.*

United States v. Seifert

351 F. Supp. 2d 926 (D. Minn. 2005)

ROSENBAUM, Judge.

Defendant is charged with arson of a building in violation of 18 U.S.C. § 844(i). Defendant objects to the government's proposed Exhibit 11, a digitally-enhanced surveillance videotape, as not the best evidence[.]

A fire of suspicious origin consumed the Cenex Co-Operative Building located in Hawley, Minnesota, during the night of December 28-29, 1999. The building was equipped with four videotape surveillance cameras. Fire investigators recovered the surveillance videotape from the burned building. Neither the chain of custody nor the original tape's accuracy and admissibility is challenged.

Defendant, however, challenges the government's subsequent treatment and enhancement of the original tape. The original analog tape was digitally copied and contrast-enhanced.

The technician recounted the steps used to enhance the challenged image. Mr. Hunter testified that he (1) copied the original analog videotape to digital format; (2) corrected the images to real time; and (3) edited the tape to show only the images of interest. There is no objection to these three steps. Defendant objects to the technician's next steps, where he circled the selected image, enlarged it to fill the screen, and adjusted the brightness and contrast to highlight the walking figure.

The original of a writing, recording, or photograph must be used to prove its contents. Fed. R. Evid. 1002. A duplicate—defined as a "mechanical or electronic rerecording . . . which accurately reproduces the original," *see* Fed. R. Evid. 1001(4)—is admissible to the same extent as an original, unless (1) a genuine question is raised as to the authenticity of the original, or (2) under the circumstances, it would be unfair to admit the duplicate in lieu of the original. Fed. R. Evid. 1003.

Defendant claims the enhanced video no longer accurately records the surveillance images, and, as such, is no longer an admissible original recording. The Court does not agree, and finds the proffered tape may be admitted.

The government has carried its burden and laid adequate foundation showing the enhanced tape "accurately reproduce[s] the scenes that took place, [and is] . . . accurate, authentic and trustworthy." During the evidentiary hearing, the Court viewed the "before" and "after" images. The Court finds the enhanced version to be a fair and accurate depiction of the original videotaped image. The enhancements more readily reveal, but remain true to, the recorded events. As such, they may be entered into evidence before the jury.

The first image transfer—from analog to digital format—changes the image only in a metaphysical sense. The viewer's perceived image is identical. This transition has no effect on the accuracy of the image. In the Court's view, it is an "equivalent [duplication] technique[] which accurately reproduces the original." Fed. R. Evid. 1001(4).

Beyond this, the Court finds that adjustments to brightness or contrast, or enlargement of the image, while arguably a manipulation, are in fact no more manipulative than the recording process itself. The image is black and white; the world is not. In the non-digital world, a camera's lens, its aperture, shutter speed, length of exposure, film grain, and development process—all affect the image. Each of these is entirely unremarkable so long as the "image" remains an accurate recording of that which occurred before the camera. If a photographic negative were magnified by lens, and an enlarged image resulted, no one would question the larger picture. Similarly, in the event of a tape recording, no one would comment if the volume were increased to make a recorded conversation more easily heard—again, so long as the volume-increased words were accurately recorded by the recording medium.

Here, the evidence showed that the technician adjusted the digital image's brightness and contrast, but maintained the relationships between the light and dark areas of the image. As an example, if the moving figure's clothing were a certain percentage lighter or darker than the wall behind it, that light/dark relationship was maintained. The technician testified that he simply "moved" the brightness relationship on the scale, increasing the light's intensity while maintaining the image's integrity.

As a result, the Court finds that the enhanced tape accurately presents a true and accurate replica of the image recorded by the Co-Operative's security camera. It does so in a fashion which maintains the image while assisting the jury in perceiving and understanding the recorded event. *Compare* [*United States v.*] *Beeler*, 62. F. Supp. 2d [136,] 149 [(D. Maine 1999)] (admitting videotapes where enhancements omitted "extraneous frames" and "the images are larger, clearer and easier to view"); *United States v. Luma*, 240 F. Supp. 2d 358, 368 (D. V.I. 2002) (admitting videotapes where enhancements "did not change the substance of the videotape, but merely clarified the tapes.")

Accordingly, the Court finds the enhanced videotape is a duplicate admissible under the best evidence rule. Fed. R. Evid. 1001 (4), 1002, and 1003.

---

2. *Exceptions to the Best Evidence Rule*

There are two levels of exceptions to the best evidence rule.[4] One group of exceptions allows a party to introduce a "duplicate" rather than the "original." The second group allows a party to dispense with documentary proof entirely in favor of testimonial proof of what a document says.

(a) When Documents Other Than the "Original" May Be Used

The Federal Rules of Evidence have a further, two-tiered set of rules depending on the nature of the writing, recording, or photograph at issue, as follows:[5]

---

4. California also has two sets of exceptions. *See* Cal. Evid. Code §§ 1521, 1523.

5. New York has a more onerous rule that allows duplicates in lieu of originals only when the copy is of a business record that was made in the ordinary course of business, *Grand Manor Health Related Facility, Inc. v. Hamilton Equities, Inc.*, 122 A.D.3d 481, 482 (N.Y. App. Div. 2014); when the original is an optically scanned image, *People v. Gunther*, 172 A.D.3d 1403, 1404 (N.Y. App. Div. 2019); or when another statute specifically permits the use of a duplicate.

- *Official records and other publicly recorded documents.* When the writing, recording, or photograph is an "official record" or a document recorded in a public office as authorized by law, a "copy" may be admitted if (1) the record or document is "otherwise admissible" and (2) someone certifies or testifies that the copy is "correct" after "compar[ing]" to the original. FRE 1005.

Specifically, FRE 1005 provides the following:

FRE 1005. Copies of Public Records to Prove Content

The proponent may use a copy to prove the content of an official record—or of a document that was recorded or filed in a public office as authorized by law—if these conditions are met: the record or document is otherwise admissible; and the copy if certified as correct in accordance with Rule 902(4) or is testified to be correct by a witness who has compared it with the original. If no such copy can be obtained by reasonable diligence, then the proponent may use other evidence to prove the content.

- *All other documents.* When the writing, recording or photograph is *any other document,* a "duplicate" may be admitted unless (1) "a genuine question is raised about the original's authenticity" or (2) "the circumstances make it unfair to admit the duplicate." FRE 1003, 1001(e).[6]

Specifically, FRE 1003 sets forth the exception and FRE 1001(e) defines a "duplicate":

FRE 1003. Admissibility of Duplicates

A duplicate is admissible to the same extent as the original unless a genuine question is raised about the original's authenticity or the circumstances make it unfair to admit the duplicate.

FRE 1001. Definitions That Apply to This Article

In this article:

(e) A "duplicate" means a counterpart produced by a mechanical, photographic, chemical, electronic, or other equivalent process or technique that accurately reproduces the original.

Consider the following examples.

---

6. Florida has a third "exception to the exception" for negotiable instruments or other writings evincing a right to the payment of money under certain conditions. Fl. Stat. § 90.953(1).

Examples

1. Plaintiff sues Defendant for breach of contract and introduces a photocopy of the contract instead of the original. Is that a "duplicate"? The answer is "yes," because photocopies are exact reproductions of the original. Thus, it is admissible unless there is some question as to its authenticity or it would be unfair to admit it for some reason.
2. Defendant is charged with solicitation of a minor. Prosecutor seeks to introduce the chat room conversation between Defendant and the victim. Prosecutor introduces a transcript "cut and pasted" from the original chat log, which is now unavailable. There are gaps in the conversation. Is that a "duplicate"? The answer is "no," because it is not an accurate reproduction.

Graphically, the exception allowing for the use of alternate documents can be illustrated as follows:

Official Records & Publicly Recorded Documents	All Other Writings, Recordings, & Photographs
• "Copy" is OK if: • Record or document is otherwise admissible; *and* • Copy is certified or accompanied by testimony that it is "correct" as compared with original	• "Duplicate" is OK if: • There is no genuine question rasied about the original's authenticity; *and* • The circumstances do not make it "unfair" to admit the duplicate

The exception for official records and publicly recorded documents is more flexible than the exception for all other documents. For the former, a "copy" will suffice—and that can be established by someone testifying that a document is "correct" as compared to the original. For the latter, however, a "duplicate" is required—and that requires an "accurate[] reproduc[tion]" of the original. Why the difference? There seem to be two reasons: It is not helpful to have the originals of public documents pulled from the public files, FRE 1005 Adv. Comm. Note, and it is safer to trust a visual comparison made by a public employee because such employees are presumed to discharge their official duties appropriately.

(b) When Testimonial Evidence or Other Evidence Aside from Duplicates and Copies May Be Used

The best evidence rule also has several exceptions that allow a party, when trying to prove the content of a writing, recording, or photograph, to introduce testimonial or other evidence.

(i) When all the originals are lost or destroyed

If a party establishes that all the originals of a writing, recording, or photograph have been lost or destroyed—and not by the party "acting in bad faith"—the best evidence rule does not stand in the way of the party proving the content of that writing, recording, or photograph with testimonial or other evidence of its content. Specifically, FRE 1004(a) provides the following:

FRE 1004. Admissibility of Other Evidence of Content

An original is not required and other evidence of the content of a writing, recording, or photograph is admissible if:

(a) all the originals are lost or destroyed, and not by the proponent acting in bad faith.

Examples

1. Defendant is charged with importing drugs across the U.S. border after his speedboat is intercepted in the Gulf of Mexico. Defendant seeks to have a witness testify that the GPS unit on the speedboat showed that he did not originate in Mexico and thus did not import drugs into the United States. Prosecutor objects on best evidence grounds. The objection should be sustained because the content of the GPS unit is being admitted without the data from the original unit.
2. Same as Example 1, but Defendant responds that the GPS unit's data was destroyed. Prosecutor agrees the data was destroyed, but calls an officer to testify that the data was deleted by someone with Defendant's initials moments before the Coast Guard boarded the speedboat. The objection should be sustained because the original was lost or destroyed, but due to the proponent's intentional actions.
3. Same as Example 1, but the GPS unit's data was deleted by someone whose initials match another passenger on the boat. The objection should be overruled because the originals are gone, but it was a third party—not Defendant—who destroyed them (unless there is proof that Defendant directed the third party to delete the data).
4. Same as Example 1, but the GPS unit's data was accidentally deleted many hours before the speedboat was intercepted. If the deletion is truly accidental, the best evidence rule is not a bar to admission.

One lingering question remains: How much effort must be expended to find an original before it is deemed to be "lost"? The Advisory Committee Note does not answer this question. Further, cases that interpret FRE 1004 have focused more on whether the original was lost or destroyed *in bad faith* rather than whether it was, in fact, "lost."

(ii) When the original is beyond the reach of the court's process

If a party establishes that all the originals of a writing, recording, or photograph "cannot be obtained by any available judicial process," the best evidence rule will not bar the admission of alternate evidence of the content of that writing, recording, or photograph. Specifically, FRE 1004(b) provides the following:

> **FRE 1004. Admissibility of Other Evidence of Content**
>
> An original is not required and other evidence of the content of a writing, recording, or photograph is admissible if:
>
> **(b)** an original cannot be obtained by any available judicial process.

(iii) When the evidence is to be admitted against a party who had control over the original

Based on the notion that "you are not in a position to complain," the best evidence rule does not apply when the original of a writing, recording, or photograph was (1) within the control of the party against whom its content is to be introduced, (2) that party was put on notice that the original would be "a subject of proof at the trial or hearing," and (3) the party failed to produce it at that trial or hearing. Specifically, FRE 1004(c) provides the following:

> **FRE 1004. Admissibility of Other Evidence of Content**
>
> An original is not required and other evidence of the content of a writing, recording, or photograph is admissible if:
>
> **(c)** the party against whom the original would be offered had control of the original; was at that time put on notice, by pleadings or otherwise, that the original would be a subject of proof at the trial or hearing; and fails to produce it at the trial or hearing.

(iv) When the evidence is pertinent only to a "collateral" issue

The best evidence rule also will not bar evidence if the writing, recording, or photograph is "not closely related to a controlling issue"—that is, if it is *collateral* to any key issue in the case. Specifically, FRE 1004(d) provides the following:

FRE 1004. Admissibility of Other Evidence of Content

An original is not required and other evidence of the content of a writing, recording, or photograph is admissible if:

(d) the writing, recording, or photograph is not closely related to a controlling issue.

This is a practicality-based exception: If the issue is not that important, it is not worth the effort of insisting upon an original or duplicate of the writing, recording, or photograph.

(v) Summaries of voluminous writings, recordings, or photographs

This practicality-based exception allows a party to summarize voluminous writings when they are more pertinent in the aggregate than individually. To avail itself of this exception, a party must show that (1) the writings, recordings, or photographs are too voluminous to be "conveniently examined in court"; and (2) the originals or duplicates were made available for copying by other parties at a reasonable time and place. Specifically, FRE 1006 provides the following:

FRE 1006. Summaries to Prove Content

The proponent may use a summary, chart, or calculation to prove the content of voluminous writings, recordings, or photographs that cannot be conveniently examined in court. The proponent must make the originals or duplicates available for examination or copying, or both, by other parties at a reasonable time and place. And the court may order the proponent to produce them in court.

Must the underlying documents be admitted into evidence? The answer is "no." But must those documents be admissible? The answer is "yes," and they must also be made available for inspection by opposing counsel. *See United States v. Strissel*, 920 F.2d 1162, 1163-64 (4th Cir. 1990); *United States v. Rizk*, 660 F.3d 1125, 1130-31 (9th Cir. 2011).

The summary itself must be properly authenticated as an accurate summary of the underlying documents before it will be admitted into evidence.

Example

In a trial for manipulation of a company's stock, a summary chart can present—and contrast—the company's earnings per share (EPS) against its stock price.

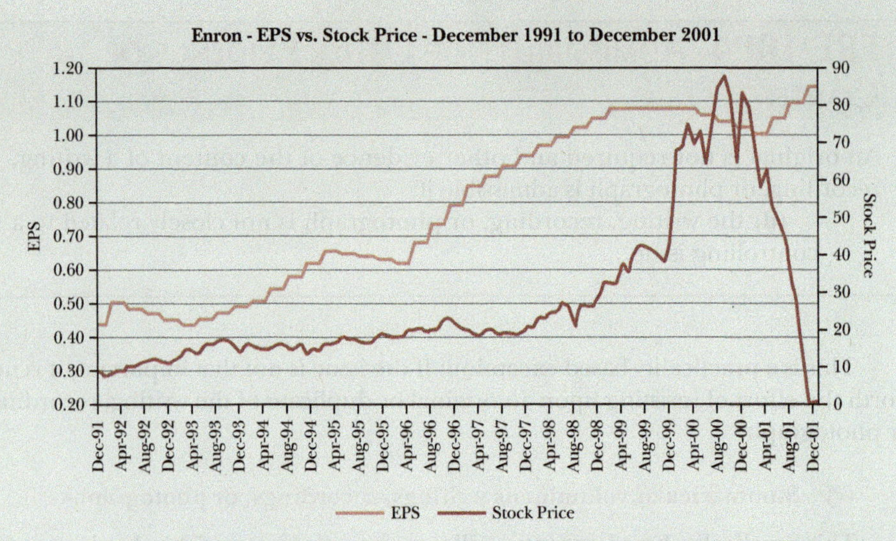

As long as the documentation of the EPS and stock price are made available for inspection in advance of trial, a party may admit this summary chart in lieu of all the individual records documenting EPS and stock price at each point during the 10-year period reflected in the chart.

(vi) "Eat your words" exception

If the content of a writing, recording, or photograph may be established through the words of the opposing party—whether while testifying, in a deposition, or in a written statement—the best evidence rule will be deemed satisfied. Specifically, FRE 1007 provides the following:

FRE 1007. Testimony or Statement of a Party to Prove Content

The proponent may prove the content of a writing, recording, or photograph by the testimony, deposition, or written statement of the party against whom the evidence is offered. The proponent need not account for the original.

Review Questions

1. **Missing will.** A brother and sister are involved in a will contest. The brother seeks to introduce what he asserts is a copy of the decedent's

trust, but the trust was not in the decedent's lawyer's file. The sister objects, "Best evidence rule."

a. Does your analysis change if there are no original copies of the trust?
b. The trial judge sustains the objection, but the brother then seeks to introduce a letter from the sister detailing the contents of the trust. Is that letter admissible?

2. **3D printer.** Defendant is charged with being a felon in possession of a firearm. The defense is that the gun was not operable. Prosecutor seeks to introduce a duplicate of the gun created by a 3D printer, as the gun itself was accidentally destroyed. Is there a best evidence problem?
3. **Plate number.** Defendant is charged with arson. Prosecutor seeks to call a witness who saw a car driving away from the burning building and then wrote down the license plate number. Prosecutor asks the witness, "What license plate number did you see?" Defendant objects, "Best evidence rule." Do you sustain or overrule the objection?
4. **Video still.** Defendant is charged with murder. The sidewalk outside of the victim's apartment had a surveillance camera, and it captured the following image of two men—one of whom is Defendant—carrying what appears to be a rolled up large area rug:

The full video is no longer available; all that remains is this still photograph. Prosecutor seeks to call one of the officers who responded to the missing persons call to testify that (a) he watched the full surveillance video, and (b) just moments after the image in the photograph, the rug tilted to the side and an arm flopped out and into view. Defendant objects, "Best evidence rule." Do you sustain or overrule the objection? What additional facts do you need to know in order to rule?

PART C: DEMONSTRATIVE EVIDENCE

It is said that a "picture is worth a thousand words," and effective trial lawyers know that. In addition to introducing evidence, the parties have the ability to add to the impact of their presentation by using demonstrative evidence.

For example, one of the most famous uses of demonstrative evidence occurred in the murder trial of football star and actor, O.J. Simpson. He was asked to try on the bloody gloves recovered at the crime scene. The prosecution claimed that the gloves fit, but the defense argued to the contrary, leading to defense lawyer Johnnie Cochran's famous adage, "If it doesn't fit, you must acquit."

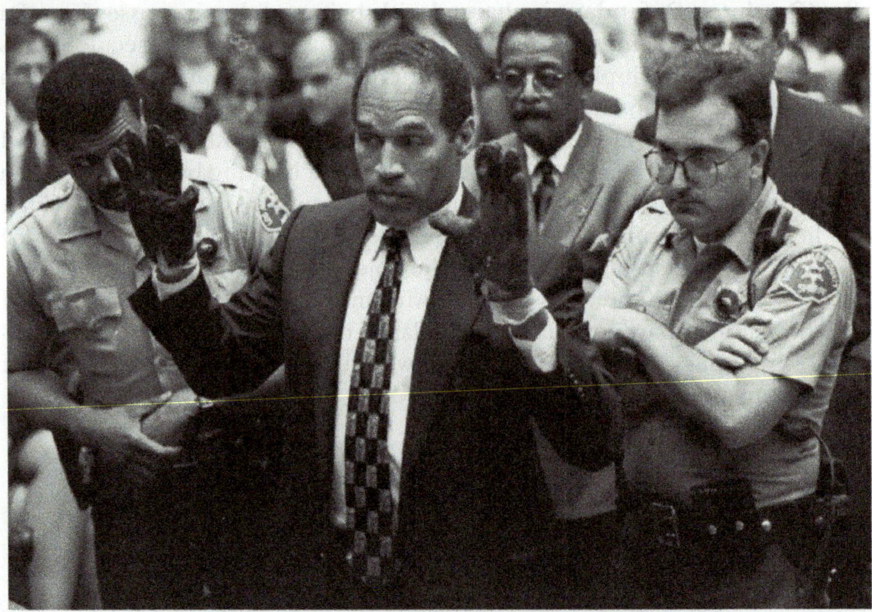

The court has broad discretion in allowing the use of objects, photographs and enlargements, charts, diagrams, models, enactments, computer simulations, and experiments in front of the jury. Sometimes, the object being used as demonstrative evidence is otherwise admitted into evidence; other times, it is not. Here are a few examples.

Examples

1. In a personal injury lawsuit, Plaintiff claims that she lost her hand in a work injury. Plaintiff's lawyer can hold up a hand in a jar during the examination of witnesses or closing argument.[7]
2. In a homicide case, Prosecutor's shaken baby syndrome expert creates a computer animation to show how shaking a baby may cause severe injuries.

---

7. The use of demonstrative evidence was spearheaded by the famous lawyer, Melvin Belli. In the article *Demonstrative Evidence: Seeing is Believing,* 16 Trial 70 (1980), Belli promoted demonstrative evidence as an important tool for engaging the jury and focusing them on "*exactly* what it is they should know." (Emphasis in original.) Demonstrative evidence appeals to the juror's senses and adds an emotional quality to the presentation of evidence.

3. A blood-spatter expert brings a board, knife, and ink into the courtroom. In front of the jury, she shows the type of pattern created by blood cast off from a knife.
4. In the film *My Cousin Vinny*, the defense counsel holds up pictures of trees and screens blocking the eyewitness's view to dramatize how the identification with these impediments was unreliable.
5. In a lawsuit involving a high-speed chase, Prosecutor seeks to display a map of the route taken during the pursuit, as seen here:

6. In a drug conspiracy trial, Prosecutor seeks to display a chart that connects how the leader of the conspiracy corresponded with various members of the conspiracy via text message, as seen here:

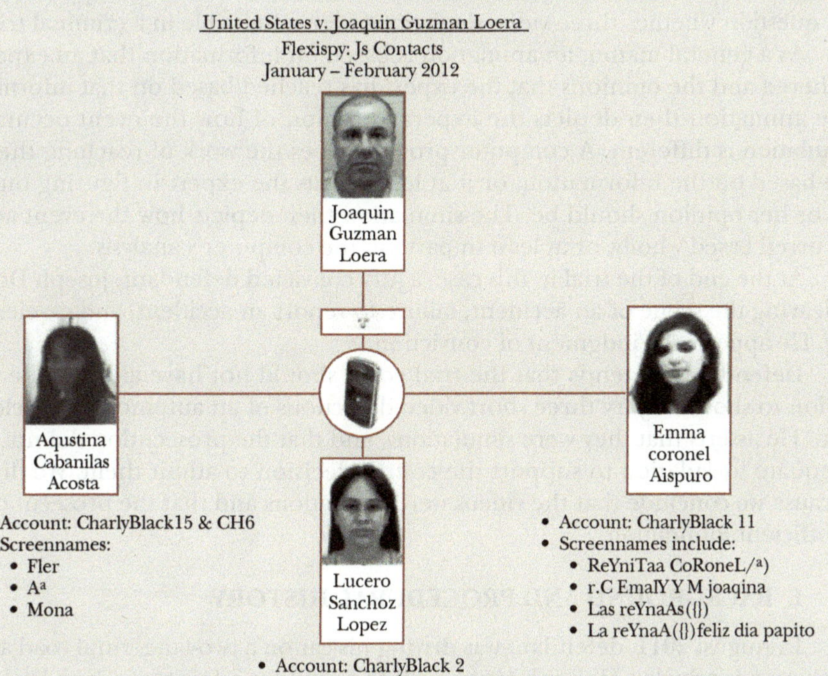

1. *Requirements for Demonstrative Evidence in General*

To be admissible, demonstrative evidence must be (1) relevant to the issues in the case, (2) based on the evidence in the case, and (3) not warranting exclusion under FRE 403 (that is, the probative value of the evidence is not substantially outweighed by the danger that the evidence is distracting, too time-consuming, or otherwise unduly prejudicial).

2. *Specific Types of Demonstrative Evidence*

(a) Experiments

If the court admits an experiment, the party offering the experiment must establish that it is being conducted under the same conditions at issue in the case. Likewise, videos must accurately reflect the facts as established by other evidence in the case.

People v. Douglas

411 P.3d 1026 (Colo. Ct. App. 2016)

BERNARD, Judge.

In our increasingly computerized world, attorneys often present video depictions of events at trial to explain how those events occurred. This appeal involves the question whether three video depictions were admissible in a criminal trial.

As a general matter, an animation is based on information that an expert has gathered and the opinions that the expert has reached based on that information. The animation then depicts the expert's opinion of how the event occurred. A simulation is different. A computer program does the work of reaching the opinion based on the information, or it at least assists the expert in figuring out what his or her opinion should be. The simulation then depicts how the event actually occurred based wholly, or at least in part, on the computer's analysis.

At the end of the trial in this case, a jury convicted defendant, Joseph Douglas, of leaving the scene of an accident, failure to report an accident, and careless driving. He appeals the judgment of conviction.

Defendant contends that the trial court should not have allowed the prosecution to show the jury three short video depictions of an automobile-bicycle collision. He asserts that they were simulations, and that the prosecution did not lay an adequate foundation to support the court's decision to admit them. We disagree because we conclude that the videos were animations and that the prosecution laid a sufficient foundation.

I. BACKGROUND AND PROCEDURAL HISTORY

In August 2011, defendant was driving his car on a two-lane, rural road around dusk on a windy day. He took his eyes off the road for a few seconds to look at his radio. The passenger side of his car struck a bicyclist who was riding in the same direction on the side of the road. She flew through the air for a distance, and she landed in a ditch, which was filled with chest-high vegetation. The collision and the resulting fall broke the bicyclist's leg and sprained her wrist. She managed to climb out of the ditch, and she then called for emergency assistance on her cell phone.

Defendant drove away. He later claimed that he had not seen the bicyclist. He had felt the side of his car strike her, but, when he stopped to look around, he did not see her or her bicycle. So he assumed that his car had struck a deer.

The prosecution informed defendant that it intended to introduce three video depictions of the collision at trial. A state trooper who was an accident reconstruction expert had prepared them. The depictions showed the collision from different angles. The trial court decided that the videos were animations and that it would allow the jury to watch them at trial. The court also found that (1) they were relevant because they would provide the jury with visual depictions of the collision and because they showed the relative positions of the car and the bicycle on the road; (2) they were fair and accurate depictions of the collision; (3) any discrepancies between the videos and other evidence went to their weight, not to their admissibility; and (4) the probative value of the videos was not substantially outweighed by any prejudice that defendant might suffer if the jury watched them.

When the prosecutor showed the videos at trial, the court gave the jury a limiting instruction. The instruction stated that the videos represented the trooper's opinion about how the collision had occurred. The court also limited the jury to watching the videos twice: once during the trooper's testimony and once during the jury's deliberations.

II. THE VIDEOS WERE ANIMATIONS

As is pertinent to this appeal computer-generated video depictions of events fall into two categories: animations and simulations. There are different foundational elements for the admission of videos based on the category in which they belong.

On the one hand, courts view animations as demonstrative evidence. The proponent of an animation must (1) authenticate it; (2) show that it is relevant; (3) show that it is a "fair and accurate representation of the evidence to which it relates"; and (4) show that its probative value is not substantially outweighed by the danger of unfair prejudice.

On the other hand, courts consider simulations to be scientific evidence. Simulations are offered as substantive, not demonstrative, evidence. A simulation depends on the proper application of scientific principles, so its admissibility hinges on whether it meets the foundational requirements of scientific evidence.

There are some similarities between animations and simulations. They can both require someone to input data into a computer program. They can both depict recreations of events. They can both use scientific principles to recreate those events. But, there are clear differences that distinguish animations and simulations. On the one hand, an animation "simply illustrates an opinion or reconstruction which an expert witness has already devised through the expert's own independent computation and analyses." Animations can be viewed as "labor saving device[s]"—they save an expert the trouble of having to draw diagrams by hand.

On the other hand, in a simulation, the computer functions independently—it is like an "expert" itself. It renders its own "opinion" based on its internal calculations. The expert may enter the data or the scientific principles, but the computer program analyzes the data to produce the conclusion.

When a computer-generated depiction does not supply missing information—meaning that an expert has arrived at an opinion without using the computer—the evidence only functions demonstratively. The depiction is demonstrative because it mirrors a witness's testimony. It is simply a more technologically savvy depiction of what the expert could have offered if he or she had used a series of explanatory drawings. The opinions depicted in the animation are the expert's, so they can then be explored and cross-examined through testimony.

If the computer-generated evidence is used to supply missing information to prove a disputed material fact in a case, it functions as substantive scientific evidence. So the validity of the conclusions that the computer drew depends on the computer's proper application of scientific principles. A computer that uses such principles to reach a scientific conclusion is a simulation.

Simulations are subject to the admissibility standards for scientific evidence because (1) they function as recreations of the *actual* event; (2) the "extreme vividness," and persuasive power of a video can create an "exaggerated aura of computer infallibility," and (3) unlike a witness, an attorney cannot cross-examine a computer about its conclusions.

Analysis

Defendant contends that the videos were simulations because the computer applied the laws of physics to depict the collision. He adds that the computer software that created the videos conducted its own internal calculations and drew its own conclusions. But we conclude that the record of how the trooper prepared the videos does not support defendant's contention. First, the record shows that the trooper, not the computer's software, supplied the calculations and the opinions that the computer used to create the videos. The videos were therefore merely graphic representations of a series of pictures that the trooper could have drawn himself.

[A] computer animation is admissible as demonstrative evidence if the party offering it can (1) authenticate it under CRE 901; (2) show that it is relevant under CRE 401 and 402; (3) establish that it is a fair and accurate representation of the evidence to which it relates; and (4) demonstrate that its probative value is not substantially outweighed by the danger of unfair prejudice under CRE 403.

As far as the third factor—fair and accurate depiction—is concerned, an animation must be substantially similar to the event that it depicts to be admissible. It need not be exact in every detail, but the important elements must be identical or very similar to the scene" as described by the evidence that the proponent of the animation introduces. But a court does not have to exclude an animation if it is "inconsistent with testimony or evidence presented by the opposing party" as long as it "fairly and accurately portrays" the proponent's "version of events."

Defense counsel adequately explored any discrepancies between the videos and defendant's description of the collision, including what defendant could see at that time and whether defendant had stopped after the collision. We conclude that these discrepancies were not so significant that the trial court should have excluded the videos.

(b) Jury Views

The trial judge also has broad discretion to determine whether to allow jurors to visit another location to personally observe a scene relevant to the case. A "jury view" is to assist the trier of fact in understanding and applying the evidence offered at trial. It is a type of real-life demonstration that helps jurors in analyzing the evidence presented at trial. As noted in Chapter One, not all courts treat a jury view as "evidence."

For example, in the O.J. Simpson criminal trial, jurors were taken to the scene of the murders and the defendant's home so that they could put into context the evidence that they had heard about how the crime occurred and the location of where evidence was found. In lieu of jury views, the court may allow a party to present a video of the location. That was the approach adopted by the judge in the trial of famed singer Michael Jackson. The defense was allowed to use as evidence a video taken of Jackson's Neverland Ranch.

The court sets the terms of a jury view. Ordinarily, it is made without commentary by the judge or counsel. The scene should also be in the same or similar condition as it was alleged to have been when the events in the case took place.

Because of the time and logistics involved, courts rarely permit jury views. There may be various reasons the court denies a request for a jury view, including possible danger by visiting a scene. However, on rare occasions, the court may permit jury views in either criminal or civil cases.

(c) Scientific Demonstrations

If the demonstrative evidence is based on scientific principles (such as physics in reconstructing the trajectory of bullet fragments to determine their point of origin), the proponent of a video visualizing that reconstruction would have to establish (1) the scientific validity of the methodology used and (2) the video's accuracy in reflecting that methodology.

Review Questions

1. **Jury view of cell.** Defendant is charged with killing his cellmate. He claims that he had nowhere to retreat when his cellmate attacked him. Defendant asks the court to take the jury to view the prison and his cell. Prosecutor has asked to build a replica of the cell in the courtroom.
2. **Runway jury.** There was a plane crash at the local airport. Defendants claim that the runway was built in a way in which a pilot cannot adequately see the end of the runway while he is trying to take off. Defendants ask for a jury view of the runway.
3. **Bank diagram.** During a bank robbery case, Prosecutor seeks to use a diagram of the bank so that the tellers can explain where they were standing and where Defendant was located during the robbery.
4. **Blow-up photos.** In closing arguments, Prosecutor seeks to use an enlarged photograph of evidence admitted in smaller form in the trial.

5. **Day in the life video.** To show the pain and suffering of his client, Plaintiff's lawyer seeks to introduce a video of a "Day in the Life" of the client that shows the client spending the day in a wheelchair.

Test Your Understanding

To test your understanding of the material in this chapter, turn to the Supplement for additional practice problems.

Chapter 14

Burdens of Proof, Presumptions, and Judicial Notice

This chapter moves away from rules of evidence to discuss instead how *much* evidence a party must present to prevail. Specifically, what are the burdens of proof in criminal and civil cases? How do presumptions and inferences affect whether this burden has been met? And can the trial judge allow the jury to consider facts that are not presented through witnesses or exhibits, but by the judge taking "judicial notice" of those facts?

Part A of this chapter discusses burdens of proof. Burdens of proof describe the *quantum* of admissible evidence that a party must produce in order to avoid an adverse ruling as a matter of law, as well as the level of proof necessary to convince the trier of fact that that party should prevail. A party may have an initial *burden of production* to present evidence in support of its claim. Then, there is the question of whether the party produced enough evidence to meet its *burden of persuasion.* Together, they are known as the *burdens of proof.*

Part B discusses inferences and presumptions. They operate as "shortcuts" that can, if applicable, lighten a party's burdens of production or persuasion. Inferences are optional. For example, if the sidewalk is wet in the morning, the jury *may,* but is not required, to infer that it rained the night before. Thus, an inference gives the trier of fact the right to infer one fact from another, if it chooses to do so. By contrast, presumptions are mandatory; they require the trier of fact to presume one fact from the existence of another. For instance, a presumption may require a fact finder to presume that a person is dead from the fact that he has not been heard from in five years; put differently, upon proof of a lack of contact for five years, the fact of death is presumed to be established without further proof. Presumptions can either be (1) rebuttable, which means that the other party can show that the presumed fact is not true in this case, or (2) conclusive, which establishes the fact being presumed *as a matter of law.* The use of presumptions is limited in criminal cases.

Finally, Part C discusses judicial notice. Judicial notice is a tool that judges may use *in lieu of* evidence in deciding a case. For instance, in a case involving an event on November 1, 2021, a judge could take judicial notice that November 1, 2021, was a Monday. The Federal Rules of Evidence set forth when a judge may, and when a judge must, take judicial notice.

PART A: BURDENS OF PROOF

The party initiating litigation bears the initial burden of presenting evidence (*burden of production*) and proving that it has sufficient evidence (*burden of persuasion*) for its claim. In a civil case, the plaintiff may have the burden by a preponderance of the evidence or, in some cases, by clear and convincing evidence. In criminal cases, the prosecution must prove its case beyond a reasonable doubt.

However, if the plaintiff or prosecution meets its burden, the burden may shift to a defendant who raises an affirmative defense (that is, a defense to the civil claim or charged crime that does more than dispute an element of the plaintiff's or prosecution's case) to prove the elements of that defense. *See Patterson v. New York*, 432 U.S. 197, 202-03 (1977). Once that occurs, the burden can shift once again to the other side to disprove that defense, depending on the nature of the defense.

1. Burden of Production

The plaintiff or prosecution must adduce sufficient evidence as to each element of their claims or charges to permit a reasonable jury to conclude that the plaintiff or prosecutor should prevail. That is the burden of production. The defense also has an opportunity to present affirmative defenses. As to affirmative defenses, the *defense* has the burden of production.

Examples

1. Defendant is charged with murder. Prosecutor must produce evidence that Defendant killed the victim with the requisite mental state. Once Prosecutor does so, Defendant may choose to argue self-defense. Then, Defendant will have the burden to produce evidence that meets each of the legal requirements for self-defense.
2. Plaintiff sues Defendant for negligence based on Defendant's violation of the basic speed law, which requires drivers to drive only as fast as conditions allow. Plaintiff must carry her burden of production to show that Defendant was driving too fast for the conditions. If she does not (perhaps because it was daylight and clear), Defendant is entitled to a directed verdict in his favor.

If a party has the initial burden of production to prove the elements of a crime or civil action but fails to carry it, the case is to be dismissed as a matter of law: In a civil case, the mechanism is a directed verdict in favor of the party who did not have the burden of production; in a criminal case, the mechanism is an acquittal for the defendant under Federal Rule of Criminal Procedure 29. There is no directed verdict *against* a defendant in a criminal case because that would cut the jury out of the process in violation of a criminal defendant's Sixth Amendment right to a jury.

2. *Burden of Persuasion*

After the party with the burden of proof carries the burden of production, that party must then convince the trier of fact that it should prevail in the litigation. This step is called the *burden of persuasion*. If the party carries its burden, it wins; if it does not, it loses.

The relationship between the burdens of production and persuasion are represented graphically as follows:

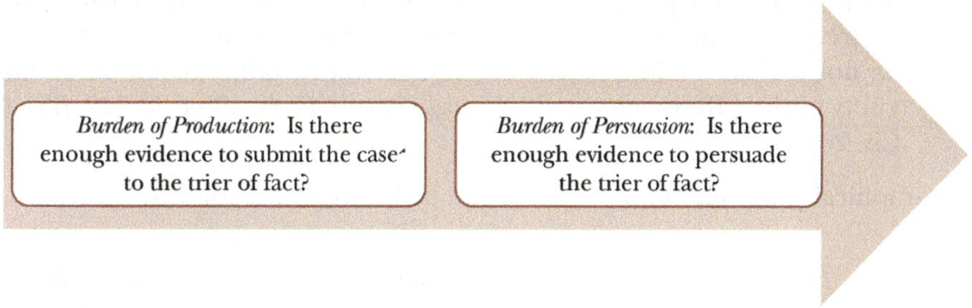

Burden of Production: Is there enough evidence to submit the case to the trier of fact? → *Burden of Persuasion*: Is there enough evidence to persuade the trier of fact?

The burdens of production and persuasion are viewed through the prism of the *standard of proof*. The standard of proof is the degree of certainty that the fact finder must have regarding the correctness of the result. There are three common standards of proof.

3. *Standards of Proof*

The three common standards of proof are preponderance of the evidence, clear and convincing evidence, and beyond a reasonable doubt. They are defined as follows:

- *Preponderance of the evidence* is the default standard of proof in civil cases. It requires that the trier of fact be convinced that a fact is more likely than not to be true. It is often thought of as "50 percent plus one." The preponderance standard is a tiebreaker: When the evidence is in equipoise and so evenly balanced that it could go either way (that is, if the evidence is "50-50"), the party with the burden of proof loses because it has not convinced the trier of fact of the "plus one" necessary to rule in its favor.
- *Clear and convincing evidence* is "an intermediate standard" that requires a greater quantum of proof than a preponderance of the evidence but less than proof beyond a reasonable doubt. "Clear and convincing evidence does not mean 'unequivocal,' or 'proof that admits of no doubt.'" Instead, it requires the trier of fact to be persuaded that a party's claim is "'highly probable'" or "reasonably certain." It is the standard of proof used in immigration proceedings, for the termination of parental rights, and for other determinations in civil cases for which public policy demands a greater degree of accuracy than the preponderance of the evidence standard can give, such as where there are fraud allegations.

- *Beyond a reasonable doubt* is the most onerous standard of proof, as it requires the trier of fact to be convinced that a party has proven the elements of the pertinent crime(s) or sentencing enhancements beyond a reasonable doubt. By the U.S. Constitution, it is the standard by which prosecutors are required to prove a defendant's guilt of any crime (as well as any sentencing allegations that affect the sentencing range). *In re Winship*, 397 U.S. 358 (1970); *Apprendi v. New Jersey*, 530 U.S. 466 (2000); *Alleyne v. United States*, 570 U.S. 99 (2013). Courts have been leery of defining this standard of proof with too much precision, but have upheld instructions defining a reasonable doubt as "when, after the careful, entire, and impartial consideration of all evidence in the case, the jurors do not feel an abiding conviction to a moral certainty that a defendant is guilty of the offense charged." *United States v. Perry*, 438 F.3d 642, 651 (6th Cir. 2006).

Graphically, the standards of proof can be illustrated as follows:

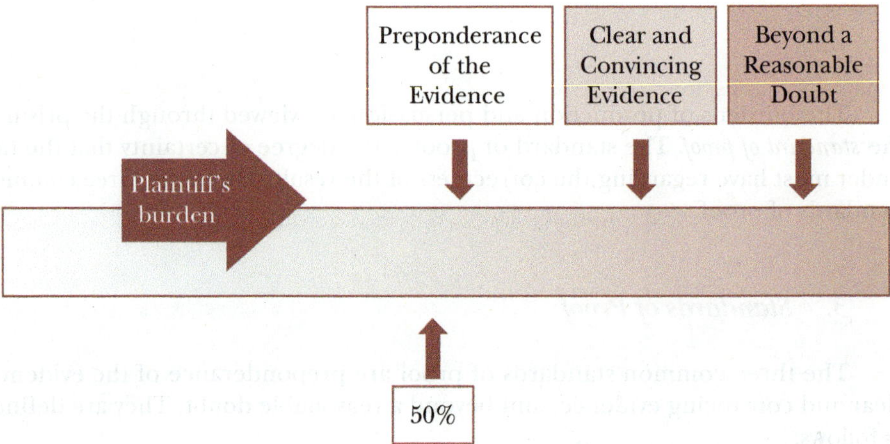

The decision as to which party bears the burden of proof and which standard of proof to apply are decisions grounded in substantive public policy. Because it is a "'substantive'" aspect of a claim, federal courts will look to federal law to define the burden and standards of proof in cases applying federal substantive law (that is, criminal cases and civil cases based on federal statutory or common law), but will look to state law to define the burden and standards of proof when federal jurisdiction is based on diversity of citizenship and the claims and defenses are grounded in state substantive law. This deference to state policy is mandated by *Erie Railroad Co. v. Tompkins*, 304 U.S. 64 (1938).

Review Questions

1. **Missing element.** Defendant is charged with bank robbery of a federally insured bank. Prosecutor rests without putting on any proof that the bank

is federally insured. Defendant moves for an acquittal. Should the motion be granted?

2. **Standards of proof.** What standard of proof applies in each of these cases?
   a. Plaintiff sues Defendant for fraudulently inducing him to sign a contract.
   b. The State seeks to terminate a mother's parental rights at the conclusion of a case involving child abuse and neglect.
   c. Defendant is charged with assault with a deadly weapon.
   d. Defendant is charged with assault with a deadly weapon, but seeks to establish that he stabbed the victim in self-defense.

PART B: INFERENCES AND PRESUMPTIONS

The rules of evidence acknowledge two mechanisms that empower the judge or jury to find a fact to be true without obligating the party with the burden of proof to affirmatively establish that fact.

1. Inferences

The first mechanism is an *inference.* It allows—but does not require—the judge or jury to infer the existence of one fact from proof of another fact. In other words, an inference tells the trier of fact, "If a party proves Fact X, you may—but are not required to—infer that Fact Y is true." Graphically, an inference operates as follows:

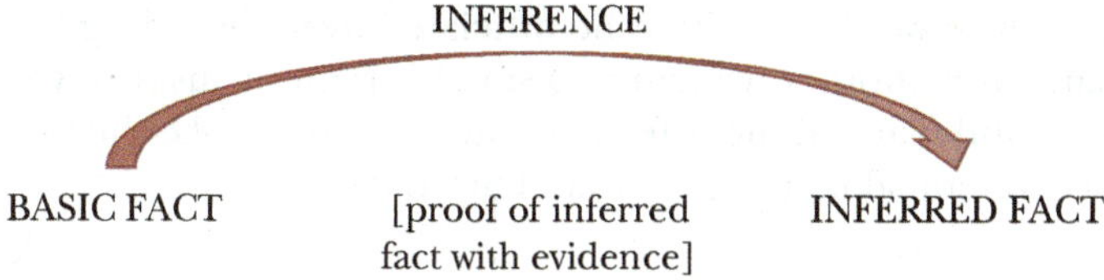

As this graphic illustrates, an inference allows the party with the burden of proof to skip over the need to *prove* the inferred fact with admissible evidence. For example, courts will often instruct juries that, if they find that the defendant has fled the scene of a crime, they may infer that the defendant has a consciousness of guilt (that is, that the defendant was aware that he has done something wrong, which tends to show that the defendant committed the crime, did it on purpose, and knew that it was wrong when he did it). Inferences are allowed in criminal cases and in civil cases as long as the connection between the fact proven and the fact to be inferred is a "rational one." *County Court of Ulster County v. Allen,* 442 U.S. 140 (1979). Thus, it is okay to infer consciousness of guilt from flight, but not to infer consciousness of guilt from the color of the perpetrator's eyes; in the latter instance, any rational connection is lacking.

2. *Presumptions*

The second mechanism is a *presumption.* A presumption operates like a mandatory inference insofar as it *requires* the trier of fact to presume the existence of the "presumed fact" from proof of a "basic fact." In other words, a presumption tells the trier of fact, "If a party proves the Basic Fact, you must presume that the Presumed Fact is true." Presumptions come in two "strengths": (1) conclusive (or mandatory) presumptions that, once triggered, cannot be refuted with contrary evidence; and (2) rebuttable (or permissive) presumptions that, once triggered, can be refuted or dispelled with contrary evidence.

Consider the following examples.

Examples

1. Plaintiff sues Defendant for breach of contract. Defendant argues that he properly rescinded the contract by mailing a notice to terminate the contract. Defendant proves that he dropped the termination notice in the mail and invokes the presumption that items placed in the mail are delivered.
2. In a will contest, the decedent's nephew challenges his exclusion from the decedent's most recent will in favor of a more distant relative. The nephew introduces a letter purporting to be from the decedent and found within the decedent's office files, dated June 16, 1988, and invokes the presumption that ancient documents (that is, those more than 20 years old) are authentic.
3. A wife sues her husband for annulment of marriage on the ground that her marriage was bigamous because her husband was already married to another woman. The wife seeks to introduce testimony from Reverend Pressley, who would state that he officiated over a wedding between the husband and another woman in a small ceremony just two years before the husband married the wife. The wife seeks to invoke the presumption that a ceremonial marriage is a valid marriage.

The trigger for any presumption is proof of the basic fact. If the evidence regarding the basic fact is conflicting, it is up to the trier of fact to decide whether that basic fact has been established. If it has, the presumption applies; if it has not, the presumption does not apply.

Why is it sometimes desirable to excuse a party from its burden of proving the presumed fact with admissible evidence? Most presumptions are justified by one or more of the following underlying rationales:

- *Efficiency.* Most presumptions have more than a seed of truth to them, so they enable proceedings to be more efficient by skipping over the need to prove something that is typically true.
- *Access to evidence.* Many presumptions exist as an acknowledgment that the party with the burden of proving that fact typically lacks access to the

evidence necessary to prove it. In such situations, it may make more sense to allow that fact to be presumed and to then place the onus on the party with better access to pertinent evidence to rebut that presumed fact.

- *Social policy.* Several presumptions exist as a way of putting the law's "thumb" on the side of the scale that leads to better social outcomes. For instance, many states presume that a child is legitimate if the child is born while his or her parents are married. This presumption is usually but not always accurate, but the outcome—presuming that children are the legitimate offspring of their married parents—furthers the societally beneficial goal of assigning both lawfully married parents the duty to care for the child. Some statutes presume that waste found within a certain distance of a factory is presumed to come from that factory, as a means of ensuring that businesses properly dispose of their waste.

Because presumptions to some extent reflect and implement public policy, they are considered "substantive" for choice of law purposes. *Raleigh v. Illinois Department of Revenue*, 530 U.S. 15, 20-21 (2000). FRE 302 provides the following:

FRE 302. Applying State Law to Presumptions in Civil Cases

In a civil case, state law governs the effect of a presumption regarding a claim or defense for which state law supplies the rule of decision.

Thus, in a case resting on federal question jurisdiction (such as federal criminal prosecutions and civil cases grounded in federal substantive law), federal courts will look to the presumptions recognized by federal statutory and common law. But in a case resting on diversity jurisdiction, federal courts will look to the pertinent state's law regarding presumptions pursuant to *Erie Railroad Co. v. Tompkins*, 304 U.S. 64 (1938).

Both mandatory and permissive presumptions are permitted in civil cases. However, neither type of presumption is generally permitted in criminal cases because they create shortcuts that can relieve the prosecution of its burden of proving every fact with evidence and thus run the risk of empowering a jury to convict a defendant of a crime without having to first find the existence of each element of the offense (and the facts supporting those elements) beyond a reasonable doubt. This possibility presents significant constitutional problems, as *Sandstrom v. Montana* reaffirms.

Sandstrom v. Montana

442 U.S. 510 (1979)

Justice Brennan delivered the opinion of the Court.

The question presented is whether, in a case in which intent is an element of the crime charged; the jury instruction, "the law presumes that a person intends the ordinary consequences of his voluntary acts," violates the Fourteenth Amendment's requirement that the State prove every element of a criminal offense beyond a reasonable doubt.

I

On November 22, 1976, 18-year-old David Sandstrom confessed to the slaying of Annie Jessen. Based upon the confession and corroborating evidence, petitioner was charged on December 2 with "deliberate homicide," in that he "purposely or knowingly caused the death of Annie Jessen." At trial, Sandstrom's attorney informed the jury that, although his client admitted killing Jessen, he did not do so "purposely or knowingly," and was therefore not guilty of "deliberate homicide" but of a lesser crime. The basic support for this contention was the testimony of two court-appointed mental health experts, each of whom described for the jury petitioner's mental state at the time of the incident. Sandstrom's attorney argued that this testimony demonstrated that petitioner, due to a personality disorder aggravated by alcohol consumption, did not kill Annie Jessen "purposely or knowingly."

The prosecution requested the trial judge to instruct the jury that "[the] law presumes that a person intends the ordinary consequences of his voluntary acts." Petitioner's counsel objected, arguing that "the instruction has the effect of shifting the burden of proof on the issue of" purpose or knowledge to the defense, and that "that is impermissible under the Federal Constitution, due process of law." . . . The instruction was delivered, the jury found petitioner guilty of deliberate homicide, and petitioner was sentenced to 100 years in prison.

II

The threshold inquiry in ascertaining the constitutional analysis applicable to this kind of jury instruction is to determine the nature of the presumption it describes. See *Ulster County Court* v. *Allen.* That determination requires careful attention to the words actually spoken to the jury, for whether a defendant has been accorded his constitutional rights depends upon the way in which a reasonable juror could have interpreted the instruction.

[W]e are convinced that a reasonable juror could well have been misled by the instruction given, and could have believed that the presumption was not limited to requiring the defendant to satisfy only a burden of production. Petitioner's jury was told that "[*the*] *law presumes* that a person intends the ordinary consequences of his voluntary acts." They were not told that the presumption could be rebutted. . . . [W]e cannot discount the possibility that the jury may have interpreted the instruction in either of two more stringent ways.

First, a reasonable jury could well have interpreted the presumption as "conclusive," that is, not technically as a presumption at all, but rather as an irrebuttable direction by the court to find intent once convinced of the facts triggering the presumption. Alternatively, the jury may have interpreted the instruction as a direction to find intent upon proof of the defendant's voluntary actions (and their "ordinary" consequences), unless *the defendant* proved the contrary by some quantum of proof which may well have been considerably greater than "some" evidence — thus effectively shifting the burden of persuasion on the element of intent.

III

It is clear that under Montana law, whether the crime was committed purposely or knowingly is a fact necessary to constitute the crime of deliberate homicide.

Thus, the question before this Court is whether the challenged jury instruction had the effect of relieving the State of the burden of proof enunciated in *Winship* on the critical question of petitioner's state of mind. We conclude that under either of the two possible interpretations of the instruction set out above, precisely that effect would result, and that the instruction therefore represents constitutional error.

We consider first the validity of a conclusive presumption. This Court has considered such a presumption on at least two prior occasions.

In *Morissette* v. *United States*, 342 U.S. 246 (1952), the defendant was charged with willful and knowing theft of Government property. Although his attorney argued that for his client to be found guilty, "the taking must have been with felonious intent," the trial judge ruled that "[that] is presumed by his own act." After first concluding that intent was in fact an element of the crime charged, and after declaring that "[where] intent of the accused is an ingredient of the crime charged, its existence is . . . a jury issue," *Morissette* held:

> *"It follows that the trial court may not withdraw or prejudge the issue by instruction that the law raises a presumption of intent from an act.* It often is tempting to cast in terms of a 'presumption' a conclusion which a court thinks probable from given facts. . . . [But] [we] think presumptive intent has no place in this case. *A conclusive presumption which testimony could not overthrow would effectively eliminate intent as an ingredient of the offense.* A presumption which would permit but not require the jury to assume intent from an isolated fact would prejudge a conclusion which the jury should reach of its own volition. A presumption which would permit the jury to make an assumption which all the evidence considered together does not logically establish would give to a proven fact an artificial and fictional effect. In either case, *this presumption would conflict with the overriding presumption of innocence with which the law endows the accused and which extends to every element of the crime."*

As in *Morissette* and *United States Gympsum Co.*, a conclusive presumption in this case would "conflict with the overriding presumption of innocence with which the law endows the accused and which extends to every element of the crime," and would "invade [the] factfinding function" which in a criminal case the law assigns solely to the jury.

A presumption which, although not conclusive, had the effect of shifting the burden of persuasion to the defendant, would have suffered from similar infirmities. If Sandstrom's jury interpreted the presumption in that manner, it could have concluded that upon proof by the State of the slaying, and of additional facts not themselves establishing the element of intent, the burden was shifted to the defendant to prove that he lacked the requisite mental state. Such a presumption was found constitutionally deficient in *Mullaney* v. *Wilbur*, 421 U.S. 684 (1975). In *Mullaney*, the charge was murder, which under Maine law required proof not only of intent but of malice. The trial court charged the jury that "'malice aforethought is an essential and indispensable element of the crime of murder.'" However, it also instructed that if the prosecution established that the homicide was both intentional and unlawful, malice aforethought was to be implied unless the defendant proved by a fair preponderance of the evidence that he acted in the heat of passion on sudden provocation. *Ibid.* As we recounted just two Terms ago in *Patterson* v. *New York*, "[this] Court . . . unanimously agreed with the Court of Appeals that Wilbur's due process rights had been invaded by the presumption casting upon him the burden of proving by a preponderance of the evidence that he had acted in the heat of passion upon sudden provocation." And *Patterson* reaffirmed that "a State must prove every ingredient of an offense beyond a reasonable doubt, and . . . may not shift the burden of proof to the defendant" by means of such a presumption. Because David Sandstrom's jury may have interpreted the judge's instruction as constituting either a burden-shifting presumption like that in *Mullaney*, or a conclusive presumption like those in *Morissette* and *United States Gypsum Co.*, and because either interpretation would have deprived defendant of his right to the due process of law, we hold the instruction given in this case unconstitutional.

Sandstrom and its logic means that presumptions cannot operate in criminal cases to excuse the prosecution from having to prove every element—and hence every fact necessary to each element—beyond a reasonable doubt *with evidence.* But presumptions may still be used in criminal cases when they do not relieve the prosecution of its burden. For instance, the federal government and states may presume that a criminal defendant is competent to stand trial and even shift the burden onto the defendant to prove his incompetence as long as the burden does not exceed a preponderance of the evidence. *Medina v. California*, 505 U.S. 437 (1992); *Cooper v. Oklahoma*, 517 U.S. 348 (1996).

As noted above, presumptions come in two strengths, conclusive (or mandatory) and rebuttable (or permissive).

(a) Conclusive (or Mandatory) Presumptions

The first and more powerful type of presumption is a *conclusive (or mandatory) presumption.* As its name suggests, once a party proves the basic fact, the presumed fact is *conclusively* deemed to be true and cannot be contradicted by introducing contrary evidence. Because conclusive presumptions effectively dictate a rule of decision as to the presumed fact, conclusive presumptions operate more like a substantive rule of law than a rule of evidence. Graphically, a conclusive presumption can be illustrated as follows:

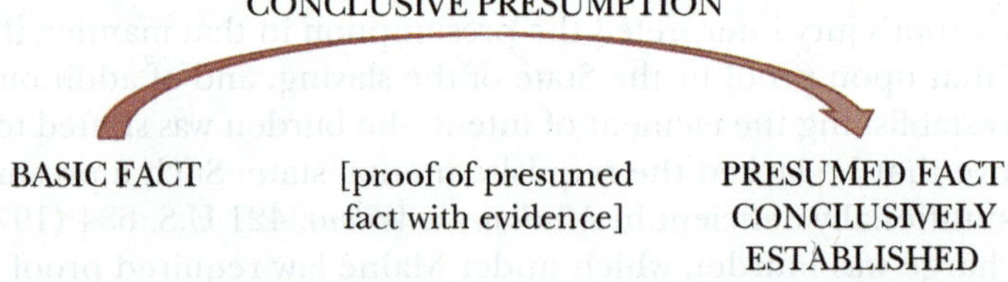

Viewed in a slightly different fashion, a conclusive presumption "moves the needle" in a way that carries the plaintiff's burden once the plaintiff establishes the basic fact.

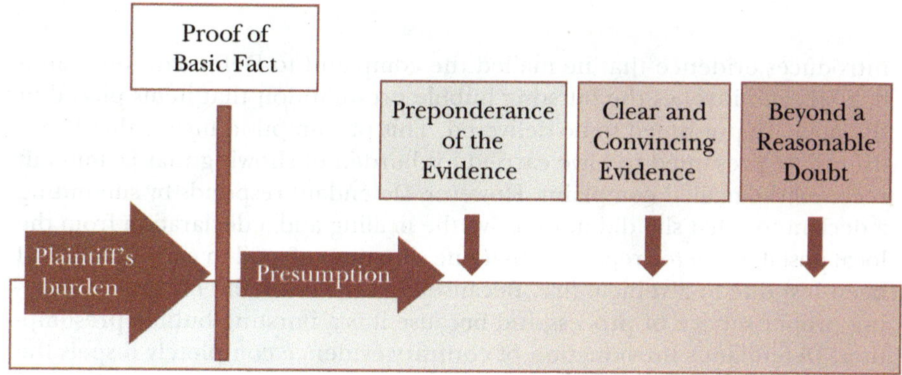

(b) Rebuttable (or Permissive) Presumptions

The second and less powerful type of presumption is a *rebuttable (or permissive) presumption.* As its name suggests, even after a party proves a basic fact and the presumption kicks in to establish the presumed fact, the party opposing the presumed fact can still attempt to rebut the presumption by introducing contrary evidence.

Rebuttable presumptions can affect either the burden of production or the burden of persuasion.

(i) Affecting the burden of production ("bursting-bubble" presumptions)

Some rebuttable presumptions only affect a party's burden of production. Here is how such a presumption operates. A party first introduces evidence of the basic fact. This showing triggers the presumption and thus presumptively establishes the presumed fact. The opposing party then has the opportunity to introduce evidence to rebut that presumed fact. Once it does, the presumption disappears entirely and is entitled to no further weight in the judge's assessment of whether the presumed fact has been established. Instead, the judge weighs the evidence supporting the basic fact, as well as any other evidence introduced by the party trying to prove the presumed fact, against the evidence introduced to rebut the presumed fact. Because this type of presumption disappears entirely, it is called a "bursting-bubble" presumption. And because this type of presumption disappears entirely upon the introduction of contrary evidence, it affects only the burden of producing evidence as to the presumed fact and does not at all alter the burden of *persuasion* as to that fact.

Example

Plaintiff sues Defendant for injuries sustained in an auto accident, but Defendant does not respond to Plaintiff's complaint, and a default judgment is entered against Defendant. Immediately after learning of the default judgment, Defendant files a motion to set aside the judgment on the ground that she did not receive the service of process through the mail. Plaintiff introduces evidence that he mailed the complaint to Defendant on March 8, 2021, and invokes the bursting bubble presumption that items placed in the mail are presumed to be delivered. This presumption means that Plaintiff will be presumed to have carried his burden of showing that Defendant received the mailed complaint. However, Defendant responds by submitting a declaration that she did not receive the mailing and a declaration from the local postal inspector reporting that one shipment of mail in early March had been lost due to a vehicle fire. Because Plaintiff bears the burden of showing proper service of process and because it is a bursting-bubble presumption, Defendant's introduction of contrary evidence completely dispels the presumption, and the burden remains on Plaintiff to prove that Defendant received the complaint through the mail.

FRE 301 erects a default rule that all presumptions under federal law are bursting-bubble presumptions unless a federal statute or other rule of evidence provide otherwise.[1] Specifically, FRE 301 provides the following:

FRE 301. Presumptions in Civil Cases Generally

In a civil case, unless a federal statute or these rules provide otherwise, the party against whom a presumption is directed has the burden of producing evidence to rebut the presumption. But this rule does not shift the burden of persuasion, which remains on the party who had it originally.

A good illustration of how a bursting-bubble presumption operates is *McCann v. George W. Newman Irrevocable Trust.*

McCann v. George W. Newman Irrevocable Trust

458 F.3d 281 (3d Cir. 2006)

Scirica, Chief Judge.

In this appeal . . . the issue is whether plaintiff established diversity of citizenship based on a change of domicile.

1. In Illinois, all presumptions are bursting-bubble presumptions. Ill. R. Evid. 301. In California and Florida, presumptions can either be bubble bursters *or* presumptions affecting the burden of persuasion. *Compare* Cal. Evid. Code §§ 630-47 (presumptions affecting burden of production) *with id.* §§ 660-70 (presumptions affecting the burden of persuasion); *see also* Fl. Stat. § 90.302-90.304. In New York, the courts are split over the effect of a rebuttable presumption.

I.

[After William E. McCann (McCann) died, his estate sued a New Jersey-based trust on the ground that it had not paid McCann properly for his work. McCann's estate sued in federal court in New Jersey, and asserted subject matter jurisdiction based on diversity, contending McCann had changed his domicile from New Jersey to New Hampshire prior to his death. Defendants filed a motion to dismiss for lack of subject matter jurisdiction under Fed. R. Civ. P. 12(b)(1), contending diversity of citizenship was lacking because all parties were domiciled in New Jersey.]

The material facts regarding McCann's domicile are undisputed. In 1969, he and his wife, Virginia, purchased a house in Short Hills, New Jersey, where they resided for over thirty years. In 1990, they purchased a second house in North Hampton, New Hampshire. In June 2000, they sold their New Jersey house and moved their furniture and personal belongings to New Hampshire. Virginia became a full-time resident of New Hampshire, but McCann rented an apartment in Springfield, New Jersey, and continued to live and work in New Jersey during the week. He spent weekends in New Hampshire.

McCann stopped commuting to New Jersey in November 2001, when he stopped receiving a salary from Secaucus Connection, L.L.C. During the three months between November 2001 and his death in February 2002, he traveled to New Jersey four times to attend meetings regarding the development project. He did not use his New Jersey apartment after January, but he did not cancel or break the lease or sublet the apartment.

McCann had ties to both states. He registered to vote in New Jersey in August 2001 and voted in the New Jersey general election on November 6, 2001. He registered to vote in New Hampshire at the end of November, but never actually voted there prior to his death. On July 30, 1999, he obtained a New Hampshire driver's license, but he maintained a New Jersey license, which he renewed after receiving the New Hampshire license. When Virginia became a full-time New Hampshire resident, the McCanns registered and insured all of their personal vehicles in New Hampshire. McCann had use of a company car in New Jersey.

McCann transferred his personal bank accounts to New Hampshire, but maintained a brokerage account in excess of $ 2.6 million in New Jersey. His federal income tax returns filed during his life represented he was a New Jersey resident. But his 2001 federal income tax return, prepared by Virginia and filed after his death, represented he was a New Hampshire resident. Virginia's application for continued health insurance coverage after McCann's death represented he was a New Jersey resident. McCann's funeral was held in New Jersey, but he was buried in New Hampshire.

In a letter opinion dated the same date, the court explained, "the burden here rests squarely on Plaintiff to demonstrate by clear and convincing evidence that McCann 1) took up residence in New Hampshire, and 2) intended to remain there." The court concluded the estate had not met this burden and accordingly, had not established McCann changed his domicile to New Hampshire prior to his death.

The estate contends on appeal that the District Court erred in applying a clear and convincing evidence standard of proof, in concluding McCann was not a domiciliary of New Hampshire, and in failing to hold an evidentiary hearing prior to dismissing the complaint.

III.

A.

Federal district courts are vested with original jurisdiction over civil actions where the matter in controversy exceeds the sum or value of $75,000 and is between "citizens of different States." 28 U.S.C. § 1332(a)(1).

Several principles guide our analysis of a party's citizenship for purposes of subject matter jurisdiction. The party asserting diversity jurisdiction bears the burden of proof. A party generally meets this burden by proving diversity of citizenship by a preponderance of the evidence. Citizenship is synonymous with domicile, and "the domicile of an individual is his true, fixed and permanent home and place of habitation. It is the place to which, whenever he is absent, he has the intention of returning." In determining an individual's domicile, a court considers several factors, including "declarations, exercise of political rights, payment of personal taxes, house of residence, and place of business." Other factors to be considered may include location of brokerage and bank accounts, location of spouse and family, membership in unions and other organizations, and driver's license and vehicle registration.

An individual can change domicile instantly. To do so, two things are required: "[h]e must take up residence at the new domicile, and he must intend to remain there." But "[a] domicile once acquired is presumed to continue until it is shown to have been changed." This principle gives rise to a presumption favoring an established domicile over a new one.

Here, the estate—the proponent of federal jurisdiction—bore the burden of establishing diversity of citizenship. The District Court required it to carry this burden by proving a change in domicile by clear and convincing evidence.

We are not convinced the proper standard is proof by clear and convincing evidence. There are two distinct elements of the burden of proof—the burden of production and the burden of persuasion.

Under Fed. R. Evid. 301, a presumption in a civil case imposes the burden of production on the party against whom it is directed, but does not shift the burden of persuasion. We have interpreted Rule 301 to express the Thayer-Wigmore "bursting bubble" theory of presumptions. Under this theory, "the introduction of evidence to rebut a presumption destroys that presumption, leaving only that evidence and its inferences to be judged against the competing evidence and its inferences to determine the ultimate question at issue." In other words, the presumption shifts the burden of producing sufficient evidence to rebut the presumed fact. Once that burden is met, the presumption "disappears from the case." This view of Rule 301 is widely accepted.

Under Rule 301, the presumption favoring an established domicile places the burden of production on the party alleging a change in domicile, but does not affect the burden of persuasion, which remains throughout with the proponent of federal jurisdiction. Accordingly, the presumption's only effect is to require the party asserting a change in domicile to produce enough evidence substantiating a change to withstand a motion for summary judgment or judgment as a matter of law on the issue.

When the party claiming a new domicile is the opponent of federal jurisdiction, the effect of the presumption in favor of an established domicile is straightforward. The party claiming a new domicile bears the initial burden of producing sufficient evidence to rebut the presumption in favor of the established domicile. If the party does so, the presumption disappears, the case goes forward, and the party asserting jurisdiction bears the burden of proving diversity of citizenship.

When the party claiming a new domicile is the proponent of federal jurisdiction, the effect of the presumption is less straightforward. One of the parties will bear both burdens—the burden of production regarding domicile and the burden of persuasion regarding federal jurisdiction. The District Court followed other courts in concluding the effect of placing both burdens on one party was to raise the relevant standard of proof. We are not so certain. We believe the effect of placing both burdens on one party is to require the party to initially carry the burden of production to rebut the presumption in favor of an established domicile. If and when the party does so, the presumption falls out of the case and the party is required to carry the burden of persuasion by proving that a change of domicile occurred, creating diversity of citizenship. Whether the party asserting a change of domicile is asserting or contesting federal subject matter jurisdiction, the appropriate standard of proof is preponderance of the evidence.

A bursting-bubble presumption can be illustrated as follows:

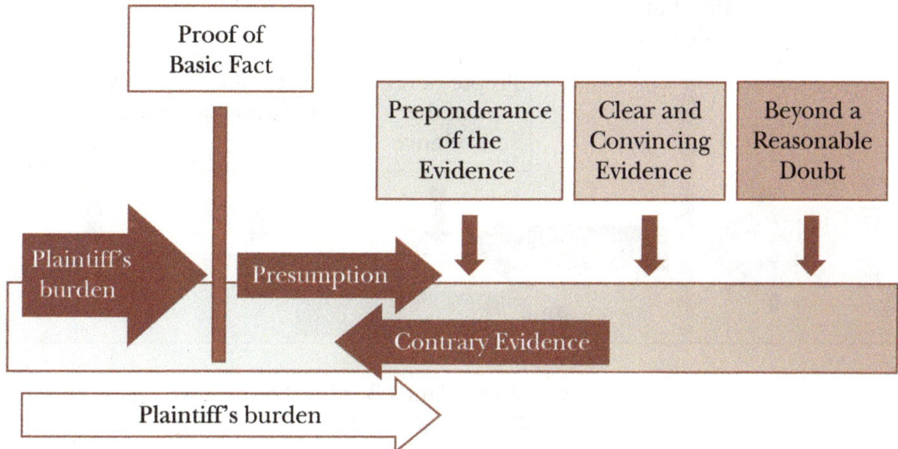

(ii) Affecting the burden of persuasion

Other rebuttable presumptions affect the burden of persuasion. Here is how they operate. A party first introduces evidence of the basic fact. This showing triggers the presumption and thus presumptively establishes the presumed fact and, at the same time, shifts the burden of persuasion to the opposing party to disprove the presumed fact. The opposing party then has the opportunity to introduce evidence to rebut that presumed fact. However, the introduction of the contrary showing does not entirely dispel the effect of the presumption (as it does with a bursting-bubble presumption) because the burden of persuasion still remains on the opposing party. In a close case where the evidence is in equipoise, the jury would have to side with the party invoking the presumption because the opposing party did not carry its burden of persuasion in rebutting the presumption.

Example

Plaintiff sues Defendant for injuries suffered when Defendant's car hit Plaintiff's car. Plaintiff introduces evidence that Defendant was traveling at 60 miles per hour in a 25 mile per hour zone. Plaintiff invokes the presumption that a person who violates an ordinance (including one setting the speed limit) is acting negligently. This presumption is one affecting the burden of persuasion. Defendant responds by introducing evidence that he was traveling that fast because his wife was in the backseat and about to give birth; he was driving her to the hospital. Because this presumption is one affecting the burden of persuasion, Plaintiff's invocation of the presumption shifted the burden of persuasion to Defendant, who now bears the burden of proving that he was *not* negligent.

A presumption affecting the burden of persuasion can be graphically represented as follows. As the illustration shows, the introduction of contrary evidence does not eliminate the presumption because the presumption has shifted the burden of persuasion to the party opposing the presumption.

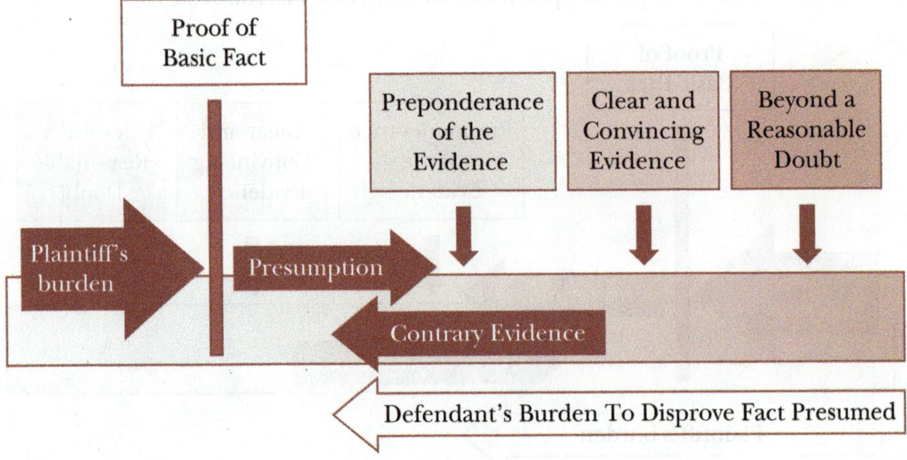

Review Questions

1. **"The threat's in the mail."** Defendant is charged with making criminal threats based on several threats made through the mail. The victim did not remember one of the threats, and Prosecutor seeks to invoke the presumption that a letter placed in the mail is presumed to be received. May Prosecutor invoke this presumption?
2. **Returned promissory note.** Plaintiff sues Defendant for failure to repay a promissory note. Defendant introduces evidence that Plaintiff returned

to him the original note for that debt. Defendant seeks to invoke the presumption that an obligation or debt returned to the debtor is presumed to be paid.

a. If this presumption is a conclusive presumption, may Plaintiff introduce contrary evidence?
b. If this presumption is a rebuttable presumption affecting the burden of persuasion, what effect, if any, does Plaintiff's introduction of contrary evidence have?
c. If this presumption is a rebuttable presumption affecting the burden of production, what effect, if any, does Plaintiff's introduction of contrary evidence have?

PART C: JUDICIAL NOTICE

Judicial notice is a mechanism courts may use to make factual findings that do *not* involve the admission of "evidence" under the rules. Instead, the trial judge simply "takes judicial notice" of those facts, and they become part of the universe of facts—along with other evidence admitted at the trial—that the trier of fact may use to make its decision. In this fashion, judicial notice is another type of "shortcut" because it dispenses with the need to otherwise formally introduce evidence under the rules of evidence.

Examples

1. Defendant is charged with murder. Defendant argues that he could not have been the killer because he was out sailing at the time of the killing. Prosecutor seeks to disprove this alibi on the ground that the tide was coming in at the time Defendant said he was sailing and wishes to use this tidal data to argue that the incoming tide would have made it impossible for Defendant to row out of the harbor (as he claimed he did). Prosecutor asks the trial judge to take judicial notice of the time of high tide on the date of the killing.
2. Plaintiff sues Defendant for injuries suffered when she and Defendant had a head-on collision on the nearby Rock Creek Parkway. Plaintiff calls witnesses to testify that Defendant was driving southbound on the Parkway at 5:30 p.m. Plaintiff asks the trial judge to take judicial notice that, on weekday afternoons from 4:00 p.m. to 7:00 p.m., the parkway changes from a traffic pattern of two lanes in each direction to four lanes in the northbound direction.
3. Plaintiff sues Defendant ambulance company for negligence in transporting him to a hospital after he had a heart attack. The ambulance company transported Plaintiff to the Cloven Hooves Hospital rather than the Pearly Gates Hospital. Plaintiff asks the trial judge to take judicial notice

of the fact that the Cloven Hooves Hospital is 6.66 miles from his house (where the ambulance company picked him up) and that the Pearly Gates Hospital is 0.77 mile from his house.

Assuming that the procedural prerequisites for taking judicial notice were met, the trial judge in each of these examples above would be able to take judicial notice of the facts requested in each of the examples.

Understanding judicial notice requires an understanding of the following topics:

- What types of facts qualify for judicial notice?
- What must a trial judge determine before taking judicial notice?
- What procedures must a trial judge follow before taking judicial notice?
- What weight must the trier of fact give a judicially noticed fact?

Each of these questions is addressed in FRE 201, the rule governing judicial notice.

FRE 201 provides the following:

FRE 201. Judicial Notice of Adjudicative Facts

(a) Scope. This rule governs judicial notice of an adjudicative fact only, not a legislative fact.

(b) Kinds of Facts That May Be Judicially Noticed. The court may judicially notice a fact that is not subject to reasonable dispute because it:

(1) is generally known within the trial court's territorial jurisdiction; or

(2) can be accurately and readily determined from sources whose accuracy cannot reasonably be questioned.

(c) Taking Notice. The court:

(1) may take judicial notice on its own; or

(2) must take judicial notice if a party requests it and the court is supplied with the necessary information.

(d) Timing. The court may take judicial notice at any stage of the proceeding.

(e) Opportunity to Be Heard. On timely request, a party is entitled to be heard on the propriety of taking judicial notice and the nature of the fact to be noticed. If the court takes judicial notice before notifying a party, the party, on request, is still entitled to be heard.

(f) Instructing the Jury. In a civil case, the court must instruct the jury to accept the noticed fact as conclusive. In a criminal case, the court must instruct the jury that it may or may not accept the noticed fact as conclusive.

Excerpts from Advisory Committee Notes to FRE 201

- Adjudicative facts are simply the facts of the particular case.
- Legislative facts . . . are those which have relevance to legal reasoning and the lawmaking process, whether in the formulation of a legal principle or ruling by a judge or court or in the enactment of a legislative body.

1. *To What Types of Facts Does the Mechanism of Judicial Notice Apply?*

For purposes of the rules of evidence, the universe of facts can be divided into two pertinent categories—"legislative" and "adjudicative."[2]

- *Legislative facts* are facts "which have relevance to legal reasoning and the lawmaking process." FRE 201, Adv. Comm. Note. When a court declines to create a new tort duty because, in its view, doing so would create perverse incentives, that court is judicially noticing facts about human behavior in the course of its reasoning. A classic example is the Supreme Court's decision in *Brown v. Board of Education*, 347 U.S. 483 (1954), where the court consulted various social studies in concluding that segregated (and hence separate) education of African Americans and Whites was inherently inequitable (and hence "not equal"). The facts that the Court relied on in its reasoning are legislative facts. Legislative facts also include facts that legislatures rely on in justifying the statutes they enact. Legislative facts also include dictionary definitions. *Robinson v. Liberty Mutual Ins. Co.*, 958 F.3d 1137, 1142 (11th Cir. 2020). They are *not* the focus of FRE 201.
- *Adjudicative facts* are "simply the facts of the particular case." FRE 201, Adv. Comm. Note. If, for instance, it matters to a case that a particular paper was filed within a certain number of days that excludes holidays, a court may take judicial notice of the adjudicative fact that October 11, 2021, was Indigenous People's Day (and hence a holiday). Or if it matters to a case how light or dark it was at the time of a gang shooting that occurred at 8:03 p.m. on a particular day (because it might affect what an eyewitness was able to see), a court may take judicial notice of the time of sunset on that particular day.

Because FRE 201 focuses solely on "adjudicative facts," we will do the same.

2. *What Showing Does FRE 201 Require Before a Court May Judicially Notice an Adjudicative Fact?*

Because judicial notice is a shortcut that sidesteps those rules of evidence that allow parties to present contradictory evidence to the trier of fact, the subset of

---

2. Some commentators also recognize additional categories of information that can be "judicially noticed" by judges in the course of deciding cases, such as the meaning of a word or what the law is in a different jurisdiction. However, a judge's recognition of these types of information is not regulated by the Federal Rules of Evidence.

adjudicative facts that may be judicially noticed is limited to those facts that are, by their nature, not subject to reasonable dispute. Specifically, FRE 201(b) limits judicial notice to adjudicative facts[3] that are "not subject to reasonable dispute" because they either:

- Are generally known within the trial court's territorial jurisdiction, or
- Can be accurately and readily determined from sources whose accuracy cannot reasonably be questioned.

When is a fact generally known within a trial court's territorial jurisdiction? It is not enough that the trial judge personally knows the fact. And it is also not required that *everyone* in the jurisdiction know the fact. Instead, as long as the fact is *generally known*, it is an appropriate fact for judicial notice. For example, the fact that the 405 Freeway in west Los Angeles has heavy traffic most of the time is a fact generally known in California (or at least in Southern California).

What types of facts may be accurately and readily determined from sources whose accuracy cannot reasonably be questioned? The classic example are facts listed in a farmer's almanac, such as the time of moonrise, moonset, sunrise, and sunset on any given day. But they also include other facts such as facts regarding geography (for example, the distance between two places or the depth of a lake), politics (for example, who was the president at any given point in time or which presidents have been impeached), science (for example, the gravitational pull of Earth), or the existence of public records (for example, that the surgeon general issued a notice advising against smoking in May 1965). By contrast, the number of COVID-19–related deaths in 2020 and 2021, as calculated by the Centers for Disease Control and Prevention, may be "reasonably in dispute" in a particular case if the methodology used to determine what constitutes a COVID-19–related fatality is contested in—and material to—that case. Whether something is "reasonably in dispute" can also change over time: The number of planets in our solar system was *not* in dispute for many years (and included nine planets), then was "reasonably in dispute" for several years as it was debated among astronomers, and now is no longer in dispute because the governing authorities all agreed that Pluto no longer qualifies as a planet.

When it comes to public records from any jurisdiction, a court may take judicial notice of the existence of the record, the date it was issued, and the action it purported to accomplish (for example, a trial court order denying a motion to dismiss). But the court cannot take judicial notice of the *truth* of any facts contained in the public record. For example, and as noted above, a trial judge can take judicial notice of the fact that the surgeon general issued a notice advising against smoking in May 1965, but cannot take judicial notice of the findings from various reports on the health effects of smoking that are set forth in the notice. Those findings are hearsay, and the power to take judicial notice does not include the power to take judicial notice of the truth of hearsay contained within documents that are themselves judicially noticeable. Such hearsay is admissible only if there is an applicable hearsay exception, which makes sense because the hearsay may be subject to

---

3. Other jurisdictions do not limit their judicial notice rules to adjudicative facts. *See* Fl. Stat. § 90.201-90.207; Cal. Evid. Code §§ 451-59; Tex. R. Evid. 201-04.

dispute, even though the existence of the document as a whole and the fact that the document sets forth certain conclusions are not.

Basank v. Decker illustrates the types of adjudicative facts that may be judicially noticed.

Basank v. Decker

449 F. Supp. 3d 205 (S.D.N.Y. 2020)

Torres, Judge.

Petitioners, Vasif "Vincent" Basank, et. al. are currently detained by Immigration and Customs Enforcement ("ICE") in county jails where cases of COVID-19 have been identified.

Last night after 11:00 p.m., Petitioners filed an amended petition for a writ of habeas corpus under 28 U.S.C. § 2241, seeking their release from ICE custody because of the public health crisis posed by COVID-19.

Petitioners were detained by ICE in connection with removal proceedings pending at the Varick Street Immigration Court. They are housed in New Jersey county jails where either detainees or staff have tested positive for COVID-19.

Each Petitioner suffers from chronic medical conditions, and faces an imminent risk of death or serious injury in immigration detention if exposed to COVID-19.

DISCUSSION

I. Legal Standard

"A plaintiff seeking a temporary restraining order must establish that he is likely to succeed on the merits, that he is likely to suffer irreparable harm in the absence of preliminary relief, that the balance of equities tips in his favor, and that an injunction is in the public interest."

A. Irreparable Harm

In the Second Circuit, a "showing of irreparable harm is the single most important prerequisite for the issuance of a preliminary injunction." That harm must be "actual and imminent" rather than speculative. Petitioners have met their showing of irreparable harm, in establishing the risk of harm to their health and constitutional rights.

1. Risk of Death

On March 11, 2020, the World Health Organization ("WHO") declared COVID-19 a global pandemic. At that time, there were more than 118,000 cases in 114 countries, and 4,291 people had died. Merely two weeks later, there have been at least 458,927 cases identified in 172 countries and at least 20,807 people have died. New York and its surrounding areas have become one of the global epicenters of the outbreak. Petitioners are held at detention facilities located in northern New Jersey.

As of March 26, 2020, New Jersey has 4,407 confirmed cases of COVID-19—the second highest number of reported cases by any state after New York.

Niko Kommenda and Pablo Gutierrez, *Coronavirus map of the US: latest cases state by state*, THE GUARDIAN (Mar. 26, 2020), https://www.theguardian.com/world/ng-interactive/2020/mar/26/coronavirus-map-of-the-us-latest-cases-state-by-state. New Jersey also has the fourth most COVID-19 related deaths in the country. *Id.* The three counties where the jails are located—Bergen, Essex, and Hudson counties—comprise one third of the confirmed cases of COVID-19 in New Jersey, with Bergen County reporting 819 positive results, Essex reporting 381 positives, and Hudson 260. The jails are no exceptions. Each of the jails where a Petitioner is being housed has reported confirmed cases of COVID-19. This includes two detainees and one correctional officer in the Hudson County Jail; one detainee at the Bergen County Jail; and a "superior officer" at the Essex County Jail.

The nature of detention facilities makes exposure and spread of the virus particularly harmful. Jaimie Meyer M.D., M.S., who has worked extensively on infectious diseases treatment and prevention in the context of jails and prisons, recently submitted a declaration in this district noting that the risk of COVID-19 to people held in New York-area detention centers, including the Hudson, Bergen County, and Essex County jails, "is significantly higher than in the community, both in terms of risk of transmission, exposure, and harm to individuals who become infected."

Moreover, medical doctors, including two medical experts for the Department of Homeland Security, have warned of a "tinderbox scenario" as COVID-19 spreads to immigration detention centers and the resulting "imminent risk to the health and safety of immigrant detainees" and the public. "It will be nearly impossible to prevent widespread infections inside the Hudson, Bergen, and Essex County jails now that the virus is in the facilities because detainees live, sleep, and use the bathroom in close proximity with others, and because '[b]ehind bars, some of the most basic disease prevention measures are against the rules or simply impossible.'"

Petitioners face serious risks to their health in their confinement. Each has underlying illnesses, including asthma, diabetes, heart disease, hypertension, obesity, and respiratory problems including COPD. The Court takes judicial notice that, for people of advanced age, with underlying health problems, or both, COVID-19 causes severe medical conditions and has increased lethality.

A number of courts in this district and elsewhere have recognized the threat that COVID-19 poses to individuals held in jails and other detention facilities. *See United States v. Stephens*, 447 F. Supp. 3d 63 (S.D.N.Y. 2020) ("[I]nmates may be at a heightened risk of contracting COVID-19 should an outbreak develop.") (collecting authorities); *United States v. Garlock* (N.D. Cal. Mar. 25, 2020) ("By now it almost goes without saying that we should not be adding to the prison population during the COVID-19 pandemic if it can be avoided. Several recent court rulings have explained the health risks—to inmates, guards, and the community at large—created by large prison populations. The chaos has already begun inside federal prisons—inmates and prison employees are starting to test positive for the virus, quarantines are being instituted, visits from outsiders have been suspended, and inmate movement is being restricted even more than usual." (citations omitted))[.]

Addressing the situation in New Jersey specifically, the New Jersey Supreme Court has held that "reduction of county jail populations, under appropriate conditions, is in the public interest to mitigate risks imposed by COVID-19" in light of "the profound risk posed to people in correctional facilities arising from the spread of COVID-19," and has ordered the release of many individuals serving sentences in New Jersey county jails. At least one court has ordered the release on bail of an inmate facing extradition on the basis of the risk to his health the pandemic poses. *Matter of Extradition of Toledo Manrique* (N.D. Cal. Mar. 19, 2020) ("These are extraordinary times. The novel coronavirus that began in Wuhan, China, is now a pandemic. The nine counties in the San Francisco Bay Area have imposed shelter-in-place orders in an effort to slow the spread of the contagion. This Court has temporarily halted jury trials, even in criminal cases, and barred the public from courthouses. Against this background, Alejandro Toledo has moved for release, arguing that at 74 years old he is at risk of serious illness or death if he remains in custody. The Court is persuaded. The risk that this vulnerable person will contract COVID-19 while in jail is a special circumstance that warrants bail.").

The risk that Petitioners will face a severe, and quite possibly fatal, infection if they remain in immigration detention constitutes irreparable harm warranting a TRO.

---

3. *What Procedures Must a Trial Judge Follow Before Taking Judicial Notice?*

A trial judge or an appellate court may take judicial notice on its own initiative or at the request of a party. FRE 201(c). The judge may do so at any point in the proceedings—before trial, during trial, or even in post-trial proceedings. FRE 201(d). No matter whose idea it is and no matter when the court takes judicial notice, the trial judge must give the parties the opportunity to be heard on whether it is appropriate to take judicial notice. FRE 201(e).

The trial judge generally has discretion whether to take judicial notice. FRE 201(c)(1). However, if a party requests judicial notice and supplies the information necessary to satisfy the showing required by FRE 201, the trial judge *must* take judicial notice of the requested fact. FRE 201(c)(2).

4. *What Is the Effect of Taking Judicial Notice?*

The effect of taking judicial notice depends on whether a case is civil or criminal:

- *Civil cases.* If a trial judge takes judicial notice of a fact in a civil case, that fact is conclusively established, and the jury must be so instructed. FRE 201(f).
- *Criminal cases.* Because a criminal defendant has a constitutional right to have every fact essential to his guilt established by evidence beyond a reasonable doubt, judicial notice of a fact cannot be conclusive; if it were, the prosecution's burden would be lightened in violation of the defendant's constitutional rights. Even though this consideration would appear to apply

only when judicial notice is taken *against* the defendant, FRE 201 sweeps more broadly. In criminal cases, FRE 201 leaves it up to the jury—no matter against whom the fact is to be judicially noticed—whether to accept the judicially noticed fact as conclusive, and the trial judge must so instruct the jury. FRE 201(f). A defendant's right to have the jury consider all facts would also seem to preclude a judge from taking *post-trial* judicial notice of any facts because, by definition, the jury never had the opportunity to consider those facts.

Review Questions

1. **Official findings.** Plaintiff sues Defendant for a design defect in her SUV. Plaintiff asks the trial judge to take judicial notice of (a) the fact that the National Highway Traffic Safety Administration issued a warning regarding the drivetrain used in Defendant's SUV and (b) the truth of the various studies set forth in the warning detailing the likelihood of injury arising from the defective drivetrain.
   a. May the trial judge take judicial notice of the warning? May she also take judicial notice of the study findings contained within the warning?
   b. If any judicial notice is permitted, what is the effect of taking notice of that fact? May Defendant introduce contrary evidence on the fact(s) judicially noticed?
2. **Maps and distances.** Defendant is charged with robbery. Prosecutor introduces cell phone records indicating that Defendant's cell phone pinged off a cell tower located at the corner of 4th and Main Streets at the time of the robbery. Prosecutor asks the trial judge to take judicial notice of the fact that the bank that was robbed was located just 800 feet away, on the intersection of 4th and Spring Streets.
   a. May the trial judge take judicial notice of this fact?
   b. What procedures must the trial judge follow?
   c. What must the trial judge instruct the jury about the fact to be judicially noticed?

Test Your Understanding

To test your understanding of the material in this chapter, turn to the Supplement for additional practice problems.

Chapter 15

Privileges

In the preceding chapters, we have discussed the various rules of evidence that are designed to ensure that the evidence presented at a proceeding is both relevant and reliable. But are relevance and reliability the sole criteria for admissibility? Consider the following examples.

Examples

1. Defendant is charged with a murder committed on New Year's Eve. At the trial, Prosecutor calls Defendant to the stand and asks him, "Where were *you* on New Year's Eve?"
2. Defendant is charged with a murder committed on New Year's Eve. At the trial, Prosecutor calls Defendant's wife as a witness and asks, "So Defendant came home a few hours after the New Year, correct? What did he tell you about what he had been doing that night?"
3. Defendant is charged with a murder committed on New Year's Eve. At the trial, Prosecutor calls the lawyer who initially represented Defendant in the case. Defendant is now represented by different counsel. Prosecutor asks, "So when you first met with your client and discussed the case, what did he tell you about what he was doing on New Year's Eve?"

In each example above, the evidence to be elicited by the prosecutor's question is both relevant and reliable. Indeed, it is hard to think of evidence *more* relevant and reliable than hearing the accused's explanation, under oath, as to what he was doing at the time of the charged crime(s). What the accused told his spouse and his lawyer about that night is only slightly less probative evidence.

But the prosecutor is not allowed to ask those questions. Why not? The exclusion of this evidence is not without cost: The trier of fact is deprived of relevant and reliable evidence that could only enhance the accuracy of its verdict.

The only thing that could possibly trump the public policy in favor of accurate verdicts are other competing—and more compelling—public policies. The public policy against forcing a person to incriminate themselves is so fundamental that it is enshrined in the Bill of Rights. And the public policies in encouraging honest and open dialogue between spouses, as well as between lawyers and their clients, are also compelling enough to justify excluding their confidential communications from evidence.

The Federal Rules of Evidence implement these competing and overriding public policies in a number of ways. As discussed in Chapter Four, competing public policies are what animate the special rules that define how to assess relevance for certain categories of evidence (such as subsequent remedial measures, compromise negotiations, humanitarian gestures, plea negotiations, and insurance). This chapter discusses the second mechanism for giving effect to competing public policies, namely, the recognition of *privileges* that, if applicable, render evidence inadmissible and, in many cases, not subject to pretrial discovery at all.[1]

Part A of this chapter discusses the mechanics of privileges under the rules of evidence, including which body of privilege law to apply (federal versus state), how a privilege is to be asserted, how a privilege can be waived, and when a privilege can itself be overridden by constitutional imperatives. Whether a particular communication is privileged is a preliminary question for the trial judge. FRE 104(a). The remaining parts of this chapter discuss the particulars of the main privileges affecting the rules of evidence. As discussed more fully below, the Federal Rules of Evidence do not themselves define privileges; instead, they leave that task to the federal courts to develop as part of federal common law.[2] FRE 501. That was no accident. The Judicial Conference Advisory Committee on Rules of Evidence responsible for drafting the rules proposed nine specific privileges to be codified in the Federal Rules of Evidence. But Congress took up the rules in the early 1970s, at a time when President Richard Nixon had invoked the concept of executive privilege to shield internal documents that might shed light on the Watergate scandal from public scrutiny. *See United States v. Nixon*, 418 U.S. 683 (1974). Reluctant at that time to engraft a set of privileges into the Federal Rules of Evidence that would shield further information from public scrutiny, Congress opted to leave the task of defining the law of privileges to the courts. This common law-based approach also had the advantage of not "freez[ing] the law" of privileges and instead "provid[ing] the courts with the flexibility to develop rules of privilege on a case-by-case basis" under the common law. 120 Cong. Rec. 40891 (1974). Often, however, the federal courts have looked to the Uniform Rules of Evidence drafted by the National Conference of Commissioners on Uniform State Laws as a bellwether when fashioning the federal common law on privileges. *E.g., United States v. Zolin*, 491 U.S. 554, 569 (1989); *Trammel v. United States*, 445 U.S. 40, 48-49 (1980).

Part B of this chapter discusses the two privileges applicable to lawyers—the attorney-client privilege and the work product "privilege." Part C discusses both

---

1. *See* Fed. R. Civ. P. 26(b)(5) (authorizing party to "withhold[] information otherwise discoverable" if that information is "privileged"); Fed. R. Crim. P. 16 (authorizing discovery in criminal cases); *United States v. Bryan*, 339 U.S. 323, 332 (1950) ("privilege[s]" can provide an "exemption from testifying or producing records").

2. This approach is also the one adopted by Illinois and, because it has not codified its rules of evidence, New York. Ill. R. Evid. 501. However, it is not the universal approach. California, Texas, and Florida, for instance, have codified all their privileges and affirmatively prohibit the development of new privileges by the courts. Cal. Evid. Code § 911 (requiring that privileges be "provided *by statute*"); Tex. R. Evid. 501 (same); Fla. Stat. § 90.501 (requiring that privileges be provided by "statute" or constitutional provision).

aspects of the spousal privilege. Part D discusses the psychotherapist-patient privilege. Part E discusses a number of other privileges that are commonly encountered, including the journalist-confidential source privilege, the physician-patient privilege, and the clergy-penitent privilege. Finally, Part F discusses the constitutionally grounded privilege against self-incrimination.

PART A: THE MECHANICS OF PRIVILEGES

Although, as Parts B through F make clear, the substantive requirements of each privilege are different, they share many commonalities. This part will discuss those commonalities.

We start with FRE 501 itself.

FRE 501. Privilege in General

The common law—as interpreted by the United States courts in the light of reason and experience—governs a claim of privilege unless any of the following provides otherwise:

- the United States Constitution;
- a federal statute; or
- rules prescribed by the Supreme Court.

But in a civil case, state law governs privilege regarding a claim or defense for which state law supplies the rule of decision.

1. Choice of Law

Because, as noted above, privileges operate as public policy-based exceptions to the general rules of evidence, and because public policy is by definition *substantive* rather than *procedural* in nature, FRE 501 incorporates the federal-state comity principles of *Erie R.R. v. Tompkins*, 304 U.S. 64, 78 (1938):

- When a case is in federal court on diversity jurisdiction, such that state law provides the rule of decision on substantive law, FRE 501 dictates that the *pertinent state's* privilege law applies.
- When a case is in federal court on federal question jurisdiction (that is, in any criminal case and in any civil case based on a federal statute or federal common law doctrine), such that federal law provides the rule of decision on substantive law, FRE 501 then looks to the federal common law of privileges.

2. FRE 501 and the Common Law of Privileges

As FRE 501's plain text makes clear, the Federal Rules of Evidence look primarily—although not exclusively—to the common law to define privileges and their contours.

At its point of origin, the federal common law regarding privileges starts with the dual principles that "there is a general duty to give what testimony one is capable of giving" and that "'the public . . . has a right to every man's evidence.'" *United States v. Bryan,* 339 U.S. 323, 331 (1950). Because the invocation of a privilege blocks the duty to provide evidence as well as the public's right to hear it, privileges thus are to be "strictly construed and accepted 'only to the very limited extent that . . . [a privilege serves] a public good transcending the normally predominant principle of utilizing all rational means for ascertaining truth.'" *Trammel v. United States,* 445 U.S. 40, 50 (1980) (citation omitted). FRE 501 empowers the federal courts to "continue the evolutionary development of" the law of privileges under these principles "in the light of reason and experience."

3. Prerequisites/Elements, Assertion, and Waiver of Privileges

In examining each privilege, it is critical to ask several questions:

What are the prerequisites or elements of the privilege?

Each privilege applies only when certain preconditions are met. It is important to know what those requirements are and whether they have been satisfied. If they have not, the privilege is—by its own terms—inapplicable. If those prerequisites have been met, it is then important to proceed to the next three questions.

Was the privilege properly asserted?

Privileges generally "belong" to a particular individual or entity, and that person is the only person holding the power to assert or to waive that privilege. The person to whom the privilege belongs is typically called the holder of the privilege. For example, the holder of the attorney-client privilege is the client (rather than the attorney). Thus, only the client may elect not to assert the privilege or may affirmatively waive the privilege; the attorney cannot take these actions because the attorney is not the holder of the privilege. In certain instances, however, the holder's representative or even the trial judge may be required to assert a privilege on behalf of the holder in order to ensure that the privilege is not waived. Thus, an attorney ordinarily has an obligation to assert the attorney-client privilege on her client's behalf. A privilege will be enforced only if it is asserted.

Was the privilege waived?

Even if the requirements are met and the privilege is properly asserted, there are instances in which the assertion of privilege will not be recognized because the privilege has been waived. Waiver can exist in the following situations:

When the privilege holder sues the other party to the privilege.

If a client sues her lawyer for legal malpractice or a patient sues his psychotherapist for medical malpractice, any privilege that may have attached to communications between the lawyer and client or the psychotherapist and patient, has been waived by the privilege holder's decision to sue the professional for malfeasance. *Accord* Uniform Rule of Evidence, Rule 502(d)(3). Any other rule would deprive the defendant-professional of the ability to rebut the claims of malfeasance.

When the privilege holder voluntarily discloses a significant part of the privileged information.

If the privilege holder voluntarily discloses a significant part of privileged information to someone who is not covered by that or some other privilege, the disclosure may constitute a waiver of the privilege.[3] For example, if the client hands his best friend a memo that the client's attorney prepared summarizing their discussion of the theft of trade secrets lawsuit they plan to file against a competitor, the memo is no longer protected by the attorney-client privilege because the client's voluntary disclosure of the memo to his best friend waived the privilege otherwise attaching to the memo.

There is no such thing as "selective disclosure"; disclosure of a significant part of a privileged communication is a waiver of the privilege as to the *whole* of the communication (although the waiver may not extend to *other* separately privileged communications). To qualify as a waiver, a significant portion of the *content* of the information must be disclosed.[4] A holder's disclosure that he consulted a psychotherapist does not waive the privilege attaching to confidential communications between the two. And to qualify as a waiver, the disclosure must be voluntary. The fact that eavesdroppers overhear a privileged communication does not effect a waiver because the holder did not voluntarily share that information with the interlopers. If there is more than one privilege holder (such as when an attorney has multiple clients), one holder's voluntary disclosure does not waive the privilege as to the other holders.

What about a voluntary—but inadvertent—disclosure of privileged information during pretrial discovery? Does *that* constitute a waiver, or can the privileged documents be "clawed back" to the discloser's custody without any waiver? This situation arises often enough that the Federal Rules of Evidence contain a rule for this precise situation in the context of the attorney-client and work-product privileges. In pertinent part, FRE 502 provides as follows:

FRE 502. Attorney-Client Privilege and Work Product; Limitations on Waiver

The following provisions apply, in the circumstances set out, to disclosure of a communication or information covered by the attorney-client or work-product protection.

3. That is the rule in California, Illinois, Florida, and Texas. Cal. Evid. Code § 919(a); *In re Marriage of Slomka*, 397 Ill. App. 3d 137, 142 (Ill Ct. App. 2009); Fl. Stat. § 90.507; Tex. R. Evid. 511(a).

4. However, the disclosure of documents in the course of a state proceeding does not constitute a waiver of the federal privilege if the disclosure would not qualify as a waiver under that state's law or would not qualify as a waiver "if [the disclosure] had been made in a federal proceeding." FRE 502(c).

(a) Disclosure Made in a Federal Proceeding or to a Federal Office or Agency; Scope of a Waiver. When the disclosure is made in a federal proceeding or to a federal office or agency and waives the attorney-client privilege or work-product protection, the waiver extends to an undisclosed communication or information in a federal or state proceeding only if:

(1) the waiver is intentional;

(2) the disclosed and undisclosed communications or information concern the same subject matter; and

(3) they ought in fairness to be considered together.

(b) Inadvertent Disclosure. When made in a federal proceeding or to a federal office or agency, the disclosure does not operate as a waiver in a federal or state proceeding if:

(1) the disclosure is inadvertent;

(2) the holder of the privilege or protection took reasonable steps to prevent disclosure; and

(3) the holder promptly took reasonable steps to rectify the error, including (if applicable) following Federal Rule of Civil Procedure 26(b)(5)(B).

. . .

(g) Definitions. In this rule:

(1) "attorney-client privilege" means the protection that applicable law provides for confidential attorney-client communications; and

(2) "work-product protection" means the protection that applicable law provides for tangible material (or its intangible equivalent) prepared in anticipation of litigation or for trial.

FRE 502 provides that an inadvertent disclosure will not constitute a waiver as long as the privilege holder (1) took reasonable steps to prevent inadvertent disclosures *before the disclosure* and (2) took prompt and reasonable steps to rectify the inadvertent disclosure at issue *after that disclosure.*[5] A rule allowing a party to retain the privilege on a document that was inadvertently disclosed is commonly called a "clawback" rule because it allows the party to "claw" back the disclosed document for which the privilege is seemingly waived and return it to its predisclosure status as a privileged document. Critically, FRE 502 is only a *default* "clawback" rule: Parties can negotiate different conditions governing when inadvertent disclosures of documents during discovery constitute a waiver. When it comes to voluminous electronic discovery (e-discovery), many practitioners strongly encourage the use of such agreements.

---

5. Illinois and Texas have a similar codified rule, Ill. R. Evid. 502(b), Tex. R. Evid 511(b), and California, Florida, New York, and Texas have adopted a similar rule through judicial precedent. *Ardon v. City of Los Angeles*, 62 Cal. 4th 1176, 1182-88 (Cal. 2016); *State Comp. Ins. Fund v. WPS, Inc.*, 70 Cal. App. 4th 644, 652-54 (Cal. Ct. App. 1999); *O'Mary v. Mitsubishi Electronics America, Inc.*, 59 Cal. App. 4th 563, 577 (Cal. Ct. App. 1997); *Nova Southeastern Univ., Inc. v. Jacobson*, 25 So. 3d 82, 86 (Fla. Dist. Ct. App. 2009); *John Blair Communications, Inc. v. Reliance Capital Group, L.P.*, 182 A.D.2d 578, 579 (N.Y. App. Div. 1992); *Paxton v. City of Dallas*, 509 S.W.3d 247, 263 (Tex. 2017).

When the privilege holder uses a privileged document to refresh his recollection while he is testifying.

Waiver might also flow from using a document to refresh recollection. If the holder of a privilege is testifying on the stand and uses a privileged document to refresh his recollection, FRE 612(b) provides that the "adverse party is entitled to have the writing produced at the hearing, to inspect it, to cross-examine the witness about it, and to introduce in evidence any portion that relates to the witness's testimony." Does this right override the privilege that previously attached to that document? The federal courts are currently split on the issue.[6]

What are the exceptions to the privilege?

Some privileges have well-established exceptions where they will be deemed not to apply, even though their elements are met, they are asserted, and they are not waived. The applicable exceptions vary for each privilege.

4. *The Constitutional Override*

With the exception of the privilege against self-incrimination, which is contained in the U.S. Constitution, most privileges are grounded in statute or in the common law. What happens when these nonconstitutionally based privileges bump up against a criminal defendant's constitutional rights? There are three instances in which this situation typically arises:

- Brady *rights.* Pursuant to *Brady v. Maryland*, 373 U.S. 83 (1963), due process obligates the prosecution team to disclose any information in its possession that is both favorable and material to the defense. What if that material is privileged? In *Pennsylvania v. Ritchie*, 480 U.S. 39 (1987), a plurality of the Supreme Court rejected the argument that the defendant was entitled to see all privileged information held by another. Instead, *Ritchie* held that the trial judge is obligated to conduct an *in camera* hearing (that is, a hearing outside the presence of the defense) where it can review the assertedly privileged material to determine if (1) the material is, in fact, privileged; and, if it is privileged, (2) the defendant's need for the information to mount a defense outweighs that privilege.
- *Rights to obtain information from third parties.* Sometimes, a criminal defendant subpoenas information from a third party, and the third party asserts that the information is privileged. Trial judges will typically follow the same procedures here as they do with information in the prosecution team's possession.

---

6. *Compare, e.g., Timm v. Mead Corp.*, 1992 U.S. Dist. LEXIS 1411 (N.D. Ill. 1992) (detailing cases finding waiver); *Audiotext Communs. Network, Inc. v. U.S. Telecom, Inc.*, 164 F.R.D. 250 (D. Kan. 1996) (same) *with Suss v. MSX Int'l Engineering Servs., Inc.*, 212 F.R.D. 159 (S.D.N.Y. 2002) (no waiver). The California courts are also split. *Compare Kerns Constr. Co. v. Superior Court*, 266 Cal. App. 2d 405 (Cal. Ct. App. 1968) (waiver) *with Sullivan v. Superior Court*, 29 Cal. App. 3d 64 (Cal. Ct. App. 1972). New York law provides that a waiver occurs in this situation. *See Slotnik v. State*, 129 Misc. 2d 553, 554-55 (N.Y. Ct. Cl. 1985).

- *When the information sought is relevant solely to impeachment.* When a criminal defendant seeks to obtain privileged information relevant only to cross-examination, the most pertinent constitutional right is the Sixth Amendment's Confrontation Clause. As noted in Chapter Nine, however, "the right to confrontation is basically a trial right." *Barber v. Page,* 390 U.S. 719, 725 (1968). Thus, the defendant's right to confront witnesses trumps a state law-based privilege when the defendant seeks the privileged information during trial. *Davis v. Alaska,* 415 U.S. 308 (1974).

Review Questions

1. **Choice of law.** Plaintiff sues Defendant for fraud in federal court; the two are from different states. In response to a discovery request, Defendant asserts the attorney-client privilege. Which jurisdiction's law of privilege applies?
2. **Protecting the privilege.** Defendant is charged with assaulting a child. Defendant subpoenas documents from the victim's therapist. If the victim is not present in court when the subpoenaed documents are sent to the court, may the trial judge disclose those documents to the defense? What privilege might apply? Who may assert it? If the privilege is asserted and Defendant insists that the information is essential for his defense, what procedures must the trial court follow? Does it matter if the sole purpose of this information is to impeach the victim?
3. **Inadvertent disclosure.** Plaintiff sues Defendant for theft of trade secrets in federal court. In discovery, Plaintiff inadvertently sends attorney-client privileged documents to Defendant. Does that constitute a waiver of the privilege as to those documents? What must Plaintiff show in order to preserve the privilege?

PART B: LAWYER-RELATED PRIVILEGES

There are two privileges potentially applicable when lawyers are involved: (1) the attorney-client privilege and (2) the work-product "privilege".[7]

1. Attorney-Client Privilege

As FRE 502 implies, the federal rules and every state's law recognize the existence of an attorney-client privilege. The public policy behind this privilege is

7. These lawyer-related privileges are similar to, but distinct, from a lawyer's ethical duties of confidentiality to the client. Privileges relate to the admissibility of evidence. Confidential duties may go beyond privileges and are beyond the scope of this book.

straightforward: "The privilege is intended to encourage 'full and frank communication between attorneys and their clients and thereby promote broader public interests in the observance of law and the administration of justice.'" *Swidler & Berlin v. United States,* 524 U.S. 399, 403 (1998). This policy is critical: If a potential civil plaintiff is not sure that what she tells her lawyer will be kept confidential, she may opt not to consult a lawyer and let a civil wrong go unaddressed; if the defendant in a civil suit is not sure that what he tells his lawyer will be kept confidential, he may not give the lawyer the information needed to mount a valid defense; and, perhaps more critically, if a criminal defendant is not sure that what he tells his lawyer will be kept confidential, he may not be fully honest about what happened, and the lawyer's ability to defend him—and to ensure that he is not unjustly deprived of his liberty or life—will suffer. The privilege implements this critical public policy by creating a bubble around those communications that prevents them from ever being discovered or admitted into evidence at a legal proceeding.[8]

---

8. Although the Federal Rules of Evidence leave the development of the attorney-client privilege in federal court to common law development, Uniform Rule of Evidence 502 (as last amended in 2005) codifies that privilege in a way that can provide helpful guidance. In full, Uniform Rule of Evidence 502 provides as follows:

(a) Definitions. In this rule:

(1) "Client" means a person for whom a lawyer renders professional legal services or who consults a lawyer with a view to obtaining professional legal services from the lawyer.

(2) A communication is "confidential" if it is not intended to be disclosed to third persons other than those to whom disclosure is made in furtherance of the rendition of professional legal services to the client or those reasonably necessary for the transmission of the communication.

(3) "Lawyer" means a person authorized, or reasonably believed by the client to be authorized, to engage in the practice of law in any State or country.

(4) "Representative of the client" means a person having authority to obtain professional legal services, or to act on legal advice rendered, on behalf of the client or a person who, for the purpose of effectuating legal representation for the client, makes or receives a confidential communication while acting in the scope of employment for the client.

(5) "Representative of the lawyer" means a person employed, or reasonably believed by the client to be employed, by the lawyer to assist the lawyer in rendering professional legal services.

(b) General rule of privilege. A client has a privilege to refuse to disclose and to prevent any other person from disclosing a confidential communication made for the purpose of facilitating the rendition of professional legal services to the client:

(1) between the client or a representative of the client and the client's lawyer or a representative of the lawyer;

(2) between the lawyer and a representative of the lawyer;

(3) by the client or a representative of the client or the client's lawyer or a representative of the lawyer to a lawyer or a representative of a lawyer representing another party in a pending action and concerning a matter of common interest therein;

(4) between representatives of the client or between the client and a representative of the client; or

(a) Prerequisites/Elements

The attorney-client privilege protects (1) confidential communications (2) between a lawyer and a client. Uniform Rule of Evidence 502(b).

(i) Confidential communications

The privilege attaches only to "confidential communications" between a lawyer and client, namely, (1) a communication (that is, what the client tells the lawyer and what the lawyer tells the client) that is (2) made in confidence.

By negative implication, the privilege does *not* extend beyond what is communicated and thus does *not* reach the following:

- The existence of the attorney-client relationship as well as the incidentals of that relationship, such as the identity of the client and the billing records. However, if the client's identity or the billing records might, by implication, reveal confidential communications, they may be privileged. For instance, the client's identity might be privileged when the content of the communication has been disclosed but not its source, such as when the client gives

---

(5) among lawyers and their representatives representing the same client.

(c) Who may claim privilege. The privilege under this rule may be claimed by the client, the client's guardian or conservator, the personal representative of a deceased client, or the successor, trustee, or similar representative of a corporation, association, or other organization, whether or not in existence. A person who was the lawyer or the lawyer's representative at the time of the communication is presumed to have authority to claim the privilege, but only on behalf of the client.

(d) Exceptions. There is no privilege under this rule:

(1) if the services of the lawyer were sought or obtained to enable or aid anyone to commit or plan to commit what the client knew or reasonably should have known was a crime or fraud;

(2) as to a communication relevant to an issue between parties who claim through the same deceased client, regardless of whether the claims are by testate or intestate succession or by transaction inter vivos;

(3) as to a communication relevant to an issue of breach of duty by a lawyer to the client or by a client to the lawyer;

(4) as to a communication necessary for a lawyer to defend in a legal proceeding an accusation that the lawyer assisted the client in criminal or fraudulent conduct;

(5) as to a communication relevant to an issue concerning an attested document to which the lawyer is an attesting witness;

(6) as to a communication relevant to a matter of common interest between or among two or more clients if the communication was made by any of them to a lawyer retained or consulted in common, when offered in an action between or among any of the clients; or

(7) as to a communication between a public officer or agency and its lawyers unless the communication concerns a pending investigation, claim, or action and the court determines that disclosure will seriously impair the ability of the public officer or agency to act on the claim or conduct a pending investigation, litigation, or proceeding in the public interest.

his attorney money to pay illegally withheld back taxes and the IRS seeks to learn the client's identity. *See, e.g., United States v. Strahl*, 590 F.2d 10 (1st Cir. 1978); *Baird v. Koerner*, 279 F.2d 623 (9th Cir. 1960). Along similar lines, billing records might be privileged to the extent they reveal the client's motive or litigation strategy; if they are privileged, the records may be redacted to eliminate the disclosure of such confidential communications. *United States v. Amlani*, 169 F.3d 1189, 1195 (9th Cir. 1989).

- The lawyer's observations about the client (because such observations do not involve communications). For example, a lawyer's observation that her client appeared to be intoxicated during a meeting is not covered by the privilege.
- The underlying facts, merely because they are repeated to a lawyer (because those facts are not communications), although the *fact* that the client relayed them to the lawyer may be covered by the privilege. Assume, for example, that a client tells his coworker that he wrote off his around-the-world vacation as a business expense on his taxes because the client checked his work e-mail one time while he was traveling. If the client subsequently tells his lawyer what he told his coworker, the fact that the client shared this story *with the lawyer* is privileged. However, what the client had previously told his coworker is not privileged: What the client previously said was not privileged at the time it was said to the coworker, and subsequently repeating that statement to the lawyer does not retroactively extend the cloak of the attorney-client privilege to that communication.

A communication is made in confidence "if it is not intended to be disclosed to third persons other than [(1)] those to whom disclosure is made in furtherance of the rendition of professional legal services to the client or [(2)] those reasonably necessary for the transmission of the communication." Uniform Rule of Evidence 502(a)(2). Thus, communications made to staff members working at the lawyer's direction or to experts retained by the lawyer as part of the representation are made in confidence. Conversely, if a client voluntarily speaks to a lawyer in a loud voice in a crowded room where it is easy to be overheard, that communication may not be in confidence. Along similar lines, if a client sends an e-mail to his lawyer over his employer's computer system when that system displays a banner that gives the employer the right to monitor all communications made over that system, that communication is also not made in confidence.

Examples

1. A client goes to an initial consultation with a lawyer and tells the lawyer, "I killed my business partner and tossed the gun I used into the East River." The client also gives the lawyer the business ledger he took from his now-deceased partner. Although the client's statement "I killed my business partner" is a privileged communication, the client cannot

assert the privilege to prevent *others* from testifying about the murder or the disposal of the gun or to keep others from obtaining the business ledger.

2. Plaintiff sues Defendant for intentional interference with a prospective economic advantage. Defendant subpoenas Plaintiff's lawyer for her billing records for this case. The records are not privileged unless the billing entries reveal information about Plaintiff's strategy.
3. Defendant is sued for causing injuries arising out of a collision that Plaintiff believes was caused by Defendant's drinking. In a deposition, Plaintiff questions Defendant's former attorney to ask whether, when they spoke, Defendant ever appeared to be drunk. The attorney-client privilege would not prevent the former lawyer from answering that question.

(ii) Between a lawyer and a client

For purposes of the attorney-client privilege, a lawyer (1) is a person (a) who is licensed to practice law or (b) whom the client reasonably believes is licensed to practice law, and (2) is consulted to provide legal advice or services. Thus, the privilege still attaches to communications made to a person who is not a lawyer but whom the client reasonably believes to be a lawyer. However, the communication must be for purposes of legal services: A communication between friends is not privileged merely because one of them happens to be a lawyer. The issue is trickier when the lawyer wears multiple "hats," as many corporate counsel do, with the lawyer acting both as an attorney *and* a business advisor. In such instances, whether the privilege applies turns on whether the communication was made at a time when the person was providing "primarily" legal services or, instead, whether the legal advice was "merely incidental" to the business advice. *United States v. Cohn*, 303 F. Supp. 2d 672, 683 (D. Md. 2003); *Brookshire Bros. Holding, Inc. v. Total Containment, Inc.*, 2006 U.S. Dist. LEXIS 22510, *8-*9 (W.D. La. 2006). Thus, when a company's in-house counsel oversees the company's telemarketing program and provides advice designed chiefly to increase profits, that lawyer is acting more in a business capacity than a legal capacity, and the privilege does not attach. *Cohn*, 303 F. Supp. 2d at 683-85. Along the same lines, when a company's in-house counsel oversees the company's environmental remediation, the privilege does not attach because the lawyer's task in overseeing the collection of data from retained engineers could be performed by nonlawyers and thus does not involve the rendering of legal services. *United States Postal Serv. v. Phelps Dodge Ref. Corp.*, 852 F. Supp. 156, 159-64 (E.D.N.Y. 1994). The privilege also does not attach to a lawyer's "activities as a business agent" for a client. *Chi. Title Ins. Co. v. Superior Court*, 174 Cal. App. 3d 1142, 1154 (Cal. Ct. App. 1985).

The privilege attaches the moment the communication is made to a lawyer in confidence; the client need not ultimately retain the lawyer. Thus, if a client consults five different lawyers trying to decide which to hire, her confidential communications with all of them during the initial consultation meetings are all privileged.

When does the privilege terminate? In federal court, the privilege survives the client's death.[9] *Swidler*, 524 U.S. at 405.[10]

There are two special situations where the privilege operates differently: (1) when the government is the client and (2) when a collective entity (such as a corporation or association or partnership) is the client.

Lawyers working for the government are differently situated from lawyers representing private entities, in part because they represent the public. Does that affect the scope of the attorney-client privilege? Some courts have said, "yes," holding that government lawyers may not assert the attorney-client privilege on behalf of their government-clients, at least with respect to possible criminal violations. *In re Lindsey*, 158 F.3d 1263 (C.A.D.C. 1998) (Deputy White House Counsel may not assert attorney-client privilege to refuse to produce information to the grand jury regarding possible criminal violations). But other federal courts have held that the privilege applies in the same way to government lawyers as it does to private lawyers. *United States v. Doe (In re Grand Jury Investigation)*, 399 F.3d 527, 532-36 (2d Cir. 2005).[11] However, if public entities hire outside counsel to represent them, those public entities still have the protection of the attorney-client privilege.

Collective entities are differently situated than individuals because a corporation cannot walk into an office and start talking to a lawyer. Instead, corporations communicate through their agents. But *which* corporate agents are covered by the privilege? Does the privilege extend only to the subset of the corporate agents who control the corporation (such as its chief executive officer, chief financial officer, and board of directors), or does it reach every employee of the corporation? The answer matters, especially when it comes to a corporation's willingness to undertake internal investigations: If what its employees say to the corporation's lawyers is not privileged, a corporation is less likely to kick that hornet's nest and uncover malfeasance that it may have to disclose to others. The Supreme Court encountered the scope of the privilege in *Upjohn Co. v. United States*.

---

9. In California, the privilege survives the client's death, but only until the client's estate is distributed; during this postdeath, predistribution period, the deceased client's personal representative becomes the holder of the privilege. *HLC Properties, Ltd. v. Superior Court*, 35 Cal. 4th 54, 66 (Cal. 2005). In Illinois, New York, Texas, and Florida, the privilege also survives the client's death. *Hitt v. Stephens*, 285 Ill. App. 3d 713, 717 (Ill. Ct. App. 1997); *Mayorga v. Tate*, 302 A.D.2d 11, 11-12 (N.Y. App. Div. 2002); Tex. R. Evid. 503(c)(3); Fla. Stat. § 90.502(3)(c).

10. *Swidler* grew out of a criminal investigation of the Office of Independent Counsel, which was looking into whether White House employees had made false statements or obstructed justice during the dismissal of several employees from the White House Travel Office in the early years of President Bill Clinton's first term. The Deputy White House Counsel at the time of the firings was Vincent Foster. Foster met with a lawyer at the Swidler law firm about the possible investigations of the firings. Nine days after this meeting, Foster took his own life. *Swidler* grew out of the Office of Independent Counsel's attempts to get the lawyer's notes of Foster's last meeting.

11. Some states have held that the attorney-client privilege does not extend to prosecutors. *People ex rel. Lockyer v. Superior Court*, 83 Cal. App. 4th 387, 399-400 (Cal. Ct. App. 2000). In such states, prosecutors instead rely on different privileges to protect the confidentiality of their ongoing investigations, such as the official information privilege, Cal. Evid. Code § 1040.

Upjohn Co. v. United States

449 U.S. 383 (1981)

JUSTICE REHNQUIST delivered the opinion of the Court.

Petitioner Upjohn Co. manufactures and sells pharmaceuticals here and abroad. In January 1976 independent accountants conducting an audit of one of Upjohn's foreign subsidiaries discovered that the subsidiary made payments to or for the benefit of foreign government officials in order to secure government business. The accountants so informed petitioner Mr. Gerard Thomas, Upjohn's Vice President, Secretary, and General Counsel. Thomas is a member of the Michigan and New York Bars, and has been Upjohn's General Counsel for 20 years. He consulted with outside counsel and R. T. Parfet, Jr., Upjohn's Chairman of the Board. It was decided that the company would conduct an internal investigation of what were termed "questionable payments." As part of this investigation the attorneys prepared a letter containing a questionnaire which was sent to "All Foreign General and Area Managers" over the Chairman's signature. The letter began by noting recent disclosures that several American companies made "possibly illegal" payments to foreign government officials and emphasized that the management needed full information concerning any such payments made by Upjohn. The letter indicated that the Chairman had asked Thomas, identified as "the company's General Counsel," "to conduct an investigation for the purpose of determining the nature and magnitude of any payments made by the Upjohn Company or any of its subsidiaries to any employee or official of a foreign government." The questionnaire sought detailed information concerning such payments. Managers were instructed to treat the investigation as "highly confidential" and not to discuss it with anyone other than Upjohn employees who might be helpful in providing the requested information. Responses were to be sent directly to Thomas. Thomas and outside counsel also interviewed the recipients of the questionnaire and some 33 other Upjohn officers or employees as part of the investigation.

[The IRS sought the questionnaires.]

The company declined to produce the documents specified in the second paragraph on the grounds that they were protected from disclosure by the attorney-client privilege and constituted the work product of attorneys prepared in anticipation of litigation. On August 31, 1977, the United States filed a petition seeking enforcement of the summons.

Federal Rule of Evidence 501 provides that "the privilege of a witness . . . shall be governed by the principles of the common law as they may be interpreted by the courts of the United States in light of reason and experience." The attorney-client privilege is the oldest of the privileges for confidential communications known to the common law. Its purpose is to encourage full and frank communication between attorneys and their clients and thereby promote broader public interests in the observance of law and administration of justice. The privilege recognizes that sound legal advice or advocacy serves public ends and that such advice or advocacy depends upon the lawyer's being fully informed by the client.

In the case of the individual client the provider of information and the person who acts on the lawyer's advice are one and the same. In the corporate context, however, it will frequently be employees beyond the control group as defined by the court below—"officers and agents . . . responsible for directing [the company's] actions in response to legal advice"—who will possess the information needed by the corporation's lawyers. Middle-level—and indeed lower-level—employees can, by actions within the scope of their employment, embroil the corporation in serious legal difficulties, and it is only natural that these employees would have the relevant information needed by corporate counsel if he is adequately to advise the client with respect to such actual or potential difficulties.

The control group test adopted by the court below thus frustrates the very purpose of the privilege by discouraging the communication of relevant information by employees of the client to attorneys seeking to render legal advice to the client corporation.

The narrow scope given the attorney-client privilege by the court below not only makes it difficult for corporate attorneys to formulate sound advice when their client is faced with a specific legal problem but also threatens to limit the valuable efforts of corporate counsel to ensure their client's compliance with the law. In light of the vast and complicated array of regulatory legislation confronting the modern corporation, corporations, unlike most individuals, "constantly go to lawyers to find out how to obey the law," particularly since compliance with the law in this area is hardly an instinctive matter.

The communications at issue were made by Upjohn employees to counsel for Upjohn acting as such, at the direction of corporate superiors in order to secure legal advice from counsel. As the Magistrate found, "Mr. Thomas consulted with the Chairman of the Board and outside counsel and thereafter conducted a factual investigation to determine the nature and extent of the questionable payments *and to be in a position to give legal advice to the company with respect to the payments.*" (Emphasis supplied.) Information, not available from upper-echelon management, was needed to supply a basis for legal advice concerning compliance with securities and tax laws, foreign laws, currency regulations, duties to shareholders, and potential litigation in each of these areas. The communications concerned matters within the scope of the employees' corporate duties, and the employees themselves were sufficiently aware that they were being questioned in order that the corporation could obtain legal advice. Consistent with the underlying purposes of the attorney-client privilege, these communications must be protected against compelled disclosure.

Upjohn helpfully lays out the two main approaches to the attorney-client privilege in the corporate context—(1) the control group test and (2) the subject matter test—and selects the subject matter test as the federal approach.[12]

---

12. New York follows this approach. *Niesig v. Team* I, 149 A.D.2d 94 (N.Y. App. Div. 1989). Not all states agree. California, Illinois, and Texas, for instance, only extend the privilege to a corporation's "control group." *D.I. Chadbourne, Inc. v. Superior Court,* 60 Cal. 2d 723, 736-37 (Cal. 1964); *Bobele v. Superior Court,* 199 Cal. App. 3d 708 (Cal. Ct. App. 1988); *Consolidation Coal Co. v. Bucryus-Erie Co.,* 89 Ill.2d 103, 112-13 (Ill. 1982); *Midwesco-Paschen Joint Venture for the Viking Projects v. Imo Indus.,* 265 Ill. App. 3d 654, 669 (Ill. Ct. App. 1994); *National Tank Co. v. 30th Judicial Dist. Ct.,* 851 S.W.2d 193, 198 (Tex. 1993); *Cigna Corp. v. Spears,* 838 S.W.2d 561, 566 (Tex. Ct. App. 1992). Florida uses a hybrid test that reaches beyond the "control group" to employees who satisfy a multipronged test. *S. Bell Tel. & Tel. Co. v. Deason,* 632 So. 3d 1377, 1383 (Fla. 1994).

(b) Mechanics

(i) Holder

The holder of the attorney-client privilege is the client. *Accord* Uniform Rule of Evidence 503(c). Thus, an attorney's voluntary disclosure of privileged material does not waive the privilege. To the contrary, and as noted above, the attorney is usually obligated to assert the privilege on the client's behalf when the client is not present to do so.

(ii) Failure to assert/waiver

As the holder of the privilege, the client's voluntary disclosure of privileged information waives the privilege.

Examples

1. Plaintiff sues her former lawyer for malpractice and, more specifically, for giving her bad advice to reject a settlement offer in an ongoing civil case. Although the confidential communications between Plaintiff and the former lawyer may have been covered by the attorney-client privilege, Plaintiff's act of filing the lawsuit premised in part on what the lawyer told her constitutes a waiver of the attorney-client privilege.
2. Plaintiff sues Defendant for breach of contract. Plaintiff seeks to discover a letter that Defendant received from his lawyer summarizing their prior conference and that Defendant forwarded to an old friend who is not a lawyer. Defendant's disclosure of that letter to the old friend constitutes a waiver of the attorney-client privilege as to that letter.
3. Same as Example 2, but Defendant gave a copy of the letter to his spouse. Because, as discussed below, communications between Defendant and his spouse are separately privileged by the marital communications privilege, Defendant's disclosure does *not* constitute a waiver.
4. Plaintiff sued Defendant for fraud. In the midst of a large discovery disclosure, Defendant disclosed a memo she wrote to her lawyer detailing what, in her view, happened and asking for advice on how to proceed. Upon realizing this error, Defendant's lawyer alerted Plaintiff's lawyer and asked to have the document returned. If Defendant's lawyer had taken reasonable steps to avoid inadvertent disclosure in the first place, Defendant may be able to "claw back" that memo without a waiver of the privilege under FRE 502.

However, what if the client discloses information to others who have separate attorneys, but all of whom are working together in litigation? Does *that* constitute a waiver? It usually does not, as courts have recognized a "common interest privilege" that precludes a waiver when privileged information is shared outside the attorney-client relationship but only with third parties who are engaged in a "joint effort with respect to a common legal interest."

(iii) Exceptions

The attorney-client privilege is subject to the following exceptions.

When a client consults a lawyer to assist with a crime or fraud, the ensuing communications are not privileged. Consider the following: A client retains a lawyer to obtain advice on how to evade taxes. Does the attorney-client privilege attach to communications aimed at committing a crime? That was the issue before the Supreme Court in *United States v. Zolin,* 491 U.S. 554 (1989).

United States v. Zolin

491 U.S. 554 (1989)

JUSTICE BLACKMUN delivered the opinion of the Court.

This case arises out of the efforts of the Criminal Investigation Division of the Internal Revenue Service (IRS) to investigate the tax returns of L. Ron Hubbard, founder of the Church of Scientology (the Church), for the calendar years 1979 through 1983.

The second issue concerns the testimonial privilege for attorney-client communications and, more particularly, the generally recognized exception to that privilege for communications in furtherance of future illegal conduct—the so-called "crime-fraud" exception. The specific question presented is whether the applicability of the crime-fraud exception must be established by "independent evidence" (*i. e.*, without reference to the content of the contested communications themselves), or, alternatively, whether the applicability of that exception can be resolved by an *in camera* inspection of the allegedly privileged material. We reject the "independent evidence" approach and hold that the district court, under circumstances we explore below, and at the behest of the party opposing the claim of privilege, may conduct an *in camera* review of the materials in question.

We have recognized the attorney-client privilege under federal law, as "the oldest of the privileges for confidential communications known to the common law." *Upjohn,* 449 U.S. at 389. Although the underlying rationale for the privilege has changed over time, courts long have viewed its central concern as one "to encourage full and frank communication between attorneys and their clients and thereby promote broader public interests in the observance of law and administration of justice." That purpose requires that clients be free to "make full disclosure to their attorneys" of past wrongdoings, *Fisher* v. *United States,* 425 U.S. 391, 403 (1976), in order that the client may obtain "the aid of persons having knowledge of the law and skilled in its practice," *Hunt* v. *Blackburn* (1888).

The attorney-client privilege is not without its costs. "[S]ince the privilege has the effect of withholding relevant information from the factfinder, it applies only where necessary to achieve its purpose." The attorney-client privilege must necessarily protect the confidences of wrongdoers, but the reason for that protection—the centrality of open client and attorney communication to the proper functioning of our adversary system of justice—"ceas[es] to operate at a certain point, namely, where the desired advice refers *not to prior wrongdoing,* to *future wrongdoing.*" It is the purpose of the crime-fraud exception to the attorney-client privilege to assure that the "seal of secrecy," between lawyer and client does not extend to communications "made for the purpose of getting advice for the commission of a fraud" or crime.

We think that the following standard strikes the correct balance. Before engaging in *in camera* review to determine the applicability of the crime-fraud exception, "the judge should require a showing of a factual basis adequate to support a good faith belief by a reasonable person," that *in camera* review of the materials may reveal evidence to establish the claim that the crime-fraud exception applies.

In many cases, the lawyer is aware that she is perpetuating a crime or fraud, such as when the lawyer is hired by the client to perpetuate the facade that a "sham transaction" is legitimate and to thereby forestall an investigation by the IRS, *United States v. A.G.E. Enterprises*, 15 Fed. App. 439, 442-43 (9th Cir. 2001) or such as when the lawyer is consulted on how to present a consistent and hence more convincing false narrative to government investigators. However, the lawyer's knowledge is not required, and the crime-fraud exception will vitiate the privilege even if the client retains the lawyer to aid in a crime or fraud but does not let the lawyer know what is really going on. *Accord United States v. Under Seal (In re Grand Jury Proceedings)*, 102 F.3d 748, 749-52 (4th Cir. 1996) (bank made loans in violation of state law but hired lawyers to prepare legal documentation that covered up the violations; crime-fraud exception applied).

Zolin establishes that the crime-fraud exception does not reach a client's communications regarding *past* crimes or frauds; those communications are still privileged. *Accord* Uniform Rule of Evidence 502(d)(1). As to *ongoing* or *future* crimes and frauds for which a client seeks the attorney's counsel, *Zolin* holds that a court may undertake an *in camera* examination of the assertedly privileged information to determine whether that information falls within the crime-fraud exception, at least upon a showing of facts sufficient to create a "good faith belief" in a "reasonable person" that the attorney was retained to commit a crime or fraud.[13]

When the client is deceased and privileged information is necessary to determine which of competing claimants is the holder of the privilege, the deceased client's communications are no longer privileged. Because the attorney-client privilege outlives the client and because sometimes more than one person claims to be the client's successor, courts have recognized an exception to the attorney-client privilege that allows disclosure of the deceased client's privileged communications if relevant to resolve who may continue to stand in the deceased client's shoes. *Accord* Uniform Rule of Evidence 502(d)(2).

When joint clients or persons with a common interest sue each other, communications relevant to the pending lawsuit are no longer privileged. As noted above, a

---

13. New York, Illinois, Florida, and Texas follow the same approach. *Matter of New York City Asbestos Litigation*, 109 A.D.3d 7, 11 (N.Y. App. Div. 2013); *In re Marriage of Decker*, 153 Ill. 2d 298, 324-25 (Ill. 1992); *Walanpatrias Foundation v. AMP Servs.*, 964 So. 2d 903, 905 (Fla. 2007); *In re Christus Santa Rosa Health Sys.*, 492 S.W.2d 276, 281 (Tex. 2016). Some states, such as California, flatly prohibit the trial judge from looking at the privileged material to determine whether an exception to the attorney-client privilege exists. Cal. Evid. Code § 915(c).

client waives the attorney-client privilege when she sues her lawyer for malpractice regarding communications. *Accord* Uniform Rule of Evidence 502(d)(3). There is a separate exception to the privilege when two clients jointly represented by the same lawyer or when two clients represented by different lawyers but under a common interest agreement sue one another. *Accord id.* 502(d)(6).

2. *Work Product "Privilege"*

When lawyers represent a client and, when necessary, prepare for trial, their work is "reflected . . . in interviews, statements, memoranda, correspondence, briefs, mental impressions, personal beliefs, and countless other tangible and intangible ways." *Hickman v. Taylor*, 329 U.S. 495, 510-11 (1947). Collectively, such work is referred to as the lawyer's "work product." The "core" of this work product is the "mental processes of the attorney" reflected in this material. *NLRB v. Sears, Roebuck & Co.*, 421 U.S. 132, 154 (1975) (work product includes "memoranda prepared by an attorney . . . which set forth the attorney's theory of the case and his litigation strategy"). Work product can be broken into (1) "fact work product," which encompasses "documents and tangible things prepared in anticipation of litigation or for trial" that are factual in nature (such as memoranda summarizing witness interviews); and (2) "opinion work product," which encompasses "materials prepared in anticipation of litigation or for trial that reflect an attorney's mental impressions, conclusions, opinions, or legal theories concerning the litigation" (such as outlines of opening and closing statements, questions to ask witnesses, observations or thoughts about the believability of witnesses who have been interviewed). *Accord Cox v. Administrator United States Steel & Carnegie*, 17 F.3d 1386, 1422 (11th Cir. 1994).

The Supreme Court has recognized a "qualified privilege for certain materials prepared by an attorney 'acting for his client in anticipation of litigation.'" *United States v. Nobles*, 422 U.S. 225, 237-38 (1975). Although it in many respects functions, as *Nobles* notes, as a "qualified privilege," the work product "privilege" is not a *true* privilege but instead is "a qualified immunity protecting from discovery documents and other tangible things prepared by a party or his representative in anticipation of litigation." *Admiral Ins. Co. v. U.S. Dist. Court*, 881 F.2d 1486, 1494 (9th Cir. 1989). The work-product "privilege" reaches materials generated by an attorney's agents (such as investigators) as well as the attorney herself. Because this "privilege" is qualified, however, a trial judge may decide that the interest in disclosing the information is more compelling than the attorney's interest in keeping the information secret; such situations include when the work product material contains "facts . . . essential to the [other parties'] case" that cannot be easily acquired from any other source. *Hickman*, 329 U.S. at 511-12.

The holder of the work product "privilege" is the attorney. The attorney may lose the privilege by not asserting it or by waiving it through voluntary disclosure of the privileged information. There are no categorical exceptions to this privilege because its qualified nature allows for exceptions to be made on a case-by-case basis. However, the crime-fraud exception is an exception to the work product "privilege" as well. *Drummond Co. v. Conrad & Scherer, LLP*, 885 F.3d 1324, 1335 (11th Cir. 2018).

Review Questions

1. **Transactional information.** Plaintiff sues Defendant for breach of contract. During a deposition of Plaintiff, Defendant asks how many lawyers she consulted, who the lawyers are, and how much she paid each of them. Is this information privileged?
2. **Reference to other professionals.** After a consultation with a lawyer, the lawyer sends Plaintiff to meet with a psychotherapist to assess Plaintiff's mental state for a possible lawsuit seeking emotional distress damages. The psychotherapist issues a report. Is this report covered by the attorney-client privilege? What if the report is given to one of the attorney's paralegals?
3. **Internal corporate investigation.** Defendant, a corporation, hires a lawyer to conduct an internal investigation of whether bribes are being paid by some of its foreign employees. The lawyer speaks with the chief executive officer, middle management, and some of the first-line workers in the various foreign locales. Are the lawyer's communications with all these groups privileged? Are the lawyer's handwritten notes, including her thoughts about the believability of the various employees, privileged?

PART C: THE SPOUSAL PRIVILEGES

Spouses have two possible privileges at their disposal: (1) the spousal testimonial privilege and (2) the spousal communications privilege.

For purposes of each privilege, spouses are defined as two individuals who are validly married under state law, including through the artifice of a common law marriage if state law so recognizes. The marriage must be a *bona fide* marriage; a "sham" marriage is insufficient.[14]

1. The Spousal Testimonial Privilege

At common law, spouses were deemed "incompetent" against each other on the theory that having spouses testify against each other would destroy "peace in the family" and "further inflame existing domestic differences." *Hawkins v. United States*, 358 U.S. 74, 75, 79 (1958).

14. The Defense of Marriage Act, 1 U.S.C. § 7, sought to limit the definition of spouses to opposite sex couples, but the Supreme Court invalidated that provision in *United States v. Windsor*, 570 U.S. 744 (2013).

(a) Prerequisites/Elements

This privilege applies (1) in criminal cases, (2) when one spouse is called as an adverse witness to the other spouse, (3) while the spouses are still married.[15] *Accord* Uniform Rule of Evidence 504(c).

(b) Mechanics

(i) Holder

At common law, the holder of this privilege was the defendant-spouse. This position was adhered to by the Supreme Court in *Hawkins*. However, the Court in *Trammel v. United States*, 445 U.S. 40 (1980) revisited the issue.

Trammel v. United States

445 U.S. 40 (1980)

CHIEF JUSTICE BURGER delivered the opinion of the Court.

On March 10, 1976, petitioner Otis Trammel was indicted with two others, Edwin Lee Roberts and Joseph Freeman, for importing heroin into the United States from Thailand and the Philippine Islands and for conspiracy to import heroin in violation of 21 U. S. C. §§ 952 (a), 962 (a), and 963. The indictment also named six unindicted co-conspirators, including petitioner's wife Elizabeth Ann Trammel.

According to the indictment, petitioner and his wife flew from the Philippines to California in August 1975, carrying with them a quantity of heroin. Freeman and Roberts assisted them in its distribution. Elizabeth Trammel then traveled to Thailand where she purchased another supply of the drug. On November 3, 1975, with four ounces of heroin on her person, she boarded a plane for the United States. During a routine customs search in Hawaii, she was searched, the heroin was discovered, and she was arrested. After discussions with Drug Enforcement Administration agents, she agreed to cooperate with the Government.

Prior to trial on this indictment, petitioner moved to sever his case from that of Roberts and Freeman. He advised the court that the Government intended to call his wife as an adverse witness and asserted his claim to a privilege to prevent her from testifying against him. At a hearing on the motion, Mrs. Trammel was called as a Government witness under a grant of use immunity. She testified that she and petitioner were married in May 1975 and that they remained married. She explained that her cooperation with the Government was based on assurances that she would be given lenient treatment. She then described, in considerable detail, her role and that of her husband in the heroin distribution conspiracy.

---

15. Texas also limits the testimonial privilege to criminal cases. Tex. R. Evid 504(b)(1). Some states, like New York, limit the testimonial privilege even further—to actions alleging adultery. *Eades v. Eades*, 83 A.D.2d 972 (N.Y. App. Div. 1981). Illinois and Florida have abolished the testimonial privilege entirely. *People v. Palumbo*, 5 Ill. 2d 409, 414-15 (Ill. 1955); *Ross v. State*, 202 So. 2d 582, 583 (Fla. Dist. Ct. App. 1967). At the other extreme, states like California, extend the testimonial privilege to civil cases. Cal. Evid. Code §§ 970-972.

After hearing this testimony, the District Court ruled that Mrs. Trammel could testify in support of the Government's case to any act she observed during the marriage and to any communication "made in the presence of a third person"; however, confidential communications between petitioner and his wife were held to be privileged and inadmissible.

The privilege claimed by petitioner has ancient roots. Writing in 1628, Lord Coke observed that "it hath been resolved by the Justices that a wife cannot be produced either against or for her husband." This spousal disqualification sprang from two canons of medieval jurisprudence: first, the rule that an accused was not permitted to testify in his own behalf because of his interest in the proceeding; second, the concept that husband and wife were one, and that since the woman had no recognized separate legal existence, the husband was that one. From those two now long-abandoned doctrines, it followed that what was inadmissible from the lips of the defendant-husband was also inadmissible from his wife.

The modern justification for this privilege against adverse spousal testimony is its perceived role in fostering the harmony and sanctity of the marriage relationship. Notwithstanding this benign purpose, the rule was sharply criticized. Professor Wigmore termed it "the merest anachronism in legal theory and an indefensible obstruction to truth in practice."

Since 1958, when *Hawkins* was decided, support for the privilege against adverse spousal testimony has been eroded further. Thirty-one jurisdictions, including Alaska and Hawaii, then allowed an accused a privilege to prevent adverse spousal testimony. The number has now declined to 24.

It is essential to remember that the *Hawkins* privilege is not needed to protect information privately disclosed between husband and wife in the confidence of the marital relationship—once described by this Court as "the best solace of human existence." Those confidences are privileged under the independent rule protecting confidential marital communications. The *Hawkins* privilege is invoked, not to exclude private marital communications, but rather to exclude evidence of criminal acts and of communications made in the presence of third persons.

No other testimonial privilege sweeps so broadly. The privileges between priest and penitent, attorney and client, and physician and patient limit protection to private communications. These privileges are rooted in the imperative need for confidence and trust. The priest-penitent privilege recognizes the human need to disclose to a spiritual counselor, in total and absolute confidence, what are believed to be flawed acts or thoughts and to receive priestly consolation and guidance in return. The lawyer-client privilege rests on the need for the advocate and counselor to know all that relates to the client's reasons for seeking representation if the professional mission is to be carried out. Similarly, the physician must know all that a patient can articulate in order to identify and to treat disease; barriers to full disclosure would impair diagnosis and treatment.

The *Hawkins* rule stands in marked contrast to these three privileges. Its protection is not limited to confidential communications; rather it permits an accused to exclude all adverse spousal testimony. As Jeremy Bentham observed more than a century and a half ago, such a privilege goes far beyond making "every man's house his castle," and permits a person to convert his house into "a den of thieves." It "secures, to every man, one safe and unquestionable and ever ready accomplice for every imaginable crime."

The ancient foundations for so sweeping a privilege have long since disappeared. Nowhere in the common-law world—indeed in any modern society—is a woman regarded as chattel or demeaned by denial of a separate legal identity and the dignity associated with recognition as a whole human being. Chip by chip, over the years those archaic notions have been cast aside so that "[no] longer is the female destined solely for the home and the rearing of the family, and only the male for the marketplace and the world of ideas."

The contemporary justification for affording an accused such a privilege is also unpersuasive. When one spouse is willing to testify against the other in a criminal proceeding—whatever the motivation—their relationship is almost certainly in disrepair; there is probably little in the way of marital harmony for the privilege to preserve. In these circumstances, a rule of evidence that permits an accused to prevent adverse spousal testimony seems far more likely to frustrate justice than to foster family peace. Indeed, there is reason to believe that vesting the privilege in the accused could actually undermine the marital relationship. For example, in a case such as this, the Government is unlikely to offer a wife immunity and lenient treatment if it knows that her husband can prevent her from giving adverse testimony. If the Government is dissuaded from making such an offer, the privilege can have the untoward effect of permitting one spouse to escape justice at the expense of the other. It hardly seems conducive to the preservation of the marital relation to place a wife in jeopardy solely by virtue of her husband's control over her testimony.

Our consideration of the foundations for the privilege and its history satisfy us that "reason and experience" no longer justify so sweeping a rule as that found acceptable by the Court in *Hawkins*. Accordingly, we conclude that the existing rule should be modified so that the witness-spouse alone has a privilege to refuse to testify adversely; the witness may be neither compelled to testify nor foreclosed from testifying. This modification—vesting the privilege in the witness-spouse—furthers the important public interest in marital harmony without unduly burdening legitimate law enforcement needs.

(ii) Exceptions

Even if a spouse invokes the spousal testimonial privilege, it does not apply when (1) the defendant-spouse is charged with a crime or alleged to be liable for a tort against the other spouse or their minor children or (2) the two spouses are jointly engaged in a crime (although the testifying spouse's privilege against self-incrimination may still apply).

2. *The Spousal Communications Privilege*

Separate and distinct from the spousal testimonial privilege, the federal common law also recognizes a privilege that attaches to the "confidential communications between husband and wife." *Blau v. United States*, 340 U.S. 332 (1951); *Wolfle v.*

United States, 291 U.S. 7 (1934). The theory behind this privilege is that honest and unimpeded communications between spouses are critical to martial harmony and longevity; a privilege that protects such communications from disclosure removes a disincentive to such honesty and, so the theory goes, increases martial harmony.

(a) Prerequisites/Elements

The spousal communications privilege applies to (1) confidential communications (2) between spouses. Because this privilege protects the *communication*, what matters is whether the spouses were married *at the time of the communication*—not whether they are still married at the time of the trial or other proceeding where the communication is sought in discovery or sought to be admitted into evidence. A communication is made in confidence "if it is made privately by an individual to the individual's spouse and is not intended for disclosure to any other person," Uniform Rule of Evidence 504(a), except perhaps minor children. And the privilege covers only *communications*, not a spouse's conduct (unless it is meant to be communicative) or the other spouse's observations.

(b) Mechanics

(i) Holder(s)

Both spouses hold the spousal communications privilege, and *either* spouse can assert it. Thus, a martial communication may be discovered or admitted into evidence only if *neither* spouse asserts the privilege or *both* spouses waive it. *Accord* Uniform Rule of Evidence 504(b). This rule has the effect of enabling either spouse to prevent the other from disclosing a confidential communication.

(ii) Exceptions

The spousal communications privilege does not apply in the following situations:

- When the communications are designed to aid in an ongoing or future crime or fraud. *Accord* Uniform Rule of Evidence 504(d)(2).
- When the spouses are adverse parties in a civil case. *Accord* Uniform Rule of Evidence 504(d)(1).
- In criminal proceedings, when one spouse is charged with a crime against the other or their minor children. *Accord* Uniform Rule of Evidence 504(d)(1), (3).

Review Questions

1. **Testimonial privilege.** Vincent and Oscar have been married since 2018. In each situation below, does Oscar have the privilege not to testify at the trial involving Vincent?
   a. Vincent is charged with murdering his business partner.
   b. Vincent is sued for wrongful death of his business partner.

   c. Vincent is charged with domestic violence against Oscar.
   d. Vincent is charged with murdering his business partner, but Vincent and Oscar divorced in 2021.
2. **Communications privilege.** Ken and Barbie have been married since 2018. In each situation below, can Ken prevent Barbie from testifying now about what he told her during a 2017 conversation?
   a. The conversation occurred in front of dinner guests.
   b. Barbie waives the spousal communications privilege.
   c. Ken is charged with domestic violence against Barbie.
   d. Ken and Barbie divorced in 2020.

PART D: THE PSYCHOTHERAPIST-PATIENT PRIVILEGE

People have sessions with psychologists and psychiatrists as a means of tending to their mental well-being or addressing past traumas. For such therapy to be effective, there must be "an atmosphere of confidence and trust in which the patient is willing to make a frank and complete disclosure of facts, emotions, memories, and fears." *Jaffee v. Redmond*, 518 U.S. 1, 10 (1996). To facilitate this necessary exchange, the federal common law has long recognized a psychotherapist-patient privilege that shields from disclosure the confidential communications between a patient and his or her psychotherapist.

1. Prerequisites/Elements

The psychotherapist-patient privilege applies to (1) confidential communications (2) between a psychotherapist and the patient. *Jaffee*, 518 U.S. at 15; *accord* Uniform Rule of Evidence 503(b). Psychotherapists include psychologists, psychiatrists, and licensed social workers providing psychotherapy. The communications must be confidential, which means "not intended to be disclosed to third persons, except [(1)] those present to further the interest of the patient in the consultation, examination, or interview, [(2)] those reasonably necessary for the transmission of the communication, and [(3)] persons who are participating in the diagnosis and treatment of the patient under the direction of the" psychotherapist. Uniform Rule of Evidence 503(a)(1). This definition raises the question: Does the privilege apply to group therapy sessions? The general concession is that it *does*, as long as the group format is part and parcel of the psychotherapy.

2. Mechanics

(a) Holder

The holder of the psychotherapist-patient privilege is the patient. *Accord* Uniform Rule of Evidence 503(c).

(b) Exceptions

The psychotherapist-patient privilege does not apply in the following situations:

- When the patient's mental health is a claim or defense in the proceeding, *accord* Uniform Rule of Evidence 503(d)(1).
- When the psychotherapist examination is court-ordered, *accord* Uniform Rule of Evidence 503(d)(1), (2).
- In some courts, when the patient poses a danger of death or serious bodily injury to himself or to others. Although *Jaffee* suggested in dicta that such an exception might exist "if a serious threat of harm to the patient or to others can be averted only by means of a disclosure by the therapist," *Jaffee*, 518 U.S. at 18 n.19, the federal courts have split on whether to recognize such an exception.[16]
- When the patient has committed a reportable offense (of child abuse and the like) under state statutes. *Accord* Uniform Rule of Evidence 503(d)(8).
- When the psychotherapist's services were sought to assist in an ongoing or future crime or fraud, *e.g.*, *In re Grand Jury Proceedings (Violette)*, 183 F.3d 71, 77 (1st Cir. 1999); *accord* Uniform Rule of Evidence 503(d)(4).

Review Questions

1. **Court-ordered evaluation.** Defendant is charged with assault with a deadly weapon. Prior to trial, the trial judge declares a doubt about Defendant's competence to stand trial and orders that Defendant be evaluated to assess her mental competency. Defendant meets with a psychologist. Are their communications privileged? Why or why not?
2. **Parental fitness.** A husband and wife are in a custody dispute regarding their four-year-old daughter. The wife wants to admit the following evidence, which she asserts will show that the husband is not a fit parent:
   a. Testimony from one of the persons who attends weekly 12-step alcohol recovery sessions with the husband.
   b. Testimony from the couple's therapist, with whom the husband, wife, and child meet every other week.
   c. Testimony from the husband's therapist.

   Which of these communications is privileged? Why or why not?
3. **Nine lives expired.** Plaintiff sues Defendant for intentional infliction of emotional distress after Defendant ran over Plaintiff's cat with his car.

---

16. *Compare United States v. Glass*, 133 F.3d 1356, 1360 (10th Cir. 1998) (recognizing exception); Uniform Rule of Evidence 503(d)(5) (same) *with United States v. Chase*, 340 F.3d 978, 981-82 (9th Cir. 2003) (no such exception); *United States v. Hayes*, 227 F.3d 578 (6th Cir. 2000) (same); *United States v. Ghane*, 673 F.3d 771, 786 (8th Cir. 2012) (same) *with United States v. Auster*, 517 F.3d 312, 315 n.5 (5th Cir. 2008) (declining to take a position).

a. Defendant seeks to call Plaintiff's therapist to the stand to testify that Plaintiff told him that the cat was dying of feline leukemia and that Plaintiff had placed the cat in the path of Defendant's tires when his car was parked so that he could sue Defendant, whom he hated.

b. Same as (a), but the therapist would also testify that Plaintiff asked the therapist to testify about the horrible trauma Plaintiff has suffered.

Which of these communications is privileged? Why or why not?

4. **Dangerous patient?** A person tells her psychologist that she *really* wants to kill her boss. May the psychologist disclose this information to the police, or does the privilege preclude him from doing so?

PART E: OTHER COMMONLY ENCOUNTERED PRIVILEGES

Although the universe of privileges is finite, it is not small, particularly when one takes into account the various privileges recognized by state law that apply when a case is in federal court based on diversity jurisdiction. That being said, some privileges are asserted more commonly than others. This section discusses some of those more commonly asserted privileges.

1. The Clergy-Penitent Privilege

The clergy-penitent privilege protects confidential communications between a religious official and a worshipper when the communication is made to the clergy person "in his or her spiritual and professional capacity" and "with a reasonable expectation of confidentiality." *In re Grand Jury Investigation,* 918 F.2d 374, 383-85 (3d Cir. 1990) (also, collecting cases); *accord* Uniform Rule of Evidence 505(b). The privilege applies to any person who is a "minister, priest, rabbi, . . . or other similar functionary of a religious organization, or an individual reasonably believed to be so by the individual consulting the" clergy person. Uniform Rule of Evidence 505(a)(1). The holder of this privilege is the penitent. *Id.* 505(c). Thus, this privilege would protect a worshipper's confessional to a priest as well as other confidential communications with a member of the clergy made for the purpose of seeking spiritual guidance. The privilege applies to penitents of any *bona fide* religion (such that the privilege does not reach communications between two people who decide, on the spot, to create "A Most Worshipful Church of Hatfield Avenue" in order to shield their communications).

How far the privilege goes beyond widely recognized religions is not entirely settled. Although courts have said as a general matter that the privilege does not reach religions that "denominate each and every member as clergy" and "proclaim that all communications have spiritual significance," *In re Grand Jury Investigation,* 918 F.2d at 384 n.13, the trial judge in the O.J. Simpson criminal trial ruled that Simpson's semiweekly scripture readings with a good friend were privileged.

Is there an exception to the privilege when clergy discover a crime that may be of interest to other congregants (such as that a member of their clergy has sexually molested one of the congregants' children)? Some courts have said "no," preferring to leave the decision whether to disclose to the clergy member. *E.g.*, *Conti v. Watchtower Bible & Tract Society of New York, Inc.*, 235 Cal. App. 4th 1214, 1229-30 (Cal. Ct. App. 2015).

2. *The Physician-Patient Privilege*

Where it exists, the physician-patient privilege protects confidential communications between a physician and a patient. Because this privilege is not part of the federal common law, the federal courts have largely declined to recognize this privilege. *E.g.*, *Whalen v. Roe*, 429 U.S. 589, 602 n.29 (1977); *Patterson v. Caterpillar, Inc.*, 70 F.3d 503, 607 (7th Cir. 1995); *Gilbreath v. Guadalupe Hosp. Foundation Inc.*, 5 F.3d 785, 791 (5th Cir. 1993); *accord* Uniform Rule of Evidence 501-12 (1974 ed.) (not including a physician-patient privilege).[17]

3. *The Journalist–Confidential Source Privilege*

Although the Supreme Court has declined to recognize a First Amendment–based privilege not to disclose one's confidential sources, *Branzburg v. Hayes*, 408 U.S. 665, 702-04 (1972), the lower federal courts have recognized a nonconstitutionally based privilege, albeit one that is qualified or conditional. *See In re Grand Jury Subpoena (Miller)*, 397 F.3d 964, 972-73 (D.C. Cir. 2005). Congress also stepped in and enacted the Privacy Protection Act, 42 U.S.C. §§ 2000aa *et seq.*, which prohibits the government from seizing a journalist's papers with a search warrant unless the journalist has committed a crime or the seizure is necessary to protect life or limb.

4. *Governmental Privileges*

National security privilege. The federal courts have recognized a privilege attaching to military intelligence, including confidential military intelligence. *United States v. Reynolds*, 345 U.S. 1 (1953).

Presidential communications privilege. The federal courts have also recognized a privilege attaching to presidential communications, albeit only those communications that at their apex involve matters of national security. *United States v. Nixon*,

---

17. Some states recognize this privilege, however, at least in civil cases. Cal. Evid. Code § 1010; *Hasan v. Garvar*, 108 So. 3d 570, 578 (Fl. 2012); *Dillenbeck v. Hess*, 73 N.Y.2d 278, 289 (N.Y. 1989). Texas and Illinois recognize it in civil and criminal cases. Tex. R. Evid. 509; 735 Ill. Comp. Stat. § 5/8-802. Where it exists, the holder is the patient, and the privilege does not apply when the patient puts his physical condition at issue, when the physician has a statutory duty to report (such as for child abuse), or when the examination is court-ordered. Thus, what a plaintiff tells her physician before suing to recover damages for her injuries is unlikely to be privileged in *any* jurisdiction.

418 U.S. 683 (1974). The contours of this privilege are still very much at issue today. In late 2021, a Select Committee of the House of Representatives subpoenaed documents from the White House regarding communications preceding the incursion into the United States Capitol on January 6, 2021; the White House responded that it would elect to exercise (or not exercise) the so-called executive privilege on a subpoena-by-subpoena basis.

5. The Official Information/Informant's Identity Privileges

Two privileges potentially shield ongoing law enforcement investigations.

Official information. Prosecutors possess a qualified privilege not to divulge communications made in the course of an ongoing investigation, at least during the pendency of that investigation. *E.g., In re United States Department of Homeland Security,* 459 F.3d 565, 568-69 (5th Cir. 2006).

Informant's identity. Prosecutors also possess a qualified privilege not to divulge the identity of an "informant" (that is, a person "who has furnished information relating to or assisted in an investigation of a possible violation of a law"). Uniform Rule of Evidence 509(a), (b). However, the privilege may be outweighed by the defendant's right to obtain that information when it is "relevant and helpful to the defense of an accused, or is essential to a fair determination of a cause." *Rovario v. United States,* 353 U.S. 53, 59-60 (1957). This privilege does not extend to the *content* of what the informant says (although that content may fall within the official information privilege).

PART F: THE PRIVILEGE AGAINST SELF-INCRIMINATION

The Fifth Amendment of the U.S. Constitution provides, in pertinent part, that "[n]o person . . . shall be compelled in any case to be a witness against himself. . . ." This language embodies the privilege against self-incrimination. The courts have construed the privilege to encompass *two* privileges: (1) a testimonial privilege and (2) an evidentiary privilege. They have separate requirements and scopes, so we will discuss each separately.

Examples

1. Defendant is charged with making a criminal threat. Prosecutor calls Defendant as a witness. Defendant has the right to refuse to testify. This right is the *testimonial* privilege against self-incrimination.
2. Defendant is charged with making a criminal threat. Prosecutor calls the victim of that threat to testify about the threat. On cross-examination, defense counsel asks, "Didn't Defendant tell you that you should 'be careful what you wish for' after you short-changed him when selling

him heroin?" The witness has the right not to answer that question because it would mean admitting that he was in the midst of an illegal drug deal. This right is grounded in the *evidentiary* privilege against self-incrimination.

1. *The Testimonial Privilege*

(a) Prerequisites/Elements

The testimonial privilege against self-incrimination precludes a person from being called as a witness *at all*. Indeed, it is called the *testimonial* privilege precisely because it protects a person from having to testify. This privilege applies only to the charged defendant in a criminal case. What is more, the privilege precludes the prosecutor from commenting on the defendant's decision not to testify. *Griffin v. California*, 380 U.S. 609 (1965).

One of the chief justifications for the testimonial privilege is the desire to avoid forcing a criminal defendant to face a "cruel trilemma": If he takes the stand and testifies truthfully, he will incriminate himself; if he takes the stand and testifies falsely, he will commit the separate crime of perjury; and if he decides not to take the stand and the prosecutor can urge the jury to infer his guilt from his failure to testify, his inaction will be viewed as evidence of his guilt. The testimonial privilege sidesteps the cruel trilemma by ensuring that the defendant may elect not to testify without legal consequence.

Thus, the elements of the testimonial privilege are (1) the criminal defendant, (2) deciding whether to testify in his or her own case.

(b) Mechanics

The holder of the testimonial privilege is the defendant.

There really is no "failure to assert" the testimonial privilege. The defense either affirmatively calls the defendant as a witness or it does not. It is an error for a prosecutor even to *try to call* a criminal defendant as a witness in the defendant's own case, so there is no opportunity for the defendant to be called and to not assert the privilege.

A defendant may elect to waive the testimonial privilege by electing to take the stand. If she does, she must subject herself to cross-examination regarding any subject within the scope of her direct testimony (plus impeachment). Courts will not allow a defendant to only give her side of the story and then refuse to be subject to testing on cross-examination; when such refusals occur, the trial judge will strike the defendant's testimony in its entirety. This precise issue came up during the 1974 federal bank robbery trial of Patty Hearst. The government charged Hearst with participating in the robbery of the Hibernia Bank as part of the Symbionese Liberation Army. Hearst's defense was that she had been brainwashed. She so testified. On cross-examination, Hearst invoked the privilege against self-incrimination in refusing to answer questions that dealt with a separate crime of which she was believed to be a suspect. The trial judge overruled the prosecutor's argument that Hearst's act of taking the stand waived her *evidentiary* privilege against self-incrimination as to questions that went beyond her direct testimony and involved a wholly separate crime. A defendant's decision to testify in a prior proceeding in the same case may also constitute a waiver.

2. *The Evidentiary Privilege*

(a) Prerequisites/Elements

The evidentiary privilege against self-incrimination protects a person from having to divulge information that may incriminate him. Unlike the testimonial privilege that only applies to criminal defendants, the evidentiary privilege may be invoked in any proceeding—civil or criminal, administrative or judicial, investigatory or adjudicatory. And unlike the testimonial privilege that potentially applies only to a criminal defendant at his own trial, the evidentiary privilege potentially applies to any *natural person*. It does not apply to collective entities such as corporations, partnerships, or associations.

As to natural persons, the evidentiary privilege applies only if three prerequisites/elements are met: (1) The information sought is *testimonial* (whether information is "testimonial" for purposes of the evidentiary privilege against self-incrimination is different from whether a statement is "testimonial" for purposes of the Confrontation Clause, as discussed in Chapter Nine); (2) someone is seeking to *compel* the information, such that information a person voluntarily discloses is not covered by the evidentiary privilege; and (3) the information sought must be *incriminating to the person invoking the privilege* (rather than incriminating to someone else). Each of these requirements is discussed separately.

(i) "Testimonial"

Information is *testimonial* only if it "disclose[s] the contents of [the] mind" by "explicitly or implicitly . . . relat[ing] a factual assertion or disclos[ing] information." *Curcio v. United States*, 354 U.S. 118, 128 (1957). Testimonial evidence is often contrasted with "real" or "nontestimonial" evidence that is *not* covered by the evidentiary privilege. Real or nontestimonial evidence includes the following:

- Fingerprints;
- Blood and breath samples;
- The sound of one's voice;
- One's appearance, including appearances in lineups;
- Handwriting and voice exemplars; and
- Other biometric information.

As this list makes clear, there are many types of information that—despite being compelled and incriminating—are still not protected by the evidentiary privilege because they do not divulge the contents of one's mind.

Examples

1. Defendant is pulled over for suspicion of drunk driving after weaving across several lanes of the highway. The police officer who pulled over Defendant administers several "field sobriety tests" designed to determine whether Defendant is under the influence. The officer arrests Defendant and takes him to a hospital to obtain a blood sample to ascertain his blood alcohol level. When Defendant refuses, the officer gets a search warrant for Defendant's blood. Defendant cannot invoke the privilege against self-incrimination to refuse to comply with the order authorizing the blood draw. Although the order compels Defendant to comply and although his blood alcohol level may incriminate him, the alcohol content of Defendant's blood does not reveal the content of Defendant's mind. *Schmerber v. California,* 384 U.S. 757 (1966).
2. Same as Example 1, but after the blood draw, Defendant is taken to the jail. During the booking process, the booking officer asks Defendant what day and year he turned six years old. If called as a witness at trial, the booking officer can testify to the fact that Defendant was slurring his words because the manner of Defendant's speech does not reveal the content of his mind. However, the officer cannot testify that Defendant was unable to calculate his sixth birthday because his answer reveals his impaired mental process and hence the content of his mind. *Pennsylvania v. Muniz,* 496 U.S. 582 (1990).

(ii) "Compelled"

Information is "compelled" if it is divulged in response to the following:

- A subpoena;
- A threat of being held in contempt; or
- A grant of immunity.

Fisher v. United States, 425 U.S. 391, 409-10 (1976).

(iii) "Incriminating"

To be "incriminating," information need not be a "smoking gun" sufficient by itself to convict the privilege holder of a crime. Instead, information is "incriminating" as long as it "furnish[es] a link in the chain of evidence" against the person. *Hoffman v. United States,* 341 U.S. 479, 486 (1951).

Example

Defendant is charged with murder. If a witness to the murder saw a light blue Infiniti driving away from the scene of the shooting, Defendant may refuse to answer the question, "Did you have access to a light blue Infiniti on the day of the shooting?" Although Defendant's access to the car at issue is not as incriminating as answering the question, "Did you shoot the victim," his answer is "incriminating" within the meaning of the evidentiary privilege because it can be used to place him at the scene of the crime and thus is one "link" in the "chain" that can result in his conviction.

Information that meets this definition may nonetheless lose its incriminating character if any of the following are true:

- The statute of limitations has run for all the crimes to which the information is incriminating.
- The prosecutor has granted the person immunity. Under federal law, prosecutors have the statutory authority to obtain a court order that grants a person immunity, called "use and derivative use" immunity. This type of immunity precludes the prosecution from (1) using the information the person directly provides and (2) using any information the prosecutor indirectly derives from the information directly provided. *See* 18 U.S.C. §§ 6002, 6003. If a person is granted "use and derivative use" immunity, what they disclose (as well as what is learned from what they disclose) cannot be used against them, so disclosure is no longer incriminating, the evidentiary privilege no longer applies, and they may be compelled to answer. *Kastigar v. United States*, 406 U.S. 441, 453 (1972). Only prosecutors may offer immunity, which makes sense because a grant of immunity is essentially a promise not to prosecute, and prosecutors are the ones exclusively vested with making such decisions. What if the defense encounters a witness who has information vital to the defendant's defense but that is incriminating to the witness? Can the defendant confer immunity upon that person in order to compel their answers? The Supreme Court has not answered that question, but lower federal courts have held that defendants do *not* have that power, although a prosecutor's refusal to grant immunity (in order to prevent the defendant from obtaining and presenting information critical to his defense) may sometimes constitute prosecutorial misconduct.

(b) Mechanics

(i) Holder

The holder of the evidentiary privilege is the person who may be "incriminated by *his own* compelled testimonial communications." *Fisher v. United States*, 425 U.S. 391, 409 (1976) (emphasis added). A person cannot assert the privilege to prevent the compelled disclosure of information *prepared by someone else* just because it incriminates that person. For instance, as the Supreme Court held in *Fisher*, a taxpayer cannot assert the privilege to prevent his accountant from responding to a subpoena demanding documents, even if those documents—which are the accountant's statements—incriminate the taxpayer.

This principle has special significance when it comes to collective entities. What if the target of a criminal investigation is the CEO of a corporation and prosecutors subpoena the corporation's records? As we know, the evidentiary privilege does not apply to collective entities like the corporation. And because the corporation is legally distinct from the CEO, the CEO cannot assert the privilege to stop the corporation from being compelled to disclose *the records* that incriminate the CEO. *United States v. Doe*, 465 U.S. 605, 611-12 (1984).

But is that the end of the analysis? Because it is a legal fiction, the corporation has to act through its officers. In other words, *some person* has to physically prepare the corporate records and produce them to the prosecutors. With small corporations, this person will often be the CEO. Can the CEO/corporate custodian's "act of production" itself be protected by the evidentiary privilege? In *Fisher* and subsequent cases, the Supreme Court held that the answer is "yes." Specifically, *Fisher* held that a custodian's compelled "act of production" can sometimes be testimonial because the custodian's conduct in producing corporate records responsive to a subpoena and potentially being subject to cross-examination about their production can constitute admissions "that the papers existed, were in [the custodian's] possession or control, and were authentic." *Doe v. United States*, 487 U.S. 201, 209 (1988); *Fisher*, 425 U.S. at 409-10. The scope of this "act of production" doctrine was discussed in *United States v. Hubbell*, 530 U.S. 27 (2000).

United States v. Hubbell

530 U.S. 27 (2000)

JUSTICE STEVENS delivered the opinion of the Court.

This proceeding arises out of the second prosecution of respondent, Webster Hubbell, commenced by the Independent Counsel appointed in August 1994 to investigate possible violations of federal law relating to the Whitewater Development Corporation. The first prosecution was terminated pursuant to a plea bargain. In December 1994, respondent pleaded guilty to charges of mail fraud and tax evasion arising out of his billing practices as a member of an Arkansas law firm from 1989 to 1992, and was sentenced to 21 months in prison. In the plea agreement, respondent promised to provide the Independent Counsel with "full, complete, accurate, and truthful information" about matters relating to the Whitewater investigation.

The second prosecution resulted from the Independent Counsel's attempt to determine whether respondent had violated that promise. In October 1996, while respondent was incarcerated, the Independent Counsel served him with a subpoena *duces tecum* calling for the production of 11 categories of documents before a grand jury sitting in Little Rock, Arkansas. On November 19, he appeared before the grand jury and invoked his Fifth Amendment privilege against self-incrimination. In response to questioning by the prosecutor, respondent initially refused "to state whether there are documents within my possession, custody, or control responsive to the Subpoena." Thereafter, the prosecutor produced an order, which had previously been obtained from the District Court pursuant to 18 U.S.C. § 6003(a), directing him to respond to the subpoena and granting him immunity "to the extent allowed by law." Respondent then produced 13,120 pages of documents and records and responded to a series of questions that established that those were all of the documents in his custody or control that were responsive to the commands in the subpoena, with the exception of a few documents he claimed were shielded by the attorney-client and attorney work-product privileges.

The contents of the documents produced by respondent provided the Independent Counsel with the information that led to this second prosecution. On April 30, 1998, a grand jury in the District of Columbia returned a 10-count indictment charging respondent with various tax-related crimes and mail and wire fraud.

[It] is [a] settled proposition that a person may be required to produce specific documents even though they contain incriminating assertions of fact or belief because the creation of those documents was not "compelled" within the meaning of the privilege. Our decision in *Fisher v. United States* (1976), dealt with summonses issued by the Internal Revenue Service (IRS) seeking working papers used in the preparation of tax returns. Because the papers had been voluntarily prepared prior to the issuance of the summonses, they could not be "said to contain compelled testimonial evidence, either of the taxpayers or of anyone else." Accordingly, the taxpayer could not avoid compliance with the subpoena merely by asserting that the item of evidence which he is required to produce contains incriminating writing, whether his own or that of someone else. It is clear, therefore, that respondent Hubbell could not avoid compliance with the subpoena served on him merely because the demanded documents contained incriminating evidence, whether written by others or voluntarily prepared by himself.

On the other hand, we have also made it clear that the act of producing documents in response to a subpoena may have a compelled testimonial aspect. We have held that "the act of production" itself may implicitly communicate "statements of fact." By "producing documents in compliance with a subpoena, the witness would admit that the papers existed, were in his possession or control, and were authentic." Moreover, as was true in this case, when the custodian of documents responds to a subpoena, he may be compelled to take the witness stand and answer questions designed to determine whether he has produced everything demanded by the subpoena. The answers to those questions, as well as the act of production itself, may certainly communicate information about the existence, custody, and authenticity of the documents. Whether the constitutional privilege protects the answers to such questions, or protects the act of production itself, is a question that is distinct from the question whether the unprotected contents of the documents themselves are incriminating.

Acting pursuant to 18 U.S.C. § 6002, the District Court entered an order compelling respondent to produce "any and all documents" described in the grand jury subpoena and granting him "immunity to the extent allowed by law." In *Kastigar* v. *United States*, 406 U.S. 441 (1972), we upheld the constitutionality of § 6002 because the scope of the "use and derivative-use" immunity that it provides is coextensive with the scope of the constitutional privilege against self-incrimination.

The Government correctly emphasizes that the testimonial aspect of a response to a subpoena *duces tecum* does nothing more than establish the existence, authenticity, and custody of items that are produced. The question, however, is not whether the response to the subpoena may be introduced into evidence at his criminal trial. That would surely be a prohibited "use" of the immunized act of production. But the fact that the Government intends no such use of the act of production leaves open the separate question whether it has already made "derivative use" of the testimonial aspect of that act in obtaining the indictment against respondent and in preparing its case for trial. It clearly has.

It is apparent from the text of the subpoena itself that the prosecutor needed respondent's assistance both to identify potential sources of information and to produce those sources. Given the breadth of the description of the 11 categories of documents called for by the subpoena, the collection and production of the materials demanded was tantamount to answering a series of interrogatories asking a witness to disclose the existence and location of particular documents fitting certain broad descriptions.

It is abundantly clear that the testimonial aspect of respondent's act of producing subpoenaed documents was the first step in a chain of evidence that led to this prosecution. The documents did not magically appear in the prosecutor's office like "manna from heaven." They arrived there only after respondent asserted his constitutional privilege, received a grant of immunity, and—under the compulsion of the District Court's order—took the mental and physical steps necessary to provide the prosecutor with an accurate inventory of the many sources of potentially incriminating evidence sought by the subpoena.

For these reasons, we cannot accept the Government's submission that respondent's immunity did not preclude its derivative use of the produced documents because its "possession of the documents [was] the fruit *only* of a simple physical act—the act of producing the documents." It was unquestionably necessary for respondent to make extensive use of "the contents of his own mind" in identifying the hundreds of documents responsive to the requests in the subpoena. The assembly of those documents was like telling an inquisitor the combination to a wall safe, not like being forced to surrender the key to a strongbox. The Government's anemic view of respondent's act of production as a mere physical act that is principally non-testimonial in character and can be entirely divorced from its "implicit" testimonial aspect so as to constitute a "legitimate, wholly independent source" (as required by *Kastigar*) for the documents produced simply fails to account for these realities.

While in *Fisher* the Government already knew that the documents were in the attorneys' possession and could independently confirm their existence and authenticity through the accountants who created them, here the Government has not shown that it had any prior knowledge of either the existence or the whereabouts of the 13,120 pages of documents ultimately produced by respondent.

As *Hubbell*'s discussion indicates, in a few potential situations a custodian's otherwise privileged act of production might nevertheless fall outside of the evidentiary privilege, namely, (1) when the records to be produced are records that the collective entity would ordinarily maintain and which the government requires the entity to produce for "essentially regulatory" purposes, *Grosso v. United States*, 390

U.S. 62, 68 (1968);[18] or (2) when the existence, the custodian's possession and control, and the authenticity of the documents are "foregone conclusions."

(ii) Failure to assert and waiver

A person's decision to answer a question and thereby voluntarily disclose incriminating information is both a failure to assert and a waiver of the privilege. That is true no matter when the waiver occurs. Thus, if a person answers a question during a deposition in a civil case, he cannot later claim that the information is covered by the privilege; once it is waived as to certain information, it is waived forever.

Review Questions

1. **Biometric locks.** Police pull over Defendant, and a police dog alerts to drugs in the trunk of Defendant's car. Police do a pat down of Defendant and seize her cell phone. Police ask Defendant for her passcode to unlock her phone. Is the passcode covered by the privilege against self-incrimination? What if she has enabled the "biometric reading" function that unlocks her phone upon capturing an image of her face and police merely hold the phone up to her face? Does *that* violate the privilege?
2. **Acts of production.** A corporation is being investigated for tax evasion. Prosecutor issues a subpoena to the corporation for the corporation's tax returns. The CEO/custodian of those records objects on the grounds of privilege. Are those records privileged? Is your analysis any different for the internal corporate documents used to prepare the tax returns?
3. **Dear diary.** Defendant is charged with murder. Pursuant to a search warrant, the police seize Defendant's diary from his house. The diary lays out Defendant's hatred for the victim and his plans to bring about his death. Is the diary privileged?

18. Under this so-called required records doctrine, information that might otherwise be privileged is deemed to be outside the privilege if (1) the government seeks this information for "essentially regulatory" reasons, (2) the information "is to be obtained by requiring the preservation of records of a kind which the regulated party has customarily kept," and (3) "the records themselves . . . have assumed 'public aspects' which render them at least analogous to public documents." Thus, in *Shapiro v. United States* 335 U.S. 1 (1948), the Supreme Court held that vendors' documentation of their sales required by the Emergency Price Control Act in effect during World War II was not privileged. *See also United States v. Chabot,* 793 F.3d 838 (3d Cir. 2015) (records that government agencies require be maintained to participate in foreign banking are "required records" exempt from the privilege). However, the doctrine does not apply where the regulatory program is "directed almost exclusively to persons inherently suspect[ed] of criminal activity," such as a requirement that people engaged in illegal wagering—but no others—must file "excise tax" documentation; *Grosso* held that this documentation fell outside the "required records" doctrine.

Table of Common Privileges

Name	Prerequisites/ Elements	Holder	Inapplicable When
	Constitutional privileges recognized in all courts		
Testimonial privilege against self-incrimination	(1) Criminal defendant (2) In own case	Defendant	Waived (by testifying)
Evidentiary privilege against self-incrimination	Seeks to elicit information from a natural person that is: (1) Testimonial (2) Compelled (3) Incriminating	Person with information	(1) Not asserted (2) Waived (by voluntarily divulging information)
	Federal court privileges		
Attorney-client privilege	(1) Confidential communication (2) Between a client and lawyer	Client	(1) Not asserted (2) Waived (3) Crime-fraud exception (4) Multiple claimants through a deceased client (5) Litigation between joint or common interest clients
Work product "privilege"	Mental impressions of attorney or attorney's agent to aid in litigation	Attorney	Case-by-case balancing
Spousal testimonial privilege	(1) Criminal case (2) *Bona fide* spouses are married at the time of testimony	Witness spouse	(1) Not asserted/ waiver (2) Defendant-spouse accused of crime/tort against other spouse or their minor children (3) Spouses jointly participate in crime

Name	Prerequisites/ Elements	Holder	Inapplicable When
Spousal communications privilege	(1) Confidential communication (2) Between spouses married at time of communication	Both spouses	(1) Crime-fraud exception (2) One spouse accused of crime/ tort against the other
Psychotherapist-patient privilege	(1) Confidential communication (2) Between psychotherapist and patient	Patient	(1) Mental condition is a claim or defense (2) Session is court-ordered (3) Psychotherapist is a required reporter (4) (In some courts) patient is dangerous to others
Clergy-penitent privilege	(1) Confidential communication (2) Between clergy and penitent	Penitent	
Privilege not recognized in federal court			
Physician-patient privilege	(1) Confidential communication (2) Between physician and patient	Patient	(1) Physical condition is a claim or defense (2) Examination is court-ordered (3) Physician is a required reporter

Test Your Understanding

To test your understanding of the material in this chapter, turn to the Supplement for additional practice problems.

Chapter 16

Pulling It All Together

As previewed in Chapter One, this book has laid out the key rules of evidence individually. It started with the general definition of relevance. From there, the book covered other doctrines setting up categorical rules of relevance such as the rules governing character evidence and the specialized rules governing the admission of subsequent remedial measures and the like. The book then shifted to doctrines aimed at assuring the reliability of evidence, such as the rule against hearsay and the constitutional overlay that most directly affects hearsay. At that point, the book turned to the reliability-focused rules that affect testifying witnesses, such as the rules of competency, the rules governing the impeachment of witnesses and then lay and opinion testimony, and the best evidence rule. The book covered the rules governing the admission of documentary and other physical evidence, such as authentication and demonstrative evidence. Last, the book turned to the "meta" rules governing substitutes for evidence (such as inferences, presumptions, and judicial notice) as well as the privileges that exclude otherwise relevant and reliable evidence in order to further other public policies.

As Chapter One also previewed, studying these rules individually is both necessary to understanding their intricacies *and* wholly artificial because, in the real world, these various rules operate simultaneously to dictate the admission or exclusion of items of evidence.

So how do you apply the rules *as an integrated whole* to determine whether a particular item of evidence is likely to be considered by a jury? A helpful starting point is to ask (1) what type of evidence is at issue and (2) which rules of evidence must that type of evidence satisfy in order to be admissible?

As this book has noted time and again, the types of evidence can be grouped into four broad, general categories:

- Testimony from witnesses;
- Documentary evidence;
- Nondocumentary physical evidence;
- Demonstrative evidence.

The following chart illustrates which rules of evidence must typically be satisfied before each type of evidence will be deemed admissible. Shown here are just the *key* questions to ask; they are not the *only* questions to ask.

Testimony
- Is it relevant?
- Is the witness competent to testify?
- If the testimony contains hearsay, does that hearsay satisfy the hearsay rule?
- If the testimony contains opinion, are the rules regarding lay or expert opinion testimony satisfied?
- If the testimony regards a writing, recording, or photograph, is the best evidence rule satisfied?
- Is any of the testimony privileged?

Documentary evidence
- Is it relevant?
- Has the document been authenticated?
- If the document contains hearsay, does that hearsay satsify the hearsay rule?
- If it is not the original, does the document satisfy the best evidence rule?
- Is the document privileged?

Non-documentary physical evidence
- Is it relevant?
- Is the object properly authenticated?

Demonstrative evidence
- Is it relevant?
- Is it properly authenticated as being based on the other evidence presented in the case?
- If it is based on any scientific principles or expert opinion, are the rules regarding such opinion satisfied?

As the proponent of the evidence, you should run through these questions for each item of evidence you hope to admit; ideally, you should do so *before* the hearing at which that evidence will be presented so that you can know when the rules of evidence may not be satisfied and whether you can present additional evidence to shore up those deficiencies. As an opponent of the evidence, you should ensure that these questions have been addressed; otherwise, an objection may be in order. (Whether you choose to forgo an objection as a matter of trial strategy is better examined in a trial advocacy course and is far beyond the scope of this text.)

To illustrate how the rules of evidence work together, see Chapter Sixteen of the Supplement. That chapter contains a number of short answer questions and longer essay questions that test the interaction of the various rules of evidence. That final chapter of the Supplement also contains a Case Study that demonstrates the interconnectivity of the rules.

Test Your Understanding

To test your understanding of the material in this chapter, turn to the Supplement for additional practice problems.

Table of Authorities

Anderson, Michelle J., From Chastity Requirement to Sexuality License: Sexual Consent and a New Rape Shield Law, 70 Geo. Wash. L. Rev. 51 (2002), 89
Belli, Melvin, Demonstrative Evidence: Seeing is Believing, 16 Trial 70 (1980), 552
Capers, Bennett, Evidence Without Rules, 94 Notre Dame. L. Rev. 867 (2019), 21
Epstein, Jules, Is Evidence Law Race "Neutral?" https://www2.law.temple.edu/aer/is-evidence-law-race-neutral, 2
Faigman, David L., Admissibility Regimes: The "Opinion Rule" and Other Oddities and Exceptions to Scientific Evidence, the Scientific Revolution, and Common Sense, 36 Sw. U. L. Rev. 699 (2008), 500
Fenner, G. Michael, The Daubert Handbook: The Case, Its Essential Dilemma, and Its Progeny, 29 Creighton L. Rev. 939 (1996), 500
Galvin, Harriett R., Shielding Rape Victims in the State and Federal Courts: A Proposal for the Second Decade, 70 Minn. L. Rev. 763 (1986), 89
Gonzales Rose, Jasmine B., Toward a Critical Race Theory of Evidence, 101 Minn. L. Rev. 2243 (2018), 2
Green, E. & Nesson, C., Problems, Cases, and Materials on Evidence (1983), 494
Joseph, Gregory P., "Internet and Email Evidence," *The Practical Lawyer* (Feb. 2012), 529
Kommenda, Niko & Gutierrez, Pablo, Coronavirus map of the US: latest cases state by state, The Guardian (Mar. 26, 2020), 580
The Legal Concept of Evidence, Stanford Encyclopedia of Philosophy (2015), 1
Levenson, Laurie L., Courtroom Demeanor: The Theater of the Courtroom, 29 Minn. L. Rev. 573 (2008), 5
Maguire, The Hillmon Case—Thirty-Three Years After, 38 Harv. L. Rev. 709 (1925), 249
Overturning Wrongful Convictions Involving Misapplied Forensics, https://innocenceproject.org/overturning-wrongful-convictions-involving-flawed-forensics (2021), 46
Tillers, Peter, What Is Wrong with Character Evidence, 49 Hastings L. J. 781 (1998), 56
Wellborn, Olin Guy, III, Demeanor, 76 Cornell L. Rev. 1075 (1991), 447
Wells, Christina E. & Motley, Erin Elliott, Reinforcing the Myth of the Crazed Rapist: A Feminist Critique of Recent Rape Legislation, 81 B.U. L. Rev. 127 (2001), 96
Wilson, Erin, Let's Talk Specifics: Why STI Evidence Should Be Treated As a "Specific Instance" Under Rape Shield Laws, 98 N.C. L. Rev. 689 (2020), 89
Wright, Charles Alan & Miller, Arthur R., Federal Practice and Procedure § 7013 (2018 ed.), 333

TABLE OF CASES

Principal cases are indicated by italics.

D

E

F

G

H

I

J

K

Y

Z

Table of Rules, Statutes, and Constitutional Provisions

INDEX

Tables are indicated by "t" following the page number.

B

C

D

T